BALTIC YEARBOOK OF INTERNATIONAL LAW

Baltic Yearbook of International Law

Volume 6, 2006

Baltic Yearbook of International Law

Volume 6, 2006

MARTINUS NIJHOFF PUBLISHERS
LEIDEN/BOSTON

A C.I.P. Catalogue record for this book is available from the Library of Congress.

Printed on acid-free paper.

ISBN 90 04 15430 2

Koninklijke Brill NV incorporates the imprints Brill Academic Publishers, Martinus Nijhoff Publishers and VSP.

http://www.brill.nl

Printed and bound in The Netherlands.

BALTIC YEARBOOK OF INTERNATIONAL LAW

Contents

Use of Force

Human Rights

History of International Law in the Baltic States

Materials on International Law: 2005

Book Reviews

Information: Legal Journals in the Baltic States

Editorial Note

On 13–15 May 2004 the Inaugural Conference of the European Society of International Law took place in Florence, Italy. It brought together international lawyers from various parts of Europe and the world with an aim to discuss 'International Law in Europe: Between Traditional and Renewal'.

The conference involved participants from 29 different States of Europe, including almost thirty participants from those States which acceded to the EU only two weeks before the Conference such as Cyprus, the Czech Republic, Estonia, Hungary, Latvia, Poland and Slovenia. Others came from Albania, Bulgaria, Belarus, Romania, the Russian Federation, and the former Yugoslavia. Less than 15 per cent of the total number of participants came from outside Europe with the United States, Australia, Canada, Israel, Brazil and Japan sending the largest contingents.

The conference consisted of keynote speeches, fora and agorae panels. The panelists at the conference also reflected a significant diversity in terms of nationalities. The largest number of speakers came from France (nine) and the United Kingdom (six). Countries which were represented by two to four panelists were: Austria, Germany, Belgium, Spain, Finland, Italy, the Netherlands, Hungary, Romania and the United States.

The participants debated the role of Europe in the past and today in the development and enforcement of international law, concluding among other things that its legacy has been mixed. Some theorists have long written glowingly about the 'European tradition in international law', and highlighted the unique contributions which it has made to the field. Europe's critics have derided it for its aspirations of universality in this area partly on the grounds that its focus has been quintessentially European and not universal, and partly that it has all too often been motivated by its own self interest. But whatever the perspective, the historical contribution has been great. European theorists have been central to the evolution of the discipline, and promotion of an international rule of law continues to feature prominently in much of Europe's foreign policy.

Volume 6 of the Baltic Yearbook of International Law in co-operation with the European Society of International Law publishes keynote speeches by professors Alain Pellet and Michael Reismann and selected papers of the panelists. The ESIL therefore continues its tradition of bringing together and reaching into different corners of Europe the debate on international law.

Baltic Yearbook of International Law, Volume 6, 2006, pp. xi–xii.

Editorial Note

The Baltic Yearbook is honoured to publish the historical proceedings in Florence where the European Society of International Law was founded.

Ineta Ziemele

Member of the Editorial Board

Proceedings of the Inaugural Conference of the European Society of International Law, Florence, 14-15 May 2004

Introduction

Bruno Simma[*]

As Ineta Ziemele, a Member of the Editorial Board of the Baltic Yearbook of International Law, has announced, the present volume publishes keynote speeches and selected papers read at the Inaugural Conference of the European Society of International Law (ESIL/SEDI), held in Florence on 13–15 May 2004.

I have had the privilege of serving as the first President of this Society, from the Florence Conference until May 2006, when, at the occasion of the Society's second General Conference in Paris, the ESIL/SEDI Executive Board elected Professor Hélène Ruiz-Fabri as my successor. Let me therefore take this opportunity to describe, in a few brief words, the 'object and purpose' of the European Society, to express things in professional terms.

At the beginning, dating back to the mid-1990s, stood the idea born among the founding editors of the *European Journal of International Law*, itself existing since 1990, that we needed a general European network to bring together international lawyers, academics and practitioners, and establish a forum for the discussion of key issues in international law. We wanted to establish a motor, as it were, driving a deeper understanding of such issues among all of those working in the field, be they government officials, diplomats, legal advisers in international organizations, academics, or practising lawyers. Despite the increasing importance of seeking to facilitate Europe-wide debates on international law, there existed previously no organisational framework within which to pursue these goals on a Europe-wide basis. This was the case notwithstanding the large number of

[*] Judge at the International Court of Justice; First President of the European Society of International Law.

Baltic Yearbook of International Law, Volume 6, 2006, pp. 1–5.

international lawyers in Europe and the significant number of international law associations at the national level.

The International Law Association performs a very special, but limited, range of functions and is not specifically European in any sense. In fact, the only comparable international umbrella grouping of importance at present is the American Society of International Law. While many European international lawyers participate in its annual deliberations, we felt a strong need to develop an effective forum for the discussion of issues of mutual concern within Europe itself and to address a European rather than an American agenda.

The increasing globalization of law and the growing importance of developing a shared understanding within Europe in relation to a wide range of international legal issues served to emphasize the desirability of creating a forum designed to foster greater interaction among European international lawyers. Current developments in a wide range of areas served to highlight the need for more concerted attention to the development of shared positions within Europe. This is demonstrated by issues ranging from the war in Iraq and the debate over the appropriate limits of international intervention, through the resolution of international trade disputes and the shape of the future international economic regime, to the role of multilateralism in general. These and many other issues have served to emphasize the desirability of developing much closer links between those working in the international law field in Western Europe and their counterparts in Eastern and Central Europe. This need became all the more marked in response to the expansion of membership of the European Union.

In many of the countries of the enlarged EU and elsewhere in Europe there is no national association of international lawyers (other than the ILA). In others, there are important national societies. The ESIL was to be established in such a way as to enable it to complement the invaluable roles played by any existing or potential national societies. Competition and duplication will be avoided and every effort will be made to work through the national societies in order to ensure a much greater degree of interaction among the different national groups. There is no other forum which undertakes this function at present and the European Society will not in any significant way overlap or compete with the role played by the other major professional groupings of international lawyers, the ILA and the Institut de Droit international.

The principal goals of ESIL are to contribute to the rule of law in international relations and to promote the study of public international law. For these purposes its Constitution provides that it will organize and support in-depth exchanges of ideas on matters of common interest to public international lawyers in Europe and elsewhere; encourage high-level scholarship and analysis and provide a forum for European-wide discussions thereon; promote a greater awareness and understanding of international law not only amongst lawyers but within the community at large; and foster a greater appreciation of the role of the European tradition and develop European perspectives for addressing the problems of the twenty-first century.

All this is to be achieved with a strong emphasis, first, on giving the younger generation of international lawyers, many still in the course of or having just completed their doctoral studies, an opportunity to air their ideas before an eclectic audience, including many of their more senior colleagues, and, second, on involving, and supporting, members of the profession from the new democracies in Central and Eastern Europe.

Let me mention a number of activities through which ESIL intends to pursue its aims.

In a more traditional vein, it will hold bi-annual conferences, like the Inaugural Conference in Florence 2004 and the second General Conference held in Paris in May 2006. The third will take place in Heidelberg in 2008, co-organized with the Max Planck Institute for Comparative Public Law and International Law.

At these occasions ESIL will discuss topics of great interest in a critical spirit. Ineta Ziemele has described briefly the main theme around which the Inaugural Conference 2004 turned, 'International Law in Europe: Between Tradition and Renewal'. If you regard the table of contents of the present volume, you might already get a good idea of what some of the concerns of the Society were right at the moment of its birth: the shadow of the American empire under which Europe finds itself, as well as its colonial past, and the totalitarian legacy left by half a century of communism in an important part of Europe.

In between these large events, the Society will endeavour to organize more focused, research-oriented meetings, like the ESIL Research Forum which took place at the Graduate Institute of International Studies in Geneva in May 2005. A second event of this nature is planned to be held in Budapest in 2007.

We plan to publish the proceedings of these conferences as well as to initiate a monograph series under the auspices of the Society. In addition, the *European Journal* will provide a forum for the quick distribution of outstanding results of the Society's academic undertakings.

Then I am proud to introduce two innovative projects.

The first is the 'Mapping of International Law in Europe'. The idea behind this undertaking is to create a database of all the universities, departments and centres involved in international law in Europe. To launch the project, ESIL sought the collaboration of a number of people to act as rapporteurs. The response was impressive, both in terms of people volunteering and the quality of the reports provided. A lot of hard work, the bulk of it done on a voluntary basis in 'spare' time, has more recently gone into collating all the information gathered and organizing it into a format which will soon be ready to go 'live' on the ESIL website.

'Mapping International Law' will be one of the very first databases of this kind and will undoubtedly be a widely sought resource for those organizing events and conferences, or those who simply want to know who is doing what and where. On a more personal level, it is also an important landmark for the ESIL, being the first tangible service it will offer to the international law community.

The second project consists in the creation of ESIL Interest Groups. In order that members of the Society, many of whom have met and kept in contact following attendance at one or more of the Society's events, have the opportunity to interact with colleagues along thematic lines on an ongoing basis, the Society has been developing the idea of ESIL interest groups. These groups will provide for discussion, networking, and joint activities within the various sub-fields of international law, thus helping to build a common-knowledge base of actors, institutions, and research in international law in Europe and beyond. The guidelines for the interest groups are now finalized and in the last few months there has been growing interaction among ESIL members to solicit interest in establishing formal interest groups. The first such group came into existence in May 2006.

Thus my brief description of the purpose of the Society and its main activities. I still remember its Inaugural Conference in Florence as a hugely successful and thoroughly enjoyable event for all who participated. The question on everyone's lips however, as the Florentine sun sank below the horizon after the closing speeches was 'what next?' As with all successful inaugural events there then remained the legacy of the hard act to follow – for a very young society with very little funds and a precedent set which would be hard to maintain. However, ESIL has risen, and risen admirably to the challenge, both through the events which it has organised or participated in – particularly the magnificent second General Conference held at the Sorbonne in May 2006 – and in the various projects, some initiated and others further developed, in the course of the last two years. As I have emphasized before, ESIL will make every effort to complement the roles played by national societies while avoiding duplication and competition. I urge all members of our profession to meet it with the good will I sincerely think it deserves.

Finally, my thanks go to Ineta Ziemele, herself a member of the Executive Board of ESIL, for having made the publication of the major contributions to the Florence Inaugural Conference possible. The *Baltic Yearbook* is a great example of the very efforts which the European Society of International Law is designed to pursue.

INTERNATIONAL LAW IN THE SHADOW OF EMPIRE

The Shadows Looming over International Law

W. Michael Reisman[*]

"The Security Council works just fine; the problem is that the rest of the world doesn't."
– A senior diplomat at the Security Council, April, 2004

I share the sense of the conveners of this meeting that, at this critical moment for international law and world order, the European college of international lawyers will be well served by a new trans-European forum which will enable its members collectively to identify and analyze problems, devise and promote new law where necessary, and appraise current and proposed constitutive decisions of the international legal system based on their contribution to minimum order and human dignity. I am an American, but am not here as a self-appointed emissary, apologist or defender, at this moment of acute tension in the Atlantic community. I approach the issues and challenges facing Europe and the international system, of which Europe is a part, as an independent intellectual committed to world order and human dignity. Judge Simma, in opening this meeting, remarked that "Europe is not a certificate of origin, but a state of mind, *une region de l'âme*". On that basis, I feel comfortable and privileged to be addressing the European Society of International Law at this moment of its founding.

As you may have surmised, I had no hand in composing the title of this panel. If the title was designed to intimate the nature of the major crises we face, I find it misleading. The transposition of the term 'empire' to the United States in contemporary international politics is inaccurate and, more seriously, unhelpful, in my view, in that it misrepresents both the problem of world order at the outset of the twenty-first century and the roles, responsibilities, and capacities of the United States in it.

---

[*] (C) W. Michael Reisman. Myres S. McDougal Professor of International Law at the Yale Law School. This paper is part of a larger project on the failure of international law. Mahnoush Arsanjani, Anna Skotko and Andrew Willard gave me helpful criticism and suggestions.

Baltic Yearbook of International Law, Volume 6, 2006, pp. 7–25.

Rather than operating *in* the shadow of a single political empire, international law operates in a world emerging *from* that shadow. As a result, it is contending with forces that have been unleashed by the retreating and dissolving empires. Let us look back for a moment. One hundred years ago, in 1904, most of our planet was controlled by empires: the British Empire, the French Empire, the Dutch Empire, the Belgian Empire, the German Empire, the Austro-Hungarian Empire, the Italian Empire, the Portuguese Empire, the Russian Empire, the Spanish Empire, the Ottoman Empire, the Japanese Empire, and the Chinese Empire. The United States, then in the midst of its own imperial estrous, had just wrested the Philippines, Cuba and Puerto Rico from the Spanish Empire and had 'detached' Panama from Colombia. The 'scramble for Africa', twenty-five years earlier, was comparatively orderly. But many of the then-extant empires were poised to dismember and absorb parts of Imperial China in a process that promised to be far less orderly. Indeed, the great empires of that moment would have done so but for the 'open door' policy initiated, albeit for less than altruistic reasons, by the United States.

Each of the powerful and expanding behemoths of the time earned what was the then coveted title of 'empire' by virtue of the fact that it controlled and directly governed significant territories geographically separate from its metropolitan areas and containing significant numbers of peoples who were racially, ethnically or religiously distinct from the populations of its metropolitan. With the exception of the Ottoman *millet* system, these various empires, whenever it served their respective interests, routinely suppressed indigenous cultures and especially political aspirations whether it was the Boxers in China, the Mahdi in the Sudan, or Somalia's 'Mad Mullah', to cite only a few examples. In their place, the empires imposed their own institutional practices and values, ostensibly to fulfil their self-defined *mission civilisatrice.*

To regulate their relationships *inter se*, these empires also established a system of international law, congenial to their common interests. In their version of the *corpus juris gentium*, war was an honorable part of statecraft, conquest was its prize and, not surprisingly, the inhabitants of the imperial lands were, for the most part, assimilated to their flora and fauna. All this pre-dated the Porter Convention, the League of Nations and, of course, the United Nations.

The last one hundred years have witnessed the collapse of almost all of these various empires and their replacement, in the diverse territories they had controlled, by independent States governed by indigenous elites. The most recent empire to topple was the Czarist Empire, which had morphed into the Soviet Union and belatedly self-destructed a decade ago. The demise of the Soviet Union also ended a bipolar dimension to international politics that had, until then, acted as something of a 'post-colonial' restraint on the actions of States that found themselves in the magnetic fields of one or the other pole of the world's superpowers.

The collapse of the empires, their retraction to their respective metropolitans, and the coincident reduction in their military capacity, began the re-emergence of indigenous cultural and political forces, often amidst great disorder and violence. This is a process which has become more pronounced as the first and second generation of elites, who had been educated and acculturated by their former 'colonial masters', have been replaced by indigenous elites with no such acculturation.

The title "International Law in the Shadow of Empire", is not only historically misleading. If the dual implication of the title of our meeting is that the United States is the world's current empire and that that fact is the major problem facing international law, I disagree. To be sure, the United States' economy is the largest in the world, larger than the *combined* economies of Japan, Germany, France and Britain. There is a comparable disproportion with respect to the military. The United States is not simply the largest single military force in the world. It accounts for 38 percent of all defense budgets and in two years its defense budget is projected to equal the combined budgets of every other nation in the world.

These are, to be sure, big numbers, but they are isolated statistical indicators of assets and not indicators of power. Power is a *relational* concept: it is the capacity of one putatively dominant actor to influence other actors so that they are constrained to adjust their behavior in critical ways that are favorable to the dominant actor. The political bean-counter simply totes up assets without looking at factors such as the capacity to form and sustain a political will, the ability to mobilize and deploy the assets of both the presumptively more powerful actor and its target, the environments of likely conflict, the utility of the assets in those environments, whatever legal and functional controls are operating and, in particular, the constraints arising from interdependence.

The truism that 'more powerful' actors exercise 'power' over 'less powerful' actors who exercise power over still 'less powerful' actors *ad infinitum*, like all truisms, tells us little. The practical question at the micro-political level is whether one actor's predominance in certain asset categories translates, in particular contexts, in relation to other specific actors, and with respect to specific issues, into some measure of power. In other words, whether it is actually powerful or simply 'muscle-bound'.

Factors such as legal institutions, organizational procedures and patterns of interdependence may temper or reduce the effectiveness of an actor with apparently greater assets or so increase the cost of using its assets as to effectively preclude it. Internal political, legal or bureaucratic arrangements as well as the dynamics of culture may introduce comparable restraints from within the putatively 'powerful' actor.

The critical question for the statesman and the international lawyer, looking at macro-politics – at the 'big picture' – is not whether one actor is stronger than another and whether this generates down-stream emotions of anxiety, envy and anger. That is so obvious and inescapable as to be trite; whether you are a human being, an orangutan or a goose, no one particularly likes to be down the line in a pecking order. The critical question is, rather, whether the assets *collectively* available to the organized community for the defense of public order constitute, in relation to the threats to public order at that time, sufficient power to protect it. Here, again, context is critical. Our French colleagues will well remember the Maginot Line. It teaches a grim lesson: an actor's assets that cannot meet an actual, as opposed to an imagined, threat but loom so reassuringly large in its eyes that, like a packrat, it continues frantically to accrue more, will prove to have a negative security value. Such assets lull the actor hunkering down behind them into a false sense of security so that it remains unprepared for the actual threats it faces. A Maginot Line's illusion of power arises from the non-contextual identification of quantities of assets per se as power.

I believe that many commentators are confusing two things. The first is what at the moment seems to be an irredressible shift in military and economic assets between the United States and Europe, which commenced 50 years ago but can only now, with the Soviet Union gone, be the subject of complaint by States that formerly depended on the United States for their ultimate security. In my view, this is more a blow to the *amour propre* of certain States than a blow to world order. The second is a real and grave problem: the lack of power of the organized international community, which includes the considerable assets of the United States, to collectively confront the critical and inter-related challenges to contemporary world public order.

I

Power is an indispensable component of law. The worlds of ethics and morality are chock-a-block with normative formulations, on the order of 'you ought to do this' or 'you ought to refrain from that'. The distinctive character of law is that its normative formulations are accompanied by an indication that they are not only authoritative, but also that the power requisite to their implementation is available and forthcoming. Power without law is, of course, tyranny. Law, without power, is semantics.

Insofar as the international legal system is effective, it must have the power to maintain minimum order through time, not simply with respect to the formal institutions of law, but also with respect to the processes of production and distribution that sustain a global civilization of science and technology. This necessarily involves the capacity to respond to the full range of contemporary conventional and unconventional threats to that civilization. It also involves the ability to sustain and improve processes of production and distribution of valued outcomes at a level sufficient to maintain the infrastructure of a technological and science-based civilization.

For 50 years, students of the United Nations have expressed admiration for the legal and political architecture of the Charter with respect to the need to maintain international peace and security, but they have lamented the inability of the critical actors in the system to agree on how and when to apply the great authority vested in the Council by the Charter. The consequence of this bottleneck was the recurring exercise of power, ostensibly to support policies of the United Nations, by an unauthorized State or group of States, as in NATO's bombardment of Serbia and Kosovo and the U.S.-led coalition against Iraq, to cite two recent examples. These unauthorized uses of force have themselves generated a secondary international legal industry devoted to the question of the lawfulness of such actions.

Scholars who have worked in this field have focused much of their discussion on the problem of the possible lawfulness or unlawfulness of unilateral action. Less attention has been given to the perennial and quintessential political problem: whether the international community, operating in an organized or unorganized fashion and operating with full authority or plurilaterally or unilaterally without it, has the *power* to deal with the contemporary configuration of threat posed to the global civilization of science and technology. I submit that neither the architecture of the United Nations nor the power available to the international community, whether operating collectively or unilaterally, is sufficient to deal with the major security challenges to world public order: Mass murder and genocide, the HIV/AIDS pandemic and the Jihadist or militant Islamic assault on the civilization of science and technology.

The mass murder and genocides in Africa have been properly recognized as a responsibility of the international community, but the community has proved itself unable to arrest or even contain them. The pretense that the establishment of an International Criminal Court can have any significant effect on these awful events is either self-delusion or hypocrisy. The carnage whirls on, in Congo, Uganda, Sudan. Efforts in Liberia and Sierra Leone have been either feeble or minimal and have been marked by an unseemly haste to declare success and to turn attention and resources elsewhere. Each disaster seems to generate some new international political agency or office, as if the engrafting of additional layers of bureaucratic tissue is a solution.

The prospect of the breakdown of order in States ravaged by HIV/AIDS, the political inability to arrest this process and the lack of resources to remedy it after the fact poses, wholly aside from the humanitarian disaster, a number of threats to international order itself.

The rise of militant Islam or Jihadism now operates in and against Islamic States as well as against Western countries and in those Western countries in which there are significant Moslem immigrant communities. In many of these States, the Moslem populations are increasing more rapidly than their counterparts, making the relation between Jihadism, which is assumed by Western leaders to be an extreme fringe, and mainstream Islam of growing importance to internal order. Both President Bush and Prime Minister Blair have carefully distinguished what they believe to be the real Islam of a majority of Moslems from the Islam of Osama Bin Laden. There is no question that Jihadism is not the faith of the majority of Moslems, but the uncertainty is the attraction of Jihadism to parts of the Moslem majority, in general or under given circumstances and Jihadism's capacity to win the passive acquiescence of the majority or to mobilize cadres from within it who are willing to make great sacrifices. Non-experts, like myself, have difficulty resisting the uneasy feeling that Osama Bin Laden may know more about Islam than Messrs. Blair and Bush. I will speak about these matters in more detail in a moment.

In myriad ways, these apparently distinct challenges are inter-related and inter-stimulating. To cite only one example, the formation of an African Union peacekeeping force, with United Nations' assistance and an African Union Peace Facility with the help of the European Union are indispensable enterprises for stemming humanitarian catastrophes and stabilizing shaky States so that they do not become platforms for terrorism. But these initiatives cannot ignore HIV/AIDS, for, in Africa, the disease is decimating military and police forces, who are also, it appears, prime carriers of the disease. One terrifying scenario which can no longer be dismissed as implausible is the breakdown of both public administration and social order in key States in Africa.

The United Nations was not tooled to deal with these types of threats and some adaptations have been under consideration since then Secretary General Boutros Ghali issued his Agenda for Peace "on ways of strengthening and making more efficient within the framework and provisions of the Charter the capacity of the United Nations for preventive diplomacy, for peacemaking and for peace-keeping".[1] Neither his initiatives nor those of the current Secretary General have produced major changes. The collective decision-making, which international lawyers extol, may be unable to retrofit the Security Council to enable it to deal with these problems. No institution always works and when the United Nations has been unable to rise to a task, individual or groups of States have filled the vacuum. So it is all the more serious to contemplate the possibility that the international community, whether acting collectively, plurilaterally through the so-called 'coalitions of the willing' or unilaterally, may simply lack the power to deal with these dangers. These are the real shadows over contemporary international law. Today I will only address the problem presented by militant Islam.

II

Although Al Qaeda and groups loosely affiliated with it do not now control a State and may, at the moment, see no strategic advantage in doing so, the Afghanistan chapter demonstrates the utility to Al Qaeda of maintaining territorial bases, for training, planning, mounting and directing operations. The effort to deny these adversaries a secure base in which to train and from which to mount operations has demonstrated a disturbing lack of congruence between the assets in the collective arsenal of the international community and the threats to which they must be directed. The internationally authorized intervention in Afghanistan to expel the Taliban government, which provided haven and support to Al Qaeda, and the unauthorized action in Iraq which purported to justify itself, *inter alia*, on similar grounds, have demonstrated a further lack of congruence between assets and challenges. The reasons for this relate to fundamental and inter-stimulating changes in weapons technology, their proliferation, the asymmetry of adversaries, and the decay of much of the law of armed conflict. The current situation in Iraq is instructive but hardly unique.

In environments as different as Peru, during the Shining Path insurrection, and Sri Lanka, during the continuing insurrection of Tamil Eelam, it has become painfully clear that a relatively small but highly

[1] UN Doc. S/23500, January 31, 1992, 3–4.

organized force is capable of bringing a very large country to a state of paralysis. Shining Path never numbered more than 12,000 people in a country of more than 25 million; Tamil Eelam was less than 20,000 in a country of 19 million. In both cases, a coherent counter-ideology, intense discipline, ruthlessness in the selection of targets and the execution of operations, the ready availability of mobile and highly destructive weapons and the inculcation of an ethos of self-sacrifice were sufficient to counter the forces of a much larger body politic. Indeed, one wonders what would have happened if Shaka, the Mahdi and Mohammed Abdullah Hassan had had RPGs.

Faced with an adversary using this *modus operandi*, a forceful response by the targeted government or its allies is often counter-productive, for it drives more of the general population to the adversary. A more discriminating response may not succeed. In any case, it cannot, in the circumstances of these types of internal conflicts, avert collateral damage and is sure to be decried by those parts of the international human rights community that focus on human rights deprivations by governments rather than human rights deprivations per se. The inevitable violation of human rights in massive exercises of violence – one thinks of the appalling treatment of some Iraqi prisoners in Baghdad by a contingent of prison guards – further erodes legitimacy and popular support within and outside the political community that is trying to act.

The Iraqi imbroglio demonstrates, once again, the effect of this strategy. It is tempting to believe that had the United States action against Iraq been international rather than effectively unilateral, one blessed by or even directed by the United Nations, the outcome would have been different. I wish it had been truly international, but I doubt that the result would have been different. The situation in Afghanistan, in which there was unequivocal international authorization, is being played out on a much smaller scale, but it is not, in my view, materially different from Iraq and even less likely to culminate in an outcome that can be characterized as successful.[2] Even if the so-called 'coalition of the willing' in Iraq had been much broader than it was in fact and the actual military contribution of the United States had been minimal and external, there is no reason to assume that those in or entering Iraq who are opposed to the expulsion of Saddam and a replacement of the Baath regime, this mysterious 'counter-coalition of the willing', would be acting differently than they are now. The brutal destruction of United

[2] *See*, in this regard, K. Gannon, Afghanistan Unbound, 83:3 *Foreign Affairs* (May, June 2004) p. 35.

Nations headquarters in Baghdad on 19 August 2003 demonstrates with hideous vividness that (as those who have carefully studied UN peace-keeping operations knew) the symbol of the United Nations is not necessarily positive or politically effective with all local groups and factions in this type of conflict. The Blue Helmet, by itself, provides no protection against individuals and groups who calculate that a UN action is going to oust them from or severely reduce their power.

In a technological and science-based civilization, modes of warfare evolve, as each side looks for an edge. Your advances – your 'edge' –is called military evolution; your adversary's advances are called asymmetrical warfare. It seems that one aspect of asymmetric military development has to be painfully relearned, in each generation, by the asset-heavy protagonist. In one of his briefings to President Reagan, ironically about Afghanistan, William Casey, then director of the CIA, observed that "[f]ar fewer people and weapons are needed to put a government on the defensive than are needed to protect it".[3] The insight, which is exemplified most recently by the Afghani and Iraqi strategies, being applied this time against the United States, demonstrates a fact about military power in the modern world, which some contemporary strategists in the United States (and, for that matter, in Russia with regard to Chechnya) have resisted and which has broad implications for world order as it faces its current challenge. That fact is that the enormous American military assets translate into what has been aptly called 'fate control' but not 'behavior control'. The United States is capable of obliterating an adversary, as a theoretical if not a practical matter, but it is, effectively, unable to control the adversary's behavior through the application of military means. It is certain that the U.S. could completely destroy Iraq in a few hours, literally eradicate it. It is not certain that it can, at a nationally or internationally acceptable price, control Iraq's behavior. In other words, in the contexts which the adversary has selected for confrontation, military and economic assets do not translate into *effective* power. The reasons for this inability are to be found in the characteristics and availability of modern weaponry, modes of waging war, the role of the media and civil society in shaping perspectives about the use of violence and unilateral restraints deriving from dynamics within modern democracies.

There are, alas, many other 'failed', 'failing' or feckless States which could serve as bases for Jihadist action. Jihadists will gain immeasurably if they have secure territorial bases, such as Al Qaeda had in Afghanistan. Even assuming domestic political will, the prospects of the United States and

---

[3] S. Coll, *Ghost Wars* (Penguin Press, New York, 2004) p. 97.

a fortiori other States intervening in order to establish an effective government in failed States in order to deny Jihadists access to the territory seem, in light of the military assets available to the world community and the techniques available to the adversary, less and less promising.

III

If one cannot speak of a single global imperial power, one may speak, in the manner of Gramsci, of an essentially *European/American* culture operating worldwide. Bernard Lewis has recently observed:

> "In every era of human history, modernity, or some equivalent term has meant the ways, norms and standards of the dominant and expanding civilization. Every dominant civilization has imposed its own modernity in its prime. The Hellenistic kingdoms, the Roman Empire, the medieval Christendoms, and Islam, as well as the ancient civilizations of India and China, all imposed their norms over a wide area and radiated their influence over a much broader one, far beyond their imperial frontiers. Islam was the first to make significant progress toward what it perceived as its universal mission, but modern Western civilization is the first to embrace the whole planet. Today, for the time being, as Atatürk recognized and as Indian computer scientists and Japanese high-tech companies appreciate, the dominant civilization is Western, and Western standards therefore define modernity."[4]

More is involved, of course, than the prescription of technological standards or the competence to assign names and addresses on the Internet. Key values of western civilization have been installed in the international human rights program. As I will explain in a moment, by *establishing* them as *the* international standard, they pathologize *ipso facto* all those surviving and reviving cultures which are coherent and self-sustaining, but are different and do not embody those international human rights values. This is not imperial control by a single State, establishing the rules of the game, in Gramsci's sense, but the installation, as world law, of the values and institutional standards of the European Enlightenment by those States that were decisively shaped by it. This world law is designed to function as a normative environment that operates on every actor within or affected by the civilization of science and technology which now covers much of the planet. This is the "empire of law" as Martens used the term. It has positive and

---

[4] B. Lewis, *What Went Wrong: Western Impact and Middle Eastern Response* (Oxford University Press, New York, 2002) p. 150.

negative implications and is an important key to the Jihadi problem facing world order. I will return to it in a moment.

In their recent book, Ian Buruma and Avishai Margalit examine the perspectives held by Jihadists and their sympathizers with respect to the rest of the world, Foucault's "other".[5] The authors flip the term 'Orientalism', made famous by the late Edward Said, and coin the term 'Occidentalism' to refer to the congeries of images and attitudes toward the West held by the Islamic world. Though I have some difficulties with Said's thesis, it is fair to say that our civilization does entertain certain 'Orientalist' views of the Islamic world or, equally distorting and demeaning, has sometimes cultivated the self-serving notion that there are no cultural differences and that the 'other' is not different from 'us'. But, of course, cultures are different and have a profound influence on the images of past and future, identifications and disidentifications and demands of those who have been acculturated within them. One should expect deep commitments to values quite different from those espoused by other cultures.

I should like to return to Gramsci and his notion of cultural imperialism. Since 1945, the international legal system, at the initiative of leading Western modernizing States, has established a set of political, economic and social ground rules of political and other social organization based upon what it considers to be universally valid and self-evident principles. It is the Universal Declaration of Human Rights,[6] concluded by the United Nations General Assembly in 1948, which are now presented as the universal 'standard of achievement'. With minor variations, regional human rights treaties in Europe and the Americas have adopted the principles and even the language of the Universal Declaration. Since 1948, a network of institutions of varying degrees of compulsoriness and effectiveness has worked to implement them. These legal formulations of rights and duties are manifestations of a larger worldview, reflecting key value goals of western civilization. In dealing with the traditional societies to which the international mechanisms are trying to apply them, five values are critical: power, respect, enlightenment, affection and rectitude or religion:

- As for power, the human rights system insists on democratic and representative forms of governance,

---

[5] I. Buruma and A. Margalit, *Occidentalism: The West in the Eyes of its Enemies* (Penguin Press, New York, 2004).

[6] *Universal Declaration of Human Rights*, G.A. Res. 217A (III), U.N. GAOR, 3d Sess., pt. 1, at 71, U.N. Doc. A/810 at 71.

effective equality and equal access to power for men and women, and freedom of expression without prior restraint, even in matters that are of great sensitivity to others.

- As for respect, it insists on the inherent dignity of all people without regard to race, religion, color, sex or sexual orientation and the entitlement of all to equal respect.
- As for enlightenment, it insists on the freedom of inquiry which may and, indeed, must go into anything of interest to the inquirer; there is no forbidden knowledge.
- As for affection, it insists, as a matter of legal right, on the freedom of the individual to cultivate agapic and erotic relations, whether homosexual or heterosexual, and have developed technologies that can separate sexual activity from procreation, allowing sexual pleasure to be cultivated for its own sake. Western civilization enforces the right of a woman to abort her fetus entirely by her own choice.
- As for the development of personal codes of rectitude, the human rights system insists on the freedom of all religions; the obligation to respect them; the separation of the state from religion and the prohibition on the state from supporting any particular religion; and the right of religions to seek to proselytize and convert members of other religions. It views the act of voluntary conversion not as apostasy but as an important exercise of an individual human right.

Europe and the United States are not only proud of their democracies but, through these instruments, they are committed to a globalization of their values. They have, in Gramsci's sense, written the rules of the game into international law. And the reach of these rules is virtually boundless. Although the United Nations Charter purported to reserve the domestic jurisdiction of States from international concern, Western governments and the human rights lobby have vigorously and progressively diminished the scope of domestic jurisdiction so that it no longer buffers the internal legal arrangements of States from the application of international human rights law. Organizations, governments and NGOs press these values as a precondition for regional and world peace, because they believe that democracies do not wage war against each other, (a hypothesis which, in my view, is unconfirmed). They press them as a precondition for economic development, because they assume that a free and open society is necessary in order for its economy to flourish. These instrumental calculations aside, they also advance these values for their own sake. So quite naturally, many of the cultural practices in other parts of the world that deviate from them are characterized as pathological and pathogenic.

The values that the organs of international law designate as 'universal' are, indeed, 'universalizable', in contrast with tribal or other ethnically or religiously restrictive values which limit their reach and confine their benefits to members of a particular group. But 'universalizable' values are not necessarily universally held. Nor are they 'natural'. Many of the values that have been incorporated into modern international law are the result of momentous conflicts in western civilization. It was the Reformation, an event attended by great violence, that laid the basis for the idea, not self-evident to true believers then or, I daresay, even now, that different religions are equally legitimate, can flourish side by side and require the concept of freedom of expression. Civilizations that have not gone through something comparable to the Reformation – including the systems of public order in Latin America and Asia, not simply in Islam – have great difficulty even understanding the notion of freedom of religion and freedom of expression, let alone implementing it. Indeed, in certain parts of the world, freedom of religions, in the plural, is viewed as a contradiction in terms: allowing other faiths to proselytize your co-religionists is complicity in apostasy. As for sexual equality and sexual freedom, now so central to individual self-expression in the West's civilization of science and technology and where sexual frontiers are still being expanded, these values are viewed in other civilizations as the official installation of a policy of promiscuity, constituting, in their view, a particularly pernicious form of evil, both corrupt and corrupting. After one year in America, Sayyed Qutb, whose work continues to influence Jihadists long after his execution by the Egyptian Government, wrote: "Humanity today is living in a large brothel. One has only to glance at its press, films, fashion shows, beauty contests, ballrooms, wine bars and broadcasting stations".[7]

It is not simply that the civilization of the West makes its commitment and practice of these values manifest and that their often extravagantly

---

[7] S. Qutb, *Fi Zilal al-Quran* (Beimt, Dar al-Shuruq, 1981) vol. I 510 - 11 cited by Y. M. Choueriri, *Islamic Fundementalism* (Twayne, Boston, 1990) p. 124.

enlarged images are aggressively exported as part of the global commoditization of the goods and services they produce or sell. Nor is it only that a globalizing entertainment industry, under the constant imperative of efficiency, must try to operate in every possible market and, with its products, inevitably brings many of these values along. These are, after all, private efforts. The critical factor is that many of these values are also aggressively pressed by Western governments and the international institutions they have established as *the* international legal standard. Having universalized the values of western civilization through human rights treaties, the organs of international law do not simply, as in the European context, make the adoption of their values a precondition to acceptance into 'Europe'. The organs of international law actively try to enforce these values upon other States through the international and national institutions that have become the infrastructure of the international human rights system. Those parts of the planet in which these values are not being implemented are, by definition, deviant and backward and are targeted for development and social change and, at its most grandiose, for 'nation-building'. While the words 'development and social change' have a very positive resonance for those who use them, because they imagine that they augur a greater and greater approximation of 'universal' standards, what they mean to many of those who are being targeted for 'development' is a coercive dismantling of their own cultural system, amputations or "self-amputations of [their] own being", to use Marshall McLuhan's vivid expression.[8] McLuhan wrote:

> "All social changes are the effect of new technologies . . . on the order of our sensory lives. It is the shift in this order, altering the images that we make of ourselves and our world, that guarantees that every major technical innovation will so disturb our inner lives that wars necessarily result as misbegotten efforts to recover the old images."[9]

Yet the aggressive exportation of Western values has been only partial. In Western Europe and North America, the values of liberal democracy do not exist in a political vacuum, but in a social and an economic context, for which many international rights have also been prescribed. Yet those rights, whose realization abroad, would be achieved at the expense of domestic economic arrangements, have not been pressed. As a result, the partial

---

[8] M. McLuhan and Q. Fiore, *War and Peace in the Global Village* (Bantam, New York, 1968) p. 5.
[9] *Ibid.*

universalization has often undermined order in developing countries and made democratic processes susceptible to appropriation by extremists.

While the West may support modernizing elites in the Islamic world for programmatic political reasons, it presses Western values for ideological ones. And it is hard to see how the West can stop without changing who it is and how it is organized, for while Islam historically allowed for and accommodated itself to zones of believers and zones of non-believers, the West's conception of human dignity is inherently universalized and presses its exponents to project and demand those values worldwide.

As for the Fundamentalist conservatizers, they are fighting a war in which they may destroy their adversary, but they cannot win. Even if Fundamentalist conservatizers try to resist what they think of as Westernization, they must somehow modernize. Like it or not, populations increase and peoples migrate to ever larger cities, the cradle of modernization. Urbanization breaks down traditional society and the process of modernization inexorably begins. And even the iron curtains of authoritarian systems cannot stop the penetration of modern information technologies, which present alternative images of possibility to each new generation. In a global system, it is, alas, not possible to pick and choose your modernization. It is an inseparable package, a syndrome. But the very futility of the Fundamentalist conservatizers' struggle may make it all the more violent.

IV

The strategy that has been selected by the United States and its coalition partners for confronting Jihadism is one in which it is principally the military strategy which is to be applied, unilaterally if necessary, to dismantle the Jihadist apparatus. This strategy faces formidable difficulties, given the nature of the conflict, the diffusion of modern armaments, the dispersal of adversaries and, not the least, the fact that much of the strategy may have to be pursued in the domestic arenas of the targeted democracies where constitutional and international human rights norms may act as significant restraints. If this strategy continues to be the principal one, even more adjustments in the *jus ad bellum* and the *jus in bello* will be demanded. The costs of such adjustments to other values will be great.

In his *magnum opus*, "World Politics and Personal Insecurity", Harold D. Lasswell observed that when the individual perceives himself or herself to be in great personal insecurity, there is a powerful impulse to resort to violence as a catharsis, even though it may not be the contextually appropriate strategy for achieving extant goals. It is useful to explore whether non-violent modes of action are more likely to respond to the individual's goals. Since 'hard power' is not brilliantly effective in this type of conflict, it is tempting to turn to what is now known as 'soft power'. But in this conflict, non-coercive alternatives do not appear promising. The issue is not the familiar argument about whether one should ever reward terrorists. The dismal fact is that techniques of terror have been used successfully by political groups seeking political change. The transformation of Rhodesia into Zimbabwe, of the colony of Kenya into an independent State and of South Africa from an apartheid to a multi-racial State were all accomplished, in no small part, by the use of terrorism. Notable terrorists such as Yasser Arafat and Nelson Mandela have received Nobel Peace Prizes. Representatives of the provisional IRA have been treated as diplomats in order to secure a political solution to an ongoing civil war. These many examples indicate that though, in the course of war, adversaries may be called terrorists and be vigorously denounced, and though official *post hoc* narratives insist that terror was not an effective weapon, in the final analysis, political accommodations were often reached with the terrorists who then enjoyed the political fruits of their violence.

Is such a solution possible in the war between Jihadism and the civilization of science and technology? At an earlier phase such an accommodation might have been possible. This all began as a war *between* Moslems in the Islamic world about the future control and social structure of the Islamic world, stretching from the Maghreb of North Africa and the largely Islamicized areas of sub-Saharan Africa, through the Middle East and the Anatolian landmass, through Central Asia and the Islamic States of the sub-continent, through the Islamic areas of China, and through the archipelagos of South Asia. It was a war about who, among contending Islamic groups, will gain power and control the *dar al Islam*, the values that will govern it and how it will be organized.

On one side of that Islamic world stand modernizing elites and those strata of the Islamic world who wish to become part of the expanding global civilization based upon science and technology. On the other side stand Fundamentalist conservatizing counter-elites – variously called Militant Islamists or Jihadists – whose members' views cover a spectrum but at the core share the common belief that the civilization of science and technology is antithetical to the true values of their faith; that it will deprive them, individually and collectively, of power; that it will hollow out their religion; and that it will contaminate and corrupt their lives and the lives of their children. The United States was singled out for violent attacks – its embassies in Nairobi and Dar es Salaam, the USS Cole in the harbor of

Aden, the World Trade Center in New York and the Pentagon in Washington – for quite rational political reasons. To be sure, the United States has been viewed as the very symbol of modernity, of power sharing and personal freedom. American support for Israel is an aggravating factor, but in my view, not a central cause of enmity. Modern Jihadism existed before the creation of Israel and if Israel were defeated and transformed into Palestine tomorrow, I do not believe that Jihadism's war against America and the West would cease.

The more compelling rationale of hatred of America was that the United States was seen as the indispensable supporter for the erstwhile modernizing elites or, at least, elites resisting greater fundamentalization. American policy of support for the modernizers has not always been consistent – in the real world, few polices can be – but it is public and certainly not episodic. Consider the Carter Doctrine which President Carter declared in January, 1980:

> "An attempt by any outside force to gain control of the Persian Gulf region will be regarded as an assault on the vital interests of the United States of America, and such an assault will be repelled by any means necessary, including military force."[10]

On 1 October 1981, President Reagan issued statements that the White House promptly characterized as "The Reagan Codicil to the Carter Doctrine".[11] In response to a question, the President said, ". . . Saudi Arabia we will not permit to be an Iran".[12] In clarification, the President added that "in Iran I think the United States has to take some responsibility for what happened".[13] Immediately afterwards, a White House aide explained to the New York Times that "the President was now pledging to support the Saudi monarchy against internal as well as external threats".[14] That codicil is still an essential plank in American foreign policy. In 1991, the United States expelled Iraq from Kuwait and, as part of the operation, established a garrison in Saudi Arabia.

---

[10] 16 Weekly Comp. of Pres. Doc. 197 (23 January 1980).

[11] *See* W. M. Reisman, *Critical Defense Zones and International Law: The Reagan Codicil*, 76 *American Journal of International Law* (AJIL) (1982) pp. 589, 590 (editorial comment).

[12] Transcript of President's News Conference on Foreign and Domestic Matters, *New York Times*, 2 October 1981, at A26.

[13] *Ibid.*

[14] *See* Reisman, *supra* note 11, pp. 590–91.

Fundamentalists had two broad war objectives. First, the withdrawal of American support for the modernizing elites, including Israel, whereupon the conservatizers believe the modernizers would flee westward. With Fundamentalist conservatizers at the helm, true Islamic States could then be established in a type of second Caliphate, reviving the old glory of Islam. Second, and this should not be underestimated, recognition of the independent and autonomous legitimacy of Islam and, as a result, an end to the characterization of parts of Islamic dogma and many Islamic mores as violations of universal human rights standards.

In the midst of conflict, it was unthinkable to broach the possibility of reaching an accommodation with the FLN, the MauMau, the PLO, ZANU, the ANC, the IRA, etc. But in each case, it proved to be feasible and was ultimately done. It might have been feasible in this war. A victory by the Fundamentalist conservatizers would not have signaled the end of economic relations between the *dar al Islam* and the *dar al harb*. After all, the suspension of commercial relations between Iran and United States was neither demanded nor sustained by revolutionary Iran. The Islamic Republic is desperate to trade with the U.S. In a possible future in which Jihadism might have prevailed in this war, oil would still be sold and investments might still be made by each side in the 'world' of the other. But Jihadist victory would mean a suspension of the vision of a global community based upon a common conception of human dignity.

Is such an outcome possible now? Arabic distinguishes between *Salaam* and *Sulh*. *Salaam* is a truce, *Sulh* is an ultimate peace that resolves differences. Perhaps an accommodation might have been reachable in which the international legal system suspended its efforts to apply many of the norms in the international human rights program to the Islamic lands, while the militant Islamic conservatizers, for the their part, suspended hostilities in and against the civilization of science and technology.

In my view, such a hypothetical arrangement is not reachable. Even if it could be put in place, it would be inherently unstable and unlikely to last, as there are dynamics within each community seeking to universalize its own values. In each community, there is a type of 'civil society', which operates independently of and often against the wishes of the governments in their States and is a critical part of the aggressive program that each civilization pursues. Equally important, the pervasiveness of modern communications mean that the protagonist seeking to resist its influence must maintain an intense internal mobilization against the 'enemy'.

If the mode of violence by destruction and self-destruction in Islam has already reached the 'tipping point', a negotiated suspension may no longer be attainable. And that is the future most to be feared. For the foreseeable future, I would expect the war in which we find ourselves engaged to continue. I am uncertain of the outcome but tremble for the shadows looming over the fragile but nonetheless vital international law and public order we have achieved. Surely, learned societies, like the one being founded today, will be called upon to help to meet these challenges by reinforcing and, if necessary, refashioning international law and hopefully dispelling the shadows looming over all of us.

Le droit international dans l'ombre de l'empire

*Alain Pellet**

Le titre même que les organisateurs de cet indispensable colloque ont retenu pour cette "séance inaugurale" témoigne de l'urgence qu'il y avait à créer une Société européenne de droit international : pour irremplaçables qu'elles soient, les sociétés nationales des États de notre chère vieille Europe doivent rassembler leurs forces et redoubler leurs efforts pour, non pas seulement "contrer" les dangers que l'impérialisme américain fait peser sur le droit international, mais aussi, mais d'abord, pour constituer un cadre de débat, ouvert à tous ceux qui, sur le vieux continent, croient encore que le droit international existe et une force crédible de propositions pour l'adapter aux nouvelles donnes internationales.

La composition de ce panel ne doit évidemment rien au hasard : en me demandant d'« affronter » Michael Reisman, les organisateurs de cette « joute » savaient bien sûr que nous présenterions des vues largement, peut-être même radicalement, opposées. Je crains de ne pas les décevoir : je ne puis, en effet, souscrire qu'à très peu des choses qu'a dites mon ami Michael – dont je tiens à dire au demeurant, que je l'aime beaucoup et le respecte profondément, pas parce que c'est poli, mais parce que c'est vrai. Mais des amis peuvent diverger sur des choses importantes. C'est le cas.

En premier lieu, contrairement à lui, je pense que le titre retenu pour ce débat est parfaitement choisi. Certes, les États-Unis d'Amérique ne sont pas le premier empire de l'histoire du monde si l'on définit l'« empire », par opposition à l'État, comme une société politique qui nie l'existence des autres, des « barbares », en tant que sociétés politiques (en paroles – je pense aux Empires orientaux, du Milieu ou du Soleil levant, ou aux empires totalitaires, nazi ou soviétique – ou dans les faits – les empires coloniaux européens). Mais, jusqu'à présent, toutes les aspirations impériales ont échoué – tous les « empires » qui se sont auto-proclamés dans l'histoire se sont, en fait, heurtés aux réactions d'autres forces ou d'autres « empires » et sont restés confinés à une ou quelques parties du monde. Ce n'est pas le cas

* Professeur à l'Université Paris X-Nanterre, Membre et ancien Président de la Commission du droit international (C.D.I.). J'ai conservé le style oral de cette intervention et n'en ai pas modifié le contenu.

Baltic Yearbook of International Law, Volume 6, 2006, pp. 27–37.

des États-Unis en ce début de siècle : leur champ d'action, c'est le monde et nul, dans l'état actuel des choses, ne peut prétendre équilibrer leur pouvoir, contrairement à ce qui s'est toujours produit aussi longtemps qu'a duré la lutte acharnée que se sont livrées les puissances européennes pour le *leadership* européen d'abord, colonial ensuite – et ceci pendant un millénaire.

Sûrement sincèrement (mais adroitement quand même) Michael Reisman nous a dit qu'après tout, les valeurs que les États-Unis défendent ne sont pas les leurs propres, mais celles de l'« Occident » tout entier. Ce n'est qu'en partie vrai. Qui aurait affirmé, qui aurait osé affirmer, il y a 50 ans, 20 ans seulement sans doute, que le libéralisme à tout crin et ses fins exclusivement commerciales, financières, mercantiles, étaient les « valeurs de l'Occident » ? Bien sûr, ce n'est pas ce que dit mon contradicteur et ami ; il parle « droits de l'homme », respect mutuel, non-discrimination – mais qui ne voit que les moyens ont éclipsé les objectifs ? Que le « libéralisme » économique est devenu un but en soi ? Que la liberté (des opérateurs économiques) supplante toutes les autres ? Et, pour dire les choses encore plus crûment, que l'invocation des valeurs est une feuille de vigne qui cache mal une réalité plus obscène : les intérêts des marchands qui se confondent avec ceux des États-Unis (ou que les États-Unis croient, à tort, être les leurs même si, à terme, ceci est loin d'être certain…).

Ce dessein douteux est servi par un phénomène dont il est indissociable : la « globalisation » économique et, dans une moindre mesure sans doute (et l'Astérix gaulois n'est sans doute pas étranger à cette nuance…), culturelle. Ce qu'aucun empire n'avait réalisé, la mondialisation de son influence, les États-Unis sont en voie de le réussir par le biais de l'hégémonisme économique. Oh certes, celui-ci est moins visible, moins spectaculaire, moins immédiatement choquant, que le rôle de gendarmes du monde affranchis de la règle juridique que ses nouveaux maîtres se sont octroyés ; il n'est pas moins efficace. Mais il y a une grande différence : il passe par le droit.

En ce qui concerne ce que j'appellerai le « droit politique » (ou le «droit de la politique » : le recours à la force, le règlement des différends entre États, les règles applicables aux traités ou à la responsabilité internationale) les États-Unis mettent à mal les normes traditionnelles sans avoir (encore ?) imposé de nouvelles règles. Au contraire, en matière économique, un nouveau droit, et un droit certainement positif, est d'ores et déjà né, sert les intérêts de l'empire et renforce son hégémonisme : l'abandon, dès les années 1970, des règles de Bretton Woods en matière monétaire qui avaient pourtant si formidablement servi les intérêts américains; l'affermissement de la *lex mercatoria*, la généralisation du « nouveau » droit des investissements par la multiplication de conventions bilatérales ultra-libérales, la création de l'O.M.C., en sont les manifestations les plus éclatantes.

Je n'y insisterai pas, sinon pour relever que, même si je pense que les juristes peuvent critiquer ces évolutions et les considérer comme de regrettables dérives, ils ne peuvent, en tant que juristes, que s'en accommoder.

Sur un point au moins (quand même !), je suis d'accord avec Michael Reisman pour penser que « *power is an indispensable component of law* ». J'irai même plus loin : le droit est le résultat de rapports de force. Il est, comme on l'a dit « une politique qui a réussi »[1] ou pour dire cela dans un jargon plus marxisant, une « superstructure » reflétant les tendances, les équilibres (et les déséquilibres) profonds d'une société. Les juristes, par essence, ne peuvent être que conservateurs en ce sens qu'ils doivent prendre acte des nouvelles normes résultant des modifications qui se sont produites dans les rapports de force entre les acteurs politiques. L'effacement politique de l'Europe, la chute de l'empire soviétique, la quasi-disparition (sans doute corrélative) du Tiers Monde de la scène internationale, l'avènement des États-Unis comme la seule super-puissance sont des faits – et des faits qui ne pouvaient pas demeurer sans effet dans la sphère du droit. L'avènement du « droit de la globalisation économique » en est un symptôme particulièrement net.

Au demeurant, même dans ce domaine, il n'y a pas de fin à l'histoire. Et le réveil spectaculaire de la Chine, le sursaut possible du Tiers Monde – dont les conférences de Seattle ou de Cancun constituent peut-être des manifestations – voire de la Russie, portent sans doute en eux les germes d'un changement du droit – ou, ce qui serait plus inquiétant, d'une montée en puissance du non-droit si, comme on peut le penser, ces évolutions conduisent à un blocage des mécanismes d'adaptation des normes juridiques aux besoins de la société internationale dont, pour l'instant, le processus de Doha semble être victime. Dans ce cas, on risque de voir se développer des zones de non-droit, autant dire, la loi de la jungle, impitoyable pour les faibles et les démunis. Pour paraphraser la célèbre formule de Lacordaire, entre le fort et le faible, c'est le droit (aussi imparfait soit-il) qui protège et le non-droit qui accroît les inégalités. L'Afrique, en particulier, pourrait sortir meurtrie et encore plus affaiblie d'une telle situation : au contraire, en fin de

[1] Émile Giraud, "Le droit positif – ses rapports avec la philosophie et la politique", *Hommage d'une génération de juristes au Président Basdevant*, Pedone, Paris, 1960, p. 234.

compte, les États-Unis pourraient s'en féliciter, même si, formellement, leur hégémonisme en serait sans doute amoindri.

De toutes manières, nous n'en sommes pas (encore?) là. Pour l'instant, dans ce domaine économique, la réalité est celle que j'ai décrite ; la globalisation est inscrite dans le droit et elle sert l'impérialisme américain et sans doute, relativement, mais relativement moins, l'intérêt des autres puissances qui ont les moyens de profiter du libéralisme économique. Mais si dans « impérialisme » il y a « empire », ce ne sont pas des concepts tout à fait superposables : l'impérialisme traduit une aspiration à l'empire, il ne signifie pas que le processus a abouti. Et, dans le cas des États-Unis, en 2004, il ne l'est pas : l'hyper-puissance peut envahir un État, menacer tel autre, se jouer des règles de droit, elle ne peut, seule, les modifier. Alors qu'en matière économique une conjoncture très particulière a permis la généralisation des normes d'inspiration ultra-libérale à laquelle elle aspirait (notamment parce que cette aspiration était partagée par ses principaux partenaires et du fait de l'effondrement du socialisme), il en va différemment au plan politique.

Et pour une raison d'abord : les aspirations à la souveraineté des peuples du monde sont, sans doute, plus vivaces que jamais comme en témoignent l'exacerbation des nationalismes de tout poil – sauf peut-être dans la vieille Europe, quoique la construction européenne ait du mal à dépasser le schéma confédéral et que, au sein de l'Union, les soubresauts souverainistes demeurent vigoureux. Du coup, ce qui est accepté au plan économique où le droit a été largement « dé-territorialisé », ne l'est pas aussi facilement dans le domaine, plus sensible, plus conflictuel, des relations plus directement politiques (ou ressenties comme telles).

Une petite parenthèse (qui pourrait être grande d'ailleurs) à ce sujet. Peu de mots sont aussi ambigus que le terme « souveraineté », dont la définition varie d'une école à une autre, d'un auteur à un autre, d'un « homme de la rue » à un autre. Je peux donc, comme tout un chacun, donner la mienne ! Pour moi, il ne s'agit nullement d'un pouvoir absolu et inconditionné, mais seulement de la caractéristique « essentielle » de l'État, celle qui fait qu'il peut exercer toutes les compétences reconnues par le droit international – dans les limites imposées par celui-ci. Dans ce sens le concept me semble respectable et est loin, en tout cas, d'avoir disparu de l'arène juridique internationale. Tous les États y demeurent attachés et c'est au nom de leur « souveraineté » qu'ils résistent aux tentations impériales des États-Unis.

Celles-ci, il faut en avoir conscience, et Michael Reisman l'a d'ailleurs rappelé, ne sont pas nouvelles. Pensez seulement au titre de l'un des plus célèbres ouvrages de Raymond Aron qui, dès 1974, qualifiait les États-Unis de « République impériale ». Les choses se sont d'ailleurs aggravées depuis lors, notamment durant les présidences de Reagan puis de George Bush père, qui ont fait preuve d'un grand activisme (paradoxalement non exempt d'isolationnisme) sur la scène mondiale et ont multiplié les interventions dans les affaires intérieures des autres États. Mais les conditions étaient très différentes de celles du monde actuel :

- au moins s'agissant de l'ère Reagan, l'Union soviétique n'avait pas encore disparu et contre-balançait, même si artificiellement (mais on ne le savait pas encore…) la puissance des États-Unis et au début des années 1990 encore, les décideurs américains n'avaient toujours pas intégré dans leurs évaluations stratégiques la nouvelle et inégalissime distribution du pouvoir à l'échelle du monde ;
- dans les deux cas, les Nations Unies demeuraient un acteur (ou un « réacteur ») influent à l'occasion des crises qui émaillaient les relations internationales :
- de plus, le fameux système des "*checks and balances*" jouait pleinement son rôle aux États-Unis mêmes, ce qui n'est plus le cas depuis le 11 septembre, même si le sursaut des média américains à la suite des révélations sur les tortures en Iraq (moins anodines ou « collatérales » que ne l'a dit Michael Reisman…) peut donner des raisons d'espérer, même si l'on attend toujours une décision de la Cour suprême condamnant le scandale de Guantanamo.

En outre – et peut-être surtout en ce qui nous concerne – les apparences étaient sauves : le droit international était parfois – trop souvent – violé par les États-Unis (pas par eux seuls, mais ils étaient déjà les plus puissants et leurs violations avaient, dès lors, une résonance particulière), mais ils tentaient au moins de s'en justifier. Et, comme on l'a souvent relevé : la violation d'une règle de droit n'est pas le signe qu'elle n'existe pas – au contraire même, en tout cas si elle entraîne des réactions de la part des victimes ou des tiers : et c'était le cas, comme le montre, exemple parmi bien d'autres, l'affaire du *Nicaragua* qui a au moins permis à la Cour internationale de Justice de rendre un arrêt important sur des points de droit fondamentaux (c'est le cas aussi, à un degré moindre, de celle des *Plates-formes pétrolières* : même si l'arrêt date de l'an dernier, l'affaire qui en a été l'occasion remonte à la guerre Iran/Iraq)…
Aujourd'hui, les États et les opinions publiques réagissent encore – mais les choses ont changé à maints égards :

- les États-Unis de George W. Bush manifestent la plus superbe indifférence à l'égard des règles les mieux établies du droit international, à commencer par l'interdiction du recours à la force armée contrairement à la Charte des Nations Unies ; à l'image de l'Empire napoléonien qui, comme la Révolution française dont il était, sur ce point l'héritier, prétendait « délivrer tous les peuples, [ses] frères » pour mieux les asservir, l'Amérique « messianique » de George W. Bush entend s'affranchir de toutes les règles pour imposer sa propre loi – celle de ses intérêts particuliers – au reste du monde ;

- ils ne prennent plus même la peine de se défendre des violations commises : la lutte contre le terrorisme justifie tout ;
- ils bloquent les réformes les plus indispensables (je pense à leur opposition dramatique au Protocole de Kyoto) ; et, surtout peut-être,
- ils modifient les règles du jeu en imposant les normes qui leur paraissent aller dans le sens de leur intérêt, sans aucune considération pour ceux des autres États et, parfois, de leur dignité.

L'exemple le plus frappant de cette attitude est sans doute la conclusion des accords par lesquels les États-Unis ont obtenu (et continuent d'obtenir) de certains États parties au Statut de la C.P.I. que leurs nationaux soient à l'abri de la juridiction de la Cour en violation des engagements conventionnels de leurs partenaires – et ceci pour ne rien dire du concept très faussement nouveau de légitime défense « pré-emptive », lorsque l'on ne peut raisonnablement pas redouter la moindre agression, ou des conditions évidemment contraires au droit international de la détention des prisonniers de Guantanamo. Plus largement, la combinaison de l'« unilatéralisme » et de l'« extra-territorialité » (pour faire court) auxquels la super-puissance recourt systématiquement depuis l'élection de George W. Bush menace évidemment non seulement les règles du droit international héritées de l'après-guerre mais aussi sans doute l'existence même du droit dans les relations internationales. Et il n'est nullement exagéré d'affirmer qu'à maints égards les États-Unis manipulent le droit international de la même manière que les États européens l'ont fait à l'égard des peuples non-européens pour mener à bien l'entreprise coloniale.

Il me semble pourtant que ni le pire, ni l'achèvement de l'empire mondial sous la bannière étoilée, ne sont sûrs: le droit international est menacé : il n'est pas encore complètement détruit; et, à certains égards, il progresse même … sans les États-Unis.

En premier lieu, ceux-ci n'en sont pas encore arrivés à se passer complètement du droit international. Par exemple, alors qu'ils n'avaient ratifié les accords de Marrakech que conditionnellement et menacé de les répudier en cas de condamnations répétées, ils les respectent *grosso modo*, y compris en cas de condamnation par l'Organe de règlement des différends de l'O.M.C. De même, embourbés en Iraq, les États-Unis ont été obligés de réintroduire, tant bien que mal (et plutôt mal et peu que bien et beaucoup) les Nations Unies dans le jeu.

En deuxième lieu, certains progrès du droit international s'accomplissent sans les États-Unis, souvent malgré eux. L'Union européenne s'élargit et s'approfondit cahin-caha : le rôle de la Cour internationale de Justice est plus fourni qu'il ne l'a jamais été : l'Assemblée générale des Nations Unies s'est montrée raisonnablement réceptive au (bon) projet de la C.D.I. sur la responsabilité des États et la C.P.I. se met en place malgré les menaces absurdes qu'ils adressent aux États (faibles) qui les défient en ratifiant le Statut de Rome.

En troisième lieu – et je m'attarderai un peu plus sur ce point – pour dangereuse et irresponsable que soit l'attitude des États-Unis face au droit international, il est essentiel que, nous, les internationalistes du vieux continent, ne nous voilions pas la face et ne nous cantonnions pas dans le rôle bougon de vestales d'un droit international auquel nous pouvons demeurer attachés mais dont il nous faut constater que des pans entiers n'existent plus ou sont, d'ores et déjà, profondément transformés. Et j'irais même plus loin : aussi exaspérante que soit la manière dont les États-Unis revendiquent et exercent leur *leadership*, certaines (certaines seulement) des craintes qu'ils expriment ne sont pas infondées ; et certains (certains seulement) des changements qu'ils ont, d'ores et déjà, maladroitement et « arrogamment » imposés au droit international sont, tout bien pesé, plutôt positifs ou, en tout cas, pourraient le devenir s'ils étaient infléchis dans la bonne direction. J'en prendrai, pour terminer, quatre exemples.

La consécration du concept de *jus cogens* dans la Convention de Vienne de 1969, la création des tribunaux pénaux *ad hoc* puis de la C.P.I., l'inclusion dans le projet d'articles de la C.D.I. sur la responsabilité des États et de la notion de « violations graves d'obligations découlant de normes impératives » et de droits d'action ouverts à des États qui ne sont pas les victimes directes d'un fait internationalement illicite ou même l'action de l'OTAN en faveur de la population kosovar - tout ceci témoigne des préoccupations de plus en plus affirmées de « la communauté internationale [des États?] dans son ensemble » au sujet des violations graves du droit humanitaire. Un premier début de réponse leur a été donné avec l'élargissement par le Conseil de sécurité de la notion de « menace à la paix » en cas de « catastrophes humanitaires ». Mais force est de reconnaître que ce n'est pas suffisant – en tout cas lorsque le Conseil de sécurité est paralysé par le veto ou la menace de son usage. D'un autre côté, l'utilisation unilatérale de la force n'est pas une réponse acceptable et le désastre de plus en plus évident auquel a conduit l'agression américano-britannique en Iraq n'encourage assurément pas à chercher une issue dans cette direction – qui d'ailleurs, sonnerait le glas d'un siècle de progrès du droit international en matière d'interdiction du recours à la force armée et entraînerait, pour reprendre l'expression de Tom Franck, la « seconde mort » de l'article 2, paragraphe 4, de la Charte[2]. En revanche, dans des cas de ce genre, le recours à des mesures collectives ou unilatérales n'impliquant pas l'usage de la force armée pourrait être utilisé plus largement, dans l'esprit d'ailleurs de l'article 54 du projet d'articles de la C.D.I. que j'ai déjà mentionné à plusieurs reprises. Dans cet esprit *et dans ces limites*, l'intervention humanitaire me paraît respectable et défendable.

De même les préoccupations américaines au sujet de la dissémination des armes de destruction massive, que ce soit entre les États ou aux mains d'acteurs non-étatiques (et d'abord, bien sûr, des groupes terroristes) doit être prise au sérieux. Certes, le précédent iraquien (dont il est maintenant établi qu'il a été une « guerre de menteurs ») n'ouvre pas non plus une voie prometteuse à cet égard. Toutefois, les résultats obtenus, par la négociation, avec la Libye et, dans une moindre mesure, l'Iran, ouvrent des perspectives encourageantes. Quant à la toute récente résolution 1540 du Conseil de sécurité, elle témoigne du consensus mondial qui se fortifie sur ce point – mais, au même titre que la résolution 1373 (2001) sur le terrorisme, elle appelle bien des critiques car le Conseil sort de son rôle en se comportant comme un législateur international. En revanche, je suis convaincu qu'il s'acquitterait de sa « responsabilité principale » s'il décidait de mesures au titres de l'article 41, *dans des situations particulières*, lorsque des négociations « à la libyenne » ou « à l'iranienne » ont échoué alors qu'il existe une certitude –pas un mensonge délibéré..., une certitude – qu'un État détient de telles armes et risque d'en faire un mauvais usage.

Plus généralement, la lutte contre le terrorisme est devenue à juste titre une préoccupation majeure pour la société internationale. J'ai déjà dit les réserves que m'inspire la résolution 1373 (2001) du fait de la fonction quasi-législative qu'elle illustre alors que cette fonction n'appartient pas au Conseil de sécurité et que cela court-circuite de manière discutable les

---

[2] See Thomas M. Franck, « Who Killed Article 2 (4)? or: Changing Norms Governing the Use of Force by States », *American Journal of International Law* (*AJIL*) (1970), pp. 809-837 and « What Happens Now? The United Nations After Iraq », *AJIL* 2003, pp. 607-620.

mécanismes de contrôle démocratique des engagements internationaux des États. D'un autre côté, il faut admettre que le terrorisme est, dorénavant, reconnu à juste titre comme constituant une menace contre la paix. Compte tenu de ces considérations contradictoires, il me semble que, « l'un dans l'autre », le précédent de la résolution 1373 ne peut être rejeté catégoriquement même s'il est loin d'être enthousiasmant.

J'ai, je dois dire, les mêmes sentiments mitigés en ce qui concerne l'utilisation de la force armée pour riposter (*ex post*) à une action armée qui n'atteint pas la gravité d'une agression. Dans son arrêt de 1986 dans l'affaire du *Nicaragua*, la C.I.J. a très justement rappelé que la légitime défense ne pouvait être invoquée que face à une agression[3]; mais elle a laissé ouverte la question de savoir si un État avait le droit de riposter à une intervention par une autre intervention, y compris en recourant à la force armée[4]. Le récent arrêt rendu par la Cour dans l'affaire des *Plates-formes pétrolières* n'apporte pas de réponse très ferme à cette question[5], mais, dans son opinion individuelle, le juge Bruno Simma a très clairement répondu par l'affirmative[6]. Je suis loin d'être sur que cela soit évident ; mais je conviens que la question se pose et qu'elle mérite d'être étudiée et débattue sérieusement.

En revanche, s'il y a une chose dont je suis certain, c'est qu'un État, quel qu'il soit, même impérial, ne peut se substituer à la communauté internationale pour décider du bien et du mal. Sans doute, la légitimité du Conseil de sécurité est-elle contestée. Il n'en est pas moins l'émanation de cette communauté toute entière. Au surplus, quoiqu'on en dise, sa composition, même si elle peut (peut-être) être modifiée et améliorée donne des gages au réalisme et n'est pas si inéquitable qu'on le dit : les principales « sensibilités » internationales y sont représentées (y compris, bien sûr, les États-Unis) et y ont un droit de veto, formel et individuel (pour les cinq prétendus « grands ») ou collectif et de fait s'agissant du Tiers Monde. En outre, s'il est paralysé soit par le veto soit, ce qui est plus rare, par l'absence d'une majorité, la résolution 377 (V) (« Union pour le maintien de la paix ») offre une « alternative souple » au chapitre VII : certes, l'Assemblée générale ne peut prendre de décisions, ni imposer des mesures impliquant

---

[3] Arrêt du 27 juin 1986, *Activités militaires et paramilitaires au Nicaragua et contre celui-ci*, *Rec.* 1986, p. 103, par. 195.

[4] *Ibid.*, p. 110, par. 210.

[5] Arrêt du 6 novembre 2003; *Rec.* 2003, pp. 198-199, par. 77.

[6] V. le par. 13 de son opinion individuelle, *ibid.*, p. 333.

une action coercitive[7] : elle n'en peut pas moins, selon les termes de la résolution Dean Acheson, faire aux Membres des Nations Unies « les recommandations appropriées sur les mesures collectives à prendre, y compris, s'il s'agit d'une rupture de la paix ou d'un acte d'agression, l'emploi de la force armée en cas de besoin pour maintenir et rétablir la paix et la sécurité internationales »[8].

En dehors des Nations Unies également, il existe des instruments et des institutions qui peuvent être utilisées à la fois pour prendre en compte et canaliser les préoccupations justifiées des États-Unis et pour s'opposer à leurs *diktat.* L'O.M.C. par exemple, au sein de laquelle aucun État, aussi puissant soit-il ne peut imposer ses vues ni au plan normatif (du fait des règles de vote), ni en ce qui concerne le règlement des différends grâce à l'O.R.D. De même, pour prendre un exemple dans un domaine différent, les États-Unis, mais aussi la Chine et d'autres États imprudents ont ratifié le Pacte des droits civils et politiques de 1966. Mais, c'est bien connu, les traités sont des « pièges à volonté » et le Comité des droits de l'homme pourrait à l'avenir marquer moins de compréhension pour ces États qu'il n'en a manifestée jusqu'à présent – en tout cas à l'occasion de l'examen du rapport américain.

Certes, de tels mécanismes ne résolvent pas tous les problèmes: d'abord il n'en existe pas dans tous les domaines; ensuite, ils ne sont pas toujours efficaces. C'est là, Mesdames et Messieurs, mes chers collègues et amis, qu'intervient non pas seulement le « *European College of Jurists* » auquel Michael Reisman s'est adressé, mais, plus largement « *the invisible college of lawyers* » dans son ensemble – et d'abord nos collègues « impériaux » qui ont une responsabilité particulière à cet égard car, plus que nous, ils peuvent – en étant un peu optimiste… – influencer les « maîtres du monde » et j'espère de tout cœur qu'ils joindront leurs efforts aux nôtres aussi bien pour dénoncer les menaces que l'Empire fait peser sur le droit international et les graves violations qu'il commet que pour réfléchir à des solutions constructives, réalistes, respectueuses des droits et des intérêts des autres nations, lorsque les États-Unis font valoir des préoccupations raisonnables – comme cela leur arrive parfois…

Faute de quoi, l'Empire aura pavé la voie aux « invasions barbares » qu'il prétend endiguer mais que, pour le moment, il ne fait qu'encourager et préparer.

---

[7] Cf. C.I.J., Avis consultatif, 20 Juillet 1962, *Certaines dépenses des Nations Unie*, *Rec.* 1950, p. 164.

[8] Résolution 377 (V) du 3 novembre 1950, par. 1.

INTERNATIONAL LAW IN EUROPE: BETWEEN TRADITIONAL AND RENEWAL

La tradition européenne du droit international

Monique Chemillier-Gendreau[*]

Je me réjouis de participer à l'acte fondateur de cette Société européenne de Droit International et d'avoir à y parler de la tradition européenne de ce droit. Je ne vais pas me livrer ici à une simple synthèse de ce qui avait été élaboré jusqu'à nous. Il faut à mes yeux, à la fois prendre une distance critique à l'égard de cette tradition et imaginer aussi ce qu'elle recèle comme possibilités d'avenir. La réflexion sur le terme même de tradition valide cette option car la tradition est l'acte de transmettre et elle est liée à l'enseignement. Mais ce n'est pas seulement un mécanisme pédagogique. La tradition ne se réduit pas à la conservation et à la transmission de quelque chose de préalablement élaboré. Elle intègre au cours de l'histoire des éléments nouveaux en les adaptant à d'autres qui sont anciens. C'est une démarche dialectique et ontologique. La tradition fait être de nouveau ce qui a été, mais elle agit sur l'héritage qu'elle transmet.

On se donnera ici la facilité de faire naître cette "tradition" dans l'Europe de la Renaissance, celle qui, en affinant l'indépendance des Princes, dégage l'espace d'une société internationale à la recherche de son droit. Mais ce serait renier le mot même de tradition que de croire qu'il y eut alors apparition du droit international. L'héritage était déjà là avec la pensée gréco-romaine, l'apport considérable de la scolastique, puis la construction de l'idée de souveraineté au cours de la deuxième partie du Moyen Âge. Toutefois, c'est l'accumulation d'idées, de concepts, de réalités sociales dégagées des relations entre communautés politiques depuis le XVè siècle qui forment le noyau essentiel de cette tradition.

Elle ne présente aucune homogénéité à aucune période. Y concourent des tendances diverses, les unes centrales, les autres latérales. Jusnaturalisme, positivisme et sa branche normativiste, objectivisme, volontarisme, réalisme, plus tard marxisme, structuralisme se mêlent parfois jusque dans la pensée d'un même auteur. S'il n'y a jamais homogénéité, en

[*] Professeur émérite à l'Université Paris VII-Denis Diderot.

Baltic Yearbook of International Law, Volume 6, 2006, pp. 37–48.

revanche, dans la dernière période, le positivisme s'est affirmé comme le courant dominant et c'est sur ce point que, personnellement, j'entends exercer une distance critique. Larguant le droit naturel pour s'affirmer comme seule doctrine du droit international, le positivisme en se déployant de manière formelle a appauvri la science du droit en dépit des efforts de courants de pensée minoritaires féconds mais sans influence concrète. Cette évolution s'est affirmée au XIXè siècle alors que l'Europe étendait son pouvoir politique sur le monde entier par le truchement des administrations coloniales que les États européens établissaient sur tous les continents. La pensée européenne du droit international se veut alors une pensée pour le monde. Elle sera essentiellement une pensée de la domination, étouffant les courants « exotiques », ignorant des pensées de longue profondeur historique et de tradition savante comme la pensée arabe ou les pensées extrême-orientales.

La science du droit et la pratique sociale désignée sous le terme de droit sont indissociables. Mais l'évolution mentionnée a amené un certain isolement de la science juridique dans l'espace académique et à bonne distance du réel car le positivisme a conduit à une perte du lien dialectique entre la théorie et l'action. Sans doute, bien des courants minoritaires se sont souciés de se fonder sur la pratique, la pratique sociale des hommes, pour construire une théorie juridique et non de construire celle-ci dans l'abstrait pour l'imposer ensuite aux sociétés humaines. Mais cela n'a pas été la tendance dominante, laquelle a cultivé les fictions de manière abusive.

Or la fonction du droit est d'énoncer ce que doivent être les rapports entre les êtres, qu'il s'agisse des individus ou des êtres sociaux, de manière à éviter que ces rapports ne soient réglés par la seule violence. Comment ne pas rappeler, nous trouvant à Florence, la remarque de Machiavel : « *Toujours, d'aussi loin que je me souvienne, ou bien on a fait la guerre ou bien on en a parlé* ». Pour ne pas que les hommes la fassent, le droit doit en parler utilement. Or, l'Europe est au cœur d'un étrange paradoxe. Elle a réussi le pari de se doter de la paix pour elle-même en dépassant par l'intégration la tradition européenne de l'État souverain et les affrontements entre États alors inévitables. Mais cela s'est fait de manière pragmatique en dehors de la théorie du droit international général. De la même manière, l'Europe a fait entrer l'individu dans la catégorie des sujets du droit international en lui ouvrant un recours contre les États. Et elle a bâti un ordre juridique européen en fixant la hiérarchie des normes entre elles. Mais cela n'a pas été le fait d'une application de la théorie du droit international et la tradition européenne de ce droit n'a pas légué pour le moment à la société mondiale des moyens efficaces de garantir la paix. C'est que la pensée du droit qui a émergé de l'ensemble européen est restée celle d'une société interétatique basée sur la souveraineté de chacun et sur le volontarisme, donc nécessairement le relativisme du droit la régissant. Et c'est bien pour le moment cette pensée-là qui entrave le mouvement européen.

À l'échelle universelle, les perspectives de maîtrise de la guerre par le droit étaient dans ce contexte très limitées. Elles l'étaient d'autant plus que bien des communautés humaines n'étaient pas des États et ne le sont pas devenues même si on leur en a prêté le nom. Ces sociétés sont le lieu d'extrêmes violences. Parallèlement, la société mondialisée par relations directes, transnationales entre individus et groupes a fait son chemin accompagnée d'un droit sommaire lorsque ce n'est pas sans aucun droit. Pourtant la pensée des origines prenait en compte les deux aspects de la communauté mondiale, en recherchant à la fois un *jus gentium* et un *jus inter gentes*. Elle a ensuite été réduite à la prise en compte des seules relations entre les États[1]. Mais le dualisme de la société mondiale persiste aujourd'hui en même temps que l'insuffisance de son droit. Comment nier devant la situation planétaire actuelle l'échec du droit international? Savonarole, pour rester à Florence et dans l'Europe de la Renaissance, disait du haut de la chaire de l'église San Marco en 1494 qu'il fallait tenir compte des « *mutationi e diversita dei tempi* » et en fonction de ces changements et de la diversité des temps, ne pas hésiter à changer les lois et les formes de la vie en commun. L'évolution considérable des formations socio-économiques et culturelles depuis la seconde guerre mondiale engendre un basculement du monde entraînant d'extrêmes dangers. Le droit international se doit d'y répondre. Mais l'Europe a innové pour elle (et il faudrait soumettre ces innovations à une pensée critique) et non pas pour le monde. Nous devons nous interroger sur ce phénomène. Je vais l'examiner ici à travers la tradition doctrinale et son ambition d'élaborer une science du droit et ensuite à travers les principaux concepts produits par la doctrine dominante.

I La construction européenne de la science du droit et l'élimination de la question du fondement.

L'Europe qui entre dans la modernité au XVè siècle, le fait à travers l'amorce d'un processus de sécularisation. Il est en germe dans l'indépendance conquise par les princes sur l'Empereur, mais surtout sur le Pape. Et si l'on accorde autant d'importance à l'œuvre de Grotius, c'est parce qu'il prend acte du fait que des communautés politiques que l'on

---

[1] Voir Emmanuelle Jouanet, « *L'idée de communauté humaine* » *in* Archives de philosophie du droit, Tome 47 (2003) pages 191 sq.

nomme alors entités étatiques, passent d'une subordination désormais révolue à la double figure du pouvoir impérial et papal, à une coordination entre elles qui va se constituer comme droit. Cette coordination, Grotius cherche à en établir les règles indépendamment de la foi, même s'il ne liquide pas encore toute trace de droit divin. À l'universalisme chrétien, nécessairement fondé sur la domination puisqu'il s'agit d'imposer une croyance subjective à un monde qui ne la partage pas et de l'imposer par la guerre juste, répond alors dans les pointillés du possible un nouvel universalisme fondé sur la seule appartenance à l'humanité comme espèce biologique douée de conscience. Mais cette humanité déjà perçue comme réalité globale, n'a pas de réalité politique. Cette dernière est dans le pluralisme des États et l'opposition parfois violente entre eux. Bien avant le XVIIè siècle et avant Grotius, les théologiens espagnols de la deuxième scolastique confrontés à l'idée de communauté mondiale comme expression du pouvoir de l'Empire chrétien, n'avaient pas eu d'autre réponse que celle d'une société d'États. Ainsi la communauté mondiale n'est prise en compte qu'à travers les entités qui la gouvernent fragmentairement. Cet écran nécessaire et contingent va confisquer la pensée de l'universel à son profit et laissera l'universalisme réel qui ne cessera pourtant de produire des relations sociales accélérées pendant des siècles, sans droit pour l'encadrer.

Selon Grotius le droit se divise en deux branches, le droit naturel et le droit volontaire. Les obligations qui découlent de ce droit naturel procèdent d'un rapport inhérent aux êtres et non d'un acte fut-il divin. C'est alors qu'entre en scène la raison, puisque c'est elle qui va permettre aux humains qui en sont doués, de découvrir ces rapports « naturels ». C'est là l'expression d'une pensée idéaliste peu propice à rendre compte des réalités humaines et sociales. Plutôt que de permettre un accès direct aux lois naturelles, il semble plus modestement que la raison humaine conduise à la « *disputatio* », cet exercice si cher aux juristes qui permet de débattre et de trancher sur des intérêts contradictoires perçus subjectivement. La raison est la clef d'accès toute relative à une certaine forme d'objectivité. Rien que cela. Quoiqu'il en soit des capacités de la raison dans ce domaine, le droit international des origines combine le volontarisme par lequel les États se donnent à eux-mêmes les contraintes que l'on nommera droit et la référence à la nature comme une source d'obligations s'imposant à eux. Que les individus, membres de l'espèce humaine appartiennent à la nature, on ne peut en disconvenir. Je ne vois pour autant aucun argument permettant d'assurer que les rapports entre eux seraient à déduire de la nature et non de la conscience ou de la volonté. Le message de la nature sur nous-mêmes est souvent illisible et le surnaturel n'est jamais bien loin de l'évocation de la nature. Mais dès lors qu'il s'agit d'êtres sociaux, dont le surgissement provient d'une évolution des sociétés, il est assuré que les règles régissant les rapports entre eux ne peuvent pas davantage être découverts dans la nature qu'ils n'en proviennent eux-mêmes. Se référer au droit « naturel » que l'on découvrirait par la raison pour indiquer le fondement d'un droit s'imposant aux États, c'est présupposer que les États seraient un phénomène naturel, ce qu'ils ne sont pas. Est-il naturel que les humains se regroupent en communautés politiques qui prendraient nécessairement cette forme-là et seraient nécessairement souveraines? Rien n'est moins sûr. Quant à savoir si les États, dans leur détermination historique sont des phénomènes naturels, la réponse est claire. Nés dans la contingence, objets de découpages et redécoupages incessants, les États souverains, répartition hasardeuse et temporaire des peuples sous un même gouvernement, n'ont rien d'une donnée naturelle. Ils ne le sont pas davantage que l'État cosmopolitique universel dessiné par Kant plus tard alors qu'il y voyait pourtant un dessein de la nature.

L'évolution à travers laquelle se construit la tradition, conduit les auteurs à privilégier l'un ou l'autre fondement. La transition avec le positivisme moderne dans ses formes radicales, se fait par des courants qui, combinant dans le sillage de Grotius droit naturel et droit volontaire, accordent une importance grandissante aux règles découlant des usages ou admises par les traités. Dans le cours du XVIIIè siècle, Bynkershoek, Mably ou de Martens, sans éliminer totalement le droit naturel, donnent la prépondérance au droit découlant des traités et en font le fondement principal du droit international[2].

On a prêté à Vattel la responsabilité d'un ancrage plus radical du droit international dans le positivisme. Il aurait privilégié la volonté de l'État en soutenant que les États étaient détenteurs de droits subjectifs absolus. Sans entrer ici dans le débat sur la paternité du positivisme internationaliste, il suffit de constater l'accent mis peu à peu de manière dominante sur le consentement de l'État, entité donnée pour souveraine, comme unique fondement du droit international. Cette évolution-là est à n'en pas douter au cœur de la tradition européenne. Armés de la souveraineté et des fonctions régaliennes de l'époque classique, les États pouvaient donc se faire la guerre jusqu'à se dévorer entre eux et l'on ne compte plus les disparitions et résurgences d'États. Et si le droit naturel a résisté comme source éventuelle des droits individuels, il s'est évanoui comme base des relations entre États au profit du positivisme se contentant de prendre acte des entités existantes et de donner pour normes valides entre eux le produit de leur consentement.

---

[2] Dionisio Anzilotti. *Cours de droit international*. 1929. Paris. L.G.D.J. 1999.

Mais en l'absence d'un fondement naturel introuvable, le consentement ferait-il l'affaire et suffirait-il à affirmer l'existence d'un droit commun aux États? L'idée a semblé être que les États par les traités ou les usages, constituaient une sorte de volonté collective créatrice des normes s'imposant à eux et pouvant contrer leurs volontés individuelles. Roberto Ago dans son cours à Paris en 1958 a pointé l'impossibilité à tenir sur cette logique. Le triomphe des volontés particulières est un obstacle à toute formation d'un droit international. Si celui-ci procède de la volonté, cela doit être d'une volonté collective qui transcenderait les vouloirs individualisés. Mais comme il n'y a pas d'être supérieur aux États, la souveraineté étant la norme centrale, on est dans une volonté collective indéterminée, c'est-à-dire sans être qui veuille, du moins tant que l'on s'en tient au formalisme organique, à ce qu'Ago nomme le préjugé étatiste[3].

Le volontarisme étatique approché de la sorte n'avait pas d'autre issue que le relativisme. La liberté des États fait obstacle à leur soumission à une règle supérieure universellement commune qui ne pourrait provenir que d'une volonté collective distanciée, fruit d'une communauté politique universelle, horizon à peine ébauché. Dans le droit international élaboré sous cette pensée, il n'y a que les règles confirmées par des volontés rapprochées et ce rapport direct enregistre et amplifie les inégalités. Il ne permet plus de différencier le droit d'un champ de bataille. L'échec du *jus cogens* en droit positif et les réticences des positivistes à l'égard de cette notion témoignent de leur inéluctable retranchement dans le relativisme. De la sorte et alors que l'universalisme économique, social, culturel progressait fortement depuis le XIXè siècle, l'universalisme juridique a été paralysé. Engagée dans cette voie, la doctrine dominante a posé comme postulat de libérer la sphère du droit de tout élément explicatif qui lui serait extérieur, de s'arrêter à la norme hypothétique et finalement d'évacuer l'explication de la norme. Celle-ci est une donnée de l'organisation sociale et cela doit suffire. Les notions formelles et procédurales envahiront le champ du droit en toute exclusivité. La démarche est liée à celle qui est menée en droit constitutionnel européen. L'État est supposé par sa seule existence garantir les libertés individuelles de ceux qui le composent sans avoir à produire le lien unifiant qui précède cette liberté. On en arrive ainsi à laisser la question des fondements à l'extérieur de la sphère du droit. Certains résistent à cette approche comme Bockenförde qui, reprenant Wilhem Henke, affirme : « *Le fondement du*

[3] Roberto Ago, « *Le problème du fondement du droit international* », Cours à l'Institut des Hautes Études Internationales. Paris. 1958.1959.

droit fait aussi partie du droit »[4]. Et il reprend l'idée du chaînon manquant entre normativité et facticité.

Le positivisme a ainsi ouvert la voie à diverses conséquences dont la principale est l'inévitable dérive vers le formalisme. Peu importe que l'État soit fantoche, qu'il n'ait aucun des attributs réels de l'indépendance, les insignes suffiront. Et l'on plaquera la fiction d'une volonté sur un corps social sans conscience de soi comme cela est le cas de bien des États déstructurés qui se trouvent cependant sur la liste des membres de l'Organisation des Nations Unies. Ne suffit-il pas que l'on soit convaincu d'être en présence de ce que Simone Goyard Fabre nomme « *l'épure rationnelle de l'État* »[5]? Une autre conséquence de l'évacuation de la question du fondement, c'est l'arrivée en force de l'effectivité et le brouillage de la ligne qui doit séparer le droit du fait. Que la tension dialectique entre ces deux éléments de la réalité sociale soit inévitable, nul ne peut en disconvenir. Mais si l'on ne garde pas les éléments d'une différenciation suffisante, cela signifie que le processus juridique comme processus d'obligations disparaît recouvert par de nouvelles effectivités.

Mais la tradition n'est pas homogène. Il est vrai que si le positivisme est devenu le courant principal, d'autres approches n'ont pas manqué. Je ne peux que mentionner l'objectivisme dominé par la grande figure de Georges Scelle, le réalisme de Quadri ou Jenks, la méthode dialectique remise à l'honneur par Charles Chaumont et qui est à mes yeux la piste la plus éclairante pour résoudre la question des fondements du caractère obligatoire de la norme. Mais je dois rendre compte ici de la tradition et non imposer mes propres conclusions sur la meilleure manière d'analyser le droit international. Je dirai donc seulement que l'évacuation de la question du fondement a été et est encore une carence considérable. Je montrerai dans les points suivants à quelles conséquences négatives cela peut mener. Disons pour conclure sur la méthode, que la norme pour être distinguée du fait, ne peut se passer d'une référence, la référence à laquelle les énoncés prétendument normatifs seront rapportés pour être confirmés comme normatifs. Le droit international a besoin d'une référence à son échelle, c'est-à-dire valable pour tous les peuples. Pour être universelle, cette référence ne peut pas être extra-sociétale. Ni Dieu, ni la nature, souvent indéchiffrable, ne peuvent livrer un message universel. La référence doit être

---

[4] Ernst Wolfgang Böckenförd. Le droit, l'État et la constitution démocratique. Bruylant. L.G.D.J. Paris. 2000. Page 206.

[5] Simone Goyard -Fabre. « L'État, figure moderne de la politique ». Paris. Armand Colin. 1999. Page 171.

intra-sociétale et ne peut pas être trouvée dans les volontés soi-disant concordantes des États, organes formels. Les volontés collectives restent importantes, mais elles ne se réduisent pas, et de moins en moins, à celles des États. C'est dans le rapport contradictoire entre les volontés étatiques mises en tension elles-mêmes avec les volontés des peuples et des individus qui en sont l'infrastructure humaine et qui sont eux-mêmes divers jusqu'au conflit, que se dégage peu à peu un sentiment universel d'obligation. Celui-ci entre en interaction avec d'autres données sociales pour fonder les règles du droit international.

II La crise des concepts comme résultat des insuffisances de la méthode.

Quelques exemples montreront comment des bouleversements considérables ont échappé à l'emprise du droit international tel qu'il s'était construit et ont ouvert le danger d'une société sans droit.

Lorsque Hobbes prône l'État pour sauver les individus de leur sauvagerie naturelle par un Pacte entre eux, il soutient que les rapports entre États, bien que placés sous le signe de la guerre, n'engendrent pas le même malheur que celui provenant de la liberté sauvage des individus. L'histoire a démenti le philosophe. Guerres interétatiques et internes se mêlent désormais dans une barbarie inouïe. Dans la notion d'État souverain, tout est en crise, la souveraineté et l'État qui ne correspondent plus aux sociétés différenciées très inégales de notre monde. La souveraineté qui était le bouclier d'un peuple garantissant son indépendance à travers des fonctions régaliennes et représentant la conscience que ce peuple avait de son unité, est désormais plus souvent à l'origine d'immenses souffrances des peuples que de leur liberté. C'est la souveraineté des puissances coloniales qui a permis l'oppression des colonisés, c'est celle des souverains gagnés par la tentation dictatoriale qui a exposé des peuples comme ceux de l'Amérique latine ou de certaines parties de l'Afrique à des crimes de masse, c'est la souveraineté des États-Unis qui leur permet de refuser tout regard sur Guantanamo ou les prisons irakiennes, comme la souveraineté d'Israël le met à l'abri des contrôles sur ses méthodes avec le peuple palestinien. C'est la souveraineté des pays européens qui leur permet de réduire le droit d'asile à presque rien et celle de la France d'interdire les contrôles sur ses centres de rétention pour étrangers. Ainsi se constitue un immense rebut humain, que le philosophe italien Giorgio Agamben désigne sous l'expression *homo sacer*[6], ces humains qui ne sont plus rien, ombres peuplant les camps, les bidonvilles,

[6] Giorgio Agamben. « *Homo sacer. Le pouvoir souverain ou la vie nue* ». Paris. Seuil. 1997.

les zones dévastées. La souveraineté est devenue dans bien des circonstances lorsqu'elle exprime l'existence de ces hordes faméliques un attribut grotesque et non plus glorieux et libérateur. Mais la souveraineté était la notion consubstantielle de l'État. À la question : qu'est-ce qu'un État ? le droit international répond : une entité souveraine. Mais comment sait-on qu'une entité est devenue souveraine ? On ne le sait pas. La Palestine est souveraine pour les uns et non pour les autres, comme le peuple sahraoui. Le Tibet ou la Tchéchénie restent des fractures sans réponses autres que répressives.

La tentation est forte de prétendre à un substrat « naturel » de l'État à travers la Nation. Mais celle-ci, expression collective des « natifs » ferme la communauté politique au lieu de l'ouvrir. Cela donne de nouvelles violences comme celles des Balkans ou celle engendrée par l'ivoirité en Côte d'Ivoire. La norme de l'égale souveraineté des États ne produit plus de pacification par le droit, dès lors que celui-ci ne sait pas résoudre l'identification d'un État lorsque c'est cette question qui est l'enjeu du conflit. Ainsi avant la question : comment régler par le droit international les risques de guerres entre États, faut-il se demander comment on identifie les États.

Le concept de guerre est lui-même obscurci et brouillé notamment par le terrorisme. L'on sait que pour Grotius cette question devait être résolue par les principes relatifs à la guerre juste. L'embryon d'un droit international supérieur aux États est bien là, dans ce butoir à leur droit régalien de faire la guerre, ce dernier ne devant être employé que pour parer à la violation d'un droit. Et la grande différence entre le droit international de la première époque et celui de la seconde dominée par le positivisme est dans le renoncement à un critère élaboré de la guerre juste. La conception prévalante de la souveraineté à partir du XIXè siècle n'a plus permis de contester la guerre qui devient licite par le postulat qu'elle serait un acte d'auto-défense ou un moyen d'extension de la civilisation. Ainsi disparaît la limite de la guerre juste et au début du XXè siècle, une guerre d'agression n'est pas contraire au droit international. Les Nations Unies n'interviendront dans ce contexte que par des modalités procédurales, mais sans progrès sur le fond. La légitime défense reste autorisée et sans contrôle véritable de son usage, en sorte que l'on voit apparaître la notion de légitime défense préventive. L'autre modalité de la guerre autorisée est celle qui est décidée par le Conseil de sécurité comme utilisation de la sécurité collective. Mais le Conseil détient la maîtrise des qualificationset l'appréciation du caractère juste d'une guerre est ainsi entre les mains des cinq grandes puissances qui en décident à leur gré ou renoncent à en décider. L'agression est interdite par les articles 2, par. 4 et 39 de la Charte. Mais elle l'est sans définition préalable. Il n'y a pas de péché avant la loi disait Spinoza. Aussi a-t-on adopté, non sans une longue gestation, la définition de l'agression en 1974. Mais, les catégories juridiques produites par des décennies de doctrine positiviste de la souveraineté l'empêchent de porter ses fruits. L'égale souveraineté a engendré de plus en plus d'inégalités et l'agression d'une grande puissance n'a soulevé qu'une faible protestation chez les juristes et des réprobations bien molles de la part des autres États sourds à ce que disaient leurs peuples. Anticipant le veto (produit de l'inégalité institutionnelle entre les souverainetés), ils ont fait l'économie d'une tentative d'application de la Charte et de la définition de l'agression à la guerre en Irak. On avait cru combler le vide de la loi et le péché a continué. La tradition n'ayant pas favorisé la poursuite de la réflexion sur les limites posées à la guerre, la notion d'agression connaît une difficile implantation, non seulement dans les rapports interétatiques, mais aussi dans le règlement pénal des crimes internationaux, puisqu'il a été jugé utile à propos du Statut de la Cour Pénale Internationale de reprendre la question de la définition.

La quasi-disparition du débat sur la guerre juste à partir du XIXè siècle a ouvert la porte par une sorte d'effet compensateur à la nécessité du *jus in bello*. Mais, comme les événements les plus récents et les plus dramatiques nous le montrent, les catégories juridiques et l'interétatisme dominant y font obstacle. Dès les premières réflexions sur la guerre, à l'entrée dans les Temps Modernes, il n'a été question de limites aux moyens de la guerre qu'entre entités politiques autonomes. Les brigands et les pirates ne sont pas dignes d'être traités en ennemis. Les hôtes du camp de Guatanamo ou de la prison d'Abou Ghraib en savent quelque chose. Et l'histoire des Protocoles de 1977 qui ont tenté d'introduire un statut de la guérilla en est l'illustration. La règle d'humanité que l'on croyait universelle bute sur la volonté des États. L'on se réjouissait de la quasi universalité des adhésions aux Conventions de Genève de 1949. Mais il y manquait un mécanisme de contrôle. Celui-ci, la Commission d'établissement des faits, introduit dans les Protocoles de 1977, est la cause de bien des refus d'adhésions et est restée pour le moment une institution au placard. La prohibition de certaines armes n'est pas mieux encadrée juridiquement. La doctrine de la dissuasion nucléaire imposée dans l'exercice de leur souveraineté par les grandes puissances a pesé lourd dans l'avis rendu par la Cour internationale sur la licéité de l'arme nucléaire (1996).

Enfin, le droit de résistance, nécessaire contrepoids de tout pouvoir, n'avait pas sa place dans la théorie classique de la souveraineté. Admis par les partisans du droit naturel comme un droit du peuple si ceux qui sont chargés du gouvernement trahissent la communauté, ce droit était surtout à usage interne. Grotius, cependant, admettait qu'un peuple formant lui-même un État autarcique puisse résister au souverain qui l'exploite. Puis il y eut une longue parenthèse et l'on a pu penser sous les Nations Unies que le droit de la décolonisation et le contenu de la résolution 2625 confirmaient un droit de résistance défini et encadré au profit des peuples en lutte contre les différentes formes d'oppression. Mais la décolonisation achevée, la page du droit de résistance s'est refermée et l'intervention humanitaire n'en remplit pas la fonction. Ce droit a disparu au profit des peuples en lutte dont le combat est partout qualifié de terrorisme et disqualifié comme tel, ce qui amplifie la dérive vers des actions aveugles. Ainsi les droits de l'homme et des peuples, comme version actuelle d'un universalisme souple, sont-ils revus, corrigés et limités par l'interétatisme qui reste le présupposé indépassé de la pensée du droit international. L'humain qui ne détient pas ses droits d'un État, ou le peuple non reconnu, sont rejetés des catégories juridiques comme le déplorait Hannah Arendt il y a plusieurs décennies et comme le fait aujourd'hui Agamben.

Autre effet pervers: les présupposés de base du droit international fondés sur l'interétatisme, ne permettent pas de construire les outils juridiques d'un droit mondial adapté à la société complexe et bouleversée qui est la notre. Si l'ordre juridique naît de mécanismes de justiciabilité assortis d'une articulation entre les normes qui permettent de trancher en cas de contradictions entre celles-ci et d'attribuer tout manquement à son auteur par des mécanismes de responsabilité, alors l'ordre juridique est absent de la société internationale. Et l'on se perd dans les marécages du droit mou, impropre à ordonner les comportements. L'expression « *ordre juridique international* » n'apparaît pas d'ailleurs dans la littérature avant le milieu du XXè siècle. La cause en est bien la réalité de droit positif de la souveraineté comme norme centrale et de ses conséquences et la pensée du droit qui en éliminant la question des fondements a permis une coupure radicale entre la norme et la réalité sociale. La souveraineté est une entrave aux progrès de la justice internationale et par conséquent aux mécanismes de mise en œuvre de la responsabilité internationale. Qu'un justiciable puisse se soustraire à la compétence de la justice est le fait d'une société inachevée qui permet donc que des manquements soient impunis. C'est bien ce à quoi nous assistons. Et les progrès escomptés d'une justice pénale internationale sont entravés de ce fait. Les positivistes, partisans de la souveraineté, peuvent-ils s'en réjouir? Restent-ils avec Anzilotti sur l'idée que la responsabilité internationale n'est que la réparation (éventuelle) d'un acte illicite, qu'elle doit donc être coupée de la notion de faute et ne résulter que de l'étroite mesure entre le comportement de l'État et le contenu de l'obligation à laquelle il avait souscrit ? Sans doute l'idée de faute progresse-t-elle, mais à échéance lointaine dans le droit positif.

L'outil nous fait défaut pour avancer vers un autre monde, ce monde qui pointe à travers les annonces d'une conscience commune qui serait l'embryon d'une communauté politique globale. Les dangers communs obligent à presser le pas. Le faire par les institutions serait long et dangereux. Le faire par un droit commun est davantage à notre portée. Mais devant l'ouverture irréversible des sociétés, il nous faut des règles universelles et indérogeables garantissant un bien commun à l'échelle du monde. L'espace en est dessiné avec la coutume et le droit impératif général. Seule une justice obligatoire, convaincue d'avoir à appliquer des normes au-dessus de la volonté des États, peut leur donner corps.

L'humanité ne peut être protégée soit contre les crimes qui la menacent, soit par la mise à l'écart du marché des biens comme l'eau ou les connaissances qui sont la condition de sa survie, que si le droit international sort d'un schéma uniquement contractualiste. Si les crimes contre l'humanité sont punis au gré de l'acquiescement des États, le droit pénal international rate son objectif. Si le patrimoine commun de l'humanité est protégé par certains États et non par tous, il n'est plus le Patrimoine de l'Humanité. Si le terrorisme est combattu lorsqu'il est le fait des individus et non lorsqu'il est celui des États, la communauté mondiale n'a pas d'avenir. Il nous faut un droit au-dessus du contrat.

La tradition européenne, longtemps féconde, l'a été remarquablement dans la dernière période pour le droit européen lui-même, sans toutefois les renouvellements théoriques attendus. Et le droit international général reste figé sous l'effet du positivisme. Il est urgent d'être à nouveau inventif, par les méthodes et par les concepts. Le droit international ne peut plus, sauf à maintenir le désordre et à s'affirmer comme un droit de la domination, être seulement celui des États souverains profondément inégaux que nous avons sous les yeux. Il ne peut pas non plus être un droit entièrement mondialisé dont Kant disait que c'était la question la plus difficile qui serait résolue en dernier par l'espèce humaine. Seule une nouvelle percée dialectique permettra au droit d'exprimer les contradictions particulièrement complexes de notre temps et de prendre en compte tous les particularismes en les confrontant les uns aux autres après avoir renoncé à ce que l'universalisme soit l'hégémonie de l'une des particularités qui coexistent et fondent, toutes ensemble, l'humanité.

EUROPE'S PAST AND INTERNATIONAL LAW

Colonialisme européen et néo-colonialisme contemporain

(Notes de lecture des manuels européens du droit des gens entre 1850 et 1914)

Emmanuelle Jouannet[*]

Il y a aujourd'hui plusieurs manifestations de ce que l'on pourrait appeler un phénomène de néo-colonialisme contemporain mais c'est surtout l'une de ses formes spécifiques qui retient ici notre attention car elle est particulièrement délicate à gérer au sein du système juridique international actuel et interpelle directement, nous semble-t-il, notre héritage européen. Il s'agit de l'attitude de certains Etats qui sont aujourd'hui tentés d'imposer aux autres un système de valeurs et de droits qui leur semblent plus justes et qui *grosso modo* s'articule autour des notions de démocratie et de droits de l'homme. Certes il ne s'agit pas de colonisation au sens strict du terme, car il n'y a pas de phénomène direct d'extension de la souveraineté, mais il s'agit d'une de ces formes latentes dans la mesure où l'on assiste à la volonté de domination et d'imposition – au besoin par la force – d'un système juridique sur un sol étranger[1]. On ne peut également ignorer que les valeurs juridiques revendiquées – et quels que soient les motifs sous-jacents qui peuvent les accompagner – sont toutefois suffisamment décisives et fondamentales pour que la prétention à les imposer demande une réflexion plus approfondie qu'une simple condamnation sans appel ou la dénonciation d'une violence de domination. Et c'est à ce titre qu'il est sans aucun doute particulièrement intéressant de revenir sur notre passé d'européen pour contribuer à éclairer les enjeux contemporains de cette question.

---

[*] Professeur à l'Université Paris I (*Panthéon-Sorbonne*).

[1] Pour la définition *juridique* du colonialisme et du néo-colonialisme, v. *Dictionnaire de droit international*, J. SALMON (dir.), Bruxelles, Bruylant, 2001, pp. 193-194. Pour une définition plus large, v. E. LE ROY, « Colonies », *Dictionnaire de la culture juridique*, S. RIALS et D. ALLAND (dir.), Paris, PUF, 2003, p. 231.

Baltic Yearbook of International Law, Volume 6, 2006, pp. 49–77.

Nul n'ignore que les phénomènes de colonisation ne sont pas une invention récente et remontent loin dans notre histoire[2]. Mais si chaque colonialisme a sa propre histoire et s'enracine dans un univers intellectuel particulier qui l'a conditionné, il est peut-être, pour nous, plus riche d'enseignements de réévaluer les ressorts profonds de la dernière grande vague d'expansion coloniale européenne qui a eu lieu au cours du 19ème siècle et jusqu'au milieu du 20ème siècle. Elle s'est en effet établie et déployée dans un cadre juridique intellectuel qui, en dépit de la décolonisation et des grands mouvements de pensée qui l'ont accompagnée, a peut-être encore des prolongements dans la pensée juridique internationaliste contemporaine. Autrement dit la question que nous nous sommes posé est de savoir si certaines nouvelles formes du néo-colonialisme contemporain ne s'inscrivent pas encore, inconsciemment ou non, dans des structures et des fondements théoriques qui étaient déjà clairement présents au 19ème siècle dans la pensée internationaliste occidentale, principalement européenne. Et pour aider partiellement à répondre à cette interrogation, on se propose de procéder à une analyse de la structure de la pensée internationaliste de cette époque. On s'est efforcé de repérer, dans le discours doctrinal des internationalistes, les différents fondements et justifications théoriques, historiques et juridiques, qui y sont présents, de façon explicite ou non, en faveur du colonialisme européen, en se demandant – en écho à notre propre interrogation contemporaine et à notre propre statut d'internationaliste – pourquoi et comment les juristes ont admis l'idée d'un devoir à coloniser –civiliser – l'autre partie du monde ? Quel déplacement ou quel ressort a pu se produire au sein de la pensée internationaliste classique pour justifier, légitimer et accompagner sa volonté de projection au sein de l'ensemble du monde et sa traduction concrète comme appropriation et exploitation d'une partie de la planète ?

L'hypothèse de départ de cette étude, qui n'est pas en soi très surprenante, est donc qu'il existe un fond commun de pensée du discours européen – voire euro-américain – de cette période, qu'il est justement nécessaire de mettre en exergue afin de montrer en quoi s'enracine de façon cardinale et ultime la pensée internationaliste classique du colonialisme[3]. Il est vrai qu'une telle analyse peut paraître profondément réductrice en ce

---

[2] Selon E. LE ROY, « Colonies », *op.cit*, c'est sans doute un phénomène universel et perpétuel.

[3] Il ne s'agit pas pour autant de rechercher une structure de la pensée ou du langage suivant la méthode structuraliste mais de montrer seulement un contenu commun de pensée qui fonde la représentation du droit des gens de cette période.

qu'elle homogénéiserait à tort plusieurs courants spécifiques défendus par des auteurs venant de pays et de traditions juridiques, philosophiques et politiques différentes. Mais si l'on est conscient de ce possible écueil, il ne nous a pas semblé suffisamment décisif pour abandonner cette recherche car il ne s'agit pas de nier une évidente diversité de traditions doctrinales mais simplement de faire ressortir ce qu'elles ont justement en commun et d'insister sur ce qui les rassemble plutôt que sur ce qui les divise. On ne prétend donc pas gommer leurs spécificités mais les laisser provisoirement de côté pour mieux faire ressortir leur structure juridique et intellectuelle fondamentale commune.

Partant de là, la recherche que nous avons ainsi menée nous conduit à penser que la structure intellectuelle de la pensée internationaliste du 19ème siècle et du début du 20ème se décompose en trois représentations majeures du droit des gens qui ont trait à son histoire (I), son fondement (II) et sa valeur (III). Ces trois représentations traduisent elles-mêmes un arrière-plan théorique combinant de façon principale l'historicisme, le rationalisme et l'humanisme juridique et c'est, selon nous, cette configuration générale qui a alimenté, d'un point de vue philosophique, au cœur même de la pensée internationaliste, la grande vague d'expansion coloniale européenne de cette époque. Il va de soi cependant que dans le cadre de cette très brève étude, on se bornera à indiquer de façon successive et très succincte ces représentations, sans pouvoir les détailler de façon approfondie, mais du moins en les posant comme telles et en clarifiant leurs implications en terme de justification de l'hégémonie coloniale européenne. Le but n'est d'ailleurs pas celui d'une minutieuse reconstitution historique des origines de cette structure intellectuelle ou des représentations du droit des gens qui en résultent, mais de révéler de façon plus générale le dispositif philosophico-juridique dans le cadre duquel vont s'épanouir les certitudes de la bonnes conscience coloniale. L'objet de cette étude est aussi de faire apparaître quelques uns des problèmes les plus fondamentaux que charrie avec elle une certaine forme de la pensée internationaliste actuelle. Nous terminerons donc sur ce point en essayant de tirer les enseignements du passé et de mettre en exergue les difficultés et les enjeux de l'humanisme juridique contemporain (IV).

I. L'Histoire du droit des gens pensée en terme de progrès accompli par les Etats civilisés

Historicité, rationalisme et colonialisme

Il n'est ni anodin ni fortuit que la plupart de ces traités du droit des gens commencent par la reconstitution de l'histoire du droit international que complète bien souvent sa propre historiographie[4]. C'est un peu comme si toute cette discipline avait définitivement franchi le pas de l'historicité et pris réellement conscience du caractère historique du droit qui lui échappait jusqu'à présent ; si bien que le droit des gens devient histoire et la science du droit se transforme partiellement en histoire du droit[5]. Or comment ne pas voir combien cette nouvelle lecture historique du droit va permettre au colonialisme d'y trouver une première fondation ? Non seulement parce qu'elle est évidemment présentée de telle sorte qu'elle va justifier l'expansion coloniale, en opposant l'homme blanc civilisé des arts et de la science aux barbares cannibales et aux sauvages, mais plus profondément par ce simple fait qu'elle démontre combien la croyance au progrès historique du droit des gens européen est à l'époque une certitude intimement partagée par tous. Cette solide conviction est d'ailleurs relayée par les remarques conclusives de ces manuels qui, en écho aux jalons historiques et théoriques posés en chapitre préliminaire, sont le plus souvent particulièrement optimistes quant à l'évolution du droit international. Bien entendu ce style de conclusion ne se retrouvera pas une fois passée la première guerre mondiale et encore moins après la seconde guerre mondiale où le désarroi issu du profond traumatisme subi par l'Europe est patent[6].

---

[4] On voit se succéder une floraison d'ouvrages qui entremêlent, parfois jusque dans leurs intitulés, les perspectives historique, théorique et pratique comme ceux par exemple de C. CALVO, *Le droit international historique et pratique, précédé d'un exposé historique du droit des gens*, Paris, Durant, Guillaumin et Amyot, 1870-1872, d'H. WHEATON, *Histoire du progrès du droit des gens en Europe et en Amérique depuis la paix de Westphalie jusqu'à nos jours, avec une introduction sur le progrès du droit des gens en Europe avant la paix de Westphalie*, Leipzig, F. A Brockhaus, 1846 ou d'E. CAUCHY, *Le droit maritime international considéré dans ses origines et dans ses rapports avec le progrès de la civilisation,* Paris, Guillaumin, 1862.

[5] En ce sens, G. FASSO, *Histoire de la philosophie du droit. XIXè et XXè siècles,* Paris, LGDJ, 1974, p. 40.

[6] Pour comp. après 1914, v L. LE FUR, *Précis de droit international public*, Paris, Dalloz, 1933, pp. 18ss, et après 1945, R. REDSLOB, *Traité de droit des gens*, Paris, Sirey, 1950, pp. 4ss. V. aussi sur ces question, R. CHARVIN, « Le droit

Mais à cette époque, antérieure à 1914, l'optimisme domine incontestablement et se fonde en priorité dans la mise en exergue du déroulement socio-historique de la civilisation européenne et de son droit des gens vers le progrès, tel qu'il apparaît de façon immédiate à leurs yeux quant à son essence et sa teneur particulière et tel qu'il est conforté par la science rationaliste historique du moment.

Quant à sa teneur, cette représentation de l'histoire va pouvoir être lue comme propice à une justification de l'expansion coloniale dès lors qu'elle se fonde sur la croyance, parfois très exaltée, en l'incarnation insensible et progressive d'un principe de raison – de civilisation – dans l'histoire. Cette histoire est en effet pensée comme celle du progrès de l'humanité grâce au développement et au rayonnement de la civilisation européenne dont le droit des gens est l'un des principaux instruments ; tant et si bien que les améliorations continues du droit sont considérées comme un élément du développement moral de l'humanité. Les internationalistes classiques se sont d'ailleurs tout naturellement appuyés sur la considération des sciences sociales de leur époque comme la géographie, l'ethnologie ou encore la science de l'évolution des espèces (darwinisme) pour étayer le principe de cette supériorité et du nécessaire rayonnement de la civilisation de l'homme blanc européen[7]. Selon ce grand encyclopédiste que fut l'allemand F. de Holtzendorf, il existe ainsi une « base ethnographique du droit des gens »[8]. En outre les faits historiques, l'histoire européenne elle-même, ont pu paraître leur confirmer cette irrésistible ascension dans la mesure où, avant les deux guerres mondiales, on n'a pas encore pris conscience – ou voulu prendre conscience – de la propre barbarie des européens. Au contraire la conviction profonde de ces auteurs est que l'histoire européenne illustre à

---

international tel qu'il a été enseigné. Notes critiques de lecture des traités et manuels (1850-1960) », *Mélanges offerts à Ch. Chaumont*, Paris, Pedone, 1984, pp. 136ss.

[7] Notamment parmi les plus cités par les auteurs, J. DENIKER, *Les races et les peuples de la terre. Eléments d'anthropologie et d'ethnographie*, 1900 ; C.DARWIN, *L'origine des espèces*, 1859 et A. de QUATREFAGES, *Histoire générale des races humaines. Introduction à l'étude des races humaines*, 1889 ; Sir Henry SUMMER MAINE, *Etude sur l'histoire des institutions primitives*, 1880 et Sir Edward BURNETT TYLOR, *La civilisation primitive,* 1876-78. La complicité entre sciences sociales et pensée coloniale est amplement analysée par R. GIRARDET, *L'idée coloniale en France. 1871-1962*, Paris, La table ronde, 1972, pp. 90ss et G. LECLERC, *Anthropologie et colonialisme*, Paris, Fayard, 1972, pp. 20ss.

[8] F. de HOLTZENDORF, *op.cit*, p.10.

merveille la façon dont les nations européennes se sont progressivement civilisées et détachées de la sauvagerie des temps anciens.

Toutefois la représentation de l'histoire véhiculée par ces manuels nous semble décisive pour l'intégration du colonialisme dans la mesure, surtout, où elle se présente sous la forme logique d'un certain nombre de principes qui s'emboîtent les uns aux autres de manière à fonder l'optimisme historique : le principe, tout d'abord, d'une vision très souvent vitaliste et organiciste des peuples, des Etats, de l'humanité, sinon de l'histoire elle-même, qui sont donc conçus comme des organismes vivants se déployant dans le monde ; le principe d'une vision uni-linéaire et progressiste du déroulement de l'histoire le plus souvent présenté de façon ternaire (les trois âges du droit des gens) ; le principe d'une profonde continuité historique qui, en dépit de certains obstacles, guerres par exemple – ou grâce à eux selon les auteurs –, se déroule pour amener les hommes à un mieux-être général ; le principe également que l'histoire a un sens, une unité et une finalité, qu'elle est donc intelligible et compréhensible ; enfin l'idée décisive selon laquelle cette finalité historique est pensée en terme de progrès. Comme le Belge G. Rolin-Jacquemyns n'hésite pas à le souligner, il y a une « loi du progrès » car chaque phase de l'histoire est supérieure aux phases précédentes et traduit une amélioration continue[9]. Or si telle est la configuration générale dans le cadre duquel doit être resituée et repensée l'évolution du droit des gens, on comprend sans peine qu'elle va permettre de tout justifier dans cette évolution avec pour effet prévisible d'y englober naturellement la colonisation européenne en cours. Sont ainsi considérés comme légitimés et fondés à cette époque la politique de l'expansion commerciale et du développement des européens, l'accroissement de leurs territoires et de leurs zones d'influences ainsi que la non-application du droit des gens à l'ensemble du monde et sa réduction aux seules nations civilisées. Ils ne sont pas traités comme les manifestations d'une politique extérieure, arrogante, arbitraire et hégémonique, mais, bien au contraire, comme étant le produit d'un processus historique en devenir, où l'on peut démontrer les filiations et les emprunts justifiés entre chaque grande époque de telle sorte que l'on puisse arriver un jour à cette finalité ultime qu'est la consécration et l'acceptation par tous des bienfaits de la civilisation européenne et de son droit. A cet égard la métaphore organiciste et vitaliste qui est souvent utilisée à titres divers est fort intéressante à repérer car elle permet de rejeter un trop

[9] G. ROLIN-JACQUEMYNS, « Les principes philosophiques du droit international », *RDILC*, V. XVIII, 1886, p.292.

grand individualisme social, de hiérarchiser les peuples comme les espèces animales et de refuser toute discontinuité historique.

On perçoit donc comment cette lecture particulièrement optimiste et très confortable de l'histoire réinsère le colonialisme comme un moment nécessaire, voire obligé, du développement du droit et de l'amélioration morale des hommes, sans avoir ainsi à s'exposer à de douloureuses remises en question. Sans doute ne s'agissait-il pas pour autant de nier les errements de certaine actions passées de la conquête coloniale, qui se laissaient peut-être plus difficilement intégrer dans ce schéma, mais d'assumer ce passé en indiquant l'horizon futur qui rétrospectivement pouvait les légitimer. Or s'il est assez aisé de comprendre le fil conducteur de cette nouvelle lecture historique du droit et de ces implications dans la justification du colonialisme européen, il est sans doute plus important encore de faire ressortir la racine intellectuelle profonde qui en est à l'origine. En fait cette façon d'historiciser le droit des gens est nouvelle au sein de la pensée internationaliste du 19ème siècle, on l'a dit, mais elle n'implique pas pour autant une rupture radicale à l'égard de la pensée antérieure. Elle se fonde en effet sur une forme particulière de rationalisme historique qui s'alimente au rationalisme antérieur de l'Ecole du droit naturel et à l'historicisme introduit par la nouvelle Ecole historique du droit allemand dont on connaît l'extraordinaire rayonnement en Europe[10]. Certes, comme A. Dufour l'a excellemment montré[11], certains représentants de l'Ecole du droit naturel avaient déjà intégré l'histoire dans le domaine du droit naturel, mais ce n'est réellement qu'avec le mouvement de Savigny, amorcé en 1814-1816, que va être consacré ce rôle de l'histoire par la pensée internationaliste dans la formation et la compréhension du droit des gens. En effet, à l'Ecole du droit de la nature et des gens, qui proposait une version statique du droit des gens dont les principes fondamentaux étaient déduits de la seule nature humaine ou de la nature (en soi) des Etats, l'Ecole historique oppose l'idée d'un droit issu d'une histoire dynamique et évolutive des peuples, un droit qui est moins le produit de la raison que de la conscience populaire nationale, un droit vivant, propre à chaque communauté constituée, et donc un droit des gens particulier à cette communauté que les nations civilisées forment entre elles. Toutefois le fait que la majorité des internationalistes semble reprendre

---

[10] Sur ce point, E. CASSIRER, *La philosophie des Lumières,* Paris, PUF, 1991, pp. 142ss et surtout A. DUFOUR, *Droits de l'homme, droit naturel et histoire*, Paris, PUF, 1991, pp. 154ss. V aussi par ex. F. de HOLTZENDORF, *Introduction au droit des gens*, 1ère part., Paris, Fischbacher, 1889, p. 22 et E. NYS, *op.cit*, pp. 70-71, qui citent Savigny de façon très élogieuse.

[11] A. DUFOUR, *op.cit*, pp. 142ss.

en partie cette nouvelle perception du rôle de l'histoire introduite par Savigny, ne veut pas dire pour autant qu'ils versent dans un complet rationalisme historique ou dans un complet irrationalisme.

Leur représentation de l'histoire est plus subtile même si elle pourra paraître inaboutie ou partiellement incohérente ; elle rejoint l'évolution prise par l'Ecole historique où subsiste toujours l'idée d'une certaine part de mystère, d'irrationnel dans les origines et l'évolution du droit, mais sans que la prise en compte de cet aspect plus irrationnel empêche toute tentative de rationalisation ou de systématisation du droit. On sait bien qu'une partie de l'Ecole du droit historique a ainsi débouché sur un véritable droit des savants et il est intéressant de voir que l'on retrouve exactement la même approche chez la plupart de ces auteurs internationalistes. Ils vont ainsi plaquer une méthode rationaliste et systématique sur les données historiques de l'observation du droit international : si le droit des gens est historicisé, c'est-à-dire s'il est resitué dans un mouvement socio-historique dont il est désormais considéré comme étant le produit, il n'en demeure pas moins un droit explicable, rationalisable, lorsqu'il est correctement décrypté et codifié par le travail scientifique du juriste.

C'est ce dont témoigne de façon exemplaire la part que s'accordent ces internationalistes dans le développement de la science du droit international dès lors qu'ils partagent tous l'idée qu'ils ont une mission fondamentale à exercer en ce qui concerne l'ordonnancement et l'articulation des règles du droit issues du bouillonnement de l'histoire[12]. L'internationaliste russe, D. I Katchenovsky, n'a-t-il pas été jusqu'à intituler son manuel de droit des gens comme étant l'*Exposé scientifique du droit international*[13]? Certains internationalistes ne se considèrent-ils pas eux-mêmes comme étant « l'organe de la conscience juridique civilisée » du monde[14] ? C'est aussi la formulation utilisée par les membres de l'Institut du droit international lors de sa fondation en 1873 à Gand où l'on retrouve notamment l'Italien

[12] Sur la certitude de l'importance et du caractère scientifique de leur travail, v. H. BONFILs et P. FAUCHILLE, *Manuel de droit international public (droit des gens)*, 4ème ed., Paris, Rousseau, 1905, p. 29 ; P. FIORE, *Nouveau droit international public suivant les besoins de la civilisation moderne*, Paris, A. Durand et Pedone-Lauriel, 1885, pp. 199ss et R. PIEDELIEVRE, *Précis de droit international public ou droit des gens*, Paris, F. Pichon, 1894, p. V.

[13] D.I. KARCHENOVSKY, *Exposé scientifique du droit international*, Kharkov, 1863.

[14] V. M. KOSKENNIEMI, *The Gentle Civilizer of Nation. The Rise and Fall of International Law*, Cambridge, University Press, pp. 42ss.

Mancini, le Belge G. Rolin-Jacquemyns et le Français De Parieu[15]. Or une telle expression est la traduction fidèle de cette conception éminente que les internationalistes se font de leur propre travail et s'adosse à leur représentation particulière du droit et de l'histoire. L'idée de *conscience* qui revient si souvent sous leur plume, semble être directement issue de l'Ecole du droit historique qui l'a très largement popularisée en en faisant la source du droit naturel et humain et des convictions juridiques des membres d'une même communauté. Elle permet de concilier l'origine humaine du droit tout en réagissant contre les excès du courant rationaliste de l'Ecole du droit naturel puisque ce faisant le droit est considéré comme issu de la conscience des hommes (ou des peuples) et non pas de la raison abstraite et désincarnée des jusnaturalistes.[16].

Toutefois la plupart des auteurs restent éclectiques et l'idée de conscience juridique issue de l'Ecole historique est très souvent rattachée à la raison des jusnaturalistes. Professeur aux Universités de Berne et de Bruxelles, A. Rivier déclarait ainsi en 1896 que la « conscience juridique commune », qui est la source primaire du droit des gens, « procède elle-même des deux éléments intimement liés l'un à l'autre : la nécessité et la raison »[17]. Leur conception foncièrement dualiste du droit international traduit cet éclectisme et interdit de réduire leur pensée internationaliste classique à un strict positivisme. Le droit des gens est en effet toujours divisé par ces auteurs en deux catégories : un droit théorique et un droit positif, qui tous deux expriment, quoique de façon différente, les principes juridiques et les valeurs des Etats européens civilisés[18]. Il y a donc, sur ce point précis,

---

[15] « L'institut du droit international…1° Doit favoriser le progrès du droit international en s'efforçant de devenir l'organe du monde civilisé », *Annuaire de l'IDI,* 1877, Session de Gand 1873, p. 18.

[16] La notion d'*organe* de la conscience juridique civilisée est, quant à elle, révélatrice d'une conception organiciste de la société internationale où l'internationaliste, envisagé comme étant véritablement l'organe et non pas le simple représentant de la communauté des Etats civilisés, ne peut qu'exprimer les intérêts et principes juridiques fondamentaux de cette communauté. Cette notion suggère ainsi, dans des termes comparables à ceux que l'on retrouve au sein des théories française et allemande de l'Etat de cette époque, l'insertion, voire l'intégration, complète du savant juriste dans cette communauté d'Etats et la façon dont il est dès lors nécessairement amené, en tant que partie organique, à en exprimer la conscience.

[17] A . RIVIER, *Principes du droit des gens,* T. 1, Paris, A. Rousseau, 1896, p. 28.

[18] Avec évidemment de nombreuses nuances que l'on ne saurait ici retracer : quelques uns sont plus jusnaturalistes comme par exemple J. LORIMER, *Principes du droit international*, T. 1, p. 72 ; R. PIEDELIEVRE, *op.cit*, pp. 12ss ; H. BONFILS et P. FAUCHILLE, *op.*cit, p. 15 et E. CHAUVEAU, *Le droit des gens ou*

une convergence paradoxale des courants rationaliste jusnaturaliste et historique allemand. Elle vient d'ailleurs renforcer ces auteurs dans leur conviction commune de l'évidente nécessité et scientificité de leur travail de systématisation du droit ; et elle s'explique par le fait que la pensée internationaliste européenne n'a pas, à l'évidence, complètement basculé dans un complet historicisme et relativisme des valeurs. Ce point de vue est même consolidé par la perspective historique profondément optimiste qui s'y déploie quant aux capacités de l'homme et des peuples à se rationaliser et se perfectionner (donc se civiliser).

On peut en effet aller plus loin dans la logique de cette représentation et montrer que cette lecture de l'histoire non-déterministe et ouverte au travail de systématisation du juriste est, de la même façon, ouverte et prédisposée à l'action des Etats civilisés. En effet, si l'histoire du droit des gens est souvent décomposée en trois temps, il n'y a pas dans ces manuels de vision réellement dialectique, de sorte de ruse de la raison historique par le biais de laquelle le droit se réaliserait par son contraire, et où chaque événement serait totalement explicable et déterminé par une causalité extérieure. Bref, on ne saurait, cette fois-ci, y voir la consécration d'une conception hyper-rationaliste au sens hégélien du terme car l'histoire se veut simplement explicative et non pas entièrement déterministe[19]. Or puisque le mouvement historique du droit des gens, de la civilisation et du progrès, ne s'ancre pas dans un projet hyper-rationaliste, on légitime alors la nécessité d'une intervention de l'homme civilisé pour réaliser ce progrès, d'une obligation des Etats civilisés à imposer les bienfaits de la civilisation. Si bien que la loi du progrès s'identifie insensiblement à la loi d'action des Etats européens[20].

---

droit international public, Paris, A. Rousseau, 1889, p. 28 et d'autres plus « civilisationnistes » ou positivistes comme par ex. L. RENAULT, *Introduction à l'étude du droit international,* Paris, L. Larose, 1879, p. 4 ; E. NYS, *op.cit*, pp. 70ss, Sir Robert PHILIMORE, *Commentaries Upon International Law*, Londres, Butterworths, 1879, I, pp. 27ss et D. ANZILOTTI, *Cours de droit international*, Paris, Sirey 1919 (1ère ed. 1912), pp. 17-20.

[19] A l'exception sans doute de T. FUNCK-BRENTANO et A. SOREL, *Précis du droit des gens*, Paris, Plon, 1887, p. 490, qui développent une vision historique beaucoup plus dialectique et déterministe que les autres.

[20] G. ROLIN-JACQUEMYNS, « le droit international… », *op.cit*, pp. 292-293, exprime cela de façon particulièrement claire : «…les agents du développement lui-même sont des êtres libres et responsables (…) et leurs actes doivent être jugés, non point au vue de ces lois finales (de l'histoire), mais au point de vue de l'usage individuel qu'ils font de ces lois finales ».

La représentation de l'histoire du droit des gens pensée en terme de progrès accompli par l'homme civilisé aura évidemment des conséquences non-négligeables sur l'idée d'un devoir à civiliser les autres peuples et on y reviendra peu après. Cette figure renouvelée du droit des gens, considéré comme produit et moteur de l'histoire, entretient de toutes façons déjà des liens étroits avec le colonialisme puisqu'elle fait de celui-ci un moment nécessaire du développement historique de la civilisation européenne.

Encore faut-il comprendre pourquoi le droit des gens issu des nations européennes civilisées reste alors circonscrit à ces seules nations européennes et pourquoi les bénéfices et droits qu'il accorde ne peuvent être que très rarement étendus aux autres peuples ? Autrement dit, qu'est-ce qui, au delà de cette représentation historique, vient philosophiquement fonder l'origine et la restriction constante du droit des gens aux nations civilisées de telle sorte qu'elles soient seules considérées comme sujets de droit et que les autres peuples soient inévitablement réifiés ou marginalisés[21]? En fait, ce second aspect caractéristique d'une pensée internationaliste exclusiviste et discriminatoire, qui de façon typique va jouer comme un mécanisme d'exclusion de l'autre, s'ancre à une autre grande racine intellectuelle de la pensée européenne qui est l'humanisme juridique, mais tel qu'il sera profondément remanié et projeté, par anthropomorphisme, aux Etats.

II. Le fondement du droit des gens et sa restriction aux Etats civilisés

Humanisme juridique, anthropomorphisme et colonialisme

On vient de voir que la prise de conscience d'une certaine historicité du droit des gens n'implique pas le rejet du rationalisme juridique mais une simple réintégration de cette vision rationaliste dans une représentation spécifique de l'histoire. Or il résulte également de l'influence croisée des grands courants antérieurs de pensée, une conception du fondement du droit international qui est particulièrement significative de ce fond commun de pensée que nous cherchons à identifier et qui va fonder la restriction du cercle des sujets aux seuls Etats civilisés. Cette réduction historique prend sa source dans une déformation progressive de l'humanisme juridique rationaliste qui imprègne toute la pensée juridique européenne depuis deux

[21] Rappelons peut-être qu'il ne s'agit d'appréhender cette réduction du cercle des sujets du droit international classique que point de vue de la pensée internationaliste européenne et non pas au regard des autres Etats ou peuples de l'époque qui pouvaient avoir leur propres raisons pour refuser l'application du droit des gens européen.

siècles. Il n'est pas question bien entendu de revenir sur le développement de l'humanisme européen déjà très longuement analysé par d'autres et sous de multiples aspects[22]. On se bornera ici à rappeler que, de manière très générale, l'humanisme juridique repose sur l'idée fondamentale selon laquelle l'homme, et non pas la nature ou Dieu, est sujet et créateur du droit ; qu'il peut donc proposer et se donner des normes juridiques et éthiques qui vont gouverner son existence en prenant la nature humaine à la fois comme fondement et comme fin en soi du droit. H. Bonfils, puis P. Fauchille qui lui succéda, expriment cela très bien en disant que le droit international public « a ses racines maîtresses et profondes dans la nature même de l'homme »[23]. Mais si cet humanisme naît aux alentours du 17ème siècle et s'épanouit pleinement au 18ème , il se transforme au 19ème siècle.

On repère en effet un glissement très suggestif de la notion de nature humaine au fondement du droit car ce n'est plus réellement la nature humaine universelle, mais la nature civilisée qui va fonder le droit des gens. Personne mieux que F. de Holtzendorf n'expliquera cette mutation essentielle en disant que le « droit des gens doit … être envisagé comme un produit, non de la nature, mais de la civilisation »[24]. Du reste les présentations qu'en font les auteurs sont rarement rigoureuses. Elles laissent le lecteur quelque peu désemparé car elles traduisent souvent une certaine ambiguïté latente de leur notion dualiste du droit des gens et de leur compréhension de la nature humaine : d'un côté, certains ne semblent pas avoir abandonné l'idée d'une nature humaine rationnelle et universelle, mais d'un autre côté, ils la transforment tous radicalement pour en faire une nature civilisée. Quand les auteurs du 18ème siècle fondaient le droit des gens sur les principes de la raison, ils envisageaient une nature commune à tous, sans trancher de façon très nette la question des tribus sauvages, mais du moins en affirmant l'universalisme originaire, de principe, de leur droit naturel. En revanche quand la nature – où plutôt la conscience – civilisée va devenir le

---

[22] On se bornera ici à indiquer les auteurs sur lesquels nous nous sommes appuyés car ils ont, selon nous, le mieux mis en exergue -quoique avec des perspectives philosophiques profondément différentes- la façon dont le rapport de l'homme à la nature et au droit s'est transformé à partir du 17ème siècle sous l'influence de l'humanisme et la métaphysique de la subjectivité : M. HEIDEGGER, *Nietzsche*, Paris, Gallimard, 1971, pp. 353ss ; L. STRAUSS, *Droit naturel et histoire,* Paris, Plon, 1954, pp. 52ss ; M. VILLEY, *Le droit et les droits de l'homme*, Paris PUF, 1983, pp. 22ss ; L. FERRY, *Philosophie politique*, I, Paris, PUF, 1984, pp. 43ss et A. RENAUD et L. SOSOE, *Philosophie du droit*, Paris, PUF, 1991, pp. 96ss.

[23] H. BONFILS et P. FAUCHILLE, *op.cit*, p. 4.

[24] F. de HOLTZENDORF, *op.cit*, p. 31.

fondement du droit des gens rationnel, elle ne fait plus référence à cette simple raison commune, à cette identité minimale qui pouvait rassembler les hommes quels que soient leur race ou leur degré d'organisation. Elle ne correspond pas plus à la condition humaine primitive qui rappelle la condition originelle de l'homme et qu'incarne pour les hommes du 18ème siècle la figure du bon sauvage. Elle est devenue la nature – la conscience – de l'homme civilisé et c'est donc à l'aune désormais de cette conscience que seront élaborées et jaugées les règles du droit des gens théorique et pratique. Elle devient alors un idéal non-universellement partagé, ce vers quoi doivent tendre les hommes et les peuples, et à laquelle ils sont arrivés quand ils sont civilisés, c'est-à-dire, selon eux, éduqués et organisés. Contrairement donc à la nature humaine universelle qui était le pilier intangible et intemporel sur lequel s'élevait l'humanisme juridique des Lumières, la nature civilisée des internationalistes du 19ème siècle est en partie historicisée et particularisée. Du même coup le droit des gens, qu'il soit droit théorique rationnel ou droit positif volontaire, demeure essentiellement le droit fondé, issu et constitué par la communauté des Etats civilisés : puisque le droit est fondé sur l'homme civilisé, c'est-à-dire sur l'homme sociable vivant en société, le droit des gens ne peut être déduit ou estimé qu'en considération d'une communauté d'Etats civilisés et vivant en société[25].

La notion de « communauté des Etats civilisés » éclaire particulièrement ici ce mouvement réductionniste du droit des gens en raison de la jonction sous-jacente établie entre droit et communauté organisée. On y décèle à nouveau l'influence de tout le courant historique allemand qui amène à fonder le droit sur la nécessité intrinsèque et la particularité de chaque communauté historique. « Quand nous affirmons qu'il y a un droit international », explique le très actif avocat anglais J. Westlake en 1894[26], « nous affirmons qu'il y a une société d'Etats, quand nous affirmons qu'il y a une société d'Etats, nous reconnaissons qu'il y a un droit international. ». D'où cette fameuse communauté historique des Etats civilisés européens – puis euro-américains – régie par le droit des gens civilisés, qui va fonctionner comme un parfait modèle d'exclusion des peuples considérés comme sauvages et des Etats non-civilisés, ou d'inclusion de certains autres considérés comme étant suffisamment civilisés pour accéder à cette

[25] Le célèbre juriste russe, F. F MARTENS, *Le droit international actuel des peuples civilisés*, Saint-Pétersbourg, 1882, est cependant l'un des seuls à transcrire directement cette idée dans l'intitulé de son traité du droit des gens.

[26] J. WESTLAKE, *Chapters on The Principles of International Law*, Cambridge, University Press, 1894, I, p. 5.

communauté et bénéficier des bienfaits de l'application du droit des gens européen[27]. Et si quelques auteurs soutiennent que la loi morale d'humanité du droit des gens rationnel doit s'appliquer aux rapports avec les peuples indigènes, ils excluent toute application du droit des gens positif ou du droit rationnel inter-étatique[28] et de telle sorte que l'idée même d'un droit des gens qui puisse, à terme, s'appliquer à tous les peuples demeure une pure illusion pour certains[29]. On retrouve donc bien, à ce stade plus précis, le glissement imperceptible qui avait conduit d'un droit des gens universel, car fondé sur la nature humaine commune à tous, à un droit historique et donc particulier aux membres de cette communauté.

La notion d'Etat civilisée est également fort intéressante à creuser. Le droit international est en effet défini par tous comme un droit entre Etats égaux qui ne fonctionne que par acceptation par les Etats de la logique synallagmatique des obligations réciproquement partagées et acceptées. Partant, le fait que l'on parle d'Etat signifie, selon ces auteurs, que l'on envisage des entités politiques suffisamment organisées pour avoir une volonté et une conscience leur permettant de suivre les préceptes du droit international fondés sur cette idée fondamentale de réciprocité. Le juriste français R. Piédelièvre résume ainsi l'opinion générale de ses contemporains en 1894 en affirmant que « le droit international suppose essentiellement la réciprocité c'est-à-dire une conscience suffisamment développée chez les nations dont il gouverne les relations extérieures, ainsi que leur volonté réfléchie et persistante d'appliquer à leurs rapports mutuels les préceptes du droit et de la justice »[30]. Les auteurs de tous ces traités de droit des gens vont donc s'appuyer sur une figure anthropomorphique de l'Etat, bâtie directement sur le modèle de l'individu, où l'Etat n'est pas ramené à ses seuls éléments constitutifs (territoire, population et gouvernement), mais

---

[27] J. KENT, *Commentary on International Law*, New-York, 1866, p. 11; J. HORNUNG, "Civilisés et barbares", *RDILC*, T. XVII, pp. 129ss; E. NYS, *op.cit*, I, p. 53 ; H. BONFILS et P. FAUCHILLE, *op.cit*, p. 5.

[28] P. FIORE, *op.*cit, I, pp. 301ss, F. de HOLTZENDORF, *op.cit*, p. 11; R. PIEDELIEVRE, *op.cit*, p. 19 et A. PILLET, « Le droit international public. Ses éléments constitutifs, son domaine, son objet… », *RGDIP,* 1, p. 20.

[29] H. BONFILS …, *op.cit,* m. 899, selon qui « l'universalité intégrale ne se réalisera jamais car un fossé séparera toujours les Etats européens et américains des Etats musulmans et de l'Empire du milieu… »

[30] R. PIEDELIEVRE, *op.cit*, p. 19. V. Aussi J. G BLUNTSCHLI, *Le droit international codifié*, Paris, Guillaumin et cie, 1868, p. 71 ; E. NYS, *Le droit international. Les principes, les théories, les faits,* T.2, Bruxelles, M. Nijhoff et Paris, M. Rivière, 1912, p.501 et A. RIVIER, *op.cit*, II, pp. 34ss.

caractérisé par une volonté et une conscience spécifiques à l'homme et à laquelle ne sauraient prétendre les animaux ou les êtres humains et les peuples sous-développés. Ceci expliquant cela, et vice versa, c'est pourquoi également seuls les Etats sont considérés comme dotés de la personnalité juridique. La notion de personne juridique vient ici traduire cet humanisme juridique anthropomorphique et consolider directement le processus colonisateur en spécifiant au niveau juridique ceux qui sont aptes à être sujets du droit des gens[31]. Elle joue ainsi comme un facteur d'exclusion et de différenciation juridique très simple puisqu'elle va permettre d'exclure du cercle des sujets du droit des gens tous les peuples non organisés dit sauvages et barbares. Considérés comme incapables de vouloir les normes du droit international, ils ne peuvent être assimilés à des personnes juridiques[32]. Et s'ils ne sont pas des personnes juridiques, ils ne peuvent ni créer, ni être titulaires, ni utiliser les règles du droit international. Mais dans ces conditions, les tribus et les colonies, dont les territoires sont occupés par les Etats civilisés, sont traitées alors, *au mieux*, comme des objets du droit des gens – de même bien entendu que les territoires qu'elles habitent. La plupart du temps, elles sont intégrées dans les biens immeubles de l'Etat colonisateur ou dans son territoire et relèvent alors principalement de son doit public interne et non pas du droit des gens lui-même[33]. C'est la raison pour laquelle leur régime juridique n'est pas abordé dans les manuels de droit européen, qu'il n'y a donc pas de véritable système juridique international du colonialisme à cette époque[34] et que l'on entrevoit une partie des questions relatives à la colonisation à travers les chapitres consacrés au

[31] Pour certains, cet anthropomorphisme s'élabore directement sur la notion de personnalité elle-même par analogie entre la personnalité de l'homme et celle de l'Etat. V. A. PILLET, « Le droit international public.. .», *op.cit*, p. 2 : «..l'homme dont on retrouve la personnalité au fond de toute conception du droit ». Sur le mouvement anthropomorphique en général comme conséquence de la métaphysique de la subjectivité, qui serait elle-même un corollaire de l'humanisme : v. M. HEIDEGGER, *Nietzsche, op.cit,* pp. 353ss et sur la notion de sujet dans ce cadre philosophique de l'humanisme, v. S. GOYARD-FABRE, « Sujet de droit et objet de droit : défense de l'humanisme », *Sujet de droit et objet de droit, Cahiers de philosophie politique et juridique,* Caen, 1992, n°22, pp. 9-30.

[32] D. ANZILOTTI, *Cours de droit international, op.cit,* (1912), p. 128.

[33] Selon T. FUNCK BRENTANO et A. SOREL, *op.cit*, p. 45, l'Etat peut traiter les colonies « comme bon lui semble ».

[34] Tout au plus trouve-t-on chez A. RIVIER, *op.cit*, p. 160, l'idée d'un « système colonial », mais pour indiquer brièvement qu'il « n'a rien d'illicite…et que le droit des gens l'autorise ».

territoire ou aux droits patrimoniaux de l'Etat sur lesquels il dispose d'un pouvoir souverain exclusif. La réification – transformation en objet – des peuples, leur assimilation à des biens immeubles de l'Etat ou leur identification à un territoire[35], et non à une communauté d'individus, les excluent et les disqualifient totalement.

En revanche, les entités politiques qui sont considérées comme des Etats et donc des personnes juridiques peuvent prétendre à l'application du droit des gens. Mais cette fois-ci, il ne suffit pas qu'elles soient des Etats, elles doivent faire preuve également d'un niveau adéquat de civilisation. Force est en effet de constater que, par le biais du même mouvement anthropomorphique issu de l'humanisme juridique sous-jacent à toutes ces constructions, le mécanisme de substitution du civilisé au rationnel *stricto sensu* est ainsi également transposé aux Etats. L'inclusion éventuelle de ces Etats dans le cercle des sujets du droit des gens euro-américain est alors basée sur la technique décisive de la reconnaissance d'un degré acceptable de conscience civilisée par les membres de la communauté des Etats[36]. Et s'il appert qu'ils n'ont pas acquis cet état de civilisation, on envisage alors d'autres modalités pour régir leurs relations avec les Etats pleinement civilisés. Le statut d'Etats semi-civilisé, la pratique des accords de protectorat, des zones d'influence, le bail ou encore le recours à un droit spécial sont autant de techniques juridiques, abondamment commentées par ailleurs, qui entérinent la dissociation de statut entre l'Etat civilisé et les autres[37].

Or comment ne pas voir combien ce déplacement de la pensée est particulièrement inquiétant ? Le lien entre droit des gens et colonialisme s'opère ici par l'effet pervers de la restriction du cercle des sujets du droit des gens aux Etats considérés comme civilisés et par toutes les pratiques discriminatoires qui en découlent ; mais il s'explique de façon beaucoup plus

[35] H. BONFILS et P. FAUCHILLE, *op.cit*, p. 261 et P. FIORE, *op.cit*, II, p. 4.

[36] V. la systématisation de cette idée avec les trois types de reconnaissance inventés par J. LORIMER, *Principes de droit international*, Bruxelles, C. Muquardt et Paris, A. Marescq aîné, 1885, p. 104.

[37] P. FIORE, *op.*cit, p. 64 : « ..pour les relations avec l'Orient un droit exceptionnel et restreint est souvent rendu nécessaire…justifié par l'inégalité de civilisations ». *Ibid* T. FUNCK-BRENTANO et A. SOREL, *op.cit,* p. 23. Après la révolution russe de 1917, certains auteurs vont aller jusqu'à soutenir qu'un Etat civilisé comme l'ancienne Russie peut régresser et sortir de la civilisation ainsi que le démontre, selon eux, la « sauvagerie communiste » (A. BONDE, *Traité élémentaire de droit international*, Paris, Dalloz, 1926, déjà cité et souligné par R. CHARVIN, *op.cit*, p. 141).

profonde par le réaménagement insensible qui affecte l'humanisme juridique au fondement de ce droit des gens et sa projection anthropomorphique aux Etats. Et il faudra attendre la fin de la seconde guerre mondiale pour que les peuples non-civilisés soient au moins considérés comme des « communautés », et la fin de la seconde guerre mondiale pour que tout Etat, quel que soit son niveau de développement et sans rechercher son niveau de « conscience » civilisée, soit considéré comme un sujet du droit international et membre, selon les termes de C. W. Jenks, d'une « communauté universelle »[38].

Reste quand même une dernière interrogation qui n'a pas encore trouvé de réponse alors même qu'elle va conforter de façon définitive l'expansion coloniale européenne de l'époque. Si le droit des gens européens est conçu comme un droit ne pouvant s'appliquer qu'à un petit nombre d'Etats, comment peut-on justifier que l'on doive l'imposer aux autres, de même que les valeurs qu'il recèle ? Certes, on ne saurait ignorer, on l'a dit, que le développement des différentes sciences sociales de l'époque ne pouvait que conforter ces internationalistes dans l'intime conviction de leur propre supériorité, mais cette considération des données de la science et de l'histoire n'est pas suffisante en soi et ne suffit pas à justifier pleinement l'hégémonie coloniale. Le destin de l'expansion coloniale européenne ne s'est pas joué du seul fait de raisons externes bien connues comme les considérations scientifiques de l'époque et d'autres raisons de tous ordres – économique, commerciale, politique… – mais il procède aussi de la philosophie européenne du droit, notamment telle qu'elle s'est manifestée dans le cadre de la pensée internationaliste classique. Or qu'en est-il ici de ce point de vue ? Quelle est la base philosophico-juridique, et le singulier raisonnement, par lesquels les internationalistes classiques ont pu fonder leur volonté de projection du droit des gens et de ses valeurs fondamentales à l'ensemble du monde ? Comment ont-ils développé une pensée qui est à la fois discriminatoire et hégémonique ?

---

[38] C. W. JENKS, *The Common Law of* Mankind, Londres, 1958, p. 62. Pour l'usage du mot communauté, l'évolution s'est faite en raison notamment du système des mandats qui se réfère à ces « communautés » (article 22 du Pacte de la SDN). V sur ce point un lapsus très révélateur de H. ACCIOLY, *op.cit,* p. 135 : « ..dans la catégorie A (des mandats), sont inclus les territoires, ou plutôt, comme le dit l'article 22 lui-même, « certaines communautés… ». On peut d'ailleurs noter que les populations indigènes de la catégorie C sont toujours, quant à elle, présentées comme des territoires..

III. La valeur du droit des gens et sa projection comme modèle du monde civilisé

Ethique du droit, moralisme et colonialisme

C'est en fait dans la capacité et la possibilité de cette pensée internationaliste à développer cette idée de projection que l'on trouve la justification de l'hégémonie européenne mais aussi ce qui révèle ses inévitables apories et d'une certaine façon ses plus cruelles désillusions. La valorisation du droit est au coeur de cette problématique : le droit des gens civilisé, théorique et positif, rationnel et volontaire, est présenté comme un modèle dont les principes fondamentaux, sinon les règles du droit, doivent être transposables au reste du monde, car il est conçu comme une valeur particulièrement éminente et donc supérieure aux autres systèmes juridiques non européens ; si le droit des gens est ainsi projeté à la face du monde ce n'est donc pas seulement parce qu'il est instrument particulièrement utile de la politique économique et politique, hégémonique et discriminatoire, des Etats européens, mais c'est aussi parce qu'il représente pour tous ces internationalistes une référence éthique essentielle du monde civilisé, en particulier, et de tout être humain, en général. Fort d'une culture historique impressionnante qui faisait autorité auprès de tous ses contemporains, E. Nys assurait ainsi en 1912 que le droit international était une magnifique « création du génie européen »[39]. Et l'on voit sans peine, dans les formulations utilisées par les auteurs, combien cette idée de valorisation du droit des gens est pour eux décisive. Elle vient conforter de façon définitive l'idée de la supériorité de la civilisation européenne dont le droit des gens est un des plus précieux fleurons ; elle consolide par là-même indirectement la légitimité de l'expansion coloniale car elle participe de la conviction morale –et non plus seulement juridique– de faire le bien en cherchant à universaliser ces principes. Et comme d'autres auteurs l'ont déjà montré de façon plus générale, ce mouvement de valorisation du droit s'inscrit tout naturellement dans la logique de cet humanisme rationaliste et historiciste européen dont nous avons déjà discuté et dont il achève d'en dessiner les contours et les implications. Le droit des gens s'y trouve doublement valorisé, d'un point de vue formel et matériel, comme définissant un *juste* que les Etats civilisés européens ont le devoir moral de défendre comme seul système juridique international valable auprès des autres Etats civilisés et d'en imposer les principes humanistes aux peuples non-civilisés.

---

[39] E. NYS, *op.cit*, p. 3.

Formellement tout d'abord, c'est-à-dire en tant qu'ensemble de règles objectives applicables aux rapports entre Etats, le droit des gens est considéré comme une valeur. Il représente en effet de ce seul point de vue formel, une valeur d'organisation, d'ordre, de stabilité que l'on oppose à la barbarie considérée comme rebelle à toute loi et toute société organisée. Et la distorsion parfois réelle de degré d'organisation entre Etats européens et peuples non-européens, tout comme la méconnaissance complète à cette époque de la signification réelle des us et coutumes existants parmi les tribus ou peuples colonisés, ramenés à l'état de barbares ou sauvages, viennent conforter cette distinction entre état de droit et de non-droit. Ce faisant, le droit des gens est donc perçu comme un signe mais aussi comme une condition du progrès de l'humanité, de par ce seul fait d'exister et de régir une communauté[40].

Le droit international est également une valeur par sa teneur, par les principes fondamentaux qui le déterminent, le fondent et en même temps représentent un horizon vers lequel les hommes doivent tendre. De ce point de vue, la dualité du droit des gens maintenue par tous ces auteurs entre droit théorique et droit positif pratique va jouer à plein afin de montrer, à travers le droit des gens théorique, naturel ou rationnel, ce que doit être le droit des gens positif, contingent et relatif. Or, d'un point de vue matériel, le droit des gens civilisés de cette époque, tel qu'il est présenté dans les différents manuels, est un droit qui vise non seulement à organiser la coexistence des souverainetés des Etats mais aussi à faire prévaloir une certaine conception de la justice humaine. On voit se déployer ainsi les valeurs fondamentales d'un humanisme juridique à la fois libéral, car respectueux de la souveraineté et l'égalité des Etats, et solidariste, car fondé sur les principes de sociabilité, de justice et d'équité des hommes vivant en société. Selon les termes quasi-prophétiques du célèbre professeur de l'Université de Heidelberg J. G. Bluntschli, « Le droit international dépend de la conscience que l'humanité a de ses droits »[41]. On relève alors non sans intérêt comment l'idée de justice, et non celle de paix, est constamment postulée comme

---

[40] A vrai dire, ce lien entre droit et civilisation date du 18ème siècle lorsque le mot civilisé est réellement apparu dans la langue européenne. V sur ce point L. FEBVRE, M. MAUSS, E. TONNELAT, A. NIEFORO et L. WEBER, *Civilisation. Le mot et l'idée*, Paris, Centre international de synthèse, La renaissance du livre, 1930, pp. 12ss.

[41] J. G BLUNTSCHLI, *op.cit, lo.cit.* V. aussi A. PILLET, *op.cit*, p. 10 ; R. PIEDELIEVRE, *op.cit*, p. 19 ; H. BONFILS et P. FAUCHILLE, *op.cit*, p. 5 ; P. FIORE, *op.cit,* I, p. 211 et T. FUNCK-BRENTANO et A. SOREL, *op.cit*, p. 499 et *Annuaire de l'IDI,* Session de Gand, 1873, p. 19.

ultime idéal à atteindre du droit des gens. En effet cette primauté qui est ainsi conférée à la justice dans l'ordre des valeurs éthiques véhiculées par le droit des gens a une portée que l'on ne saurait sous-estimer. Elle résonne étrangement pour un lecteur des jurisconsultes de la fin du 18ème siècle qui, à l'instar de Wolff et Vattel, avaient justement déterminé des priorités inverses et privilégié le respect absolu de la souveraineté de chaque Etat afin de garantir la paix et la stabilité de l'Europe, en évitant que les querelles européennes soient envenimées par les questions de justice et de juste cause dont personne ne peut établir objectivement les principes. Un siècle plus tard, la justice redevient une priorité même si elle donne lieu à des droits d'action limités ; et les juristes du 19ème siècle résolvent la difficulté qu'avait soulevée Vattel en prétendant, on l'a vu, pouvoir formuler de manière objective et scientifique ces principes de justice.

Le droit des gens des traités classiques est donc bien considéré comme une valeur éthique fondamentale, comme étant juste sous un angle formel et matériel, du moins lorsque le droit positif est conforme aux principes du droit rationnel. Pour cette raison, il consacre sa propre supériorité en tant que droit international et droit inter-étatique[42]. Il est donc conçu par tous les internationalistes européens comme devant nécessairement s'imposer face aux autres formes de droit des relations extérieures pratiquées par des Etats civilisés ou semi-civilisés comme la Chine, le Japon et la Turquie. Il est même intéressant de voir qu'à une époque où la meilleure connaissance de vieux Etats comme la Chine ou le Japon obligeait les européens à pluraliser la notion de civilisation, et donc à reconnaître l'existence de plusieurs civilisations non-européennes, le droit des gens devient l'une des manifestations exemplaires de la supériorité de la civilisation européenne sur les autres.

Corrélativement, émerge également l'idée d'un droit, voire d'un devoir, à diriger totalement la conduite des peuples sauvages, à instaurer la civilisation dans les territoires inhabités ou auprès des peuples semi-civilisés[43]. Selon J. de Hornung, « les civilisés doivent donner l'exemple d'une justice supérieure…les nations civilisées doivent aider les « races inférieures » à entrer dans le système politique des Etat »[44]. Cette idée bien connue, qui sera codifiée à l'article 22 du Pacte de la SDN, est déjà diffusée

---

[42] V cet impérialisme excellemment décrit par Y. ONUMA, « When was the law of International Society Born ? –An Inquiry of the History of International Law from an Interciviliational Perspective", *Journal of the History of International Law*, 2000, 2, pp. 1-66.

[43] H. BONFILS et P. FAUCHILLE, *op.cit,* p. 17

[44] J. HORNUNG, « Civilisés et barbares », *op.cit*, p. 552.

à cette époque à travers toute une littérature innombrable relative au colonialisme[45]. Elle emporte avec elle une signification de la notion de civilisation qui elle-même est loin d'être neutre car elle est porteuse d'un jugement de valeur fondé sur le rationalisme et l'humanisme évoqués plus haut où l'on assiste à un glissement allant des principes de la raison abstraite vers ceux de la conscience civilisée européenne. La civilisation européenne dont il est question représente le triomphe de la raison européenne dans tous ses possibles domaines d'activité mais aussi la défense de valeurs qui se veulent consubstantielles à l'homme vivant en société. Représentant un bien à la fois individuel et collectif, cette notion de civilisation traduit donc de manière générale – et à l'instar du droit des gens qui en est issu – quelque chose de moralement bon et désirable qui pare les européens de l'époque d'une forme éminente de prestige et les destine naturellement à en être les propagateurs auprès de tous ceux qui ne la connaissent pas et qui de ce fait sont catégorisés par le célèbre titulaire de la chaire d'Edimbourg, J. Lorimer, en sauvages, barbares et semi-civilisés[46]. Elle s'appuie aussi sur l'idée, incluse également dans la philosophie européenne, selon laquelle la nature humaine et la nature des peuples est perfectible. Cette vieille idée aux multiples conséquences extrêmement fécondes, fut théorisée en son temps par J.J. Rousseau puis pleinement développée par J. G. Fichte comme étant le signe même, le trait distinctif essentiel de la nature humaine, comme ce qui différencie l'homme de l'animal et l'humanité de la naturalité. Or elle est reprise ici de manière à fonder les conditions de possibilité de toute mission de civilisation : civiliser les autres est possible car, comme les hommes, les peuples barbares ou semi-civilisés sont susceptibles d'évoluer, d'apprendre et de se perfectionner.

---

[45] V. Pour l'Europe, P. GUILLAUME, *Le monde colonial,* Paris, A. Colin, 1974, pp. 38ss et pour la France, M. ASTIER-LOUFTI, *Littérature et colonialisme. L'expansion coloniale vue dans la littérature romanesque française, 1871-1914*, Paris, La Haye, Mouton, 1971, pp. 139ss. V. notamment quelques ouvrages décisifs comme ceux de J. DUVAL, *Les colonies et la politique coloniale de la France*, Paris, A. Bertrand, 1864, p. VI : « la colonisation constitue l'une des faces les plus brillantes de l'humanité. Elle est le rayonnement extérieur des familles humaines… », E. LEROY-BEAULIEU, *De la colonisation chez les peuples modernes*, Paris, Guillaumin, 1874, p. 26, selon qui la colonisation « est une des fonctions les plus élevées des sociétés parvenues à un état avancé de la civilisation ».

[46] Suivant toujours les catégories de J. LORIMER (*op.cit, loc.cit*) qui ont eu énormément de succès auprès de ses contemporains, même si ceux-ci n'ont pas toujours repris le fondement jusnaturaliste de cette théorie.

Toutefois cette mission de civilisation n'est pas toujours explicitement traitée comme telle dans les manuels de droit international que nous avons étudiés car elle n'est presque jamais présentée sous la forme d'un droit ou devoir juridique de l'Etat[47]. Elle n'est pas non plus partagée par tous et certains juristes – très peu nombreux il est vrai – vont même jusqu'à dénoncer l'arrogance que pourraient avoir les nations chrétiennes à prétendre imposer aux autres leur civilisation[48]. Il faut d'ailleurs comprendre que si cette mission de civilisation avait été conçue comme un véritable devoir juridique, elle aurait passablement embarrassé les Etats européens dès lors que son non-accomplissement devrait engager logiquement leur responsabilité internationale : construction juridique si déstabilisatrice que les juristes ne l'ont pas reprise à leur compte. Il est vrai que le droit, et non le devoir, des Etats à civiliser les peuples barbares aurait pu être plus facilement introduit comme simple droit mais il ne transparaît pas non plus sous cette forme dans la plupart des manuels et ne fait donc pas partie de la liste des droits fondamentaux ou secondaires des Etats. Mais s'ils ne consacrent pas expressément ce droit comme droit fondamental des Etats, les internationalistes vont en codifier certains autres qui lui sont directement voisins. Ainsi en est-il du droit au développement de chaque nation qui permet aux Etats européens d'étendre singulièrement leur propre civilisation ou encore du droit au commerce qui depuis fort longtemps déjà était considéré comme un instrument particulièrement propice au rayonnement de la civilisation européenne[49]. Quant à la mission de civilisation proprement dite, elle est plutôt envisagée au cours des chapitres introductifs comme un devoir moral, et non pas *stricto sensu* juridique, et de telle sorte que le progrès historique de l'humanité soit bien présenté comme lui étant consubstantiellement lié. Beaucoup d'auteurs rappellent ainsi que les Etats européens ont pour devoir éthique, non seulement de faire respecter et d'imposer leur propre droit des gens aux Etats suffisamment civilisés, mais également d'éduquer les tribus barbares et les peuples sauvages ; même s'ils

---

[47] Une exception avec C. CALVO, *Dictionnaire de droit international public et privé*, Paris, 1885, I, p. 154 : « Une nation a le droit d'explorer et de coloniser par elle-même et par ses nationaux tout territoire non compris dans le domaine d'une nation civilisée »

[48] R. PIEDELIEVRE, *op.cit*, p. 274. V également les débats sur cette question *in Annuaire de l'IDI,* 1880, Session d'Oxford, pp. 464ss.

[49] Nonobstant également, une fois sur place, les devoirs moraux que l'Etat peut avoir à l'égard des populations soumises. Par ex. E. NYS, *op.cit*, II, p. 93. Pour le droit au développement, *op.cit*, II, p. 1.

doivent pour ce faire, imposer un système juridique particulier garantissant cette évolution.

Mais ce faisant il y a ici un moralisme en embuscade qui est lourd de menaces puisque du même coup la mission de civilisation devient un impératif moral qui légitime toutes les institutions ou règles juridiques allant dans ce sens[50]. Ce moralisme juridique se transforme en effet en une véritable apologie de la bonne conscience coloniale ; laquelle se perçoit littéralement et de façon immédiate dans l'utilisation constante et non fortuite du terme « civiliser » à la place du terme « coloniser » comme si le premier pouvait occulter la réalité du second. Comme l'indiquait A. Truyol y Serra, cette bonne conscience explique aussi que ces auteurs se préoccupent peu des titres pouvant justifier la colonisation mais beaucoup plus de l'encadrement juridique de son établissement[51]. En revanche on peut mettre au crédit de la plupart de ces auteurs, la façon dont ils rejettent tout fondement religieux du droit des gens. Se situant résolument dans le domaine de la science dont ils ne doutent encore aucunement, ils se félicitent en effet de la lutte contre tous les fanatismes religieux et du mouvement de sécularisation du droit opéré avant eux par l'Ecole du droit de la nature et des gens. Comme l'explique le professeur italien de l'Université de Padoue, E. Catellani, l'ère de la suprématie pontificale est bien finie ainsi que toute idée de guerre juste qui pourrait prendre peu ou prou l'allure de croisade[52]. Il n'y a donc pas de droit des gens chrétien qui soit nommément imposé comme tel ou d'un droit des gens basé sur la révélation divine ; et cela quand bien même certains vont parler de droit des nations chrétiennes pour rappeler son origine historique et la confusion occasionnelle entre valeurs chrétiennes et valeurs juridiques. Et si cette identité éventuelle d'origine et de contenu pourra permettre de consolider d'une autre façon le colonialisme, elle ne transforme pas pour autant ce moralisme juridique en intégrisme religieux. *A contrario*, il peut sembler d'autant plus préoccupant de voir parfois invoquer aujourd'hui un humanisme contemporain prétendant se ressourcer à la loi religieuse.

Toujours est-il que, dans une telle perspective, qui tout à la fois préserve et justifie la supériorité du droit des gens en le fondant sur les valeurs

---

[50] Un moralisme juridique revendiqué expressément par P. FIORE, *op.cit*, I, p. 211, selon qui l'ensemble du droit des gens repose sur la « morale universelle ».

[51] A. TRUYOL Y SERRA, *Histoire du droit international public*, Paris, Economica, 1995, p. 109.

[52] E. CATELLANI, "Le droit international au commencement du XXème siècle », *RGDIP*, 1901, pp. 569 et 576. *Ibid* A. PILLET, « Le droit international... », *op.*cit, p. 24 et P. FIORE, *op.cit*, I, p. 527

fondamentales de l'humanisme juridique, demeure, il est vrai, la question toute aussi décisive des moyens d'action pouvant être déployés au service de la projection de ce droit et de ces principes fondamentaux. A cet égard, on ne saurait méconnaître que les manuels de l'époque ne reconnaissent que très rarement un droit direct d'intervention pour imposer la civilisation européenne et son système de valeurs car – et cela demeure un point fondamental – la notion de guerre juste est abandonnée depuis le 18ème siècle, laquelle ne faisait parfois que masquer sous un autre nom un droit de conquête des territoires étrangers[53]. Cet abandon de tout droit d'intervention, même pour une juste cause, ne doit pas cependant faire illusion. D'abord la guerre n'est pas disqualifiée comme elle le sera après 1945. Elle est le plus souvent associée à un mal nécessaire, « une nécessité pour les Etats », selon les termes de l'ouvrage commun de T. Funck-Brentano et A. Sorel[54], voire considérée comme un facteur de progrès car la priorité n'est pas la stabilité du monde, on l'a dit – même si cette préoccupation demeure – mais la réalisation de la justice des gens civilisés. Ensuite, si le droit d'intervention est condamné, ce n'est qu'entre Etats civilisés égaux et non pas pour les Etats protégés ou vassaux et *a fortiori* encore moins pour les territoires occupés puisqu'ils font désormais partie du territoire de l'Etat. Simplement, dans ce dernier cas, on ne parle plus d'intervention au sens internationaliste du terme mais d'action de police intérieure. Enfin on voit consacré par les mêmes traités de l'époque, un droit à l'occupation effective des territoires sauvages qui sera entériné pour l'Afrique avec la fameuse Conférence de Berlin de 1884-85 ; si bien qu'en réalité, si les mots ont changé de même que la nature des titres juridiques – droit à l'occupation effective et non pas droit de conquête ou de juste guerre – le résultat est le même, à savoir l'expansion de la souveraineté par appropriation des territoires sauvages ou non-civilisés et la colonisation des populations qui y sont installées.

IV. Enseignements : des difficultés de l'humanisme juridique contemporain entre tradition et renouveau

Décisives lorsqu'elles s'agencent les unes aux autres, ces trois représentations de l'histoire, du fondement et de la valeur de ce droit des gens européen –combinant historicisme, rationalisme et humanisme juridiques- font de lui un droit qui est à la fois rationnel et historiquement constitué, limité aux Etats européens et définissant un modèle de justice humaniste et libérale transposable aux autres. C'est pourquoi, si la

[53] R. PIEDELIEVRE, *op.cit*, p. 271.
[54] T. FUNCK-BRENTANO et SOREL, *op.cit*, p. 435.

découverte de l'historicité du droit des gens devait rendre profondément problématique à terme l'idée d'universel juridique, on n'en est pas encore là au 19ème siècle car les auteurs de ces manuels n'en assument pas moins la défense d'un certain rationalisme universaliste hérité des Lumières. Sans doute aussi perçoit-on aujourd'hui assez facilement ce que peut avoir de discutable une telle configuration car si ces caractéristiques étaient poussées à leur extrême, elles révèleraient mieux leurs prémisses contradictoires. Nous n'avons cependant pas cherché à introduire de la cohérence là où il n'y en avait pas, mais simplement tenté de montrer le fond commun de pensée hétéroclite et complexe qui innerve l'ensemble des manuels de cette époque. Et il n'en résulte pas moins que la logique des rapports et des implications de cette pensée internationaliste avec le colonialisme est à cet égard aisément perceptible. Non pas que l'on soutienne ici que ces internationalistes ont délibérément déployé un arsenal conceptuel destiné directement à justifier l'entreprise coloniale européenne ; ce qui serait selon nous une véritable erreur d'interprétation. Leur propos est ailleurs. Il est de nature scientifique et consiste avant toute chose à codifier et systématiser toutes les règles du droit des gens, théorique et pratique, sous la forme d'une doctrine des droits et devoirs fondamentaux des Etats[55]. Mais, en réalité, c'est peut-être en cela justement que la pensée de ces internationalistes est la plus inquiétante : s'il n'y a pas de volonté subjective de défendre la colonisation en cours – ni de la condamner – la question est cependant posée de savoir s'il existe une complicité *objective* entre leur dispositif intellectuel et le colonialisme, une complicité qui s'établirait de façon nécessaire et inévitable. Ou pour préciser les termes de cette interrogation : savoir si l'arrière-plan philosophico-juridique que nous avons essayé de mettre en exergue contenait en lui-même, de façon intrinsèque, les linéaments du colonialisme ou bien si le colonialisme n'en est seulement que l'un des effets pervers, non-nécessaire ou voisin ?

Face à cette interrogation qui semble absolument décisive pour nous aujourd'hui, de nombreuses solutions ont été déjà apportées et ont alimenté l'évolution même de la pensée internationaliste contemporaine. Dans un premier temps, c'est-à-dire vers les années 1960-70, l'affaire a pu paraître

---

[55] La colonisation ne constitue donc pas pour eux un sujet spécifique d'étude mais, on l'a vu, elle est quand même inévitablement traitée dès lors que tous ces internationalistes demeurent, à n'en point douter, profondément convaincus de la grandeur de l'entreprise coloniale (T. FUNCK-BRENTANO et A. SOREL, *op.cit*, p. 431 et aussi E. NYS, *op.cit*, p. 62) et qu'en tout état de cause, ils ne pouvaient esquiver de parler de ce qui représentait une des activités les plus importantes des relations internationales de leur époque.

réglée au vu des réfutations très dures portées à l'encontre du rationalisme, de l'humanisme juridique et du moralisme européens qui avaient accompagné la pratique du colonialisme. Les travaux de C. Levi-Strauss nous semblent singulièrement éclairants sur ce point[56]. Au vu de ce que nous avons précédemment exposé, on comprend d'ailleurs fort bien la logique de cette déconstruction systématique et pourquoi certains auteurs ont préféré miser sur la nature (naturalisme), la vie (vitalisme) ou le jeu des structures (structuralisme) plutôt que sur l'humanisme et ressourcer le droit à d'autres configurations intellectuelles que le rationalisme et le subjectivisme modernes. La déconstruction du droit international sous toutes ses formes (sociologique, marxiste, fonctionnaliste, linguistique et réaliste) et la montée en force d'un positivisme radical, de l'historicisation devenue complète des concepts du droit et du profond relativisme des valeurs juridiques qui en ressort, étaient autant de coup portés à cette ancienne configuration intellectuelle européenne. Loin d'être considéré, ainsi qu'il l'était auparavant, comme doté d'une réelle vertu émancipatrice et civilisatrice, le droit a été dénoncé tour à tour comme un instrument mystificateur et pervers de la lutte des classes, des rapports de force, du pouvoir de domination des Etats colonisateurs etc… Du même coup le droit international, qui était une valeur éthique fondamentale de la pensée internationaliste européenne d'avant la première guerre, a pu sembler brutalement dévalorisé à la suite des enseignements doctrinaux tirés des convulsions tragiques de ce droit et de la société internationale. Mais en fait ce retournement n'était que partiel car, alors même que se déployaient les critiques déconstructivistes en tous genres, se forgeait aussi, dans la réalité des textes conventionnels d'après guerre, un *renouveau* paradoxal du droit international. N'est-ce pas en effet en 1945 que les droits de l'homme et des peuples étaient inscrits pour la première fois dans un traité de portée universelle comme la Charte des Nations Unies et n'est-ce pas à ce moment-là que prenait naissance un courant de pensée, multiforme et peu structuré, mais très large et nettement déterminé en faveur d'une revalorisation implicite du droit international ?

---

[56] En particulier *Race et Histoire*, Paris, Unesco, 1952 ; *Tristes tropiques*, Paris, Plon, 1955 et *L'homme nu*, Paris, Plon, 1971 : « Jamais mieux qu'au terme des quatre derniers siècles de son histoire, l'homme occidental ne peut-il comprendre qu'en s'arrogeant le droit de séparer radicalement l'humanité de l'animalité, en accordant à l'une tout ce qu'il retirait à l'autre, il ouvrait un cycle maudit et que la même frontière, constamment reculée, servirait à écarter des hommes d'autres hommes, et à revendiquer au profit de minorités toujours plus restreintes, le privilège d'un humanisme corrompu aussitôt né pour avoir emprunté à l'amour propre son principe et sa notion »

Et dans la foulée de cette tendance originaire, la pensée internationaliste, dans un second temps que caractérisent ces vingt dernières années, s'est faite remarquer par un activisme sans précédent en faveur d'un certain contenu du droit international. Il y a une volonté manifeste de défendre un mouvement de réévaluation du droit international et des valeurs qu'il peut traduire ou protéger, en particulier les droits fondamentaux de l'individu, la justice pénale ou la démocratie. Ceux-ci sont alors fréquemment invoqués comme nouveaux fondements et finalités de l'ordre juridique international et donc parfois, comme devant être imposés unilatéralement à certains Etats en raison d'un devoir moral à intervenir. Or comment ne pas voir que, lorsqu'elles s'articulent autour des droits fondamentaux de la personne humaine, ces valeurs sont précisément fondées sur l'humanisme juridique ? Et qu'on le veuille ou non, il y a bien en cela une idée du Juste, fondée sur cet humanisme juridique, qui est véhiculée par le droit international contemporain et qui le soumet à des mutations indiscutables.

Or cette évolution paradoxale et complexe de la pensée internationaliste contemporaine – et du droit des gens sur lequel elle porte – fait apparaître des enjeux essentiels aujourd'hui. Elle montre que certains aspects de notre pensée internationaliste actuelle s'articulent plus ou moins directement, plus ou moins consciemment, autour de la problématique du siècle précédent et se fondent en partie sur son dispositif intellectuel. Ce faisant la pensée internationaliste contemporaine est, par là même, placée devant une interrogation très profonde, qui est héritée de son passé colonialiste proche et qui nourrit de nombreux débats car c'est le destin d'une certaine conception du droit international qui s'y joue et celui de l'homme lui-même : comment rester sur le terrain de l'humanisme et du rationalisme juridiques en droit des gens, d'une prétention à l'universalité et l'intangibilité de certaines valeurs éthiques fondamentales, sans tomber dans les errements du colonialisme ou de l'impérialisme? Comment penser l'universalisme sans tomber dans les pièges de l'hégémonie et de l'européocentrisme ? Certes, on peut récuser la prétention à l'universalité comme à l'intangibilité de ces valeurs juridiques et décréter leur relativisme historique, géographique et culturel, mais il serait alors particulièrement délicat de fonder philosophiquement les conditions de pensabilité (possibilité) de leur statut de droits fondamentaux et on nierait également ce que représente leur réalité juridique elle-même. En effet, on peut faire à ce stade le constat immédiat que la pratique juridique internationale contemporaine a plutôt tendance à reconnaître et déclarer des droits universels, en tenant compte de leur adaptation nécessaire à chaque type de culture mais sans remise en cause de leur caractère intrinsèquement universel. Il est vrai aussi que la question de l'humanisme occidental est loin d'être nouvelle mais encore faut-il prendre conscience que la pratique actuelle de certains Etats, dont nous avons parlé en introduction, transporte justement la question sur le terrain concret de l'action et nous met directement aux prises avec les dérives néo-coloniales qu'un certain humanisme moraliste peut susciter ; que cette pratique actuelle fait donc ressurgir avec beaucoup de force une vieille question doctrinale jamais résolue et à laquelle nous devons à nouveau réfléchir en tant qu'internationalistes.

Or, face à la question posée, les termes de la réponse peuvent peut-être être formulés sous la forme d'une alternative facile à identifier mais particulièrement délicate à résoudre. Soit on considère que c'est impossible (impensable au sens strict) et qu'il faut nécessairement abandonner l'humanisme juridique, la prétention à l'universalisme de certaines valeurs éthiques, pour échapper à tout danger d'une pensée impérialiste propice à la mise en place d'une forme contemporaine de néo-colonialisme. Soit on considère que c'est possible (pensable) et on s'efforce de conserver cet humanisme juridique mais en faisant le pari de le reconstruire. Ou encore, soit on reprend tout simplement les critiques déjà effectuées et on se cantonne au déconstructivisme ainsi qu'à la défense d'un strict relativisme, multiculturalisme ou inter-civisationnel comme étant fondateurs d'un nouvel ordre juridique international, oit on refuse cette voie qui peut sembler beaucoup trop ruineuse au regard d'un humanisme juridique universaliste et on cherche à fonder le droit international sur une pensée humaniste et rationaliste, mais renouvelée car devenue critique d'elle-même et consciente, grâce aux errements du passé et aux apports indiscutables de la déconstruction, des fausses illusions qu'elle a pu susciter et des dérives auxquelles elle a pu s'exposer comme la vision continuiste de l'histoire, la réduction de l'humanisme juridique à celui de l'homme occidental et le moralisme du droit. Cette seconde voie est la nôtre. Elle nécessite que l'on continue d'explorer les éléments de réponse induits par des pratiques juridiques et politiques des Etats en trouvant des solutions comme celle du multilatéralisme face à l'unilatéralisme et celle de la délibération intersubjective de la norme par rapport au décisionisme masqué de certaines grandes résolutions ; elle requiert aussi que l'on s'interroge sur le sens que peuvent prendre certaines notions comme celles de devoir d'ingérence humanitaire et de guerre juste et sur les périodes de la pensée qui permettent d'ouvrir des pistes pour cette réflexion – la philosophie juridique des

Lumières n'a-t-elle pas suscité un humaniste rationaliste anti-colonialiste[57] ? ; elle demande donc enfin que l'on s'interroge beaucoup plus profondément sur le dispositif intellectuel qui, cette fois-ci, les fonde et les légitime. En tant qu'internationalistes, on ne peut plus se contenter de faire comme nos prédécesseurs du 19ème siècle et se borner à exposer ou défendre des règles et des institutions fondées sur l'humanisme juridique car on court justement le risque de voir se reproduire les dérives néo-coloniales et impérialistes actuelles, lesquelles ne suscitent que suspicion et rejet et emportent avec elles la condamnation de l'humanisme lui-même. Si bien que contrairement parfois à ce que l'on peut peut-être penser intuitivement en tant que juriste, la difficulté ne réside pas seulement dans le choix de la meilleure technique juridique à mettre en œuvre – aussi difficile que soit également ce travail – dans la combinaison plus ou moins réussie de l'universalisme avec le relativisme, mais également dans la fondation philosophique de cette pratique car c'est la structure intellectuelle elle-même de notre discours internationaliste qui doit être renouvelée.

[57] Ceci n'est évoqué qu'à titre indicatif d'un mouvement de pensée qu'au demeurant il ne s'agit pas de retrouver intégralement dès lors qu'il véhicule justement un humanisme « naïf » auquel il faut échapper. Sur ce point A. Renaut et L. Sosoe, *Philosophie du droit*, Paris, PUF, 1991, pp. 38-39.

Europe and International Law's Colonial Present

Antony Anghie[*]

It was only fitting that one of the first panels of the inaugural Conference of the European Society of International Law should be devoted to the theme of 'Europe and International Law's Colonial Past'. As the very stimulating key note presentations by Professors Pellet and Reisman on the topic of 'International Law in the Shadow of Empire' suggested, however, the topic of imperialism has once again emerged as a source of keen interest to scholars of international law; empire is not a thing of the past. The purpose of this brief paper is to present, in very broad and somewhat summary terms, an overview of some key themes relating to this complex relationship and to suggest some ways in which we might attempt to understand the relationship between 'Europe and International Law's Colonial Past' and 'International Law in the Shadow of Empire'.

How is colonialism understood within the traditional histories of international law? Generalizing very broadly, conventional approaches to international law assert that international law is a European creation: the fundamental doctrines and principles of international law were a product of European history, practice and thinking.[1] For instance, the model of modern sovereignty that acts as a basis for international law derives from the Peace of Westphalia, and the universalization of international law resulted from the process by which these European doctrines were transferred to, or imposed upon, the non-European world, principally through the mechanism of colonialism. Colonialism, then, has certainly been the subject of extensive inquiry by European legal scholars. However, much of this scholarship was concerned to understand and resolve the various practical problems posed by non-European societies – the problem, for instance, of how a non-European state is to be arrogated to European sovereignty and thereby placed within the international system. Colonialism, then, was treated as peripheral to the major theoretical debates that profoundly shaped the character of the discipline of international law. It is interesting to note, for example, that

* Antony Anghie is the Samuel D. Thurman Professor of International Law at the S. J.Quinney School of Law at the University of Utah.

[1] *See e.g.,* J. H. W. Verzijl, *International Law in Historical Perspective* (Vol. 1, A.W.Sijthoff, Leiden, 1968) pp. 435–436.

Baltic Yearbook of International Law, Volume 6, 2006, pp. 79–84.

while Sir Hersch Lauterpacht has written extensively on colonial issues,[2] none of these issues appear in his great works on the basic problems and fundamental character of international law. In this way, colonialism is relegated to the peripheries of theoretical inquiry about international law. An examination of the relationship between colonialism and international law, according to the traditional view, reveals very little about the fundamental character of the discipline.

This tendency to elide the significance of colonialism to the discipline has been reinforced by the great theoretical questions that the discipline has formulated for itself and then attempted to resolve. At least since the nineteenth century, the major problem that has haunted the discipline – and that was presented in its most powerful form by John Austin – is the problem of 'how is order to be achieved among sovereign states'. This way of examining international law, of course, presumes the existence of sovereign equality. It thereby completely excludes from inquiry the situation of the non-European world, for non-European societies were regarded as not being sovereign, or only partially sovereign. The question that is posed by the non-European states, then, is: how was it decided that these states lacked sovereignty? And what are the terms on which they might acquire sovereignty? Rather than raise these questions – questions that could further a deeper understanding of the relationship between colonialism and international law – traditional approaches to international law assert that colonialism, while an unfortunate episode in the history of international law, has long since been overcome. While the international law of the nineteenth century legitimized colonialism, the United Nations period ushered in a new era in which international law negated colonialism through, for example, the promotion of decolonization. The old colonial doctrine of conquest is no longer recognized by contemporary international law.

I argue that this traditional understanding of the relationship between colonialism and international law is inadequate, if not, simply wrong. I would argue that colonialism, far from being peripheral to the discipline, was central to the very creation of international law. It was only through colonialism that international law became universal; and fundamental doctrines of the discipline, such as sovereignty itself, were profoundly shaped by the colonial encounter, because, I would argue, sovereignty was formulated in such a way as to exclude and subordinate the non-European

[2] *See e.g.,* H. Lauterpacht, 'The Mandate Under International Law in the Covenant of the League of Nations' in H. Lauterpacht and E. Lauterpacht (eds.), *International Law* (Vol. 3, Cambridge, Cambridge University Press, 1970) pp. 29–84.

world.[3] Further, the civilizing mission, that was such an integral aspect of European imperialism and that was furthered through international law, continues to be an integral aspect of contemporary international law – as suggested by doctrines relating, for example, to 'good governance' and now, the War against terror.

This is the background to the resurgence of Empire in the form of the United States' policies that animate its 'global war on terror' – the policies of pre-emptive self-defense and the attempt to transform societies into democracies. The US led war against Iraq of course, evokes images of imperialism in its most blatant form and it is evident that Europe perceives itself as needing to unite to face the challenges presented by an imperial United States. This concern is exemplified by the manner in which very prominent European intellectuals, who belong to sharply contrasting, if not opposing, intellectual traditions, Jurgen Habermas and Jacques Derrida, united to urge the development of a common European foreign policy.[4] The powerful document concludes:

> "Each of the great European nations has experienced the bloom of its imperial power. And, what in our context is more important still, each has had to work through the experience of the loss of its empire. In many cases this experience of decline was associated with the loss of colonial territories. With the growing distance of imperial domination and the history of colonialism, the European powers also got the chance to assume a reflexive distance from themselves. They could learn from the perspective of the defeated to perceive themselves in the dubious role of victors who are called to account for the violence of a forcible and uprooting process of modernization. This could support the rejection of Eurocentrism and inspire the Kantian hope for a global domestic policy."[5]

The broad assertion is that Europe is somehow 'post-imperial' and, as a consequence, is in a better position to develop the sorts of policies necessary to achieve a cosmopolitan peace.

How are we to understand these new developments? As a scholar who has an interest in the relationship between imperialism and international law, I would argue that these developments are somewhat bewildering. Whatever

---

3 I have developed these arguments in A. Anghie, *Imperialism, Sovereignty and the Making of International Law* (Cambridge, Cambridge University Press, 2005).

4 J. Habermas and J. Derrida, 'February 15, or What Binds Europeans Together: A Plea for a Common Foreign Policy, Beginning in the Core of Europe', 10:3 Constellations (2003) p. 291

5 Habermas and Derrida, p. 297.

the divisions between the United State and Europe over the war in Iraq, it is extremely implausible for European intellectuals to attempt to suggest that Europe has somehow transcended imperialism. Europe's practices and policies are profoundly imperial, and continue to be so – as reflected by its practices, not only within NATO, but also in extremely important international institutions such as the World Bank, the IMF and the WTO.[6] The new European posture might be understood as a response to the imperial threat that is perceived to arise as a consequence of the United States invasion of Iraq. But, I would argue, the Iraq episode is simply a very explicit and obvious example of imperial practices. Imperialism is experienced in the Third World, I would suggest, in a much more everyday way through, for example, international economic regimes, supported and promoted by international law and institutions, that systematically disempower and subordinate the people of the Third World. This is the 'everyday' imperialism, the quotidian and mundane imperialism that is accepted as somehow normal and that is furthered and promoted, in various ways, by Europe. For the Third World, then, I suspect, imperialism is not an aberration, an extraordinary event that has emerged with the US actions in Iraq. Rather, imperialism is an integral and enduring aspect of day to day international relations. What is missing in this analysis of the international situation is a clear and powerful sense of how the third world might understand and experience the ongoing relationship between colonialism and international law.

And the supposed divisions between Europe and the United States, and their contrasting visions on how to conduct international affairs, is also a familiar spectacle to non-Western peoples. It occurred at the Berlin Conference in 1884–85, where the United States representative joined for the first time with major European powers in discussing colonial problems. It occurred again in Paris in 1919, when President Wilson of the United States – speaking now with the authority of a Great Power – fought European skepticism and British Commonwealth manipulations to create the Mandate System of the League of Nations which was supposed to present an

6 For an examination of the contribution made by various European initiatives towards the furtherance of neo-imperial economic policies, for instance, *see* B. S. Chimni, 'International Institutions Today: An Imperial Global State in the Making', 15(1) *European Journal of International Law* (2004) p. 1.

entirely new way of managing relations between advanced and backward, civilized and uncivilized states.[7]

By this time, the ranks of the civilized had expanded. Japan and various Commonwealth countries such as Australia seized the opportunity presented by the disruptions of the Great War and the succeeding Paris peace talks to establish themselves firmly in the ranks of the civilized in this system. My basic point, then, is that, historically, differences between the United States and Europe on how to run the world have been a fairly constant feature of international relations. And these differences cannot always be characterized as a conflict between two parties, one of which is for imperialism and the other against. Rather, it is often a conflict between what sort of imperial policy might be the best approach.

In the current circumstances, formalism, an insistence on affirming and upholding the Law of the Charter, may be the best approach to deal with the more egregious forms of imperialism that are now being attempted by the United States.[8] And yet, there is a fear that the United Nations itself, through the Security Council in particular, may become an imperial institution. And a study of nineteenth century international law reveals how positivist formalism was used to further imperialism. Formalism, then, may provide a provisional and necessary defense against imperialism, but it is by no means a final and comprehensive answer. Indeed, the whole question of the adequacies of formalism raises a much larger issue. As international lawyers we would like to believe that international law provides us with a defense against imperialism. But this position is open to a serious challenge because, I would argue, *we do not as yet have an adequate understanding of the relationship between imperialism and international law.* For if, as I have argued, the relationship between imperialism and international law was, and continues to be, one of complicity rather than opposition, then profound problems accompany attempts to use international law to negate imperialism. What this suggests to me is that it is crucially important for our discipline to identify and understand the imperial aspects of international law, to grasp the relationship between 'Europe and International Law's Colonial Present'. It is only if we seek to understand that multiple forms of imperialism that are still an integral part of international relations and the role that international law plays in furthering these imperial systems that we

7 *See* Q. Wright, *Mandates Under the League of Nations* (Chicago, University of Chicago Press, 1930) pp. 24–63

8 A. Orford, 'The Gift of Formalism', 15 *European Journal of International Law* (2004) pp. 179–195.

might aspire to construct an international law that can truly aspire to promote international justice.

European Tradition and the European Society of International Law: Some Remarks about the Totalitarian Legacy

Iulia Voina-Motoc[*]

Contents

1. Introduction

From where do we come? How can we trace back a European tradition of international law? In our attempt to do so, we may identify two sources of this tradition, which goes as far as the Greek-Roman culture.

If we follow the Greek line of the European tradition, we notice that many of its concepts and ideas prepared the ground for the European key-concepts that we now call *tradition*: for example, *paidea* anticipates the modern philosophy of education and the tragedy, originally a literary term, informs many of the European concepts that followed.

Paidea, which conceptualized beauty and social good, developed into a trend in education that aimed to shape citizens devoted to the aforementioned values. *Paidea* represented the cultural formation of individuals and contrasted with learning a trade or an art. It helped the

[*] Professor of Public International Law, University of Bucharest. I thank Mona Momescu for the help with the preparation of the article in English.

Baltic Yearbook of International Law, Volume 6, 2006, pp. 85–109.

tradition of European international law to define itself within an intellectual context.[1]

According to the interpretation given by Nietzsche to the key concepts of ancient Greek thinking, the tragedy, the Apollonian vocation, which was inherent to the normativeness of the *paidea* received its complementary concept in the Dionysian sublimation of violence and irrationality.[2] This opened the path of the willpower that reinvents itself and glides on its own reflection, like Narcissus, demanding the apparition of the *Übermensch* and the rise of radical politics.

The Romans bequeathed the formalism of Roman civil law, as it had been codified under the Emperor Justinian in the *Corpus Juris Civilis*; it relied on the distinction between *jus civile* and *jus gentium*, later rediscovered at the edge of the Middle Ages by the French and Italian interpreters of Bartolus, the forefather of international private law.

Nevertheless, if we look back at the tradition the way we have, we interpret it from a meta-historic and mythological perspective. Tradition means the history of a domain that developed its own methods and means of investigation; within its margins, it continuously questions its very own methods previously invented.

Which tradition does the European Society of International Law, constituted in 2003 follow? What kind of questions should it answer and what type of problems is it supposed to solve? In the face of globalization and devastating perils the main voices of political philosophy have called for a planetary response involving the transition from classical international law, still anchored in the nineteenth-century model of the nation-State, to a new cosmopolitan order in which multilateral institutions and continental alliances would become the chief political orders.[3] The rise of international institutions after the end of the Cold War and their growing influence on the behaviour of international subjects bring up the question of the legitimacy of international governance. This line of thinking automatically leads to questions about the nature of the boundary between regimes, international

---

[1] *See* regarding the intellectual tradition of European International Law M. Koskenniemi, *The Gentle Civilizer of Nations, The Rise and Fall of International law, 1870–1960* (Cambridge University Press, Cambridge, 2004) *passim*.

[2] "That life is at the bottom of things, despite all the changes of appearances, indestructibly powerful and pleasurable . . . With this chorus the profound Hellene, uniquely susceptible to the tenderest and deepest suffering, comforts himself . . . Art saves him, and through art – life", Nietzsche, *The Birth of Tragedy*, section 7.

[3] G. Borradori, *Philosophy in time of terror, dialogues with J. Habermas and J. Derrida* (The University of Chicago Press, 2003) p. XVI.

organizations and governance. The debate about the legitimacy of international governance has to be conducted in a broader way, even if the actual proposals address the international organizations or certain political regimes. The European Society of International Law appeared in such a moment of historic importance when, mirroring the birth of the 1873 Institute, international law should have acted as a "consciousness of humanity".[4]

In order to attempt to answer some questions about the European Society of International Law, which started its activity in 2003, we launched several hypotheses, which can be only sketched in this article but which require further in-depth analysis. We define the recent European tradition on which the society relied as scarred in part by totalitarianism. Eastern Europe experienced communist totalitarianism, while Western Europe experienced reconstruction after the Holocaust and World War II. This is why we prefer to use European law as a branch of the once united international law in order to support our arguments. We examine some of the characteristics of communist international law and especially the distance between the theory and the practice, which is the most difficult question to answer within the communist regime. In its attempt to wipe out totalitarianism European law has formulated some pertinent but partial answers to the nation-State crisis. Until now, international law has not come up with plausible responses also because it has and does refuse to rely on theory. Another question refers to the deontological foundations of the society. European international lawyers have to assert their intellectual vocation – as it has been defined since the Dreyfuss affair more forcefully. This means that they have to intervene actively in society, and to make public any flaw of the instated power.

Whereas the Fascist period[5] benefited from a small and still marginal number of studies on the history of law no such studies were undertaken about the Communist period. The history of law during the Communist period is considered irrelevant to the Communist doctrine.[6] Or, the omission

---

[4] Koskenniemi, *supra* note 1, *passim.*

[5] C. Joerges and N. Singh Ghaleigh, *Darker Legacies of Law in Europe, The Shadow of National Socialism and Fascism over Europe and its Legal Traditions* (Hart, 2004) *see also* M. Koskenniemi, 'By Their Acts You Shall Know Them . . .' (And Not by Their Legal Theories) 15:4 *European Journal of International Law* (*EJIL*) (2004) *passim.*

[6] C. Mieville, 'The Commodity-Form Theory of International law: An introduction', 17 *Leiden Journal of International Law* (2004) pp. 276–277, *see also* C. Mieville, *Between Equal Rights: A Marxist Theory of International Law* (Brill, 2005). It is worthwhile to notice that the debate between fascism and communism was highly

of the study of the tradition of communist law had various and important effects as violations of human rights to knowledge and justice. This omission resulted into the refusal to acknowledge the past of a part of Europe recently integrated into the EU. This also prevents a correct and complete revaluation of Marxism, which can be accomplished only by relating Marxist theory to Marxist political practice. As Dérrida wrote: "*Finally the scene of our times, dominated by the specter of defeated communism that has come to haunt the future of a unified world under globalization and the triumph of the market economy . . . incapable of mourning over what it claims to have put to death*".[7] We will try to outline some lines of development of international law under communism. It is impossible to define the recent European tradition of international law while ignoring its Marxian praxis in Eastern Europe.

The first part examines international law in Communist Europe. Europe's sad experience of colonialism is common knowledge, whereas the failure of political modernity as recorded by the communist experiment has not been studied sufficiently.

The second part deals with the ways in which the consequences of totalitarianism were taken into account in Western Europe. European law has developed original thinking related to the nation-State. Is it possible that international law should develop in this direction, or is it the same old history of 'conceptual re-colonization'?

The third part is a synthesis of the first and the second, presenting friendship and hospitality in international law. The narrative of friendship is based on Hannah Arendt's assessment that the lack of this civic friendship is a characteristic of totalitarianism. Thus, the civic friendship should be at the core of international law in Europe.

Our study is not a systematic one; it is meant to endear more profound studies regarding the question of totalitarianism, especially communist totalitarianism and the way it was reflected in international law. We will use an approach which is *subjective* (it relies on individual opinions of authors) and *objective* alike, i.e. it also relies on general conceptions and ideas.

---

politised *see e.g.*, F. Furet and E. Nolte, *Fascisme et communisme* (Ed. Hachette, Paris, 1998). A. Besançon, *Le malheur du siècle* (Paris, Ed. Fayard, 1998), S. Courtois *et al.*, *Le livre noir du communisme* (Paris, Ed. Robert Laffont, 1997). S. Courtois, *Du passé faisons table rase! Histoire et mémoire du communisme en Europe* (Paris, Ed. Robert Laffont, 2002).

[7] J. Derrida and E. Roudinesco, *For what tomorrow. A Dialogue*, p. 78, *see also* Specters of Marx, *Specters of Marx, the state of the debt, the Work of Mourning, & the New International*, translated by Peggy Kamuf, (Routledge, 1994) *passim*.

Another issue may be the difficult choice between theory and practice in describing the analyzed tradition. We have chosen both, according to their importance in relation to our discourse. To schematize this extremely vast theme, we had to restrict our investigation to two cases of Western European law and two of Eastern European law.

2. The Eastern European Tradition

There are elements of commonality and elements of difference in the region. Most commonalities in the outer empire of the USSR were the result of policies imposed by the USSR. Indeed, in Eastern Europe between 1948 and 1989, the Soviet military presence was a clear and determinative factor in beating back the impressive range of heterogeneous resistance these satellites still managed to generate.[8] Without a domestic change of the hegemon it was extremely difficult for both Central and Eastern European elites and people to initiate new political processes that might have led to transformations.[9]

Much of the pre-1989 literature from the countries of the region suffered from two analytical problems. Initially a major strand of the literature began with such an exclusive focus on the region's shared status as 'satellites' that the significant heterogeneity of the pre-communist and communist State-society relations of each country was played down. Later many scholars began to emphasis the uniqueness of the countries they specialized in.[10]

The corpus of Marx's work is very large and intricate. It is not our intention to analyze the Marxist doctrine in international law; we would rather follow Habermas and examine the relation among the various aspects of Marxism: genuine Marxism, Marxist-Leninism and the social practice.[11]

---

[8] During the GDR riots in 1953, during the Hungary revolution in 1956, and after Prague spring of Czecholsovakia in 1968, Soviet troops were used to alter the course of domestic politics. J. J. Linz and A. Stepan, *Problems of Democratic Transition and Consolidation* (John Hopkins University Press, 1996) p. 237.

[9] *Ibid.* p. 238.

[10] *Ibid.*

[11] The philosophical discourse of justice lacks its institutional dimension, toward which the sociological discourse on law is directed from the outset. Without the view of law as an empirical action system, philosophical concepts remain empty. However, insofar as the sociology of law insists on an objective view from the outside, remaining insensitive to the symbolic dimension whose meaning is only internally accessible, sociological perception falls into the opposite danger of remaining blind. J. Habermas, *Between Facts and Norms Contributions to a*

As we stated in the introduction, we will examine the tradition of European international law as it is today; in this context, we are interested in the Marxist project as a failed utopian project of modernization.[12]

We will further demonstrate that there is an unquestionably direct relation between Marxian philosophy and the creation of communist society. If one denies this, then there is little chance, if any, to redeem anything from Marxian thinking. Even if, as Brad Roth observed, Marx dismissed utopian political thought and he was interested in the scientific development society,[13] we cannot deny that the very project of a society without social classes, and, ultimately, a society which exists in the absence of a State was a utopian project. It is more than that, it is the most utopian project of modernity; a project that, according to Krygfier, has furnished few resources to struggle against usurpation and brutalities.[14]

2.1. The Delegalization

2.1.1. Law as Superstructure – the Cult of Inconsistency

Zdanow, one of the great theorists of Soviet Marxism, made a famous declaration cited on every possible occasion by Soviet writers as a politico-philosophical directive and also used to explain the sudden and arbitrary changes in Soviet political practice and theory "[o]ne and the same idea, under different circumstances, can be, depending on the case, reactionary or progressive". The cult of change persisted in Soviet theory as truly consistent with the interest of the proletariat. The Soviet government felt authorized to decide unilaterally whether and what change was necessary to carry out.[15] This lack of consistency appears obvious in the frequency of controversies and in the arbitrary changes in international law. It was rather frequent that Soviet authors changed their opinions in compliance with the interests of the USSR.

Discourse Theory of Law and Democracy (Translated by William Rehg. MIT Press 1996) p. 32.

[12] As pointed out by Anne Orford.

[13] B. Roth, 'Retrieving Marx for the Human Rights Project', 17 *Leiden Journal of International Law* (2004) p. 32.

[14] M. Krygier, 'Marxism and the Rule of law: reflections After the Collapse of Communism', 15 *Law and Social Inquiry* (1990) p. 633.

[15] M. S. Korowicz, 'Present aspects of sovereignity', 1 *Recueil des cours* (*Rdc*) (1961) p. 30.

2.1.2. Totalitarianism: International Law – The 'Weapon of the Enemy'

During the early years of the Soviet system, there was much to make the Soviet leaders distrust international law. The world was hostile to the new Soviet government, and favourable arguments were frequently retrieved from international law. Payment of debts of the Tsarist regime were required; Soviet decrees nationalizing industrial and commercial establishments were resisted whenever this property was in the non-Soviet courts; Western governments were participating in the war against the Soviet government.[16]

It is nonetheless true that the quality of jurisprudence was also weak. The lack of confidence in international law reflected a more general and widely spread lack of confidence in the power of law. The Manifesto already prepared an answer: "The proletariat will use its domineering role in politics in order to snatch the capital from the hands of the bourgeoisie, step by step . . . It goes without saying that in the beginning we can do that only by despotically breaking the rule of right to property and of the bourgeois work and production relations".[17] From this perspective, the Constitution became a temporary legal instrument, useful only until the State as a form of government ceases to exist.[18]

For example, the Constitution of the People's Republic of Romania, 1952, one of the most evidently revolutionary Communist constitutions, tackled the fundamental human rights and liberties in chapter seven. "He who would not work, would not eat" is one of the legal principles stipulated in this Constitution.[19] The right to work comes first in a hierarchy of human rights, which is at par with equality in the hierarchy of rights. The core of the communist constitution lies in the transformation of the right to private property. The rights to work, study, and association were protected, as were the freedoms of speech and assembly in the 1952 Polish Constitution. However, the Constitution provided no mechanism, for the individual to put into effect these rights and freedoms. The government claimed that no requirement for an enforcement mechanism existed since the necessary benefits of those governing and those governed were the same. The

---

[16] J. Hazard, 'The Soviet Union and International law', 1:3 *Soviet Studies* p.189.

[17] K. Marx and F. Engels, *Manifesto of the Communist Party 1848* <www.anu.edu.au/polsci/marx/classics/manifesto.html>.

[18] For the interpretation that the absence of the rule of law during communism can be traced in the Marx analysis of liberal State and society *see* Krygier, *supra* note 13.

[19] <www.cdep.ro/pls/legis/legis>.

Communists rejected as basically defective the notion of an independent, politically neutral judiciary. Judges in a socialist system constituted part of the State's coercive apparatus, consequently no procedures were essential to control the constitutionality of statutes. Judicial review was rejected because it would constitute a limitation of the sovereign rights of Parliament.[20]

Deprived of any specific meaning or autonomy, the law including international law looses its normative status (*sollen*). In Kant's words, the legal system in totalitarian societies is reduced to its material reality (*sein*). This is why the subjects of totalitarian societies are as submissive to official law as they are to the laws of nature. As Hannah Arendt commented, the rule of law during totalitarianism became like the law of nature described by Hobbes.[21]

2.2. Post-Totalitarianism:[22] Dynamics and Movement

We consider communist post totalitarian law as characterized by a significant gap between State law and the applied law. This gap is the result of adopting a legal framework which is entirely incompatible with the legal culture of a certain State.[23]

---

[20] I. Motoc, 'Manifestul Partidului Comunist, Totalitarismul, Statul de drept posttotalitar, trei fete ale refuzului modernitatii politice' ('The Manifesto of the Communist Party, Totalitarism and Post-Totalitarian Rule of Law – Three Dimensions of Political Modernity Rejection') in K. Marx, F. Engels, *Manifestul Partidului Comunist* (*Manifesto of the Communist Party*) (commented Ed), Nemira Publishing House, Bucharest, 1998.

[21] H. Arendt, *Le systeme totalitaire* (Paris, Points-Politique, 1972) p. 40 *et seq*.

[22] Post-totalitarism is considered by J. J. Linz and A. Stephan to be the late evolution of the totalitarian regime where the regime elites "may collectively decide to constrain the completely arbitrary powers of the leader, to reduce the role of leader and to begin to tolerate some non-official organizations to emerge in what had been virtually a complete flattened civil society. Starting with '70 the communist regime was considered to be posttotalitarian". J. J. Linz and A. Stepan, *supra* note 8 p. 293.

[23] One of the most important differences among States does not pertain to the difference in their constitutions or in their law systems, but to the extent to which the official law is applied. The almost complete ignorance in this respect is a result of the positivist approach, for which all norms with no juridical relevance have been ignored. The organization of society based on legal rules relies on the assumption that these rules are objective in some sense while political ideas, views, or personal preferences are not. To show that law is objective – one may act on two levels. On the one hand, it aims to ensure the *concreteness* of the law by distancing it from theories of natural justice; on the other hand, it aims to guarantee the *normativeness*

In our attempt to demonstrate the gap between theory and practice, we choose to present two relevant doctrines for international law: that of the relation between the State and the capitalist world and that of human rights. The evolution of human rights during communism has deeper effects than one may guess. At the end of the eighties, under the influence of the political upheaval in Eastern Europe, Western European thinking agreed to "return to law" ("le retour au droit").[24]

2.2.1 The State and the Capitalist World Economy

For the Marxist theory of international law, the formal definition of the State laid down in the 1932 *Montevideo Convention on Rights and Duties of States* fails to recognize that the State is a function and form of social relations. As it was interpreted by Marxism, the Montevideo Convention failed to acknowledge that the modern State emerged in response to certain fundamental social transformations that accounted for the transition from feudalism to capitalism. The same Marxist interpretation postulated that in international law the bourgeois State coexisted from the beginning with the colonial State in an evolving capitalist world economy, which laid an indelible mark on the body of international law.[25]

It is true that socialist ideology supports a hostile attitude towards capitalism, the destruction of private property and the fusion between politics and economy. In the post-totalitarian age, the influence of the totalitarian State on economic activities weakens, while the formerly centralized State economies turn into negotiated economies. The State appears more and more vulnerable when facing the pressure of new economic patterns. The totalitarian State is now replaced by a weak State, which finds itself incapable of managing a well functioning fiscal system that provides an equitable redistribution of income.

After the totalitarian period there is no longer any totalitarian interference of the State in the economic sphere. The economies which were formally planned became 'negotiated' between the communist leaders and the leaders of State enterprises. The weak State seems to be common to all

---

of the law by creating distance between it and actual State behaviour, will, or interest. *See* M. Koskenniemi, 'The politics of law', *EJIL* (1990) pp. 1–2.

[24] A. Renaut and L. Sosoe, *Philosophie du droit* (Paris PUF, 1991) p. 21.

[25] B. S. Chimini, 'An Outline of a Marxist Course on Public International Law', 17 *Leiden Journal of International Law* (2004) p. 5.

utopian societies. Corruption is a characteristic of all post-totalitarian societies.[26]

The creation of an economic class from the political class is taking place and it is exploiting the legislative amorphousness characteristic of the prerogative State. An example of this is the dual ownership of fixed assets in the State sector: sometimes these assets are regarded as being assigned group ownership, at other times they are considered State property. The communist leadership became 'bourgeoisified'. What had been developed was 'Brezhnevism', 'goulash communism' and an implicit social pact in which elites offered the prospect of social welfare in exchange for silence.[27]

In 1848, Marx and Engels explained this to their contemporaries: "you are frightened because we want to abolish private property. But, in the society you lead and in which you live now, private property is non-existent for nine tenth of its members."[28] Public law completely colonized the territory of private law except for one last relic: the right to personal property. The history of the right to personal property makes one of the most interesting histories of totalitarianism.[29]

---

[26] A. Prezworski, *Democracy and the market, political and economical reforms in Eastern Europe and Latin America* (Cambridge University Press 1991) *passim*

[27] *Ibid.*, p. 2.

[28] Marx and Engels, *supra* note 17.

[29] I. Motoc, 'Manifestul Partidului Comunist, Totalitarismul, Statul de drept posttotalitar, trei fete ale refuzului modernitatii politice' ('The Manifesto of the Communist Party, Totalitarism and Post-Totalitarian Rule of Law – Three Dimensions of Political Modernity Rejection') in K. Marx and F. Engels, *Manifestul Partidului Comunist* (*Manifesto of the Communist Party*) (commented Ed), Nemira Publishing House, Bucharest, 1998. According to Marx and Engels, the expansion of public law to the detriment of private law was supposed to put civil and political rights into practice. This objective seemed so unfeasible that no Communist constitution included it among its principles. In the communist State this resembles the fruit seller portrayed by Havel, who displayed the motto "Workers from all the world, unite" in the window of his small fruit shop. To the citizens of the communist State, the Constitution shares the status of the Communist Manifesto, namely it is an external object, a special type of law. Havel explained the exercise of daily opportunism of the grocer by the fact that he was corrupted by means of "small advantages", offered by communism in its consumerist stage. If the grocer did not display the motto on a daily basis, he would be refused the "small advantages": to own a summer house, to spend long vacations with his family. This minor key and trivial consumerism really corrupts. Individuals do something very powerful and dangerous when they 'live within a lie'. They thereby contribute to the general panorama of ideology which maintains the structure of power. Small affirmations

2.2.2. Human Rights

Even for those who argue that the Marxist vision is compatible with human rights movements it is clear that Marx's project cannot be reconciled with a natural rights approach, nor can Marx be interpreted to embrace the view that 'moral rights' are a distinctively useful construct in reasoning about political morality.[30]

In practice, the USSR's representatives in the Human Rights Commission of the United Nations have stated that several rights of the UDHR constitute infringements of sovereignty. It was argued that to let the United Nations itself, or other nations enforce human rights would constitute an infringement of sovereignty. The USSR accepted the UDHR adopted by the General Assembly in 1948 but was cautious concerning the provisions relating to enforcement. It wanted no other State or international tribunal to enforce the provisions. It wanted no other State or international tribunal to act as a policeman or court enabled to prosecute a State for violating a principle of the UDHR. Considerations of the Genocide Convention by the United Nations brought forth similar hesitations. Again, a breach in the wall was accepted by the USSR at Nuremberg.[31]

In the Soviet Union and Central and Eastern European countries, international law could not be directly invoked before and enforced by domestic courts. Under the Soviet system, international obligations were applicable domestically only if they were transformed by the legislature into a specific statute or administrative regulation. As a result, the Soviet Union was able to sign the various United Nations human rights treaties and yet still avoid any implementation of these rights in domestic law.

Nevertheless, after the Final Helsinki Act was signed, there was an incontestable evolution in the conception of human rights in Eastern Europe. This new broadening of views was profoundly beneficial to the human rights movements; the activists in the field understood they had recourse first to the regulations in international law and to the human rights stipulated in the Constitution.

---

and compliances with this ideology serve to confirm this panorama. Because of this, Havel observes, each and every individual bears a portion of guilt for the functioning of the system. Everyone thus functions as both victim and oppressor. One's position of power only determines one's degree of implication; as Havel puts it, "the fault lines run through each individual".

[30] B. Roth, 'Retrieving Marx for Human Rights', 17 *Leiden Journal of International Law* (2004) p. 32.

[31] J. Hazard, *supra* 16, p. 194.

But 'modern' Soviet human rights law did not come together until the early 1970s. This new law was intended to be a careful response to the wave of dissident movements inside the USSR in the late 1960s. The Soviet government sought to achieve two interrelated goals: to give the characteristic bases for its contemplated counterattack against its dissidents at home and to create the appearance of aligning its laws with the evolving international standards on human rights.

'Modern' Soviet human rights law differentiates between: moral rights and legal rights; human rights and natural rights; positive rights and inalienable rights; group rights and individual rights; obligatory (peremptory) rights and discretionary (optional) rights; and socio-economic and cultural rights on the one hand and civil and political rights on the other. This law also expresses the general principles governing the relationship between the citizen and the State on the one hand and between the individual and society on the other. It must always be borne in mind that Soviet constitutional law concerning human rights operates against the backdrop of two fundamental principles of Soviet law: the doctrine of abuse of rights and the principle of the interdependence of rights and duties of citizens.[32]

The section of the 1977 constitution dealing with the bill of rights is considerably more extensive than the corresponding sections of the earlier Soviet constitutions; chapter 7 contains thirty separate provisions. This does not mean that the Soviet citizen possesses new substantive rights or that he has been saddled with new obligations. Rather, those rights that in the past had been treated merely as statutory rights have now been elevated to the constitutional level. It is true, however, that some of the old constitutional rights have been broadened. Professor Voevodin of Moscow State University Law School, a leading Soviet constitutional scholar, dispels the notion of any intended difference between the two groups of enumerated liberties with the following explanation:

> "By individual rights or freedoms, in a strictly legal sense, one means the legally recognized opportunity of an individual to choose the form or mode of his conduct, to utilize those blessings afforded him by law both in his self-interest as well as in the interest of society at large . . . Such legally recognized opportunities sometimes are traditionally referred to as 'rights', whereas at other times they are referred to as 'freedoms'. Between these two concepts, it is difficult to draw any meaningful distinction, because the same opportunity may be interchangeably characterized both as a right and

---

[32] C. Osakwe, 'Soviet Human Rights Law Under the USSR Constitution of 1977: Theories, Realities and Trends', 56 *Tulane Law Review* (1981) p. 249.

> as a freedom . . . In other words, there are two forms that express the legally recognized opportunity of an individual to choose his mode of conduct. When such an opportunity is linked with the exercise of a specific social blessing the law traditionally speaks of a 'right', whereas when the reference is to a degree of choice of mode of conduct the law speaks of 'freedom'. Compare, for example, the right of education, the right of medical care, with the freedom of conscience and the freedom of creativity."[33]

The position towards human rights has also changed because of the concept of *jus cogens*. As stated by Tunkin the delegation of Socialist States and most of the delegations of the Afro-Asian countries firmly supported the article concerning the principle of *jus cogens*. Their representative stated that the rule of *jus cogens* is a cornerstone of the progressive development of contemporary international law and is essential for the stability of international relations.[34]

The human rights issue has acquired special importance in Poland and Czechoslovakia because of the large-scale repression in Czechoslovakia after the defeat of Prague in the spring and in Poland during the student unrest in 1968 and then in the wake of the workers' riots in Ursus, Radom and other localities in 1976. The Polish opposition groups which at first concentrated on the defense of workers persecuted for the June 1976 riots, now concerned themselves with human rights and at the same time with the need for change in the country's governance and social life. A reform program was formulated by an impressive array of former politburo and central committee members. In the spring of 1981, a character in A. Wajda's film, *The Iron Man*, explained this strategy: the unjust laws must be criticized, but the State had to respect at least the constitutional rights of citizens.[35] Kundera, by means of Mirek, the character from *The Lost Letters*, presents the same hypostasis of the communist subject in the same sense as *The Iron Man*. Mirek, who ends his life in prison, is invented as a result of the relation between the novelist and his novel; at the same time, by his constant relation with his personal life, the character relates to the Constitution.[36]

---

[33] *Ibid.*

[34] G. Tunkin, International Law in the International System, *Rdc* (1975) p. 323.

[35] A. Renaut and L. Sosoe, *Philosophie du droit, supra* note 22, p. 21.

[36] Mirek is the only character influenced by political modernity: his relation with his own life is rational and he always requires the protection of law. Thus, he acts as an authentic anti-Marxian. In the post-totalitarian universe, Mirek is caught between the fruit seller, who exerted his Communist rights, and the poet, who did the same, in

According to Adam Michnik, dissidence had a special status in Eastern European economies: the radicals and the exiled cultivated the illusion that dictatorship was solely a result of constraints. Long-term dictatorial regimes created their particular state of sub-normality and a culture associated with it. They also created a human type who had lost the sense of freedom, truth, dignity and self-consciousness.[37] The rebels were no more than a minority that counted for very little. In the aftermath of the reforms in the sixties, most intellectuals sided with the official power. Had Soljenitsyne lived in Hungary, he would have never written *The Gulag Archipelago*; instead, he might have enjoyed the privileges of having been elected president of the Hungarian writers' association, Miklos Haraszti wrote.[38]

The communist intellectual as a typology was described by C. Milosz, who compared them with the Islamic *ketman.* Similarly, the intellectual whose most precious possession is the truth, shouldn't have his person and wealth exposed to all those who follow an immoral code, however, if this is the case he must hide his thoughts. When confronted with the representatives of political power, the *ketman* knows he possess the truth, which is ignored by those acting as agents of power and the very knowledge of this truth makes him happy.[39] In post-totalitarian societies we may speak of a national, esthetic and metaphysical *ketman.*[40]

This practice is evident in Kundera's literature. There it is the case of Jaromil, the poet from *Life Is Elsewhere.* A wonder kid, he becomes a national poet at the end of the games of privileges and compensations granted to him by *The Party.* Jaromil is then capable of any compromise with power. It is the case of Sabrina, from *The Unbearable Lightness of Being*, she finds kitsch more detestable than communism. The communist drama in Central Europe, as it appears in Kundera's novels, resides more in revisiting national culture than in the lost individual freedom in the name of communist ideology.[41]

---

the name of a pre-modern hierarchic moral order. I. Motoc, *The Manifesto of the Communist Party, supra* note 20.

[37] A. Michnik, *Letters from Prison and Other Essays* (University of California Press, Berkley, 1985) *passim.*

[38] M. Harastzi, *The Velvet Prison: Artists under State Socialism* (Basic Books, New York, 1987) p. 178.

[39] C. Milosz, *The Captive Mind* (Vintage Books, New York, 1990).

[40] I. Motoc, 'L'Europe unie et l'Europe après le communisme: rationalite et ethique de l'elargissement' in E. Barnavi and P. Goossens, *Les frontieres de l'Europe* (Bruxelles De Boeck, 2001) p. 174.

[41] *Ibid.*

Jan Patocka, who dominated the spirit of the Charter 77, was also a critic of political modernity, much in the tradition of Husserl and Heidegger. His work analyzed the philosophy of the Enlightenment, the utilitarianism and the excessive role of technocracy.[42] As opposed to the other intellectuals, Patocka understood that a destructive social climate, as was the case in totalitarian societies, could not shelter and support arts and philosophy. For him, communist totalitarianism was the sum of individual alienation; a life based on dignity should have been protected at any price. Even with the price of one's own life, as it happened with Patocka himself.[43]

The Charter 77 was created and has survived from 1977 to 1992 as a movement exposing victimization practices, i.e. violations of human rights and international commitments. The human rights orientation was dominant in the sense of a demand that the regime should bring its legal system in line with its own constitution and the United Nations covenants on rights and freedoms.[44]

The publications from that period showed us that the Polish movement was constantly related to law by the Western intelligentsia. Suddenly, there was a consensus that revolved around legal values. In the seventies, under the influence of the postmodernist paradigm, law was conceived in terms of a war and there was no clear demarcation between law and politics. Once the social movements in Eastern Europe extended, Western subjects began to understand that the reference to law could coexist with a variety of forms of democratic consciousness.[45]

The years that followed were devoted to the interpellation of force in the name of law; the left enthusiastically adopted this practice, as well. Thus, the Soviet intervention in Afghanistan was denounced in the name of the rights of peoples; in other times, we would have probably relied on a harsh critique of imperialism followed by references to a philosophy of history that promoted the perspective of a socialist future. At the same time, the interpellation of force in the name of law moved to the reports presented by smaller groups, such as *Amnesty International* or *Médecins sans frontières*.[46]

---

[42] J. Patocka, *Essais eretiques sur la philosophie de l'histoire* (Lagrasse, Verdier, 1999) *passim*.

[43] I. Motoc, 'L'Europe Unie et l'Europe d'apres le communisme', *supra* note 40.

[44] H. Rigby, 'Politics in the Mono-organizational Society', in A. Janos, *Authoritarian Politics in Communist Europe* (Berkely, 1970).

[45] Renaut and Sosoe, *supra* note 24.

[46] *Ibid.*

3. The Western European Tradition

There are two reasons why we have chosen European law as a descriptor of the European tradition of international law.[47] On the one hand European law had an answer for totalitarianism at the end of World War II; on the other hand, with the help of political theory and political science, it offered answers to the problems of federalism, constitutionalism and to international legitimacy.

3.1. The Search for Peace in the Process of European Integration

As Haltern wrote: "the Union born from the ashes of Auschwitz, millions dead and indescribable destruction was a reaction to the destructive force of politics, eroticism".[48] In the immediate aftermath of World War II, the cause of European integration was sustained by the United Europe Movement and by the US and the Marshall Plan. The movement reached a high in 1948 when the European Congress imposed the creation of the Council of Europe. As an intergovernmental organization, it soon disappointed the promoters of the movement and the US alike. The US then insisted on continuing the Marshall Plan within the Organization for European Economic Cooperation (OEEC).[49]

Five years after the end of WWII, sensing the danger of a Cold War, Monnet proposed a new plan for reconciliation. The European unification efforts started in 1950 with the Schuman plan and led to the treaty of Rome in 1957. This meant a very deliberate overcoming of the racist imperialism of the Nazi regime. Immediately after WWII, peace was the most explicit and evocative ideal of the European Union.

---

[47] The publication of Stein's article, 'Lawyers, Judges and the Making of Transnational Constitution' in the *American Journal of International Law* in 1975 marked the separation between European law and international law. At the same time, European law has enough efficient means to comply with international legal standards: accession, legal succession, autonomous references (e.g. Article 6(2) EU), and general principles of law. The Community institutions are, however, quite reluctant to limit their scope of action and to compromise the autonomy of EU law.

[48] U. Haltern, 'Pathos and Patina: The Failure and Promise of Constitutionalism in the European Imagination', Web-Papers, ConWEB No. 6/2002 <http://les1.man.ac.uk/conweb/> p. 19

[49] J. D. Donahue and M. Pollack, 'Centralization and its Discontents: the Rhythms of Federalism in the United States and the European Union', in K. Nicolaidis and R. Howse (eds.), *The Federal Vision: Legitimacy and Levels of Governance in the United States and the European Union* (Oxford University Press, 2001) pp. 73–118.

The Schuman Declaration of 9 May 1950 which attempted to unify the nations of Europe required the elimination of the age-old opposition of France and the Federal Republic of Germany; the first concern in any action undertaken must be these two countries. This solidarity made it plain that any war between France and Federal Republic of Germany became, not merely unthinkable, but materially impossible.[50]

The discourse on peace occurred again only at the end of the Cold War, mostly when the relations with the former Yugoslavia were re-established. The discourse of the European Commissioner for Enlargement in Sarajevo stands as a proof: "You may think that I ask for the impossible, just ten years after the violent break-up of Yugoslavia but let me remind you that Robert Schumann made his declaration on European unity in May 1950, just five years after the Second World War. Thus, when the founding fathers of Europe decided to bury their swords and set up the peace project that is nowadays called the European Union, the memories of terror, death and fear were still vivid in the minds of these political leaders, as well as the peoples of Europe".[51]

The Draft Treaty establishing a Constitution for Europe's preamble lacks any obvious reference to the genesis of European integration: the catastrophes of the 20th century and particularly World War II. The architects of Europe emerged from the horrors of the Second World War determined to thwart even the possibility that another war could occur. One might object that the Convention's preamble does refer to "the ancient divisions" which are to be "transcended", and Article I-3, para. 1 declares that the "Union's aim is to promote peace".[52]

The Intergovernmental Conference introduced into the Convention's third reading of the preamble the words "after bitter experiences". With these words, "bitter experiences", the TeCE links the catastrophic events of the 20th century with its formation; they appear to be a possible ground for a

---

[50] <www.diplomatie.gouv.fr/archives.gb/dossiers/schuman/module03.html>.

[51] In that regard the EU is a victim of its own success. I believe young Europeans do not appreciate the EU as a peace project as naturally and as profoundly as their parents or grandparents do. After 60 years of peace they take it for granted. But peace or democracy can never be taken for granted – they have to be constantly pursued, and new generations won over Speech Commissioner Rehn delivered to students at Sarajevo University on July 11 2005 <http://europa.eu.int>.

[52] Armin van Bogdandy, The European Constitution and European Identity: Potentials and Dangers of the IGC's Treaty Establishing a Constitution for Europe in Symposium: Altneuland: The EU Constitution in a Contextual Perspective No5/04 <www.jeanmonnetprogram.org>.

common interpretation of crucial historic events that might also permeate the European Union with deep significance.[53]

3.2. Nomos: Federalism and Constitutionalism

The principle of federalism should not be mistaken for the specific manifestations of a certain federation. When certain idealists believed that a shift from the nation-State system to federalism could be accomplished at the global level via the UN, the rivalries between Cold War actors stifled their enthusiasm. Additionally, the recently de-colonized States did not want to give up their newly acquired statehood this way. The model of the United States of Europe was perceived as being too revolutionary at the time. Functionalism seemed a more attainable and practical solution. The new approach was made possible by transferring the collective security issue to another organization, NATO.[54]

At the end of the sixties, it appeared obvious that the European Communities began to make arrangements based on functionalism. The actualization of this confederation may be perceived in two ways: a union of States, each of which may be constructed in the form of statism but which together pooled certain powers for mutual advantage; or as a union of unions in which sovereignty was vested in the people of each member unit and through them to its whole.[55]

It is true that the history of federalism and constitutionalism in the EU has been examined so many times that it has become boring. In spite of this, we have to agree with Haltern when he examined the weary old judicial review debate from another angle, however, Europe's constitutionalism debate has, I believe, not even reached the heart of the matter. A contributing element of this may be the uncertainty about what 'constitutionalism' means. For example, Professor Craig's essay on European constitutionalism suggests no less than five different meanings of 'constitutionalism' and 'constitutionalization'.[56]

We will try to present three perspectives on European constitutionalism, encompassing three different points of view;

Tucked away in the fairyland Duchy of Luxemburg and blessed, until recently, with benign neglect by the powers that be and mass media, the Court of Justice of the European Communities has fashioned a constitutional

[53] *Ibid.*
[54] Donahue and Pollack, *supra* note 49.
[55] *Ibid.*
[56] Haltern, *supra* note 48.

framework for a federal-type structure in Europe. It is true that, as pointed out in J.H.H. Weiler,[57] beginning in 1963 and going through the seventies, the ECJ stated the four doctrines that founded European constitutionalism: the doctrine of direct effect, the doctrine of supremacy, the doctrine of implied powers and the doctrine of human rights.

The mid-seventies and the eighties did not bring much to European constitutionalism; it happened because of the international situation and because of the ascent of new States that shared varying ideas as far as integration was concerned. What was really important in this period was the deepening of the differences between the competences of the Member States and the Community. Whereas in the case of a federal State this is explicitly stipulated in the Constitution, in the case of the EU it appeared and developed implicitly.[58]

The Treaty on European Union, which formally moved the European polity beyond the previous incremental approach to integration and took a fundamental step towards economic and monetary union, as well as moving towards political union, is at present usually perceived as being abrupt and associated with the first genuine sign of a popular legitimacy crisis.[59]

Constitutional tolerance is encapsulated in the original expression of its meta-political purpose in the preamble of the EC Treaty. In political terms, this principle of tolerance finds its manifestation in the political organization of the Community and Union, which defies the normal premise of constitutionalism. In the Community, the European peoples are subject to constitutional authority although the peoples are different. Constitutionally, the principle of tolerance finds its expression in the understanding which has now come under discussion: a federal constitutional authority, which is not entrenched in a "statist formalized constitution".[60]

Ante Winer has identified three stages of the constitutional construct of the European Union: first, integration through supranational institution-building, second Europeanization through domestic institutional adaptation and third, late politicization as the more complex process of socio-cultural and legal institutional adaptation in vertical and horizontal dimensions. The particular organs of the Union are treated as 'hard' institutions. The appearance of so-called 'soft' institutions such as ideas, social and cultural

---

[57] J. H. H. Weiler, *The Constitution of Europe – do the New Clothes have an Emperor?* (Cambridge University Press, 1998) pp. 10–101

[58] *Ibid.*

[59] *Ibid.*

[60] *Ibid.*

norms, rules and/or routine practices and their respective relation with the appearance and resonance of the institutions of constitutional law are at the center of this interpretation. The phases are distinguished by reference to significant changes in *type*, *place* and *dynamics* of integration that caused institutional change within the European multi-level governance system.

The first stage is characterized by bottom-up institution building. Center theories were involved in the discussion over 'grand theory' among neo-functionalist and inter-governmentalist approaches in international relations theories.[61]

The second stage is distinguished for Wiener by a top-down research perspective on institutional adaptation. At this time the focus of study is the question of more or less Europeanization. Theoretical orientation for this viewpoint is provided by the hodgepodge of the explanatory and increasingly all-encompassing multi-level governance methods, organization theories, the various neo-institutionalisms, and regime theories as well as constructivist research; theoretically this phase brought a shift from international relations to comparative governance and public administration.[62]

The third stage is made up by the increasingly complex challenge of reintegrating bottom-up institution building, i.e. the changing institutional basis of the European political organs, as well as the parallel and interrelated process of top-down Europeanization of formal institutions in politics, the market, and the legal and administrative structures in the respective candidate countries. Furthermore, in the face of bulky enlargement this third phase also involves the requirement of rethinking, reassessing and rearticulating the position and sense of values and norms that lie at the center of European governance and – most importantly – the possibilities of their eventual expression within a distinctly defined constitutional framework. During this phase, interdisciplinary theoretical work bringing together law, political science, sociology and cultural studies has begun to examine the considerable normative, functional, legal and political questions of European integration as a procedure that might have surpassed its dynamics of institution-building and expansive potential as a process of consolidation both in domestic and world political matters.[63]

---

61 A. Winer, *Towards a Transnational Nomos – The Role of Institutions in the Process of Constitutionalization*, Jean Monnet Working Papers, 9/03 <www.jeanmonnetprogram.org/papers/papers03.html>.

62 *Ibid.*

63 *Ibid.*

The third perspective was exposed by Ulrich Haltern in his article *Pathos and Patina: The Failure and Promise of Constitutionalism in the European Imagination.* He considered that legal studies act in response to the Union's social legitimacy deficit either by being channelled into the puzzle through empirical sociology, or by paying no attention to it on the whole. Haltern argues that the difficulty of social reception can be traced back to the texture of EU law. Law is more than a quantity of rules: it is a social practice, a structure of meaning and a system of beliefs. National law is supported by a deep foundation in cultural practices. In contrast, EU law is exemplified by the flowing facade of consumer characteristics. The Union's counter-measures – adding *pathos* and *patina* to counteract our distrust – have been demonstrated ineffective. The forward thinking after that, is coming to terms with the market citizen, more willingly than believing in, and forcing upon the consumer, stories of joint values in times gone by. Haltern maintains that such treatment of one of the core problems of European integration is inadequate. Social skepticism is not limited to the area of empirical sociology. It is intimately linked with the area of law. Social legitimacy, then, is a matter of legal consideration, and deserves attention from the perspective of the law.

And yet, what is the relevance of this debate for public international law? As Anne Orford has shown, international law is not a knight clad in white armor, waiting in some (European) capital to intervene when politics goes wrong. It is always *already* there structuring the private and public relations within which material and spiritual resources are distributed throughout the world.[64]

Though there are many features of European integration that imply that global processes will not duplicate European processes, there are prominent similarities between contemporary international law and European law. Equally, international law and European law are no longer limited jurisdictionally to their respective spheres. Equally in European and international law the link connecting State consent and the appearance of legal obligations is frequently eased. The spread of non-consensual international obligations created by separated groups of actors has meaningfully increased. Constitutional arguments invoking democracy are beginning to be articulated in Western liberal democracies to challenge the

[64] Martti Koskienniemi on Anne Orford, *Reading Humanitarian Intervention. Human Rights and the Use of Force in International Law* (Cambridge University Press, 2003).

legitimacy of international law, in much the same way as discussion of the democratic deficit has dominated European debates in the last decade.[65]

The first lesson learned from European law is methodological. European law examined the problem of the nation-State in an appropriate manner, as it constantly co-operated with political theory; this happened only accidentally in international law after 1950. It goes without saying that international law cannot copy the European model. Beyond the moral and political status of a prospective conceptual reformulation, there are more practical arguments. As it has been demonstrated repeatedly, European law cannot be reproduced on any different regional scale. On the other hand, in most of the contemporary States the rule of law is weak, they keep *nomos* at their margins, and thus they survive in contradiction with the European model of integration.

4. Friendship in International Law

The European Society of International Law appeared at a critical moment; on the one hand, it was the moment of reunification of a Europe previously divided by totalitarianism, on the other hand there was the ascent of international law. What is the deontological background of the society? In academia, friendship is a word that one may hear frequently, almost a catchword. We then ask, what does friendship mean in international law? Can it be the deontological background in international law?

Aristotle was the first philosopher who wrote extensively on the importance of friendship. For Aristotle, ethics is essentially the art of living well. Only those who have friends can achieve the successful pursuit of excellence because friendship provides the ideal conditions for this. "Complete" friendship is an essential part of what Aristotle calls "the good life".

Aristotle divides friendship into three species: friendship of *good* people, friendship based on *utility* and friendship based on *pleasure*. Friendship based on utility and/or pleasure *alone* is described by Aristotle as incomplete, while friendship of good people, similar in virtue, are *complete* friendships. The reason friendships based on utility are incomplete, is that they are motivated by short-term considerations and are contingent on changeable circumstances. Similarly, friendships based on pleasure are

---

[65] Kathrin Blanck *et al.*, 'Conference Report – Europe's Constitutionalization as an Inspiration for Global Governance? Some Viennese Conference Impressions', 6 *German Law Journal* (2005) p. 227, M. Kumm, 'The Legitimacy of International Law: A Constitutionalist Framework', 15:5 *EJIL* (2004) p. 907.

contingent on feelings and accidental conditions. The friendship of good people is most enduring, and complete, because they "wish goods to each other for each other's own sake", in addition to being useful and pleasant to each other.[66]

Cicero in *Laelius de Amicitia* proposed a vision of friendship that differentiated between friendship of ordinary folk, or of ordinary people – although even these are sources of pleasure and profit – and the true and perfect friendship, the kind that is possessed by those few men who have gained names for themselves as friends.[67]

We may continue with the history of friendship but, in order to find some common ground between friendship and normativeness we have to return inside the citadel. Thus, Hannah Arendt's interpretation of Ancient Greek thinking is most relevant to our case. She believed that the Greek acceptance of friendship was inseparably related to life in society; if this was lacking, as Rousseau also wrote in his time, the modern man risks alienation. This is why friendship becomes of public importance. For Aristotle, friendship meant more than the abandonment of civil wars; the essence of friendship consisted in discourse. Citizens can be united only by dialogue. As opposed to private conversations, dialogue envisaged public wellness first. For Arendt, the world is humane because it is created by humans and it becomes humane only when the voice of humanity resonates harmoniously. Humanity is created by friendly conversations in the ancient Greek tradition of *philanthropia*, love for people "amour de l'homme".[68] Arendt wrote that the lack of this civic friendship is a characteristic of totalitarianism.

At the beginning of this study we wrote that *paidea* is one of the European sources of international law. As Koskenniemi wrote, the tradition of European law was an intellectual one; the jurists define themselves as a "consciousness of humanity''.[69] What happened after 1960? According to Koskenniemi, this type of tradition disappeared as a result of public international law losing interest in problems without practical value. However, within European law the interest of jurists in theory and political sciences did not fade. The 1980s meant social engagement for the European jurists. They also tried to analyze and interpret the law in particular political, economic and historical contexts.

---

[66] D. Thunder, Friendship in Aristotle's Nichomachean Ethics: An essential component of the Good Life <www.nd.edu/~dthunder/Articles/Article4.html>.

[67] Cicero, *Laelius de amicitia* (University of Michigan Press, 1971).

[68] H. Arendt, *Vies politiques* (Paris, Gallimard, 1974) pp. 34–35

[69] Koskenniemi, *supra* note 1.

The European University Institute was created in 1972 by the Member States of the founding European Communities. Its main objective was "to provide advanced academic training to Ph.d students and to promote research at the highest level".[70] It carries out research from a European perspective (fundamental research, comparative research and Community research) in history, law, economics, political and social science.

An analysis of the 'law in context' was also the message of the editors of the European Journal of International Law (EJIL) founded in 1990.[71] In terms of its orientation the EJIL is distinguished by its emphasis upon critical and theoretical approaches, its commitment to publishing contributions from a diverse range of contributors and its continuing interest in the historical origins of the 'European tradition' (in the best and broadest sense) in international law.

The ever-increasing numbers of Western human rights centers that cooperate closely with the NGOs share the same vision. More and more jurists have now become involved in the activity of international NGOs,[72] however, these lawyers are not vocal enough on the European intellectual scene.

This intellectual vocation of the European jurist is now menaced by the managerial vocation of contemporary organizations. As the universities are increasingly subjected to and transformed by the management system, the bureaucratic structures in which the jurist becomes involved menace his/her intellectual vocation. As they are part of the 'management structures', the jurists are less inclined to speak out on events in his immediate surrounding. If we paraphrase the Italian polemics between Antonio Tabucchi and Umberto Eco, we may say that: if something important takes place in my town or in the wide world, the intellectual jurist will hurriedly participate in the events. The manager will say that unfortunately, he/she cannot participate, as he/she is too busy organizing a conference or preparing a new issue of a review. The most important quality of the intellectual, according to Tabucchi, is the Cartesian doubt. Undoubtedly, the manager-jurist will adopt the model of friendship, where friendship means utility. In this case, he/she will act in a manner promoting public relations and not towards authentic friendship.

---

[70] <www.iue.it>.

[71] <www. ejil.com>.

[72] P. M. Dupuy, 'Some Reflections on Contemporary International Law and the Appeal to Universal Values: A Response to Martti Koskenniemi', 16:1 *EJIL* (2005).

Is the European jurist tempted to spread his own model, as Anne Orford rightly observed? And how can he/she escape this temptation? In order to find a solution to this, we believe that the acceptance of hospitality according to Dérrida is a useful argument.

For Derrida hospitality is a flexible concept comparable with tolerance, that represents the motivation of the strongest and powerful. If somebody thinks he's hospitable because he is tolerant it is because 'I', the interlocutor, want to limit myself, to retain power and maintain control. To Derrida, tolerance means conditioned hospitality. By being tolerant one accepts the other on their own terms, such as authority, law and hospitality. Pure and unconditional hospitality opens or is opened in advance to someone who is neither expected, nor invited; it opens to a new arrival, non-identifiable and unforeseeable, in short, a complete otherness. Derrida would call this a hospitality of visitation rather than an invitation. The visit might be actually very dangerous and we must not ignore this fact, but hospitality without risk would not be true hospitality.[73]

Beyond conceptual queries that the European Society of International Law needs to take up, there remain the deontological ones. Will friendship within the Society mean more than utility and utilitarianism? Will the Society manage to impress the intellectual and – more than that – theoretical approach to international law without which it is impossible to answer today's questions regarding the disintegration of the nation-State? Will the West be capable of relating to Eastern Europe in a manner other than 'tolerant'? Will European international lawyers be able to think and relate to the world outside Europe with all the risks incumbent with 'hospitality'?

---

[73] Derrida in Borradori, *supra* note 3.

The Definition of Genocide and the Role of Soviet International Lawyers:

Reflections on the Socialist Legacy in International Law[*]

Lauri Mälksoo[**]

Contents

1. Introduction

A ghost is wandering around in Central and Eastern Europe, the ghost of the *Historikerstreit*. Although some time ago Ernst Nolte and Jürgen Habermas completed their heated arguments, scholars and commentators living in the countries of the former Eastern block are passionately revisiting the history of the mass crimes of the 20th century. What was suppressed during the socialist period has now come to the surface and in several instances radically moved the pendulum of the historical consciousness. This has happened notwithstanding the somewhat paradoxical fact that former (transformed) socialist elites continue to hold parts of political and economic power in Central and East European countries. The "end of Yalta"[1] in 1990/1991 has not just completely changed the European political landscape;

---

[*] Revised Presentation at the Inaugural Meeting of the European Society of International Law, May 2004, Florence.

[**] Dr.iur., Associate Professor of International Law, Faculty of Law, University of Tartu.

[1] *See* K. Skubiszewski, 'The End of Yalta', in K. Wellens (ed.), *International Law: Theory and Practice. Essays in Honour of Eric Suy* (Martinus Nijhoff, The Hague, 1998) pp. 107–119.

Baltic Yearbook of International Law, Volume 6, 2006, pp. 111–124.

it has also given impetus to new interpretations and understandings of the history, spreading its impact also to the context in which post-Cold War and post-Maastricht international legal theory is thought.

This is the current background of our carefully titled panel "The Legacy of Socialism in International Law". The topic of this panel is both ambitious and ambiguous. It is ambitious because it sets out to appraise the significance for international law of (depending on how one counts) at least seventy years of very turbulent world history.

The topic is at the same time ambiguous since 'socialism' means different things to different people. There was a disillusioned anecdote in the USSR (i.e. Union of . . . *Socialist* Republics), which claimed that the only country where socialism had been achieved in practice, not just in theory, was . . . of course not the USSR itself but Sweden. Indeed, it is possible to argue that Sweden's traditional social democracy is an interpretation or application of 'socialism'. Even before the collapse of the Communist block caused a serious identity crisis to the socialist movement generally, it was often argued that the Soviets 'got it all wrong', that Russia was in 1917 not prepared to move on from quasi-feudalism to socialism, and in particular Soviet mass persecutions had nothing in common with the *real* teachings of the founding fathers of socialism. In other words: it has been claimed that the Soviet interpretation and/or application of socialism was incorrect which was why one should not put an equation mark between the terms 'socialist' and 'Soviet'. Perhaps it reflects this terminological confusion and the uncertainty about whether Soviet crimes have or have not discredited 'communism' or 'socialism', that Council of Europe educational materials when addressing the crimes committed in Europe during the 20th century and before its own creation, refer euphemistically to crimes committed by "fascism *and totalitarianism*".[2]

International law is generally a pragmatically oriented discipline in the sense that it takes as its basis what is significant in State practice. Ideological interpretations that are 'right' but have little or no practical impact on State practice, are generally not of much interest for international legal studies. For that reason, I would not have to lose myself here in the debate about which form of socialism was the 'correct one', whether there has yet been

[2] *See* P. Brander *et al* (eds.), COMPASS. A Manual on Human Rights Education with Young People (2nd ed., Council of Europe Publishing, 2003) p. 31, under the heading "[w]hat and where is Europe?" explains that "[t]he continent is associated with the birth of democracy and, at the same time, with some of the worst examples of fascism and totalitarianism that the world has ever seen".

such or whether one has to yet wait for its coming. I would thus turn to the historical-political phenomenon that identified itself with the concept of socialism and decisively influenced the 20th century world history: the existence of first Soviet Russia (since 1917) and then the USSR (since 1922) in the European political and legal landscape until 1991, with its dramatic increase of power and influence following the defeat of Nazi Germany and the formation of the socialist Eastern block in 1945. In this sense, my contribution to the panel could also be phrased as "The Soviet Legacy in International Law". As my interpretation today is more historically than theoretically oriented, it should be seen independently from topics like the legacy of Marxism in international law.[3]

Asking about the socialist legacy in international law poses several problems. As we all remember, socialism as a political system came to its end in Europe only recently, in 1989–1991. This is a significant aspect, also for international legal analysis. When Henry Kissinger asked Zhou Enlai how he estimated the impact of the French revolution of 1789 for world history, Zhou famously replied: "It is too early to say". Certainly, one's perspective of the socialist history in Central and Eastern Europe today is shaped by the fact that we all, in one or other way as participants or at least contemporaries, lack sufficient time perspective and neutrality for analyzing the past. In this sense at least, it is too early to say what the socialist legacy in international law is. Yet paradoxically, at the same time it is also too *late* to ask what the socialist legacy has been – when, for example, not much can be done about the Soviet crimes.

As socialism means different things to different people, it follows that so does its legacy. It can even mean different things for the same individuals. A discussion of ideological concepts such as 'socialism' may raise the temptation to see a legacy as something overwhelmingly negative (socialism as 'bad') or, for that matter, overwhelmingly positive (socialism as fundamentally 'good'). The future's judgment will probably be more balanced. In any case, there are positive aspects of the socialist legacy in international law. Consider the idea of social and economic rights – would those rights play such an increasingly significant role in today's human rights law, if there would not have been Marxist thought or a Soviet-led socialist Eastern block constantly insisting on those rights? (Which is, on the other hand, one of the reasons why conservative opponents of social and

---

[3] *See* contributions by Martti Koskenniemi, Anthony Carty, B.S. Chimni and Brad R. Roth at the 2003 symposium 'Marxism and International Law' in 17 *Leiden Journal of International Law* (2004).

economic rights claim that those rights should not be trusted.) Moreover, there are countries in the world outside Europe that link their decolonization and the exercise of their right to self-determination after World War II to socialist ideas and liberation movements influenced by Marxism-Leninism. When we disapprove of the legacy of colonialism, we cannot deny the progressive transformatory role that was played by socialist critical ideas.

It seems that the legacy of socialism (also for international law) can be appraised differently in different historical and geographical contexts. Therefore, I am aware that my own perspective is not necessarily universal – rather, it is an East European or perhaps even more distinctly a Baltic perspective. But this is also a feature of international law and its applications: while striving to be universal, international law can be seen from different perspectives. Since I know many people who want what I am going to say to be expressed, I almost feel as an agent of history (and I do of course say it with a degree of self-irony) when presenting at this historic inaugural conference of the European Society of International Law.

In the following, I will argue that the biggest socialist/Soviet legacy in international law is silence. This silence concerns legal and practical responses to the crimes that were committed by the USSR in the name of socialism against its own citizens and against citizens of its neighbouring countries in Central and Eastern Europe. International law, reflecting power relations between its main constituents, States, has not responded adequately to those crimes. This non-responsiveness has had two dimensions. First, existing definitions of crimes (in particular crimes against humanity) were in practice not applied to Soviet crimes. Second, other definitions of crimes (genocide) were shaped in such a way that the experiences of the GULAG[4] and Soviet mass repressions were on purpose left out of the scope of the definition. Thus, the way crucial legal concepts were drafted and applied as a response to Nazi crimes only, simultaneously reflected post-Second World War power relations and did hardly correspond to the Aristotelian maxim of justice suggesting that like cases must be treated alike.

2. Regarding the Pain of Others: The Nuremberg Trials and the 1948 Definition of Genocide in International Law

No matter how hard one would try, it is impossible not to compare the Soviet socialism with the Nazism/fascism when thinking about the history of the 20th century. British leaders, for example, inevitably had to ask in 1939

[4] For a recent history of GULAG, *see* A. Applebaum, *Gulag: A History* (Doubleday, New York, 2003).

which power, the USSR or Nazi Germany, constituted a bigger threat, geostrategically and morally. It was an unpleasant choice between two evils and there are several indications which imply that the choice lay primarily on the basis of geostrategic necessities rather than moral calculation. Nazi Germany simply constituted a larger and more immediate threat to the West while the Soviet threat seemed further away from the center of the West. As the alliance for the defeat of Nazism succeeded, it was not in the West's immediate interest to announce that Stalin's USSR had also committed heinous crimes against international law. Having been allied with a power with no less a criminal record than Nazi Germany could have relativized the moral significance of the victory over Nazism. If the price for one person's liberation is another person's slavery, the very act of liberation might reduce the importance of its moral power.

The French historians under the leading editorship of Stèphane Courtois who recently published "*Le livre noir du communisme*" have claimed that approximately 20 million people fell victim to Soviet mass crimes from the 1920s to 1950s.[5] In addition, historians claim that the Soviet occupation and *de facto* control in Central and Eastern Europe resulted in approximately one million victims. Even those historians critical of the accuracy of Stèphane Courtois' and his co-authors' interpretations and in particular their ideas about attributability, do agree that the number of Soviet victims reaches many millions.

Not surprisingly, this kind of historical evidence was suppressed during the first international criminal trial in human history, at Nuremberg. The Soviet attempt to ascribe their own mass murder of arrested Polish officers in Hatyn (Katyn) forest to the Nazis has by now received much public attention. An equally significant incident happened when a German defence lawyer, Dr. Seidl, wanted to elaborate on the secret protocols of the Nazi-Soviet Pact of 23 August 1939, and was abruptly cut off by the Soviet prosecutor, Major Rudenko. But with these secret protocols Hitler's Germany and Stalin's USSR effectively divided Eastern European countries between themselves. It was the territorial compensation offered to the USSR that enabled Hitler to start the Second World War by attacking Poland on 1 September 1939. On 17 September 1939 Soviet troops invaded the Eastern Polish territories accorded to it in the Pact's secret protocols. To the extent that the Nuremberg judgment suppressed the evidence of the Hitler-Stalin Pact's secret protocols, it gave a historically inaccurate account of the issue

---

[5] *See* S. Courtois, *et al.*, *The Black Book of Communism: Crimes, Terror, Repression* (Harvard University Press, 2000).

of causality and the genesis of the Second World War and the *Soviet* crimes against peace that were committed during it.

As far as war crimes were concerned, the defence of '*tu quoque*' ('you too') found a certain recognition at the Nuremberg trials. In the application of crimes against humanity,[6] the argument 'tu quoque' would have of course been an absurd defence. Mass persecution of civilians could hardly be justified with the defence that the enemy did the same. Nevertheless, it was in particular in this account that the Soviet presence at Nuremberg was most disturbing. For "murder, extermination, enslavement, deportation, and other inhumane acts committed against any civilian population, before or during the war; or persecutions on political, racial, or religious grounds in execution of or in connection with any crime within the jurisdiction of the Tribunal" [7] was widely practiced in the USSR already in the 1930s, both against 'hostile' social classes and 'hostile' ethnic groups. As lawyers we should also note the once very important debate about the "link with the crimes against peace or crimes against humanity" in the London statute's definition of crimes against humanity. (In the post-Nuremberg period,[8] and most recently in the Rome statute of the International Criminal Court, it has been eliminated from the definition of crimes against humanity.) Bertold Brecht's "thinking worker"[9] (academic one) would ask whether the link of crimes against humanity with war crimes and/or (Nazi) crimes against the peace was established for Nuremberg due to the fact that in the 1920s and 1930s, millions of civilians were persecuted in the USSR already before the Nazi aggressions were committed in the Second World War?

When the Second World War ended, the need to single out the worst kind of crimes against humanity was widely felt. Raphael Lemkin, a criminal

---

[6] *See* Article 6 (c) of the Charter of the International Military Tribunal, annexed to the Four-Power Agreement of 8 August 1945. *See also* United Nations War Crimes Commission, *History of the United Nations War Crimes Commission and the Development of the Laws of War* (UN War Crimes Commission, London, 1949) p. 192 *et seq*. and E. Schwelb, *Crimes against Humanity*, 23 *British Year Book of International Law* 1946, pp. 178–226 and C. M. Bassiouni, *Crimes Against Humanity in International Criminal Law* (2nd ed., Kluwer, The Hague-Boston-London, 1999).

[7] *See* the London Charter of the International Military Tribunal, 8 August 1945, Article 6 (c).

[8] *See* already Control Council for Germany, Law No. 10, 1946.

[9] *See* Brecht's poem "Fragen eines denkenden Arbeiters".

law scholar who had emigrated from Poland, coined the term "genocide".[10] Genocide was conceptualized as the gravest form of crimes against humanity, with particular emphasis on the intent to destroy specific groups (the subjective component in the definition of a crime or *mens rea*). The legal definition of genocide very interestingly reflects hierarchies of power established after the end of the Second World War. During the *travaux préparatoires* of the Convention for the Prevention and Punishment of the Crime of Genocide,[11] a heated political debate ensued about how this "crime of the crimes" was to be defined.[12] While the initial UN draft defined genocide as "the intentional destruction of a group of human beings", including racial, national, linguistic, religious or political groups, the USSR strongly opposed the inclusion of the destruction of social and political groups, arguing that genocide was a crime that was "organically bound up with fascism-nazism". As the USSR threatened otherwise to block the adoption of the convention, other UN States of that time finally gave in and agreed to exclude the intentional destruction of social and political groups from the definition of genocide.

Arguments presented in favour of this discriminating legal definition of genocide have failed to cover the fact that the exclusion was carried out on the basis of power politics rather than on morally (or even logically) defendable grounds. One of the arguments in favour of the exclusion was that racial, religious, ethnic and national groups were somehow more permanent and stable than political groups. It was argued that you could give up your social class or political convictions, however, the Nazis did not give such a chance to the groups hated by them, e.g. Roma – if you were one, you were meant to be annihilated. But looking for instance how insignificant a percentage of pre-1940 Estonian, Latvian and Lithuanian politicians and officers survived the 1940–1941 year of the Soviet occupation, one has to conclude that no such chance for 're-education' was given by the Soviets to hostile political classes either (albeit in this case the policy of annihilation was connected with foreign occupation, i.e. it was not a pure case of class

[10] *See* R. Lemkin, *Axis Rule in Occupied Europe: Laws of Occupation – Analysis of Government – Proposals for Redress* (Carnegie Endowment for International Peace, Washington, DC, 1944).

[11] Adopted by the UN General Assembly Res. 260(iii)A on 9 December 1948, 78 UNTS 277 (1951).

[12] *See* W.A. Schabas, *Genocide in International Law* (Cambridge University Press, Cambridge, 2000).

conflict but constituted also national conflict).[13] Membership in a certain political class or organization meant quasi-automatically one's death sentence. Furthermore, social scientists have demonstrated that all groups tend to be social constructions rather than 'objectively' existing entities.[14] In principle at least, to give up or change one's religion would not be more difficult than for example to give up one's conviction that private property or a non-Soviet nation State was a good idea.

One negative consequence of those asymmetric definitional hierarchies has been the reluctance of the State-continuator of the USSR, the Russian Federation, to unequivocally condemn the Soviet crimes. The argument "but the USSR was the primary force in beating Nazi Germany" unfortunately still sometimes serves as justification for the relativization of Soviet crimes and occupations in Eastern Europe. This attitude has been nourished by the fact that although German Nazism received the judgment it deserved in Nuremberg, no international legal decisions or instruments have been delivered in the case of Soviet mass crimes.[15]

Another negative consequence was that the mass murder committed by the Khmer Rouge against hostile classes among the Cambodian people in the 1970s could not be qualified as genocide according to the restrictive definition adopted by the Convention against Genocide.

Thirdly, the unity of international law has not been served by the unconvincing justification of the exclusions in the 1948 definition of genocide, many States have adopted a broader definition of genocide in their criminal codes, including the purposeful destruction of political groups in their domestic definition of the crime.

---

[13] *See further* L. Mälksoo, *Soviet Genocide? Communist Mass Deportations in the Baltic States and International Law*, 14 *Leiden Journal of International Law* (2001), pp. 757–787.

[14] B. Anderson, *Nations – Imagined Communities: Reflections on the Origin and Spread of Nationalism* (Verso, London, 1991). For a literary adoption of the idea of how race can be a social construction, *see* P. Roth, *The Human Stain* (Vantage, New York, 2000).

[15] It could happen only on the basis of such an asymmetric culture of impunity that when a Latvian court convicted in 2000 a former Soviet partisan for having committed war crimes against Latvian civilians in the village of Malye Baty in 1944, the Russian president sent a letter to the Latvian president asking for the acquittal of the former partisan, with the justification that the latter had been fighting against Nazi Germany.

3. Choices, Threats and Temptations of Academic Lawyers in Socialist Countries

In the third part of my part presentation, I want to draw your attention to a fascinating field of study for the future: biographies of (international) leading lawyers and legal scholars under socialism. Significant research has already been produced about leading international legal scholars and academic collaborators under Nazism.[16] My own preliminary research on leading legal academics under socialism indicates that legal scholars in socialist countries often faced similar challenges, threats and temptations as lawyers under the Nazi regime.

Already in the 1930s, legal commentators noticed striking similarities between the Nazi and Soviet legal systems.[17] The Estonian legal philosopher, Artur-Tõeleid Kliimann, wrote in 1939 that the Soviet and the Nazi legal systems were characterized by a number of common undemocratic features that were not compatible with legal systems found in liberal democracies[18] (Kliimann's native country, Estonia, along with most other Central and Eastern European countries had ceased to be liberal democracy in 1934, following a *coup d'état* that established a form of authoritarianism). After the Second World War, it was the philosopher Hannah Arendt who explained the German Nazism and the Soviet Communism as two sides of the same destructive illiberal current in European politics.[19]

Returning now to Kliimann. I would argue that the way Kliimann's life and arguments entered into a dialogue with the life and arguments of the German legal theorist Carl Schmitt carry a significant symbolic weight about ideological clashes and paradoxes of the 1930s in Europe.[20] Kliimann's attack against Schmitt was a predecessor of the German *Historikerstreit* of the 1980s. Kliimann's and Schmitt's intertwined story symbolizes dilemmas faced and choices made by continental European legal thinkers in the face of

---

[16] *See especially* C. Joerges and N. Singh Ghaleigh with a Prologue by M. Stolleis and an Epilogue by J. H. H. Weiler, *Darker Legacies of Law in Europe: The Shadow of National Socialism and Fascism over Europe and its Legal Traditions* (Hart Publishing, Oxford and Portland, 2003).

[17] *See e.g., Emil* v. *Hofmannsthal, Some Similarities Between Russian and German Law*, in 21 *Transactions of the Grotius Society* (1936) pp. 23–25.

[18] *See* A.-T. Kliimann, *Õiguskord* (Akadeemiline Kooperatiiv, Tartu, 1939).

[19] H. Arendt, *The Origins of Totalitarianism* (Harcourt Brace Jovanovich, New York, 1951).

[20] *See further* L. Mälksoo, 'Von der Demokratie bis zur Diktatur: ein verborgener Dialog zwischen A.-T. Kliimann und Carl Schmitt', 43 *Der Staat* (2004) pp. 57–82.

the rising antagonistic Nazi and Communist ideologies. First, there was a certain similarity between the intellectual profiles of Schmitt and Kliimann. Just as in the early 20th century, criminal law had been to Professor Franz von Liszt (in his own words) a "wife" and international law a "lover", so did both Schmitt and Kliimann, theoreticians of constitutional law, develop a keen side interest in aspects of international law and its theory. Kliimann had been a student of Hans Kelsen in Vienna in the 1920s and became in 1932 law professor at the Estonian national university in Tartu (formerly Dorpat). In 1939, Kliimann published an ambitious book on legal theory "Õiguskord" (The Legal Order) in which he denounced with the harshest possible words Carl Schmitt's brief career as the crown jurist of Nazi Germany.[21]

While Schmitt's collaboration with the Nazis may have been opportunistic, his anti-Communism was genuine. Schmitt had expressed in the late 1920s idiosyncratic views about why anti-religious and anarchically inclined Communist Russia was a threat to Europe and the European 'idea' that in Schmitt's view was embedded in Catholicism. In 1929 Schmitt made it clear that Soviet Russia was the enemy for German-led Central Europe: "We in Central Europe live under the eyes of the Russians".[22] Schmitt complained that Soviet Russia was possessed by the spirit of technology, the compulsion toward mastery for mastery's sake. He also insisted that if European intellectuals continued to indulge their passively aesthetic enrapture with the *status quo*, they abdicated their duty and privilege to lead, and invited domination by their more radical brother.[23] Later on, in 1939, Schmitt presented a theory of international legal *Grossraum*, the immediate political consequence of which was that Germany was destined to control and lead Eastern Europe as its historical "greater space".[24]

---

[21] A.-T. Kliimann, *Õiguskord* (Akadeemiline Kooperatiiv, Tartu, 1939).

[22] C. Schmitt, Das Zeitalter der Neutralisierungen und Entpolitisierungen, 1929, reprinted in Schmitt, Der Begriff des Politischen: Text von 1932 mit einem Vorwort und drei Corollarien (Duncker and Humblot, Berlin, 1963).

[23] For a recent critical discussion, *see* J. P. McCormick, 'Carl Schmitt's Europe: Cultural, Imperial and Spatial, Proposals for European Integration, 1923-1955', in C. Joerges and N. Singh Ghaleigh, *Darker Legacies of Law in Europe. The Shadow of National Socialism and Fascism over Europe and its Legal Traditions* (Hart Publishing, Oxford and Portland, 2003) pp. 137.

[24] *See* C. Schmitt, *Völkerrechtliche Grossraumordnung mit Interventionsverbot für raumfremde Mächte*, (Hamburg, Hansischer Gildenverlag, 1941). *See also* M. Schmoeckel, *Die Großraumtheorie. Ein Beitrag zur Geschichte der Völkerrechtswissenschaft im Dritten Reich* (Duncker and Humblot, Berlin, 1994).

Kliimann criticized Schmitt's views about law as unethical, suggesting that Schmitt used it merely as an instrument for the imperialist and militarist politics of the German Nazi regime. Kliimann himself was destroyed by the clash of Communist Russia and Nazi Germany in Eastern Europe. When Estonia was occupied by the Soviet army in June 1940 and annexed in August 1940, Kliimann, the decisively liberal, antifascist and anti-Communist voice of 1939, turned into an active intellectual collaborator of the Soviets. It is unclear whether Kliimann did this in the hope of advancement of his career or perhaps out of fear. He may have become disillusioned by the fact that East European countries had been 'betrayed' by the West and carved up between Hitler's Germany and Stalin's USSR. Kliimann's writings from 1940–1941 indicate that he collapsed as a moral agent. In his articles between 1940–1941, Kliimann praised the progressiveness of Stalin's constitution and in the eyes of many of his readers endorsed the Soviet arrests, executions and mass deportations in the Baltic republics when he recommended that the "bourgeois poisonous snake be destroyed by hitting a knife into his throat".[25] Nevertheless, it remained nothing else but extra-judicial murder when a group of Estonian partisans and later Nazi collaborators shot (arguably for personal reasons) Kliimann while the Red Army retreated from Estonia during the summer of 1941.

It is not my purpose here to tell Kliimann's tragic story as perhaps interesting *per se*. I am also not interested here in Kliimann as a victim (what he undoubtedly was) but in Kliimann as a collaborator with the occupying Soviet regime. To the extent that Kliimann's words in 1940–1941 could be understood as an endorsement of Soviet crimes, he as an intellectual and lawyer deserves similar criticism as Schmitt for his anti-Semitic outbreaks and intellectual endorsement of aggressive Nazi foreign policy.

It took, of course, quite a long time after the end of the Second World War until books and articles about Nazi international and constitutional lawyers became published.[26] Commentators have been rightly critical about not just outright Nazi lawyers such as Reinhard Höhn but also of more subtly 'theoretical' international law collaborators of the Third Reich such as Carl Schmitt or Friedrich Berber. One can predict that the question of how to relate to the writings and professional activities of Soviet (or 'socialist')

---

[25] *See* A.-T. Kliimann, *Anname surmava teravlöögi kodanluse üritusele*, Tartu Kommunist, 8.01.1941, p. 2.

[26] *See e.g.*, B. Rüthers, *Entartetes Recht – Rechtslehren und Kronjuristen im Dritten Reich* (Beck, München, 1988) and D. Vagts, 'International Law in the Third Reich', 84 *American Journal of International Law* (1990) pp. 661–704.

international law scholars in Eastern Europe and Russia will continue to trouble the affected countries and probably also the international legal scholarship for some time. To the extent that such issues are suppressed now (and they still undoubtedly are), a similar situation to the protests of 'sons against the fathers' in the style of 1968 cannot be ruled out. Of course, already Solzhenitsyn has condemned notorious Soviet lawyers like Andrei Januar'evitch ('Jaguar'evitch') Vyshinski who, besides theorizing about Soviet international law, directed Stalin's show trials.[27] But problematic cases may go further than that. For example, to the extent that the USSR continued to be an internally repressive and externally aggressive State in the post-Stalinist era, how 'neutrally' should we today relate to Soviet international legal doctrines and their leading exponents, e.g. Grigory Tunkin?[28] I definitely do not intend to suggest any need for a 'witch hunt' or Orwellian 'think police' that would be so incompatible with the idea of academic freedom. Neither should scholars be punished for having lived and thought in a certain time period. However, the question of the responsibility of lawyers for their role in the legitimization of State crimes (including crimes committed in the name of socialism) is an issue that must inevitably be addressed. When we ask critically "how could Carl Schmitt endorse *this*?", we must also be prepared to ask similar questions about leading Soviet international lawyers and ask how Jean-Paul Sartre could fail to see *that*? It is also in this sense that there is a certain degree of symbolism in Kliimann's assault against Schmitt: just as Kliimann, many liberal left-leaning lawyers opposing Nazism (for good reasons), have at the same time been somewhat blind towards crimes committed in the name of socialism.

Balanced and well-researched biographies of leading interpreters and appliers of socialist (international) law may help us in the future to better understand not only the socialist legacy in international law but also the history of Europe in the 20th century and will thus remain a promising research topic.

Postscript

After lengthy debates and not without opposition, the Parliamentary Assembly of the Council of Europe adopted on 25 January 2006 Resolution

---

[27] *See* A. Solzhenitsyn, *The Gulag Archipelago 1918–1956. An Experiment in Literary Investigation* (HarperCollins Publishers, 1975).

[28] *See* W. Butler, 'The Learned Writings of Professor G.I. Tunkin', 4 *Journal of the History of International Law* (2002) pp. 394–424.

1481 (2006) entitled "Need for International Condemnation of Crimes of Totalitarian Communist Regimes". The resolution states:

"1. The Parliamentary Assembly refers to its Resolution 1096 (1996) on measures to dismantle the heritage of the former communist totalitarian systems.

2. The totalitarian communist regimes which ruled in central and eastern Europe in the last century, and which are still in power in several countries in the world, have been, without exception, characterised by massive violations of human rights. The violations have differed depending on the culture, country and the historical period and have included individual and collective assassinations and executions, death in concentration camps, starvation, deportations, torture, slave labour and other forms of mass physical terror, persecution on ethnic or religious grounds, violation of freedom of conscience, thought and expression, of freedom of the press, and also lack of political pluralism.

3. The crimes were justified in the name of the class struggle theory and the principle of dictatorship of the proletariat. The interpretation of both principles legitimised the 'elimination' of people who were considered harmful to the construction of a new society and, as such, enemies of the totalitarian communist regimes. A vast number of victims in every country concerned were its own nationals. It was the case particularly of the peoples of the former USSR who by far outnumbered other peoples in terms of the number of victims.

4. The Assembly recognises that, in spite of the crimes of totalitarian communist regimes, some European communist parties have made contributions to achieving democracy.

5. The fall of totalitarian communist regimes in central and eastern Europe has not been followed in all cases by an international investigation of the crimes committed by them. Moreover, the authors of these crimes have not been brought to trial by the international community, as was the case with the horrible crimes committed by National Socialism (Nazism).

6. Consequently, public awareness of crimes committed by totalitarian communist regimes is very poor. Communist parties are legal and active in some countries, even if in some cases they have not distanced themselves from the crimes committed by totalitarian communist regimes in the past.

7. The Assembly is convinced that the awareness of history is one of the preconditions for avoiding similar crimes in the future. Furthermore, moral assessment and condemnation of crimes committed play an important role in the education of young generations. The clear position of the international community on the past may be a reference for their future actions.

8. Moreover, the Assembly believes that those victims of crimes committed by totalitarian communist regimes who are still alive or their families, deserve sympathy, understanding and recognition for their sufferings.
9. Totalitarian communist regimes are still active in some countries of the world and crimes continue to be committed. National interest perceptions should not prevent countries from adequate criticism of current totalitarian communist regimes. The Assembly strongly condemns all those violations of human rights.
10. The debates and condemnations which have taken place so far at national level in some Council of Europe member states cannot give dispensation to the international community from taking a clear position on the crimes committed by the totalitarian communist regimes. It has a moral obligation to do so without any further delay.
11. The Council of Europe is well placed for such a debate at international level. All former European communist countries, with the exception of Belarus, are now members, and the protection of human rights and the rule of law are basic values for which it stands.
12. Therefore, the Assembly strongly condemns the massive human rights violations committed by the totalitarian communist regimes and expresses sympathy, understanding and recognition to the victims of these crimes.
13. Furthermore, it calls on all communist or post-communist parties in its member states which have not yet done so to reassess the history of communism and their own past, clearly distance themselves from the crimes committed by totalitarian communist regimes and condemn them without any ambiguity.
14. The Assembly believes that this clear position of the international community will pave the way to further reconciliation. Furthermore, it will hopefully encourage historians throughout the world to continue their research aimed at the determination and objective verification of what took place."

CUSTOMARY LAW: ARE RUMOURS OF ITS DEATH EXAGGERATED?

The Collective Factor as a Promoter of Customary International Law

Lauri Hannikainen[*]

Contents

1. Pros and Cons of Customary Norms in International Law

In recent years, doubts have been expressed about the continuing relevancy of customary law as a source of international law. It has been argued that treaty law has become the overwhelming source of norms of international law and has significantly lessened the need of customary norms which are vague and difficult to identify. Could one argue that it would be enough to have treaty law supplemented by standards created by international organizations and conferences – non-binding 'soft law' standards, which representing consensus, have proved to be of practical significance? However, those standards are not binding and can be disregarded by States.

Treaty law is factually the most important source of present day international law. It covers many fields with multilateral and regional treaties (conventions) and a huge number of bilateral treaties. Treaties create identifiable obligations and rights in written texts. It is known which States

[*] Professor of International Law, University of Turku (Åbo), Finland

Baltic Yearbook of International Law, Volume 6, 2006, pp. 125–141.

are bound by any given treaty. Many treaties have created international monitoring organs and mechanisms in order to ensure respect for them.

A customary norm is defined in Article 38 (1) (b) of the Statute of the International Court of Justice as "custom, as evidence of general practice accepted as law". The constitutive elements of this definition are 1) practice and 2) the acceptance of this practice as obligatory (*opinio juris*). The Statute of the Court is an expression of universal international law.

Customary law was the most important source of international law in the 18th century and in the first part of the 19th century, when virtually the only multilateral treaties among States were peace treaties which were dictated by the victorious side. Customary norms developed slowly in the course of State practice, the acceptance of such practice as obligatory could be identified in the course of the consolidation of this practice. The number of States was limited and a small number of great powers led the international society of States. It was possible to identify the practice of this limited number of States; especially significant was the practice of great powers.

Customary law has a number of inherently problematic elements in international law. It may be difficult to identify customary norms: whether there exists any customary norm at all, what its content is, when has it entered into force, and whom does it obligate? It is difficult to amend a customary norm with a new customary norm in an orderly way. What are the most relevant forms of practice, do written and oral statements of State representatives on the international arena constitute both State practice and *opinio juris*, or can they merely be proof of *opinio juris*? The significant increase of the number of States in recent decades complicates the possibility of identifying the practice of over 190 States, even in the face of important developments in the means of communications.

Notwithstanding these problematic features there is a continuous need of customary international law:

- The international community of States has not been able to adopt multilateral treaties in all fields of international law. There are important problem areas which are not covered and regulated by treaty law. Customary international law fills gaps left uncovered by treaty law.

- Customary norms contribute to the universality of norms, since treaties only obligate the parties to them. There are only a limited number of truly universal treaties. During the process of formation of a customary norm only such a State which expressly manifests its opposition to the new rule does not become bound by that norm. Silence is interpreted as consent. Most existing universal norms of international law would not exist without the role of customary law.

- Customary norms are significant in increasing stability in international law, because their denunciation is difficult; to give an example, a State's denunciation of a treaty does not release that State from such obligations in that treaty which are also customary norms.[1]

The International Court of Justice (ICJ) continuously treats treaty law and customary law as sources of equal rank.

A number of customary norms of the pre-UN era have been replaced by more recent norms of international law, a number have been modified and a number continue to be in force as customary norms – they may also have been codified in treaty law.

2. Three Relevant Factors in the Contemporary International Community

When one looks at the international community of States and international law at the beginning of the 21st century, one can note beside the *increase of the number of States* to nearly 200 and the *increasing importance of treaties* as a source of international law also the *increasing role of intergovernmental organizations* in the development and administration of, as well as in the supervision of respect for, international law. The number of these intergovernmental organizations exceeds the number of States being roughly 300; in the following they are called 'international organizations'. Most of them are subjects of international law, i.e. they are holders of international legal rights and obligations and have defined competences in international affairs. This article concentrates especially on the role of international organizations in the formation of customary international law.

3. Different Contemporary Approaches to Customary International Law

Those three factors – increase of the numbers of States, treaties and international organizations – have an effect on customary international law. However, very different conclusions have been drawn by legal experts:

One approach takes a *cautious and traditional approach* to the creation of customary norms in international law. The emergence of a new customary norm requires that there is widespread material practice by individual States and proof that this practice is accepted as law. Thus, customary law as a

[1] *See* Article 43 of the 1969 Vienna Convention on the Law of Treaties.

source of international law is factually in a secondary position when compared with treaty law.[2]

There are authors who take quite a *negative view*: the traditional requirements make customary law broadly an outdated relic as a source of international law.[3]

Another approach also takes a *critical and even negative view* on customary international law. It is very difficult to identify in a reliable way the actual practice of over 190 States. Regularly the contemporary examination of State practice with regard to allegedly universal customary norms by courts and legal experts is a selective examination, paying attention only to certain forms of State practice and only to the practice of a limited number of States. The outcome is a gap that exists between many claimed norms of customary international law and State practice; customary international law has become a tool of political abuse. Often the claimed norms of new customary international law are legal equivalent to a "wish list for Santa Claus".[4]

One variation of the above critical approach is connected to the place of customary norms in the domestic law of a monistic system. It has been given expression especially in the United States.[5] According to its legal system, customary international law is part of the 'law of land'. Thus, if new customary norms are declared without having a solid basis in State practice, why should they be recognized as customary international law in the domestic law of the United States? The legal character of such false customary norms should be objected to.

Many other experts take a more *positive and dynamic approach*, they are of the opinion that international law has to recognize, and adjust to, the changes and tailor the criteria of customary international law accordingly. Because of the large number of States it is difficult to identify reliably the practice of individual States; therefore one important way to create customary norms is norm-creation in a multilateral process, collectively in

---

[2] *See* D. P. Fidler, 'Challenging the Classical Concept of Custom: Perspectives on the Future of Customary International Law', 37 *German Yearbook of International Law* (1996) pp. 216–220.

[3] *Ibid.*

[4] *Ibid.*, pp. 224–228; J. L. Goldsmith and E. A. Posner, 'Understanding the Resemblance between Modern and Traditional Customary International Law', 40 *Virginia J. of International Law* (Winter 2000) pp. 640–672; S. Estreicher, 'Rethinking the Binding Effect of Customary International Law', 44 *Virginia Journal of International Law* (Fall 2003) pp. 5–17.

[5] *See* Fidler, *supra* note 2, pp. 229–231.

international organizations. The affirmative voting and statements by State representatives in the preparation of resolutions of international organs constitute relevant State practice and *opinio juris* of States – they also constitute relevant practice of international organizations and *opinio juris communis*. Words are not less important than deeds. However, many experts of this group still point out that if material State practice is different from the expressions of States in international organizations, it would be unrealistic to support the emergence of a new customary norm.[6]

The ICJ's position is *closest to the positive and dynamic approach* but also supports the statement contained in the last sentence. It has given considerable weight to the declarations and resolutions of international organizations, but it also has stressed the necessity of material practice. In the *Nicaragua* case in 1984 the Court stated that "the mere fact that States declare their recognition of certain rules is not sufficient for the Court to consider these as being part of customary international law, and as applicable as such to those States . . . The Court must satisfy itself that the existence of the rule in the *opinio juris* of States is confirmed by practice." Regarding practice, the Court did not

> "consider that, for a rule to be established as customary, the corresponding practice must be in absolutely rigorous conformity with the rule . . . The Court deems it sufficient that the conduct of States should, in general, be consistent with the rules, and that instances of State conduct inconsistent with a given rule should generally have been treated as breaches of that rule, not as indications of the recognition of a new rule."[7]

In the *North Sea Continental Shelf* cases in 1969 the ICJ commented on the emergence of a customary norm from a provision of a multilateral treaty:

> "even without the passage of any considerable period of time, a very widespread and representative participation in the convention might suffice itself, provided it included that of States whose interests were specially affected . . . Although the passage of only a short period of time is not necessarily, or of itself, a bar to the formation of a new rule of customary international law on the basis of what was originally a purely conventional rule, an indispensable requirement would be that within the period in question, short though it might be, State practice, including that of States

[6] *Ibid.*, pp. 220–224.

[7] *Military and Paramilitary Activities in and against Nicaragua, Nicaragua* v. *United States* (Merits), International Court of Justice: Reports of Judgments, Advisory Opinions and Orders, 1986, paras. 183–186.

whose interests are specially affected, should have been both extensive and virtually uniform . . . and should moreover have occurred in such a way as to show a general recognition that rule of law or legal obligation is involved."[8]

4. The Role of International Organizations in Contemporary International Law and Relations

What are the essential functions of international organizations in the globalizing world which is characterized by increasing interdependence of nations? Many international problems would be hard to settle by States in bilateral arrangements – multilateral solutions are needed. International organizations are created by States to tackle multilateral problems, to develop cooperation among States and to constitute forums for multilateral communication and negotiation. According to Bennett, the chief function of international organizations is to provide the means of cooperation among States in areas in which cooperation provides advantages for a large number of nations. In many cases they furnish not only a place where decisions to cooperate can be reached but also the administrative machinery for translating the decisions into action. At best international organizations are dynamic instruments for governments to develop cooperative executive- and legislative-type actions.[9] International organizations and organs as a whole have become an essential actor for the development of and creation of international law.[10]

The rising importance of international organizations does not mean that they have risen above States or constitute a serious challenge to State sovereignty. States continue to be the leading actors in the international arena; as the founders and members of international organizations they are able to control these institutions created by them – even to dissolve them. At the same time it should be kept in mind that States have purposefully given international organizations different kinds of powers, even supranational powers to certain international organizations in which States by majority can make decisions binding on all members. Such supranational powers give the

---

[8] *North Sea Continental Shelf Cases*, *Federal Republic of Germany* v. *Denmark, Federal Republic of Germany* v. *the Netherlands*, International Court of Justice: Reports of Judgments, Advisory Opinions and Orders, 1969, paras. 73–74.

[9] A. LeRoy Bennett, *International Organizations, Principles and Issues* (6th ed. Prentice Hall, Englewood Cliffs, New Jersey, 1995) pp. 3–7.

[10] *See* N. D. White, *The Law of International Organizations* (Manchester University Press, Manchester, 1996) p. 2 *et seq.*

organization itself a strong position in the international arena. Usually, however, decisions of international organizations are formally recommendations only.[11] (A natural exception is decision-making concerning the internal affairs of an international organization, for example, acceptance of the annual budget of the organization or selection of the membership of the organs of the organization.)

Some factors enhance the role of international organizations in international law and in their relations with the member States:

- The member states are under an obligation to respect the charter of an international organization in good faith.

- In the course of recent decades the stature of many international organizations has become stronger and the scope of their activities broader in accordance with the theory of implied powers of the organization, and their secretariats have acquired more independent functions.

- In general terms it is not an exaggeration to say that international organizations and organs are the upholders of respect for international law. They have a leading role in the international supervisory work. They are the leading international force trying to maintain respect for international law.

- There are organs composed of individual experts in many international organizations. Altogether the role of these organs has proved to be very positive for the promotion of the common good, including development and respect for international law.

- The role of non-governmental international and national organizations has increased in the international arena; in many cases these organizations cooperate actively with intergovernmental organizations.

There are fields of international relations in which States have many disagreements, especially in fields where political interests are paramount. The outcome may be that the charter of an international organization is not well observed by all members. There are also examples of situations where one State or a small number of powerful States and their close allies have grabbed factual power in an international organization, after which that organization's role in the international field has had many negative characteristics. As examples one can mention the Warsaw Pact organization

[11] *See* J. Klabbers, *An Introduction to International Institutional Law* (Cambridge University Press, Cambridge, 2002) p. 200 *et seq.*

dominated by the Soviet Union and the Organization of American States at the time when it was dominated by the United States.

On the other hand, there are other fields of international relations where States' mutual interests are strong. As telling examples one can mention the need to control the spread of diseases across national boundaries or to facilitate the interchange of mail. In many international organizations cooperation is proceeding well and their charters and other regulations are well observed by members.

It should also be noted that to an increasing extent international organizations cooperate directly with each other. The center of attention is no more just on the question of the powers of an international organization vis-á-vis its members, but international organizations as a logical consequence of their strengthened role cooperate directly with each other for the solution of diverse problems.

The present-day network of international organizations with their different organs, mechanisms and programs is a vast and manifold network. There are many examples of well functioning organs and mechanisms. As examples one can mention the dispute settlement mechanism of the World Trade Organization; the monitoring of the Covenant on Civil and Political Rights by the Human Rights Committee, which handles and comments on the periodic reports of (some 150) ratifying States as well as complaints by individuals; and the European and American Courts of Human Rights.

A certain stagnation of the central organization of the international community, the UN, is well known. It has not been able to modernize itself in accordance with the requirements of the post cold war circumstances due to disagreements among its members and to the excessive powers of the individual permanent members of the Security Council. This organ has strong powers, but it is not able to safeguard international peace and security efficiently. Another example: The powers of the International Court of Justice have not been increased during its 60 years of existence.

Some conclusions from the perspective of customary international law appear *uncontestable*: Consolidated practices in the internal affairs of given international organizations can well develop to customary norms of those international organizations. Customary norms can also develop in the mutual relations of given international organizations. In such international organizations where mutual interests are highly valued by the members without much disagreement, adopted resolutions are often duly observed by the members and form a major source of new customary norms.

My question: Since international organizations are the second category of subjects of international law, how important is the practice and *opinio juris* of international organizations in the creation of norms of customary international law – as factors separate from the practice and *opinio juris* of individual States?

5. Five Examples of Contemporary Custom Formation and Identification

Let us proceed further and have a look at five examples of the (potential) contemporary formation of customary international law with substantial contributions by international organizations.

The *first example* is from an organization where common interests are strong, the International Telecommunication Union (ITU). This organization is concerned with the maintenance and extension of cooperation with regard to the use of telecommunication in the international arena. It also promotes development of facilities and efficiency of services. The basic structure of the ITU is as follows: The Plenipotentiary Conference is the supreme organ, whereas the Council acts on behalf of the Plenipotentiary Conference as the executive organ. Then there are world conferences on international telecommunications and the Secretariat. Much of the substantial work is concentrated in three sectors, the Radio Communication Sector, the Telecommunications Standardisation Sector and the Telecommunications Development Sector. The resolutions, decisions or recommendations of these Sectors are non-binding in character. The ITU's enforcement system is weak.

Hinricher writes that restrained by the laws of physics, not by the laws of politics, cooperation is vital and unavoidable, thus turning simple recommendations and other legally non-binding decisions into powerful and authoritative 'law', which is, to use the words of a former ITU Secretary-General, "almost universally followed". A State's non-compliance could in all three ITU Sectors lead to severe consequences up to complete isolation from the 'telecommunication-world'. Hinricher refers to Skubiszewski that the overall compliance of States with non-binding recommendations issued by international organizations such as the ITU "slowly evolve into binding customary rules and practices".[12]

[12] J. Hinricher, 'Law-Making of the International Telecommunication Union (ITU) – Providing a New Source of International Law?', 64 *Zeitschrift für ausländisches öffentliches Recht un Völkerrecht* (2004) pp. 489–501. Hinricher also reports on and analyzes in an interesting way binding decisions within ITU. K. Skubiszewski, 'Forms of Participation of International Organizations in the Lawmaking Processes', 18 *International Organization* (1964) p. 795.

The *second example* is from the UN. Chapter XI of the Charter deals (dealt) with non-self-governing territories, in practice most colonies, and Chapter XII with trusteeship territories, in practice more advanced colonies. The former Chapter calls upon those member States which have assumed responsibilities for the administration of non-self-governing territories to guide their peoples towards self-government, whereas the latter calls for the promotion of development towards self-government or independence. However, in the massive process of decolonization these two Chapters, especially Chapter XI, were fundamentally superseded by a declaration of the General Assembly, the 1960 Declaration on the Granting Independence to Colonial Countries and Peoples (res. 1514 (XV)).

This Decolonization Declaration became the 'Magna Charta' of the decolonization process; it called for speedy realization of the right of full self-determination by colonial peoples. In subsequent practice national independence became the main form of realization of self-determination by colonial peoples. The Declaration was referred to as authoritative in hundreds of resolutions by UN organs. It cannot be said that the Declaration constituted an (authoritative) interpretation of the Charter, because it went beyond the Charter. It is more appropriate to conclude that the Declaration became expression of customary international law. The ICJ in the *Western Sahara* case stated that the Decolonization Declaration provided the basis for the process of decolonization which resulted since 1960 in the creation of many new States.[13] By referring to eight legal experts, I wrote in 1988 that the UN practice is so widespread and the number of resolutions so vast that new customary law, going beyond the Charter in sanctioning the right of dependent peoples to self-determination, has developed.[14]

In this case the reason for the great significance of the Decolonization Declaration was the strong political and moral thrust to dissolve the fundamentally suppressive colonial domination. This was a matter of universal significance. It was the practice and strongly expressed *opinio juris communis* of the UN which was the most important legal ground of the customary norm on the right of peoples to self-determination from alien domination and suppression.

---

[13] *Advisory Opinion on Western Sahara*, International Court of Justice: Reports of Judgments, Advisory Opinions and Orders, 1975, para. 57.

[14] L. Hannikainen, *Peremptory Norms (Jus Cogens) in International Law – Historical Status, Criteria, Present Status* (Finnish Lawyers' Publishing Company, Helsinki, 1988) pp. 361–367.

The *third example* also comes from the UN. When the UN has been ready to launch a peacekeeping operation in a given country or countries, it wants to make an agreement with the receiving State(s) on the status of the international troops and other personnel. A practice has developed to conclude so-called status-of-forces agreements (SOFAs). In 1990 the UN Secretary-General issued a model status-of-forces agreement (UN Model SOFA). It was explicitly stated that the model agreement was based "upon established practice drawing extensively upon earlier and current agreements" and was intended to function as a model for future individual agreements between the UN and host States. In a detailed study on the SOFAs Engdahl, referring to the views of the Security Council, Secretary-General, States and legal experts, comes to the conclusion that the UN Model SOFA has relevancy for the development of customary international law. He points out that a SOFA has been concluded in almost all operations between the UN and host nations. With minor changes and additions the content of these SOFAs has been virtually uniform. He concludes:

> "A body or practice has emerged which forms part of the concept of peace operations . . . Norms of the UN Model SOFA relating to the protection of personnel form an integral part of a concept of peace operations and are therefore applicable in the territory of the host state, even when at the material time an individual SOFA had yet to be concluded. Some basic norms relating to the protection of personnel would have developed into the status of customary law. Such essential requirements, that military personnel be allowed to wear uniform and carry weapons, if their function so requires, are undisputable. The right to freedom of movement, the right to set up a communication system, functional immunity for such personnel, and exclusive criminal jurisdiction for sending states over their military forces, is also regarded as rules of customary law."[15]

In this example customary norms have developed from the initiative of the UN with the acceptance of troop-receiving and troop-sending States.

The *fourth example* deals with an organ of the Council of Europe, the European Commission against Racism and Intolerance (ECRI).[16] I have chosen this organ, because as a member I know it well. This organ was established in 1993 and its membership is composed of independent experts. It is not a treaty monitoring organ but has a general mandate to combat racism, xenophobia, discrimination, anti-semitism and intolerance at the

---

[15] O. Engdahl, *Protection of Personnel in Peace Operations* (Stockholm University, Stockholm, 2005) pp. 171–226, 346–347.

[16] *See* <www.ecri.coe.int>.

level of greater Europe. The most essential form of ECRI's work is its preparation of country reports. At present ECRI is in the middle of the third round of country reporting; in the third round ECRI's country reports make 25–30 tightly packed pages. ECRI makes many targeted proposals to the government concerned on means to tackle problems and improve the situation. ECRI takes as its basic standards the standards established in convention-based human rights law, but on many occasions it has called upon the members States of the Council of Europe to apply somewhat higher and more demanding standards. With the help of its proposals ECRI wishes to engage in constructive dialogue with governments and civil society in order to intensify action against racism, xenophobia, etc. As an organ composed of individual experts and with a non-definite mandate ECRI cannot be characterized as a strong international organ. States' engagement in dialogue and positive responses to ECRI's proposals are important measuring sticks when the success of ECRI's performance is assessed.

Among other forms of ECRI's activities one should mention general policy recommendations, wherein ECRI collects standards and principles, which it regards relevant in the fight against racism, xenophobia, etc. and applies them in its country reports. Examples include the recommendations on combating racism and intolerance against Roma/Gypsies, Muslims and anti-semitism, as well as the recommendation on combating the dissemination of racist, xenophobic and anti-semitic material via the Internet and another on national legislation to combat racism and racial discrimination.

Mark Kelly, an external expert who was commissioned by ECRI to make an assessment of its first ten years, makes the following concluding remark in his study:

> "ECRI has itself contributed to the development of standards, in an innovative way: starting from the bottom-up. ECRI's primary concern has been to make useful and concrete proposals, and these proposals have gradually come to form a corpus of standards. Without necessarily having this aim at the outset, ECRI has, through its empirical approach, helped to create new standards in the fight against racism and racial discrimination."[17]

[17] M. Kelly, *ECRI – 10 years of combating racism: A review of the work of the European Commission against Racism and Intolerance* (Council of Europe, Strasbourg, 2004) p. 138. *See also* L. Hannikainen, 'Reflections of the Country Report on Finland by the European Commission against Racism and Intolerance

My experience confirms that Kelly has reached the right conclusion. However, it is most evident that the new standards formulated by ECRI remain non-binding standards. In many cases this may be so, but ECRI is not the only international organ addressing questions of racism, discrimination, xenophobia, etc. Recommendations based on a similar philosophy as ECRI have been made by a number of other international organs, such as the Parliamentary Assembly of the Council of Europe, the European Parliament and the UN Committee on the Elimination of Racial Discrimination (CERD). At least some new standards, which are well received by States may, in the course of time, develop into regional customary norms in Europe. States are ready to develop laws and rules which will be effective in combating racism, discrimination, xenophobia, etc.

The *fifth* example is of a different kind. It does not deal with the formation of a certain customary norm but is a relevant example of how to study the existence of customary norms, i.e. how to identify them. The study – *Customary International Humanitarian Law* – was organized by the International Committee of the Red Cross and published in three parts (circa 5000 pages) in 2005.[18] Several hundred experts of international humanitarian law (IHL) were involved in the preparation of the study. The study identified 161 customary norms in IHL, most of them obligatory both in international and non-international armed conflicts. The 1949 Geneva Conventions on the protection of war victims with over 190 ratifications and their 1977 Additional Protocols with 162 and 157 ratifications respectively (at the time of the completion of the study) formed a solid basis of the study.

In its research the study relied on various forms of the practice of 47 States as well as on the practice of international organizations – studying the relevancy of this practice and *opinio juris*. The States were selected on the basis of geographical representation as well as on the basis of recent experience with armed conflict: nine from Africa, eleven from the Americas, sixteen from Asia (including several from the Middle East, as well as Australia), and eleven from Europe.[19] The authors of the study were convinced that the practice of the carefully selected 47 States was enough, since other sources were also relied on.

(ECRI)', in M. Scheinin and R. Toivanen (eds.), *Rethinking Non-Discrimination and Minority Rights* (Åbo Akademi University, Åbo, and German Institute for Human Rights, Berlin, 2004) pp.48–50.

[18] *Customary International Humanitarian Law*, Volume I: Rules, Volume II: Practice – Part 1, and Volume II: Practice – Part 2, ed. by J-M. Henckaerts and L. Doswald-Beck (Cambridge University Press, Cambridge, 2005).

[19] *Ibid.*, Volume I, pp. xlix-l.

In more detail, the study identified six sources to be checked: 1) treaties and other instruments; 2) national practice (especially military manuals, national legislation, national case law) as the most substantial source; 3) practice of international organizations and conferences (especially resolutions of the Security Council and General Assembly of the UN but also practice of various regional organizations); 4) the practice of international judicial and quasi-judicial bodies; 5) the practice of the International Red Cross and Red Crescent movement; 6) other practice.[20]

The study is not immune from criticism, but it is perhaps the most serious attempt to systematically identify the existence of customary norms in a given field of international law.

6. Analysis: The Increasing Importance of the Collective Element in the Contemporary Formation of Customary Norms in International Law

The overwhelming majority of resolutions of international organizations are formally recommendations only. This is well known to States – they may have very different reasons to vote for a resolution. Those reasons may include political expediency and the desire not to be singled out as a dissenter. Even if a resolution employs legal terminology and speaks of all States' obligations, a State's affirmative vote cannot be taken as a definitive proof of *opinio juris*.

A resolution's 'story' can imply different legally relevant consequences. Resolutions formulate the opinion of the international community of States or at least of the majority of States on various international questions and problems. They are a handy way to react to newly emergent problems. Let us concentrate here on resolutions by an inter-State organ 1) using legal terminology and speaking in normative way on legal obligations and rights of States or other actors and 2) being adopted unanimously or nearly unanimously or by consensus. There are, indeed, many such resolutions. Especially relevant in this context are such universal organs as the General Assembly of the UN in which all UN member States are represented.[21]

---

[20] *See ibid.*, Volume I, pp. xxv-li, but especially Volume II where the customary law status of different rules is studied in detail, for example, Part 1, pp. 3–66 regarding rule 1 on the distinction between civilians and combatants.

[21] R. Müllerson points out that the ICJ on various occasions and in different manners has emphasized the role of General Assembly resolutions in the process of custom formation – *see* his *Ordering Anarchy – International Law in International Society* (Martinus Nijhoff Publishers, The Hague, 2000) pp. 233–240. O. Schachter states that the judgment of the ICJ in the *Nicaragua* case reflects the widespread

It is quite common that in matters of importance a given international organ adopts several similar resolutions in consequent years, thus repeating the existence of certain obligations. It is also quite common that organs of more than one international organization adopt resolutions with similar tones. The repetition of resolutions and the adoption of resolutions by several international organs are multilateral manifestations that the subject matter needs regulation. If a State consistently votes for such resolutions, it cannot start from, and rely on, the assumption that this affirmative expression has no legal consequences.

The international community may be satisfied to have at its use non-binding standards created by resolutions of international organizations. But often there is a need to cement the most essential standards into more binding rules. If the conclusion of a multilateral treaty with good prospects of a respectable number of ratifications does not appear possible, then the alternative is customary law. Repetitive resolutions by an inter-State organ and/or resolutions by several different international organs may well be taken as practice of the international organizations concerned and *opinio juris communis*, and also as practice and an expression of *opinio juris* of yes-States.[22] The international organizations have received such a meaningful position in the international community and in the development of international law that a State's repetitious affirmative voting for juridical-type resolutions can be taken as acceptance of the legal significance of the main obligations identified by those resolutions.

However, the ICJ, in the *Nicaragua* case, pointed out that resolutions are not sufficient for the emergence of new customary norms, but there has to be actual practice of States confirming the legal relevancy of the resolutions in question. Resolutions can be the motivating force but actual State practice must confirm that there, indeed, is *opinio juris*. Uniform practice is not required – it is not necessary to examine the practice of every State. Cassese

---

professional opinion that law-making resolutions particularly when adopted by unanimous decisions of the General Assembly could have a creative role in the formation of custom – *see* his 'New Custom: Power, *Opinio Juris* and Contrary Practice', in J. Makarczyk (ed.), *Theory of International Law at the Threshold of the 21st Century* (Kluwer Law International, The Hague, 1996) pp. 531–532. *See also* J. Charney, 'Universal International Law', 87 *American Journal of International Law* (1993) pp. 543–545.

[22] Article 38 of the ICJ Statute does not speak of State practice but of general practice. It is logical to submit in the circumstances of the 21st century that the practice in question is practice by the full subjects of international law, i.e. States and intergovernmental organizations.

points out that no national or international court dealing with the question of whether a customary norm had taken shape on a certain matter has examined the views of all the States of the world. For a rule to take root in international dealings it is sufficient for a majority of States to engage in consistent practice corresponding with the rule and to be aware of its imperative need.[23] Regarding the scope of 'practice', there is much support for the view that verbal acts can be relevant State practice. According to the International Law Association, "verbal acts, and not only physical acts, of States count as State practice".[24]

Resolutions are not the only important form of activity of international organizations for the creation of customary norms. Many international organs conduct dialogue with States with the purpose of persuading them to adopt certain good practices or forms of conduct. There are strong international organs which may not limit themselves to persuasion but can also employ forms of pressure vis-à-vis a member State. According to Cassese, general consent of the least common denominator often evolves: the majority of States eventually succeed in overcoming opposition by individual States and in achieving general standards of behavior.[25]

Taking different sources of international law together, individual sources often do not function in isolation but interact. It is not uncommon that leading provisions in (the first articles of) well-ratified conventions develop into universal customary norms, most often with the help of resolutions of international organizations. Basic principles and general principles of international law may also play a prominent role in the creation of customary norms in international law; they may offer a base to build on.

---

[23] A. Cassese, *International Law* (Oxford University Press, Oxford, 2001) p. 123. The Introduction to *Customary International Humanitarian Law*, *supra*, note 18, assesses as follows (p. xlii): "It appears that international courts and tribunals on occasion conclude that a rule of customary international law exists when that rule is a desirable one for international peace and security or for the protection of the human person, provided that there is no important contrary *opinio juris.*"

[24] Report of the Sixty-Ninth Conference of the International Law Association (London 2000) pp. 725–726. M. Villiger in *Customary International Law and Treaties* (Martinus Nijhoff Publishers, Dordrecht, 1985) p. 6, after a thorough study of State practice in international conferences, concludes that "there is much merit in qualifying verbal acts as state practice", since "states themselves regard comments at conferences as constitutive of state practice". Thus, international conferences can effectively contribute to customary law-making with the help of statements of governments and conference declarations.

[25] Cassese, *supra* note 23, p.125.

7. Final Observations

When efforts are taken to create new specific customary norms in international law, the starting point often is not zero. There may already exist a base to build on. An individual State's opposition to intensive efforts of the international community to create new norms may be interpreted as a *mala fide* attitude which cannot prevent the entry into force of a new customary norm. The example above of the Decolonization Declaration is revealing in this sense.

The development of the international community and international law in the UN era calls for the modification of the criteria regarding the creation of customary norms – or the broadening of those criteria. Increasingly customary law-making has become a multilateral process with collective statements. Material State practice is not pushed away as irrelevant but it may have a lesser, confirmative role.

However, with the intensification of international cooperation the need of treaty law with far-reaching and detailed norms will increase.[26]

---

[26] *See* W. Friedmann, *The Changing Structure of International Law* (Stevens & Sons, London, 1964) pp. 121–123.

USE OF FORCE

Nouvelles questions sur le principe de l'interdiction du recours à la force

Oriol Casanovas[*]

Contents

1. Les nouvelles menaces à la paix et la sécurité internationales

Le principe de l'interdiction de l'emploi de la force consacré à l'article 2, num. 4 de la Charte des Nations Unies est un élément d'un système mondial pour le maintien de la paix, complété par le mécanisme de sécurité collective établi dans le chapitre VII et le droit de légitime défense reconnue à l'article 51. Très souvent, on oublie que la Charte des Nations Unies appartient à une époque pré-atomique puisqu'elle fut signée à San Francisco le 26 juin de 1945 et les explosions d'Hiroshima et Nagasaki n'ont eu lieu, respectivement, que le 6 et le 9 août suivant. La période de la « guerre froide », avec la confrontation Est-Ouest, bloqua pendant des décennies le fonctionnement du mécanisme de sécurité collective prévu dans la Charte, mais – d'une façon paradoxale – la dissuasion nucléaire empêcha une nouvelle confrontation armée à l'échelle mondiale. Malgré tout, des conflits armés et l'emploi de la force se sont produits à maintes reprises dans plusieurs lieux. Dans chaque situation on s'est prévalu pour justifier l'emploi de la force de divers arguments justificatifs ou on a allégué des exceptions à la règle. Vingt-cinq ans après la consécration du principe de la prohibition de

[*] Professeur à l'Université Pompeu Fabra , Barcelone, Espagne.

Baltic Yearbook of International Law, Volume 6, 2006, pp. 143–156.

l'emploi de la force, un auteur bien connu écrivait un article avec le titre provocateur « Qui a tué l'article 2, num. 4 ? »[1]. A ce moment-là, quand le principe recevait une reconnaissance universelle lors de l'adoption de la Déclaration des principes du droit international, annexe à la résolution 2625 (XXV) de l'Assemblée générale des Nations Unies, il était encore possible de répondre que les nouvelles sur la mort de l'article 2, num. 4, étaient « très exagérées »[2]. L'évolution ultérieure n'autorise pas une réponse aussi optimiste.

Aujourd'hui, après la chute du mur de Berlin et, surtout, après les attaques du 11 septembre 2001, la situation est beaucoup plus préoccupante. Il y a de nouvelles menaces à la paix et la sécurité internationales qui ne pouvaient être prévues : réseaux terroristes à l'échelle mondiale, dissémination des armes de destruction massive, crime et corruption globalement organisés, etc. Le mot « guerre » qui semblait effacé, au moins dans le langage juridique international au profit de l'expression « conflit armé », a acquis de nouveau un usage quotidien. Le président George W. Bush dans son message sur l'état de l'Union du 20 de janvier 2003 disait : « les terroristes et ceux qui leur donnent appui ont déclaré la guerre aux Etats-Unis, et ils l'ont eue. »

Les cas les plus récents d'emploi de la force (Kosovo (1999), Afghanistan (2001), Irak (2003)) ont soulevé un débat très vif, non seulement sur la légalité de ces interventions, mais aussi sur la portée du principe de l'interdiction de l'emploi de la force en général. Le principe de l'égalité souveraine chancelle aussi avec la qualification de certains états comme des « états en décomposition » (*failed states*) et « états voyous » (*rogue states*). L'ordre juridique international même est en cause. Dans ce débat, on discute le projet internationaliste de paix mondiale convenu notamment entre les Etats-Unis et les pays européens après la deuxième Guerre mondiale. Certains analystes perçoivent que la fameuse « brèche transatlantique » entre les Etats-Unis et les états européens est si profonde qu'elle met face à face deux conceptions antithétiques de l'ordre mondial. D'après cette opinion, l'internationalisme américain prônerait l'extension au reste du monde de la liberté, de la démocratie et du droit enracinés dans le constitutionnalisme américain. L'internationalisme européen, par contre,

---

[1] Th. M. Franck, « Who killed article 2, (4) ? or Changing Norms Governing the Use of Force by States », 64 *American Journal of International Law* (*AJIL*) (1970) pp. 809–837.

[2] L. Henkin, « The Reports of Death of Article 2 (4) are Greatly Exaggerated », 65 *AJIL* (1971) pp. 544–548.

serait fondé sur des principes universels qui auraient des sources en dehors des processus démocratiques constitutionnellement établis. La conclusion, derrière laquelle on peut soupçonner une justification de la politique unilatéraliste, est une question aussi provocante qu'erronée : le droit international est-il une menace pour la démocratie ?[3]

Sans doute, il est trop tôt pour cerner dans toute sa portée la dimension des changements intervenus dans les dernières années, mais il y a des points de vue qui, du côté de la réflexion de la philosophie politique ou de la théorie des relations internationales, jettent un regard qui permet d'entrevoir leur transcendance. D'après un point de vue politico-philosophique, on peut considérer la situation actuelle à la lumière de la doctrine de l'état d'exception[4]. L'ordre juridique international général, à la différence de certains ordres internes, ne règle pas la situation de l'état d'exception. Seul le Conseil de sécurité a des pouvoirs reconnus pour prendre des décisions dans les cas d'une « menace contre la paix, d'une rupture de la paix ou d'un acte d'agression. » Les décisions en dehors de ce cadre de légalité pour la défense de l'ordre juridique menacé sont ou bien une violation de l'ordre international établi, ou bien une décision de fait prise en marge du système juridique que l'on pourrait considérer constitutive d'un état d'exception qui lui enlève sa vigueur. Comme l'avait mis en relief Carl Schmitt, celui qui décide l'état d'exception et qui déclare qui est l'*hostis* est le souverain[5]. La conduite des États-Unis après le 11 septembre pourrait être analysée comme un changement du système international qui aurait, bien que l'idée sonne un peu grandiloquente et que ce n'est pas la première fois qu'elle a été avancée, mis fin à l'ordre westphalien pour inaugurer une nouvelle modalité d'impérialisme ou d'hégémonie. Dans ce nouveau cadre, le principe de la prohibition de l'emploi de la force n'aurait pas de place, puisque l'état d'exception ne serait pas temporel comme il doit être conçu, mais serait un état d'exception permanent qui supposerait la guerre permanente contre le terrorisme mondial et les nouvelles menaces à la paix et la sécurité internationales[6] auxquelles il est très difficile de faire face et qui peuvent rebondir au moment et dans le lieu où on les attend le moins.

---

[3] J. Rubenfeld, « Te Two World Orders », 27 *The Wilson Quarterly* (Autumn 2003) pp. 22–36.

[4] *Cf.* G. Agamben, *Etat d'exception*, trad. J. Gayraud, Paris, Ed. du Seuil, 2003.

[5] C. Schmitt, *Die Diktatur*, 4ème ed., Berlin, Duncker & Humblot, 1978 et *Politische Theologie. Vier Kapitel zur Lehre von der Souveränität*, 4ème ed., Berlin, Duncker & Humblot, 1985.

[6] P. Hassner, « Vers l'état d'exception permanent ? », *Le Monde*, 24 juin 2003.

D'autres analystes des relations internationales considèrent qu'au cours des dernières années s'est produit un changement de système dû aux différences apparues entre les États à cause de l'émergence d'un nouveau type d'État : « l'État post-moderne »[7]. Les relations entre les États postmodernes, dont l'Union européenne est l'exemple le plus abouti, ont comme caractéristiques le refus de la violence et la sécurité fondée sur la transparence, l'ouverture entre eux, l'interdépendance, la vulnérabilité mutuelle. Mais, comme les États postmodernes coexistent avec des États pré-modernes dans lesquels règne le chaos et qui menacent la sécurité des États post-modernes, « il est besoin d'un impérialisme de type nouveau, qui soit compatible avec le respect des droits de l'homme et les valeurs cosmopolites : un impérialisme dont les objectifs soient apporter de l'ordre et de l'organisation »[8].

Ces approches pour depasser l'ordre international établi et y substituer un nouveau *jus gentium* ne sont pas une réalité avérée, mais témoignent d'une tendance forte qui peut et doit être contrecarrée[9]. Pour ce faire, il faudrait que l'ordre juridique international remplisse deux conditions préalables : a) qu'il y ait un système cohérent de régles et, b) qu'il y ait une distinction claire entre ce qui devrait être et ce qui est. L'impact des attaques du 11 septembre sur l'ordre international n'a pas seulement concerné le principe de la prohibition de l'emploi de la force ou la doctrine de légitime défense, mais sur fondements du système international : la cohérence de ses régles et la distinction entre ce qui devrait être et ce qui est.[10]

2. L'intervention en Iraq de 2003 et le principe de l'interdiction de l'emploi de la force armée

L'application du principe de la prohibition de l'emploi de la force (art. 2, num. 4) présente des difficultés particulières de cohérence à cause de la

---

[7] R. Cooper, *The post modern State and world Order*, London, The Foreign Policy Center, 2000.

[8] R. Cooper, « Why we still need empires », *The Observer*, Sunday 7th April 2002.

[9] S. Laghmani, « Du droit international au droit impérial ? Réflexions sur la guerre contre l'Irak », *Actualité du droit international*, avril 2003 [http://www.ridi.org/adi]

[10] F. Hoffmann, « Watershed or Phoenix From the Ashes ?- Speculations on the Future of International Law After the September 11 Attacks », 2 *German Law Journal*, No. 16, 1st October 2001. Sur les repercussions du 11 septembre 2001 sur le droit international en général *cf.* aussi K. Zemanek *et al.* "Is the Nature of the International Law System Changing?", 8 *Austrian Review of International and European Law* (2003) pp. 3–246.

rédaction même des dispositions de la Charte des Nations Unies et de la pratique des États. Les notions d' « emploi de la force » qui se trouvent dans l'article 2, num. 4, d' «agression » (art. 49) comme condition pour l'adoption de mesures collectives ou d'«agression armée » (art.51) comme fait préalable à l'exercice du droit de légitime défense ne sont pas des concepts équivalents et la réglementation internationale est clairement asymétrique. L'article 51 n'admet pas la légitime défense dans les cas de « menace ou emploi de la force » auxquels se réfère l'article 2, num. 4, ni ne l'admet non plus en relation à « toute menace à la paix ou acte d'agression » comme le dit l'article 39. L'article 51 règle le droit de légitime défense seulement dans une circonstance précise : « en cas d'agression (*armed attack*) », de façon que ce droit existe par rapport à une modalité spécifique d'emploi de la force. L'interdiction du recours à la force de l'article 2, num. 4, a une portée beaucoup plus générale puisqu'il se réfère à l'emploi de la force par des États dans n'importe laquelle de ses modalités. Emploi de la force et « agression » ou « armed attack » ne sont pas des notions équivalentes.

Le Conseil de sécurité, comme est bien connu, dispose d'un large pouvoir de qualification non seulement dans les cas d'agression mais aussi dans ceux de « menaces à la paix » ou de « ruptures de la paix ». Ce pouvoir est, toutefois, conditionné par la procédure de vote envisagée à l'art. 27, num. 3 (droit de veto). Ces dispositions affectent non seulement le fonctionnement du système de sécurité collective, mais aussi la qualification des situations dans l'ordre international, laquelle ne dépend pas exclusivement de l'application des régles, mais de la décision d'un organe politique. D'un autre côté le défaut de conclusion des « accords spéciaux » prévus à l'article 43, en vertu desquels les États membres mettraient à la disposition du Conseil de sécurité les forces armées nécessaires pour l'adoption des mesures collectives à caractère militaire de l'art. 42, a empêché le fonctionnement du système de sécurité collective dessiné à San Francisco.

L'intervention au mois de mars 2003 en Iraq des forces de la coalition internationale formée par les États-Unis, le Royaume-Uni et la Nouvelle Zélande ne trouve pas d'appui dans les dispositions de la Charte des Nations Unies. Avant que l'intervention se soit produite, des groupes de spécialistes en droit international ont dénoncé collectivement son illégalité. D'après un manifeste promu par des juristes de l'Université libre de Bruxelles, l'éclatement d'une guerre généralisée en Iraq « constituerait une rupture de la paix et un crime international qualifié comme tel par le droit international. » Un groupe nombreux d'internationalistes espagnols rendirent public un *Manifeste contre la guerre* dans lequel on peut lire qu'à défaut d'une autorisation expresse du Conseil de sécurité « les États qui emploieraient la force en Iraq violeraient les règles internationales, notamment l'article 2, num. 4, de la Charte des Nations Unies, et leurs actions pourraient être considérées, dans certaines conditions, comme un crime d'agression. »

La pratique des organes des Nations Unies et des États membres a dérivé vers une modalité de la sécurité collective dans laquelle la coercition est exercée, non pas sur la base de l'article 42, mais en vertu de résolutions prises sur l'invocation générique du chapitre VII qui « autorisent » l'emploi de « tous les moyens nécessaires »[11]. La résolution 678, adopté par le Conseil de sécurité le 29 novembre 1990, créa « un précédent complètement nouveau »[12].

La raison d'être de cette pratique est que les États autorisés, en particulier les États-Unis, n'avaient pas souhaité que les opérations militaires fussent sous le contrôle du Conseil de sécurité ou que cet organe put décider de la fin de ces opérations au moment ou il l'aurait voulu. L'autorisation de l'emploi de la force par le Conseil de sécurité a reçu un large appui de la communauté internationale est, d'exception, s'est transformée en une nouvelle règle. La Déclaration de Bruges sur l'emploi de la force, approuvée par l'Institut du droit international le 2 septembre 2003, consacre cette évolution en admettant qu'on puisse faire recours à la force « en vertu de l'autorisation du Conseil de sécurité ».

Le mécanisme, une fois ouverte la voie à une interprétation flexible de la Charte, se prête à des prétentions qui fondent l'emploi de la force sur une « autorisation implicite » qui aurait son origine dans des résolutions antérieures du Conseil de sécurité. Ainsi on a justifié la légalité de l'intervention en Iraq sur la base que la résolution 1441 (2002) du Conseil de sécurité renvoyait aux résolutions 687 (1991) et 678 (1990), qui établissent les obligations de l'Irak et autorisent l'emploi de tous les moyens nécessaires pour assurer leur exécution[13]. À travers l'autorisation implicite « on a contourné les mots des résolutions et l'on a ignoré les débats qui ont eu lieu

---

[11] *Cf.* L.-A Sicilianos, « L'autorisation par le Conseil de Securité de recourrir a la force : une tentative d'évaluation » 106 *Revue générale de droit international public* (*RGDIP*) (2002) pp. 5-48

[12] B.W. Weston, « Security Council resolution 678 and Persian Gulf Decision Making : Precarious Legitimacy », 85 *AJIL* (1991) p. 522.

[13] John Yoo, « International Law and the War in Iraq » 97 *AJIL* (2003) pp. 573-576 ; Romualdo Bermejo Garcia, « El debate sobre la legalidad internacional tras la crisis de Irak y las Naciones Unidas », 19 *Anuario de Derecho Internacional* (2003) pp. 52–53.

auparavant pour proclamer que l'on agit au nom de la communauté internationale »[14] et l'on a ouvert la voie d'une nouvelle modalité de la sécurité collective.

On a aussi considéré que la résolution 1244 (1999) du Conseil de sécurité adoptée après l'intervention de l'OTAN en Yougoslavie lors du conflit au Kosovo ou les résolutions 1483 (2003) et 1511 (2003) relatives à l'intervention de la coalition internationale en Irak pouvaient être considérées comme une forme de légalisation *ex post facto* de l'emploi de la force[15]. Certains auteurs rétorquent que s'il s'agissait d'un acte de délégation en faveur des intervenants celui-ci devrait cependant avoir eu lieu *ex ante*[16], mais cette discussion envisage le problème d'un point de vue très formel puisque la légalisation pourrait aussi être intervenue comme une validation *ex post ipso* et non comme une autorisation préalable. Mais même cet argument doit être rejeté avant tout parce qu'il ne s'appuie pas sur le texte des résolutions du Conseil de sécurité qui à aucun moment ne se prononcent sur la légalité des conduites qui ont eu lieu avant leur approbation et se limitent à adopter après coup des mesures pour faire face à la situation créée une fois les hostilités terminées.

3. Le droit de légitime défense et les nouvelles menaces à la paix

Le droit de légitime défense réglé à l'article 51 de la Charte des Nations Unies admet l'emploi de la force à la condition qu'un État ait été victime « d'une agression armée » (*armed attack*). Cette expression ne couvre pas n'importe quel emploi de la force par un autre État. La Cour internationale de Justice dans l'affaire des *activités militaires et paramilitaires au Nicaragua* distinguait entre les formes plus graves d'emploi de la force, qui donnaient lieu à une agression armée (*armed attack*), et d'autres formes moins graves[17]. Ainsi, dans le but de limiter l'exercice du droit de légitime

---

[14] Ch. Gray « From Unity to Polarization: International Law and the Use of Force Against Iraq », 13 *European Journal of International Law* (*EJIL*) (2002) No. 1, p. 9.

[15] C. Gutierrez Espada, « La *contaminación* de Naciones Unidas o las Resoluciones 1483 y 1511 (2003) del Consejo de Seguridad », 19 *Anuario de Derecho Internacional* (2003) pp. 81–85.

[16] O. Corten et F. Dubuisson, « L'hypothèse d'une regle émergente fondant une intervention militaire sur une *autorisation implicite* du Conseil de securité » 104 *RGDIP* (2000) pp. 905–907 et M.G.Kohen, « L'emploi de la force et la crise du Kosovo : vers un nouveau désordre international » 22 *Revue Belge de droit international* (1999) pp. 141–142.

[17] *Activités militaires et paramilitaires au Nicaragua et contre celui-ci (Nicaragua c. Etats-Unis d'Amérique) Décision sur le fond, Jugement, CIJ Recueil 1986*, par. 191.

défense aux cas les plus graves d'emploi de la force, les cas qu'on a nommés des « emplois mineurs » de la force demeurent en dehors de l'exception. Ces cas ne pouvaient faire l'objet d'une réponse armée puisque le droit international actuel interdit les représailles ou contre-mesures armées (art. 50, 1, a des articles de la CDI sur la responsabilité internationale des États). En outre, d'après le droit international coutumier la légitime défense doit être une réponse « immédiate, necessaire et proportionnelle » à l'agression, comme il a été dit dans l'affaire de l'incident du *Caroline* par une formule que l'on a répété maintes fois par la suite [18].

À la suite des attentats terroristes du 11 septembre 2001, l'intervention armée en Afghanistan a été considéré comme un acte de légitime défense. Cette justification, examinée au regard de la réglementation internationale de la légitime défense, soulève d'emblée plusieurs questions.

1) Les actes terroristes réalisés par des personnes privées de nationalité étrangère peuvent-ils être considérés comme une « agression » ou «armed attack » au le sens de l'article 51 de la Charte des Nations Unies autorisant la légitime défense ?
2) Le droit de légitime défense autorise-t-il l'emploi de la force contre d'autres États, tout au moins dans le territoire d'autres États, auxquels on ne peut imputer, directement ou indirectement, aucune agression ou attaque armée ?
3) Est-il nécessaire pour l'exercice du droit de légitime défense contre un État que celui-ci ait donné protection aux auteurs de l'attaque ?
4) Peut-on décider de l'emploi de la force en légitime défense même s'il n'y a aucun danger immédiat que se produise une attaque ou un acte de terrorisme massif ?

La résolution 1368 du Conseil de sécurité, du 12 septembre 2001, témoigne de ces difficultés. Elle fait référence aux « attaques » terroristes du 11 septembre mais ces derniers sont qualifiés de « menace contre la paix » et non d' « agression armée » (*armed attack*) pouvant donner lieu à une action de légitime défense au titre de l'article 51. La résolution 1373, du 23 septembre suivant, fait tout de même référence au droit de légitime défense des États-Unis. Il semble que la communauté internationale a voulu élargir la notion de légitime défense et considérer les attaques terroristes comme incluses dans la notion d' « agression armée » (*armed attack*). Le problème

---

[18] R. Y. Jennings, « The *Caroline* and *McLeod* Cases » 32 *AJIL* (1938) pp. 82–99 et *Collected Writings of Sir Robert Jennings,* Vol. 2, Kluwer Law International, The Hague *et al.*, 1998, pp. 1195–1217.

posé par le droit de légitime défense face aux attaques terroristes est que le droit de légitime défense est reconnu contre d'autres Etats et non contre des réseaux terroristes et pourrait être exercé uniquement, le cas écheant, contre des États qui abriteraient ces organisations terroristes[19]. Une partie de la doctrine considère que les résolutions du Conseil de sécurité adoptées à l'occasion des attentats terroristes du 11 septembre 2001 témoignent de l'approbation de la communauté internationale d'une extension du droit de légitime défense en réponse à des actes terroristes d'une portée considerable[20].

En suivant une conception de la légitime défense dépourvue de tout fondement tant dans la Charte des Nations Unies que dans le droit international, le président George W. Bush a annoncé en septembre 2002 une nouvelle doctrine stratégique des États-Unis fondée sur la « légitime défense préventive » (*pre-emptive self-defense*) préconisant l'attaque armée « même si nous ne savons pas quand et comment attaquera l'ennemi »[21]. Le terrorisme international altère les catégories juridiques essentielles de la Charte des Nations, mais il ne peut pas amener à des positions politiques et stratégiques contraires à tout ordre international comme c'est le cas de cette doctrine stratégique de la « légitime défense préventive ».

4. Le recours à la force dans le cadre du droit international général

Avec l'appui des résolutions du Conseil de sécurité adoptées après la « guerre froide » et de la campagne de l'OTAN au Kosovo (1999), on a plaidé en faveur d'une nouvelle exception à l'interdiction de l'emploi de la force qui devrait être admise dans le contexte d'une « intervention humanitaire » dans des cas extrêmes qui auraient pour but de mettre fin à de graves violations massives des droits de l'homme. On ne peut pas conclure que ce droit est généralement admis dans le droit international actuel, mais il semble s'amorcer une tendance à justifier l'emploi de la force dans ces cas

---

[19] A. Cassese, « Terrorism is Also Disrupting Some Crucial Legal Categories of International Law » 12 *EJIL* (2001) num. 5 pp. 993–1001.

[20] L. Condorelli, « Les attentats du 11 septembre et leurs suites : Ou va le droit international ? », 105 *RGDIP* (2001) p. 843 ; S. Ratner, « *Jus ad bellum* and *Jus in Bello* after September 11 », 96 *AJIL* (2002) p. 914.

[21] The *National Strategy of the United States of America*, The White House, Washington, September, 2002.

exceptionnels[22]. C'est un domaine ou la distinction entre ce qui devrait être et ce qui est ; les décisions doivent se rapprocher si on veut un ordre juridique qui mérite son nom. La Commission internationale indépendante sur l'intervention et la souveraineté des États, promue par le gouvernement du Canada, a publié un rapport qui donne à cette tendance la forme d'une « responsabilité de protéger » et précise les conditions rigoureuses dans lesquelles l'emploi de la force pourrait être justifié dans des cas exceptionnels[23]. L'Acte constitutif de l'Union africaine adopté à Lomé (Togo) le 11 juillet 2000 reconnaît conventionnellement le droit de l'Union à intervenir dans un État membre dans les cas graves « en particulier : crimes de guerre, génocide ou crimes contre l'humanité » (art. 4, lit. h). Le principe de l'égalité souveraine des États et le principe de non-intervention n'autorisent pas à changer le régime dictatorial d'autres États pour y étendre la démocratie (*regime change*), mais qu'en est-t-il lorsque le seul moyen de mettre fin à une situation très grave de violation massive des droits de l'homme est, précisément, la déposition du despote et le changement de régime ?

Une autre façon de justifier le recours à la force, qui a des liens avec celle que l'on vient d'exposer et qui a également un fondement sur le droit international général, est la doctrine qui préconise la possibilité d'adopter des contre-mesures généralisées ou, le cas écheant, l'adoption de mesures avec le recours à la force, décidées sans l'autorisation du Conseil de sécurité, en réponse á la violation des obligations essentielles pour la protection des intérêts généraux de la communauté internationale. Cette possibilité serait toujours ouverte si ces obligations avaient été indiquées dans des résolutions préalablement approuvés par le Conseil de sécurité et l'inaction ultérieure de celui-ci pourrait légitimer une action décentralisée de la part des États qui recoureraient à l'emploi de la force en défense de ces intérêts fondamentaux[24].

---

[22] O. Casanovas. *De l'ajuda humanitària al dret d'ingerència humanitaria, Lliçó inaugural del curs acadèmic 1993-1994, 28 de septembre de 1993,* Barcelona, Universitat Pompeu Fabra, 1993.

[23] *La responsabilité de protéger*, Rapport de la Commission internationale de l'intervention et de la souveraineté des états, Ministère des Affaires étrangers et du Commerce international, Canada, décembre, 2001.

[24] N. Krisch, « Unilateral Enforcement of Collective Will : Kososvo, Iraq and Security Council » *Max Planck Yearbook of United Nations Law* (1999) pp. 59–103 et V. Gowlland-Debbas, « The Limits of Unilateral Enforcement of Community Objectives in the Framework of UN Peace Maintenance » 11 *EJIL* (2000) pp. 361–383

5. Vers l'effacement de la distinction entre « jus ad bellum » et « jus in bello »

Le droit international actuel part de la distinction entre *jus ad bellum*, où se pose la question de la légalité du recours à la force et le *jus in bello,* formé par les règles applicables dans les conflits armés et le droit international humanitaire. Les nouvelles menaces qui pèsent sur les États (terrorisme global, armes de destruction massive, crime organisé à l'échelle planétaire, etc.) perturbent aussi les conditions dans lesquelles cette distinction a un sens. Le droit international humanitaire part de conditions préalables telles 1) la visibilité des combattants, encore qu'elle ait été réduite au minimum par l'article 44, num. 3 du Protocole Additionnel I de 1977 aux Conventions de Genève de 1949 ; 2) la portée limitée des armements, puisque le droit des parties en conflit à choisir les moyens de combat « n'est pas illimité » (art. 35, num 1 du Protocole Additionnel I) et que l'emploi des armes que causent « des maux superflus » est interdit (art. 35, num 2 du Protocole Additionnel I) et 3) les armes sont des moyens de combat qui se trouvent entre les mains des armées ou des combattants. Le terrorisme international échappe à ces conditions préalables et la possibilité que des organisations terroristes de portée globale puissent disposer d'armes de destruction massive crée une menace d'une extrême gravité. Dans l'avis consultatif sur la *licité de la menace ou de l'emploi des armes nucléaires* la Cour internationale « ne peut conclure de façon définitive que la menace ou l'emploi d'armes nucléaires serait licite ou illicite dans une circonstance extrême de légitime défense dans laquelle la survie même d'un Etat serait en cause »[25]. L'avis de la Cour met en relief que la distinction entre *jus ad bellum* et *jus in bello* n'est pas aussi rigide que l'on pourrait être amené à penser. Dans le silence des règles se pose à nouveau, d'une nouvelle façon, la question de la guerre juste[26]. La réglementation actuelle des armes de destruction massive part de la considération préalable de leur possession par un nombre réduit d'États qui partagent une même conception de la sécurité. Cette situation est radicalement altérée si d'autres États qui ne partagent cette conception possèdent ou aspirent à posséder des armes nucléaires. Le problème est beaucoup plus aigu si ces armes passent aux mains d'acteurs non-étatiques. C'est en regard de ce type de menace à la sécurité internationale que l'on

---

[25] *Liceité de la menace ou de l'emploi d'armes nucleaires dans un conflit armé, avis consultatif, CIJ Recueil 1996,* p. 266.

[26] R. Ranjeva, « L'avis consultatif sur la liceité de la menace ou l'emploi des armes nucléaires et le problème de la guerre juste », 2 *Cursos Euromediterráneos Bancaja de Derecho internacional* (1998) pp. 21–33.

prétend justifier juridiquement la cause de la légitime défense préventive (*pre-emptive self defence*) [27] Mais l'Assemblée Générale des Nations Unies, tout en reconnaissant que « les actes de terrorisme nucléaire peuvent avoir les plus graves conséquences et peuvent constituer une menace contre la paix et la sécurité internationales », envisage les mesures à adopter par le renforcement de la coopération judiciaire internationale[28].

En outre, les actes terroristes restent en dehors du domaine d'application des régles du droit international humanitaire et même de celles applicables dans les conflits internes. Le Protocole Additionnel II de 1977 se borne à régler les conflits armés sans caractère international sous leur forme la plus classique de guerres civiles et exclut de son domaine d'application les « situations de tensions internes et de troubles intérieurs, tels que les émeutes, les actes sporadiques et isolés de violence et d'autres actes semblables » (art. 1, num 2), situations qui comprennent évidemment les actes de terrorisme.

Même si les traités de droit international humanitaire ne s'appliquent pas aux actes de terrorisme, ces actes et leurs auteurs sont soumis aux règles du droit international général et aux ordres juridiques étatiques. D'une part le caractère légal ou illégal de l'emploi de la force est sans rapport avec l'application des règles essentielles de protection internationale des droits de l'homme et du droit international humanitaire. D'autre part les mesures adoptées par les législations nationales pour prévenir et sanctionner le terrorisme sont des mesures de nature policière et pénale, ainsi que la poursuite judiciaire de ses sources de financement. Dans ces matières, on ne peut pas dépasser le domaine de la coopération internationale, particulièrement en ce qui concerne dans l'arrestation et l'extradition des responsables.

6. Nouveaux problèmes et nouvelles réponses : interprétation ou changement normatif ?

Devant ces nouvelles menaces l'on peut, évidement, adopter la position de maintenir que le droit international tel qu'il a été généralement conçu pendant la deuxième moitié du XXe siècle apporte une réponse suffisante. On a soutenu que la pratique récente et l'alignement de l'OTAN, de l'Union européenne et des pays du Pacte de Rio à une conception large de la légitime

[27] W.M. Reismann, « Assessing Claims to Revise the Laws of War », 97 *AJIL,* (2003) pp. 82–90.
[28] Res. 59/290, de 13 avril 2005, Convention internationale pour la répression des actes de terrorisme nucleaire, UN Doc. A/RES/59/290.

défense adoptée par les États-Unis s'écarte clairement du droit international et ne peut éviter de soulever des contradictions[29]. Mais l'opinion la plus répandue est que des changements s'imposent dans l'ordre international. Le Secrétaire Général Kofi Annan, dans son discours d'ouverture du débat général de l'Assemblée Générale au mois de septembre dernier, disait : « nous sommes à la croisée des chemins (*we have reached a fork in the road*)[30] Le Secrétaire Général a mandaté un groupe de personnalités de haut niveau pour examiner le problème des nouvelles menaces à la paix et la sécurité internationales. Le rapport présenté par ce groupe sous le titre *Un monde plus sûr : notre affaire à tous* considère que le Conseil de sécurité, pour déterminer s'il doit approuver ou autoriser l'usage de la force armée, devrait toujours examiner au moins cinq critères de légitimité : a) la gravité de la menace ; b) la légitimité du motif de l'intervention ; c) si c'est une mesure de dernier ressort ; d) la proportionnalité des moyens par rapport à la menace et e) mettre en balance les conséquences.[31]

Aux États-Unis l'unilatéralisme de l'administration actuellement au pouvoir est critiqué au motif que l'intérêt même du pays est mieux défendu par une politique orientée vers le multilatéralisme.[32] Mais une approche multilatérale des crises et les coalitions *ad hoc* ne sont pas des solutions adéquates. Le problème consiste en ce que la communauté internationale doit faire front face aux nouvelles menaces. Les Nations Unies sont le forum dans lequel la communauté internationale doit s'exprimer. L'ordre international est un ordre évolutif et dans les décennies passées il a montré une grande flexibilité. L'adaptation de la communauté internationale aux mesures « autorisées » par les Nations Unies en est la preuve. La réforme de la Charte des Nations Unies semble un objectif très difficile à atteindre. Il y a des propositions intéressantes qui ne passent par cette voie. Une des possibilités est le renforcement de la tendance dejà envisagée que le droit international coutumier développe une *lex specialis* qui autoriserait la

---

[29] M.G. Kohen, « The use of force by the United States after the end of the Cold War and its impact on international law », *United States Hegemony and the Foundations of International Law,* M. Byers et G. Nolte (eds.) Cambridge University Press, Cambridge, 2003, p. 230.

[30] Communiqué de presse SG/SM/8891 (23/09/03).

[31] *Un monde plus sur: notre affaire à tous*, Rapport du Groupe de personnalités de haut niveau sur les menaces, les défis et le changement. UN Doc. A/59/565, par. 207.

[32] B.W. Jentleson, « Tough Love Multilateralism », 27 *The Washington Quarterly* (Winter 2003-04) No. 1, pp.7–24.

légitime défense contre des attaques terroristes[33]. On a aussi proposé que le Conseil de sécurité adopte une résolution qui établisse les conditions qui pourraient justifier l'emploi de la force dans certaines situations comme : 1) la possession d'armes de destruction massive ou, le cas écheant, la une preuve claire et convaincante de la volonté d'en disposer ; 2) les abus graves et systématiques des droits de l'homme qui manifestent qu'il n'y a pas de limites à la conduite des gouvernements dans l'ordre interne ; 3) la preuve qu'on cherche à attaquer d'autres nations[34]. Le Secrétaire Général, pour sa part, recommande au Conseil de sécurité d'adopter une résolution établissant les principes de légitimité recommandés par le Groupe de haut niveau dont il devrait s'inspirer lorsqu'il décidera d'autoriser ou de demander le recours à la force.[35]

Tout changement des régles en vigueur doit partir d'un nouveau consensus et le cadre dans lequel il doit se produire est celui des Nations Unies. La voie vers un nouveau consensus est ouverte mais elle est plus difficile que jamais à suivre. Par le passé, les grands changements dans l'ordre international se sont produits après de grandes confrontations armées. Maintenant il s'agirait du changement d'une règle comme celle qui interdit l'emploi de la force et qui, de surcroît, est considérée comme une norme de *jus cogens*. Cela n'empêche pas sa modification et, même avec des changements, elle ne perdrait pas sa nature impérative, mais ceci nous indique la difficulté de l'entreprise.

---

[33] L. Condorelli, « Les attentats du 11 septembre et leurs suites : Où va le droit international ?, » 105 *RGDIP* (2001) No. 4, p. 843.

[34] A.M. Slaughter, « A Chance to Reshape the UN », *The Washington Post*, Sunday, April 13, 2003.

[35] *Dans une liberté plus grande : développement, sécurité et respect des droits de l'homme pour tous*, Rapport du Sécretaire général, 24 mars 2005. UN Doc. A/59/2005, para. 126.

The Normative Underpinnings of the Use of Force. Doctrinal Foundations and Ambiguities in the CFSP/ESDP Discourse

Barbara Delcourt[*]

Contents

Abstract

As has often been pointed out, the "EU's legitimacy relies on its ability to contribute to the strengthening of universal norms of human rights and democracy at the international level". But are all EU Members ready to become involved in armed conflicts (and eventually accept human losses) to uphold or defend these values? Setting my work in the context of current debates in academic and political circles about the use of force in

[*] Professor at the Faculty of Social, Political and Economic Sciences and at the Institute of European Studies and Associate Member of the Centre of International Law (Free University of Brussels). This contribution is mainly drawn from a text published in French by the review *Etudes internationales* (vol. XXXIV, n° 1, Mars 2003, pp. 5–24.).

Baltic Yearbook of International Law, Volume 6, 2006, pp. 157–183.

international relations, I will seek to trace the emergent normative foundations of the EU's common security and defence policy.

The first part of the paper is mostly dedicated to an empirical investigation. It shows the evolution of the European position on the use of force, from the early days of the European Political Cooperation (EPC) through the post-Cold War developments. It consists of an overall review of EC declarations related to the use of force. This discourse analysis is justified, from a methodological point of view, by the need to avoid common bias. Indeed, by mixing factual and normative statements, some analyses lead to a re-interpretation of the past that does not reflect all cases. Moreover, those analyses are mostly focused on the political debates surrounding the contemporary development of European Security and Defence Policy (ESDP). On the whole, a close reading of the documents highlights the EC insistence on the necessity to severely limit the use of force, in accordance with the UN Charter. Nevertheless the end of the Cold War, and especially the Yugoslav crisis, raised fresh questions about humanitarian intervention and the necessity, for the EU, to back diplomacy by force. This brought about a new type of discourse, more 'robust' in its character, even if references to the principles of international law and the specific authority of the UN Security Council concerning the use of force are still present. As a result of these changes, the image of a 'civilian power' that used to characterise the EC's external policy seems to a certain extent, old-fashioned.

In the second part of the paper, I attempt to identify the doctrinal foundations of such declarations in order to understand how changes in conceptions pertaining to the use of force by European States could be justified from a normative point of view. In order to produce a more stringent analysis, I have focused on two different kinds of justification for the use of force. The first is provided by the liberal paradigm inspired by the Kantian doctrine and the second is grounded in the realist paradigm influenced by Hobbes. This choice is motivated by the degree of congruence of each of these paradigms with the European discourse and not by a personal or scientific conviction as to their intrinsic value or relevance. Indeed, all of the EC/EU's and individual Member States' declarations surrounding the question of European Defence and the Petersberg tasks relate, in one way or another, to these two schools of thought in international relations. The European discourse on the use of force appears to be suffering from chronic inconsistency. The texts produced in the European institutional framework are ambiguous. At a first glance, they appear to endorse a traditional liberal view by legitimising the use of force on humanitarian grounds. On the other hand, modes of action and reasons for action are still justified in realistic terms, mainly through references to the specific interests of the Union and its Member States. This testifies to the enduring difficulty in defining a common political project based on common foundations, in particular when values and interests are at stake.

1. Introduction

Trying to identify the core values of the external action of the Union is either a very simple or a very complicated task. A brief look at the Common Foreign and Security Policy (CFSP) objectives in the Treaty reveals what it is about: promoting democracy, rule of law, human rights and so on. Values and norms seem to be intrinsically linked to the interests of Europe and the world altogether.[1] This assessment is rarely questioned, as demonstrated by Mr Dehaene's presentation of the work on 'external action' undertaken in the framework of the convention, even in the academic field (with a few notable exceptions!).[2] Most of the time, discussions are dedicated to institutions and competences that could be more suitable for Europe to perform its historical task: to contribute to world peace and security and achieve lasting development.[3] The lack of debates or questioning of these 'European' values and interests renders the identification of the normative underpinnings of CFSP an elusive task. As Martti Koskenniemi noticed: "In addition to repeating norms to which Members are already bound through the UN Charter, the objectives remain abstract . . . Peace and security are by themselves meaningless postulates".[4]

My main hypothesis is that the identification of the normative underpinnings of the EU's external action could be achieved by questioning the way the use of force in international relations is justified (by international norms and values) in the European discourse. The mere fact that Europe as a whole has not yet developed a genuine Common European Defence Policy should not prevent us from analysing its conception of the

[1] TEU, Title V, Article 11 §1.

[2] R. Youngs indicates that an analysis of ESDP must begin to pay greater attention to the question: what is it for? 'The European Security and Defence Policy: What Impact on the EU's Approach to Security Challenges?', 11:2 *European Security* (Summer 2002) p. 103.

[3] *European Convention,* Doc. 6 December 2002 < wwww.europakonvent>

[4] M. Koskenniemi, 'International Law Aspects of the Common Foreign and Security Policy', in M. Koskenniemi (ed.), *International Law Aspects of the European Union* (Martinus Nijhoff, The Hague, 1998) p. 28.

use of force in international relations. From the early days of the European Political Cooperation (EPC) in the 1970s until the present Gulf crisis, the Foreign Affairs ministers have regularly taken positions on this matter. But most analyses have not based their findings on an overall empirical study of what was actually *said* and which kind of norms emerged from these declarations. The first part of this paper will therefore explain the main features of the European position regarding the use of force and its evolution.

Trying to conduct an overall assessment of the empirical evidence without a theoretical framework can lead to nowhere but up a blind alley.[5] I will therefore explain changes in the discourse by reference to some of the political and juridical doctrines that underpin the external political aspects of European integration.

2. The Critical European Standpoint Concerning the Use of Force in International Relations

Until now Europe has often been presented as a 'civilian power'. Its desire to distinguish itself from traditional State behaviour in the field of international relations, particularly its reluctance to resort to coercive means in order to impose its own priorities and interests is deemed to contribute to its genuine identity.[6] If we examine the positions taken in this regard, we ascertain that, most of the time, declarations sought to enhance United Nations resolutions while at the same time recalling obligations under the Charter, in particular the principle of peaceful resolution of conflicts. With the fall of the Berlin Wall, military actions under the auspices of the UN were made possible to respond to different international crises. The fratricidal wars in the Balkans (and elsewhere) were in this respect a challenge for the Europeans who wanted to develop a more political project for Europe. By that time, Europe had begun to change its position on external intervention including by means of force although one cannot speak of a total reversal of its previously restrictive interpretations.

---

[5] *See* H. Patomaki, 'Cultivating the Mood of "Grieving Delight" The Moral Lessons of the Study of Narratives and Metaphors in the 1990–1991 Gulf War', *Paper prepared by the second EuPRA-Conference in Budapest,* Hungary, 12–14 November 1993, p. 14.

[6] C. Hill, *The Actors in Europe's Foreign Policy* (Routledge, London, 1996); F. De La Serre, 'La communauté, acteur international?', 69 *Pouvoirs* (April 1994) pp. 107–116.; K. Nicolaidis and R. Howse, '"This is my Eutopia…": Narrative as Power', 40:4 *Journal of Common Market Studies* pp. 767–792.

2.1. The Necessity to Respect the UN Charter and the Prohibition of the Use of Force between States

The 1973 *Document on European Identity* expresses the initial ambitions of Europe as a 'whole':

> "L'Europe des Neuf est consciente des devoirs internationaux que lui impose son unification. Celle-ci n'est dirigée contre personne *ni inspirée par une quelconque volonté de puissance*. Au contraire, les Neuf sont convaincus que leur union sera bénéfique pour la communauté internationale tout entière, en constituant un élément d'équilibre et un pôle de *coopération avec toutes les nations, quels que soient leur dimension, leur culture et leur système social*. Ils entendent jouer un rôle actif dans les affaires mondiales et contribuer ainsi, dans le *respect des buts et des principes de la Charte des Nations Unies*, à ce que les relations internationales soient fondées sur plus de justice, à ce que l'indépendance et l'égalité des États soient mieux préservées, la prospérité mieux partagée et la sécurité de chacun mieux assurée . . .".[7]

In fact, the basic principles of the United Nations concerning peaceful coexistence between its Member States have frequently been used in order to condemn or criticize military interventions all over the world, with a few exceptions, mainly involving US military interventions. Many reasons could explain such an attitude. European States were no longer colonial powers in pursuit of territorial expansion, and they were aware of the dangerous consequences of unilateral interventions conducted on 'moral' or political grounds.[8] This attitude explains Europe's firm condemnations of South Africa's interventionism[9], Israel's military campaigns[10], invasion of Afghanistan by soviet troops[11] and Vietnamese intervention in Cambodia

---

[7] Copenhagen, 14 December 1973, pt. 9 (emphasis added).

[8] O. Corten, 'Droit, force et légitimité dans une société internationale en mutation', 37 *Revue interdisciplinaire d'études juridiques* (1996) pp. 86–87; U. Schwarz, *Confrontation and Intervention in the Modern World* (New York, Oceana Publications Inc., 1970) p. 89.

[9] *Bulletin de la Communauté européenne* 7 August 1985, p. 112; *ibid.,* 9 (1985), pp. 84–85; *ibid.,* 2 (1986) pp. 91–92; *ibid.,* 5 (1986) p. 81; *ibid.,* 4 (1987) p. 65; *ibid.,* 6 (1987) p. 109.

[10] *Bull. CE,* 2 (1977) p. 69; *ibid,* 6 (1979) p. 100; *ibid,* 12 (1981), p. 76; *ibid.,* 4 (1982) pp. 50–51; *ibid.,* 6 (1982) pp. 84–85.

[11] *Bull. CE,* 1 (1980), p. 7; *ibid.,* 2 (1980) p. 85; *ibid.,* 3 (1981) p. 10. ; *ibid.,* 6 (1981) p. 9; *ibid.,* 12 (1985) p. 118.

against the Khmer Rouge regime.[12] A thorough examination of the texts produced in the framework of EPC reveals that no humanitarian concerns were ever used to justify the unilateral use of force.[13] By the same token, it should be noted that intervening States themselves rarely justify their actions on the basis of humanitarian concerns and prefer to motivate intervention with an extensive interpretation of the principle of self-defence. But this was not sufficient to convince European States of the well-founded nature of military operations led by Vietnam in Cambodia or India in Pakistan, or even Tanzania in Uganda.[14]

In the case of traditional interstate wars, such as those opposing Iraq and Iran or India and Pakistan, the EC and its Member States have repeatedly recalled the prohibition of the use of force and the necessity to solve conflicts by peaceful means.[15] On the other hand they never condemned the use of force by the United States against Libya, the capture of Noriega during the military operation in Panama or the bombing of Nicaragua's harbours in the 1980's (and the military training of the contras). This absence of official reactions left groundless any kind of justification for exceptions to the prohibition on the use of force (such as in the case of intervention against terrorism and narco-trafficking, to promote the restoration of democracy or making respect for human rights more effective).[16]

We can therefore state that, until the 1990s, the EC and its Member States refused to accept military interventions for the "sake of Humanity" or in order to "project a Hexagon of civilisation" (rule of law, democratic participation, peaceful resolution of conflicts, social justice, interdependence and State monopoly of violence).[17] If Europe has had a tendency to portray

---

[12] *Bull. CE,* 7/8 (1980) p. 91; interventions in Thailand have also been condemned, *Bull. CE,* 4 (1983) p. 68; 1 (1984) p. 55.

[13] This is the case of most Members of the UN, N. J. Wheeler, 'Pluralist and Solidarist Conceptions of International Societies: Bull and Vincent on Humanitarian Intervention', 21:3 *Millennium: Journal of International Studies* (1992) p. 472.

[14] *Ibid.*

[15] *Bull. CE,* 4 (1986) p. 115; *ibid.,* 7/8 (1986) p. 109, *ibid.,* 1 (1987) p. 694; *ibid.,* 4 (1990) pp. 77–78. *See also* the positions defended in the name of Europe in front of the General Assembly of the UN, *ibid.,* 9 (1987) p. 117.

[16] As S. Hoffmann states, during the cold war, interventionist doctrines like those of Brejnev or Reagan, did not actually rely on humanitarian concerns, 'The Politics and Ethics of Military Intervention', 37:4 *Survival* (Winter 1995/6).

[17] L. Goetshel, 'L'Union européenne et la sécurité collective', 86 *Relations internationales* (Eté 1996) pp. 143–161; H.-G. Ehrart, 'Quel modèle pour la PESC ?', 55 *Cahiers de Chaillot* (October 2002), pp. 10–11 and pp. 12–13.

itself as an original security actor, it is largely due to its identification with alternative dimensions of security (e.g., social, political, environmental, etc.) alongside with the development of a so-called "genuine pacific culture".[18]

2.2. From the Attempt to Extend the Scope of the Rule Concerning the Prohibition on the Use of Force, to the Temptation to Use Military Means

In the aftermath of 1989, some changes began to appear in the European discourse, while foreign ministers continued to condemn aggressive actions[19] such as the occupation of Kuwait by the Iraqi regime.[20] During this period, the most remarkable thing to point out is the tendency to consider as 'illegal' the use of military force *within* a country.[21] For instance in the case of Yugoslavia, Europeans recalled the principle prohibiting the use of force even before recognising the independence of the Republics.[22] This was

---

[18] H. Sjursen, 'New Forms of Security Policy in Europe', 01:4 *Arena Working Papers WP*; A. Deighton, 'The European Security and Defence Policy', 40:4 *Journal of Common Market Studies* p. 722; Goetshel, *supra* note 17, p. 159; M. Bacot-Decriaud, 'L'UE confrontée aux interventions d'humanité: une délicate conceptualisation', in J-F. Rioux, *La sécurité humaine. Une nouvelle conception des relations internationales* (L'Harmattan, Paris, 2001) pp. 205–244; Ehrart, *supra* note 17, pp. 23–25.

[19] Like the ones in Nagorno-Karabach, *Bull. CE,* 5 (1992) p. 115; *Bull. UE,* 9 (1993) p. 84; *ibid.,* 1 (1994) pt. 1.3.7.; the military intervention of Yugoslavian army in Bosnia-Herzegovina, *Bull. CE*, 4 (1992) p. 87; *ibid.* 5 (1992) pp. 112–113. The EU seemed to develop a more understanding attitude towards the Turkish military actions in northern Iraq in 1995, *Bull. UE,* 4 (1995) pt. 1.4.17 and 5, (1995) pt. 1.4.15. But the EU has a more critical position against military interventions in Congo, *Bull. UE,* ½ (1997) pt. 1.3.19. In the conflict between Ethiopia and Eritrea, the UE Presidency has constantly been recalling the principle of pacific resolution of conflicts, *see* for instance, *Bull. UE,* 5 (1998) pt. 1.3.7.

[20] *Bull. CE,* 7/8 (1990), pp. 127–130; *ibid.,* 9 (1990), pp. 84–86; *ibid., 1*/2 (1991) pp. 107 *et seq.*

[21] In the Baltic States for example, *Bull. CE,* 3 (1990) pp. 81–82; *ibid.,* 1/2 (1991) pp. 109–110; in Sri-Lanka, *ibid.,* 10 (1990) p. 105; *see also* the condemnation of military actions against the Karen population in Myanmar, *ibid.*, 4 (1992) p. 88. On the 1991 events in Lithuania, *see* article by Zalimas in this volume – ed.

[22] Déclaration commune du 26 mars 1991, *Bull. CE,* 3 (1991) p. 77 ; Déclaration commune du 8 mai 1991, *Bull. CE,* 5 (1991) p. 90. In the common statement delivered on 5 July, the EC and its Member states declared: "[q]u'il appartient aux seuls peuples de la Yougoslavie de décider de l'avenir de leur pays. Ils soulignent, par conséquent, leur ferme opposition à tout usage de la force", *Bull. CE,* 7/8 (1991) p. 117.

clearly a change in relation to their traditional stand on civil warfare, partly motivated by the need to protect individual and minority rights. This is still the case when they want to strengthen a cease-fire or a process of internal pacification.[23] In such cases the declarations amount to criticism of the *excessive* use of force by a State against its own population rather than an actual wish to extend the scope of the traditional rule.[24] The reason for this prudence lies certainly in the necessity to avoid an upheaval of the principle that characterises modern States, that is the 'state monopoly of legitimate violence'. The events in Côte d'Ivoire seem to confirm this interpretation.[25]

This 'liberal' attitude has not led to a radical departure from the non-interference rule enshrined in the UN Charter. Even if the 'right to interfere' ranked high on the agenda by the early 1990s, no European foreign minister has ever pledged support for the unilateral use of force in international *fora* and has never endorsed it or understood it as being an emergent norm in international law.[26] In fact they have shown a remarkable consistency in

---

[23] Declaration by the Presidency on behalf of the EU on recent developments in Côte d'Ivoire, Brussels, 22 September 2003, *12745/03 (Presse 277) P 115/03;* Declaration by the Presidency on behalf of the EU on the Peace Process in Sudan, Brussels, 8 August 2003, *11973/03 (Presse 238) p 96/03* ; Declaration by the Presidency on behalf of the EU on the Peace Process in Liberia, Brussels, 28 July 2003, *11832/1/03 REV (Presse 223), p 92/03 ;* Declaration by the Presidency on behalf of the EU on Peace Agreement in Liberia, 22 August 2003, *12062/03 (Presse 246) P 101/03*; Declaration by the Presidency on behalf of the EU on the latest military attacks in Bujumbura (Burundi), Brussels, 10 July 2003, *11367/03 (Presse 206) P85/03.*

[24] *See* the EU Declaration on Chechnya, *Bull. UE,* ½ (1995) p. 94 and the Press release delivered in Brussels on the 17th of January 1995, *Documents d'actualité internationale (D.A.I.),* no.5 (1er mars 1995) pt. 61.

[25] *See also* the tremendous efforts of the international community to restore a monopoly of force in Afghanistan and the way Europeans tried to cope with the Albanian rebels (UCK) in Macedonia, C. Piana, 'La PESC après Saint-Malo: de la diplomatie à la défense', Colloque du CERI "l'Union europénne, acteur international", 20–21 June 2002, <www.ceri-sciences-po.org/themes/europe /home.htm>: *see also* the request made by the Council to the illegal armed group in Columbia "to cease all hostilities", 25 59th Council meeting "External Relations", Brussels, 26 January 2004.

[26] Even during the Kosovo War, *see* O. Corten, 'La référence au droit international comme justification du recours à la force : vers une nouvelle doctrine de la guerre juste?', in A-M. Dillens, *L'Europe et la guerre* (Facultés Universitaires Saint-Louis, Bruxelles, 2001) pp. 69–94.

condemning unilateral military intervention.[27] In their repeated demands for the neighbours of Congo and Burundi to stop their military aid to the belligerents, they clearly stick to the traditional rules prohibiting indirect interventionism.[28]

As a matter of fact, they did not really need such a 'new legal basis'. Since the end of the cold war the Security Council has been able to manage some international crises without being paralysed by a veto. Insofar as massive human rights violations in internal conflicts may be qualified as "threat to international peace and security", the Security Council can authorize States to "use all necessary means" to enforce peace agreements, the delivery of humanitarian assistance, no-fly zones, etc.[29] In these circumstances, European States have participated with their armed forces to multilateral peacekeeping or peace enforcement missions.[30]

Nevertheless the Yugoslav conflicts have raised some questions about the legitimacy of the very restrictive rules concerning the use of force in international relations. On one hand, Europe was incapable of ending the slaughter that was taking place in its own backyard. While its economic power is undeniable, it was insufficient to ensure that respect for fundamental principles of human and minority rights were upheld. The UN itself was losing its credibility as a result of its involvement in the area whilst NATO made a 'bold' display of its capacity to 'project power' vis-à-vis the Serbs in Bosnia. At that time, more and more Europeans were

---

[27] Declaration by the Presidency on behalf of the EU on the recent massacres in and around Drodro, North-Eastern part of DRC, Brussels, 14 April 2003, *8433/03 (Presse 115) P47/*03; Declaration by the Presidency on behalf of the EU on the withdrawal of Ugandan people's Defence Forces from the Ituri region of DRC, Brussels, 30 April 2003, *8827/03 (Presse 121) P52/03.*

[28] Declaration by the Presidency on behalf of the EU on the situation in the East of the DRC, Brussels, 27 June 2003, *11016/1/03/REV 1 (Presse 192) P77/03*; Declaration by the Presidency on behalf of the EU on the massacres in the province of Ituri in the DRC, Brussels, 13 October 2003, *13526/03 (Presse 301) P 127/03*; Declaration by the Presidency on behalf of the EU on the latest military attacks in Bujumbura (Burundi), Brussels, 10 July 2003, *11367/03 (Presse 206) P85/03.*

[29] O. Corten and P. Klein, *Droit d'ingérence ou obligation de réaction?* (Bruylant, 2ème éd., Bruxelles, 1996) and Rapport de la Commission internationale de l'intervention et de la souveraineté des Etats, *La responsabilité de protéger,* December 2001, <www.crdi.ca>.

[30] M. Ortega, 'L'intervention militaire et l'Union européenne', 45 *Cahiers de Chaillot* (2001), <www.iss-eu.org/chaillot/chai45.html>; J. Howorth, 'L'intégration européenne et la défense: l'ultime défi?', 43 *Cahiers de Chaillot,* (Novembre 2002) pp. 1–101.

becoming convinced of the need to develop new military capabilities within the EU, so it was not very surprising that during the Kosovo crisis, European Heads of State and government chose to endorse military action against Yugoslavia without the due authorization of the Security Council.[31]

However at the end of the Kosovo war, some European ministers like Joschka Fischer, Louis Michel and Hubert Védrine expressed their refusal to endorse such a permissive regime, pointing out the potential dangers of such a 'precedent' for the global security system.[32] France, Germany and Belgium used the same kind of argument to convince their partners (the so-called 'New Europe') not to engage in or sustain a military operation against Iraq without the formal approval of the Security Council. They succeeded in some way when, in February 2003, all the participants of the extraordinary European Council stated: "We [as members of the European Union] are committed to the United Nations remaining the centre of the international order. We recognise that the primary responsibility for dealing with Iraqi disarmament lies with the Security Council".[33] Even in light of subsequent events this remains a very important official statement that deserves attention, especially when *opinio juris* is to be taken into consideration for assessing the emergence of a new norm governing the use of force.

It is noteworthy that when it comes to the right to self-defence the EU is more prone to an extensive and permissive interpretation of it. For instance it has accepted the American argument for exercising their right of self-defence against Afghanistan after the 11 September attacks even if the American argument provided a very extensive interpretation of it. Europeans did not even mention the obligation enshrined in Article 51 of the Charter to work closely with the Security Council when exercising this right.[34] Whether this move is symptomatic of a shift to a less formalistic view regarding the use of force in international relations is worth questioning.

---

[31] At that moment, there were also divergences among Europeans on the question of the legal basis, *see* O. Corten and B. Delcourt, *Droit, légitimation et politique extérieure: l'Europe et la guerre du Kosovo* (Bruylant, Bruxelles, 2000/1) p. 310.

[32] B. Delcourt and F. Dubuisson, 'Contribution au débat juridique sur les missions 'non-article 5' de l'OTAN", 1–2 *Revue belge de droit international* (2002) pp. 439–467.

[33] *Extraordinary European Council*, Brussels, 17 February 2003; *Presidency Conclusions, Brussels*, 20–21 March 2003, §§ 67 and 69.

[34] *See* O. Corten and F. Dubuisson, "'L'opération 'liberté immuable': une extension abusive du concept de légitime defense", 1 *Revue générale de droit international public* (2002) pp. 51–77.

The evolution of the European discourse – that is the discourse shaped in the framework of the European institutions – on the use of force is therefore not free of ambiguity. At first glance, it seems quite obvious that it reveals an orthodox view; and some will qualify it as being 'legalistic'. But the more European governments have developed political ambitions at the international level (encompassing the development of a security and defence policy), the more they seem to have introduced elements of distortion. This growing discursive instability can be traced back to the traditional doctrinal debates about the use of force in international relations.

3. The Normative Underpinnings of Debates Surrounding the ESDP

The development of a common European defence and security policy has been justified by the need to provide adequate institutions in order to implement the norms and the values Europe is fighting for. Europe's essentially declaratory external policy has been considered as the main reason explaining its failures in the Balkans. The link between *norms* and force has always been a concern for philosophers, especially those who embrace a cosmopolitan view. But some arguments used in order to sustain the European endeavour have to be understood in light of a different kind of doctrine. As a matter of fact, a lot of arguments are more or less related to the *interests* of the State (or Europe). This kind of justification can also be found in modern doctrines that are, unlike the former, more anchored in a 'statist' tradition.

3.1. Coercion as a Condition to Achieve the Rule of Law: The 'Kantian' Paradigm[35]

If law needs institutions to be implemented, coercion appears to be a condition for the operability of a legal system – be it internal or

[35] From a theoretical perspective, it seems relevant to establish a link between Kant, Kelsen and Habermas. They share a common conviction on the necessity to assure that law is prevailing over politics in international relations. In their views, persons and social groups must be the first beneficiaries of a kind of cosmopolitan order in which supranational institutions are capable of implementing individual and collective rights and to maintain order. This school of thought has been presented as the doctrine *par excellence* that underlines European integration. *See* I. Manners 'Normative Power Europe: A Contradiction in Terms?', 40:2 *Journal of Common Market Studies* (2002) pp. 240 *et seq*; A. Colonomos, 'L'éthique de la politique étrangère', in F. Charillon, *Politique étrangère. Nouveaux regards* (Presses de Sciences Po, Paris, 2002) p. 130.

international.[36] In the 18th century, Emmanuel Kant expressed this conceptual link between law and coercion, surmising that only coercion could bring the inherent rights of a person into existence.[37] In this regard, it is the public constraint – the State – that is in charge of implementing the law. With the prospect of an emerging cosmopolitan State – that is to say a community of free States bound by law – the legitimate constraint must rely on a cosmopolitan constitution and a coercive apparatus. In any event, this constraint is only applicable inside the 'society of nations'. Unlike some 'neo-Kantian' authors who support a broader interventionist concept, the German philosopher seems to criticize intervention by principle[38], even if he considers that war could sometimes be a "*ruse de la raison*" enabling people to converge around republican values.[39] Above all, he takes a radical stand against the 'just war' doctrine as he considers that law cannot be used to justify war. Only self-defence could imply the resort to force.[40]

Hans Kelsen is clearly inspired by the Kantian doctrine. As a positivist, but also a fervent militant for an international democracy based on a global security system, he has criticized the concept of State sovereignty insofar as it prevents regulation by international law. The principle of the primacy of international law he has fought for is grounded on the 'unity of mankind'; this is the reason why he considers that international norms have to prevail upon internal norms written by States.[41] Moreover, to be effective the international legal system must develop international jurisdictions that must rely on an international police force for enforcing their judgments.[42]

---

[36] B. Conforti, 'Humanité et renouveau de la production normative' (*Mélanges René-Jean Dupuy,* Paris, Pedone, 1991) p. 119.

[37] E. Kant, *Idée de l'histoire universelle d'un point de vue cosmopolitique* (*Œuvres philosophiques, t.2,* Paris, Gaillard, 1996).

[38] E. Kant, *Projet de paix perpétuelle* (Hatier, Paris, 1988) principe V des articles préliminaires, p. 28; C. Duflo, *Kant. La Raison du droit* (Michalon, Paris, 1999) p. 51; W. B Gallie, *Philosophers of Peace and War* (Cambridge University Press, Cambridge) 1978, pp. 23 *et seq*. According to I. Manners, norms and values can be diffused without resorting to military tools, *supra* note 35, pp. 244–245.

[39] S. Goyard-Fabre, *Kant et le problème du droit* (Librairie philosophique Vrin, Paris ,1975) pp. 239 *et seq*.

[40] G. L. Negretto, 'Kant and the Illusion of Collective Security', 46:2 *Journal of International Affairs* (1993) pp. 506 *et seq*.

[41] D. Zolo, 'International Peace through International Law', 9:2 *European Journal of International Law* (1998) pp. 306 *et seq*.

[42] C. Leben, 'Hans Kelsen and the Advancement of International Law', 9:2 *European Journal of International Law,* (1998) pp. 287–305; C. Tournaye, *Kelsen et la sécurité collective,* (L.G.D.J., Paris, 1994) pp. 9–14.

Sanctions are viewed as a condition for the normativity of the international legal order, which will otherwise long remain 'primitive law'. For Kelsen the 'just war' principle is intended to support the idea that ethical norms (like human rights) must be enforced by military means to be considered as positive laws.[43]

Some of the writings of Jurgen Habermas could also be understood in reference to this cosmopolitan tradition. In the book he has written for the bicentenary of the Perpetual Peace Treaty (Kant 1795), he states that human rights will never be fully respected unless the international community establishes an executive force. By the same token, the rule of non-interference must be revised to enable humanitarian actions.[44] In this respect, Habermas defended the NATO operation against Yugoslavia in 1999. He considered that the Kosovo war enhanced the cosmopolitan values and norms pitted against traditional international law.[45] He justified the non-observance of procedures on humanitarian grounds – in this case the Security Council's authority – on account of the uneven progress of international institutions.[46]

Could ESDP be seen as an instrument for fulfilling the requirements of this kind of cosmopolitan doctrine? As a matter of fact, some declarations seem to be pointing in this direction. For example, EU External Relations Commissioner Chris Patten has declared: "An independent foreign policy is an empty slogan if it is not used to some purpose and to some effect . . . The EU in short has every reason to strut its stuff: boasting its achievements, shaping events and spreading its values".[47] Unlike European governments, the European Parliament has explicitly supported the implementation of a 'right to interfere' to protect people around the world from the curse of

---

[43] H. Kelsen, *Théorie pure du droit* (L.G.D.J./Bruylant, Paris/Bruxelles, 1999) pp. 311–313; F. Rigaux, 'Hans Kelsen on International Law', 9:2 *European Journal of International Law* (1998) p. 335.

[44] J. Habermas, *La paix perpétuelle. Le bicentenaire d'une idée kantienne* (Ed. du Cerf, Paris, 1996) pp. 61–62. *See also* J. Rawls, for whom the non-intervention principle does not apply in the case of massive human rights violations, *Le droit des gens* (Ed. Esprit, Paris, 1996) pp. 59, 78, and 82.

[45] J. Habermas, 'Bestialité et humanité: une guerre à la frontière du droit et de la morale', *Revue PESC, Forum franco-allemand,* <www.le forum.de/fr/fr-revue-pesc08.htm>. All web pages have been visited on in April 2004.

[46] *Ibid.*

[47] '*A Voice for Europe? The Future of CFSP*', <www.europa.eu.int/comm/external_relations/ news/patten/speech01_111.htm>.

human suffering.[48] Javier Solana (the High representative for the EU) has argued that "CFSP is the means to an end, namely to promote the values and principles for which the European Union is respected worldwide. We should increasingly be able to ensure that the rule of law and human rights are respected and that the people throughout the world can, like ourselves, enjoy the benefit of freedom, democracy and prosperity".[49] The lessons of Europe's failures in the Balkans and the relative success of the US-led NATO military intervention in Bosnia seem to have determined the course of the European defence project, to be understood as a 'projection of European values'. Tony Blair declared in 1998 that "the only thing that was ever going to work in Kosovo was diplomacy backed up with a credible threat of force",[50] expressing what most of the European governments thought at that time.

Very enthusiastic comments were made around the initiative launched by the French and the British governments pointing out the fact that military interventions that will be undertaken within the framework of the ESDP would only be justified by reference to the universal values and international norms enshrined in the UN Charter. As a consequence strictly ideological or imperialist concerns are no longer supposed to motivate Europe's external action.[51] As stated during the European Council in Thessalonica, the EU "will contribute relentlessly to strengthening and reshaping the institutions of global governance, regional cooperation and *expanding the reach of*

---

48 *Bull. UE,* 4 (1994) p. 96. In the last report pertaining to the relations between the EU and the UN, the 'right to interfere' is not used anymore. But it is suggested that in case of mass murder, crimes against humanity or genocide, it should be possible to by-pass a veto issued in the Security Council if an 'impartial institution' acknowledges that there is a danger regarding the above mentioned crimes, *A5-0480/2003*, p. 13 § 18.

49 Address by J. Solana, *Forschunginstitut der Deutschen Gesellschaft für Auswärtige Politik*, Berlin, 47 *Cahier de Chaillot* (14 November 2000) p. 113.

50 T. Blair, Press conference in Pörtschach, 47 *Cahier de Chaillot*, (24 and 25 October 1998) p. 8; *see also* J. Solana: "There is no inherent opposition between power, supposedly to the US method, and law, the 'European method'. Law and Power are two sides of the same coin. Power is needed to establish law and law is the legitimate face of power. Sometimes European countries have tended to forget that law and international norms have to be backed by force", in 'The Future of transatlantic Relations: Reinvention or Reform?', Published by *Progressive Governance Conference* (11–13 July 2003) <www.ue.eu.int>.

51 Ortega, *supra* note 30, p. 28; Ehrart, *supra* note 17, p. 26; J. Solana, 'Europe. Security in the Twenty-first Century', *The Olof Palme Memorial Lecture*, Stockholm, 20 June 2001, p. 7

international law".[52] This position followed a decisive stand in favour of the establishment of the International Criminal Court,[53] whose Statute, by the way, clearly rejects the unilateral use of force for implementing the objectives laid down by the signatories.[54]

Besides what can appear to be a concrete step to the establishment of a cosmopolitan order, there are other arguments used in the debates surrounding the ESDP that could not be understood by reference to this specific school of thought.

3.2. The Convergence between Values and Interests as a Prerequisite for the Use of Force: The 'Realist' Paradigm

Those who consider that every community has its own system of values question the existence of universal ethics.[55] Pluralist conceptions of international society are anchored in a realist tradition rather than on the idea of natural law that actually sustains the claims towards universal justice.[56] In the hobbesian doctrine, for example, the notion of 'justice' is intrinsically linked to the existence of a Sovereign who is the sole interpreter of the norms derived from natural law. At the international level, the absence of a unique decision-making centre prevents any possibility of defining universal norms for the community of nations. Since international law (that is natural law) is not deemed to regulate international relations, only few cautionary rules should exert a civilizing effect on relations between States.[57] Max Weber would later argue that attempts to limit State sovereignty through reference to universal values would nevertheless fail to overcome the

[52] *Presidency Conclusions*, Thessaloniki, 19–20 June 2003, §54 (emphasis added).
[53] *Bull. EU*, 4 (2002) 1.6.18.
[54] Preamble of the Statute of the International Criminal Court, §§8–9.
[55] D. Boucher, *Political Theories of International Relations* (Oxford University Press, Oxford/New York, 1998) pp. 340, 344 and D. Morrice, 'The Liberal-Communitarian Debate in Contemporary Political Philosophy and its Significance for International Relations', 26:2 *Review of International Studies* (2000) pp. 236–237.
[56] Wheeler, *supra* note 13, p. 464 ; A. J. Bellamy, 'Humanitarian Intervention and the Three Traditions', 17:1 *Global Society* (2003) pp. 9–11. For didactic purpose, we only focus on the two main traditions, considering that authors inspired by the 'rationalist' tradition could either be 'pluralist' or 'solidarist' in certain circumstances.
[57] S. Goyard-Fabre, 'Les silences de Hobbes et de Rousseau devant le droit international', tome 32 *Archives de philosophie du droit* (1987) pp. 59–69

irrational nature of domination. On the contrary, it would instead lead to a "war of the gods"[58] or, to put it in other terms, a 'clash of civilizations'.

Modern realists consider that international politics is by nature determined by power relations. That is the reason why they tend to focus on the question of interests to explain the international system.[59] In this respect, only national interests can explain military interventionism, while humanitarian concerns are seen as secondary motivations. Stephen Krasner has thus demonstrated that powerful States have only defended 'universal values' when their specific interests were at stake.[60] No general or abstract concern has ever been decisive in such a matter.[61]

We should keep in mind that in the EU Treaty the primary objective of the CFSP is:

> " - to safeguard the common values, fundamental interests, independence and integrity of the Union in conformity with the principles of the United Nations Charter;
> - to strengthen the security of the Union in all ways;
> - to preserve peace and strengthen international security, in accordance with the principles of the United Nations Charter, as well as the principles of the Helsinki Final Act and the objectives of the Paris Charter, including those on external borders;
> - to promote international cooperation;

[58] P. Raynaud, 'La guerre et le droit: les limites de la rationalisation. Max Weber et sa postérité', tome 32 *Archives de philosophie du droit* (1987) pp. 104–105.

[59] D. Battistella, 'L'intérêt national. Une notion, trois discours', in Charillon, *supra* note 35, pp. 143–147.

[60] *For* Youngs: "Ministerial statements have frequently suggested that more forceful military intervention is necessary to reaffirm the EU's identity and bestow it with enhanced credibility in the eyes of the European citizens disillusioned with their government's dismal failure in the Balkans", *supra* note 2, p. 106.

[61] S. Krasner, 'Sovereignty, Regimes, and Human Rights', in V. Rittberger (ed.), *Regime Theory and International Relations* (Clarendon Paperbacks, Oxford University Press, Oxford, 1995) pp. 141, 143. Inside the pluralist paradigm, some authors do not agree with tough realist analyses considering that only egoistic interests can motivate military intervention by powerful States. But they consider that the international society is not mature enough as to provide consensual and universal definition of the 'good life', Wheeler, *supra* note 13, p. 467. It is then unlikely to have a 'right to interfere' for the sake of 'Humanity', Morrice, *supra* note 55, pp. 233–251.

> - to develop and consolidate democracy and the rule of law, and respect for human rights and fundamental freedoms."[62]

During the Kosovo war, some statements made by the British and French foreign ministers assumed that, in democratic regimes, interests can also have a "moral" dimension.[63] Javier Solana recalled a very popular idea concerning Europe's international role when he said: "CFSP is about making a difference in international politics. It is about the European Union being able to project its values and interests – the core of its political identity – effectively beyond its own borders."[64] In a comment published by the *Financial Times*, he stated that the new capabilities of Europe

> "will help the EU to advance its core objectives: the alleviation of poverty, the promotion of democracy and the rule of law; and the protection of human rights. *It will allow us to make a greater contribution to the development of international stability and the preservation of peace and security. This will serve our own interests: a more stable, safer world helps create buoyant markets, together with the scope for greater trade and fewer displaced persons.*"[65]

---

[62] TEU, Title V, Article 11.

[63] This kind of 'narrative' clearly appears in Bush's Declarations concerning the US global policy, *see* E. Rhodes, 'Onward Liberal Soldiers? The Crusading Logic of Bush's Grand Strategy and what is Wrong with it', <www.ciaonet.org/special-_section/iraq/analysis> p. 15. The 'natural' congruence between universal values and US interests is also resumed in a presidential statement delivered by Clinton in 1994 and in most arguments underlying American interventionism in the 1990s, Ortega *supra* note 30, pp. 31–33. In a conference given in Chicago on the 22 April 1999, T. Blair has proposed five criteria or questions for sustaining military intervention that revealed a more utilitarian than moral or legal approach: 1) Are we sure of what we are going to do? 2) Have we exhausted all available means? 3) Are there military operations that could be implemented in a rationalistic and cautious way? 4) Are we ready to undertake a long lasting operation? 5) Are our national interests at stake? Howorth, *supra* note 30, p. 93, note 170 (author's translation).

[64] Address by J. Solana, *supra* note 49, p. 111; N. Gnesotto, 'Guerre et paix: la prévention des conflits en Europe', 11 *Cahiers de Chaillot,* (1993) p. 2 ; A. de Vasconcelos, 'La politique extérieure d'une Europe ouverte', in M.-F. Durand and A. De Vasconcelos (eds.), *La PESC. Ouvrir l'Europe au monde* (Presses de Sciences Po, Paris, 1998) pp. 25 *et seq*.

[65] J. Solana, 'Why Europe needs the military option', *Financial Times* (29 September 2000) (emphasis added); *see also* A. JK Bailes, 'The Security Challenges for the European Union', *A Talk at Copenhagen*, 25 September 2003.

Texts and declarations from inside the EU undoubtedly reflect the idea of developing an autonomous capacity to manage international crises, or to restore peace and security in troubled areas. At the same time, they also suggest there are some political limits to the actions that the EU could undertake, which suggest that realist theory rings true. The following facts can support this assertion:

- Firstly, European Defence is mainly dedicated to protecting Western European populations.[66] Broader security issues – including societal, environmental or economical aspects – often concern events and threats (like terrorism) that could undermine the well being of Europeans themselves.[67] Here, interests are likely to be collective and not defined in a strictly national framework.[68] But are they intrinsically different? The use of force is still envisaged when Europeans are in danger. Many hypotheses of military planning are related to the European theatre or its immediate neighbourhood (the "near abroad"), even if some faraway operations are also envisaged.[69]

---

66 D. Mahncke, 'Les paramètres de la sécurité européenne', 10 *Cahier de Chaillot* (1993) p. 5.

67 "La PESD, grâce aux capacités militaires et civiles qu'elle développe pour la gestion de crise, doit contribuer à la prévention et à la maîtrise de la menace terroriste, et ce faisant à la protection de *nos populations*", Franco-German Defence and Security Council, Nantes, 47 *Chaillot Paper* (23 November 2001) p. 119. Declarations concerning ESDP and the fight against terrorism actually put more weight on the preservation of *our* security, even if the development of European capabilities in this field is supposed to benefit the populations concerned, *see* Annex V, Presidency Conclusions, Seville, 21 and 22 June 2002; J. Solana, 'A European route to security', *Eurohorizon*, 5/03/04, <www.euro-horizon.com/isolana.html>.

68 *See* anyway the speech of J. Chirac, "France, of course, intends to retain her capacity to act alone if her *own interest and bilateral commitments so demand*", 47 *Chaillot Paper*, p. 35.

69 47 *Cahier de Chaillot,* p. 79; Howorth, *supra* note 30, pp. 80–81. The former colonial States are more prone to extend the geographic limits of military interventions in order to cover their traditional zones of influence, Déclaration de J. Chirac, T. Blair and L. Jospin in London, 29 November 2001, 2 *D.A.I.,* 15 January (2002) p. 76; Youngs, *supra* note 2, pp. 110–111. W. Wallace recalled that in 1998, when the British and French governments launched their initiative for ESDP, they were silent on where beyond south-eastern Europe joint forces might be used, *Financial Times* (27 June 2003).

- The Petersberg Tasks include humanitarian missions and rescuing of EU nationals abroad. The White papers published by the European national defence administrations clearly emphasize the rescue of EU nationals. They do not seem to share the 'sacred' mission mentioned above, namely the spread of values and democracy all over the world.[70] Moreover, the tasks enshrined in Article 17 are not interpreted in the same way across the EU.[71]
- From the beginning, ESDP has been conceived as a means for Europe to become a major actor on the international scene and to face new threats with up-to-date armed forces.[72] Since the European Council in Helsinki, Heads of State and government have consistently underlined the necessity for Europe to "play its full role on the international stage"[73] and to be able to influence events outside its borders.[74] This concern increasingly appears as an inherent objective of ESDP, whereas the reference to universal norms and values seems to be more a mean to attain this specific goal.[75]
- In including the Petersberg Tasks in the Amsterdam Treaty, European States have expressed their wish to participate in peacekeeping, peace enforcement missions, etc., in accordance with the goals and principles of the UN Charter.[76] To some extent, the EU

---

[70] A. Dumoulin, R. Mahieu and V. Metten, 'Présentation comparative et thématique des politiques de défense des États membres de l'Union européenne', 68 *Sécurité et Stratégie* (Décembre 2001).

[71] A. Missiroli, 'Ploughshares into Swords? Euros for European Defence', 8 *European Foreign Affairs Review* (2003) pp. 8–9.

[72] Déclaration sur la défense européenne, Sommet franco-britannique, Saint-Malo, 3 and 4 December 1998, 47 *Cahier de Chaillot,* pt. 1 and pt. 4, *see also* the strategic debate surrounding the definition of the 'headline goal' in Helsinki, *ibid.,* p. 77.

[73] Göteborg European Council, Presidency Report on the European Security and Defence Policy, Brussels, 11 June 2001 (Nr: 9526/1/01); 'Summary of the remarks by Javier SOLANA', *Informal Meeting of Defence ministers*, Brussels, 5–6 April 2004, S0097/04.

[74] European Council, Vienne, 11 and 12 December 1998, pt. 76, 47 *Cahier de Chaillot,* p. 14 and European Council, Cologne, 3 and 4 June 1999, pt. 1, *ibid.,* p. 34.

[75] Annexe IV, rapport de la présidence, 47 *Cahier de Chaillot,* p. 63; Déclaration de Mayence, Conseil franco-allemand de défense et de sécurité, 9 June 2000, *ibid.,* p. 87.

[76] Sommet italo-britannique, Londres les 19 et 20 juillet 1999, 47 *Cahier de Chaillot,* p. 38; Conseil Européen de Nice, 47 *Cahier de Chaillot* (7, 8 et 9 décembre 2000) p. 121.

considers itself to be a regional security organization and this does not fit the archetype of a 'global policeman' driven by a messianic vision.

- From a more general point of view, the texts produced by the Europeans put more weight on practical and institutional aspects of the security policy than 'interventionist doctrine' that mainly focuses on the social and political conditions for legitimating the use of force.[77]

Finally, it appears that references to European actions to protect human rights and to implement the rule of law lie mainly in documents dealing with *civil* aspects of crisis management and preventive diplomacy.[78] And by definition, preventive *diplomacy* does not rely on military tools but rather on non-military forms of coercion, including economic sanctions.[79] Nonetheless, various presidency conclusions of the European council reveal a tendency to integrate civil and military aspects of crisis management under the head of the ESDP,[80] and this is perhaps the sign of a progressive move towards a more coercive policy on behalf of the EU. But until now, ESDP operations (EUPM in Bosnia, CONCORDIA in FYROM and ARTEMIS in RDC) are clearly undertaken under the authority of the UN.[81]

To some extent, the realist school of thought could shed some light on the real motivations of European governments in developing a common security and defence policy, but it fails to explain the significance of legalistic arguments that limit the pursuit of European interests.

---

[77] Ortega, *supra* note 30; *see also* arguments sustaining the 'just war' doctrine as they appeared in 'Lettre d'Amérique, les raisons d'un combat', *Le Monde,* 14 February 2002 or in R. Cooper's pledge for 'The New Liberal Imperialism', *Observer Worldview* (7 April 2002).

[78] Rapport présenté par Secrétaire général/Haut représentant et la Commission, Nice, 8 December 2000, *Cahier de Chaillot 47*, p. 156; Message from J. Solana to the EU Conference of National Police Commissioners, Brussels, 10 May 2001, *Chaillot Paper 47,* pp. 17–19 ; Howorth, *supra* note 30, p. 92.

[79] "Commission officials openly concerned at the shift in power towards the PSC, comforted themselves with the prediction that, in the words of one, '95 per cent if future action will be civilian'", Youngs, *supra* note 2, p. 109.

[80] *Presidency Conclusions*, Thessaloniki, 19–20 June 2003, § 57.

[81] Internet source: <www.ue.eu.int/pesc>.

4. Conclusion

There are certainly no clear-cut answers to the question of what exactly constitute the normative underpinnings of Europe's position on the use of force. The European discourse seems to be torn between two traditions. One is more messianic in its tonality and expresses an enduring trend to project values Europeans consider to be universal and to resort to the use of military coercion if necessary. The other tradition is more anchored in a realist or pragmatic vision and is linked to the interests of the Europeans themselves and the tasks Europe has to handle in order to become a credible international actor. From this perspective, the use of force is more motivated by political opportunities than moral concerns.[82]

Almost every text about European defence stresses the main responsibility of the UN Security Council for the maintenance of international peace and security and insists on the fact that any likely European contribution must uphold the goals and principles of the United Nations.[83] It therefore appears that, at the European level at least, the Member States are unprepared to accept what a certain doctrine has been suggesting for a long time: to give Europe the necessary means to defend democracy, market economy, fundamental rights and liberties all over the world regardless of legalistic concerns.

But at the same time, the Commission and the European Parliament do not seem ready to abandon what has long been considered as a specific feature of the EC: the civil nature of its power.[84] Moreover, the debates

---

[82] Ex.: Conclusions de la présidence (5/57), *Bull. UE,* 6 (2000) pt. 1.6.8 ; *ibid.,* 12-2001, pt. I.28.

[83] Ex.: Speech by J. Chirac, President of the French Republic, to the Institute for Higher Defence Studies, 47 *Chaillot Paper* (Paris, 8 June 2001) pp. 29–34; On EU-UN cooperation, *Bull. EU,* 6 (2001), I.31.53; Franco-British Summit, London, 47 *Chaillot Paper* (29 November 2001); Presidency Conclusions, Brussels, 24 and 25 October 2002, point III/20, SN 14702/02; Youngs, *supra* note 2, p. 110; Communication de la Commission au Conseil et au Parlement européen. Union européenne et Nations Unies: le choix du multilatéralisme, *COM (2003) 526 final*, pp. 7, 8 (s'agissant de la lutte contre les armes de destruction massive, il est rappelé que le Conseil de sécurité doit rester *l'arbitre suprême en cas d'infraction*) pp. 9–16.

[84] *Bull. UE,* 6 (2000), pt.1.6.9.; *Bull. UE,* 4 (2000), pt.1.6.1.; Résolution du PE sur l'établissement d'une politique européenne commune en matière de sécurité et de défense après Cologne et Helsinki, *A5-0339/*2000; Résolution du PE sur l'établissement d'une politique européenne commune en matière de sécurité et de défense, *A5-0340/2000*; Rapport sur les progrès réalisés dans la mise en œuvre de la

around the Kosovo and Iraqi wars reveal important divergences among Member States. In some way, these tensions affect the coherence of the European discourse, as the Laeken Declaration testifies:

> "What is Europe's role in this changed world? Does Europe not, now that is finally unified, have *a leading role to play in a new world order, that of a power able both to play a stabilising role worldwide* and to point the way ahead for many countries and peoples? Europe as the continent of human values, the Magna Carta, the Bill of Rights, the French Revolution and the fall of the Berlin Wall; the continent of liberty, solidarity and above all *diversity*, meaning respect for other's languages, cultures and traditions. The European Union's one boundary is democracy and human rights. The Union is open to countries which uphold basic values such as free elections, respect for minorities and respect for the rule of law. Now that the Cold War is over and we are living in a globalised, yet also highly fragmented world, Europe needs to shoulder its responsibilities in the governance of globalisation. The role it has to play is that of a *power resolutely doing battle against all violence, all terror and fanaticism,* but which also does not turn a blind eye to the world's heartrending injustices"[85].

In this text, we can identify some influences from the political pluralism that inspired the Copenhagen Declaration on European Identity in 1973,[86] but also a form of seduction for a more messianic project based on the promotion of a specific form of liberal democracy.[87] In this regard, the

---

politique étrangère et de sécurité commune, Commission des affaires étrangères, des droits de l'homme, de la sécurité commune et de la politique de défense, *A5-0296/2002*, 11 septembre 2002; Communication de la Commission au Conseil et au Parlement européen. Union européenne et Nations Unies: le choix du multilatéralisme, *COM (2003) 526 final* (the European Council has welcomed this document, *see Presidency Conclusions,* Brussels, 12/13 December 2003, p. 23 §91); *see also* the *European Union/African Joint Declaration on Effective Multilateralism*, Annex I of the *EU-Africa Ministerial meeting*, Dublin, 1 April 2004, 8230/04 (Presse 104); for A. Moravcsik, militarisation would betray European ideals and interests, 'One Year on: Lessons from Iraq', 68 *Chaillot Paper* (March 2004) p. 190.

[85] Laeken Declaration, 15 December 2001 (*SN 273/1*), (emphasis added).

[86] *See also* the comments of Nicolaidis and Howse, *supra* note 6, p. 783; De Vasconcelos, *supra* note 64, p. 24; Manners, *supra* note 35, p. 240 point 8; Meeting of the Heads of State or Government of the EU and the President of the Commission, Ghent, 19, 47 *Chaillot Paper* (October 1991); Conclusions and plan of action of the extraordinary European Council meeting on 21 September 2001, SN 140/1.

[87] Rhodes, *supra* note 63, Nicolaidis and Howse, *supra* note 6, p. 769; P. Allott, 'European Foreign Policy : After-Life of an Illusion', in Koskenniemi (ed.), *supra*

replacement of the 'civil' adjective traditionally used in conjunction with the term 'power' is certainly significant.[88]

The coexistence of different forms of rhetoric in the European discourse is not a new phenomenon.[89] In this case, the inconsistency of the European discourse is the result of the difficulty of defining a common and coherent political project based on common normative underpinnings.[90] Fighting terrorism or preventing the spread of weapons of mass destruction will perhaps become the core project around which Europeans will converge;[91] but it would be presumptuous to assume that, besides a firm condemnation of terrorist acts, European governments do agree on the concrete means to

---

note 4, pp. 215–229; A. Bartholomew and J. Breakspear, 'Human Rights as Swords of Empire', in L. Panitch and C. Leys (eds.), *The New Imperial Challenge* (Socialist Register 2004).

[88] According to N. Gnesotto: "L'Europe comme pure puissance civile est morte", 9 *Bulletin,* Institut d'études de sécurité de l'UE (January 2004).

[89] This is sometimes a sign of an internal tension between the Council and the Commission for "control of the policy 'spaces' within the security framework", Deighton, *supra* note 18, p. 730; Youngs, *supra* note 2, p. 105.

[90] B. Delcourt, *Droit et souverainetés. Analyse critique du discours européen sur la Yougoslavie* (Peter Lang, Bruxelles, 2003); J. Zielonka, 'Paradoxes of European Foreign Policy. Policies without Strategy: the EU's Record in Eastern Europe', 2 *Yearbook of Polish European Studies* (1998) pp. 25–42. *See also* Ehrart, *supra* note 17, p. 71; S. Duke, 'ESDP and the EU Response to the 11 September: Identifying the Weakest Link', 7:2 *European Foreign Affairs Review* (Summer 2002) pp. 16 *et seq.*; J. Howorth, 'The CESDP and the Forging of a European Security Culture', in B. Irondelle and P. Venesson, 'L'Europe de la défense: institutionnalisation, européanisation', 8 *Revue Politique européenne* (Automne 2002) pp. 88 *et seq.*

[91] *See* Presidency Conclusions, Seville, 21 and 22 June 2002, SN 200/1/02 REV 1, in particular Annex V: 'Declaration by the European Council on the contribution of the CFSP, including the ESDP, to the fight against terrorism'; European Council Declaration on Iraq, Presidency Conclusions, Copenhagen, 12 and 13 December 2002, Annex IV, SN 400/02; Speech to the EP, Chris Patten, 29 January 2003, speech: 03/34; Extraordinary European Council, Brussels, 17 February 2003, 6466/03; Presidency Conclusions, Thessaloniki, 19–20 June 2003, Annex II; *Declaration on combating terrorism*, Brussels, 25 March 2004. I agree with A. Deighton saying that "it is too soon to say whether the campaign against terrorism will become a 'new paradigm' for international relations", *see* her article, *supra* note 18, p. 727. As a matter of fact, debates inside the convention show that there is no agreement on the fact that the fight against terrorism has to be a priority for the ESDP. Inside the convention, there were some divergences on the opportunity to concentrate on the issue of terrorism as the main threat for the European security; *see also* Bailes, *supra* note 65.

put an end to these particular threats. Divergences between the 'old' and the 'new' Europe on Iraq testify of the enduring challenge for Europe to be an 'actor' on the international stage.

On the other hand, we can understand this absence of a single 'utopian vision' in a positive way:

> "[t]he actual institutions of European integration always fall short of the underlying utopian vision, which leads some to dismiss the vision as largely irrelevant dreaming. This gap *is* in some sense the legitimacy crisis of the European Union. But the attempt to close the gap has enormous risks. What exactly does constitute the European level of governance as a political community, what common projects, ends or value? Many would argue that the very fact of asking the questions denies the open-ended, experimental essence of the European project. Equally problematic, an explicit answer to this question would risk defining much more explicitly than today insiders and outsiders within Europe and raise the possibility of what must be avoided – drawing new exclusionary boundaries, this time around 'Europe' itself. This would in turn deny, for better or for worse, the EU's biggest project of all, its *mission civilisatrice,* to export its miracle to the rest of the world."[92]

What could be a sensible position on a philosophical ground might be untenable on a political one. As Michael Smith notices, the 'European foreign policy space' lacks the key central institutions and instruments characteristic of foreign policies based on statist ('modernist') assumptions. Therefore, in a situation of crisis and 'hard security', the collective action is hard to pursue given the dispersal of preferences among Member States.[93] Most of the time the problem of 'procedure' serves as a substitute for policy, the 'layer' of policy itself (which consists of a sustainable balance between interests, commitments and capabilities) being indeed very feeble or unclear.

This is certainly a problem Javier Solana wanted to cope with when he proposed a kind of strategic vision for Europe.[94] But did he really add some flesh to the bones? At this stage, his core message is twofold. We, as Europeans, are facing the same new threats as the ones identified by the American administration (mainly international terrorism, WMD

---

[92] Nicolaidis and Howse, *supra* note 6, pp. 781–782.

[93] M. Smith, 'The framing of European Foreign and Security Policy: Towards a Post-Modern Policy Framework?' 10:4 *Journal of European Public Policy* (August 2003) pp. 558–559.

[94] 'A Secure Europe in a Better World', European Council, Thessaloniki, 20 June 2003.

proliferation, failed States and organised crime). In order to offer a brighter prospect to mankind, the EU has to develop three strategic objectives: extending the zone of security around Europe, strengthening the international order and countering old and new threats.[95]

Jean-Yves Haine rightly points to the fact that the discourse on the new threats looks like Bush's, even if the means to counter them are kept distinct from those prescribed in the US strategy.[96] On the other hand, the (legal) conditions under which Europe would eventually resort to a 'preventive' or 'pre-emptive' action remain unclear. Does it mean that Europe might definitely adopt the American normative standards? Or, in order to be more authentically 'European', the double standard attitudes that Robert Cooper advocates?

> "The challenge to the post-modern world is to get used to the idea of double standards. Among ourselves, we operate on the basis of laws and open cooperative security. But when dealing with more old-fashioned kind of states outside post-modern continent of Europe, we need to revert to the rougher methods of an earlier era-force, pre-emptive attack, deception, whatever is necessary to deal with those who still live in the nineteenth century world of every state for itself".[97]

It is for sure a kind of post-modern thinking that more closely resembles anti-modern thinking (as updated by the neo-conservative lecture of Leo Strauss).[98] To that extent, it seems difficult to merge a modernist and pluralist vision of the international society (as enshrined in the UN Charter) and this so-called 'liberal imperialism'.

It is anyway noteworthy that the issue of pre-emptive action caused much trouble to some governments, in particular the German and the French ones, which have tried to amend the draft in order to remove the ambiguity regarding the power of the Security Council.[99] In the last version presented by the High Representative in December 2003, the reference to 'pre-emptive

---

[95] J. Solana, 'Europe; Security in the Twenty-first Century', *The Olof Palme Memorial Lecture*, Stockholm, 20 June 2001.

[96] J-Y. Haine, 'Les premiers pas d'une Europe stratégique', 7 *UE-IES Bulletin* (July 2003).

[97] Cooper, *supra* note 77.

[98] This 'idea' is not that new, *see* C. Schmitt, *Le Nomos de la terre (dans le droit de gens du* Jus Publicum Europeanum), (P.U.F., Paris, 2001) p. 15 (P. Haggenmacher's Presentation).

[99] J. Dempsey, 'Words of war: Europe's first security doctrine backs away from a commitment to US-style pre-emption', *Financial Times* (5 December 2003).

action' has been removed,[100] whereas the necessity to act in partnership with the USA in order to "be a formidable force for *good* in the world" remains.[101]

The existence of a perpetual conversation between different paradigms or traditions helps to explain the paradoxes lying in state discourses when governments argue differently on the same subject (i.e. humanitarian intervention).[102] As Jan Zielonka reminds us, the Union is not the only international actor with a foreign policy agenda dominated by internal, parochial concerns:

> "However there are at least three crucial factors that make this problem greater for the Union than for 'traditional' international actors such [sic.] nation states . . . the Union prefers to maintain an ambiguous profile in terms of its basic purposes and interests. But in the absence of a clear hierarchy of collective interests, parochialism has a greater chance of asserting itself. Moreover, the Union is a collection of still largely sovereign states with largely diverging agendas, and the Union's decision-making process is still based on intergovernmental bargaining. No wonder that parochialism has good chances to prevail over strategic arguments . . .".[103]

As far as the resort to force is concerned, ambiguity will probably remain the main feature of the European discourse. Commenting on the last version of the 'European Security Strategy' document, Steven Everts wondered how long Europe could evade the "contentious issue of the conditions for the use of force, which cannot be eliminated by semantic fudge".[104] In other words, if preventive diplomacy or multilateralism failed, would Europe be ready to

---

[100] The focus is now on conflict prevention, which has a different meaning and does not imply *per se* the use of military tools, 'A Secure Europe in a Better World', *European Security Strategy*, Brussels, (12 December 2003) sp. p. 7; Dempsey *supra* note 99.

[101] *Ibid.*, p. 13; for M. Leonard, this second version "remains almost Rumsfeldian in its warning about terrorism and rogue states", he also stated that "the significance of the document is that it moves on from traditional idea of multilateralism for its own sake to a determination to achieve results", *see* 'The Dream of a Mighty Europe', *The Wall Street Journal Europe*, (5 February 2004); *see also* S. Everts, 'Two cheers for the EU's new security strategy. Soft power and hard power', *International Herald Tribune* (9 December 2003).

[102] This the reason why Bellamy uses the expression "pragmatic solidarism"2, Bellamy, *supra* note 56, pp. 17–20.

[103] Zielonka, *supra* note 90, p. 37.

[104] Everts, *supra* note 101.

resort to force? That's the "acid test of the security doctrine"[105] and for sure, it is quite difficult to deliver clear answers.

[105] Mr Shöpflin's interview in Dempsey, *supra* note 99.

Globalization and Jurisdiction: Lessons from the European Convention on Human Rights

Olivier De Schutter[*]

Contents

---

[*] Professor of Human Rights Law, University of Louvain (Belgium); Global Law Professor at New York University School of Law; Visiting Professor, Univ. of Paris I-Panthéon-Sorbonne; Co-ordinator of the EU Network of Independent Experts on Fundamental Rights.

Baltic Yearbook of International Law, Volume 6, 2006, pp. 185–247.

1. Introduction

Our era has witnessed a spectacular redeployment of the functions of the State and a concomitant redefinition of the relationship of the State to its national territory as one of its constituent elements.[1] There are different facets to this redeployment. On the one hand, States have extended the assertion of their power beyond the national territory, as illustrated both by the 'global war on terrorism' and by the development of extra-territorial jurisdiction. On the other hand, the sovereignty of the State is questioned by the emergence of powerful transnational actors, both private and intergovernmental, affecting in many instances the ability of the State to assert its authority even on its national territory and leading to calls for a global administrative law better capable of controlling these actors which, although they are seen as competing with the State, are not subjected to the same legitimacy tests.[2] Whether it is interpreted as an expansion of the influence the State exercises in the era of globalization or as a sign of its decline, if not marginalization, the interdependency of States is more important than ever, explaining for instance the popularity of the concept of global public goods[3] and the calls for the affirmation of an extra-territorial responsibility of States, towards populations other than their own.[4]

---

[1] *See*, among many others, G. Kreijen *et al.* (eds.), *State, Sovereignty, and International Governance*, (Oxford Univ. Press, 2002); H. Ruiz Fabri, 'Immatériel, territorialité, Etat', *Archives de philosophie du droit*, (1999) pp. 187–212; A. Tita, 'Globalization: A New Political and Economic Space requiring Supranational Governance', 3 *Journal of World Trade* (1998) p. 47.

[2] This is the main intuition behind the Global Administrative Law project launched by the Institute for International Law and Justice at New York University School of Law: *see* <www.iilj.org> and, for a presentation of the main themes, B. Kingsbury, N. Krisch and R. Stewart, 'The Emergence of Global Administrative Law', *IILJ Working Paper* (2004) p.1.

[3] *See in particular* W. D. Nordhaus, *Managing the Global Commons* (MIT Press, Cambridge, MA, 1994), and the contributions emanating from the United Nations Development Programme, in particular I. Kaul, I. Grundberg and M. A. Stern, *Global Public Goods: International Cooperation in the 21st Century* (Oxford Univ. Press, New York, 1999); Office of Development Studies, *Global Public Goods: Taking the Concept Forward*, Discussion Paper 17, (UNDP, New York, 2001); and I. Kaul, P. Conceicão, K. Le Goulven and R. U. Mendoza (eds), *Providing Global Public Goods: Managing Globalization* (Oxford Univ. Press, New York and Oxford, 2003).

[4] *See, for instance*, U.N. Committee on Economic, Social and Cultural Rights, General Comment No. 14 (2000), *The right to the highest attainable standard of*

The most important questions facing the international law of human rights today relate to this renegotiation of the position of the State and to the renewed understanding of its links to the events it may or may not influence.[5] Are States obligated under the human rights treaties they have ratified when they act beyond their national territory, or when they fail to act beyond their national territory although they could influence events abroad, for instance by better controlling their nationals operating on foreign territory?[6] Conversely, may States escape their responsibility where events

---

health (article 12 of the International Covenant on Economic, Social and Cultural Rights), U.N. Doc. E/C.12/2000/4 (2000), para. 39: "States parties have to respect the enjoyment of the right to health in other countries, and prevent third parties from violating the right in other countries, if they are able to influence these third parties by way of legal or political means, in accordance with the Charter of the United Nations and applicable international law"; U.N. Committee on Economic, Social and Cultural Rights, General Comment No. 15 (2002), *The right to water (arts. 11 and 12 of the International Covenant on Economic, Social and Cultural Rights),* U.N. Doc. E/C.12/2002/11 (26 November 2002), para. 31: "To comply with their international obligations in relation to the right to water, States parties have to respect the enjoyment of the right in other countries. International cooperation requires States parties to refrain from actions that interfere, directly or indirectly, with the enjoyment of the right to water in other countries. Any activities undertaken within the State party's jurisdiction should not deprive another country of the ability to realize the right to water for persons in its jurisdiction"; *The right to food*, Report submitted by the Special Rapporteur on the right to food, Jean Ziegler, in accordance with Commission on Human Rights resolution 2002/25, U.N. Doc. E/CN.4/2003/54 (10 January 2003), para. 29. These references are discussed in a paper by S. Narula, 'The Right to Food: Closing Accountability Gaps under International Law', forthcoming in the *Columbia Journal of Transnational Law.*

[5] *See*, among many others, the essays collected in F. Coomans and M. Kamminga (eds), *Extraterritorial Application of Human Rights Treaties* (Intersentia, Antwerp-Oxford, 2004); and Michael J. Dennis, 'Application of Human Rights Treaties Extraterritorially in Times of Armed Conflict and Military Occupation', 99 *American Journal of International Law* (2005) p. 119; T. Meron, 'Extraterritoriality of Human Rights Treaties', 89 *American Journal of International Law* (1995) p. 78.

[6] *See e.g., The Realization of Economic, Social and Cultural Rights, Final report on the question of the impunity of perpetrators of human rights violations (economic, social and cultural rights)*, prepared by Mr. El Hadji Guissé, Special Rapporteur, pursuant to Sub-Commission resolution 1996/24, U.N. Doc. E/CN.4/Sub.2/1997/8, 27 June 1997, para. 131: "The violations committed by the transnational corporations in their mainly transboundary activities do not come within the competence of a single State and, to prevent contradictions and inadequacies in the remedies and sanctions decided upon by States individually or as a group, these

take place on their territory which however they are unable to influence? May the acts of intergovernmental organisations States have set up and delegated powers to be imputed to the States? May they be held responsible for the acts of other States with whom they cooperate? And if we agree they might incur responsibility for the acts of such organisations or for those of such other States, may States be held responsible for *not* using their powers, affirmatively, in order to influence the behaviour of those other entities? At a fundamental level, the question is whether the responsibility of States towards the human rights they are internationally committed to uphold should be aligned with this contemporary redefinition of the State and of its relationship to national territory, or whether the understanding of this responsibility should instead be based on the reaffirmation of the classical functions of the State and of its role as the territorial sovereign. In the era of globalization, the tension is heightened between law and fact,[7] between the temptation to hold on to a classical definition of the State as the territorial sovereign and the contemporary realities of its redeployment: the slogan of 'effectiveness' of human rights might mean, either that the State must reaffirm its control of events which it should be held accountable for, whether or not it is in a position to effectively exercise that control; or that the determination of the international responsibility of States should be made more realistic, indexed on the evolution of the influence it may (or may not) exercise in fact.[8]

The recent case-law of the European Court of Human Rights constitutes an excellent laboratory to test the relationship between the facts of

---

violations should form the subject of special attention. The States and the international community should combine their efforts so as to contain such activities by the establishment of legal standards capable of achieving that objective"; M. Sornarajah, *The International Law on Foreign Investment* (Cambridge Univ. Press, 2nd ed. 2004), chap. 4 (arguing at p. 169 that "developed States owe a duty of control to the international community and do in fact have the means of legal control over the conduct abroad of multinational corporations").

[7] It is by this 'tension' that Ch. de Visscher defined its notion of 'effectiveness in action'. *See* Ch. de Visscher, *Les effectivités du droit international public* (Pedone, Paris, 1967) p. 15 (defining 'l'effectivité en action' as a situation where "le rapport du fait avec le droit prend le caractère d'une tension").

[8] *See e.g.*, J. Lenoble, 'Responsabilité internationale des Etats et contrôle territorial', *Revue belge de droit international*, 1981–1982, p. 95, para. 109 (explaining, about the principle of effectiveness, that the rule "traduit une transparence du fait et du droit qui fait que la règle contient en elle-même les éléments qui assurent son évolution").

globalization and interdependency and the evolution of international law away from its classical adherence to a territorial concept of the State. Article 1 of the European Convention on Human Rights provides that the Contracting Parties "shall secure to everyone *within their jurisdiction*" the rights and freedoms of the Convention, a condition which also concerns the Additional Protocols to the Convention. Whether or not the alleged victim of the violation was under the jurisdiction of the defending State when the violation was committed thus precedes the two questions which Article 2 of the International Law Commission's Articles on State Responsibility defines as the two constituent elements of an internationally wrongful act of a State,[9]

---

[9] As adopted by the ILC on 9 August 2001; the UN General Assembly has taken note of the Articles in Res. 56/83 adopted on 12 December 2001, 'Responsibility of States for internationally wrongful acts'. Of course, the presentation of the question of 'jurisdiction' as logically preceding the questions of attribution and compliance *vel non* with the international obligations of the State is contestable. Some authors would be tempted to equate the question of whether an individual is under the jurisdiction of the State with the question of attribution (under the theory that an individual may be said to be under the jurisdiction of the State to the extent that this individual has been directly affected by the act or the omission of the State); others would see the question of 'jurisdiction' as defining the scope of the State's obligations, and thus as having to be analyzed, once the question of attribution has been answered in the affirmative, as part of the question whether the State has breached its international obligation. But treating the question of 'jurisdiction' as a threshold question describes better the approach followed by the European Court of Human Rights: *see* M. O'Boyle, 'The European Convention on Human Rights and Extraterritorial Jurisdiction: A Comment on "Life After Bankovic"', in F. Coomans and M. Kamminga (eds), *Extraterritorial Application of Human Rights Treaties* (Intersentia, Antwerp-Oxford, 2004), p. 131 ("[i]n the Convention system the concepts of jurisdiction and state responsibility are not interchangeable. They are separate concepts though the former is necessarily the pathway to establishing the latter") (responding to the critique of the methodology followed by the Court in the inadmissibility decision it adopted in the case of *Bankovic*, *see* text corresponding to *infra* notes 12–28, by R. Lawson, 'Life After Bankovic: on the Extraterritorial Application of the European Convention on Human Rights', in the same volume, pp. 83–123). In judgments it delivered respectively on 8 July 2004 in the case of *Ilascu and Others* v. *Moldova and Russia*, and on 16 November 2004 in the case of *Issa and Others* v. *Turkey*, the Court notes: "The exercise of jurisdiction is a necessary condition for a Contracting State to be able to be held responsible for acts or omissions imputable to it which give rise to an allegation of the infringement of rights and freedoms set forth in the Convention" (*Ilascu and Others* v. *Moldova and Russia*, 8 July 2004, ECHR (GC), no. 48787/99, para. 311; *Issa and Others* v. *Turkey*, 16 November 2004, no. 31821/96), para. 66 (final on 30 March 2005). It is

i.e., 1) whether the measure complained of (an act or an omission) may be attributed to that State and 2) whether that measure constitutes a breach of an international obligation of that State. In this sense, the requirement of 'jurisdiction' stipulated in Article 1 ECHR is preliminary to the question of State responsibility for a breach of the Convention. In principle, the imputability of a situation to a State is therefore not a substitute for this situation falling under its jurisdiction. Rather, the question of imputability is only raised at a second stage, after it has been determined that the event occurred under that State's 'jurisdiction'.

However, the fact that States may affect situations beyond their national borders, by adopting acts which are clearly attributable to them in the meaning of Chapter II of the ILC's Articles on State responsibility, raises the question of the relationship between this notion of 'jurisdiction' and the notion of national territory. It is this question which this paper explores, in three different directions which the following sections address in turn. A number of States parties to the European Convention on Human Rights have been allegedly committing violations of this instrument by undertaking activities beyond their national territory, raising the question whether the Convention does apply to such 'extra-territorial' situations (Section 2. The Extra-territorial Applicability of the European Convention on Human

---

however possible to identify instances where the questions of 'jurisdiction' in the meaning of Article 1 ECHR and of imputability to the State of the acts complained of were treated as identical, to the extent that 'jurisdiction' was described as being either 'territorial' or, alternatively, 'personal': *see e.g.*, *Drozd and Janousek* v. *France and Spain,* 26 June 1992, ECHR, Series A no. 240, para. 91 (where, confronted with the allegation that France and Spain were responsible for the alleged violation of the ECHR committed by courts of Andorra where French and Spanish judges were sitting, the Court remarks that "[t]he term 'jurisdiction' is not limited to the national territory of the High Contracting Parties; their responsibility can be involved because of acts of their authorities producing effects outside their own territory. The question to be decided is whether the acts complained of by Mr Drozd and Mr Janousek can be attributed to France or Spain or both, even though they were not performed on the territory of those States"); *Al-Adsani* v. *the United Kingdom,* ECHR 2001-XI, no. 35763/97, para. 40 (where, in a case where an applicant with joint British and Kuwaiti nationality complained about having been abducted and tortured in Kuwait, the Court notes that "[t]he applicant does not contend that the alleged torture took place within the jurisdiction of the United Kingdom or that the United Kingdom authorities had any causal connection with its occurrence"). These cases are discussed hereunder. All the decisions and judgments of the European Court of Human Rights may be found via the HUDOC database: *see* the website of the European Court of Human Rights, <www.echr.coe.int/echr>.

Rights). The European Court of Human Rights has also been confronted with situations where events occurred on portions of the territory which *de facto* escaped control by the organs of the defending State (Section 3. The 'Jurisdiction' of the State on its National Territory). Perhaps even more significantly, the Court is faced on the European continent with an extraordinary proliferation of cooperation between States, of which the expansion of the European Union and the progress of its integration constitutes perhaps the most spectacular, but by no means unique, manifestation. It therefore is confronted with the discrepancy between the individual character of the responsibility of States under the Convention and the reality of inter-State cooperation, resulting in situations where the alleged violation of the rights of the individual has its source, in fact, not in the acts of any single State party to the Convention, but in the combination of acts of two or more States (Section 4. State Jurisdiction and Intergovernmental Cooperation).

In the context of the European Convention on Human Rights, these questions are made significantly more complex by the recognition that certain positive obligations may be imposed on the Contracting States, i.e., obligations to adopt measures which ensure the protection of the rights of individuals, and that they are not simply bound to respect those rights by abstaining from the adoption of measures which could infringe those rights in violation of the Convention. Indeed, the identification of positive obligations in the Convention implies that, where a situation falls under the 'jurisdiction' of a State party, that State must act through its organs, and may not remain passive even in the face of events for which it bears no direct responsibility. But the ability of the State to fulfil those positive obligations is severely curtailed where the situation calling for State action either occurs on foreign territory, or is a situation which is affected by the combined action of a number of States, parties or not to the Convention, and therefore does not depend on the adoption of a measure by the defending State alone. Where the exercise of the sovereign powers of this State clashes with competing sovereignties, or with the powers attributed by treaty to an international organisation of which it is a member, how can the State be required to fulfil its positive obligations? Which limits to the identification of such obligations does the existence of competing sovereignties impose? If we consider that the requirement according to which the situation where a violation of the Convention is alleged to have occurred must be under the 'jurisdiction' of the State concerned does not in principle constitute an obstacle to imposing on the States parties to the Convention 'extra-territorial' obligations extending beyond their national territory, is the implication that they must seek to influence the situation of human rights in territories other than their own?

The case-law of the European Court of Human Rights is exemplary in a number of ways. First, despite the professed willingness of the Court to examine the issues it is presented with within the framework of general public international law – a position it has emphasized in particular in cases where the limits imposed by the requirement of 'jurisdiction' have been tested[10] – it cannot fully escape the tension between that framework and the specificity of human rights treaties – a specificity which, indeed, also has been emphasized during the early stages of the development of the case-law of the European Convention on Human Rights' supervisory bodies.[11] Second, nowhere to a larger extent than on the European continent has inter-State co-operation been developed, and has State sovereignty been restricted,

---

[10] *See e.g.*, *Al-Adsani* v. *the United Kingdom,* 21 November 2001, ECHR (GC), no. 35763/97, *Reports of Judgments and Decisions* 2001-XI, paras. 52–56. For a discussion of *Al-Adsani* in the light of public international law, *see* L. M. Caplan, 'State Immunity, Human Rights, and *Jus Cogens*: A Critique of the Normative Hierarchy Theory', 97 *American Journal of International Law* (2003) p. 741; *see also* M. Emberland, 'Case Report: McElhinney v. Ireland, Al-Adsani v. United Kingdom, Fogarty v. United Kingdom', 96 *American Journal of International Law* (2002) p. 699.

[11] The European Commission of Human Rights emphasized as early as in 1961 that "the purpose of the High Contracting Parties in concluding the convention was not to concede to each other reciprocal rights and obligations in pursuance of their individual national interests, but to realize the aims and ideals of the Council of Europe, as expressed in its Statute, and to establish a common public order of the free democracies of Europe . . . [The] obligations undertaken by the High Contracting Parties in the European Convention are essentially of an objective character, being designed rather to protect the fundamental rights of individual human beings from infringements by any of the High Contracting Parties than to create subjective and reciprocal rights for the High Contracting Parties themselves": European Commission on Human Rights, *Austria* v. *Italy ('Pfunders'* case*)*, no. 788/60, *Yearbook of the ECHR*, 1961-IV, p. 116. On the specificities of human rights treaties, *see* B. Simma, 'International Human Rights and General International Law: A Comparative Analysis', 4 *Collected Courses of the Academy of European Law* (1995) p. 153; M. Craven, 'Legal Differentiation and the Concept of the Human Rights Treaty in International Law', 11: 3 *European Journal of International Law* (EJIL) (2000) pp. 489–519. For a broader analysis of the coexistence of specific, treaty-based regimes, and general public international law, *see* P.-M. Dupuy, 'L'unité de l'ordre juridique international. Cours général de droit international public', 297 *Recueil des Cours de l'Académie de Droit International* (RCADI) (2002), esp. at pp. 428–478.

especially – for the Member States of the European Union – due to the supranational character of the Union. This requires not only that we address the question of the 'jurisdiction' which States may be said to exercise over situations which are affected, not by measures they have adopted (or could have adopted) unilaterally, but by the combined acts of a number of States, whether or not in the framework of an international organisation. It also requires that we ask whether any positive obligation may be imposed on States to develop further these modes of inter-State cooperation, where this is required for the effective protection of the rights of the individual, and whether this may be reconciled with the principle of specialty of international organisations. These features justify calling the European Convention on Human Rights a laboratory for the understanding of the evolving notion of "jurisdiction" in the era of globalization.

2. The Extra-Territorial Applicability of the European Convention on Human Rights

2.1. The Territorial Understanding of the Notion of 'Jurisdiction'

In the case of *Bankovic and Others* v. *Belgium and Others*,[12] the Grand Chamber of the European Court of Human Rights was confronted with the question whether the States parties to the European Convention on Human Rights could be held responsible under that treaty for the bombing of the building of the Serbian Radio and Television on 23 April 1999 by NATO forces. In the view of the applicants, who were injured or whose relatives had been killed in the event, this had led to a number of the provisions of the Convention being violated, including the right to life protected under Article 2. They contended that the aerial strike brought them under the jurisdiction of the defending States. Their contention was, specifically, that "the extent of the positive obligation under Article 1 of the Convention to secure Convention rights would be proportionate to the level of control in fact exercised".[13] They relied in particular on the decisions of the European Court of Human Rights in *Loizidou* v. *Turkey*. There, finding that the applicant

[12] For a critical commentary, *see* K. Altiparmak, 'Bankovic: An Obstacle to the Application of the European Convention on Human Rights in Irak?', 9:2 *Journal of Conflict and Security Law* (2004) pp. 213–251.

[13] *Bankovic and Others* v. *Belgium and Others,* 12 December 2001, ECHR (GC), no 52207/99, decision (inadmissibility), *Reports of Judgments and Decisons* 2001-XII, para. 42 (hereafter referred to as '*Bankovic*').

should be considered as falling under the jurisdiction of Turkey although the acts complained of occurred not on Turkish territory but on the territory of the 'Turkish Republic of Northern Cyprus', which Turkey (and Turkey alone in the international community) had recognized as an independent State, the Court had concluded that "the responsibility of a Contracting Party may . . . arise when as a consequence of military action – whether lawful or unlawful – it exercises effective control of an area outside its national territory. *The obligation to secure, in such an area, the rights and freedoms set out in the Convention derives from the fact of such control* whether it be exercised directly, through its armed forces, or through a subordinate local administration".[14] In the *Bankovic* Court was not persuaded. It considered instead that there existed no "jurisdictional link between the persons who were victims of [the aerial bombing] and the respondent States", and that accordingly, it was "not satisfied that the applicants and their deceased relatives were capable of coming within the jurisdiction of the respondent States on account of the extra-territorial act in question".[15]

This reading of Article 1 of the Convention, restricting in principle the applicability of the Convention to the national territory of the States parties, was based primarily on two considerations. First, seeking reliance on the preparatory works of the Convention,[16] the Court considered that the Contracting Parties never intended the Convention to apply beyond the national territories of these States. The Convention, the Court emphasized, has an essentially regional vocation, and was not meant to apply beyond the Council of Europe Member States "[t]he Convention was not designed to be applied throughout the world, even in respect of the conduct of Contracting States".[17] We shall return to this argument later.[18] Second, and more

[14] *Loizidou* v. *Turkey,* 23 March 1995 (preliminary objections), no. 15318/89 of, Series A no. 310, para. 62 (my emphasis). *See also Loizidou* v. *Turkey,* (merits) 18 December 1996 no. 15318/89, *Reports of Judgments and Decisions* 1996-VI, p. 2234, para. 52.

[15] *Bankovic*, *supra* note 13, para. 82.

[16] The Court recalls in paras. 19 and 63 of its decision that the Expert Intergovernmental Committee which drafted the Convention replaced the words "all persons residing within their territories" originally proposed with a reference to all persons "within the jurisdiction" of the States parties with a view to expanding the Convention's application to those who are not legally residing, but who are, nevertheless, present on the territory of the Contracting States. The preparatory works are in fact not conclusive on the issue and commentators have understandably disagreed on their interpretation.

[17] *Bankovic*, *supra* note 13, para. 80.

decisively, the Court referred to a number of writings from which it concluded that,

> "from the standpoint of public international law, the jurisdictional competence of a State is primarily territorial. While international law does not exclude a State's exercise of jurisdiction extra-territorially, the suggested bases of such jurisdiction (including nationality, flag, diplomatic and consular relations, effect, protection, passive personality and universality) are, as a general rule, defined and limited by the sovereign territorial rights of the other relevant States".[19]

This second argument is unconvincing. It confuses two entirely different understandings of the concept of jurisdiction. Indeed, it is one thing to say that a State may, under public international law, exercise its 'jurisdiction' vis-à-vis certain situations not confined to its national territory, for example under the principles of nationality, passive personality or universality for certain internationally recognized crimes, or even, as some would argue, in the absence of a specific prohibition imposed by international law on States adopting legislation with extra-territorial reach.[20] It is quite another to say

---

[18] *See hereafter*, text corresponding to notes 45–66.

[19] *Bankovic*, *supra* note 13, para. 59.

[20] Although the answer to the question of which acts with an extra-territorial scope (affecting situations beyond the national territory) a State *may* adopt obviously may have repercussions on the question of which obligations may be *imposed* on a State to adopt such acts (and thus influence situations outside its national territory), I am not entering here into the controversy about which limits general public international law imposes on the adoption by States of acts which will affect events situated outside its territory. It is clear that the exercise of *executive* (or *enforcement*) extra-territorial jurisdiction is limited by the sovereign rights of the territorial States and, conversely, that the exercise of *adjudicative* extra-territorial jurisdiction, whereby a State confers upon its jurisdictions a competence to decide cases originating in events located outside its national territory while applying the *lex loci*, is in principle unlimited. More controversial are the limits to *prescriptive* extra-territorial jurisdiction, i.e., to the adoption by a State of legislative norms which seek to influence behavior outside its national territory. In the *Lotus Case (France* v. *Turkey)* (Series A no. 10, pp. 18–19), the Permanent Court of International Justice remarked that "[f]ar from laying down a general prohibition to the effect that States may not extend the application of their laws and the jurisdiction of their courts to persons, property and acts outside their territory, it leaves them in this respect a wide measure of discretion which is only limited in certain cases by prohibitive rules; as regards other cases, every State remains free to adopt the principles which it regards as best and most suitable". This *obiter dictum* of its judgment of 27 June 1927 has

that certain acts or failures to act may or may not be imputed to a State, such as, for instance, the violations of the right to life resulting from aerial strikes on civilian targets. Conflating the two amounts to the paradoxical result that a State acting beyond its 'jurisdiction' in the former sense, i.e., beyond its powers as recognized under international law, could not be held responsible for the consequences resulting from these acts under the treaties it has agreed to. This would be unacceptable in both political and legal terms. It is inconsistent with the position of the International Court of Justice that "[p]hysical control of a territory, and not sovereignty or legitimacy of title, is

---

sometimes been interpreted as affirming a freedom of States to act in this regard – although of course, "the permissive rule [enunciated in *Lotus*] only applies to prescriptive jurisdiction, not to enforcement jurisdiction: failing a prohibition, State A *may,* on its own territory, prosecute offences committed in State B *(permissive rule)*; failing a permission, State A *may not* act on the territory of State B" (dissenting opinion of *ad hoc* judge Van den Wyngaert to the judgment of the International Court of Justice delivered on 14 February 2002 in the case relating to the *Arrest warrant of 11 April 2000 (Democratic Republic of Congo* v. *Belgium)*, para. 49) . However, both the interpretation of this decision and its contemporary relevance are debated. On the distinction between these three manifestations of extra-territorial jurisdiction, *see* C. Scott, 'Translating Torture into Transnational Tort: Conceptual Divides in the Debate on Corporate Accountability for Human Rights Harms', in C. Scott (ed), *Torture as Tort. Comparative Perspectives on the Development of Transnational Human Rights Litigation* (Hart Publ., Oxford, 2001), pp. 45–63, p. 54; and *see also* Jennings and Watts (ed.), *Oppenheim's International Law*, (Longman, New York, 9th ed., 1992) para. 137; R. Higgins, 'The Legal Basis of Jurisdiction', in C. J. Olmstead, *Extra-territorial Application of Laws and Responses Thereto* (I.L.A. & E.S.C. Publ. Ltd., Oxford, 1984) p. 4. On the controversies about prespective extra-territorial jurisdiction in the face of current developments, *see* O. De Schutter, 'L'incrimination universelle de la violation des droits sociaux fondamentaux', in *La compétence universelle* (*Revue de droit de l'ULB-Annales de Droit de Louvain*, Bruylant, Bruxelles, 2004) pp. 218–223. F. A. Mann and B. Stern have significantly contributed to the doctrinal progress in this field: *see* F. A. Mann, 'The Doctrine of Jurisdiction in International Law', 82 *RCADI*, 1964-I, pp. 9–162; F.A. Mann, 'The Doctrine of International Jurisdiction Revisited after Twenty Years', *RCADI*, 1984-III, pp. 9–115; B. Stern, 'Quelques observations sur les règles internationales relatives à l'application extra-territoriale du droit', *Annuaire Français de Droit International* (AFDI), 1992, pp. 239–313; B. Stern, 'Une tentative d'élucidation du concept d'application extraterritoriale', *Revue québecoise de droit international* (1986) pp. 49–78.

the basis of State liability for acts affecting other States",[21] which the European Court of Human Rights relied on in *Loizidou* in order to consider that Turkey should be considered internationally liable for the acts of the authorities of the 'Turkish Republic of Northern Cyprus': if the illegality under international law of the invasion by Turkish forces of the Northern part of the Island of Cyprus in 1974 may not be invoked to restrict the responsibility of Turkey for the events occurring on the territories it occupied after that invasion, why then should the responsibility of the States parties to the Convention be limited, in other situations, with regard to events where they might be acting beyond the scope of their 'jurisdiction' as recognized under international law ?

The argument that State responsibility under international law should be limited to the acts by which it is acting within its 'jurisdiction' under international law is untenable.[22] Indeed, it is amply refuted by the international courts and human rights bodies which have decided similar issues in recent years. Under Article 2(1) of the International Covenant on Civil and Political Rights, a State party to this treaty undertakes "to respect and to ensure to all individuals within its territory and subject to its jurisdiction" the rights it recognizes. In the famed case of *Lopez Burgos* where it was confronted with the forcible abduction in Argentina by the Uruguayan security forces of a trade-unionist and political opponent, from where he was clandestinely transported to Uruguay, the Human Rights Committee considered that neither Article 2(1) ICCPR, nor Article 1 of the Optional Protocol which provides that the Committee may receive communications from individuals 'subject to [the] jurisdiction' of the State concerned, may be read to imply that this State "cannot be held accountable for violations of rights under the Covenant which its agents commit upon the territory of another State, whether with the acquiescence of the Government of that State or in opposition to it". Indeed, the Committee stated "it would be unconscionable to so interpret the responsibility under article 2 of the Covenant as to permit a State party to perpetrate violations of the Covenant

---

[21] International Court of Justice, *Legal Consequences for States of the Continued Presence of South Africa in Namibia (South West Africa) notwithstanding Security Council Resolution 276 (1970), I.C.J. Reports* 1971, pp. 16 *ff.*, p. 54, para. 118.

[22] Unfortunately, the European Court of Human Rights appears to hold to this confusion between the notion of 'jurisdiction' as a source of potential State responsibility under Article 1 ECHR and the notion of (prescriptive) 'jurisdiction' as the scope of the powers to legislate which public international law recognizes to a State, despite the absence of any logical connection between these two concepts: *see Assanidze* v. *Georgia,* 8 April 2004, ECHR no. 71503/01, para. 137.

on the territory of another State, which violations it could not perpetrate on its own territory".[23] The term 'jurisdiction', in the view of the Committee, refers "not to the place where the violation occurred, but rather to the relationship between the individual and the State in relation to a violation of any of the rights set forth in the Covenant, wherever they occurred".[24] Since the Committee initially adopted this position, it has been amply confirmed:[25] the States parties to the Covenant must respect and ensure the rights laid down in this instrument to "anyone within the power or effective control of that State party, even if not situated within the territory of the State party".[26] The same position has been adopted by the Committee on Economic, Social and Cultural Rights under the International Covenant on Economic, Social, and Cultural Rights.[27] These views have been spectacularly endorsed by the International Court of Justice in the Advisory Opinion it delivered on 9 July 2004 regarding the *Legal Consequences of the Construction of a Wall in the Occupied Palestinian Territory*.[28]

---

[23] Human Rights Committee, *Lopez Burgos* v. *Uruguay* (communication no. 52/1979 final views 29 July 1981 (thirteenth session)) (UN doc. CCPR/C/13/D/52/1979), para. 12.3. *See also*, for an identical statement in a twin case, Human Rights Committee, *Celeberti de Casariego* v. *Uruguay* (communication no. 56/1979 final views of 29 July 1981 (thirteenth session)) para. 10.3.

[24] *Ibid.*, para. 12.2.

[25] *See* in particular the Concluding Observations/Comments on Israel, (1999) (UN doc. CCPR/C/79/Add. 93), para. 10; Concluding Observations/Comments on Israel (2003) (UN doc. CCPR/CO/78/ISR), para. 11: "the provisions of the Covenant apply to the benefit of the population of the Occupied Territories, for all conduct by the State party's authorities or agents in those territories that affect the enjoyment of rights enshrined in the Covenant and fall within the ambit of State responsibility of Israel under the principles of public international law".

[26] Human Rights Committee, *General comment No. 31: The Nature of the General Legal Obligation Imposed on States Parties to the Covenant*, adopted on 29 March 2004 at 2187th meeting of the Committee (eightieth session), in *Compilation of General Comments and General Recommendations adopted by Human Rights Treaty Bodies*, 12 May 2004 (HRI/GEN/1/Rev.7) para. 10.

[27] Committee on Economic, Social, and Cultural Rights, Concluding Observations of the Committee on Economic, Social and Cultural Rights: Israel, 23 May 2003 (E/C.12/1/Add.90), para. 31 (reaffirming the view "that the State party's obligations under the Covenant apply to all territories and populations under its effective control").

[28] International Court of Justice, *Legal Consequences of the Construction of a Wall in the Occupied Palestinian Territory*, para. 102–113.

2.2. The Exception to the Territorial Understanding of the Notion of 'Jurisdiction'

A later case, *Issa and Others* v. *Turkey*, implicitly overrules *Bankovic* insofar as this latter decision seemed to imply that a State party to the Convention could not be held responsible for the consequences of acts going beyond the jurisdiction it might legitimately exercise under public international law, unless it occupied foreign territory where it exercises *de facto* governmental powers.[29] Six Iraqi nationals, acting on their own behalf and on behalf of deceased relatives, alleged the unlawful arrest, detention, ill-treatment and subsequent killing of their relatives in the course of a military operation conducted by the Turkish army in northern Iraq in April 1995. In its judgment of 16 November 2004, the Court stated that, under the principles established in its case-law,

> "a State may . . . be held accountable for violation of the Convention rights and freedoms of persons who are in the territory of another State but who are found to be under the former State's authority and control through its agents operating – whether lawfully or unlawfully – in the latter State . . . Accountability in such situations stems from the fact that Article 1 of the Convention cannot be interpreted so as to allow a State party to perpetrate

---

[29] In the *Bankovic* the court mentions in this regard (now operating on the confusion between *prescriptive* extra-territorial jurisdiction which was at the basis of its reasoning and *enforcement* extra-territorial jurisdiction) that in addition to the case where "the respondent State, through the effective control of the relevant territory and its inhabitants abroad as a consequence of military occupation or through the consent, invitation or acquiescence of the Government of that territory, exercises all or some of the public powers normally to be exercised by that Government", "other recognised instances of the extra-territorial exercise of jurisdiction by a State include cases involving the activities of its diplomatic or consular agents abroad and on board craft and vessels registered in, or flying the flag of, that State. In these specific situations, customary international law and treaty provisions have recognised the extra-territorial exercise of jurisdiction by the relevant State" (ECHR (GC), *Bankovic and Others* v. *Belgium and Others,* 12 December 2001, ECHR (inadmissibility dec.) no. 52207/99, *Reports of Judgments and Decisons* 2001-XII, paras. 71 and 73). A situation such as that presented by *Issa and Others* – where a State conducts military operations on the territory of a foreign State without the latter's consent, but without this turning into *de facto* control over an occupied portion of the territory equivalent to the exercise of governmental powers – does not fall under these categories, thus excluding, in the approach adopted in *Bankovic*, the applicability of the European Convention on Human Rights, as the individuals affected would not be under the 'jurisdiction' of the State concerned.

> violations of the Convention on the territory of another State, which it could not perpetrate on its own territory".[30]

The Court considered however that the conditions for the applicants' relatives to be under the "jurisdiction" of Turkey in this sense were not satisfied. It distinguished the situation in *Issa* from that in *Loizidou* in the following terms:

> "notwithstanding the large number of troops involved in the aforementioned military operations, it does not appear that Turkey exercised effective overall control of the entire area of northern Iraq. This situation is therefore in contrast to the one which obtained in northern Cyprus in the *Loizidou v. Turkey* and *Cyprus v. Turkey* cases . . . In the latter cases, the Court found that the respondent Government's armed forces totalled more than 30,000 personnel (which is, admittedly, no less than the number alleged by the applicants in the instant case . . . but with the difference that the troops in northern Cyprus were present over a very much longer period of time) and were stationed throughout the whole of the territory of northern Cyprus. Moreover, that area was constantly patrolled and had check points on all main lines of communication between the northern and southern parts of the island."[31]

This, however, did not necessarily exclude the imputability to Turkey of the acts complained of in *Issa and Others*. Indeed, the Court proceeds to examine whether the allegation that the Turkish troops could be held responsible for the abductions and killings of the Iraqi shepherds whose relatives had brought the application before the Court could be proven. As the Turkish troops did not exercise *de facto* control over the Northern part of Iraq comparable to that exercised by Turkey on the Northern part of the Island of Cyprus, such imputability could not be presumed. It had to be verified whether at the relevant time Turkish troops conducted operations in the area where the killings took place, or whether other elements could be seen as evidence that those killings could be attributed to them. The Court arrived at the conclusion that "it has not been established to the required standard of proof that the Turkish armed forces conducted operations in the area in question, and, more precisely . . . where, according to the applicants' statements, the victims were at that time"[32]; therefore "the Court is not

[30] *Issa and Others* v. *Turkey*, 16 November 2004, ECHR (2nd sect.) no. 31821/96, (final on 30 March 2005), para. 71.
[31] *Ibid.*, para. 75.
[32] *Ibid.*, para. 81.

satisfied that the applicants' relatives were within the 'jurisdiction' of the respondent State for the purposes of Article 1 of the Convention".[33]

In sum, this line of the case-law of the European Court of Human Rights, concerning the extra-territorial applicability of the Convention, leads it to distinguish between two situations. Where the alleged violation has occurred either on the territory of the defending State party to the Convention, or on a territory on which that State exercises *de facto* control equivalent to that it exercises on its national territory – equivalent, that is, insofar as it has at its disposal a governmental apparatus making it possible to secure the rights of the Convention for the benefit of the persons on that territory – it is under an obligation both to respect and to protect the rights and freedoms guaranteed in the Convention to all persons present within those territories. It is in this sense that, in the case of *Cyprus* v. *Turkey*, the Court made it clear that, Turkey having effective overall control over northern Cyprus,

> "its responsibility cannot be confined to the acts of its own soldiers or officials in northern Cyprus but must also be engaged by virtue of the acts of the local administration which survives by virtue of Turkish military and other support. It follows that, in terms of Article 1 of the Convention, Turkey's 'jurisdiction' must be considered to extend to securing *the entire range of substantive rights* set out in the Convention and those additional Protocols which she has ratified, and that violations of those rights are imputable to Turkey".[34]

The applicability of the European Convention on Human Rights is not limited, however, to those situations of territorial control. As *Issa* shows, the extra-territorial acts of the States parties to the Convention – i.e., the acts of those States which allegedly lead to violations of the rights afforded under the Convention in situations not located on its territory or on a territory on which it exercises *de facto* control – may also engage their responsibility provided those acts may be directly attributed to the State organs. This has been the position traditionally adopted by the monitoring bodies of the European Convention on Human Rights. In the first case presented to the European Commission of Human Rights concerning the situation created by the invasion of Northern Cyprus by Turkish forces in 1974, the Commission noted that "nationals of a State, including registered ships and aircrafts, are partly within its jurisdiction wherever they may be, and that authorized

[33] *Ibid.*, para. 82.

[34] *Cyprus* v. *Turkey*, 10 May 2001, ECHR (GC), no. 25781/94, *Reports of Judgments and Decisons* 2001-IV,. para. 77.

agents of a State, including diplomatic and consular agents and armed forces, not only remain under its jurisdiction when abroad but bring any other persons or property 'within the jurisdiction' of that State, to the extent that they exercise authority over such persons or property. Insofar as, by their acts or omissions, they affect such persons or property, the responsibility of the State is engaged".[35] It took this view also in *Ilse Hess* v. *the United Kingdom*, where the Commission noted that the United Kingdom could in principle be held responsible for the situation of the Spandau prison, located in the British sector of West Berlin, and which the four allied powers controlled jointly. The Commission saw "no reason why the acts of British authorities in Berlin should not entail the liability of the United Kingdom under the Convention", as "a State is under certain circumstances responsible under the Convention for the actions of its authorities outside its territory"; it dismissed the application as inadmissible *ratione personae*, however, as the United Kingdom alone could not, without the consent of the other three allied powers, modify the regime applied in the prison.[36] These statements have never been overruled.[37] Indeed, also *post Bankovic*, the Court in *Öçalan* – where the applicant, the leader in exile of the Workers' Party of Kurdistan (PKK), had been brought by the Kenyan authorities to an aircraft in the international transit area of Nairobi Airport, in which Turkish officials were waiting for him, and from where he was brought to Turkey in order to face trial – confirmed that, in such a situation, a person brought under the effective authority of officials of a State party to the Convention is "within the jurisdiction' of that State for the purposes of Article 1 of the Convention. The Court distinguished *Bankovic* by emphasizing that, *in Öçalan*, "the applicant was physically forced to return to Turkey by Turkish

[35] European Commission on Human Rights, *Cyprus* v. *Turkey*, 26 May 1975, no. 6780/74 and no. 6950/75, 2 DR 136.

[36] European Commission on Human Rights, *Ilse Hess* v. *the United Kingdom,* no. 6231/73, 2 DR 73, 18 *Yearbook of the ECHR* 174 (1975).

[37] For instance, in *Ramirez Sanchez* v. *France*, the European Commission of Human Rights considered that the applicant, the terrorist 'Carlos' abducted from Sudan and surrendered to the French authorities, was "under the authority, and therefore the jurisdiction", of France upon the moment of his surrender, for the purposes of the applicability of Article 5 ECHR which guarantees the right to liberty and security, even though this authority was exercised in a foreign country: European Commission on Human Rights, *Illich Sanchez Ramirez* v. *France*, 24 June 1996 (inadmissibility dec.), no. 28780/95.

officials and was subject to their authority and control following his arrest and return to Turkey".[38]

In other terms, where the State party to the Convention does not occupy a territory, exercising powers equivalent to those of a local government, it may still be bound to respect the Convention when acting beyond its national territory, but its obligations are limited: the State is under an obligation to respect the rights of the individuals who are under the effective control of its organs. However, it is not bound under the Convention to protect the rights of the population of territories where its organs occasionally deploy their activities. One obvious consequence is that the State is not under an obligation to control the activities of its nationals operating in foreign territories, even where the activities of those nationals would lead to violations of the rights of others. Although, under the active personality principle, the State could impose a liability, in particular a criminal liability, on its nationals wherever they conduct their activities,[39] a failure by a State party to the Convention to exercise this power would not engage its responsibility under the Convention, even though certain individuals' human rights could be affected by this failure to act.[40] Another consequence is that individuals affected by the conduct of the organs of a State party to the Convention which it has put at the disposal of another State may not be considered as placed under the "jurisdiction" of the former State, which excludes the imposition of any obligation on that State to control the way such organs will behave.[41] The judgment delivered by the Court in 1992 in

---

[38] *Öçalan* v. *Turkey*, 12 March 2003, ECHR (1st sect.), no. 46221/99, para. 93. This position was confirmed upon referral by the Grand Chamber of the Court: *Öçalan* v. *Turkey*, 12 May 2005, ECHR (GC), no. 46221/99, para. 91.

[39] This constitutes an exercise of the prescriptive (or normative) jurisdiction of the State; it is of course without prejudice of the limits which the exercise of its executive (or 'enforcement', sometimes also referred to as 'prerogative') jurisdiction encounters, due to the need to respect the sovereign rights of the territorial State. *See supra* note 20.

[40] Indeed, the very broad language used by the European Commission of Human Rights in the first *Cyprus* v. *Turkey* case (*see* text corresponding to *supra* note 35), where it refers to the fact that "nationals of a State . . . are partly within its jurisdiction wherever they may be", would seem to imply such a possibility.

[41] The question whether, in any case, such conduct of the organs of a State party to the Convention which are put at the disposal of another State may be *attributed* to the former State, is a distinct question from that of whether or not the individuals affected by that conduct are 'under the jurisdiction' of this State: *see* text corresponding to *supra* note 4. The ILC's Draft Articles on State Responsibility answer negatively to the question whether a State which has put its organs at the

the case of *Drozd and Janousek* v. *France and Spain* exemplifies this well.[42] The applicants, a Spanish and a Czechoslovak national, had been convicted by a court of the Principality of Andorra (at a time when Andorra was not a party to the Convention), under conditions which, they alleged, were in violation of the fair trial requirements of Article 6 of the Convention. The *Tribunal de Corts* before which the trial had taken place had been presided over by a French magistrate, another French magistrate was sitting in the three-members court, and the third member was designated by the Bishop of Urgel. The Court nevertheless considered that the responsibility of France nor that of Spain could be engaged for the administration of justice in Andorra:

> "Whilst it is true that judges from France and Spain sit as members of Andorran courts, they do not do so in their capacity as French or Spanish judges. Those courts, in particular the Tribunal de Corts, exercise their functions in an autonomous manner; their judgments are not subject to supervision by the authorities of France or Spain."[43]

---

disposal of another State may be imputed to the former State, "where the organ is acting in the exercise of elements of the governmental authority of the State at whose disposal it is placed" (Article 6). This however does not preclude that the European Convention on Human Rights could in the future impose on the State which places its organs at the disposal of another State an obligation not to contribute to a violation of the rights and freedoms guaranteed by the ECHR. This would not lead to attributing directly to the State the conduct of those organs affecting individuals in foreign territories when put at the disposal of another State; the conduct which could lead to international responsibility would be that of the national legislator, for having failed to impose such an obligation on the organs put at the disposal of another State.

[42] Indeed, the rapporteur of the International Law Commission J. Crawford cites the case of *Drozd and Janousek* in order to illustrate the rule of Article 6 of the ILC's Articles on State Responsibility (*The International Law Commission's Articles on State Responsibility. Introduction, Text and Commentaries*, (Cambridge Univ. Press, 2002), p. 15 (*infra* note 141); and the comparison *a contrario* with, *X and Y* v. *Switzerland,* no. 7289/75 and no. 7349/76, 9 D.R. 57 (exercise by the Swiss police, in Liechtenstein who was not at the time party to the ECHR, of 'delegated powers', however customs and immigration jurisdiction was exercised in Liechtenstein by Swiss police officers governed exclusively by Swiss law and exercising the public authority of Switzerland, leading J. Crawford to conclude that they were not organs of the Swiss State 'placed at the disposal' of Liechtenstein)).

[43] *Drozd and Janousek* v. *France and Spain*, 26 June 1992, ECHR (plenary Court), Series A no. 240, para. 96.

In this two-tiered approach to the question of the so-called 'extra-territorial' applicability of the Convention, the notion of territorial control therefore has a crucial regulating function to fulfil. Whenever an event, allegedly constituting a violation of the Convention, occurs on the territory of a State party to the Convention, the responsibility of that State is potentially engaged, either because the violation has been committed directly by one of its organs, or because the State has failed to prevent the violation from occurring by adopting reasonable measures which could have been expected and by providing adequate remedies for the reparation of the victim if and when those preventive measures fail. The situation where an event occurs not on the national territory of the State but on a portion of foreign territory where it *de facto* exercises elements of sovereignty is assimilated to this first hypothesis, because it would be unacceptable for States to be allowed to escape their liability by refusing to consider as part of their national territory certain zones on which, in effect, they retain the governmental powers.[44] The regime applicable to the second hypothesis is the result of two, partly conflicting, concerns. It is necessary, of course, to constrain the exercise of powers by the State even when they are exercised outside the national territory. Again, a State should not be allowed to evade its responsibility simply because, for instance, it persecutes political opponents living abroad rather than within its national territory. On the other hand, however, because the degree of control of any State on events occurring on foreign territory is much more limited – restrained as it is, indeed, by the need to respect the sovereign rights of the territorial State – it would be unrealistic to impose on a State (with respect to events occurring on foreign territory) obligations similar to those imposed with respect to events occurring on its national territory. In this hypothesis, the 'presumption of control' is lacking, on which the regime of human rights obligations of States with respect to events occurring on their national territory or on territories on which they exercise governmental powers is based.

Thus, two principles emerge: (i) on the national territory of a State party to the Convention or on territory where it has assumed governmental powers, that State must ensure that the full range of the rights recognized under the Convention are ensured, and must comply with the corresponding obligations, both to respect and to protect those rights, which the Convention imposes, (ii) where the organs of the State act beyond the national territory

---

[44] *See*, *mutatis mutandis*, *Amuur* v. *France,* 25 June 1996, ECHR, para. 42 (so-called 'international zone' of the international airport of Paris-Orly falls under the jurisdiction of France notwithstanding its status under national law).

or territory assimilated to national territory, they remain bound to respect the rights set forth in the Convention, to the extent that they exercise effective control over certain persons or property.

2.3. *The 'Espace Juridique' of the Convention*

The reader will have noted that, in the definition of the two above principles, no distinction is made between the potential liability of a State party to the Convention in extra-territorial situations where that State occupies a territory in which the Convention was previously in force or where its agents perform acts on such territory, and situations which occur outside the territory of States parties to the Council of Europe. As we have seen however,[45] this distinction did seem to play an important role in the inadmissibility decision adopted unanimously by the Grand Chamber in *Bankovic*. The applicants had argued before the Court that "any failure to accept that they fell within the jurisdiction of the respondent States would defeat the *ordre public* mission of the Convention and leave a regrettable vacuum in the Convention system of human rights' protection".[46] The answer of the Court to this contention was that:

> "the Convention is a multi-lateral treaty operating . . . in an essentially regional context and notably in the legal space (*espace juridique*) of the Contracting States. The FRY clearly does not fall within this legal space. The Convention was not designed to be applied throughout the world, even in respect of the conduct of Contracting States. Accordingly, the desirability of avoiding a gap or vacuum in human rights' protection has so far been relied on by the Court in favour of establishing jurisdiction only when the territory in question was one that, but for the specific circumstances, would normally be covered by the Convention."[47]

There are powerful arguments in favour of this distinction, and thus, for limiting any extra-territorial applicability of the Convention to territories situated within the '*espace juridique*' – in the geographical sense of the expression – of the Council of Europe Member States. First, in the decision of 26 May 1975 in the first *Cyprus* v. *Turkey* case – a decision which would twenty years later lead to *Loizidou* – the European Commission of Human Rights appears to have been guided by its concern that, if it did not find Turkey to have jurisdiction on the occupied territory of Northern Cyprus, it

---

[45] *See supra* notes 17–18.
[46] *Bankovic*, *supra* note 13, para. 79.
[47] *Ibid.*, para. 80.

would have allowed the Convention to have become ineffective on that part of the island: the military occupation would have deprived the inhabitants of the Northern part of Cyprus from protection under the Convention which they otherwise would have enjoyed.[48] If the Court found otherwise it would result in a 'vacuum' being created in the protection that the instrument affords. This surfaces again in the judgment of the Court delivered on 10 May 2001 in the case of *Cyprus* v. *Turkey*. The Court notes that if it were to consider that the 'jurisdiction' of Turkey does not extend to this territory, this would result in "a regrettable vacuum in the system of human-rights protection in the territory in question by removing from individuals there the benefit of the Convention's fundamental safeguards and their right to call a High Contracting Party to account for violations of their rights in proceedings before the Court . . .". [49] Second – and this again is an argument the *Bankovic* Court puts forward[50] – the inclusion in the Convention of a clause[51] enabling a Contracting State to declare that the Convention shall extend to all or any of the territories for whose international relations that State is responsible demonstrates that, at least in the view of the drafters, the applicability of the Convention beyond the national territories of the States parties was not presumed, even where they might effectively control certain (non-European) territories.

However, also on this point, it would appear that the case-law of the Court may be seen as having overruled *Bankovic*. As to the argument that the Northern Cyprus cases led to an extensive understanding of the notion of 'jurisdiction' in order to ensure that there would be no 'vacuum' created, it cannot but be remarked that this argument was not made, explicitly at least, in the judgment of 8 July 2004 delivered by the Grand Chamber in the case of *Ilascu and Others* v. *Moldova and Russia*. This is remarkable, insofar as

[48] *See* text corresponding to *supra* note 35. The European Commission on Human Rights notes specifically: "The operation of the Convention in the occupied part of Cyprus would become ineffective if one accepted [Turkey's] submission that alleged violations of the Convnetion in that area could not be examined by the Commission. It followed from Art. 17 that the Convention did not allow such a vacuum in the protection of its rights and freedoms". Article 17 ECHR states in particular that nothing in the Convention "may be interpreted as implying for any State . . . any right to engage in any activity or perform any act aimed at the destruction of any of the rights and freedoms set forth [in the Convention] or at their limitation to a greater extent than in provided for in the Convention".

[49] *Cyprus* v. *Turkey, supra* note 34, para. 78.

[50] *Bankovic*, *supra* note 13, para. 80.

[51] Article 56 para. 1 ECHR (previously Article 63 para. 1).

the circumstances of that case, which are examined in more detail below, would seem to call for a similar reasoning. In this case the individuals situated on the territory of the separatist 'Moldavian Republic of Transdniestria' whose authorities had proclaimed their independence from Moldova and were not under the effective control of the Moldovan central authorities, would in effect be deprived of the protection of the Convention if they were not allowed to impose on the Federation of Russia – whose 'jurisdiction' was seen to extend to that territory because of the decisive influence it exercises on the authorities of the separatist regime – that it assumes its obligations under the Convention also with respect to that zone. The omission of this argument in the context of *Ilascu* by the fact that, as we shall see, Moldova was considered by the Court to still have 'jurisdiction', albeit limited in fact, on the zone of the separatist republic – a zone on which, indeed, it continued to claim sovereignty and the control of which it sought to retain. Thus, the 'vacuum' in the system of protection of the Convention would not be complete, as the population of the 'Moldavian Republic of Transdniestria' still, in principle, may call upon Moldova to ensure that the Convention is complied with within that territory. The 'vacuum' argument nevertheless could have been made, insofar as any protection the Modovan authorities could have provided in the zone on which the 'Moldavian Republic of Transdniestria' was self-proclaimed would have been essentially theoretical.[52]

More fundamentally, the judgement of the Court adopted a few months later in *Issa and Others* seems to confirm that the notion of a geographically limited '*espace juridique'* in which the Convention is to apply has lost any support it may have had in the past. Where it summarizes the principles guiding its case-law, the Court in *Issa* simply restates that:

> "the concept of 'jurisdiction' within the meaning of Article 1 of the Convention is not necessarily restricted to the national territory of the High Contracting Parties . . . In exceptional circumstances the acts of Contracting

[52] Thus, the English High Court of Justice (Divisional Court), in a widely publicized judgment of 14 December 2004, considered – rightly, in my view – that "the northern Cyprus and Moldova cases are correctly to be understood as ultimately turning on the exclusive and inclusive aspects of the rationalisation of the Convention as operating essentially only within its own regional sphere but also as permitting no vacuum to appear within that space" (*The Queen*, on the application of *Mazin Jumaa Gatteh Al Skeini and Others* v. *The Secretary Of State For Defence*, [2004] EWHC 2911 (Admin), [2004] 2 WLR 1401, para. 274). This case is examined in more detail below.

> States performed outside their territory or which produce effects there ('extra-territorial act') may amount to exercise by them of their jurisdiction within the meaning of Article 1 of the Convention."[53]

There is no allusion to the fact that such exceptional circumstances should only play a role on a territory where the Convention would otherwise have been applicable. Indeed, later in the judgment, applying the general principles to the case in dispute, the Court explicitly addresses the question of the applicability of the Convention beyond the '*espace juridique*' of the Council of Europe, and offers a quite different understanding of this notion. It says:[54]

> "The Court does not exclude the possibility that, as a consequence of this military action, the respondent State could be considered to have exercised, temporarily, effective overall control of a particular portion of the territory of northern Iraq. Accordingly, if there is a sufficient factual basis for holding that, at the relevant time, the victims were within that specific area, it would follow logically that they were within the jurisdiction of Turkey (and not that of Iraq, which is not a Contracting State and clearly does not fall within the legal space (*espace juridique*) of the Contracting States (see the above-cited *Bankovic* decision, § 80)."

Although *Issa* was adopted by a Chamber of the Court constituted within the second section, and thus in principle is less authoritative than the *Bankovic* decision – adopted unanimously by a Grand Chamber – it should not be too easily dismissed. Three of the judges sitting in *Issa*, which was adopted unanimously, were also sitting in the Grand Chamber which decided *Bankovic.*[55] This latter decision has not been overlooked. On the contrary, the reading offered of it was deliberate. We should not ignore *Issa* because it is inconsistent with *Bankovic*. Instead, we should read *Bankovic* in the light of the later case-law of the Court.

The relationship between *Bankovic* and *Issa* formed a central aspect of the very richly reasoned judgment delivered on 14 December 2004 by the English High Court of Justice (Divisional Court), when it examined the claims of relatives of Iraqi citizens who had died in Iraq at a time and within geographical areas where the United Kingdom was recognized as an

[53] *Issa and Others* v. *Turkey,* 16 November 2004, ECHR (2nd sect), no. 31821/96,) para. 68.
[54] *Ibid*., para. 74.
[55] These are judges Costa, Thomassen and Baka.

occupying power.[56] Five claimants were killed in incidents with British troops. A sixth applicant died while in the custody of British troops in a military prison. The claimants alleged violations of Article 2 of the Convention, which guarantees the right to life, and – in the case of the sixth applicant – of Article 3, which prohibits torture and inhuman or degrading treatment, as they considered that the deaths had not led to effective enquiries. Both these provisions were made applicable before British courts by virtue of the Human Rights Act 1998.

The High Court concluded that the 'jurisdiction' of the United Kingdom did not extend to the total territory occupied by the British armed forces in Iraq, even though that territory may be said to be under its effective control. Basing itself mainly on *Bankovic*, which it considers the leading authority on the interpretation of Article 1 ECHR after an extensive review of the case-law of the European Court of Human Rights,[57] the High Court took the view that

> "article 1 jurisdiction does not extend to a broad, world-wide extra-territorial personal jurisdiction arising from the exercise of authority by party states' agents anywhere in the world, but only to an extra-territorial jurisdiction which is exceptional and limited and to be found in specific cases recognised in international law. Such instances . . . are ones where, albeit the alleged violation of Convention standards takes place outside the home territory of the respondent state, it occurs by reason of the exercise of state authority in or from a location which has a form of discrete quasi-territorial quality, or where the state agent's presence in a foreign state is consented to by that state and protected by international law: such as diplomatic or consular premises, or vessels or aircraft registered in the respondent state".[58]

---

[56] *The Queen*, on the application of *Mazin Jumaa Gatteh Al Skeini and Others* v. *The Secretary Of State For Defence*, [2004] EWHC 2911 (Admin), [2004] WLR 1401.

[57] *The Queen*, on the application of *Mazin Jumaa Gatteh Al Skeini and Others* v. *The Secretary Of State For Defence*, para. 245 ("*Bankovic* is the leading authority in support of both the basic proposition [that the essential and primary nature of Article 1 jurisdiction is territorial] and the reasons for it. As such it must throw its light and its learning over all the authorities which precede and follow it"); *see also* para. 268 ("*Bankovic* is a watershed authority in the light of which the Strasbourg jurisprudence as a whole has to be re-evaluated").

[58] *The Queen*, on the application of *Mazin Jumaa Gatteh Al Skeini and Others* v. *The Secretary Of State For Defence*, at paras. 269–270.

The claims of the first five claimants failed on that basis. However, the Court did recognize that the situation of the sixth claimant, Mr Mousa, warranted a different conclusion:

> "It seems to us that it is not at all straining the examples of extra-territorial jurisdiction discussed in the jurisprudence considered above to hold that a British military prison, operating in Iraq with the consent of the Iraqi sovereign authorities, and containing arrested suspects, falls within even a narrowly limited exception exemplified by embassies, consulates, vessels and aircraft, and in the case of Hess v. United Kingdom, a prison".[59]

The judgment went on to decide that the inadequacies in the enquiries which took place following the death of Mr Mousa justify a finding of a violation of the procedural requirements of Articles 2 and 3 of the Convention.

The judgment of the High Court of Justice was substantially affirmed, on appeal, by the Court of Appeal (Civil Division), in a judgment of 21 December 2005.[60] Yet, whether its reasoning was entirely dictated by the case-law of the European Court of Human Rights may be doubted. In order to dismiss the claims for judicial review of the five first claimants, the High Court of Justice based itself on the notion of an '*espace juridique*' of the Convention expressed in para. 80 of the *Bankovic* decision. It reads this notion as implying that a State party to the Convention is not bound to ensure the rights and freedoms set forth in that instrument on foreign territories effectively under its control, unless this would result in a 'vacuum' of the system of protection of the Convention within the territories of the Council of Europe to which that instrument was intended to apply. This reading not only treats as binding authority what was merely *obiter* in *Bankovic* – where all parties agreed that the NATO forces did not exercise effective control over Serbia – it also does not take into consideration the almost explicit reconsideration of that passage in the later case of *Issa*. The High Court of Justice does recognize this tension.[61] But it adheres to a 'pick-

---

[59] *The Queen*, on the application of *Mazin Jumaa Gatteh Al Skeini and Others* v. *The Secretary Of State For Defence*, para. 287.

[60] [2005] EWCA Civ 1609. This judgment was delivered at a time when this article was already finalized. It has thus not been possible to include a detailed discussion in these pages.

[61] *The Queen*, on the application of *Mazin Jumaa Gatteh Al Skeini and Others* v. *The Secretary Of State For Defence*, para. 263. *See also* para. 277 of the judgment, where the Court candidly notes: "In Issa at para 74 the Court recognises the espace juridique doctrine but, in our respectful opinion, does not succeed in avoiding it

and-choose' jurisprudence which is manifest in the justification it offers for following *Bankovic* instead of the more recent case-law of the European Court of Human Rights:

> "in our judgment the dicta in Issa do not, for the reasons which we have sought to express, follow any 'clear and constant jurisprudence of the Strasbourg court'. On the contrary, we think that they are inconsistent with Bankovic and the development of the Strasbourg jurisprudence in the years immediately before Bankovic. In a sense Issa seems to us to look back to an earlier period of the jurisprudence, which has subsequently made way for a more limited interpretation of article 1 jurisdiction. It may well be that there is more than one school of thought at Strasbourg; and that there is an understandable concern that modern events in Iraq should not be put entirely beyond the scope of the Convention: but at present we would see the dominant school as that reflected in the judgment in Bankovic and it is to that school that we think we owe a duty under section 2(1) [of the Human Rights Act 1998]."[62]

Borrowing from Justice Scalia's flavourful qualifications,[63] we may consider that this is simply an answer to the 'never-say-never' jurisprudence of the European Court of Human Rights. And, indeed, the Strasbourg Court may have failed to provide the national courts with all the guidance they may require for this question. It has preferred to decide the questions it has been confronted with, which often are especially sensitive in situations which contain an extra-territorial element, on a case-to-case basis, wishing neither to definitively close any doors, nor to open the floodgates for fanciful and politically motivated applications.[64] Nevertheless, when confronted with two

---

implying that non-Convention territory automatically becomes Convention territory if there is effective control of an area by a state party".

[62] *The Queen*, on the application of *Mazin Jumaa Gatteh Al Skeini and Others* v. *The Secretary Of State For Defence*, para. 265.

[63] *See* the opinion of Justice Scalia, joined by the Chief Justice and Justice Thomas, concurring in part and concurring in the judgment, in *Sosa* v. *Alvarez-Machain et al.*, 542 U.S. 692 (2004) (judgment of 29 June 2004), slip op., p. 13 of the separate opinion.

[64] For one example, *see Aziz* v. *Cyprus, Greece, Turkey and the United Kingdom*, 23 April 2002, no. 69949/01, decision (partial decision of inadmissibility): the applicant, a member of the Turkish Cypriot community who could not be registered in the Greek Cypriot electoral role, considered that not only the Cypriot government was responsible for this situation, but also Greece, which "caused the military coup in 1974 against the Cyprus Government", Turkey, which "illegally invaded and still occupies nearly 40% of Cypriot territory and supports the illegal 'Turkish Republic

successive decisions of the European Court of Human Rights which contain apparently conflicting dicta, the role of the national courts is to either reconcile these decisions by identifying some overarching principle which could explain both, or to recognize the primacy of the most recent decision, which is presumed to represent the current position of the international judge. To affirm the primacy of the older decision under the pretext that the more recent ones are not adequately supported by the authorities it relies on[65] hardly seems to conform with the kind of cooperation between the English courts and the European Court of Human Rights which the Human Rights Act 1998 seems to call for.[66]

2.4. The Positive Obligation to Influence Extra-Territorial Situations

The two principles identified above require that a distinction be made between (i) the national territory of a State party to the Convention or the territory where it has assumed governmental powers, and (ii) situations where the organs of the State act beyond the national territory or territory assimilated to national territory. The determination of the scope of the State's obligations should depend on this distinction. The judgment of the Court in *Ilascu and Others* v. *Moldova and Russia*[67] concerns an intermediate situation, in which the *de facto* influence exercised by the Russian authorities on the authorities of the self-proclaimed 'Moldavian

---

of Northern Cyprus'", and the United Kingdom, which "gave support to the revolutionary Cyprus government to propose constitutional changes in 1963 and has done nothing ever since to uphold the Constitution". The Court answered that "the applicant's complaints, to the extent that are directed against Greece, Turkey and the United Kingdom, are of a political nature and have no bearing on the situation complained of by the applicant, namely the refusal of the Cypriot authorities to register him in the electoral lists".

[65] *The Queen*, on the application of *Mazin Jumaa Gatteh Al Skeini and Others* v. *The Secretary Of State For Defence*, para. 263: "in the light of our analysis of Issa . . . we do not consider that its broad dicta are consistent with Bankovic. Moreover, the authorities relied on by the Court for those broad dicta do not adequately support them . . .".

[66] As explained by Lord Bingham in the case of *Ullah*: "This reflects the fact that the Convention is an international instrument, the correct interpretation of which can be authoritatively expounded only by the Strasbourg court. From this it follows that a national court subject to a duty such as that imposed by section 2 should not without strong reason dilute or weaken the effect of the Strasbourg case law" (*Regina (Ullah)* v. *Special Adjudicator* [2004] UKHL 26, [2004] 3 WLR 23, para. 20).

[67] *Ilascu and Others* v. *Moldova and Russia, supra* note 9, no. 48787/99.

Republic of Transdniestria' was in effect considered by the Court to be such as to compensate for the absence of a territorial control of Russia equivalent to that exercised by Turkey on the Northern part of Cyprus. The 'Moldavian Republic of Transdniestria' is a region of Moldova which proclaimed its independence in 1991 but is not recognised by the international community. It has been consistently supported, first by the USSR when the Republic of Moldova proclaimed its independence in August 1991, and later by the Federation of Russia. In fact, the Fourteenth Army of the USSR, previously deployed in Moldova with its headquarters in Chisinau, retreated from most of Moldova but remained present in Transdniestria, and has actively cooperated with the separatists since. After the end of the conflict between Moldova and the separatist republic in 1991–1992, senior officers of the former Fourteenth Army participated in the public life in Transdniestria, and soldiers of the former Fourteenth Army took part in the elections in Transdniestria, military parades of the Transdniestrian forces and other public events. Strong links, both economic and legal – for instance in the field of judicial cooperation – were established between the Moldavian Republic of Transdniestria and the Federation of Russia, the successor State to the USSR. The four applicants, Moldovan nationals who were arrested in June 1992, were condemned by a Transdniestrian court to imprisonment and, in the case of Mr Ilascu, to death. The applicants alleged in particular that the court which had convicted them was not competent for the purposes of Article 6 of the Convention, that they had not had a fair trial, that their detention in Transdniestria was not lawful (in breach of Article 5), and that their conditions of detention contravened Articles 3 and 8 of the Convention. The applicants argued that the Moldovan authorities were responsible under the Convention for the alleged violations, since they had not taken any appropriate steps to end to them. They further asserted that the Russian Federation shared responsibility since the territory of Transdniestria was and is under *de facto* Russian control on account of the Russian troops and military equipment stationed there and the support allegedly given to the separatist regime by the Russian Federation. With respect to this latter question, the Court recalled that, under *Loizidou*, "a State's responsibility may be engaged where, as a consequence of military action – whether lawful or unlawful – it in practice exercises effective control of an area situated outside its national territory. The obligation to secure, in such an area, the rights and freedoms set out in the Convention derives from the fact of such control, whether it be exercised directly, through its armed forces, or through a subordinate local administration".[68] This quote is one we are already familiar with. However the Court then added: [69]

> "It is not necessary to determine whether a Contracting Party actually exercises detailed control over the policies and actions of the authorities in the area situated outside its national territory, since even overall control of the area may engage the responsibility of the Contracting Party concerned . . .
>
> Where a Contracting State exercises overall control over an area outside its national territory its responsibility is not confined to the acts of its soldiers or officials in that area but also extends to acts of the local administration which survives there by virtue of its military and other support . . .
>
> A State's responsibility may also be engaged on account of acts which have sufficiently proximate repercussions on rights guaranteed by the Convention, even if those repercussions occur outside its jurisdiction. Thus, with reference to extradition to a non-Contracting State, the Court has held that a Contracting State would be acting in a manner incompatible with the underlying values of the Convention . . . if it were knowingly to hand over a fugitive to another State where there are substantial grounds for believing that the person concerned faces a real risk of being subjected to torture or to inhuman or degrading treatment or punishment (see Soering v. the United Kingdom, judgment of 7 July 1989, Series A no. 161, p. 35, paras. 88-91).
>
> In addition, the acquiescence or connivance of the authorities of a Contracting State in the acts of private individuals which violate the Convention rights of other individuals within its jurisdiction may engage the State's responsibility under the Convention . . . That is particularly true in the case of recognition by the State in question of the acts of self-proclaimed authorities which are not recognised by the international community."

Applying those principles to the facts of the case, the Court arrived at the conclusion that the Moldavian Republic of Transdniestria, "set up in 1991-1992 with the support of the Russian Federation, vested with organs of power and its own administration, remains under the effective authority, *or at the very least under the decisive influence*, of the Russian Federation, and in any event that *it survives by virtue of the military, economic, financial and political support given to it by the Russian Federation*", and that therefore the applicants must be considered to come within the 'jurisdiction' of the

---

[68] *Ibid.*, para. 314 (citing *Loizidou* v. *Turkey* (*Merits*), 18 December 1996, ECHR, *Reports of Judgments and Decisions* 1996-VI, pp. 2234-2235, para. 52).
[69] *Ilascu and Others* v. *Moldova and Russia, supra* note 9, paras. 315–318.

Russian Federation for the purposes of Article 1 of the Convention.[70] This finding extends the notion of (extra-territorial) jurisdiction under this provision beyond what resulted from the Cypriot cases, insofar as exercising a decisive influence on a rebel regime and even an overall control on the territory cannot be assimilated to a situation of full military occupation, as the position of Turkey in the Northern part of Cyprus may be described.[71]

Nevertheless, this was the less controversial part of the judgment of the Court.[72] And, indeed, once it is recognized that the *de facto* influence exercised by the Federation of Russia on Transdniestria is comparable in effect to that exercised by Turkey in Northern Cyprus, even though the means may not be as direct, and that the Region of Transdniestria therefore is under the 'jurisdiction' of Russia in the meaning of Article 1 ECHR, the ensuing reasoning – holding Russia responsible for the acts of the authorities of the self-proclaimed Moldavian Republic of Transdniestria – is not particularly remarkable. Although we may be trained, as international lawyers, to think that the international responsibility of a State may not be engaged by the conduct of actors not belonging to the State apparatus unless they are in fact acting under the instructions of, or under the direction or control of, that State in carrying out the conduct,[73] the private-public distinction on which this rule of attribution is based is mooted (though not contradicted) by the imposition of positive obligations on the States parties

[70] *Ilascu and Others* v. *Moldova and Russia*, *supra* note 9, paras. 391–394 (my emphasis). It will be noted that, although the Court announced in the passage quoted above that "[a] State's responsibility may also be engaged on account of acts which have sufficiently proximate repercussions on rights guaranteed by the Convention, *even if those repercussions occur outside its jurisdiction*" (para. 317; my emphasis), thus presenting 'jurisdiction' and 'imputability' as *alternative* grounds for a finding of liability. Here the fact that a situation is imputable to the Russian authorities (due to the influence they may exercise on the Transdniestrian separatists) leads to a finding that the 'jurisdiction' of the Federation of Russi extends to such situations. These conceptual hesitations and even inconsistencies are a sign of the uncertainties within the Court as to how to treat such situations.

[71] *See* the dissenting opinion of judge Ress, para. 3.

[72] Although the judgment elicited no less than four partly dissenting and one dissenting opinions from altogether 13 judges of the 17-member Grand Chamber, only one member of the Court disagreed with the finding concerning the extent of the jurisdiction of Russia. This was judge Kovler, elected on behalf of Russia.

[73] To paraphrase Article 4 of the ILC's Draft Articles on State Responsibility, which itself is of course directly inspired by the position of the International Court of Justice in the case of *Military and Paramilitary Activities in and against Nicaragua (Nicaragua* v. *United States of America) (merits)*, *ICJ Reports* 1986, p. 14.

to the ECHR. Once a situation is found to fall under the 'jurisdiction' of a State party to the Convention, the State must accept responsibility not only for the acts its organs have adopted, but also for the omissions of these organs, where such omissions result in an insufficient protection of private persons whose rights or freedoms are violated by the acts of other non-State actors.

What is noteworthy in the *Ilascu* case, however, is that the applicants were directing their application not only against Russia, the 'sponsor' State of the Moldavian Republic of Transdniestria, but also against Moldova, which sought since 1991 – but failed – to assert its sovereignty on the Region of Transdniestria. They thus confronted the Court with the question whether, when a portion of the national territory escapes the effective control of the central authorities, that segment of the territory should nevertheless be considered to be under the 'jurisdiction' of the State concerned, with the obligations this entails. It is to this problem that I now turn.

3. The 'Jurisdiction' of the State on its National Territory

3.1. The 'Jurisdiction' of the State on National Territory under its Effective Control

The preceding section recalled that, where a State exercised on a foreign territory a form of control comparable to that of a territorial sovereign, assuming the governmental powers generally associated therewith, the events occurring on that territory should be considered to fall under its 'jurisdiction' in the meaning of Article 1 ECHR. It would seem to fit within that same logic that, conversely, "the presumption that persons within the territory of a State are within its 'jurisdiction' for Convention purposes is a rebuttable one and, exceptionally, the responsibility of a State will not be engaged in respect of acts in breach of the Convention which occur within its territory".[74] In both situations, 'jurisdiction' thus would derive from control,[75] and far from being determinative, the fact that a particular event occurs on the national territory only would serve to establish a *presumption of control.* Thus, whilst 'jurisdiction' should extend to the situations

---

[74] *See* the partly dissenting opinion of Judge Sir Nicolas Bratza, joined by judges Rozakis, Hedigan, Thomassen and Pantîru appended to the judgment of the Court in *Ilascu and Others* v. *Moldova and Russia* case, *supra* note 9.

[75] For an exposition of why responsibility derives from control, *see* C. Eagleton, 'International Organisation and the Law of Responsibility', 76 *RCADI* (1950) p. 385.

effectively under the control of the State which may ensure the protection of the full range of the rights protected under the Convention, it should be limited, conversely, where a State is *de facto* unable to exercise its governmental powers on some portions of the national territory. Indeed, this was the position adopted by the Court in *Cyprus* v. *Turkey*, where the Court justified reiterating its conclusion that Northern Cyprus was under the 'jurisdiction' of Turkey

> "having regard to the . . . *continuing inability [of the government of Cyprus] to exercise their Convention obligations in northern Cyprus*, [so that] any other finding would result in a regrettable vacuum in the system of human-rights protection in the territory in question by removing from individuals there the benefit of the Convention's fundamental safeguards and their right to call a High Contracting Party to account for violation of their rights in proceedings before the Court."[76]

That statement seemed to imply, first, that the 'jurisdiction' of a State party to the Convention could not be considered to extend to all its national territory if, on certain portions of that territory, the State is unable in fact to exercise its control in order to effectively guarantee the rights and freedoms set forth in the Convention; second, that the notion of 'jurisdiction' is an all-or-nothing concept, in the sense that any single event falls under the jurisdiction of either State A or of State B, depending on which State effectively could have controlled the event and, therefore, may be held internationally responsible for not having guaranteed the rights and freedoms recognized under the Convention.

This however is not to say that the responsibility of the State under whose jurisdiction a particular event occurs is necessarily engaged simply because the event which it should have prevented occurred. Rather, in the logic espoused by the Court in *Cyprus* v. *Turkey*, where an event occurs under the jurisdiction of a State party to the Convention three situations are to be carefully distinguished. No particular difficulty is raised in the first situation, where the violation has its source directly in the acts of the organs of the State – for instance, a judicial decision has been adopted in violation of the requirements of a fair trial or a law has been passed which creates an unjustifiable interference with the right to respect for private life. But it may be that the event allegedly resulting in a violation of Convention rights may not be directly attributed to the organs of the State, in that it has its source in the acts of private individuals. In this second situation, the international

[76] *Cyprus* v. *Turkey*, *supra* note 34, para. 78.

responsibility of the State will only be engaged where it appears that the State has not adopted the measures which could have reasonably prevented the event from occurring, but this infringement cannot be presumed from the simple fact that those measures have failed in a particular instance to prevent the rights of an individual from being violated: the obligation here is one of means, not of result.[77] The requirement of a prior exhaustion of the local remedies available before the European Court of Human Rights may consider an application ensures that, where the violation complained of has its source in the acts of private individuals, the international responsibility of the State will only exist where it has not only failed to prevent the event from occurring, but also where it has failed to place the individuals who are victims of the event in the situation they would have been in the absence of that event,[78] and to identify and punish those responsible for the violation.[79]

---

[77] *Plattform "Ärtze für das Leben"* v. *Austria*, 21 June 1988, ECHR, Series A no. 139, para. 34.

[78] Since the early 1980s, the case-law of the Court requires not only that the State authorities ensure reparation to the victim, but also that they adopt measures acknowledging that the Convention has been violated (*see e.g.*, *Amuur* v. *France,* 25 June 1996, ECHR, *Reports of Judgments and Decisions* 1996-III, p. 846, para. 36: "a decision or measure favourable to the applicant is not in principle sufficient to deprive him of his status as a 'victim' unless the national authorities have acknowledged, either expressly or in substance, and then afforded redress for, the breach of the Convention"). This ensures that States will not be tempted to simply 'buy off' individual victims by compensating them on a case-by-case basis but without removing the deficiencies in the national legal system or the practices which led to the violation in the first place.

[79] It is clear that, in this situation where the alleged violations have their source directly in the acts of private individuals, the local remedies rule constitutes a rule of substance (defining whether the State has violated an international obligation) rather than a rule of procedure (governing only the admissibility before the international jurisdiction of the claim of the individual aggrieved). Although, as is well known, the first qualification was favored first by E. Borchard and, later, by R. Ago as well as, generally, by the Italian doctrine; Ch. de Visscher and C. F. Amerasinghe in particular were in favor of the second qualification. *See*, among many other references, E. Borchard, 'The Local Remedies Rule', *American Journal of International Law* (1934) p. 729; R. Ago, 'Le délit international', 68 *RCADI*, 1939-II, pp. 26–554, para. 516; G. Barile, *I diritii assoluti nell-ordinamento internazionale* (Giuffrè, Milano, 1951) p. 327; F. Durante, *Ricorsi individuali a organi internazionali* (Giuffrè, Milano, 1958) p. 137; G. Gaja, *L'esaurimento dei ricorsi interni nel diritto internazionale* (Giuffrè, Milano, 1967) p. 140 (for a presentation of the local remedies rules as a rule of substance), and contrast with Ch. de Visscher, 'Notes sur la responsabilité internationale des Etats et la protection

In other terms, despite all the conceptual confusion which still continues to pervade this part of the jurisprudence of the Court, the acts of private individuals are not *as such* imputable to the State, although if they are left unpunished or unremedied, their occurrence and repetition may serve to shed light on the failure of the organs of the State to comply with its obligation to protect the rights of individuals under its jurisdiction.[80] The responsibility of

---

diplomatique d'après quelques documents récents', *Rev. dr. int. et de légis. comparée*, (1927) pp. 245 and *ff.*, at p. 252; Ch. de Visscher, 'Le déni de justice en droit international', 52 *RCADI,* 1935-II, pp. 368–442, esp. chap. III: 'Les rapports du déni de justice avec la responsabilité internationale et avec la règle de l'épuisement préalable des voies de recours internes', at pp. 421–432; and C. F. Amerasinghe, 'The formal character of the rule of local remedies', *Zeitschrift für ausländisches öffentliches Recht und Völkerrecht* (ZaöRV), vol. 25, 1965, p. 445. On the controversy as to the qualification of the rule, *see* J. Fawcett, 'The exhaustion of local remedies: substance or procedure?', *British Yearbook of International Law* (BYIL) (1954) p. 452. For more contemporary perspectives, *see especially* A. A. Cancado Trindade, *The application of the rule of exhaustion of local remedies in International law. Its rationale in the international protection of individual rights* (Cambridge Univ. Press, 1983); D. Sullinger, *L'épuisement des voies de recours internes en droit international général et dans la Convention européenne des droits de l'homme* (Imprimerie des Arts et Métiers, Lausanne, 1979). I have argued elsewhere that, while the local remedies rules may be seen as a rule of procedure where the violation has its direct source in the acts of a State organ, it should be treated as rule of substance where the responsibility of the State is alleged to arise from a failure to control the acts of private parties: *see* O. De Schutter, *Fonction de juger et droits fondamentaux* (Bruylant, Bruxelles, 1999) pp. 269–279; and O. De Schutter, 'La subsidiarité dans la Convention européenne des droits de l'homme : la dimension procédurale', in M. Verdussen *et al.* (ed), *L'Europe de la subsidiarité* (Bruylant, Bruxelles, 2000) pp. 63–130.

[80] *See e.g., X and Y* v. *the Netherlands,* 26 March 1985, ECHR, Series A no. 91, pp. 11–13, paras. 21–27 (abuse committed against a mentally disabled minor of more than 16 years of age, revealing a lacuna in the Dutch criminal legislation which in such circumstances offered insufficient protection to the victims of sexual abuse); *Stubbings and Others* v. *the United Kingdom,* 22 October 1996, *Reports of Judgments and Decisions* 1996-IV, p. 1505, paras. 62–64 (while noting that "Children and other vulnerable individuals are entitled to State protection, in the form of effective deterrence, from such grave types of interference with essential aspects of their private lives", the Court finds that "In the instant case . . . such protection was afforded" despite the fact that the applicants had been sexually abused when they were children and were barred from seeking a remedy against their alleged abusers); *A.* v. *the United Kingdom*, 23 September 1998, ECHR, para. 22 (concerning a child beaten repeatedly by his stepfather: the Court concluded that

the State is only engaged in such instances because its organs have failed to fulfil their duties to protect the human rights of individuals under the jurisdiction of the State.[81] For example, if the legislature has failed to adopt legislation which sufficiently discourages violations from being committed or the executive has failed to enforce the applicable legislation or the judiciary has failed to adequately protect the rights of the victims, even though these rights may be not only recognized under international law, but are also protected under internal legislation. Unless such failures may be identified in the behaviour of the State organs, the State will not be held responsible for an event which, although it might be described as a violation of the rights of the individual, will not be treated as a violation of the obligations imposed on the State by the European Convention on Human Rights to which it is a party.[82] A third and again very different situation is where the State is willing or sufficiently attentive to the need to prevent violations from occurring, but *unable* to effectively control actors operating on its national territory. It is this situation which the following section examines.

3.2. The 'Jurisdiction' of the State on National Territory Escaping its Effective Control

From the logic of *Cyprus* v. *Turkey*, the question of a State unable to effectively exercise control over an event occurring on its national territory should not be whether the State has deployed all the efforts which could have been reasonably expected in order to prevent violations from occurring. Rather, the preliminary question to be answered is whether the presumption that the State is in control of the events occurring on that territory may be

---

the law in the United Kingdom does not provide adequate protection to children against treatment or punishment contrary to Article 3 ECHR).

[81] L. Condorelli, 'L'imputation à l'Etat d'un fait internationalement illicite : solutions classiques et nouvelles tendances', 189 *RCADI*, 1984-IV, pp. 9–222, p. 153 ("ce qui est imputé à l'Etat n'est pas le fait de particuliers mais le comportement des organes de l'Etat ; ce dernier comportement, que la conduite de l'individu se limite à mettre en évidence, peut naturellement avoir un caractère omissif ou commissif et enclenche la responsabilité internationale de l'Etat lorsqu'il représente l'infraction à une obligation de prévention et/ou de répression").

[82] *See* O. De Schutter, 'L'intervention des autorités publiques dans les relations familiales et l'obligation de prévenir les mauvais traitements : vie familiale et droit à la protection de l'enfant dans la jurisprudence de la Cour européenne des droits de l'homme', *Revue trimestrielle de droit familial*, 3/1999, pp. 427–455.

maintained, or whether it should be replaced by a more realistic view about its capacity to influence those events. Indeed, the understanding of the 2001 *Cyprus* v. *Turkey* judgment quoted above is that where a State is unable to control a part of its national territory, it has no 'jurisdiction' over the events occurring there, and either another State party to the Convention may be identified as the State effectively exercising jurisdiction (such as Turkey with respect to Northern Cyprus) or, however regrettable it may be, there is a vacuum in the system of protection of the Convention.

This latter solution, however, is precisely the one which the *Ilascu and Others* v. *Moldova and Russia* judgment challenges. Although the Court finds that "the Moldovan Government, the only legitimate government of the Republic of Moldova under international law, *does not exercise authority over part of its territory*, namely that part which is under the effective control of the [Moldavian Republic of Transdniestria]", the Court does not conclude from this that – it being impossible for Moldova to exercise its jurisdiction on the said territory – this State may not be held responsible for what occurs in the region concerned. Instead, the Court considers that "*even in the absence of effective control over the Transdniestrian region*, Moldova still has a positive obligation under Article 1 of the Convention to take the diplomatic, economic, judicial or other measures that it is in its power to take and are in accordance with international law to secure to the applicants the rights guaranteed by the Convention".[83] In the approach the Court took to the Cypriot cases, jurisdiction was an all-or-nothing concept, which therefore could constitute a threshold question to be answered before examining whether the alleged violation may be attributed to the State and whether the State has violated its obligations under the Convention. Jurisdiction now becomes a relative concept, a matter of degree determining the scope of the obligations of the State concerned. The Court considers that:[84]

> "where a Contracting State is prevented from exercising its authority over the whole of its territory by a constraining *de facto* situation, such as obtains when a separatist regime is set up, whether or not this is accompanied by military occupation by another State, it does not thereby cease to have jurisdiction within the meaning of Article 1 of the Convention over that part of its territory temporarily subject to a local authority sustained by rebel forces or by another State.

Ilascu and Others v. *Moldova and Russia*, *supra* note 9, paras. 330–331 (my emphasis in both quotes).

[84] *Ibid*., para. 333.

> Nevertheless such a factual situation *reduces the scope of that jurisdiction* in that the undertaking given by the State under Article 1 must be considered by the Court only in the light of the Contracting State's positive obligations towards persons within its territory. The State in question must endeavour, with all the legal and diplomatic means available to it vis-à-vis foreign States and international organisations, to continue to guarantee the enjoyment of the rights and freedoms guaranteed by the Convention."

This statement is methodologically disputable. The notion of 'positive obligations', in fact, had until presently been used in an entirely different context where, precisely because a State exercised (complete) jurisdiction over a course of events (was in 'full and effective control'), it could be required to protect the rights and freedoms guaranteed to the individuals under the Convention, by adopting the necessary measures. It appears here to fulfil a different function, as if in order to compensate for extending the 'jurisdiction' of the State in the meaning of Article 1 ECHR – and thus, the scope of the obligations of the State under the Convention – beyond what would be justified by a realistic appreciation of its effective ability to influence a situation. Moldova should be considered to have jurisdiction on the region where the self-proclaimed Moldavian Republic of Transdniestria is established, but we are not to worry: its obligations with respect to the continued arbitrary detention of the applicants in the hands of the authorities of that separatist republic are strictly tailored to what may be required from the Moldovian authorities in such a situation. The 'positive obligations' imposed on them relate only to "the measures needed to re-establish [the control of Moldova] over Transdniestrian territory, as an expression of its jurisdiction" (although as the Court acknowledges, "there was little Moldova could do" in this respect),[85] and to "measures to ensure respect for the applicants' rights, including attempts to secure their release".[86] Therefore, although, as stated by judge Sir Nicolas Bratza, the reliance on the concept of 'positive obligations' may be a source of confusion ("both misleading and unhelpful in the present context" in his words), the idea behind the use of that concept is nevertheless clear: a State may not seek refuge behind its inability to control portions of its national territory in order to escape its obligation to do everything which it legally and practically can do in order to secure the rights of the Convention on all its territory.

It is useful to contrast the *Ilascu and Others* judgment with the attitude of the Court in its *Assanidze* v. *Georgia* judgment, delivered by the Grand

---

[85] *Ilascu and Others* v. *Moldova and Russia*, *supra* note 9, para. 341.
[86] *Ibid.*, para. 339.

Chamber only three months earlier. The applicant in this case had been held in custody in the 'Ajarian Autonomous Republic' in Georgia since 1993, after having been arrested and convicted for allegedly illegal financial dealings. Although the Georgian president had granted him a pardon in 1999 suspending the remaining two years of his sentence, he had remained in detention. Indeed, soon after the presidential decree granting the pardon had been adopted, the Ajarian High Court had declared the pardon null and void, and the judgments of the Georgian Supreme Court quashing that latter judgment had been ignored by the local authorities in the Ajarian Autonomous Republic. After the applicant was again convicted on another ground in 2000 by the Ajarian High Court, the Supreme Court of Georgia acquitted him. However, that acquittal judgment was also never executed. Despite the best efforts of the General Prosecutor's Office of Georgia, the Public Defender, the Georgian Ministry of Justice and the Legal Affairs Committee of the Georgian Parliament, and even the President of the Republic of Georgia, seeking the immediate release of Mr Assanidzé, the local authorities in the Ajarian Autonomous Republic refused to comply, apparently believing that he had been conspiring against the President of the autonomous Republic.

When the question of whether Mr Assanidzé was subjected to arbitrary detention in violation of Article 5(1) ECHR was presented to the European Court of Human Rights, the Georgian government "accepted that the Ajarian Autonomous Republic was an integral part of Georgia and that the matters complained of were within the jurisdiction of the Georgian Republic", and it moreover insisted that "Georgian law was duly applied in the [Ajarian Autonomous Republic] and that, apart from the present case, with its strong political overtones, there was no problem of judicial cooperation between the central authorities and the local Ajarian authorities" .[87] The Court took the view that the events complained of by the applicant fell under the 'jurisdiction' of the Georgian State:[88]

> "The Ajarian Autonomous Republic is indisputably an integral part of the territory of Georgia and subject to its competence and control. In other words, there is a presumption of competence. The Court must now determine whether there is valid evidence to rebut that presumption.
>
> In that connection, the Court notes, firstly, that Georgia has ratified the Convention for the whole of its territory. Furthermore, it is common ground

[87] *Assanidze* v. *Georgia,* 8 April 2004, ECHR, no. 71503/01, paras. 133–134.
[88] *Ibid.*, paras. 139–143.

> that the Ajarian Autonomous Republic has no separatist aspirations and that no other State exercises effective overall control there (see, by converse implication, *Ilascu, Lesco, Ivantoc and Petrov-Popa v. Moldova and the Russian Federation* [GC], no. 48787/99, decision of 4 July 2001; and *Loizidou v. Turkey* (preliminary objections) cited above). [. . .]
>
> Thus, the presumption referred to . . . above is seen to be correct. Indeed, for reasons of legal policy – the need to maintain equality between the State Parties and to ensure the effectiveness of the Convention – it could not be otherwise. But for the presumption, the applicability of the Convention could be selectively restricted to parts only of the territory of certain State Parties, thus rendering the notion of effective human-rights protection underpinning the entire Convention meaningless while, at the same time, allowing discrimination between the State Parties, that is to say beween those which accepted the application of the Convention over the whole of their territory and those which did not."

It is clear from this passage that the Court considers the 'presumption' that the jurisdiction of a State extends to all its national territory is an absolute one where no other State *de facto* occupies a portion of the territory: even where the central authorities fail to impose their will on autonomous entities within the State, the State remains fully responsible under international law, and it may not shelter behind the inability of the central authorities to impose on the subordinate levels that they comply with the rights and freedoms of the Convention.[89] Thus, although the Court does not deny in *Assanidze* that

---

[89] On the obligation to control the lower levels of the administration, *see* among many others *Ireland* v. *the United Kingdom*, 18 January 1978, ECHR, Series A no. 25, pp. 90–91, para. 239. As recalled by the European Court of Human Rights in *Assanidze* (para. 141 of the judgment), the European Convention on Human Rights contains no 'federal clause', comparable to Article 28 in the American Convention on Human Rights. This provision, which was inserted in the American Convention on Human Rights at the request of the United States, introduces a differentiation between the obligations concerning subject matters which fall under the "legislative and judicial jurisdiction" of the national (i.e., federal) government, which the central authorities must implement (Article 28(1) ACHR), and those concerning subject matter on which the constituent units of the federal state have jurisdiction, with regard to which the obligation of the central authorities is to "immediately take suitable measures, in accordance with its constitution and its laws, to the end that the competent authorities of the constituent units may adopt appropriate provisions for the fulfillment of the Convention" (Article 28(2) ACHR). On the interpretation of Article 28 ACHR by the Inter-American Court of Human Rights, *see* in particular the *Garrido and Baigorria* case, *Reparations (Art. 63(1) American Convention on*

"the central authorities have taken all the procedural steps possible under domestic law to secure compliance with the judgment acquitting the applicant, have sought to resolve the dispute by various political means and have repeatedly urged the Ajarian authorities to release him" – but have failed – and that therefore "under the domestic system, the matters complained of by the applicant were directly imputable to the local Ajarian authorities",[90] it concludes nevertheless that this should not affect the scope of the 'jurisdiction' of the State of Georgia under Article 1 ECHR: "It is only the responsibility of the Georgian State itself – not that of a domestic authority or organ – that is in issue before the Court".[91] This conclusion was adopted unanimously by the Grand Chamber.

3.3. The Positive Obligation to Exercise Effective Control on all of the National Territory

On their surface, *Assanidze* and *Ilascu* look alike: in both cases, the 'jurisdiction' of the State is presumed to extend to its entire national territory, whatever the difficulties the central authorities may be experiencing in imposing their will to other parts of the administration. In reality, not only are the factual settings of both cases very dissimilar, but moreover *Ilascu* in two important respects contradicts the reasoning of the Court in *Assanidze*. *Assanidze* was justified by the idea that no other State exercises overall control on the territory of the Ajarian Autonomous Republic; in *Ilascu* on the contrary, it is despite the fact that the Federation of Russia exercises overall control of Transdniestria that the 'jurisdiction' of Moldova is considered to extend to that territory. 'Jurisdiction' in *Assanidze* was considered an all-or-nothing concept, designating in fact the sovereign power on the portion of territory where the events complained of had

---

Human Rights), judgment of 27 August 1998, Series C, No. 39, para. 38–46, and especially the reminder that under general public international law, a State cannot in principle "plead its federal structure to avoid complying with an international obligation". In this respect, the confirmation in Article 50 of the International Covenant on Civil and Political Rights that the provisions of the Covenant "shall extend to all parts of federal States without any limitations or exceptions" is unwelcome precisely because it is redundant and simply restates the general rule (*see* on the circumstances of the introduction of this rule M. Sorensen, 'Federal States and the International Protection of Human Rights', 46 *American Journal of International Law*, p. 207).

[90] *Assanidze* v. *Georgia, supra* note 37, para. 145.

[91] *Ibid.*, para. 149.

occurred, in order to identify the potential responsibility of that power during those events. In *Ilascu*, 'jurisdiction' is seen instead as a relative concept, not only in the sense that what happens in Transdniestria is considered to be influenced both by Moldova and Russia who therefore are jointly responsible for the situation denounced before the Court, but also in the sense that, the 'jurisdiction' of Moldova on the Moldavian Republic of Transdniestria is not complete (its 'scope' is 'reduced', says the Court). The obligations of the Moldovan authorities are tailored to the extent of the jurisdiction effectively exercised, as if the European Convention on Human Rights contained a 'federal clause' similar to Article 28 of the American Convention on Human Rights.[92] The Court arrives at the conclusion that the obligations of Moldova are limited to taking all the legal and practical steps they are able to in order to secure the release of the applicants arbitrarily detained in Transdniestria. It thus reasons as if the authorities of the Moldavian Republic of Transdniestria were private actors not part of the State apparatus, which is entirely justifiable. What is more remarkable, and which the separate opinions appended to the *Ilascu* judgment rightly emphasize, is that this is accompanied by a move towards a concept of 'jurisdiction' which has become relative, tailored to the degree of control effectively exercised.

What significance should be attached to this shift? In his partly dissenting opinion in *Ilascu and Others*, judge Loucaides suggests that the position of the Court, insofar as it imposes on Moldova positive obligations to secure the rights of the Convention even with respect to situations on which it cannot exercise its effective control, would lead to absurd results as it

> "would lead, for instance . . . to the illogical conclusion that all High Contracting Parties to the Convention, would have jurisdiction and responsibility for violations of the human rights of persons in any territory of a High Contracting Party, including their own but outside their actual authority (either *de facto* or *de jure* or both depending on the territory), merely by virtue of not pressing to secure the Convention rights in that territory through action against the State which does in reality exercise such authority over these persons".

This is disingenuous and it misrepresents the position of the majority which the partly dissenting opinion criticizes. In fact, the imposition of positive obligations on Moldova cannot be dissociated from the fact that the situation

[92] *See supra* note 61.

complained of – the continued arbitrary detention of the applicants – essentially occurred on the national territory of Moldova, and should therefore be presumed to be under the jurisdiction of that State. It is *to the extent the situation occurred on its national territory*, that Moldova was under an obligation to take all the necessary steps to ensure that the rights are freedoms of the Convention are secured to all, and that it could not simply seek shelter behind an alleged incapacity to influence the situation leading to a violation of the Convention.[93]

Although the *Ilascu* judgment therefore does not represent a radical departure from a territory-based understanding of the concept of 'jurisdiction' as a condition for State responsibility under the European Convention on Human Rights, it nevertheless does mark an evolution in the case-law, insofar as the Court recognizes that 'jurisdiction', rather than being necessarily exclusive may be *shared* between two of more States parties to the Convention. This may be the case either where more than one State exercises a decisive influence on the situation potentially constituting a breach of the Convention, even by unilateral action, or where two or more States could, by their *combined* action, decisively exercise such an influence. We see, then, how the debate on the relationship between the concept of 'jurisdiction' in the meaning of Article 1 ECHR and the national territory stands in close relationship to the debate on the ability of the European Convention on Human Rights to adequately address situations where, by concluding treaties among themselves, the States parties to the Convention in fact reallocate among themselves the responsibility of ensuring compliance with the Convention. We thus arrive at the third and most difficult question addressed in this paper.

[93] Judge Loucaides describes the position of the Court as one according to which "a High Contracting Party to the Convention has 'jurisdiction' over any person outside its authority simply because it does not take the political or other measures mentioned in general terms by the majority". In fact, the positive obligations identified by the Court do not extend to "any person outside the authority of the State", but only to those on its territory, who therefore would be under its jurisdiction had the State the possibility to assert effectively its authority on those persons.

4. State Jurisdiction and Intergovernmental Cooperation

4.1. 'Jurisdiction' and the Scope of State Obligations in the Framework of Inter-State Cooperation

When it is confronted with situations where the *combined* actions of two of more States parties to the Convention have created a situation allegedly in violation of the obligations of each State under this instrument, the European Court of Human Rights has consistently adhered to three principles. First, States may not, by the conclusion of international agreements following the accession to the Convention, escape their obligations under this instrument. *Pacta sunt servanda*: unless all the States parties to the Convention agree to revising the content of the mutual obligations they have towards one another, no State individually may bind itself by international treaties which will make it impossible for that State to continue to comply with its Convention obligations, without engaging its responsibility under this instrument.[94] In particular, where certain States parties to the European Convention on Human Rights have agreed to create between themselves an international organisation, the Court has emphasized that the Convention "does not exclude the transfer of competences to international organisations provided

[94] This is of course in conformity with the rule expressed in Article 30 of the Vienna Convention on the Law of Treaties of 23 May 1969, entitled 'Application of successive treaties relating to the same subject-matter' (*see, specifically*, Article 30 para. 4, b)). As explained by Special Rapporteur Fitzmaurice: "Since anything that some of the parties to a treaty do *inter se* under another treaty is clearly *res inter alios acta*, it cannot in law result in any formal diminution of the obligation of these parties under the earlier treaty, or affect juridically the rights or position of the other parties, which remain legally intact and subsisting" (G. Fitzmaurice, 'Third Report', 2 *ILC Yearbook* (1958), p. 43). For further discussions of the rule, *see in particular* Ch. Rousseau, 'De la compatibilité des normes juridiques contradictoires dans l'ordre international', 39 *Revue générale de droit international public* (1932) pp. 133–192; E. W. Vierdag, 'The Time of the Conclusion of a Multilateral Treaty: Article 30 of thje Vienna Convention on the Law of Treaties and Related Provisions', 59 *British Yearbook of International Law* (1988) pp. 92–111; W. Czaplinski and G. M. Danilenko, 'Conflict of Norms in International Law' , 21 *Netherlands International Law Review* (1990) pp. 12–28; J. B. Mus, 'Conflicts Between Treaties in International Law' , 29 *Netherlands International Law Review* (1998) pp. 208–232.

that Convention rights continue to be 'secured'. Member States' responsibility therefore continues even after such a transfer".[95]

However, in order not to discourage the development in the future of intergovernmental cooperation, and seeking to offer a reading of the Convention, to the fullest extent possible, in the light of any relevant rules and principles of international law applicable in relations between the Contracting Parties,[96] the European Court of Human Rights has recently concluded that it would presume the compatibility with the European Convention on Human Rights of acts adopted by States in fulfilment of the obligations imposed upon them as members of an international organisation, to the extent that these acts may be adequately reviewed for their compatibility with fundamental rights in the system set up within that organisation itself. This is the second principle to which it adheres. It stated in the *'Bosphorus Airways'* case[97] that:

---

[95] *Matthews* v. *the United Kingdom*, 18 February 1999, ECHR, no. 24833/94, para. 32.

[96] In conformity with Article 31 para. 3(c) of the Vienna Convention on the Law of Treaties of 23 May 1969 and as according to the well-established case-law of the Court: *see Al-Adsani* v. *the United Kingdom*, ECHR, no. 35763/97, *Reports of Judgements and Decisions* 2001-XI, para. 55.

[97] *Bosphorus Hava Yolları Turizm ve Ticaret Anonim Şirketi* v. *Ireland, supra* note 77. The case concerned the impounding of an aircraft, which was the property of Yugoslav Airlines ('JAT'), the national airline of the former Yugoslavia, and had been leased by the applicant Turkish company. The impounding was justified as part of the implementation of UN Security Council Resolution 820 (1993) of 17 April 1993, which provided that States should impound, *inter alia*, all aircraft in their territories "in which a majority or controlling interest is held by a person or undertaking in or operating" from the FRY. That Resolution had been implemented by EC Regulation 990/93 which entered into force on 28 April 1993 (O.J.L. 102/14 (1993)), and implemented in turn in Ireland by the European Communities (Prohibition of Trade with the Federal Republic of Yugoslavia (Serbia and Montenegro)) Regulations 1993 (SI 144 of 1993). In a judgment of 30 July 1996 delivered in response to a referral from the Irish Supreme Court, the European Court of Justice confirmed that Article 8 of EC Regulation 990/93 applied to the aircraft concerned and that the impounding did not violate the fundamental rights of the applicant company. The restriction to the right to property of the company, in particular, was proportionate to the fulfilment of "an objective of general interest . . . fundamental for the international community, which consists in putting an end to the state of war in the region and to the massive violations of human rights and humanitarian international law in the Republic of Bosnia-Herzegovina".

> "State action taken in compliance with such legal obligations [deriving from commitments of a State party to the Convention under a treaty concluded subsequently to their accession to the Convention] is justified as long as the relevant organisation [set up by such subsequent treaty] is considered to protect fundamental rights, as regards both the substantive guarantees offered and the mechanisms controlling their observance, in a manner which can be considered at least equivalent to that for which the Convention provides . . . By 'equivalent' the Court means 'comparable': any requirement that the organisation's protection be 'identical' could run counter to the interest of international co-operation pursued".[98]

Such State action implementing obligations imposed under treaties entered into by States parties to the Convention after their accession to this latter instrument will be presumed compatible with the Convention "[i]f such equivalent protection is considered to be provided by the organisation, the presumption will be that a State has not departed from the requirements of the Convention when it does no more than implement legal obligations flowing from its membership of the organisation"[99] – that is, when the State is deprived of any margin of appreciation in the implementation of those obligations. However, such a presumption may not be absolute. The Court reiterates its view according to which "absolving Contracting States completely from their Convention responsibility in the areas covered by such a transfer would be incompatible with the purpose and object of the Convention: the guarantees of the Convention could be limited or excluded at will thereby depriving it of its peremptory character and undermining the practical and effective nature of its safeguards". It follows not only (according to the first principle mentioned above) that the State "is considered to retain Convention liability in respect of treaty commitments subsequent to the entry into force of the Convention",[100] but also that the presumption of compatibility with the Convention of acts adopted by States parties by which they implement obligations resulting from their membership of international organisations where fundamental rights are recognized a protection equivalent to that provided under the European Convention on Human Rights "can be rebutted if, in the circumstances of a particular case, it is considered that the protection of Convention rights was manifestly deficient. In such cases, the interest of international co-operation

---

[98] *Bosphorus Hava Yolları Turizm* v. *Ticaret Anonim Şirketi* v. *Ireland*, *supra* note 77, para. 155.
[99] *Ibid.*, para. 156.
[100] *Ibid.*, para. 154.

would be outweighed by the Convention's role as a 'constitutional instrument of European public order' in the field of human rights".[101]

This position of the Court is clearly inspired by the attitude of the German Federal Constitutional Court (*Bundesverfassungsgericht*) towards European Community law. Indeed, the German Federal Constitutional Court has agreed to recognize the supremacy of European Community law, without scrutinizing its compatibility with the fundamental rights protected under the German Basic Law (*Grundgesetz*), only after it surmounted its initial hesitations and was convinced that fundamental rights are adequately protected in the legal order of the Community.[102] It is already that attitude of the German courts which led the European Commission of Human Rights, in 1990, to develop the doctrine of "equivalent protection", according to which the monitoring bodies set up by the European Convention on Human Rights should not control acts adopted by States parties as Member States of the European Community in fulfilment of their Community obligations insofar

---

[101] *Ibid.*, para. 156.

[102] This case-law has been developing in different phases, to which judgments adopted respectively in 1974 ('Solange I') (BverfGE 37, 271 (280)), 1987 ('Solange II')(BverfGE 73, 339 (379)), 1993 (the 'Maastricht' decision) (BverfGE 89, 155 (174)) and 2000 (the 'Bananas' decision)(2 BvL 1/97, EuGRZ 2000, p. 328 (333)) correspond. The development of this case-law has been abundantly commented upon; I will therefore be excused for not describing it in detail. The main lesson is that, having been reassured by the development of a system ensuring that fundamental rights will be protected within the legal order of the European Community at a level substantially equivalent to that provided by the German Basic Law – the doubts raised by certain national constitutional courts about the compatibility of the doctrine of supremacy of EC Law with the protection of fundamental rights under national constitutions having led the European Court of Justice to develop its protection of fundamental rights as part of the general principles of European Community law – the *Bundesverfassungsgericht* now applies a presumption of compatibility with the requirements of fundamental rights of EC Law. It will therefore agree to review the compatibility of EC law with those requirements only in situations where the applicant brings forward elements tending to demonstrate that the level of protection of fundamental rights has not been maintained at the level at which it was found by the *Bundesverfassungsgericht* to be satisfactory in its 'Solange II' decision of 22 April 1987. *See* regarding these developments, *inter alia*, J. Limbach, 'La coopération des juridictions dans la future architecture européenne des droits fondamentaux. Contribution à la redéfinition des rapports entre la Cour constitutionnelle fédérale allemande, la Cour de justice des Communautés européennes et la Cour européenne des droits de l'homme', 12: 10-12 *Revue universelle des droits de l'homme* (2000) pp. 369–372.

as the legal order of the Community provided for its own system of protection of fundamental rights which could be considered to be generally satisfactory.[103] That doctrine has been relied upon in later cases by the European Court of Human Rights, even before its spectacular reaffirmation in *Bosphorus Airways*. Most notably, it appears at least implicitly in two judgments the Court delivered on 18 February 1999 where it considered that the application by the German courts of the rule on immunity of jurisdiction of the European Space Agency does not constitute a violation of Article 6 § 1 of the Convention, which guarantees in principle a right of access to court. Indeed, the Court considered there that, insofar as it corresponds to a long-standing practice established in the interest of the good working of international organisations and fits within a "trend towards extending and strengthening international cooperation in all domains of modern society",[104] applying a rule on immunity of jurisdiction of international organisations is permissible under the Convention, insofar as "the applicants had available to them reasonable alternative means to protect effectively their rights under the Convention".[105] It thus recognized that the setting up of remedies within the internal structures of the European Space Agency could ensure compatibility with the requirements of Article 6 § 1 of the Convention, although the immunity of jurisdiction of the ESA implied that it could not be sued before the domestic courts of Germany. Although the applicants in these cases were clearly under the 'jurisdiction' of Germany – the issue was not even raised before the Court –Germany could justify denying access to its courts by pointing at the alternatives open to the applicants under the rules of the European Space Agency.

Although it establishes a presumption of compatibility with the European Convention on Human Rights of State action implementing rules of an international organisation within which fundamental rights are protected at an equivalent level, the position of the European Court of Human Rights as expressed in *Bosphorus Airways* does not question that a State party to the Convention still exercises its 'jurisdiction' when it

---

[103] European Commission on Human Rights, *M. & Co* v. *Germany,* 9 February 1990, ECHR, no. 13258/87, DR 64, p. 138; European Commission on Human Rights, *Heinz* v. *the Contracting Parties also parties to the European Patent Convention,* 10 January 1994, no. 21090/92, DR 76-A, p. 125.

[104] *Beer and Regan* v. *Germany*, 18 February 1999, no. 28934/95 para. 53; *Waite and Kennedy* v. *Germany*, 18 February 1999, no. 26083/94, para. 63. Both judgments were decided by a unanimous Court.

[105] *Beer and Regan* v. *Germany*, *supra* note 104, para. 58; *Waite and Kennedy* v. *Germany*, *supra* note 104, para. 73.

implements its obligations under such rules, even where, as in the circumstances of that case, its national authorities are left no discretion whatsoever as to the means by which to comply with those obligations.[106]

Through this case-law, the Court seeks to ensure in particular that the Convention will not constitute an obstacle to further European integration by the creation among the Member States of the Union of a supranational organisation – a development which, as the representatives of the European Commission argued in their submissions to the Court, would be seriously impeded if the Member States were to verify the compatibility with the European Convention on Human Rights of the acts of Union law before agreeing to apply them, even in situations where they have no margin of appreciation to exercise . But the Court stops short of stating that because the Member States have transferred certain powers to a supranational organisation, the European Community, the situations resulting directly from the application of European Community acts would escape their 'jurisdiction' in the meaning of Article 1 of the Convention. Instead, while the Convention remains applicable to such situations, and while the States parties remain fully answerable to the supervisory bodies it sets up, it is only the level of scrutiny exercised by the European Court of Human Rights which is influenced by the circumstance that the alleged violation has its source in the application of an act adopted within the European Community. The Court considers that, insofar as the legal order of the European Union ensures an adequate level of protection of fundamental rights, and unless it is confronted with a "dysfunction of the mechanisms of control of the observance of Convention rights" or with a "manifest deficiency",[107] it may presume that, by complying with the legal obligations under this legal order, the EU Member States are not violation their obligations under the ECHR.

The *Waite and Kennedy*, *Beer and Regan*, and *Bosphorus Airways* cases, all concern situations where an international organisation was considered to have internal mechanisms offering protection of fundamental rights

[106] *See* para. 137 of the judgment: "In the present case it is not disputed that the act about which the applicant complained, the detention of the aircraft leased by it for a period of time, was implemented by the authorities of the respondent State on its territory following a decision to impound of the Irish Minister for Transport. In such circumstances the applicant company, as the addressee of the impugned act, fell within the 'jurisdiction' of the Irish State, with the consequence that its complaint about that act is compatible *ratione loci, personae* and *materiae* with the provisions of the Convention."

[107] *Bosphorus Hava Yolları Turizm* v. *Ticaret Anonim Şirketi* v. *Ireland, supra* note 77, para. 166.

equivalent to that which would have been afforded under the European Convention on Human Rights. The question whether this doctrine of 'equivalent protection' should play a similar role in the context of inter-State cooperation remains debated. The Court distinguishes the *Bosphorus Airways* situation from *Pellegrini* v. *Italy* – where Italy was found to have violated the right to a fair trial guaranteed in Article 6 § 1 of the Convention for having enforced a judgment delivered by the Vatican courts in violation of the rights of defence of the applicant[108] – on the basis that "enforcement of a judgment not of a Contracting Party to the Convention [[109]] . . . is not comparable to compliance with a legal obligation emanating from an international organisation to which Contracting Parties have transferred part of their sovereignty".[110] The implied suggestion is that, where States parties to the Convention co-operate with one another, they may subject the acts of the other States to only minimal review; instead, where they cooperate with States not parties to the European Convention on Human Rights (or when the implement secondary legislation adopted within international organisations not offering a protection of human rights at a level similar to that guaranteed by the European Convention on Human Rights), there could be no presumption that the measures adopted in the framework of such co-operation comply with the requirements of the Convention, and a strict scrutiny of such compliance therefore would be required.

Although, when faced with situations where States have cooperated with one another, the Court occasionally seems to treat Contracting Parties to the Convention the same way it treats third States, it does allow to some extent for a presumption that the behaviour of the States Parties will be in conformity with the requirements of the Convention.[111] In the case of *T.I.* v. *the United Kingdom* for instance, the applicant was facing the risk of being returned by the United Kingdom to Germany from where he feared he might be expelled to Sri Lanka where he believed his security would be threatened. In the inadmissibility decision of 7 March 2000 reached by the European

---

[108] *Pellegrini* v. *Italy*, 20 July 2001, ECHR (4th sect.), no. 30882/96, para. 40.

[109] The Holy See is not a Contracting Party to the European Convention on Human Rights.

[110] *Bosphorus Hava Yolları Turizm* v. *Ticaret Anonim Şirketi* v. *Ireland*, *supra* note 77, para. 157.

[111] *See generally* on this question O. De Schutter, 'L'espace de liberté, de sécurité et de justice et la responsabilité individuelle des Etats au regard de la Convention européenne des droits de l'homme', in G. de Kerchove and A. Weyembergh (eds.), *L'espace pénal européen: enjeux et perspectives* (éd. de l'ULB, Bruxelles, 2002) pp. 222–247.

Court of Human Rights, the Court considered that "[t]he indirect removal . . . to an intermediate country, which is also a contracting state, does not affect the responsibility of the United Kingdom to ensure that the applicant is not, as a result of its decision to expel, exposed to treatment contrary to Article 3 of the Convention".[112] However, the fact that Germany is bound by the European Convention on Human Rights does lead the Court to presume that the fears expressed by the applicant are ill-founded. Indeed, although it considers that it should not establish a blind – or absolute – presumption that the removal of the applicant to Germany will not expose him to a risk of violation of his Convention rights, the Court says that "[t]here is . . . no basis on which [it] could assume in this case that Germany would fail to fulfil its obligations under Article 3 of the convention to provide the applicant with protection against removal to Sri Lanka if he put forward substantial grounds that he faces a risk of torture and ill-treatment in that country". Therefore, the Court allows at least for a relative presumption of compatibility with the Convention of forms of inter-State cooperation between two States parties to the Convention, although that presumption may be rebutted in the face of certain specific circumstances.[113]

On the other hand, however, both because it is reluctant to be seen to impose on third States compliance with rules of the Convention,[114] and

[112] *T.I.* v. *the United Kingdom*, 7 March 2000, ECHR, no. 43844/98 (inadmissibility).

[113] *See also*, for cases where persons suspected of links with the basque terrorist organisation ETA were surrendered by the French authorities to the Spanish police: European Commission on Human Rights, *L. Iruretagoyena* v. *France*, 12 January 1998, no. 32829/96; and European Commission on Human Rights, *J. A. Urrutikoetxea* v. *France*, 5 December 1996, no. 31113/96. These decisions illustrate the fact that Spain is bound by the European Convention on Human Rights, while not conclusive, does lead to a presumption that the treatment which the applicants can expect in the hands of the Spanish authorities will be in conformity with the Convention. In the latter decision, the absence of any ill-treatment of the applicant although he had been transferred to Spain justified this conclusion *post hoc*.

[114] Of course, technically, only the States parties to the Convention against which an application is filed before the European Court of Human Rights will be responsible for breaches of the Convention, even where such breaches originate in the fact that they have cooperated with another State having adopted a certain behavior which, if that same behavior had been adopted by the State party to the Convention, would have constituted a violation of that treaty. Where State A party to the ECHR extradites an individual to State B which is not a party thereto, State A may be in violation of its obligations under the ECHR if the individual risks being subjected to treatment which would not be allowable under Article 3 ECHR, even if that

because it seeks to remain "pragmatic"[115] when imposing certain restrictions on inter-State cooperation,[116] the Court has sometimes considered that States

treatment would violate no international obligation of the receiving State. As the European Court of Human Rights has remarked, "there is no question of adjudicating on or establishing the responsibility of the receiving country, whether under general international law, under the Convention or otherwise. In so far as any liability under the Convention is or may be incurred, it is liability incurred by the extraditing Contracting State by reason of its having taken action which has as a direct consequence the exposure of an individual to proscribed ill-treatment" (*Soering* v. *the United Kingdom*, 8 July 1989, ECHR, Series A no 161, para. 91). Nevertheless, as the Court recognizes in the same paragraph, "[t]he establishment of such responsibility [of the extraditing State] inevitably involves an assessment of conditions in the requesting country against the standards of Article 3 of the Convention".

[115] In a decision on 22 June 2004, where it considered inadmissible an application by a gay man fearing persecution on grounds of his sexual orientation if returned to Iran, a Chamber constituted within the 4th section of the European Court of Human Rights explained that "[o]n a purely pragmatic basis, it cannot be required that an expelling Contracting State only return an alien to a country which is in full and effective enforcement of all the rights and freedoms set out in the Convention". The Court suggests in this case that, insofar as the persecutions feared would not lead to violations of rights protected under Articles 2 (right to life) or 3 (torture or inhuman or degrading treatment), the existence of certain risks for the person returned should not constitute an obstacle to his or her removal from the territory (*Fashkami* v. *the United Kingdom*, 22 June 2004, ECHR (4th sect.), no. 17341/03).

[116] This concern of the Court is already expressed in the 1989 judgment of *Soering* v. *the United Kingdom*, where the Court noted that "the Convention does not govern the actions of States not Parties to it, nor does it purport to be a means of requiring the Contracting States to impose Convention standards on other States. Article 1 cannot be read as justifying a general principle to the effect that, notwithstanding its extradition obligations, a Contracting State may not surrender an individual unless satisfied that the conditions awaiting him in the country of destination are in full accord with each of the safeguards of the Convention. Indeed, as the United Kingdom Government stressed, the beneficial purpose of extradition in preventing fugitive offenders from evading justice cannot be ignored in determining the scope of application of the Convention and of Article 3 in particular" (para. 86). The Court further developed this point: "As movement about the world becomes easier and crime takes on a larger international dimension, it is increasingly in the interest of all nations that suspected offenders who flee abroad should be brought to justice. Conversely, the establishment of safe havens for fugitives would not only result in danger for the State obliged to harbour the protected person but also tend to undermine the foundations of extradition. These considerations must also be included among the factors to be taken into account in the interpretation and

parties to the Convention wishing to cooperate with non-party States were only prohibited from doing so in situations of gross injustice committed in non-party States. In the *Drozd and Janousek* judgment of 16 June 1992, when examining whether the French authorities should have verified whether the procedures followed by the Andorran courts complied with Article 6 of the Convention when asked to execute the resulting criminal conviction (at a time, as has already been recalled, when Andorra was not a party to the Convention), the Court stated:[117]

> "As the Convention does not require the Contracting Parties to impose its standards on third States or territories, France was not obliged to verify whether the proceedings which resulted in the conviction were compatible with all the requirements of Article 6 of the Convention. To require such a review of the manner in which a court not bound by the Convention had applied the principles enshrined in Article 6 would also thwart the current trend towards strengthening international cooperation in the administration of justice, a trend which is in principle in the interests of the persons concerned. The Contracting States are, however, obliged to refuse their co-operation if it emerges that the conviction is the result of a *flagrant denial of justice* (*see,* mutatis mutandis, the Soering v. the United Kingdom judgment of 7 July 1989, Series A no. 161, p. 45, para. 113)."

Thus, a third principle appears: where the alleged violation has its source in a State measure which does not directly commit the violation, but is adopted in the framework of a form of inter-State cooperation where the violation is directly attributable to the other State, the State party to the Convention giving effect to that violation or facilitating it only is bound to respect a 'core content' of the Convention, roughly corresponding to its 'international public policy' component if we rely on an analogy with private international law.

The three principles thus summarized may be contested, and the scope of their applicability in the case-law of the Court remains subject to debate. That they are currently guiding the development of this jurisprudence, however, is hardly controversial: a State party to the Convention may not, by the conclusion of a later treaty – whether this treaty sets up an international organisation or whether its subject-matter is less ambitious – derogate from its prior obligations under the Convention (first principle). Nevertheless we

---

application of the notions of inhuman and degrading treatment or punishment in extradition cases" (para. 89).

[117] *Drozd and Janousek* v. *France and Spain* 16 June 1992, ECHR, *supra* note 9, para. 110.

may presume that, where precaution has been taken to ensure that human rights remain protected at an equivalent level in the framework of the inter-State cooperation under this treaty, a State party to the Convention does not violate its obligations under this instrument when it simply complies with the resulting obligations it has agreed to in the later treaty (second principle). Finally, the acts which take place in the framework of inter-State cooperation are examined under a specific level of scrutiny: where the act of State A contributes to a violation of the rights of the individual in combination with the act of State B, a lower level of scrutiny will apply than if the act were attributable exclusively to the former State. This corresponds to our intuition that State A may not be held to account for acts committed by State B as if these acts were its own, even if State A in some way participated in the adoption of those acts or gave them effect (third principle). The conclusion of a subsequent treaty or the entering into forms of inter-State cooperation does not affect the 'jurisdiction' of the State party to the Convention, which remains bound by the Convention even in situations where it has assumed obligations under another treaty and simply implements those obligations in the adoption of the measure allegedly leading to a violation of the Convention, without exercising any margin of appreciation. It is not the existence of 'jurisdiction' on a particular situation, but only the scope of the State's obligations under the Convention which will be affected by the conclusion of this later treaty, as these obligations will be examined taking into account any other (possibly competing) international agreements entered into by the State.[118]

4.2. Positive Obligations in the Framework of Inter-State Cooperation

In contrast with these three previous principles, a fourth principle is hardly ever made explicit, because it is assumed to have an obvious character and therefore does not require any justification. We may call this the principle of

[118] Indeed, the existence of other international obligations may justify that certain restrictions be brought to the rights guaranteed under the Convention. Thus, the Court has accepted that compliance with EC law by a Contracting Party constitutes a legitimate general interest objective within the meaning of Article 1 of Protocol No. 1, *Bosphorus Hava Yolları Turizm* v. *Ticaret Anonim Şirketi* v. *Ireland*, supra note 77, no. 45036/98, para. 151, and *mutatis mutandis*, *S.A. Dangeville* v. *France*, 16 April 2002, ECHR (2nd sect.) no. 36677/97, paras. 47 and 55). It has also recognized that restrictions to the right of access to a court could be justified by the existence of treaties recognizing certain immunities (*see supra* note 10, and *infra* note 122).

individual State responsibility. According to this principle, each State individually, and not States jointly, may be found in violation of the Convention: where a situation allegedly in breach of the Convention has resulted from the combination of the action of two or more States parties to the Convention, the international responsibility of each State is to be examined separately. As a result, each State may escape responsibility under the Convention if – although the alleged violation has occurred in the context of inter-State cooperation – the violation is entirely imputable to another State and could not have been avoided by the defending State before the Court. Where, for instance, delays in judicial proceedings are attributable to the slowness of a court belonging to another legal system or to that of foreign authorities, these delays may not be imputed to the defending State, whose responsibility must be examined only with respect to the acts or omissions of its organs.[119] Where the violation of the right to have witnesses cross-examined[120] is alleged in a situation where the judicial authorities failed to secure the presence of a witness at a hearing because of the lack of cooperation of another State, this failure cannot be imputed to the defending State, whose courts may not be held responsible for that failure, where they have deployed their best efforts to ensure that presence.[121] Where an

---

[119] *See e.g., Pafitis and Others* v. *Greece*, 26 February 1998, ECHR, Reports 1998-I, para. 95 ("[a]s regards the proceedings before the Court of Justice of the European Communities [as one of the additional factors which contributed to the prolongation of the proceedings concerned], the Court notes that the Athens District Court decided on 3 August 1993 to refer a question to the Court of Justice, which gave judgment on 12 March 1996. During the intervening period the proceedings in the actions concerned were stayed, which prolonged them by two years, seven months and nine days. The Court cannot, however, take this period into consideration in its assessment of the length of each particular set of proceedings: even though it may at first sight appear relatively long, to take it into account would adversely affect the system instituted by Article 177 of the EEC Treaty [now Article 234 EC] and work against the aim pursued in substance in that Article"). *See also Karalyos and Huber* v. *Hungary and Greece*, 6 April 2004, ECHR, no. 75116/01.

[120] Article 6 para. 3(d) of the Convention provides that "[e]veryone charged with a criminal offence has the following minimum rights: . . . to examine or have examined witnesses against him and to obtain the attendance and examination of witnesses on his behalf under the same conditions as witnesses against him".

[121] *See e.g., G. Calabro* v. *Italy and Germany*, 21 March 2002 , ECHR, (1st sect.), (dec.) no. 59895/00. In this case where the applicant had been convicted for cocaine trafficking on the basis, *inter alia*, of statements made by an undercover agent of the German federal police ('Jürgen') who had taken part in a joint operation of the German and Italian police, this undercover agent did not testify before the Italian

individual fails to have a judgment executed because of the immunity invoked by the foreign State against which the judgment has been delivered, the State under whose jurisdiction the individual is situated and whose courts have delivered the judgment which he seeks to enforce may not be found in violation of the right of access to a court guaranteed under Article 6 para. 1 ECHR, as such a restriction may be seen as justified by the legitimate aim of respecting the immunity of execution of foreign States[122]. Nor may the individual challenge the choice of a State before foreign courts to raise the defence of sovereign immunity, as an individual is not 'under the jurisdiction' of that State when that State is simply a defendant to an action

---

courts, as the German authorities declared that he could not be found. The European Court of Human Rights took the view that "the Italian authorities made considerable efforts to obtain oral testimony from Jürgen, having made several orders requiring him to attend court to give evidence, and issued a request for evidence on commission. However, despite those efforts, they were unable to secure his presence at the hearing as, according to the information received from Germany, he could not be found". The Court considered that "it was not for the Italian authorities to make enquiries to establish the whereabouts of a person residing on the territory of a foreign State. By making an order for Jürgen's attendance and issuing an international request for evidence on commission, the Criminal Court and the Court of Appeal used the means at their disposal under domestic law to secure the presence of the witness concerned. Moreover, they had no alternative but to rely on the information received from qualified sources based in Germany . . . Under these circumstances, the Italian authorities cannot be accused of a lack of diligence engaging their responsibility before the Convention institutions". *See* for another example, in similar circumstances, *Kostu* v. *Italy*, 9 March 1999 , ECHR, (2nd sect.), (dec.) no. 33399/96, (inadmissibility).

[122] *See Kalageropoulou and Others* v. *Greece and Germany*, 12 December 2002, ECHR (1st sect.) (inadmissibility) no. 59021/00: "measures taken by a High Contracting Party which reflect generally recognised rules of public international law on State immunity cannot generally be regarded as imposing a disproportionate restriction on the right of access to a court as embodied in Article 6 para. 1. Just as the right of access to a court is an inherent part of the fair trial guarantee in that Article, so some restrictions on access must likewise be regarded as inherent, an example being those limitations generally accepted by the community of nations as part of the doctrine of State immunity (*see Al-Adsani* v. *the United Kingdom* [GC], no. 35763/97, ECHR 2001-XI, paras. 52–56). In the light of the foregoing considerations, the Court considers that although the Greek courts ordered the German State to pay damages to the applicants, this did not necessarily oblige the Greek State to ensure that the applicants could recover their debt through enforcement proceedings in Greece".

brought before such foreign courts and may thus be likened to a private individual against whom proceedings are instituted.[123]

Although it does set limits to the scope of the 'jurisdiction' of the State party to the Convention in situations of inter-State cooperation, this fourth principle does not logically contradict the previous three. It may, however, result in neutralizing them in fact. For instance, although (under the constant case-law of the European Court of Human Rights) the EU Member States, as States parties to the European Convention on Human Rights, should ensure that the European Court of Justice will comply with Article 6 para. 1 ECHR, which includes a requirement that delays of judicial proceedings will not be unreasonable, a State may justify the length of the proceedings before the national courts, which otherwise would appear unreasonable in the light of the complexity of the case and the behaviour of the parties, by the time it took for the European Court of Justice to answer a question of interpretation of EC law referred to this Court.[124] Or to consider another example, although a State might be found in violation of the Convention for executing a judgment adopted in violation of the requirements of a fair trial, for example because a criminal conviction was based on testimony which could not be contradicted by the accused and which was not corroborated by other evidence, it is uncertain whether that State would be found in violation of the Convention for having convicted a person on the basis of such testimony where the impossibility to cross-examine the witness has its source in the refusal of another State to cooperate.[125] In sum, the fact that the responsibility of each State is considered separately from the responsibility of the other States or international organisations with which it cooperates may lead to certain restrictions to fundamental rights being justified, although the same restrictions would not be allowable if the responsibility was examined for all the States involved jointly.[126] And, more importantly,

---

[123] The Court considers that "the participation of a State in the defence of proceedings against it in another State does not, without more, amount to an exercise of extraterritorial jurisdiction": *McElhinney* v. *Ireland and the United Kingdom*, 9 February 2000, ECHR (GC), no. 31253/96.

[124] *See Pafitis and Others* v. *Greece*, 26 February 1998, ECHR, *supra* note 119.

[125] *Cf.* with Eur. Ct. HR (1st sect.), *G. Calabro* v. *Italy and Germany*, 21 March 2002, no. 59895/00, *supra* note 121. It should be added however that, in this case, the conviction of the applicant by the Italian courts was not based exclusively on the declarations of the witness which the German authorities asserted could not be found in order to testify in the Italian criminal procedure.

[126] The famous *dictum* of the *Matthews* case where the Court says that the United Kingdom, "*together with all the other parties to the Maastricht Treaty*, is

the Court has never imposed on the States parties to the Convention a positive obligation either to enter into international agreements or even to fully develop the potential of existing agreements where this would ensure an improved protection of the human rights guaranteed under the Convention.

The very silence of the Court concerning the principle according to which, under the Convention, State responsibility is to be examined for each State individually, may thus be seen as revealing. It illustrates that, while the progress of international cooperation is in principle favourably seen by the European Court of Human Rights, which seeks to read the Convention in accordance with its requirements, and progressively to develop a regime under which the obligations of the Contracting Parties under the Convention will be seen as compatible with the transferral of powers to international or supranational organisations, the Court still has not conceived a requirement of deeper international cooperation to be imposed under the Convention, even where it would benefit an effective protection of the rights on individuals under the jurisdiction of the States parties.[127] Although a State

---

responsible *ratione materiae* under Article 1 of the Convention and, in particular, under Article 3 of Protocol No. 1, for the consequences of [the Treaty on the European Union, signed in Maastricht in 1992]" (*Matthews* v. *the United Kingdom*, *cited above*, note 95, para. 33 (my emphasis)), does not contradict this. On the contrary, the responsibility of the United Kingdom – like that of each other EU Member State having concluded the Maastricht Treaty without having ensured that the residents of Gibraltar would be authorized to vote in elections to the European Parliament – results from the fact that that State, considered individually, had the choice whether or not to ratify the Treaty, and that this was a choice for each State to make, rather than for the organisation as a whole or for the States acting collectively.

[127] The Court does refer to the international agreements concluded by the States parties to the ECHR as a means to evaluate the scope of their positive obligations in certain cases. This is an *estoppel*-like argument under which a State may not argue that a particular measure it is expected to adopt in order to comply with the Convention is disproportionate, when that State has already accepted to be bound by a similar obligation under another international instrument. *See e.g.*, *Ignaccolo-Zenide* v. *Romania*, 25 January 2000, ECHR (1st sect.), no. 31679/96, para. 113 (where the Cout considers that "the positive obligations that Article 8 of the Convention lays on the Contracting States in the matter of reuniting a parent with his or her children must be interpreted in the light of the Hague Convention of 25 October 1980 on the Civil Aspects of International Child Abduction. This is all the more so in the instant case as the respondent State is also a party to that instrument, Article 7 of which contains a list of measures to be taken by States to secure the prompt return of children", and remarks that "the authorities did not take the

may not unilaterally manipulate the scope of its 'jurisdiction' by entering into inter-State cooperation in order to diminish its international responsibility, the Court does not impose that it takes responsibility for situations which call for solutions based on an expansion of inter-State cooperation.

5. Conclusion

The requirement that the situation complained of by the victim of a violation alleged before the European Court of Human Rights was under the 'jurisdiction' of the defending State constitutes a preliminary condition for a finding of State responsibility under the Convention. However, although the function this notion fulfils may be clear, its precise status between norm and fact is still subject to controversy. The notion of national territory serves to justify a differentiated approach to the notion. Where a particular situation occurs on the national territory of the State party to the Convention, 'jurisdiction' of the territorial State is presumed, in the sense that any violation resulting from that situation may in principle be imputed to the State, if this situation reveals a failure by that State to comply with its obligations under the Convention.[128] Although such a presumption is absolute – a State may not escape its obligations under the Convention by claiming that a particular portion of its territory is not under effective control and therefore is not within its 'jurisdiction' – where it is unable in fact to exercise control, the obligation of the State is limited to an obligation to do all which is practically and legally possible in order to ensure that the rights of the Convention are fully respected.[129] Here, the notion of 'jurisdiction' thus functions as a *norm*: it serves to justify imposing certain obligations on the State and in the name of effective control it is *under an obligation to exercise* effective control – and indeed, is presumed to – on its national territory. Instead, where a situation occurs outside the national territory, 'jurisdiction' becomes a question of *fact*, hardly distinguishable from imputability. It serves to designate a fact, that of effective control over a

---

measures to secure the return of the children to the applicant that are set out in Article 7 of the Hague Convention ", in order to conclude that the national authorities have not put sufficient efforts into ensuring compliance with judgments imposing that the children be returned to their mother, when the father was abroad with the children); and *Iglesias Gil and A.U.I.* v. *Spain* , 29 April 2005, ECHR (4th sect.), no. 56673/00, para. 51.

[128] *See* section 3 above.

[129] *See* text corresponding to *supra* notes 67–73.

situation, which implies that the State exercising such control should comply with its obligations under the Convention to an extent commensurate with the control actually exercised.[130] The reality of effective control produces certain normative consequences, as an identification of the obligations imposed on the State will follow from identifying its actual control over certain events. But the determination whether 'jurisdiction' exists in the first place will require an examination in fact, rather than depend on the determination of the legal status of a territory or on the identification of the territorial sovereign.

This distinction between situations located on the national territory of a State party and extra-territorial situations also may be related to the distinction between negative and positive obligations. In principle, where a situation occurs on the national territory of the State or on a territory where it exercises *de facto* governmental powers, the State should guarantee the full range of Convention rights, and it is bound by the corresponding obligations, including the obligation to protect the rights of the Convention from violations committed by third parties. Instead, where a situation occurs outside the national territory, only a negative obligation will be imposed on the State not to violate the rights of the Convention when acting through its organs. Under this framework, the potential importance of *Ilascu and Others* v. *Moldova and Russia* resides in that, for the first time, the Court – and not only certain individual members of the Court[131] – recognized that certain positive extra-territorial obligations may be imposed on a State, by stating that a State's responsibility "may also be engaged on account of acts which have sufficiently proximate repercussions on rights guaranteed by the Convention, even if those repercussions occur outside its jurisdiction".[132] However, the highly specific character of the case and in particular the closeness of the links between the Federation of Russia and the separatist

---

[130] *See* section 2 above.

[131] Referring to the obligation of France and Spain to impose on the courts of the Principality of Andorra that they respect the rights of Article 6 ECHR, judges Pettiti, Valticos and Lopes Rocha, remarked in their joint dissenting opinion to the 1992 judgment of the Court in *Drozd and Janousek* v. *France and Spain* (*supra* note 9) approved by judge Walsh and Spielmann, that "the Co-Princes should even now use their authority and influence in order to give effect in Andorra to the fundamental principles of the European Convention on Human Rights, which has the force of law or even overrides national law in their own countries, and more generally is a basic element of the rule of law in Europe".

[132] *See* text corresponding to *supra* notes 67–73.

regime set up in the self-proclaimed 'Moldavian Republic of Transdniestria' makes it difficult to generalize from this isolated holding.

Although, for obvious reasons, the limits of the 'national territory' will not play the same regulating function where the notion of 'jurisdiction' is examined in the context of inter-State cooperation – in particular by the setting up of international organisations to which States may choose to attribute certain powers – here also a clear distinction, albeit still implicit, is made between negative and positive obligations. The supervisory organs of the European Convention on Human Rights have consistently held that the rights and freedoms listed in the Convention should continue to be secured after the conclusion of such treaties or the setting up of such organisations. The conclusion of later treaties, in other terms, should not result in diminishing the level of protection of fundamental rights, or this would allow the States parties to the Convention to limit the scope of their obligations under the Convention by concluding treaties with other parties. It is therefore understandable that the Court has considered that the Convention "does not exclude the transfer of competences to international organisations *provided that Convention rights continue to be 'secured'*".[133] However, although they remain bound by the Convention when they decide to conclude later international agreements, the States parties to the Convention are not under a positive obligation either to enter into international agreements which might improve the protection of the human rights they have agreed to ensure respect of under the Convention, or, where such international agreements do exist – as those leading to the creation of the European Union and the European Communities –, to ensure that the potential of those agreements is fully realized. For instance, the international organisations they have set up exercise all the powers they have been attributed in order to effectively protect the fundamental rights for the benefit of the persons situated under the jurisdiction of the Member States. The requirements of the European Convention on Human Rights impose limits on what international agreements may be concluded and to what powers may be transferred to international organisations, and they impose that certain safeguards be built into such agreements and transferrals of powers. However, they do not influence which international agreements should be concluded or which powers should be exercised in a coordinated fashion at the international level. Although few would dispute that there may be cases where the protection of fundamental rights in a harmonized or coordinated fashion at the international level may improve the quality of this

[133] *See* text corresponding to *supra* notes 94–95.

protection – in which sense human rights may be conceptualised as global public goods calling for further intergovernmental coordination – the consequences thereof for the definition of State obligations in the European Convention on Human Rights have not been drawn yet.

The interdependency of States characteristic of the era of globalization, and further reinforced by the phenomena of regional integration as most clearly exemplified on the European continent, addresses new challenges to the international law of human rights. We have up to now witnessed a defensive reaction, which consists in refusing a dilution of State responsibility resulting from the deployment of extra-territorial activities by the State not accompanied by the imposition of human rights obligations commensurate to the effective control exercised by a State outside its national territory, and in imposing certain limits to the development of forms of intergovernmental cooperation which may result in human rights violations for which no individual State may be found directly responsible. This defensive reaction is important and, indeed, crucial to the continued relevance of the European Convention of Human Rights. The time may have come however, to ask whether a more offensive attitude should not be adopted, based on the notion that 'positive obligations' could serve to determine not only the scope of the obligations of States with regard to situations falling under their jurisdiction, but also the scope of the jurisdiction itself they ought to exercise. With regard to situations occurring on its national territory, a State party to the Convention must not only respect the rights and freedoms that instrument guarantees, but also protect those rights from the acts of others. It should now be asked which obligations the State party to the Convention owes to persons whose situation it may decisively influence, even though they might be situated outside its national territory. And it should be asked which forms of international cooperation a State may be under an obligation to develop, where this appears necessary for the effective protection of human rights in a world – and on a continent – where the interdependency of States has never been stronger, and where the situation of human rights in any particular location thus is made to depend, more frequently than before, not only on the measures adopted by the territorially sovereign State, but also on measures adopted by other States sharing with a former State a single area.

Terrorism and Human Rights: EU Anti-terrorism Measures from an ECHR Perspective

August Reinisch[*]

Contents

1. Introduction

When hearing of 'Terrorism and Human Rights' in a post-9/11 world an international lawyer's mind may immediately concentrate on issues such as the lawfulness of self-defense as a response to terrorist acts, the relationship between multilateral and unilateral measures, the applicability of humanitarian law, the treatment of detainees at Guantanamo Bay, etc.[1]

Since we are here today on the occasion of the founding conference of a European Society of International Law, I think it is worthwhile to focus on the European responses to terrorist threats from a European, international law point-of-view. I intend to speak about some EU anti-terrorism measures which I find rather problematic from a human rights point-of-view – to be precise: if looked at through the lenses of the European Convention on Human Rights as interpreted by the European Commission and Court of Human Rights.

---

[*] Professor of International and European Law at the University of Vienna and Professorial Lecturer at the Bologna Center of SAIS/Johns Hopkins University in Bologna.

[1] *See* Symposium: 'A War against Terrorism': What Role for International Law? US and European Perspectives, 14 *European Journal of International Law* (2003) p. 209.

Baltic Yearbook of International Law, Volume 6, 2006, pp. 249–261.

The direction of EU activities in this area was clearly laid out in the EU Action Plan of 21 September 2001[2] which provided, *inter alia*, for the "adoption of a common definition of terrorism 'as a matter of urgency'", the "identification of presumed terrorists in Europe and of organisations supporting them in order to draw up a common list of terrorist organisations" as well as "combating the funding of terrorism as a decisive aspect of the fight against terrorism".

The two most problematic aspects of such EU action I would like to draw your attention to are: a) the definition of terrorism and b) the freezing of assets of terrorists.

2. Definition of Terrorism

For decades lawyers and diplomats have attempted to agree on an internationally acceptable definition of terrorism. Their successes, at least on the universal level, have been rather limited.[3] While the UN General Assembly has adopted resolutions reflecting a shared understanding of the notion of terrorism,[4] the UN Comprehensive Convention on International Terrorism is still under negotiation. Thus, it was not possible to speak of a clearly defined notion of terrorism as of 9/11 2001. Nevertheless, the UN Security Council in its anti-terrorism resolution 1373 of 28 September 2001 demanded from all states to ensure that "terrorist acts are established as serious criminal offences in domestic laws and regulations".[5]

---

[2] Conclusions and Plan of Action of the Extraordinary European Council Meeting on 21 September 2001, Press Release 21/9/2001 No. 140/01. Available at <http://ue.eu.int/en/Info/eurocouncil/index.htm>.

[3] *See* R. Higgins and M. Flory (eds.), *Terrorism and International Law* (KY Routledge, London, Florence, 1997).

[4] *See* UN GA Resolution of 19 November 2002, A/RES/57/27, in which the General Assembly "2. *Reiterates* that criminal acts intended or calculated to provoke a state of terror in the general public, a group of persons or particular persons for political purposes are in any circumstance unjustifiable, whatever the considerations of a political, philosophical, ideological, racial, ethnic, religious or other nature that may be invoked to justify them."

[5] UN Security Council Resolution 1373 (2) (e) provides that all States shall "[e]nsure that any person who participates in the financing, planning, preparation or perpetration of terrorist acts or in supporting terrorist acts is brought to justice and ensure that, in addition to any other measures against them, such terrorist acts are established as serious criminal offences in domestic laws and regulations and that the punishment duly reflects the seriousness of such terrorist acts;' Available at <http://ods-dds-

This Security Council mandate has given momentum to the EU's earlier attempts[6] to reach political agreement on a common definition of terrorism and ultimately led to a Third Pillar measure, the Framework Decision on Combating Terrorism of 13 June 2002.[7] Its Article 1(1) contains a definition of terrorist crimes. These have to be made part of the domestic criminal law of the EU's Member States. It provides:

> "Each Member State shall take the necessary measures to ensure that the intentional acts referred to below in points (a) to (i), as defined as offences under national law, which, given their nature or context, may seriously damage a country or an international organisation where committed with the aim of:
>
> - seriously intimidating a population, or
> - unduly compelling a Government or international organisation to perform or abstain from performing any act, or
> - seriously destabilising or destroying the fundamental political, constitutional, economic or social structures of a country or an international organisation,
>
> shall be deemed to be terrorist offences:
>
> (a) attacks upon a person's life which may cause death;
> (b) attacks upon the physical integrity of a person;
> (c) kidnapping or hostage taking;
> (d) causing extensive destruction to a Government or public facility, a transport system, an infrastructure facility, including an information system, a fixed platform located on the continental shelf, a public place or private property likely to endanger human life or result in major economic loss;
> (e) seizure of aircraft, ships or other means of public or goods transport;
> (f) manufacture, possession, acquisition, transport, supply or use of weapons, explosives or of nuclear, biological or chemical

ny.un.org/doc/UNDOC/GEN/N01/557/43/PDF/N0155743.pdf?OpenElement>, visited 11 May 2004.

[6] Such as the 1999 Tampere European Council which identified terrorism as one of the most serious violations of fundamental freedoms, human rights and of the principles of liberty and democracy.

[7] 2002/745/JHA, OJ L 164/3, 22 June 2002. Available at <http://europa.eu.int/eur-lex/pri/en/oj/dat/2002/l_164/l_16420020622en00030007.pdf>, visited 11 May 2004.

weapons, as well as research into, and development of, biological and chemical weapons;

(g) release of dangerous substances, or causing fires, floods or explosions the effect of which is to endanger human life;

(h) interfering with or disrupting the supply of water, power or any other fundamental natural resource the effect of which is to endanger human life;

(i) threatening to commit any of the acts listed in (a) to (h)."

Although this definition includes some very broad language it reflects already a restricted version of the original Commission proposal. The proposed Framework Decision as of 19 September 2001 was even more broadly formulated with regard to both the criminal intent required and the activities incriminated.[8] As to the former, it included offences "which are intentionally committed by an individual or a group against one or more countries, their institutions or people with the aim of intimidating them and seriously altering or destroying the political, economic, or social structures of a country." With regard to the latter, the proposal included acts such as "(f) unlawful seizure of or damage to state or government facilities, means of public transport, infrastructure facilities, places of public use, and property" as well as "(j) attacks through interference with an information system".

The proposal provoked very serious criticism from human rights groups. For instance, Human Rights Watch, in an open letter to the EU Presidency, expressed its concern "that public demonstrations and protests – such as those against nuclear weapons and those in favor of more transparent procedures governing international financial institutions – could be subject to the provisions of the proposal, thus infringing on the rights to freedom of association and assembly".[9] It is also telling that with regard to the broad notion of "unlawful seizure of or damage to state or government facilities, means of public transport, infrastructure facilities, places of public use, and property" even the EC Commission stated in its explanatory note that "[t]his could include, for instance, acts of urban violence".[10]

As already mentioned, the final (June 2002) text of the Framework Decision is more limited. In addition, the EU legislator inserted a general

---

[8] Commission proposal framework decision on combating terrorism, 19/9/2001, COM(2001) 521 final.

[9] Open Letter to the President of the EU by Human Rights Watch, dated 26 September 2001. Available at <http://www.hrw.org/press/2001/09/eu-0927-ltr.htm#security>, visited on 11 May 2004.

[10] Commission proposal framework decision on combating terrorism, 19/9/2001, COM(2001) 521 final, 9.

human rights compatibility clause into its text according to which "[t]his Framework Decision shall not have the effect of altering the obligation to respect fundamental rights and fundamental legal principles as enshrined in Article 6 of the Treaty on European Union".[11]

Still, the crucial question remains whether these precautions are sufficient to guarantee that the resulting definition of terrorism conforms to the exigencies of the criminal law requirement of *nullum crimen sine lege stricta/certa*. As is well known, Article 7 European Convention on Human Rights (ECHR),[12] which might be read as a mere non-retroactivity clause, has been interpreted by the European Commission and Court of Human Rights to include a prohibition on the extensive interpretation of criminal law provisions, e.g. by analogy, and thus to require a certain minimal precision and clarity.[13]

3. Freezing of Assets

The broad aim of "combating the funding of terrorism" as stated in the EU Action Plan can be pursued by various means, among them the attempt to prevent funds from being made available to terrorists and for terrorist purposes.[14] Since this may sometimes involve the (lawful) solicitation of

---

[11] Article 1(2) Framework Decision on Combating Terrorism, *supra* note 7.

[12] Article 7(1) ECHR provides: "No one shall be held guilty of any criminal offence on account of any act or omission which did not constitute a criminal offence under national or international law at the time when it was committed. Nor shall a heavier penalty be imposed than the one that was applicable at the time the criminal offence was committed. »

[13] For instance, in *Kokkinakis* v. *Greece*, 25 May 1993, Series A No. 260-A, para. 52, available at <http://hudoc.echr.coe.int/Hudoc1doc/HEJUD/sift/412.txt>, the Court held that "Article 7 para. 1 (art. 7-1) of the Convention is not confined to prohibiting the retrospective application of the criminal law to an accused's disadvantage. It also embodies, more generally, the principle that only the law can define a crime and prescribe a penalty (nullum crimen, nulla poena sine lege) and the principle that the criminal law must not be extensively construed to an accused's detriment, for instance by analogy; it follows from this that an offence must be clearly defined in law. This condition is satisfied where the individual can know from the wording of the relevant provision and, if need be, with the assistance of the courts' interpretation of it, what acts and omissions will make him liable."
See also the recent judgement in *E.K.* v. *Turkey*, 7 February 2002, Application No. 28496/95, finding a violation of the prohibition to construe criminal law extensively by way of analogy.

[14] One may have doubts whether the EU has taken effective steps in this regard. *See* A. Reinisch, 'The Action of the EU to Combat International Terrorism', in A.

funds, e.g. by charitable institutions where donors are unaware of the illegitimate uses of their donations, the more direct approach chosen by the EU and others focuses on preventing the use of funds already at the disposal of terrorists. Such freezing of assets is also required by the UN Security Council anti-terrorism resolution 1373 which – in addition to demanding that all States shall "prevent and suppress the financing of terrorist acts"[15] – requires that all States shall

> "freeze without delay funds and other financial assets or economic resources of persons who commit, or attempt to commit, terrorist acts or participate in or facilitate the commission of terrorist acts; of entities owned or controlled directly or indirectly by such persons; and of persons and entities acting on behalf of, or at the direction of such persons and entities, including funds derived or generated from property owned or controlled directly or indirectly by such persons and associated persons and entities."[16]

The resulting EU 'freezing action' in order to implement this Security Council mandate is a further example of the complex interplay between intergovernmental Second (and Third) Pillar CFSP (and JHA, now PJCC) cooperation, on the one hand, and supranational First Pillar decision-making in the field of economic sanctions.[17] Following earlier examples, in particular with respect to freezing legislation directed against the Taliban,[18] the Council first adopted a) the Common Position of 27 December 2001 on the application of specific measures to combat terrorism.[19] On this basis it voted on b) Regulation 2580/2001 of 27 December 2001 on specific restrictive measures directed against certain persons and entities with a view

---

Bianchi (ed.), *Enforcing International Law Norms Against Terrorism* (Oxford and Portland Oregon, Hart 2004) pp. 140.

[15] UN Security Council Resolution 1373 (1) (a).

[16] UN Security Council Resolution 1373 (1) (c).

[17] *See also* P.-J. Kuijper, 'Implementation of Binding Security Council Resolutions by the EU/EC', in de Wet/Nollkaemper (eds.), *Review of the Security Council by Member States* (Antwerp – Oxford – New York, Intersentia, 2003) pp. 39–55.

[18] The original Council Regulation (EC) No 467/2001 of 6 March 2001 prohibiting the export of certain goods and services to Afghanistan, strengthening the flight ban and extending the freeze of funds and other financial resources in respect of the Taliban of Afghanistan, and repealing Regulation (EC) No 337/2000, OJ L 67/1, 09/03/2001, has been frequently amended.

[19] 2001/930/CFSP, OJ L 344/93, 28 December 2001, Available at <http://europa.eu.int/eur-lex/pri/en/oj/dat/2001/l_344/l_34420011228en0093 0096.pdf>.

to combating terrorism.[20] In addition, the Council adopted c) a separate Decision, establishing a list of targets of freezing measures.[21]

a) The Common Position defines "terrorist acts" and "terrorist groups"[22] and provides that the EC "shall order the freezing of the funds and other financial assets or economic resources of persons, groups and entities listed in the Annex."[23]

b) The Regulation provides for the freezing of "all funds, other financial assets and economic resources belonging to, or owned or held by, a natural or legal person, group or entity included in the list referred to in paragraph 3".[24] According to paragraph 3 of this provision "[t]he Council, acting by unanimity, shall establish, review and amend the list of persons, groups and entities to which this Regulation applies, in accordance with the provisions laid down in Article 1(4), (5) and (6) of Common Position 2001/931/CFSP."[25]

c) The Council Decision of December 2001 contained only the "EU external"[26] terrorists found in the Common Position. It listed 8 individuals and 2 groups. Both the Decision and the Common Position have been frequently amended since their initial adoption in 2001 and now reflect a far broader coverage.

---

[20] OJ L 344/70 28. 12. 2001, Available at <http://europa.eu.int/eur-lex/pri/en/oj/dat/2001/l_344/l_34420011228en00700075.pdf>.

[21] Council Decision of 27 December 2001 establishing the list provided for in Article 2(3) of Council Regulation (EC) No 2580/2001 on specific restrictive measures directed against certain persons and entities with a view to combating terrorism (2001/927/EC), OJ L 344/83 28. 12. 2001, lists eight individuals and two groups. Available at <http://europa.eu.int/eur-lex/pri/en/oj/dat/2001/l_344/l_34420011228en00830084.pdf>.

[22] The definition contained in Article 1(3) of the Common Position largely corresponds to the terrorism definition in Article 1(1) of the Framework Decision on Combating Terrorism, *supra* note 7.

[23] Article 2 Common Position of 27 December 2001 on the application of specific measures to combat terrorism, *supra* note 19.

[24] Article 2(1) (a) Regulation 2580/2001, *supra* note 20.

[25] Article 2(3) Regulation 2580/2001, *supra* note 20.

[26] This has to do with the perceived lack of competence of the EC to take economic sanctions against individuals and groups found within Member States.

A crucial aspect from a human rights perspective is the listing procedure provided for in the Regulation by way of referring to principles contained in the Common Position.[27] These principles state as follows:

> "The list in the Annex shall be drawn up on the basis of precise information or material in the relevant file which indicates that a decision has been taken by a competent authority in respect of the persons, groups and entities concerned, irrespective of whether it concerns the instigation of investigations or prosecution for a terrorist act, an attempt to perpetrate, participate in or facilitate such an act *based on serious and credible evidence or clues, or condemnation for such deeds*. Persons, groups and entities identified by the Security Council of the United Nations as being related to terrorism and against whom it has ordered sanctions may be included in the list."[28]

> "The Council shall work to ensure that names of natural or legal persons, groups or entities listed in the Annex have sufficient particulars appended to permit effective identification of specific human beings, legal persons, entities or bodies, thus facilitating the exculpation of those bearing the same or similar names."[29]

> "The names of persons and entities on the list in the Annex shall be reviewed at regular intervals and at least once every six months to ensure that there are grounds for keeping them on the list."[30]

This listing procedure has provoked harsh criticism. And it does not seem far-fetched to remember the concern expressed in the House of Lords debate with regard to similar provisions found in UK anti-terrorism legislation: "[T]here is something distasteful about a process which begins by convicting someone and then proceeds to inquire whether there is a case against them".[31]

Indeed, whether the presumption of innocence[32] and the criminal fair trial guarantees[33] of the ECHR are complied with by such a listing procedure

---

[27] *See* Article 2(3) Regulation 2580/2001, *supra* note 20.

[28] Article 1(4) Common Position of 27 December 2001, *supra* note 19, (emphasis added).

[29] Article 1(5) Common Position of 27 December 2001, *supra* note 19.

[30] Article 1(6) Common Position of 27 December 2001, *supra* note 19.

[31] Lord Archer of Sandwell, cited in UK Terrorism Act: 21 new proscribed organisations, available at <www.statewatch.org/news/2001/oct/01proscribed.htm>.

[32] Article 6(2) ECHR provides: "Everyone charged with a criminal offence shall be presumed innocent until proved guilty according to law."

appears highly questionable. However, one should not overlook that both guarantees have been interpreted rather restrictively in the case law of both the European Commission and the European Court of Human Rights. The European Commission, for instance, regarded Italian anti-Mafia legislation providing for the confiscation of criminal proceeds as a preventive measure, not a penal one. As a result, it considered the presumption of innocence not applicable.[34]

For the same reason, i.e. that freezing orders are preventive measures and not 'criminal charges', the criminal fair trial guarantees of Article 6(3) ECHR would also seem to be technically inapplicable.[35]

However, since the European Court of Human Rights has held that measures of confiscation of property relate to civil rights,[36] at least the

---

[33] Article 6(3) ECHR provides: "Everyone charged with a criminal offence has the following minimum rights:

a. to be informed promptly, in a language which he understands and in detail, of the nature and cause of the accusation against him;
b. to have adequate time and facilities for the preparation of his defence;
c. to defend himself in person or through legal assistance of his own choosing or, if he has not sufficient means to pay for legal assistance, to be given it free when the interests of justice so require;
d. to examine or have examined witnesses against him and to obtain the attendance and examination of witnesses on his behalf under the same conditions as witnesses against him;
e. to have the free assistance of an interpreter if he cannot understand or speak the language used in court."

[34] *M.* v. *Italy*, European Commission of Human Rights, 15 April 1991, Application No. 12386/86: 'Dans ces circonstances et à la lumière de la jurisprudence de la Cour, la Commission conclut que la confiscation litigieuse ne comporte pas un constat de culpabilité, qui suit une accusation, et ne constitue pas une peine. Dès lors, les griefs tirés de la violation des articles 6 par. 2 et 7 (art. 6-2, 7) de la Convention sont incompatibles "ratione materiae" avec ces dispositions et doivent être rejetées conformément à son article 27 par. 2 (art. 27-2).'

[35] This is at least the clear opinion of the European Court of Human Rights with regard to another preventive measure, special supervision, in *Raimondo* v. *Italy*, 22 February 1994, para. 43: "The Court shares the view taken by the Government and the Commission that special supervision is not comparable to a criminal sanction because it is designed to prevent the commission of offences. It follows that proceedings concerning it did not involve "the determination . . . of a criminal charge" (*see* the Guzzardi judgment cited above, p. 40, para. 108).' Available at <http://hudoc.echr.coe.int/Hudoc2doc/HEJUD/sift/455.txt>.

[36] *Raimondo* v. *Italy*, 22 February 1994, para. 43: "On the matter of confiscation, it should be noted that Article 6 (art. 6) applies to any action whose subject matter is

guarantees of Article 6(1) ECHR[37] appear to be applicable. In this context it is, of course, relevant that in the view of the Strasbourg organs some of the more specific criminal fair trial guarantees are part of the general notion of fair trial required under Article 6(1) ECHR.[38]

The freezing of assets also appears problematic from a right to property-perspective under Article 1 of Protocol No. 1 to the ECHR.[39] The relevant case law of the European human rights organs demonstrates, however, considerable deference to the discretion of States as regards freezing or forfeiture or similar orders affecting property rights. The Strasbourg court basically only required access to court in the sense of Article 6(1) ECHR in order to review such measures.[40]

On the basis of these precedents, one can hardly doubt that the guarantees under Article 6(1) ECHR apply to the EU freezing measures. This result is also confirmed by the Council of Europe's Guidelines on Human Rights and the Fight against Terrorism which stated, *inter alia*, that

---

'pecuniary' in nature and which is founded on an alleged infringement of rights that were likewise of a pecuniary character (see the *Editions Périscope* v. *France* judgment of 26 March 1992, Series A no. 234-B, p. 66, para. 40). That was the position in the instant case." *Supra* note 35.

[37] Article 6(1) ECHR provides: "In the determination of his civil rights and obligations or of any criminal charge against him, everyone is entitled to a fair and public hearing within a reasonable time by an independent and impartial tribunal established by law. […]"

[38] "In addition to being specifically mentioned in Article 6 § 2, a person's right in a criminal case to be presumed innocent and to require the prosecution to bear the onus of proving the allegations against him or her forms part of the general notion of a fair hearing under Article 6 § 1 . . ." *Phillips* v. *United Kingdom*, European Court of Human Rights, 5 July 2001, Application No. 41087/98, para. 40. Available at <http://hudoc.echr.coe.int/Hudoc2doc2/HEJUD/200201/phillips%20-%2041087jnv.chb4%2005072001e.doc>.

[39] Article 1 Protocol No. 1 to the ECHR provides "Every natural or legal person is entitled to the peaceful enjoyment of his possessions. No one shall be deprived of his possessions except in the public interest and subject to the conditions provided for by law and by the general principles of international law.
The preceding provisions shall not, however, in any way impair the right of a State to enforce such laws as it deems necessary to control the use of property in accordance with the general interest or to secure the payment of taxes or other contributions or penalties."

[40] *Cf. AGOSI* v. *United Kingdom*, European Court of Human Rights, 24 October 1986, Ser. A No. 108. Available at <http://hudoc.echr.coe.int/Hudoc2doc/HEJUD/sift/3.txt>. *See also* the *Raimondo* v. *Italy* case, *supra* note 35.

"[t]he use of the property of persons or organisations suspected of terrorist activities may be suspended or limited, notably by such measures as freezing orders or seizures, by the relevant authorities. The owners of the property have the possibility to challenge the lawfulness of such a decision before a court."[41]

As a result, the crucial human rights issue with regard to freezing measures seems to be the question of legal recourse against them. In this respect, it is, of course, not very promising to find that neither the Common Position nor the Regulation provide for any challenge procedure or other remedies for incorrect freezing that would be available to affected parties. The periodic review of the "names of persons and entities on the list" as provided in Article 1(6) of the Common Position[42] clearly does not give standing to persons on the list to demand changes.

This leaves, as the only alternative available, recourse to general measures of judicial review of Community acts, at least with regard to the first pillar regulation and decisions. These Community acts may be challenged according to Article 230 TEC.[43] Since the lists of targeted individuals and groups are contained in Council decisions, problems otherwise pertinent with regard to the standing of individual applicants in annulment proceedings are unlikely to arise.[44]

However, there may be a problem with the scope of review that is available before the ECJ and the Court of First Instance. According to the European Court of Human Rights Article 6(1) ECHR requires national courts to provide "full jurisdiction" and review of questions of fact and of

---

[41] Article XIV Guidelines of the Committee of Ministers of the Council of Europe on human rights and the fight against terrorism, adopted on 15 July 2002. Available at <http://www.coe.int/T/E/Communication_and_Research/Press/Theme_Files/Terrorism/CM_Guidelines_20020628.asp#TopOfPage>.

[42] *See supra* text at note 30.

[43] Article 230 (1) TEC provides: "The Court of Justice shall review the legality of acts adopted jointly by the European Parliament and the Council, of acts of the Council, of the Commission and of the ECB, other than recommendations and opinions, and of acts of the European Parliament intended to produce legal effects vis-à-vis third parties."

[44] Article 230 (4) TEC provides: "Any natural or legal person may, under the same conditions, institute proceedings against a decision addressed to that person or against a decision which, although in the form of a regulation or a decision addressed to another person, is of direct and individual concern to the former."

law.[45] The Court held, for instance, that the judicial review exercised by the Austrian Constitutional Court, which is limited to assess the conformity of legislative and administrative acts with the Austrian Constitution and which prevents the Constitutional Court from examining all relevant facts, was not sufficient to fulfil the requirements of a judicial body with full jurisdiction.[46]

In a similar way, judicial review by the EC courts in annulment proceedings is limited to specific grounds mentioned in the EC Treaty.[47] The main issues to be raised by applicants in annulment proceedings against freezing measures are likely to concern issues of fact relating to questions such as, whether the persons in the freezing lists were correctly identified, whether they were in fact involved in international terrorism, etc. and the accompanying evidentiary problems. Unless the European courts are willing to broadly review such issues, the lack of an alternative procedural safeguard for persons affected by freezing measures may violate the fundamental right of access to court. The experience of litigation challenging the similar Taliban freezing sanctions[48] shows that the European courts are very reluctant to scrutinize anti-terrorism measures. Since their requests for provisions measures were rejected by the Court of First Instance two years ago,[49] these cases are still pending. Even if the applicants may eventually receive "full jurisdiction" and review of questions of fact and of law, the time passed so far does not promise timely and effective administration of justice.

4. Conclusion

The EU's anti-terrorism measures may prove to become a tough test case for the human rights compatibility required by Article 6(1) TEU. By whatever means the EU will provide such compliance it is important to keep in mind

---

[45] *See Le Compte, Van Leuven and De Meyere* v. *Belgium*, ECtHR, 23 June 1981, Ser. A , No. 43, para. 51; *Albert et Le Compte* v. *Belgium*, ECtHR, 10 February 1983, Ser. A , No. 58, para. 29.

[46] *Zumtobel* v. *Austria*, ECtHR, 21 September 1993, Ser. A , No. 268-A, para. 29, 30.

[47] Article 230 (2) TEC provides: "It shall for this purpose have jurisdiction in actions brought by a Member State, the Council or the Commission on grounds of lack of competence, infringement of an essential procedural requirement, infringement of this Treaty or of any rule of law relating to its application, or misuse of powers."

[48] *See* Cases T-306/01, *Aden and Others* v. *Council and Commission*; T-315/01, *Kadi* v. *Council and Commission*; T-318/01, *Othman* v. *Council and Commission*.

[49] Case T-306/01 R, *Abdirisak Aden and Others against the Council of the European Union and the Commission of the European Communities*, ECR II-2387.

"that it is not only possible, but also absolutely necessary, to fight terrorism while respecting human rights, the rule of law and, where applicable, international humanitarian law".[50] Otherwise terrorism may have already achieved – part of – its aim of "seriously destabilising or destroying the fundamental political, constitutional, economic or social structures of a country".[51]

[50] Preambular para. d) Guidelines of the Committee of Ministers of the Council of Europe on human rights and the fight against terrorism, *supra* note 41.

[51] *Cf.* Article 1(1) Council Framework Decision on combating terrorism, *supra* note 7.

Inside and Outside the European Convention: The Case of Minorities Compared*

*Gaetano Pentassuglia***

Contents

1. Introduction: Fundamental Freedoms and Minority Identity

As is widely known, the European Convention on Human Rights (hereinafter, ECHR) does not contain any specific minority rights provisions. This has been reaffirmed by the Strasbourg bodies on several occasions in earlier times. Nevertheless, in recent years there has been a significant increase in the number of cases brought before the European Court of Human Rights (hereinafter, the Court) regarding minority groups, seemingly inspired by a number of important changes in the landscape of human rights and minority rights protection in Europe and beyond. As minority issues increasingly make their way into the Court's docket, the question arises as to what role, if any, this judicial forum can be expected to play within the wider post-Cold War context of the international protection of minorities.

This paper does not provide an exhaustive review of the Court's jurisprudential body. Rather, it offers a selective commentary on a set of

---

* This paper was presented at the Inaugural Conference of the European Society of International Law in Florence in May 2004. It does not consider developments subsequent to March 2005.

** Dott.re in Giurisprudenza, PhD, Senior Lecturer in Law, Liverpool Law School, University of Liverpool; e-mail: g.pentassuglia@liv.ac.uk. He previously taught international law and minority rights at the University of Munich, Germany.

Baltic Yearbook of International Law, Volume 6, 2006, pp. 263–291.

cases that, unlike other cases pointing in several ways to established case law (for example, in the area of physical integrity), seems to be pushing the Court into what has traditionally been uncharted territory for it, namely the field of minority (ethno-cultural) identity. More specifically, putting the minority question into a forward-looking judicial-like perspective, the stage of development of minority considerations under the ECHR is explored by way of a comparison with the approach taken by the United Nations Human Rights Committee (hereinafter, HRC) mostly in relation to claims of a breach of Article 27 of the International Covenant on Civil and Political Rights (hereinafter, ICCPR) brought before it pursuant to the quasi-judicial complaints procedure established by the Optional Protocol to this instrument. As argued below, the comparison may not only enhance the understanding of the ECHR through the lens of mainstream minority discourse; it also mirrors the reach of protections derived from minority rights as such under international human rights law.

The Court has importantly come to set a benchmark for minority identity in the context of freedom of expression and freedom of association, in Articles 10 and 11 ECHR. In *Young, James and Webster* v. *United Kingdom*,[1] the Court had already referred in general to the criteria of "pluralism, tolerance and broadmindedness" as hallmarks of a democratic society which implied the "fair and proper treatment of minorities" as a necessary limit to the views of the majority. However, it was only in a group of recent cases – all involving Turkish political parties with a pro-Kurdish agenda – that the Court recognised in particular that seeking solutions for the benefit of a distinctive ethno-cultural group, ranging from ways of enhancing dialogue between the minority and the rest of the population to endorsing a federal system within existing state borders to the conferral of minority language rights, could not in itself justify the dissolution of the political party that publicly advocated or embraced those solutions. The Court has gone further by stating that a call for autonomy or even secession of part of the country's territory by a group of freely associated persons or a political party, with its derivative demands for fundamental constitutional and territorial changes, cannot automatically justify a prohibition of its assemblies, let alone its compulsory dismantling or even the termination of the mandates of MPs belonging to that party.[2]

[1] *Young, James and Webster* v. *United Kingdom,* 13 August 1981, Series A No. 44.

[2] *Case of Socialist Party of Turkey (STP) and Others* v. *Turkey*, 12 November 2003 (available in French), ECHR, no. 26482/95; *Sadak and Others* v. *Turkey*, 11 June 2002, ECHR, nos. 25144/94, 26149/95 to 26154/95, 27100/95 and 27101/95; *Dicle*

However, the Court has clarified that the body in question must reject the use or propagation of violence and firmly endorse democratic principles for it to enjoy protection under the ECHR. In *Dicle for the Democratic Party (DEP)* v. *Turkey*,[3] it appeared to accept that some potential for violence seemingly conveyed by a public political speech can be tolerated provided that the ensuing threat is very limited, and therefore that the penalty of dissolving an entire political party remains in itself disproportionate under Article 11.

Other cases have gone beyond the issue of supporting minority demands politically by raising – explicitly or implicitly – the specific question whether the manifestation or assertion of minority identity through the proclaimed objectives of an association, particular public meetings or simply the general activities of the group concerned should be protected by the ECHR. While *Sidiropoulos and Others* v. *Greece*[4] linked the assertion of minority identity to the registration of an association, *Stankov and the United Macedonian Association Ilinden* v. *Bulgaria*[5] interestingly acknowledged a further space of freedom for a minority in that it led to a finding of a violation of Article 11 in banning *Ilinden* – an unregistered association claiming the recognition of a Macedonian minority in Bulgaria – from holding public meetings to commemorate certain historical events. In the case of *Gorzelik and others* v. *Poland*,[6] though, the Court accepted Poland's speculative allegation that the applicant association of Silesians, by seeking registration as an organization of the 'Silesian national minority', had tried

---

for the Democracy Party (DEP) v. *Turkey*, 10 December 2002, ECHR, no. 25141/94. For earlier landmark cases, *see e.g.*, *United Communist Party of Turkey and others* v. *Turkey*, 30 January 1998, ECHR, *Reports of Judgements and Decisions 1998-I*; *Socialist Party and others* v. *Turkey*, 25 May 1998, ECHR, *Reports of Judgements and Decisions 1998-III*; *Freedom and Democracy Party (ÖZDEP)* v. *Turkey*, 8 December 1999, ECHR, *Reports of Judgements and Decisions 1999-VIII*; *Yazar, Karatas, Aksoy and the People's Labour Party (HEP)* v. *Turkey*, 9 April 2002 (available in French), ECHR, nos. 22723/93, 22734/93 and 22725/93. In this context, recent jurisprudence also includes cases specifically concerning Article 10; *see e.g.*, *Kizilyaprak* v. *Turkey*, 2 October 2003 (available in French), ECHR, no. 27528/95.

[3] *See supra* note 2, para. 64.

[4] *Sidiropoulos and Others* v. *Greece*, 10 July 1998, ECHR, no. 57/1997/841/1047, *Reports of Judgements and Decisions 1998-IV*.

[5] *Stankov and the United Macedonian Association Ilinden* v. *Bulgaria,* 2 October 2001, ECHR, nos. 29221/95 and 292225/95.

[6] *Gorzelik and others* v. *Poland,* 20 December 2001 (Fourth Section) and 17 February 2004 (Grand Chamber), ECHR, no. 44158/98.

to circumvent Polish electoral law conferring special benefits on registered associations of national minorities. By contrast, in the quite similar *Sidiropoulos* case the Court rejected the suspicions and doubts voiced by the respondent government regarding the true intentions of the association's founders as justifying an interference with freedom of association in Article 11. The emphasis here was on actions taking priority over declarations or suppositions, irrespective of the existence of the minority in question, while the Grand Chamber in *Gorzelik* more ambiguously included the intentions 'impliedly declared' in the association's programme to justify pre-emptive state measures. *Gorzelik* arguably diluted the demanding evidentiary test established in the above cases to review the state party's margin of appreciation.

On the whole, this case law unquestionably indicates increasing endorsement by the Court of important areas of pluralism, resulting in the prohibition of arbitrary interference in the expression of minority demands and assertion of minority identity. In *Gorzelik* itself, the Court recognised the instrumental value of Article 11 in helping a minority to preserve and uphold its rights. The theme of pluralism has been extended to the sphere of religion, as is illustrated by a number of cases in which the state authorities were found to have disproportionately interfered with the activities of a minority religious community by either refusing to register the church of that community or determining its internal hierarchy.[7] The non-arbitrary interference parameter apparently resembles the equally, at least primarily, negative rationale of Article 27 ICCPR, which states that persons belonging to ethnic, religious or linguistic minorities "shall not be denied" the right to enjoy their own culture, to profess and practice their own religion, or to use their own language. At the same time, though, the hands off approach implied by the criterion of non-denial is measured against the backdrop of a marked interaction between individual rights and aspects of group protection. Irrespective of any positive action arguably attached to Article 27, this element is somewhat tentatively echoed by the reference in the provision to the communal exercise of rights.[8]

---

[7] *See e.g.*, *Metropolitan Church of Bessarabia and others* v. *Moldova*, 13 December 2001, ECHR, no. 45701/99; *Serif* v. *Greece*, 14 December 1999, ECHR, no. 38178/97; *Hasan and Chaush* v. *Bulgaria*, 26 October 2000, ECHR, no. 30985/96; *Case of Supreme Holy Council of the Muslim Community* v. *Bulgaria*, 16 December 2004, ECHR, no. 39023/97.

[8] For a general discussion about Article 27 ICCPR, *see* G. Pentassuglia, *Minorities in International Law: An Introductory Study* (Council of Europe Publishing, 2002), pp. 97–111.

In a typical Article 27 dispute the respondent state generally reveals itself as an intermediate actor between either the minority and its complaining members – as a result of legislative (or otherwise) measures adopted for the benefit of the group as a whole but wholly or partially impugned by the applicant(s)[9] – or the minority and its members, on the one hand, and private parties, on the other – as a result of legislative (or otherwise) measures benefiting the latter that allegedly affect the exercise of Article 27 rights.[10] In other words, 'non-denial' by the state is essentially defined by whether certain steps taken by a state still permit or cumulatively erode the enjoyment of a collectively construed minority identity,[11] or – alternatively – may be possibly justified by the aim of preserving this identity while producing individual restrictions on Article 27 rights themselves. By contrast, such a community dimension is precisely what is lacking in the ECHR cases mentioned above. In these cases, the spaces of freedom upheld by the Court benefit a minority group as they are construed as "necessary in a democratic society"[12] rather than necessary for the protection of minority identity, very much in line with the theme of

[9] Cases of this sort include *Sandra Lovelace* v. *Canada*, 30 July 1981, Human Rights Committee, no. 24/1977, Annual Report, 1981, p. 166 *et seq.*; Annual Report, 1983, p. 248 *et seq.*; *Ivan Kitok* v. *Sweden*, 27 July 1988, Human Rights Committee, no. 197/1985, Annual Report, 1988, p. 221 *et seq.*; *Apirana Mahuika et al.* v. *New Zealand*, 27 October 2000, Human Rights Committee, no. 547/1993, UN Doc. CCPR/C/70/D/541/1993 (1993).

[10] Examples include *Bernard Ominayak, Chief of the Lubicon Lake Band* v. *Canada,* 26 March 1990, Human Rights Committee, no. 167/1984, Annual Report, vol. II, 1990, p. 1 *et seq.*; *I. Länsman* v. *Finland,* 26 October 1994, Human Rights Committee, no. 511/1992, Annual Report, vol. II, 1995, p. 66 *et seq.*; *J. Länsman* v. *Finland,* 30 October 1996, Human Rights Committee, no. 671/1995, Annual Report, vol. II, 1997, p. 191 *et seq.*; *Anni Äärelä and Jouni Näkkäläjärvi* v. *Finland*, 24 October 2001, Human Rights Committee, no. 779/1997, UN Doc. CCPR/C/73/D/779/1997 (1997); *Jarle Jonassen and Members of the Riast/Hylling Reindeer Herding District* v. *Norway*, 25 October 2002, Human Rights Committee, no. 942/2000, UN Doc. CCPR/C/76/D/942/2000 (2000).

[11] This issue may occasionally arise involving no specific private parties. *See e.g.*, *J.G.A. Diergaardt et al.* v. *Namibia*, 25 July 2000, Human Rights Committee, no. 760/1997, UN Doc. CCPR/C/69/D/760/1996 (1996); *Tadeusz Kleczkowski (Tadeuš Kleèkowski)* v. *Lithuania,* no. 1032/2001, submitted on 3 October 2001.

[12] In *Gorzelik*, the Court (Grand Chamber) clarified that, not only political parties but also associations set up for other purposes, such as those making minority claims or asserting minority identity, play an important role to the "proper functioning of democracy" protected by Article 11 ECHR. *See supra* note 6, para. 92.

protection against abuse of majority rule underpinning *Young* with regard to the very different issue of membership in labour unions. Instead of the triangular relation which *de facto* underlies most Article 27 disputes as indicated earlier, those cases reflect a classic binary relation in which individual applicants challenge state measures which directly target their basic liberties. The issue of minorities and their complexities is not valued per se and the principle of non-arbitrary interference on which those cases are based remains an identity-blind one.

The protection is ultimately indirect in nature, and the state's margin of appreciation allowed by the Court tends to widen as more open and complex considerations of minority identity may become involved. In *Gorzelik*, which originated from an underlying controversy over the existence and status of the Silesians as a national minority, the Court embraced a doubtful interpretation of Polish electoral law by Polish domestic courts,[13] and held that there had been no breach of freedom of association per se; rather, the Silesians were not allowed to call themselves a nation or a national minority. Unsurprisingly, the positive, but generic, reference to democratic pluralism in *United Communist Party of Turkey and others* v. *Turkey*, *Stankov, Sidiropoulos* and similar cases, becomes the negative reference to the boundaries of such pluralism in *Gorzelik*, in which the Court rejected the applicants' claim by stressing that groups of individuals should be prepared to limit some of their freedoms for the sake of the stability of the country as a whole, defined by the protection of its electoral system.[14] But what if it is the state that is not prepared to do so *vis-à-vis* a minority group? In *I. Länsman v. Finland*, the HRC stated that the freedom of a state to pursue its own interests (*in casu*, development or economic activity by enterprises) should not be assessed by reference to a margin of appreciation ascribed to it, as contended by the respondent party (which recalled the Court's approach under the ECHR), but by reference to whether the exercise of that freedom amounted to a denial of Article 27 rights. Unlike the HRC, the

[13] *Ibid.*, paras. 99–102. That reading appeared all the more controversial as it was linked to merely hypothetical and future events involving the applicants.

[14] *Ibid.*, para. 66 (Fourth Section). Along broadly similar lines, in *The Gypsy Council and Others* v. *the United Kingdom,* 14 May 2002 (admissibility), ECHR, no. 66336/01, the Court held that the Horsmonden Horse Fair – a historical event in the life of the Roma/Gypsy community in the UK, prohibited by the authorities – was indeed a traditional gathering of longstanding and considerable cultural importance to the Roma/Gypsy group, but the prohibition order complained of was proportionate in terms of Article 11 as it was intended to respond to the legitimate interests of the community as a whole.

Court does not have an explicit ethno-cultural parameter on which to rely within the scope of the ECHR. And yet, can it be maintained that the Court might now have one *implicitly*?

2. Private and Family Life

Potential for some measure of direct protection of minority identity may well derive from respect for private and family life in Article 8. A first area of concern is offered by the question whether an individual defined by his or her ethno-cultural origin – and *a fortiori* a member of a minority group – may obtain protection of his or her personal name as written in accordance with the language of origin, not the language of the state in which such individual resides. The case of *Kuharec* v. *Latvia,*[15] concerning an alleged misspelling of the name of a 'non-citizen' of Latvia of Russian ethnic origin, in breach of Article 8(1), seems to match another case now pending before the HRC brought by a Lithuanian citizen of Polish origin who complains, *inter alia*, of a breach of his Article 27 rights as a result of Lithuanian legislation imposing the use of Lithuanian instead of mother tongue spelling for personal names.[16] The admissibility of neither of them has been decided yet, but they seem to suggest that an area of convergence between Article 8 ECHR and Article 27 ICCPR may arise with regard to claims to minority name spelling. Also, Article 8 might arguably be read as encompassing this minority issue in view of the right to use, and to official recognition of, one's minority name(s) and surname recognised in major international instruments.

It is the overall way of life of a minority, though, that may give Article 8 an even more specific role. This view was expressed by the Commission in *G and E* v. *Norway*[17] and *Buckley* v. *United Kingdom,*[18] and only recently endorsed by the Court in a series of similar cases involving Roma/Gypsy

---

[15] The case of *Kuharec alias Kuhareca* v. *Latvia* was declared inadmissible by the Court on 7 December 2004. See also *Mentzen alias Mencena* v. *Latvia* (inadmissibility), 7 December 2004. – ed.

[16] *See*, respectively, the report on the case by the Latvian Human Rights Committee, 40 *Minority Issues in Latvia*, 9 December 2001, accessible at <www.minelres/lv/count/latvia.htm#MinIssuesLatvia>; and *Tadeusz Kleczkowski (Tadeuš Kleèkowski)* v. *Lithuania, supra* note 11.

[17] *G and E* v. *Norway*, 3 October 1983 (admissibility), European Commission of Human Rights, nos. 9278/81 and 9415/81, 35 *Decisions and Reports 1894,* p. 35.

[18] *Buckley* v. *United Kingdom,* 11 January 1995, European Commission of Human Rights, 19 *European Human Rights Reports* (1995), p. 20; the Court reversed the Commission's finding of a breach of Article 8 in its judgement of 25 September 1996, *Reports of Judgements and Decisions 1996-IV.*

individuals, whom like the applicant in *Buckley* claimed to be able to park their caravan on their land despite the absence of planning permission.[19] Following an acknowledgement that the applicants' lifestyle, as part of their long-standing cultural identity, did attract the protection of Article 8, the Court referred to "an emerging international consensus" within the Council of Europe "recognising the special needs of minorities and an obligation to protect their security, identity and lifestyle", and identified a positive obligation under Article 8 "to facilitate the Gypsy way of life". Nevertheless, it confirmed the *Buckley* jurisprudence, particularly in regard to a wide margin of appreciation enjoyed in principle by national authorities in the choice and implementation of planning policies, and concluded that the relevant facts did not disclose any violation of Article 8 – a finding firmly opposed by a joint dissent of seven judges.

The protection of the particular way of life of a minority group has been broadly recognised within the context of Article 27 ICCPR. In a number of cases,[20] the HRC has consistently defined such way of life by the social and economic activities (whether they are adapted to modern technology or not) distinctive to the culture of the group. As hinted at earlier, the HRC has stressed that state discretion with regard to economic or other activities – benefiting either private parties or the group itself – is conditioned on respect for the way of life of minority members, although the HRC appears to give states a certain leeway on these matters before a breach of Article 27 can be actually established.

Compared to this case law, the Court has unsurprisingly been widely generous with the defendant state in assessing the impact of its measures on the way of life of Roma/Gypsy individuals. Does this suggest that states parties retain unbounded freedom under Article 8 ECHR in the name of the general community interest? As a matter of fact, the Court, while showing deference to state policies and practices, has also attempted to identify constraints on state action. In *Chapman* v. *United Kingdom*, it conceded that the implementation of certain general laws might have an effect on the Roma/Gypsy traditional lifestyle, and defined a positive obligation to facilitate the Roma/Gypsy way of life in terms of giving "some special

---

[19] *Chapman* v. *United Kingdom,* 18 January 2001, ECHR, no. 27238/95; *Beard* v. *United Kingdom,* 18 January 2001, ECHR, no. 24882/94; *Coster* v. *United Kingdom,* 18 January 2001, no. 24876/94; *Lee* v. *United Kingdom,* 18 January 2001, ECHR, no. 25154/94; *Jane Smith* v. *United Kingdom,* 18 January 2001, ECHR, no. 27238/95.

[20] *See supra* notes 9–10.

consideration" to their needs and different lifestyle "both in the relevant regulatory planning framework and in arriving at the decisions in particular cases".[21] Whereas *Chapman* is unclear as to what exactly the 'special consideration' criterion should imply in practice, the case of *Noack* v. *Germany*,[22] involving the contested relocation of a Sorbian village in order to permit mining for lignite, seems more openly to offer prior consultation and continuing protection of the minority's way of life as a possible yardstick to measure state conduct under Article 8. Interestingly, this approach comes close to that of the HRC in a stream of cases in which it applied the test of consultation and proportionality, based on economic sustainability, to development activities conducted by private parties and authorised by the state, which might arguably erode the authors' right to enjoy their own culture.[23] The HRC has thereby established its monitoring role in relation to both the decision-making process leading up to the impugned measures *and* the effects of such measures on the way of life of the people concerned once they have been implemented.

However, one should note that while the HRC's balancing act discourse (general versus minority interest) matches the Commission's line in *Buckley* and has been directly or indirectly suggested by concurring or dissenting opinions from Commission or Court members,[24] the Court's majority in *Buckley* and the set of recent cases exemplified by *Chapman* eventually shifts the focus from such an approach to the far narrower and identity-blind

[21] *Chapman* v. *United Kingdom, supra* note 19, para. 96. This line arguably adjusted the approach to Article 8 taken in *Buckley*, by implying *in principle* a link between procedural elements and substantive considerations of identity. These two perspectives re-emerged in the case of *Connors* v. *The United Kingdom*, 27 May 2004, ECHR, no. 66746/01, paras. 83–84; although the Court stressed governmental deficiencies vis-à-vis Roma/Gypsy needs and way of life (*e.g.*, paras. 90 and 94; *see also* reports of pending cases regarding Roma/Gypsies in the UK at <www.legalday.co.uk/current/humanrights.htm>), the case turned on the general issue of providing equal procedural safeguards to justify an interference under Article 8(2).

[22] *Noack* v. *Germany*, 25 May 2000 (admissibility) (available in French), ECHR, no. 46346/99, para. 1 (*En Droit*).

[23] *See* the *Länsman* cases, *supra* note 10. This approach has been confirmed in *Apirana Mahuika et al.* v. *New Zealand* (*supra* note 9) and *Anni Äärelä and Jouni Näkkäläjärvi* v. *Finland* (*supra* note 10), paras. 7.5 – 7.6, though in this latter case the HRC was unable to reach conclusions on the matter due to a lack of sufficient information before it.

[24] *See* the Commission's decision *supra* note 18, para. 84, and the concurring opinion by Ms Liddy. *See also* the joint dissent in *Chapman*, *supra* note 19.

issue whether the applicants' *right to a home* has been violated.[25] In this respect, the *Chapman* judgement does *not* advance on *Buckley* on Roma/Gypsy way of life issues.[26]

Furthermore, the HRC's reading of the minority way of life in Article 27 ICCPR is premised on the established public dimension of group identity, while "private and family life" in Article 8 ECHR would seem *prima facie* exclusive rather than inclusive in scope from the standpoint of the relationship of the affected people to larger collectivities and the essential elements of their ethno-cultural identities.[27] To be sure, Article 17 ICCPR – somewhat the counterpart to Article 8 ECHR – was indeed interpreted broadly by the HRC in the case of *Hopu and Bessert* v. *France*,[28] most notably in connection with the community's social and cultural practices and traditions. Still, this group-oriented line of interpretation outside Article 27 appears contentious.[29]

---

[25] *See* the *Chapman* judgement, *supra* note 19, para. 100, and the *Buckley* judgement, *supra* note 18, para. 76.

[26] For an equally cautious line on those issues, *see e.g.*, *Cyprus* v. *Turkey*, 10 May 2001, ECHR, no. 25781/94, paras. 352–353; compare with a partly dissenting opinion in the same case before the Commission led by Ms Liddy (and joined by Messrs Trechsel, Thure, Rozakis, Sváby, Ress and Perenic), 4 June 1999, European Commission of Human Rights, no. 25781/94, paras. 575–576; in *The Gypsy Council* case (*supra* note 14), the Court did not address the issue of Article 8 raised, *inter alia*, by the applicants.

[27] *See e.g.*, *Slivenko* v. *Latvia*, 9 October 2003, ECHR, no. 48321/99, paras. 94–95, and the opinion by Mr Klover, Section I; but compare with *Cyprus* (*supra* note 26), paras. 295–296. For a recent case involving a breach of Article 8 in connection with the internal displacement of the Kurdish population in south-east Turkey, *see Doğan and Others* v. *Turkey*, 29 June 2004, ECHR, nos. 8803-8811/02, 8813/02 and 8815-8819/02, para. 159.

[28] *Hopu and Bessert* v. *France*, 29 July 1997, Human Rights Committee, no. 549/1993, Annual Report, vol. II, 1997, p. 70 *et seq.*

[29] The HRC read 'family' in Article 17 to include members of one's ethno-cultural group and one's ancestors. Four HRC members dissented. *Ibid.*, paras. 4–5 (dissenting opinion of Messrs Kretzner, Buergenthal, Ando and Lord Colville). For a nuanced reading of this case, *see* B. Kingsbury, 'Reconciling Five Competing Conceptual Structures of Indigenous Peoples' Claims in International and Comparative Law', in Alston (ed.), *Peoples' Rights* (Oxford University Press, 2001) p. 69 *et seq.*, at p. 105.

3. Education and Language Rights

While Article 8 ECHR may well turn out to be a test for a degree of *direct* protection of minority identity, though one based on an *implicit*, progressive embrace of aspects of such identity, more specific areas like mother tongue education and mother tongue communication with public bodies are expected to highlight further difficulties in this regard. As is widely known, in the landmark *Case Relating to Certain Aspects of the Laws on the Use of Languages in Education in Belgium*[30] the Court held that there was no right to mother tongue education under Article 2 of Protocol No. 1, taken alone or in conjunction with Article 14. Yet, in the recent case of *Jeļena Grišankova and Oļegs Grišankovs* v. *Latvia,*[31] the applicants – a mother and her son, both Latvian citizens of Russian ethnic origin – complained about the Education Law passed by Latvian Parliament in 1998 providing for, in particular, a shift to public secondary education (from the 10th grade onwards) in Latvian as the only language of instruction as of 1 September 2004. They claimed a denial of the right to education in Article 2 of Protocol No. 1. The Court declared the application inadmissible because of a failure to exhaust local remedies, but left open the substantive question whether the claim as such could disclose a breach of the ECHR. In effect, in the earlier case of *Cyprus* v. *Turkey*, the Court, without reversing the *Belgian Linguistic* approach to mother tongue education, found a violation of Article 2 of Protocol No. 1 in respect of the Greek-Cypriot children living in northern Cyprus.[32] Despite the specific situation of this region, the decision may well imply more generally the possibility of finding *implicit* exceptions to the no-mother tongue rule under the ECHR, at least when the claimed mother tongue education adds to mother tongue schooling levels for which the state is responsible, represents a way of restoring the education previously available under domestic law, and is rooted in a clear wish of the community in question.[33] These elements might have arguably been established in

---

[30] *Case Relating to Certain Aspects of the Laws on the Use of Languages in Education in Belgium*, 23 July 1968, Series A no. 6.

[31] *Jeļena Grišankova and Oļegs Grišankovs* v. *Latvia,* 13 February 2003 (admissibility) (available in French), no. 36117/02.

[32] The Court held that failure on the part of the Turkish-Cypriot authorities to make continuing provision for Greek-language secondary schooling amounted to a denial of the substance of the right to education. *See supra* note 265, para. 278.

[33] *Ibid.* (*mutatis mutandis*).

Jeļena Grišankova,[34] as is further suggested by rather sharp criticisms even of later amendments to the Education Law believed to disproportionately curtail, while not completely abolishing, public minority education in Latvia.[35]

For its part, the HRC has thus far not been asked to decide Article 27 cases raising the issue of mother tongue education, nor has it offered any major indication in this area under the reporting procedure. The case of *Waldman* v. *Canada,*[36] relating to the public funding of minority religious schools, was decided on the basis of Article 26 (right to equality), not Article 27. Nevertheless, HRC member Scheinin stressed that positive obligations do exist under Article 27 to promote instruction in minority religions, and mentioned by analogy the case of publicly funded education in minority languages.[37] Still, whether and to what extent the HRC as a whole views Article 27 as embodying a duty to ensure some degree of minority education (including the sphere of religion) remains unclear.

In terms of the ECHR, the issue of using minority languages before public bodies is still being considered in line with a steady stream of earlier decisions precluding linguistic freedom in dealings with the authorities. The question whether Article 10 protected linguistic freedom implicitly was raised by some of the applicants in the *Belgian Linguistics* case,[38] but was basically sidelined by the Commission and even ignored by the Court. Interestingly, though, the Commission appeared not to exclude that freedom of expression might have an implicit linguistic component as it noted that nothing prevented the applicants from "expressing their thoughts freely in the language of their choice".[39] And indeed, in the context of the ICCPR, the HRC has come to recognise that freedom of speech in Article 19(12) does have such a linguistic component, at least in the private sphere, as it extends

[34] The case highlighted a claim to continuing provision for Russian-language secondary schooling (which had already been made available along with Russian-language primary schooling), in accordance with the wish of the parents that the schooling of their children be completed through the medium of their language.

[35] *See e.g.*, *Minority Issues in Latvia*, nos. 71 (16 August 2003), 79 (23 January 2004), and 80 (21 February 2004), accessible at <www.minelres/lv/count/latvia.htm#MinIssuesLatvia>.

[36] *Waldman* v. *Canada,* 3 November 1999, Human Rights Committee, no. 694/1996, UN Doc. CCPR/C/67/D/694/1996 (1996).

[37] *Ibid.*, para. 5.

[38] *See e.g.*, Application no. 1474/62, 6 *Yearbook of the European Convention on Human Rights* (1963) p. 332 *et seq.*, at p. 340.

[39] *Ibid.*, p. 342.

to every *form* of opinion, news and information, as well as commercial activity.[40] The Court has included commercial speech within the purview of Article 10 ECHR,[41] but has not so far covered the linguistic element implied in the HRC's reasoning in *Ballantyne et al.* v. *Canada*, nor has it generally linked freedom of expression to linguistic freedom in the private sphere. As for minority language use in the public sphere, despite the prevailing negative reading of Article 19(2) ICCPR,[42] the joint concurring opinion led by Mrs Evatt in *J.G.A. Diergaardt* v. *Namibia* argued for a more nuanced understanding of this provision in the event that the relevant public officials have the personal capacity to speak the authors' mother tongue, but refuse to do so.[43] One major point here is that the minority aspects that might ideally be shared between Articles 19(2) and 27 ICCPR could hardly coalesce in a supposedly progressive Court reading of Article 10 ECHR to facilitate the public use of minority languages.

In *Podkolzina* v. *Latvia*,[44] the applicant attempted to re-open the debate as to whether Article 3 of Protocol No. 1 (electoral rights) can be read in a way to establish a 'public' linguistic component. She argued, *inter alia*, that, as a member of the Russian-speaking minority in Latvia, she did not need to be proficient in Latvian to discharge the parliamentary mandate that she received from her Russian-speaking electors or to communicate with them. The Court did not really address the point made by the applicant, that in certain circumstances mother tongue communication might be a means of securing the effectiveness of Article 3 of Protocol No. 1 (apparently confirmed, to some extent, by the abolishment of Latvian language requirements to stand for parliamentary and local elections passed by the

---

[40] *Ballantyne et al.* v. *Canada,* 31 March 1993, Human Rights Committee, nos. 359/1989 and 385/1989, Annual Report, vol. II, 1993, p. 91 *et seq*. "A State" – the HRC held – "may choose one or more official languages, but it may not exclude, *outside* the spheres of public life, the *freedom to express oneself in a language of one's choice*" (emphasis added). *Ibid.*, para. 11.4.

[41] *Markt Intern* v. *Germany*, ECHR, 12 *European Human Rights Reports* (1989), p. 161.

[42] *See e.g., Dominique Guesdon* v. *France,* 25 July 1990, no. 219/1986, Annual Report, vol. II, 1990, p. 61 *et seq. See also supra* note 40.

[43] *J.G.A. Diergaardt* v. *Namibia*, *supra* note 11 (concurring opinion of Messrs Evatt, Klein, Kretzmer and Quiroga; c*ontra*, dissenting opinion of Messrs Bhagwati, Lord Colville and Yalden).

[44] *Podkolzina* v. *Latvia*, 9 April 2002, ECHR, no. 46726/99.

Latvian Parliament in 2002 following this case).[45] Along similar lines, in *Lagerblom* v. *Sweden*[46] the Court left unexplored the applicant's argument, which, unlike the previously dismissed arguments on language rights in court proceedings,[47] was not concerned with Article 6 per se, but with the distinct issue of facilitating public counselling in a minority language under *paragraph (c)* of that provision. The implication that may be attached to it is the improvement of the degree of effective participation of minority members as such in trials,[48] irrespective of whether they speak and understand the 'national' language, arguably in connection with the broader theme of effective participation of minorities in public life reflected in several minority rights instruments.[49]

Thus far the ECHR has been examined but, by contrast, does Article 27 ICCPR generate minority language guarantees in the public sphere? The joint dissent led by Mr Bhagwati in *Diergaardt* disagreed with the view that

---

[45] The case in fact revolved around the claim that the language skills in question had been inappropriately tested by the authorities. Compare, *e.g.*, with *Antonina Ignatane* v. *Latvia*, 25 July 2001, Human Rights Committee, no. 884/1999, CCPR/C/72/D/884/1999 (1999). However, the applicant had made not only the mother tongue communication claim but also the claim that the 'third-level knowledge' of Latvian required of prospective candidates in parliamentary elections was manifestly disproportionate to the aim pursued.

[46] *Lagerblom* v. *Sweden*, 14 January 2003, ECHR, no. 26891/95.

[47] *See e.g., Isop* v. *Austria,* European Commission of Human Rights, no. 808/60, 5 *Yearbook of the European Convention on Human Rights* (1962), p. 108 *et seq.*; *Bideaut* v. *France,* European Commission of Human Rights, no. 11261/84, 48 *Decisions and Reports* 1986, p. 232 *et seq.*; *X and Y.* v. *Belgium,* European Commission of Human Rights, no. 2332/64, 9 *Yearbook of the European Convention on Human Rights* (1966), p. 418 *et seq.*

[48] The applicant further argued that since he belonged to a large Finnish minority in Sweden, the domestic courts should have appointed for him a public counsel who could speak Finnish.

[49] *See* G. Pentassuglia *supra* note 8, *passim*. The issue whether minority groups have (or should have) a right to use their own language in court is in effect independent of whether those groups speak or understand the 'national' language. Such use includes, and yet transcends, the procedural fairness approach of classic defence rights, including entitlements to interpretation assistance (Articles 5(2) and 6(3)(a) and (e) ECHR), to make minority languages living identity tools in the public sphere. *See e.g.,* the Oslo Recommendations Regarding the Linguistic Rights of National Minorities, paras. 17–19, adopted in 1998 under the auspices of the Hague-based Foundation on Inter-Ethnic Relations and the OSCE High Commissioner on National Minorities.

Article 19(2) could raise issues in regard to the authors' allegation that they had been denied the use of their mother tongue in the public sphere, while adding that "*of course*, [they] might have argued that their language rights under Article 27 were being denied" (emphasis added).[50] As a matter of fact, whereas the HRC has indicated that Article 27 does differ from other ICCPR provisions such as Article 19(2) and Article 14(3)(f) (right to the free assistance of an interpreter where the accused cannot use the official language),[51] and has even suggested under the reporting procedure that 'public' minority language use may well be a means of complying with Article 27,[52] overall the HRC's line is tentative and its ramifications rather fluid at this stage. For example, in *Dominique Guesdon* v. *France*, the HRC stated that minority language use in court proceedings "did not raise issues" under Article 27.[53] Furthermore, it did not pick up on a similar, but broader, claim brought by members of the Rehoboth Baster community of Namibia in *Diergaardt*.[54] These uncertainties indirectly highlight – and partly justify – the even greater difficulties posed in this context by the ECHR (and ICCPR) general rights.

4. The Equality Approach

Critical spheres of minority identity might still be considered from the wider perspective of equality. *Belgian Linguistics* and, more recently, *Thlimmenos* v. *Greece*[55] have come to set the themes of the Court's discourse on Article 14 ECHR. In particular: difference in treatment that is reasonable and objective is compatible with the ECHR; distinctions that fail to pass such a

---

[50] *J.G.A. Diergaardt* v. *Namibia*, *supra* note 11, para. 3 (emphasis added) (dissenting opinion of Messrs Bhagwati, Lord Colville and Yalden).

[51] General Comment no. 23 (50) on Article 27, UN Doc. CCPR/C/21/Rev.1/Add.5 (1994), para. 5.3 (emphasis added).

[52] *See e.g.*, the Concluding Comments on Norway, Sudan and Algeria, UN Doc. CCPR/C/79/Add. 27 (1993); UN Doc. CCPR/C/79/Add. 85 (1997); UN Doc. CCPR/C/79/Add. 95 (1998).

[53] *Dominique Guesdon* v. *France*, *supra* note 42, para. 7.3.

[54] HRC member Lallah, offering his own explanation of this, maintained that "[t]he Committee presumably found no violation of Article 27 . . . Indeed, it would be stretching the language of Article 27 too far to suggest, as the Committee might in effect be perceived to have done, that public authorities must make it possible to use a non-official language (Afrikaans) in official business when the official language is different". *J.G.A. Diergaardt* v. *Namibia*, *supra* note 11, para. 5 (individual opinion of Mr Lallah).

[55] *Thlimmenos* v. *Greece*, 6 April 2000, ECHR, no. 34369/97.

test may indirectly produce discrimination although no specific breach of the substantive right in question is found; and most importantly, arbitrary failure to differentiate violates the Article 14 right. On this approach, one might arguably conceptualise three different perspectives that might be brought to bear directly, though implicitly, on the protection of minority identity:[56] First, unreasonable distinctions against a minority; second, positive distinctions in favour of a minority; and third, justificatory, case-specific reasoning on the treatment of a minority.

The Court's scrutiny of Belgian language policies under Article 14 in *Belgian Linguistics* while rejecting the claim to mother tongue education may be broadly taken to imply that the ECHR is *not* indifferent to the possible discriminatory effects on minority groups that may have been generated by official (language or otherwise) policies, but, on the contrary, prohibit them (somewhat echoing the equality discourse of the Permanent Court of International Justice in *Minority Schools in Albania*);[57] and that proactive domestic policies that appear *prima facie* in line with the ECHR must be corrected so as to remove the source of discrimination against minority groups in breach of Article 14. A largely convergent approach is reflected in the *Diergaardt* and *Waldman* cases before the HRC. Both of them led to a finding of discrimination against members of minority groups (under Article 26 ICCPR) as a result of state policies on language and religious education, respectively, that either targeted the group's language or unreasonably differentiated between minorities in providing public funding

---

[56] Interestingly, in the cases of *Yazar et al.*, *Dicle* and *Case of Socialist Party* (*supra* note 2, paras. 42, 39–40, and 15, respectively), Turkey suggested that the very recognition of the existence of an ethno-cultural minority is incompatible with the principle of equal enjoyment of citizenship rights without any distinction. The Court's line of reasoning in all those cases and the general jurisprudence on Article 14 clearly do not embrace such a traditional claim. A similar argument has been openly dismissed by the HRC (*see supra* note 51, para. 4).

[57] *Minority Schools in Albania*, Advisory Opinion, PCIJ, Series A/B, No. 64, p. 17. The Court held that the decision of the Albanian government to close all private schools, including those of the Greek minority in that country, as a result of the establishment of a generally applicable public education system, generated *de facto* consequences against this latter group's wish to maintain its own schools that were at odds with the principle of equality. Interestingly, in *Kelly* v. *United Kingdom*, 4 May 2001, ECHR, no. 30054/96, para. 148, the Court stated that "where a general policy or measure had disproportionately prejudicial effects on a particular group, it is not excluded that this may be considered as discriminatory notwithstanding that it is not specifically aimed or directed at that group".

that was not specifically required by the ICCPR.[58] A similar case against discrimination is being made in Latvia with regard to current provisions of the above-mentioned Education Law debarring minority private schools from seeking state financial support, which is open only to Latvian-speaking private schools.[59] An important question is how to remedy such discrimination. The extension of positive treatment to previously excluded minorities (for which it has also been argued with regard to measures falling within the reach of Article 27 rights)[60] does not seem to preclude the 'equalising down' option consisting in terminating the positive treatment itself.[61] In this regard, it should be noted that the Court has always been deferent towards states parties as to the most appropriate means of putting an end to a breach of the ECHR.

But perhaps the deeper aspect of the Court's jurisprudence is reflected in the very issue of looking into the existence of a breach of the duty not to produce unreasonable distinctions against minorities. Traditionally, the Article 14 question has been left aside following determination of a violation of the substantive provision and/or absent a major and clear-cut instance of discrimination, though the Court has indeed found an additional, autonomous breach of that provision in some recent cases concerning such general matters as the rights to life and to vote.[62] More importantly, the Court's overall tendency thus far has been to carefully avoid enlarging *in casu* the established boundaries of negative equality in relation to complex group (identity) situations. While *Jeļena Grišankova* – in which the applicants also advanced the argument of inequality of treatment between

[58] Indeed, the HRC observed in the second case that "the Covenant does not oblige States Parties to fund schools which are established on a religious basis", *supra* note 36, para. 10.6.

[59] *See supra* note 35.

[60] *See e.g.*, C. Tomuschat, 'Protection of Minorities under Article 27 of the International Covenant on Civil and Political Rights', in Bernhardt, Geck, Jaenicke, and Steinberger (eds.), *Völkerrecht als Rechtsordnung Internationale Gerichtsbarkeit Menschenrechte: Festschrift für Hermann Mosler* (1983) p. 949 *et seq.*, at 970; Nowak, *The UN Covenant on Civil and Political Rights: CCPR Commentary* (Springer-Verlag, Berlin, 1993) p. 504.

[61] On the option of 'equalising down', *see* S. Joseph, J. Schultz and M. Castan, *The International Covenant on Civil and Political Rights: Cases, Materials, and Commentary* (Oxford University Press, 2000), p. 570.

[62] *See Nachova and Others* v. *Bulgaria*, 26 February 2004, ECHR, nos. 43577/98 and 43579/98 (the case is currently pending before the Grand Chamber); *Aziz* v. *Cyprus*, 22 June 2004, ECHR, no. 69949/01. *See generally Airey* v. *Ireland*, 9 October 1979, ECHR, no. 6289/73, para. 30.

native Latvians and members of the Russian-speaking group in respect of mother tongue education in public secondary schools – was declared inadmissible on procedural grounds, other cases such as *Mathieu-Mohin and Clerfayt* v. *Belgium*,[63] *Jewish Liturgical Ass'n Cha'are Shalom ve Tsedek* v. *France*,[64] and *Gorzelik* illustrate this point on the merits. For example, in *Gorzelik* the Polish government argued that the act of recognising the Silesians as a national minority would produce discriminatory consequences for 'other ethnic groups' in Poland, such as the Highlanders, Kashubinas and Mazurians. Both the Chamber and the Grand Chamber accepted the notion that Poland had acted to protect, *inter alia*, the rights of others, without considering, though, the groups between which a comparison was appropriate, and the very reason for such comparison. The proposition put forward by the Court, that it was not for it to determine whether the Silesians were a national minority, was hardly an answer, because if that was indeed the case (based on a comparison not between the Silesians and those groups mentioned by Poland, but between the former and the groups that had already been recognised as national minorities),[65] an instance of discrimination against them would have to be found contrary to Article 14 ECHR (at least with regard to electoral matters), in line with the Court's above jurisprudence on domestic policies going beyond what the ECHR specifically requires.

The question whether Article 14 ECHR, besides outlawing unreasonable distinctions, can generate a positive duty to achieve equality, in a way that benefits minority identity, raises even more problematic issues. For one thing, the finding in *Thlimmenos* of a breach of Article 14 (in conjunction with Article 9) for failure by the respondent state to treat significantly different situations differently (*in casu*, by means of appropriate exemptions

---

[63] *Mathieu-Mohin and Clerfayt* v. *Belgium*, 2 March 1987, ECHR, Series A No. 113 [the Court's majority shied away from the argument, embraced by the joint dissent, that the actual functioning of the Belgian system of political representation entailed a group-based language distinction contrary to Article 14 ECHR in conjunction with Article 3 of Protocol No. 1].

[64] *Jewish Liturgical Ass'n Cha'are Shalom ve Tsedek* v. *France*, 27 June 2000, ECHR, no. 27417/95 [the Court downplayed a difference in treatment affecting a sector of the Jewish community in France compared to mainstream Jewish associations].

[65] Recognition had mostly derived from bilateral treaties entered into by Poland, and the procedure for the registration of associations. The 2002 Report submitted by Poland under the Framework Convention for the Protection of National Minorities has provided an additional source.

allowing a Jehovah Witness to have access to the profession of charter accountant despite an earlier court conviction against him arising from his religious beliefs) appears consistent with the Court's increasingly embraced understanding of the ECHR as not excluding the existence of positive obligations for the parties.[66] And yet, to interpret this particular case as the actual recognition of an automatic general duty to ensure positive equality, which may directly benefit minorities along with other groups under the ECHR, would probably amount to a misperception. First, the Court does not point to a direct entitlement to differential treatment, but rather to the effects on equality deriving from the lack of such treatment, which arguably does not necessarily exceed the view of indirect discrimination already encompassed by the *Belgian Linguistics* and other decisions. Second, the 'reasonable and objective' test, reaffirmed therein, leaves the parties a margin of appreciation in assessing the situations in question, and in practice the Court has not been keen to intrude upon the parties' assessment on issues involving Article 14. Third, the individual-oriented characterisation of the situations leading up to a differential treatment (the focus is indeed on 'persons' in analogous or significantly different situation) seems to suggest that the impact of the Court's proposition on groups considerations (if they ever exist) may be more limited. And some post-*Thlimmenos* case law provides indication of that, including *Podkolzina*, *Chapman* and *Refah Partisi (The Welfare Party) and Others* v. *Turkey*, in which the Court did not address or embrace relevant aspects of group differentiation.[67]

From a broader perspective, a fundamental distinction should be made between the sort of 'special measures' envisaged by general anti-discrimination clauses and the positive action conceptualised by the minority rights discourse. The former essentially constitute tools for temporary affirmative action treatment, whereas the latter serves *au fond* the specific

---

[66] The Court has in fact found positive duties in relation to several classic ECHR rights, such as freedom of association in Article 11, *Plattform 'Arzte für das Leben'*, 21 June 1988, Series A No. 139; freedom of religion in Article 9, *Jewish Liturgical Ass'n Cha'are Shalom ve Tsedek* v. *France, supra* note 64; and respect for private and family life in Article 8, *Chapman* v. *United Kingdom*, *supra* note 19.

[67] In *Podkolzina* and *Chapman* the Court declined to uphold special arrangements tackling the arguably 'significantly different' situation of the groups involved (Russian speakers and Roma, respectively); in *Refah Partisi*, it held that a plurality of personal law regimes along religious lines was *tout court* incompatible with Article 14; *Refah Partisi (The Welfare Party) and Others* v. *Turkey,* 31 July 2001 (Chamber) and 13 February 2003 (Grand Chamber), ECHR, nos. 41340/98, 41342/98, 41343/98 and 41344/98.

and sole objective of governing the complexities brought about by the existence of a minority as an ethno-cultural group. Thus, such positive action may well be of a permanent nature, as long as it is in tune with the principle of equality.[68] It may be argued that a reading of Article 14 ECHR that implies a direct and general duty to reasonably differentiate, though not precluding minority identity considerations, would be likely to constrain them because of the most basic character of positive discrimination under international human rights law. Having said that, it remains unclear whether Article 27 ICCPR, as the *locus classicus* of minority rights in international law, does embody a positive duty to protect minority identity in general. The HRC has appeared quite assertive on this sort of positive action (aside from protection in the private sphere),[69] but the core discourse has been mostly framed in terms of justifying, rather than systematically subsuming, positive measures under that provision. As a matter of fact, the HRC's view of Article 27 is incremental in nature, and an ever higher number of affected states parties is subscribing to the notion that Article 27 does entail positive identity obligations.[70] Clearly, the base line from which to assess existing positive measures in connection with Article 27 is the complex of anti-discrimination clauses, by analogy with *Diergaardt* and *Waldman* as commented above.

On the justificatory approach, states are normally left free to decide if and when positive action is necessary, though a solid equality benchmark is offered as to *how* such action, where it takes place, must be shaped. Whether or not the HRC will clarify its view of Article 27 in a way that favours direct and positive identity duties, the justificatory perspective may well reflect a model for looking at minority issues under Article 14 ECHR. In other words,

---

[68] G. Pentassuglia, *supra* note 8, pp. 88–93; *ibid.,* 'Minority Rights and the Role of Law: Reflections on Themes of Discourse in Kymlicka's Approach to Ethnocultural Identity', 4 *Journal of Ethnopolitics and Minority Issues in Europe* (2002) p. 1 *et seq.*, at pp. 13–15. *See* also K. Myntti, 'The Prevention of Discrimination v. Protection of Minorities – With Particular Reference to 'Special Measures'', 2 *Baltic Yearbook of International Law* (2002) 199 *et seq.*

[69] *See* especially the *Lubicon Lake Band, Länsman* and *Apirana Mahuika* decisions, *supra* notes 9–10. *See also* General Comment No. 23 (50), *supra* note 51, paras. 6.1–6.2 and 7.

[70] G. Pentassuglia, *supra* note 8, pp. 107–108. In *Jarle Jonassen and Members of the Riast/Hylling Reindeer Herding District* v. *Norway, supra* note 10, para. 4.10, Norway implicitly accepted in principle the point made by the authors, that Article 27 generated positive obligations to protect minority identity. The HRC's majority declared the case inadmissible due to a failure to exhaust local remedies.

instead of moving away from the notion of equality as solely negative in character to a broader understanding that includes an unqualified, general and positive duty to reasonably differentiate, the Court might arguably be more prepared to embrace the justificatory perspective in order to monitor *ex post facto* certain minority regimes.[71] And indeed, in the light of *Thlimmenos*, earlier case law might be read in the sense that domestic regimes of minority rights that pass the 'reasonable and objective' test are fully compatible with Article 14.[72] The *Refah Partisi* case also reminds us that the Court, while recognising the right to freedom of religion through the organisational autonomy of religious communities, may not be inclined to justify minority regimes along religious lines. It needs to be noted that the assumption discussed by the Court was that *all* fields of public and private law would differentiate between individuals according to their religion. In his concurring opinion, Judge Kovler aptly observed that, aside from the specifics of the case (involving the banning of a mainstream Muslim political party, not the outlawing of a minority group's stance), it is well-established in ancient and modern legal theory that in certain cases minority regimes of personal law, whether on religious grounds or otherwise, can be accepted as legitimate models of protection. Interestingly, he argued for a democratic compromise within society that is able to accommodate the interests of the communities concerned, rather than one that simply limits or

---

[71] The case-by-case approach that follows does not point to the inherently case-based assessment of the Court, but rather to the context-specific place of the anti-discrimination principle in the ECHR, which does not seem to guarantee that the equality dimension will always be addressed by the Court, and even more so – it might be argued – when it impinges upon groups. For comments on the 'contingency' of Article 14, *see* L. Wildhaber, 'Protection against Discrimination under the European Convention on Human Rights – A Second Class Guarantee?', 2 *Baltic Yearbook of International Law* (2002) p. 71 *et seq*., at p. 80.

[72] The Court might thus justify, through Article 14, special arrangements virtually coinciding with the positive action embodied by the international protection of minorities, despite the absence of a specific minority entitlement in the ECHR. *See e.g., Case Relating to Certain Aspects of the Laws on the Use of Languages in Education in Belgium,* 25 June 1965, European Commission of Human Rights, para. 405; *The Liberal Party, Mrs R. and Mr P.* v. *United Kingdom,* ECHR, no. 8765/79, 21 *Decisions and Reports 1981*, p. 211 *et seq*. *See also* the joint dissent implicitly justifying special electoral arrangements in *Mathieu-Mohin, supra* note 63; compare with *Diergaardt, supra* note 11, para. 10.8 and concurring opinion of Mr Scheinin; *Marie-Hélène Gillot et al.* v. *France*, 15 July 2002, Human Rights Committee, no. 932/2000, UN Doc. CCPR/C/75/D/932/2000 (2000), para. 13.4.

rejects them in the name of the general interest as implied by the theme of democratic compromise in *Gorzelik* and *Refah Partisi* itself.[73]

Importantly, the justificatory case-specific perspective seems to be in line with the logic of Protocol No. 12, entered in force on 1 April 2005. This instrument does not impose any obligation to adopt positive measures to achieve full and effective equality, while acknowledging that *de facto* inequalities suffered by certain groups or categories of persons may constitute justifications for adopting them.[74] A major assumption underlying the notion of indirect discrimination, which was already broadly reflected, albeit implicitly, in *Belgian Linguistics*, is that the lack of positive treatment does not in itself breach the equality principle, as such treatment may not be *claimed* on the basis of that principle. And yet, the Court held in *Thlimmenos* that Article 14 ECHR is also *violated* if a state fails, without a reasonable and objective justification, to treat different situations differently.[75] If *Thlimmenos* were to be read as going beyond Protocol No. 12 on this question, then the conclusion would paradoxically be that Protocol No. 12 actually marks a retreat into the more familiar pre-*Thlimmenos* jurisprudence on Article 14. On the other hand, the setting forth of an independent (as opposed to accessory) prohibition of discrimination may well suggest that the legal effects of this protocol are meant to widen, rather than deepen, those of Article 14. On this arguably more plausible reading, the functioning of the principle of equality in the ECHR and Protocol No. 12 would be in essence the same (both including the justificatory perspective), while the value added of *Thlimmenos* for anti-discrimination law may consist in not excluding case-specific positive obligations for individual categories of persons (as opposed to a general positive equality clause). But, as indicated earlier, whether and to what extent that may allow for greater consideration of minority identity per se remains controversial.

---

[73] *See supra* note 67. *See also* the dissenting opinion of Messrs Fuhrmann, Loucaides and Bratza in the Chamber Judgement of 31 July 2001, *ibid.*, maintaining that it was not necessary to examine the precise nature or effect of the plurality of personal law regimes in question.

[74] Along broadly similar lines, Article 5 of the European Community Council Directive of 29 June 2000 implementing the principle of equal treatment between persons irrespective of racial or ethnic origin, EC Directive 2000/43 of 29 June 1996, O.J. 2000 L 180, 22, provides that "[w]ith a view to ensuring full equality in practice, the principle of equal treatment shall not prevent any member State from maintaining or adopting specific measures to prevent or compensate for disadvantages linked to racial or ethnic origin".

[75] *See supra* note 55, para. 44.

5. The Problem of Interpretation

Overall, the Court's approach to minority issues brings to the fore the way in which the Court understands its interpretative role in structuring the relationship between those issues and the ECHR in general. For example, in *Gorzelik* the Court shifted the focus from the potentially abusive situation in Poland regarding recognition and classification of 'national' minorities and 'ethnic' minorities or groups under Polish law[76] to a narrow and superficial question of electoral benefits that the government suspected the applicant Silesians would be seeking following their recognition as a national minority. The Grand Chamber stressed that Polish authorities had, though, consistently recognised the existence of a Silesian ethnic minority and the right of Silesians to associate with one another. Yet, it offered no analysis as to whether there was any basis for distinguishing this group from recognised national minorities. In practice, the Court disconnected the ECHR from the deeper minority problem at stake, questionably relaxing the earlier case law on Article 11. In *Chapman*, the Court broadly argued that the complexities and sensitivity of minority issues renders its role "a strictly supervisory one", or, simply put, one of a somewhat detached observer of state policies and practices in the area. That suggested the de-coupling of the case from what more directly impinges on the position of minorities in international law, rather than the need for contextual appreciation of the minority question as indicated on several occasions by the HRC.[77] However, the substantial joint dissent firmly opposed this clear deferential line. It urged the Court to

[76] The procedure for registration of associations was the only indirect method of seeking recognition as a national minority under Polish law for those groups which had not already been recognised through international treaties. The Court acknowledged this state of affairs as a lacuna in the law generating uncertainty for individuals and discretion on the part of the authorities vis-à-vis persons claiming to belong to a minority. And indeed, the absence of an internal mechanism to seek minority status, while not required by international law, may in practice reinforce that discretion over the treatment of all or some of the groups concerned. The Katowice Court of Appeal and the Supreme Court controversially provided their own understanding of 'national or ethnic minorities' under Article 35 of the Constitution. The Court of Appeal argued that in order for a group to constitute a national minority, this group must be linked to a majority outside Poland and/or reflect the existence of a nation accepted by others. Those elements have in fact no basis in international law. Both of those courts drew a distinction between 'national minorities' and 'ethnic minorities' or groups – again, a contestable characterisation from the perspective of the core notion of minority under international law.

[77] *See e.g.*, *I. Länsman* v. *Finland*, *supra* note 10, para. 9.3.

actively embrace international legal developments on minorities – which had been downplayed by the majority by moving back to the right to a home theme – as they reflect international consensus within the Council of Europe system.[78] In fact, the competing visions of minority rights surfaced in *Chapman* go beyond contingent interpretation to conceal different understandings of the issue of minorities within the human rights framework in general, and under the ECHR in particular, thereby defining the substance of the margin of appreciation given to states parties.

6. Access to Court

Apart from the receptivity of the Court to minority issues per se under the ECHR, Article 6(1) might provide at least a procedural context within which such issues in general, or even minority rights in particular, can be determined.[79] In the case of *Muonio Saami Village* v. *Sweden*,[80] Sweden plainly recognised the minority right in question under the 1971 Reideer Husbandry Act as a 'civil right' in the sense of Article 6(1). Although the focus in *Muonio* was on domestic minority rights, the access to court issue may well arise from a claim to minority rights under international law, or a claim that is somewhat linked to such rights, as is illustrated by the two-tier structure of the complaint and decision in *Apirana Mahuika et al.* v. *New Zealand* and *Anni Äärelä and Jouni Näkkäläjärvi* v. *Finland* before the HRC

---

[78] They importantly emphasised that the protection of minorities implied both negative and positive duties upon state parties. *See Chapman* v. *United Kingdom*, *supra* note 19, dissenting opinion of Messrs Pastor Ridruejo, Bonello, Tulkens, Straznicka, Lorenzen, Fischbach and Casadevall. Compare generally with *Connors* v. *The United Kingdom*, *supra* note 21, paras. 84, 90 and 93–94.

[79] As clarified by the Court, the right recognised in Article 6(1) is not just a defendant's right, it is a plaintiff's right as well, including the right to effective enforcement of judgements. Also, the procedure about which the applicant is complaining must be decisive for the determination of the 'civil right' in question. *See e.g.*, *Golder* v. *United Kingdom,* ECHR, 1 *European Human Rights Reports* (1974) p. 524 *et seq.*; *Hornsby* v. *Greece,* 19 March 1997, ECHR, *Reports of Judgements and Decisions 1997-II*; *Fayed* v. *United Kingdom,* ECHR, 18 *European Human Rights Reports* (1994) p. 393 *et seq.* Recent case law on religious communities indirectly signals the relevance of that provision to minority groups, particularly in respect of legal personality and property matters; *see e.g.*, *Canea Catholic Church* v. *Greece*, 16 December 1997, ECHR, *Reports of Judgements and Decisions 1997-VIII*. *See* by analogy, *supra* note 7. *See also*, *mutatis mutandis*, *The Holy Monasteries* v. *Greece*, 9 December 1994, ECHR, no. 10/1993/405/483-484.

[80] *Muonio Saami Village* v. *Sweden*, 9 January 2001, ECHR, no. 28222/95.

(both establishing a connection between Article 27 claims and due process guarantees in domestic proceedings in Article 14(1) ICCPR). As long as minority issues fall within the scope of a 'civil right' for the purposes of Article 6(1) ECHR,[81] the 'strictly supervisory role' referred to by the Court in *Chapman* would thus be linked, not to any evaluation of the merits of minority claims, but to securing a fair (judicial) mechanism to settle those claims in light of domestic and international standards (somewhat echoing the *procedural* approach of Article 14(3) of ILO Convention No. 169 Concerning Indigenous and Tribal Peoples in Independent Countries).[82]

7. Conclusion

Two basic points seem to emerge from the analysis of the Court's case law within the wider international law context offered by the HRC's judicial-like

---

[81] On the prior question whether the complaint concerns the determination of an actual 'right', whether relevant aspects of that right are justiciable, and/or whether major public law issues are involved, *see e.g.*, *Masson and Van Zon* v. *The Netherlands,* ECHR, 22 *European Human Rights Reports* (1995) p. 491 *et seq.*, para. 44; *Rolf Gustafsson* v. *Sweden,* ECHR, *Reports of Judgements and Decisions 1997-IV*, p. 1149 *et seq.* (concurring opinion of Mr de Meyer). Compare with *Apirana Mahuika et al.* v. *New Zealand*, *supra* note 9, paras. 6.4 and 9.11, and the partly dissenting opinion by Mr Scheinin. On the critical distinction between civil rights and public rights for the purposes of Article 6, *see generally* Janis, Kay and Bradley, *European Human Rights Law: Texts and Materials* (Oxford University Press, 2000) p. 418 *et seq.,* citing *Feldbrugge* v. *The Netherlands,* ECHR, 8 *European Human Rights Reports* (1986), p. 425 *et seq.* A similar discussion has developed with regard to the concept of 'suit at law' in Article 14(1) ICCPR: *see* Joseph, Schultz and Castan, *supra* note 61, pp. 279–282. In general, one can assume that human rights, affecting individuals as such, fall within the purview of these provisions and prevail over other public law considerations. *But see* recently the case of *Al-Adsani* v. *United Kingdom*, 21 November 2001, ECHR, 34 *European Human Rights Reports* (2002), p. 11 *et seq.*; on this case, *see also* Orakhelashvili, 'Restrictive Interpretation of Human Rights Treaties in the Recent Jurisprudence of the European Court of Human Rights', 14 *European Journal of International Law* (2003), p. 529 *et seq*., especially pp. 561–562.

[82] 28 ILM (1989), p. 1382 *et seq.* This provision requires the parties to secure "adequate procedures" to resolve such land claims as might exist, although this treaty is not intended to establish new land claims. In particular, those problematic land issues that are left unresolved by the treaty are referred to fair domestic mechanisms for legal determination. By analogy, Article 6 ECHR might guarantee judicial review of certain minority claims that may be brought under domestic and international law.

perspective regarding the ICCPR and its Article 27. The first is that the ECHR, repeatedly referred to by the Court as a 'living instrument' to be interpreted in accordance with present-day conditions,[83] may prove more responsive to the needs of minority groups than traditionally expected or understood as a result of the lack of specific minority provisions, and the limited reference to a national minority in Article 14. The second is that the limitations implied in the Court's reading of the ECHR can paradoxically help appreciate, by contrast, those inevitably missing areas of protection that capture (or should capture) the essence of minority rights in the larger human rights canon. From a forward-looking perspective, the expanded ECHR system generated by the end of Cold-War polarities might play a substantive role (i.e. aside from the equally important, yet procedural approach mentioned above) in terms of protecting some essential preconditions for enjoying minority identity (indirect protection) and engaging with the complexities and substance of minority identity per se (direct, though implicit, protection). Whereas the former area, reflected in the Articles 10/11 case law, is ultimately defined by the absence of *legal* (as opposed to factual) autonomy of the minority question to the determination of the case, *Chapman* signals a principled, though limited, advance in the latter area, which might *potentially* be strengthened both on its own terms and by further expanding examination into certain aspects of mother tongue education, language use, and of course equality.

At the same time, though, a relatively clear understanding of the minority phenomenon in international law may well be needed if the ECHR is to work properly in regard to certain issues intersecting this area. In *Gorzelik*, the Court shied away from the definitional question absent a specific *treaty* concept of minority, while the concurring opinion led by Judge Costa annexed to the Grand Chamber's judgement characterised the Polish view of the Silesians and national minorities as a political one on which they declined to comment.[84] In fact, while lacking an explicit treaty definition, international law certainly constrains state conduct with regard to traditional ethno-cultural groups,[85] as seemingly implied at one point by the Grand Chamber's judgement itself (by pointing to a "commonly shared European view" on national minorities generated by European history),[86] and

---

[83] *See generally Tyrer* v. *United Kingdom*, 25 April 1978, ECHR, Series A No. 26; *Marckx* v. *Belgium*, 13 June 1979, ECHR, Series A No. 31.

[84] *See Gorzelik and others* v. *Poland, supra* note 6 (Grand Chamber), para. 8 (concurring opinion of Messrs Costa and Zupancic, joined by Mr Kovler).

[85] G. Pentassuglia, *supra* note 8, Chapter III. *See also supra* note 68.

[86] *See Gorzelik and others* v. *Poland supra* note 6 (Grand Chamber), para. 68.

the Court could – arguably should – have relied on this for at least discussing the position of Silesians, especially from the perspective of Article 14. Interestingly, in the case of *Acquisition of Polish Nationality*, the Permanent Court of International Justice rejected the Polish argument that it was only for Poland to define and thus place under international protection its minorities, stressing instead the autonomous role of international law on the basis of the 1919 Minority Treaty.[87] The fundamental theme of ethno-cultural identity in the Court's case law, which is relevant to traditional groups, differs from the broader question of social inclusion and full enjoyment of citizenship rights typically posed by immigrants, 'minorities by force', and others,[88] even when the pursuing of fair terms of integration arguably requires the accommodation of their (cultural, religious, or otherwise) differences.[89] Still, a degree of impact of such case law on the

---

[87] *Acquisition of Polish Nationality*, Advisory Opinion, PCIJ, Series B No. 7 (1923), pp. 13–16. To some extent, the notion of 'autonomous concepts' developed by the Court in respect of the ECHR might assist with interpreting '(national) minority' in the context of Article 14 and the treaty as a whole. On that theory, *see* recently G. Letsas, 'The Truth in Autonomous Concepts: How To Interpret the ECHR', 15 *European Journal of International Law* (2004) pp. 279–305.

[88] *See e.g.*, *Aziz* v. *Cyprus*, *supra* note 62 [access to vote]; *Zdanoka* v. *Latvia*, 6 March 2003 (admissibility), ECHR, no. 58278/00 [access to vote]; *Selim* v. *Cyprus*, 18 September 2001 (admissibility) and 16 July 2002 (friendly settlement), ECHR, no. 47293/99 [access to civil marriage]; *Sisojeva et al.* v. *Latvia*, 28 February 2002 (admissibility), ECHR, no. 60654/00 [access to legal residency]; *Al-Nashif* v. *Bulgaria*, 20 June 2002, ECHR, no. 50963/99 [access to religious teaching].

[89] *Thlimmenos* illustrates the particular question of pursuing full integration into mainstream society through the accommodation of certain religious differences, which arguably echoes Will Kymlicka's reference to fair terms of integration for ethnic and religious groups different from national minorities. W. Kymlicka, *Multicultural Citizenship: A Liberal Theory of Minority Rights* (1995) pp. 114–115; *ibid.,* 'Can Liberal Pluralism be Exported?', in W. Kymlicka and M. Opalski (eds.), *Western Political Theory and Ethnic Relations in Eastern Europe* (2001), *passim.* However, in the case of *Leyla Şahin* v. *Turkey*, 29 June 2004, ECHR, no. 44774/98, the Court held that forbidding the applicant, a young practising Muslim student, to wear the Islamic headscarf when attending the University of Instanbul did not breach the ECHR, particularly Article 9 (freedom of religion) and Article 2 of Protocol No. 1 (right to education). Contrast with the remarkable decision of a British Court of Appeal in the case of *R (Shabina Begum)* v. *Head Teacher and Governors of Denbigh High School* [2005] EWCA Civ 199, 2 March 2005, holding instead that a High School in Luton had violated the right to education and to manifest religious beliefs in refusing to allow a Muslim girl pupil to wear the

latter groups cannot be excluded, notably in the area of anti-discrimination law as suggested by *Thlimmenos*. On the other hand, it would appear that some general aspects affecting minority identity can also arise from the situation of groups or individuals whose specific international legal status as minorities or minority members (in the above sense) is remarkably questionable.[90]

No matter how the dilemmas and tensions within the Court on relevant minority identity issues will be resolved[91] – particularly whether aspects of the HRC's case law might intrude upon, or inspire advances under the ECHR – the previous assessment also suggests the importance of the 'negative' role of the ECHR in defining the areas where the international architecture of minority rights needs to be reinforced in its own right. In the Court's reading, classic ECHR non-interference rights generally do not reach out to a collectively understood minority dimension, which calls for, or highlights, a corresponding strength of such dimension in relation to the amount of non-interference freedoms that are attached to minority rights regimes. But the key question here is the protection of minority identity that surrounds the justification for the very existence and the character of minority rights as interrelated with, and most importantly *additional* to, general human rights ('public' education and language rights, positive action duties): While the Court's case law proves clearly limited (in spite of potential improvement), the HRC's case law does *not* prove terribly successful in overcoming those limitations. In fact, it might be argued that the two bodies of jurisprudence reflect more similarities than differences than might be expected, either in principle or in practice. This exposes at least some of the conceptual and legal oscillations between general

Islamic 'jilbab'. Along comparable lines, *see* further, *Raihon Hudoybergonova* v. *Uzbekistan*, 5 November 2004, no. 931/2000, U.N. Doc. CCPR/C/82/D/931/2000 (2004).

[90] *See e.g.,* the case of *Lagerblom* v. *Sweden, supra* note 44, in which the applicant claimed to belong to the Finnish-speaking minority in Sweden, despite the fact he had moved from Finland to Sweden in the second half of the 1980s. Broadly speaking, questionable minority cases in the sense of international law can nevertheless either indirectly generate principled considerations regarding the international treatment of minorities or even result in producing protection that crosscuts a wider spectrum of individuals and groups, given the general nature of the ECHR.

[91] It is not entirely clear whether those dilemmas are being defined by the perceived lack of consensus on the protection of minorities or the very (general) scope of the ECHR; *see e.g., Chapman* v. *United Kingdom, supra* note 19, paras. 93–94 and 100.

assumptions and special protections generated in different ways by the mainstream minority rights discourse (analogous oscillations inform the non-judicial discourse reflected in the Council of Europe's Framework Convention for the Protection of National Minorities), that *de facto* question the ultimate relevance and productiveness of minority rights themselves.

From the perspective of twenty-first-century Europe – nationally and sub-nationally diverse – there seems to be compelling reasons for the emergence of a general human rights framework that can partially, yet effectively, embrace minority- and group-friendly considerations while leaving the periphery of the system to minority rights that can entrench clearer, not necessarily greater, legal guarantees than the existing ones appear to entail. In other words, some sort of two-speed multicultural European human rights law designed to critically rethink ethno-cultural identity on the Continent.

History of International Law in the Baltic States

The Soviet Aggression against Lithuania in January 1991: International Legal Aspects

*Dainius Žalimas**

Contents

---

* Associate Professor, the head of the Department of International Law and the European Union Law, Faculty of Law, Vilnius University.

Baltic Yearbook of International Law, Volume 6, 2006, pp. 293–343.

1. Introduction

The year 2006 marked the 15th anniversary of the failed Soviet attempt to overthrow Lithuania's independence in January 1991. The peak of the Soviet aggressive action was reached on 11–13 January when the Soviet Armed Forces seized the press, radio and television station buildings as well as several other government buildings in Vilnius. During the night-time attack on 13 January of the television tower and national television and radio stations the Soviet military killed 13 civilians and more than 1000 were injured. However, the unprecedented massive peaceful civic resistance compelled the Soviet Union to withdraw its armed forces without achieving its main objective of overthrowing the legitimate Lithuanian Government and restoring the puppet Lithuanian SSR. A week later, on 20 January 1991, similar events on a minor scale took place in Riga, the capital of Latvia, when during the storming of the building of the Ministry of the Interior of the Republic of Latvia by the Moscow controlled Soviet militia forces seven civilians were killed. It was also a part of the USSR plan to overthrow the legitimate Latvian authorities and, in general, Latvia's very independence, by setting up a puppet communist regime identical to that attempted to be implemented in Lithuania;[1] however, probably due to the failure in Lithuania this scheme was aborted in Latvia also.

Lithuania's major achievement was stopping the Soviet aggression of January 1991 by exclusively peaceful means. The Lithuanian experience of unarmed civic resistance was later applied in a wider context, e.g. both in the other two Baltic States and in Moscow on 19–21 August 1991 when the people successfully defended their legitimate government's independence and democracy against the attempted *coup d'etat* by the Soviet reaction

[1] It was also planned to conceal direct Soviet military aggression by using the local section of the USSR Communist Party in Latvia, which as in Lithuania, created the so-called 'Rescue Committee' in order to take power with the support of the Soviet Armed Forces. These facts are confirmed *inter alia* by the European Court of Human Rights in its recent Judgment passed by the Grand Chamber in the *Ždanoka* v. *Latvia* case (in particular, *see* paras. 20–24, 116–131 of the Judgment) where the January 1991 events in Latvia are depicted in the context of similar events in Lithuania. *See also* in general this Judgment as far as it concerns the historical, political and legal context of the situation of the Baltic States in January 1991: *Ždanoka* v. *Latvia*, 16 March 2006, ECHR, no. 58278/00, <cmiskp.echr.coe.int/kp197/view.asp?item=1&portal=hbkm&action=html&highlight=&sessionid=6271375&skin=hudoc-en>, visited on 19 March 2006.

forces. This resistance by peaceful means finally finished off the Soviet Union.

Therefore, looking retrospectively from the distance of 15 years and taking into account the wider historical context, prior and subsequent events, 13 January 1991 in Lithuania could be placed side by side with such historical dates and events as the establishment of the 'Solidarity' movement in Poland and the fall of the Berlin wall. If the 'Solidarity' movement started the end of the existence of the Soviet dominated camp of socialist system countries and the unification of Germany actually finished it, then 13 January 1991 marked the start of the dissolution of the Soviet empire itself. After 13 January 1991 it became obvious even for Russia that the Soviet Union was inevitably doomed to failure. However, of course, it could be reasonably questioned whether indeed the empire has disappeared forever, for even now we can observe, e.g. the continuous genocide in Chechnya, the prolongation of the old imperialistic policy.

Despite their historical significance, the 13 January 1991 events in Lithuania are not widely known or often recalled. Therefore, this article serves as a good opportunity to bring attention to them and assess them in the light of international law. In particular, those events have never been examined by international jurists as they have focused their attention on the international legal assessment of such general issues as the 1990–1991 restoration of the independence of the Baltic States, the international recognition of the governments of the Baltic States in 1991, the development of the relationships of the Baltic States with the Soviet Union and Russia in 1990–1993, international legal responsibility for the Soviet occupation of the Baltic States, etc.[2] Thus, it is the intent of this article to deepen the previous

---

[2] *E.g. see* R. Kherad, 'La Réconnaisance Internationale des Etats Baltes', in A. Sprudzs (ed.), *The Baltic Path to Independence* (William S. Hein & Co., New York, 1994) pp. 293–322; R. Yakemtchouk, 'Les republiques baltes en droit international: Echec d'une annexation operee en violation du droit des gens', in A. Sprudzs (ed.), *The Baltic Path to Independence* (William S. Hein & Co., New York, 1994) pp. 261–291; I. Ziemele, *State Continuity and Nationality: the Baltic States and Russia* (Martinus Nijhoff Publishers, Leiden, 2005) pp. 21–43; L. Malksoo, *Illegal Annexation and State Continuity: the Case of the Incorporation of the Baltic States by the USSR* (Martinus Nijhoff Publishers, Leiden, 2003) pp. 45–77; D. Žalimas, 'Legal Issues on the Continuity of the Republic of Lithuania', 1 *Baltic Yearbook of International Law* (2001) pp. 1–21; D. Žalimas, 'Commentary to the Law of the Republic of Lithuania on Compensation of Damage Resulting from the Occupation by the USSR', 3 *Baltic Yearbook of International Law* (2003) pp. 133–141, 149–151; D. Žalimas, *Lietuvos Respublikos nepriklausomybės atkūrimo 1990 m.*

studies concerning the continuity and restoration of the independence of the Baltic States by examining in detail the January 1991 events as one of the critical dates for the statehood of Lithuania and the other Baltic States.

This article deals with the following international legal issues: 1) how the Soviet military action of January 1991 can be assessed from the standpoint of international law, whether it should be regarded as an act of aggression or, on the contrary, a kind of internal conflict; 2) what was the impact of the January 1991 events to further the development of the situation around Lithuania and the other Baltic States under international law; 3) who probably until now bears the international legal responsibility for the Soviet military action of January 1991 against Lithuania.

2. Factual and Legal Background[3]

It is reasonable to start this article by recalling the main facts and their legal context in order to depict the situation that existed at that time, which is probably not well known outside the Baltic States. Most of those facts have also been established and confirmed by the courts during the Lithuanian legal proceedings in the *January 13 Case* where several leaders of the former local section of the USSR Communist Party (hereinafter – the CPL/CPSU) were convicted for their activities against the Republic of Lithuania from 1990 to 1991.[4]

---

kovo 11 d. tarptautiniai teisiniai pagrindai ir pasekmės (Demokratinės politikos institutas, Vilnius, 2005) pp. 257–261.

[3] A short chronology of the facts can also be found in, *e.g. Lietuva, 1991.01.13/Lithuania, 13.01.1991* (State Publishing Centre, Vilnius, 1991). A chronology of the 1990–1991 events and the main documents of that period in English can be found in *The Road to Negotiations with the U.S.S.R.* (State Publishing Centre, Vilnius, 1991).

[4] Therefore, this article also relies on facts provided by the judgments of the courts in the *January 13 Case*, in particular, 23 August 1999, the Vilnius District Court, No. 1-2(1999) (a copy of the Judgment was provided by the Court), 20 February 2001, the Court of Appeal, No. 1A-43(2001) (a copy of the Judgment was provided by the Court), 28 December 2001, the Supreme Court of Lithuania, No. 2K-595/2001, the internet site of the Court <www.lat.litlex.lt>, <ovada.tic.lt/lat/nutartis.aspx?id=20347>, visited on 10 January 2006.

2.1. The Restoration of Lithuania's Independence and the Negative Reaction of the USSR

It is well known that at the end of the ninth decade of the last century the process of democratisation in the Soviet Union logically resulted in the establishment of the popular fronts in the occupied Baltic States which sought to restore justice, freedom of their people and the independence of their countries. On 24 February 1990 the first independent parliamentary elections under Soviet rule were held in Lithuania during which the people of Lithuania expressed their full support to the programme of the *Sąjūdis* (the Popular Front) of Lithuania. The main purpose of the *Sąjūdis*' programme was to restore the independence of the State of Lithuania – the Republic of Lithuania – as well as to start negotiations on the withdrawal of the Soviet Armed Forces from Lithuania, to adopt the temporary Constitution of the Republic of Lithuania, to re-establish diplomatic relations with other States, and to restore the Lithuanian Armed Forces and police force, etc. Most would realise that those goals by the same token meant the immediate independence of the State, including independence from the Soviet Union by cutting off all illegal constraints imposed by the latter.

The *Sąjūdis*, indeed, won a huge victory in the elections. No opponent of independence was elected to the Supreme Council, in particular the CPL/CPSU was completely defeated. Therefore, no vote (124 votes for and six abstentions) was cast against the restoration of independence on 11 March 1990 in the Supreme Council.

In 1990 the Lithuanian situation was substantially different from that of Latvia and Estonia in the sense that Lithuanians could move forward in a more determined manner[5] and *de jure* restore their independence on 11 March 1990 *without declaring any transitional period*. It is evident from the main legal act restoring independence, the 11 March 1990 Act on the Re-establishment of the Independent State of Lithuania[6] (hereinafter – the Act on the Restoration of Independence), that full independence and execution of State sovereignty was restored. The first paragraph of the Act, in line with the will of the Lithuanian people, proclaimed that "*the execution of the sovereign power* of the State of Lithuania, heretofore *constrained by foreign force in 1940*, is hereby restored, and henceforth Lithuania *is again* an

[5] Ziemele, *supra* note 2, p. 38.

[6] *Lietuvos Respublikos Aukščiausiosios Tarybos ir Vyriausybės žinios*, 1990, No. 9-222. *See* English text of the Act, *e.g.* in the internet site of the Seimas of the Republic of Lithuania: <www3.lrs.lt/pls/inter3/dokpaieska.showdoc_l?p_id =50850>, visited on 10 January 2006.

Independent State" (emphasis added). Additionally, the last paragraph of the Act declared that the Supreme Council "begins to realise the complete sovereignty of the State". By the same token, that also meant that no other institution could have sovereign powers on the territory of Lithuania, including any Soviet institution or the puppet bodies later attempted to be established by the Soviets.

The conclusion can be also drawn from the 11 March 1990 Act on the Restoration of Independence that "the Lithuanian State has been restored rather than proclaimed as a new State",[7] i.e. the restoration of independence took place on the basis of the *de jure* continuity of the Republic of Lithuania that had been established already in 1918 and had never legally ceased to exist. Logically the second paragraph of the Act confirmed the legal identity of the Republic of Lithuania, by stating that "the Act of Independence of 16 February 1918 of the Council of Lithuania and the Constituent Seimas (the Parliament) Resolution of 15 May 1920 on the Re-established Democratic State of Lithuania never lost their legal effect and comprise the constitutional foundation of the State of Lithuania".

Paragraph 3 of the Act on the Restoration of Independence proclaims that "*the constitution of no other State is valid*" (emphasis added) on the territory of the Republic of Lithuania. To implement that principle two accompanying constitutional acts were also adopted on 11 March 1990 together with the Act:[8] the Law on the Reinstatement of the 12 May 1938 Constitution of Lithuania,[9] whereby the effect of the constitutions of the USSR and Lithuanian SSR (as well as the fundamental laws of the Soviet Union) was terminated. Furthermore, in line with the legal continuity and identity of the State of Lithuania the last Constitution of the Republic of Lithuania was reinstated and the Law on the Provisional Basic Law of the Republic of Lithuania[10] immediately suspended the validity of the 1938 Constitution, taking into account "the necessity to harmonise the provisions of that Constitution with the changed political, economic and other social relationships" (i.e. the reality of the 1990s). The Law also approved the

---

[7] Ziemele, *supra* note 2, p. 40.

[8] D. Žalimas, 'Legal Issues on the Continuity of the Republic of Lithuania', 1 *Baltic Yearbook of International Law* (2001) pp. 12, 18. *See also* S. Jakštonytė and M. Cvelich 'Constitutional and International Documents Concerning the International Legal Status of Lithuania', 1 *Baltic Yearbook of International Law* (2001) p. 302.

[9] *Lietuvos Respublikos Aukščiausiosios Tarybos ir Vyriausybės žinios*, 1990, No. 9-223.

[10] *Lietuvos Respublikos Aukščiausiosios Tarybos ir Vyriausybės žinios*, 1990, No. 9-224.

Provisional Basic Law that had been in effect, instead of the suspended 1938 Constitution, until the new permanent Constitution of 1992 was invoked. Therefore, the Provisional Basic Law in setting out the constitutional principles of the Lithuanian State acted as a temporary constitution for Lithuania for more than two years. Indeed, it implemented and developed the principles of the Act on the Restoration of Independence, including the principles of independence, sovereignty of the Lithuanian people and democracy, and in no way implied any legal ties with any other State.

Following the 11 March 1990 Act on the Restoration of Independence, the Supreme Council of the Republic of Lithuania, started to implement the full sovereignty of the State. First of all, this is evident from the legislative activity that demonstrates full independence from the USSR and the withdrawal of the Lithuanian people and territory from the previous illegal control by the Soviet Union. For example, on 11 and 13 March 1990 the Supreme Council adopted laws, in accordance with which all authorities previously subjected to the central Soviet Union Government, as well as all other institutions, organisations, undertakings and enterprises formerly subordinated to the central Soviet Government in Moscow were then placed under the jurisdiction of the Republic of Lithuania;[11] on 12 and 14 March 1990 the Supreme Council passed the explanatory decisions,[12] which declared that Lithuanian citizens could no longer be recruited to the Soviet Armed Forces and decided to terminate the activities of the Soviet military organs for recruitment, as they were regarded to be the organs of another State; in order to strengthen the restored independence of the State, until 1991 the Supreme Council also adopted laws concerning all the main fields of organisation of the independent State structures, including demarcation of State borders, national defence forces and military service, the police, national border guards and customs services, etc.[13]

Secondly, in the field of external relations as from 11 March 1990 the Republic of Lithuania always treated the USSR as a foreign State. This is evident from the political documents of that time:[14] e.g., on 12 March 1990

---

[11] *Lietuvos Respublikos Aukščiausiosios Tarybos ir Vyriausybės žinios*, 1990, No. 9-225, 235.

[12] 1 *Lietuvos Respublikos Aukščiausiosios Tarybos ir Aukščiausiosios Tarybos Prezidiumo dokumentų rinkinys* (LR AT leidykla, Vilnius, 1990) pp. 57–58, 61.

[13] *E.g., see* 1-2 *Lietuvos Respublikos Aukščiausiosios Tarybos ir Aukščiausiosios Tarybos Prezidiumo dokumentų rinkinys* (LR AT leidykla, Vilnius, 1990–1991).

[14] There are many official documents that prove this. It is simply impossible to cite or refer to all the numerous decisions, statements and press releases made by the Supreme Council, the Chairman of the Supreme Council, the Government, the Prime

the Chairman of the Supreme Council of the Republic of Lithuania sent official letters to the Chairman of the Supreme Council of the USSR and the Chairman of the Council of Ministers of the USSR, thereby informing them about the restoration of Lithuania's independence and calling for negotiations on the bilateral issues arising thereof. On the same day the Supreme Council adopted the Appeal to the Nations of the USSR which explained the decisions on the restoration of independence and called for peaceful and amicable neighbourly relations. On 13 March 1990 the Supreme Council adopted the Appeal to the Chairman of the Supreme Council of the USSR, which reminded him of the continued illegal stationing of the Soviet Armed Forces in Lithuania from 15 June 1940 and called for negotiations on their withdrawal as well as the discontinuation of any illegal military manoeuvres or similar activities. On 18 March 1990 the Chairman of the Supreme Council of the Republic of Lithuania sent a letter to the President of the USSR, thereby informing him that the Republic of Lithuania treated as illegal any decisions of the Soviet authorities concerning the 11 March 1990 legal acts of Lithuania and that the legal interests of the USSR in Lithuania had to be defined during bilateral negotiations. On 19 March 1990 the Supreme Council of the Republic of Lithuania adopted the Statement, thereby once again defining the stationing of the Soviet Armed Forces in Lithuania as illegal, since they had been used against Lithuania as a tool of aggression and occupation. On 22 March 1990 the Supreme Council and the Government of Lithuania issued the Joint Statement, thereby protesting against the illegal, from the standpoint of international law, decisions of the Soviet authorities with regard to Lithuania.

Thus, as from 11 March 1990 only *Lithuania's State institutions were exercising exclusive legislative, executive and judicial authority within the territory of Lithuania, and no Soviet legislative, executive or judicial organ was operating there*. The only Soviet organs then operating in Lithuania were the Soviet Armed Forces illegally stationed on Lithuania's soil. However, they were incapable of exercising legislative, executive or judicial functions. They controlled only the areas in which they were located and served as the military and logistical basis for the activities of the CPL/CPSU and its daughter pro-Soviet organisations.

Minister, etc. *E.g.*, *see* 1, 2, 3 *Lietuvos Respublikos Aukščiausiosios Tarybos ir Aukščiausiosios Tarybos Prezidiumo dokumentų rinkinys* (LR AT leidykla, Vilnius, 1990–1991); *The Road to Negotiations with the U.S.S.R.* (State Publishing Centre, Vilnius, 1991).

Such developments met with a fierce reaction from the Soviet Union. The Soviet Union decided not to comply with its international obligations to cease the illegal act and apply the principle of restitution with regard to Lithuania.[15] Contrary to international law, the USSR insisted on the prolongation of Lithuania's annexation by refusing to recognise Lithuania's legal acts on 11 March 1990 concerning the restoration of independence and even declared them illegal from the standpoint of Soviet law.[16] However, there was no authority in Lithuania subordinate to the USSR and capable of carrying out the decisions of the latter. Therefore, being aware of the fact that the Soviet Constitution and laws had not been in effect in Lithuania as of 11 March 1990, the USSR demanded that Lithuania immediately reinstate the constitutions of the USSR and Lithuanian SSR, i.e. according to Soviet demands the Lithuanian SSR was to be restored and the situation prior to 11 March 1990 re-established. Those demands were supported by political, economic and military coercion as well as subversive activities within Lithuania.

First of all, instead of a peaceful resolution of all differences, as suggested by Lithuania, the Soviet Union imposed an economic blockade on Lithuania. On 14 April 1990 the President and the Prime Minister of the Soviet Union sent a Telegram to the Supreme Council and the Government of Lithuania,[17] which accused the leadership of Lithuania of alleged illegal activity and presented an ultimatum, i.e. they demanded Lithuania cancel its

---

[15] As established by customary international law and codified in the UN International Law Commission's *Draft Articles on Responsibility of States for Internationally Wrongful Acts* (in particular, Articles 30, 34 and 35) the State responsible for the internationally wrongful act is under the obligation to cease the act, if it is continuing, and to make full reparation, including re-establishment of the legal situation that existed before the illegal act. *See* Official Records of the UN General Assembly, Fifty-sixth Session, Supplement No. 10 (A/56/10), chp. IV.E.1; also available at the Internet site of the International Law Commission: <untreaty.un.org/ilc/texts/instruments/english/draft%20articles/9_6_2001.pdf>, visited on 10 March 2006.

[16] *E.g.*, on 15 March 1990 the USSR Congress of People's Deputies declared as invalid Lithuania's legal acts on 11 March 1990, thereby insisting on the sovereignty of the USSR over Lithuania and the validity of the Soviet Constitution in Lithuania. *See* the 15 March 1990 Decree on the Decrees of 10–12 March 1990 Adopted by the Supreme Soviet of the Lithuanian SSR, *The Road to Negotiations with the U.S.S.R.* (State Publishing Centre, Vilnius, 1991) pp. 72–73.

[17] *See The Road to Negotiations with the U.S.S.R.* (State Publishing Centre, Vilnius, 1991) pp. 97–98.

legal acts concerning the restoration of independence within two days and immediately re-establish "the situation of the Republic as of 10 March 1990". This demand was a precondition for any further discussions between the USSR and Lithuania. In case of refusal, the USSR threatened to suspend the delivery of goods from the USSR and other States to Lithuania. Such an economic blockade actually took place when the Republic of Lithuania refused to renounce its independence, which would have been contrary to its constitutional order and the mandate of the Lithuanian people. The blockade instituted by the USSR, *inter alia*, constituted a grave breach of the principle of non-interference into the affairs of other States, as defined in the 1970 UN General Assembly Declaration on the Principles of International Law concerning Friendly Relations and Cooperation among States in accordance with the Charter of the United Nations.[18] Namely, it is prohibited under international law to use economic and political coercion to undermine the sovereign rights of other States.

The economic blockade ended in July 1990 with Lithuania's offer of a conditional moratorium on its legislative and executive activities.[19] However, all of Lithuania's attempts to facilitate the start of negotiations with the USSR had not been successful due to the uncooperative attitude of the latter and the absence of political will to treat Lithuania on an equal footing so as to eliminate the consequences of the 1940 illegal annexation. For instance, from 12 March 1990 to 31 May 1991 the Soviet Union had not replied to more than 50 official documents sent by Lithuania with various offers concerning proposed modes of negotiation and other issues of bilateral relations.[20] On 13 December 1990 the Soviet Union informed Lithuania about its decision to postpone consultative meetings of the delegations and

---

[18] *See Resolutions Adopted by the General Assembly during its Twenty-fifth Session, 15 September – 17 December 1970*, Official Records of the UN General Assembly, Twenty-fifth Session, Supplement No. 28 (A/8028) (United Nations, New York, 1971) pp. 121–125.

[19] On 29 June 1990 the Supreme Council of the Republic of Lithuania declared a readiness to suspend temporarily the legislative and executive activities aimed at strengthening independence provided that official negotiations with the USSR were started. However, it never happened and such a conditional moratorium was not effective until 28 December 1990 when it was finally renounced. *See The Road to Negotiations with the U.S.S.R.* (State Publishing Centre, Vilnius, 1991) pp. 127–128, 199–200.

[20] *See The Road to Negotiations with the U.S.S.R.* (State Publishing Centre, Vilnius, 1991) pp. 28–67.

working groups of experts,[21] i.e. to suspend the preliminary talks on eventual official negotiations with Lithuania. In fact, the USSR had finally determined to resort to force.

Thus, secondly, the USSR had prepared in advance to forcibly impose a solution on Lithuania. The Soviet military forces illegally stationed in Lithuania refused to comply with Lithuania's laws and from 11 March 1990 carried out several violent actions; they seized and looted the former Communist Party buildings and forcibly recruited Lithuanian citizens into the Soviet Armed Forces. Furthermore, they demonstrated their strength by staging military parades. The Soviet military forces also provided military and logistical support as well as safe shelter to the CPL/CPSU and its daughter organisations in Lithuania. The Soviet chief military commanders in Lithuania had been registered in the local sections of the CPL/CPSU and were even part of its leadership.

Seeking to mask its military and subversive activities against Lithuania, the Soviet Union decided to follow its long-standing tradition of creating visible popular unrest against Lithuanian authorities. For that purpose it decided to use the CPL/CPSU, which had been completely rejected by the Lithuanian people in the 24 February 1990 elections.[22] This local section of the USSR Communist Party (the so-called 'Communist Party of Lithuania on the CPSU platform') emerged on 23 December 1989 and was formed from the remnants of the former Communist Party of Lithuania by a group of former delegates (the secessionists) to the XX Congress of the Communist Party of Lithuania. In accordance with the decisions of the Congress, on 21 December 1989 the Lithuanian section of the Communist Party of the Soviet Union legally ceased to exist as it was reorganised into and was legally replaced by the independent Communist Party of Lithuania (later – the

---

[21] *See ibid.*, p. 194.

[22] There are many documents from that time demonstrating the USSR's support to the local section of the Soviet Communist Party. For instance, on 15 September 1990 the Political Bureau of the Central Committee of the Communist Party of the Soviet Union issued the Address to Communists and to the People of Lithuania, which regarded "favourably the search for ways for the Republic (of Lithuania) *to develop within the USSR* as a sovereign republic that are being undertaken by the Communist Party of Lithuania (CPSU platform)" and based "its hopes on the 21st Congress of the Communist Party of Lithuania (CPSU platform). The Congress is called upon to prepare documents mobilising, for the realisation of the constructive programme of perestroika, communists and all the people of the Republic who are *defending socialist achievements*". *See The Road to Negotiations with the U.S.S.R.* (State Publishing Centre, Vilnius, 1991) pp. 156–157.

Democratic Labour Party) with no legal ties to the Communist Party of the Soviet Union. However, a number of delegates decided not to comply with those decisions;[23] they were determined to remain under Moscow's control by reviving the Lithuanian section of the Communist Party of the Soviet Union (the CPL/CPSU) with the aims of maintaining Lithuania under Soviet control, restoration of the Lithuanian SSR and reinstatement of the Soviet constitution.

Obviously, as of 11 March 1990 under the national law of Lithuania this communist organisation, as well as its dependent entities, was treated as an illegal anti-State organisation; active participation in the CPL/CPSU was regarded as a crime against the State. First of all, the aims and activities of the CPL/CPSU contradicted the main principles of the Provisional Basic Law.[24] In particular, the special constitutional provision of Article 5 of the Provisional Basic Law provided that "*parties, public organisations and public movements shall be created according to the procedure established by law and shall function within the limits of the Provisional Basic Law and other laws of the Republic of Lithuania*" (emphasis added).

---

[23] It should be recalled here that a convincing majority, i.e. 855 out of 1033 Congress delegates, voted for the reorganisation of the Lithuanian section of the Communist Party of the Soviet Union into the independent Communist Party of Lithuania with its own programme and statute. *See* the Declaration of the Independence of the Communist Party of Lithuania and the Resolution on the Status of the Communist Party of Lithuania. For more general information concerning the XX Congress of the Communist Party of Lithuania and its outcomes, including the formation of the CPL/CPSU and its dependence on the Soviet Armed Forces, the government and the Communist Party of the Soviet Union *see*: *Lietuvos suvereniteto atkūrimas 1988-1991 metais* (Diemedis, Vilnius, 2000) pp. 216–226, 453; *Nepriklausomybės žingsniai, 1989-1994 metų kronika* (LDDP taryba, Vilnius, 1994); *Lemties posūkis* (Diemedis, Vilnius, 1999).

[24] In this regard the most important was Article 1 ("the Republic of Lithuania shall be a sovereign democratic State expressing the general will and interests of the people of Lithuania") and Article 2 ("the sovereign State power shall belong to the people of Lithuania. The people shall express their sovereign power through the exercise of legislative initiative, the election of deputies, votes on constitutional matters, and democratic referenda. No one shall have the right to restrict this power or to appropriate it. The Supreme Council of the Republic of Lithuania, the Government of the Republic of Lithuania and the Judiciary shall exercise State power in Lithuania") of the Provisional Basic Law.

The Law on Political Parties[25] passed on 25 September 1990 by the Supreme Council implemented Article 5 of the Provisional Basic Law and also expressly outlawed the CPL/CPSU. The preamble of the Law (it declared that one of the aims of the Law was to ensure the activities of the political parties would serve the interests of the consolidation of the independent and democratic State of Lithuania) as well as Article 2 clearly confirmed that the parties of other States and the parties operating outside the framework of the Provisional Basic Law were considered illegal.

However, acting under instructions and with support from the Kremlin and the Soviet Armed Forces, the CPL/CPSU and its associate organisations actually ignored the laws of the Republic of Lithuania. Together with its puppet pro-Soviet organisation 'Jedinstvo'[26] the CPL/CPSU attempted to create alternative authorities, i.e. the so-called 'organs of the Lithuanian SSR' that no longer existed as of 11 March 1990. In April 1990 the leadership of the CPL/CPSU created 'the committees of citizens of the Lithuanian SSR' which were to become the local Soviet alternative organs to those of the Republic of Lithuania. In fact, all activities of those 'committees' had been controlled by the leaders of the CPL/CPSU and had been carried out mostly by members of that Party. The 'committees' created paramilitary militia units. Some of those units collaborated closely with the Soviet Armed Forces in the January 1991 attacks against Lithuania.

Although unsuccessful, the leadership of the CPL/CPSU also attempted to divide the Lithuanian police forces and create the alternative 'Ministry of the Interior of the Lithuanian SSR' and a Soviet militia (however, the search for 'the minister' failed as no candidate had agreed to take this 'post'). This 'Soviet militia' (actually remnants of the former OMON platoon[27]) comprised of a few dozen former policemen of the Republic of Lithuania

---

[25] *Lietuvos Respublikos Aukščiausiosios Tarybos ir Vyriausybės žinios*, 1990, No. 29-692. *See* English text of the Law on the internet site of the Seimas of the Republic of Lithuania: <www3.lrs.lt/pls/inter2/dokpaieska.showdoc_l?p_id=21180>, visited on 10 March 2006.

[26] This organisation was analogous to the pro-Soviet organisations in Latvia and Estonia, known under the name Interfronts. Those organisations had been created in order to demonstrate the alleged massive support for the Soviet authorities and opposition to the popular fronts for independence.

[27] The OMON platoons had been created within the system of the USSR Ministry of Interior and ministries of interior of the Soviet republics and had been used as a special repressive force against the population, although initially it had been directed against organised criminal activities.

who betrayed the State in January 1991. OMON had been completely dependent on the Soviet Armed Forces; until August 1991 it operated as an organised gang and was engaged in terrorist operations directed against Lithuanian police, national defence and border control forces. Furthermore, OMON participated in looting and the destruction of property of the Republic of Lithuania.

To replace the Government of the Republic of Lithuania in the economic sphere, the so-called 'Association of Free Businessmen' was created by the leadership of the CPL/CPSU and the Government of the USSR. The 'Association' united the former Soviet enterprises in Lithuania and had gradually become 'the small council of ministers'. In order to spread Soviet propaganda against the State of Lithuania, the CPL/CPSU with technical support from the Soviet military established the illegal radio station 'Soviet Lithuania'. This radio station, which broadcast from a building illegally occupied by the military, was intended to replace the Lithuanian national radio and television stations.

However, in general all the above mentioned efforts by the Soviet Union were fruitless as they could not extinguish popular support for the legitimate authorities of the Republic of Lithuania and in fact no alternative authority ever emerged. Therefore, at the end of 1990 the USSR launched the next stage of intensive military activities.

2.2. The Soviet Actions of January 1991

On 16 December 1990 the CPL/CPSU and the 'committees of citizens of the Lithuanian SSR' united into the so-called 'Congress of Democratic Forces of Lithuania', i.e. one more puppet creation led by the leader of the CPL/CPSU. The 'Congress' initiated public actions directed against the authorities of the Republic of Lithuania. It also organised 'public appeals of workers and other people of Lithuania' to promote the introduction of a direct Soviet presidential ruling, i.e. to overthrow the legitimate authorities of Lithuania.

The leadership of the CPL/CPSU prepared the plan of the Soviet presidential ruling in Lithuania and presented it to the leadership of the Soviet Union at the beginning of January 1991. In accordance with that plan, all the authorities of the Republic of Lithuania were to be dissolved and, if necessary, eliminated by force. In their place, the USSR Ministry of Defence would take actual control over the situation in Lithuania. In addition the 'Presidential State Committee' would be formed and constitute the highest 'civilian' body. This Committee would implement its powers by relying on the Soviet military, KGB and militia forces. The leadership of the

CPL/CPSU informed the Soviet leadership about its existing ties and readiness to coordinate activities with those forces so as to implement the plan. The plan also included the forcible seizure of the Lithuanian national radio and television stations, which actually took place on 13 January 1991.

Soon after the submission of the plan to the USSR authorities Soviet military forces started to intensify their activities in Lithuania and even additional special military forces were introduced into the territory of Lithuania, along with other active efforts to destabilise the internal situation. It goes without saying that the plan concerning the direct Soviet presidential ruling had already been launched.

On 8 January 1991 in Vilnius the meeting of the so-called 'working people' was organised by the 'Jedinstvo' organisation and the CPL/CPSU in collaboration with the Soviet military. The participants of the meeting demanded the resignation of the Lithuanian authorities, in particular the Supreme Council and attempted to storm the building of the Supreme Council, however, the guards of the building with the assistance of the Lithuanian people successfully withstood the attack. After the failed attempt to overthrow the Lithuanian authorities by means of a 'people's revolution' open armed attacks were launched.

On 9 January 1991 the Soviet Armed Forces began demonstrating its strength with processions of tanks, armoured vehicles and other military vehicles. Meanwhile the Lithuanian people started their massive 24 hour daily duty of surrounding government (including the Supreme Council) and other important State buildings so as to protect them peacefully against possible attacks.

In Moscow, on 8 and 9 January 1991, the leaders of the CPL/CPSU met with several high-level Soviet government officials and representatives of the President of the USSR. On 10 January 1991 the wider delegation of the so-called 'Congress of Democratic Forces of Lithuania' met with the chairman of one of the chambers of the Soviet parliament who also represented the President of the USSR and publicly urged the Soviet authorities to introduce the direct presidential ruling in Lithuania. On the same day (10 January 1991) the Soviet President M. Gorbachev sent a telegram to the Supreme Council of Lithuania,[28] whereby he accused Lithuania of violating Soviet laws and decrees, as well as the "re-establishment of a bourgeois system and regime". Similarly, as on 4 April 1990 when the economic blockade was imposed on Lithuania, he demanded

[28] *The Road to Negotiations with the U.S.S.R.* (State Publishing Centre, Vilnius, 1991) p. 205.

that Lithuania "*immediately and completely re-establish the validity of the USSR Constitution and of the Constitution of the Lithuanian SSR, and to revoke the anti-constitutional acts adopted earlier*" (emphasis added), i.e. to return to the situation that existed prior to 11 March 1990. The next day (11 January 1991) the leadership of the CPL/CPSU acting on behalf of the 'Congress of Democratic Forces of Lithuania' sent the ultimatum to the Supreme Council and the Government of the Republic of Lithuania. It gave the Lithuanian authorities until 3 p.m. to comply with the demand, otherwise it threatened to establish the 'National Rescue Committee' that would 'take care' of affairs in Lithuania.

On 11 January 1991 the Supreme Council of the Republic of Lithuania by its special Statement[29] rejected the ultimatum of the USSR on the ground that it had "neither the right, nor the mandate of the voters to renounce the sovereignty of the Republic of Lithuania", i.e. the Supreme Council could not undertake such a course of action as it would mean voluntary entry into the Soviet Union and legalisation of the 1940 annexation. The Supreme Council also reminded the USSR that Lithuania was open to negotiations, however, no positive reply to instigate negotiations was received from the Soviet Union. It also stressed that "in spite of *the USSR's aggression*, the situation in Lithuania is under control, and the great majority of its population supports the Supreme Council and the Government of the Republic of Lithuania" (emphasis added). On the same day the Supreme Council made the second special statement,[30] in which it announced that "the self-appointed 'National Rescue Committee' was intending to take power with the support of foreign armed forces" and declared that if the usurpation of power was successful the new authority would be completely illegal.

Subsequently on 11 January 1991, the 'Congress of Democratic Forces of Lithuania' announced that, due to the refusal of the Supreme Council of the Republic of Lithuania to comply with the demands of the President of the USSR, the 'Congress of Democratic Forces of Lithuania' would take control of State power in Lithuania, while the 'National Rescue Committee' would control executive power. Furthermore, the 'Congress' called for the full reinstatement of the USSR and Lithuanian SSR constitutions in Lithuania. Thus, the 'National Rescue Committee' would likely act as the 'Presidential State Committee' foreseen by the plan on the direct Soviet presidential ruling in Lithuania. Actually all the documents of the 'Congress' and the

---

[29] *Ibid.*, pp. 207–208.

[30] 2 *Lietuvos Respublikos Aukščiausiosios Tarybos ir Aukščiausiosios Tarybos Prezidiumo dokumentų rinkinys* (LR AT leidykla, Vilnius, 1991) p. 508.

'National Rescue Committee' had been prepared and issued by the CPL/CPSU leadership.

Simultaneously (on the morning of 11 January 1991) the Soviet Armed Forces began the active stage of their military operations. In various locations they forcefully seized or looted buildings of the national defence forces of Lithuania. During an attack on the press building in Vilnius a dozen people were injured by gunfire. The occupied press building was used by the CPL/CPSU. On the evening of 11 January 1991 the Soviet Armed Forces acting on behalf of the so-called strikes committees (they had been established by activists of the CPL/CPSU), forcibly seized the traffic control post of the Vilnius railway station and stopped all railway traffic through Vilnius.

On 12 January 1991 the Soviet Armed Forces occupied the base of the Lithuanian special police unit in Vilnius, during this occupation 32 policemen deserted to the enemy camp and formed a pro-Soviet criminal band (the so-called OMON). However, the attempt to seize the Police Academy building failed due to resistance by the Lithuanian police. On the same day the Soviet Armed Forces also destroyed one Lithuanian border check-point.

On 12 January 1991 the Supreme Council of the Republic of Lithuania passed the Decision on Means to Defend the Republic of Lithuania,[31] in which the activities of the USSR against the Republic of Lithuania were determined to be *open aggression* (emphasis added).[32]

On the evening of 12 January 1991 the 'National Rescue Committee' issued an ultimatum demanding the Lithuanian authorities immediately cease broadcasting of national radio and television. Soon after, the 'Committee' decided to take control of the Lithuanian national radio and television stations as well as the television tower in Vilnius. The 'Committee' also appealed to the Soviet Armed Forces for assistance in carrying out this decision. The Soviet Armed Forces complied with the

---

[31] *Lietuvos Respublikos Aukščiausiosios Tarybos ir Vyriausybės žinios*, 1991, No. 3–56.

[32] The same assessment was later repeated in many other documents passed by the Supreme Council. Among them was the 13 January 1991 Law on the Government of the Republic of Lithuania in Exile which entrusted the Minister of Foreign Affairs who then was abroad to form the Government of the Republic of Lithuania in Exile in the event of the forcible overthrow of the Supreme Council. The preamble of the Law referred to the continuing *open armed aggression* against the Republic of Lithuania. *See Lietuvos Respublikos Aukščiausiosios Tarybos ir Vyriausybės žinios*, 1991, No. 3–57.

request of the self-proclaimed authority.[33] On the night of 13 January 1991 they stormed the radio and television buildings and the television tower with tanks and attacked unarmed crowds of people at those locations, killing and injuring civilians. The bloodiest operation took place around the television tower.

On 13 January 1991 the 'National Rescue Committee' decided to establish the 'Radio and Television Committee of the Lithuanian SSR' on the basis of the occupied property. In fact, the occupied radio and television buildings and television tower were further used by the CPL/CPSU to broadcast Soviet propaganda against the Republic of Lithuania.

Additionally, on 13 January 1991 the 'National Rescue Committee' imposed a night-time curfew.[34] More people were killed and injured when Soviet Armed Forces attempted to implement the curfew.

January 13th was to be the day of the final liquidation of the Republic of Lithuania. From 12–14 January (in particular, the night of 13 January) 1991 the illegal radio station 'Soviet Lithuania' and Soviet military vehicles broadcasted the statements of the 'National Rescue Committee', whereby this 'Committee' declared that it took all power, reinstated the Soviet constitutions in Lithuania and imposed a curfew. Furthermore, it urged the Lithuanian people to comply with the orders of this 'new authority'. The same statements were later repeated in the press of the CPL/CPSU.[35]

---

[33] This is more evidence of the Soviet plot against Lithuania. It was impossible and unimaginable for the Soviet Armed Forces to act under the instructions of such self-proclaimed authorities without the prior approval of the highest USSR leadership, including the Supreme Commander of the Armed Forces M. Gorbachev. Moreover, although on 22 January 1991 the President of the USSR formally condemned the cooperation of the Soviet Armed Forces with the so-called 'committees' seeking to overthrow the government by force, he did not order the Soviet Armed Forces to retreat from the occupied buildings in Lithuania and Soviet support for the activities of the CPL/CPSU continued. *See The Road to Negotiations with the U.S.S.R.* (State Publishing Centre, Vilnius, 1991) pp. 233–234.

[34] The Supreme Council of the Republic of Lithuania declared that a curfew had been proclaimed illegally by non-authorised people. *See* 2 *Lietuvos Respublikos Aukščiausiosios Tarybos ir Aukščiausiosios Tarybos Prezidiumo dokumentų rinkinys* (LR AT leidykla, Vilnius, 1991) p. 511.

[35] After the subsequent failure of the attempted coup the CPL/CPSU ceased announcing the existence of the 'National Rescue Committee' and the seizure of power. It used only to claim that the diarchy had allegedly existed and for this reason it repeated the demand to introduce the direct Soviet presidential ruling in Lithuania.

However, the Soviet military machine choked on the blood it spilled. On the night of 13 January Soviet tanks passed near the building of the Supreme Council of the Republic of Lithuania where more than twenty thousand people surrounded the building in order to protect the authorities, independence and the democratic constitutional order in general. In the face of the Soviet Armed Forces, the people did not disperse; on the contrary, they firmly stood in defence of their parliament and started to build barricades and prepared themselves for the eventual Soviet attack. It was clear that an armed attack would result in thousands of civilian victims. Peaceful resistance had not been predicted by the Soviets and large numbers of civilian casualties would have been extremely negative for the Soviet Union and its image. Therefore, the USSR did not dare to finish its plan and after a short assessment of the situation the Soviet Armed Forces retreated from the surroundings of the Lithuanian parliament. They never came back, thus Lithuania's independence and democratic constitutional order survived.

On 14 January 1991 the Supreme Council of the Republic of Lithuania adopted the Decision on the Political and Legal Assessment of the so-called 'National Rescue Committee',[36] whereby the Committee was characterised

[36] *Lietuvos Respublikos Aukščiausiosios Tarybos ir Vyriausybės žinios*, 1991, No. 3-70. The full text of the Decision reads as follows (translation made by the author):

"On 11 January 1991 the CPSU organisation in Lithuania (CPL) announced the establishment of the so-called Lithuanian 'National Rescue Committee' in Lithuania. It was stated that this Committee 'was assuming power and would take care of the future of Lithuania', that is it would become *a tool of aggression*. It should be pointed out that the establishment of the Committee, if it exists at all, coincided with the acts of *open USSR military aggression* and the bloody violence of the Soviet Armed Forces in our country.

Due to the brutal measures people were killed and injured, the State and private property destroyed and seized, and the social peace disturbed. The so-called 'National Rescue Committee' is inciting national hatred and social disturbances, and urging people to disrupt the economy and labour collectives. Acting under the guise of this self-appointed committee and its activities and attempting to disrupt the State and public life, the occupying army has illegally declared the imposition of a curfew in the Republic of Lithuania. By those actions it has attempted *to establish the occupying authorities* and overthrow the legitimate authorities of the Republic of Lithuania as well as to mask *the continuing USSR military aggression*.

The Supreme Council of the Republic of Lithuania hereby resolves:

1. That the so-called 'National Rescue Committee' has been established *illegally*, its aims and activities are of an *anti-constitutional and anti-State character* and therefore they are *criminal*.

as a tool of *aggression* and its activity was declared illegal, anti-constitutional, anti-State and criminal.

2.3. Post-January Developments in 1991

After the January 1991 attacks on the Lithuanian people and the government buildings, the Soviet military concentrated on the occupation of the seized buildings and attempted to prevent Lithuania from controlling its borders (e.g., operations were conducted against the State border control and customs check-points). The next peak of Soviet military activities against Lithuania was reached on 31 July 1991, when the military not only destroyed the border check-point at Medininkai (Lithuania's border with Belarus), but also killed all Lithuanian police, border control and customs officers on duty at the check-point.

Against the background of the Soviet military activities, the Supreme Council of the Republic of Lithuania sought to consolidate the statehood of the independent State of Lithuania. On 16 January 1991 it decided to hold a nation-wide public opinion poll (the consultative plebiscite) on the endorsement of the fundamental provision of the Constitution of the Republic of Lithuania concerning the independence and democratic regime of the State of Lithuania.[37] On 9 February 1991 independence and democracy was endorsed by more than three-quarters of the people eligible to vote (84.52 percent of those having taken part in the plebiscite).[38] Following voting, on 11 February 1990 the Supreme Council adopted the Constitutional Law on the State of Lithuania,[39] thereby declaring that the fundamental constitutional principle that the State of Lithuania is "an

---

All orders of this 'Committee' and other similar illegal organisations have no legal force and cannot be implemented in any circumstances.

The persons and organisations, carrying out the orders of this 'Committee' and other similar illegal organisations, shall be held responsible under the laws of the Republic of Lithuania.

2. To stress that, acting together with the armed forces of a foreign State in the criminal actions against the peaceful Lithuanian people and the State institutions of the Republic of Lithuania, the so-called 'National Rescue Committee' contributes to the commitment of *an international crime*." (emphasis added)

[37] *The Road to Negotiations with the U.S.S.R.* (State Publishing Centre, Vilnius, 1991) p. 226.

[38] *Ibid*., p. 250.

[39] *Ibid*., pp. 251–252. *See also* the internet site of the Seimas of the Republic of Lithuania: <www3.lrs.lt/pls/inter3/dokpaieska.showdoc_l?p_id=21090>, visited on 10 March 2006.

independent and democratic republic" could only be changed by plebiscite if no less than three-quarters of the citizens of Lithuania eligible to vote support the amendment.

The successful defence and massive popular support of the restored independence of Lithuania finally brought positive results at the international level. Soon after the plebiscite, on 11 February 1991, the first foreign State, Iceland, recognised the restored independence of Lithuania and the full validity of the 1922 recognition of the Republic of Lithuania. It was soon followed by Denmark which recognised the restoration of the independence of the Republic of Lithuania on 28 February 1991. Thus, a diplomatic blockade had been broken, although other States followed Iceland and Denmark in late August.

The January 1991 events also helped consolidate the political coalition between the Baltic States and democratic Russia (the latter was headed by the President B. Yeltsin). On 13 January 1991 B. Yeltsin expressed his full support to Lithuania and the other Baltic States and protested against the USSR's military actions. Soon after, Lithuania and Russia started negotiations on their future relationship which resulted in the 29 July 1991 bilateral Treaty on the Fundamentals of Interstate Relations, whereby both Parties recognised the sovereignty and independence of each other. In this way, the Baltic-Russian coalition contributed substantially to the final collapse of the Soviet Union.

In addition, the January 1991 events strengthened Lithuania's position in the preliminary talks with the Soviet Union, which were resumed in February 1991. The USSR was compelled to withdraw all preconditions at the start of the negotiations with the Republic of Lithuania and accept the latter on an equal footing. However, it still lacked the political will to start the negotiations in accordance with those principles.

The Soviet Armed Forces in Lithuania and the CPL/CPSU generally supported the attempted coup d'etat in Moscow on 19 August 1991. The Soviet military also occupied several more government buildings in Lithuania, however, while waiting for further developments in Moscow, it did not dare attack the Supreme Council which, as in January, was surrounded by a huge crowd of unarmed people. After the failure of the coup in Moscow the Soviet military forces were withdrawn from all the occupied buildings in Lithuania, however, they continued to be used to shelter the leaders of the CPL/CPSU attempting to escape prosecution by the Lithuanian authorities. The 'Party' was finally dissolved and liquidated by the 22 August 1991 Decision on the activities of the CPL(CPSU) in

Lithuania,[40] it was also decided to take all property in possession of the 'Party' and to facilitate settlement of issues concerning legal responsibility of those involved in its illegal activity.

As from 23 August 1991 the universal recognition of the restored independence of Lithuania had begun. On 6 September 1991 the USSR was only the 60th State to have recognised the restoration of the independence of Lithuania and the other two Baltic States.

3. The Soviet Actions of January 1991 in the Light of International Law

There are two related aspects to be examined under international law in connection with the January 1991 Soviet actions in Lithuania. First of all, how those actions are assessed from the standpoint of international law and, secondly, whether this assessment could cover the activity of the CPL/CPSU or should it be treated in a different manner.

3.1. The International Legal Status of the Republic of Lithuania in January 1991

The crucial factor in determining the character of the January 1991 Soviet actions is the international legal status of the Republic of Lithuania at the relevant time. If it is established that the Republic of Lithuania had been an independent State and subject of international law, then the conclusion can be drawn that the Soviet Union was a foreign State with regard to Lithuania, i.e. the norms of international law governing interstate relations had to be applied to the January 1991 situation between the Republic of Lithuania and

---

[40] 3 *Lietuvos Respublikos Aukščiausiosios Tarybos ir Aukščiausiosios Tarybos Prezidiumo dokumentų rinkinys* (LR AT leidykla, Vilnius, 1991) p. 392. Taking into account the factual and legal context of the 22 August 1991 Decision, it should be concluded that *the Decision actually did not imply the alleged previous legality of the activities of the CPL/CPSU*. As was mentioned, this activity had been regarded illegal in accordance with other legal acts of superior force, such as the Provisional Basic Law, the Law on Political Parties and the Criminal Code. Additionally, the January 1991 and subsequent activities had been specifically declared as illegal by the special statements and decisions of the Supreme Council. The 22 August 1991 Decision itself, first and foremost, expressly recognised that *the previous illegal activity* (*e.g.*, that was pursued in January and August 1991) of that 'Party' *was still continuing*. Thus, the Decision only finally stopped the factual illegal activity. Lithuanian authorities had not been able to take this measure until 22 August 1991, since the 'Party' had been protected and operated under the shelter of the Soviet Armed Forces.

the USSR. Therefore it is only logical that the Soviet actions against Lithuania amounted to an act of aggression. On the contrary, if it is determined that the Republic of Lithuania was not an independent State and a separate subject of international law in January 1991, then the conclusion should be made that the Soviet actions could probably only be assessed under national law as all the events would likely have the character of an internal conflict.

Two periods relevant for the determination of the international legal status of the Republic of Lithuania have to be taken into account: the period from the loss of independence (1940) until its restoration (1990) and the period starting from 11 March 1990 when independence was restored.

3.1.1. Events prior to the 11 March 1990 Restoration of Lithuania's Independence

As to the situation, it is necessary to determine the international legal character of the relationship between the USSR and Lithuania that existed from 1940–1990. Here again the core issue is the assessment of the 1939–1940 events that led to the incorporation of Lithuania into the USSR.

There is a sufficient uniformity of views on this issue, as well as in general, on the illegality of the 1940 annexation and the legal continuity of the Baltic States.[41] The contrary point of view, i.e. Russia's attempt to justify the 1940 aggression against the Baltic States and their annexation, which denies the existence of an illegal occupation, has not gained any significant support as it is manifestly incorrect and inconsistent with both international law and State practice.[42]

---

41 *E.g.*, a comprehensive bibliography consisting of more than 100 positions on matters related to Baltic statehood is provided by Prof. D. A. Loeber in D. A. Loeber, 'Legal Consequences of the Molotov-Ribbentrop Pact for the Baltic States: On the Obligation 'to Overcome the Problems Inherited from the Past'', 1 *Baltic Yearbook of International Law* (2001) pp. 153–166. In addition, *see* the relevant articles of L. Malksoo, R. Satkauskas, I. Ziemele, and D. Žalimas in 1 and 3 *Baltic Yearbook of International Law* (2001, 2003) as well as the recent publications referred to in *supra* note 2.

42 *See e.g.*, D. A. Loeber, 'Legal Consequences of the Molotov-Ribbentrop Pact for the Baltic States: On the Obligation 'to Overcome the Problems Inherited from the Past'', 1 *Baltic Yearbook of International Law* (2001) pp. 131–135; D. Žalimas, 'Commentary to the Law of the Republic of Lithuania on Compensation of Damage Resulting from the Occupation by the USSR', 3 *Baltic Yearbook of International Law* (2003) pp. 124–125; Žalimas, *supra* note 8, pp. 4–8.

The fact of the 1940 aggression against the Baltic States and the illegality of their annexation by the Soviet Union recently have in essence been confirmed by the Grand Chamber of the European Court of Human Rights in its 16 March 2006 judgment in the *Ždanoka* v. *Latvia* case.[43] In para. 119 of the judgment, the Court expressly noted that the Baltic States lost their independence "in 1940 in the aftermath of the partition of the Central and Eastern Europe agreed by Hitler's Germany and Stalin's Soviet Union by way of the secret protocol to the Molotov-Ribbentrop Pact, *an agreement contrary to the generally recognised principles of international law*" (emphasis added). The Court also stressed that the "ensuing annexation of Latvia by the Soviet Union was orchestrated and conducted under the authority of the Communist Party of the Soviet Union (CPSU), the Communist Party of Latvia (CPL) being a satellite branch of the CPSU". While in para. 13 the Court stated that in June 1940 "the Soviet army *invaded*" (emphasis added) the Baltic States, the legitimate governments were removed and new governments were formed under the direction of the CPSU, after which in July–August 1940 the Soviet Union completed the annexation. Thus, it is obvious from the judgment that the Court considers the 1940 annexation of all the Baltic States, including Lithuania, to have been illegal and one of the consequences of the illegal protocols of the Molotov-Ribbentrop Pact as well as a result of the armed invasion undertaken in implementing the Pact. It is also worth mentioning that the reference by the Court to the June 1940 Soviet armed invasion implies recognition of the aggression against the Baltic States and of the illegal occupation as the result of the invasion.[44]

Taking that into account, it is enough for the purposes of the present article only to recall the main points relying on the documents of particular relevance to the position of Lithuania with regard to the USSR before 11 March 1990, which could also explore principal issues noted by the European Court of Human Rights. It is important that those documents had been adopted earlier by the Soviet authorities, therefore, it was incumbent on the USSR to comply with the findings set forth by those documents when dealing with Lithuania.

In particular, the Soviet Union had to comply with the decision of its highest authority, i.e. *the 24 December 1989 Resolution of the Congress of*

---

[43] *Supra* note 1.

[44] *E.g.*, Judge Zupančič in his dissenting opinion did not dispute the historical facts. On the contrary, he expressly mentioned "the long-term illegal occupation (of Latvia) by the Soviet Union".

People's Deputies of the USSR on the Political and Juridical Appraisal of the Soviet-German Non-aggression Treaty of 1939[45] (hereinafter – the 24 December 1989 Resolution of the USSR Congress of People's Deputies). By this Resolution the Soviet Union condemned the secret protocols of the Molotov-Ribbentrop Pact and declared them legally unfounded and therefore "invalid from the very moment of their signing" (para. 7 of the Resolution). Apart from that, there are also the following important statements in the Resolution. Firstly, in para. 5 it is noted that "territorial divisions into Soviet and German 'spheres of influence' . . . *from the standpoint of international law were in conflict with the sovereignty and independence of several third countries*" (emphasis added), and in this respect the Congress of People's Deputies of the USSR was referring to such third States as Latvia, Lithuania, Estonia, Poland and Finland. Secondly, in para. 7 it is stressed that although the secret protocols of the Molotov-Ribbentrop Pact had not formed a new basis for the USSR's relationships with those third countries, the protocols were used "for ultimatums and *pressure by force* on (those) other States *in breach of legal obligations* assumed (by the USSR) towards those States" (emphasis added). Since in the above mentioned para. 5 of the Resolution, the Congress of People's Deputies of the USSR specifically noted that the relationships of the USSR with Latvia, Lithuania and Estonia had been based on the 1920 peace treaties and the 1926–1933 non-aggression treaties, in accordance with which "the Parties had been obliged to respect in any circumstances the sovereignty and territorial integrity of each other", it is clear that para. 7 read in conjunction with para. 5 of the Resolution has to be understood as an acknowledgement by the USSR of the breaches of the above mentioned treaties with the Baltic States and the corresponding legal obligations towards those States. In regard to Lithuania that means an acknowledgement of the breaches of the 1920 Soviet Russian – Lithuanian peace treaty and the 1926 USSR-Lithuanian non-aggression treaty. By the same token one is simply compelled to draw the conclusion that *the USSR itself had recognised the 1940 aggression against Lithuania* (as well as against all three Baltic States), because it is the only logical way to explain the said provisions of the 1989 Resolution, i.e. it is obvious that to violate both a peace treaty and a non-aggression pact one must commit an act of aggression.

---

45 *TSRS Liaudies deputatų suvažiavimo ir TSRS Aukščiausiosios Tarybos žinios*, 1989, No. 29-579. *See* English text in 39(2) *Eesti Teaduste Akadeemia Toimetised* (Publication of Estonian Academy of Science, Tallinn, 1990) pp. 198–199.

The USSR also had to take into account two other important documents adopted by the authorities of the Lithuanian SSR which elaborated the principles laid down by the 24 December 1989 Resolution of the USSR Congress of People's Deputies, although the first of them, the 22 August 1989 Conclusions of the Commission of the Supreme Council of the Lithuanian SSR for the Examination of the German-Soviet Agreements of 1939 and Their Consequences,[46] had been adopted a few months earlier. However, the Commission of the Supreme Council of the Lithuanian SSR also found that the secret protocols of the Molotov-Ribbentrop Pact had been null and void because of their inconsistency with general international law and the international obligations of the parties to the Pact. The Commission enumerated many legal obligations under both multilateral and bilateral treaties which had been violated by the USSR and Germany in respect of Lithuania in the course of concluding and implementing the Molotov-Ribbentrop Pact. *Inter alia*, the Commission stressed that the conclusion and implementation of the Molotov-Ribbentrop Pact resulted in grave breaches by the USSR of:

- Article 10 of the Covenant of the League of Nations (the obligation to respect and preserve against external aggression the territorial integrity and political independence of other States),
- Article I and II of the 1928 Paris Treaty on the Renunciation of War as a Means of National Policy (the Briand-Kellogg Pact) (the obligation not to resort to war and the obligation to settle all disputes solely by peaceful means),
- Article I of the 1920 Peace Treaty between Lithuania and Soviet Russia (later replaced by the USSR) according to which Soviet Russia unreservedly recognised the independence of Lithuania and renounced forever all sovereign rights over the Lithuanian people and territory, Article V of the same Treaty (guarantees of Lithuania's eventual neutrality),
- Articles 1–3 and 5 of the 1926 Non-aggression Treaty between the USSR and Lithuania (the obligations to respect the 1920 Peace Treaty, "to respect in all circumstances the sovereignty and territorial integrity of each other", "to sustain from any act of aggression" and to resolve disputes between the Parties in a peaceful manner),

[46] The Lithuanian newspaper *Tiesa*, 22 August 1989.

- Article VI and VII of the 1939 Treaty on the Transfer of Vilnius and Vilnius District to the Republic of Lithuania and on Mutual Assistance between Lithuania and the Soviet Union (the obligations not to participate in any coalition directed against one of the Parties and to respect the sovereign rights of each other, including non-interference in domestic affairs).

These findings led the Commission to the conclusion that the 15 June 1940 Soviet armed invasion into Lithuania and the subsequent military occupation of its territory was to be considered *an act of aggression*, since these Soviet acts met the definition of the term "act of aggression" as defined in para. 2 of Article II of the Convention for the Definition of Aggression between Lithuania and the USSR. Namely, it was an "invasion by armed forces, with or without a declaration of war, of the territory of another State".[47] In line with the general principle of law *ex injuria jus non oritur*, the Commission stated that the acts of Lithuania's annexation, i.e. both the 21 July 1940 Declaration of the puppet Lithuanian parliament (the 'People's Seimas'), set up by the Soviets, and the 3 August 1940 USSR law concerning Lithuania's incorporation into the Soviet Union, had to be considered illegal.

Taking into account both the 22 August 1989 Conclusions of its Special Commission and the 24 December 1989 Resolution of the USSR Congress of People's Deputies, on 7 February 1990, that is shortly before the 24 February 1990 elections to the Supreme Council that restored the independence of the Republic of Lithuania, the last Supreme Council of the Lithuanian SSR adopted the Decision on the 1939 German-Soviet Treaties and the Liquidation of their Consequences for Lithuania.[48] As follows from the preamble, this decision was based on the principle *ex injuria jus non oritur* and sought to restore the violated rights of the State and people of Lithuania. After condemning the aggression against Lithuania, its occupation

---

[47] In addition to this conclusion, it is worth mentioning that this bilateral Convention was identical to the multilateral London Convention for the Definition of Aggression also signed in 1933 by the USSR and nine other States, including Estonia and Latvia. Both conventions were based on the Briand-Kellogg Pact, which,according to the Parties, as stated in the preambles of both conventions, "prohibits all aggression". Therefore, both conventions on the definition of aggression clarified the meaning of aggression as prohibited already by the Briand-Kellogg Pact, i.e. their object was to give more precision to the obligations arising from the Pact. *See*: I. Brownlie, *International Law and the Use of Force by States* (Clarendon Press, Oxford, 1963) pp. 75–76, 103.

[48] *Lietuvos TSR AT ir Vyriausybės žinios*, 1990, No. 8-182.

and annexation, as international crimes committed by the USSR, the Supreme Council of the Lithuanian SSR made the following decisions: 1) to declare unlawful and invalid the 21 July 1940 Declaration of the puppet 'People's Seimas' of Lithuania in regards to Lithuania's entry into the USSR; 2) to state that the 3 August 1940 Soviet Law on the Admission of Lithuania into the USSR was both unlawful and non-binding upon Lithuania. Thus, the 7 February 1990 Decision of the Supreme Council of the Lithuanian SSR is unique, as even the Lithuanian SSR acknowledged the illegality of its nature and establishment in 1940 resulting from the illegal incorporation of Lithuania into the USSR. After the decision declaring Lithuania's annexation null and void it became clear that the restoration of the independence of the Republic of Lithuania was inevitable and would be resolved quickly by democratically elected Lithuanian authorities.

Of course, it is regrettable, that after acknowledging the 1940 aggression against the Baltic States, the USSR did not have sufficient political will to move forward following the pattern of the Lithuanian SSR, i.e. the Soviet Union had neither declared Lithuania's annexation illegal nor positively responded to numerous Lithuanian offers to negotiate on the modes of liquidation of the illegal situation and its consequences for Lithuania. Instead, even after 11 March 1990, the USSR continued to rely on its existing constitution and address the Lithuanian authorities as the authorities of the non-existing Lithuanian SSR. This state of affairs existed even though the USSR was aware that the 7 February 1990 Decision of the Lithuanian SSR recognized the illegality of its formation and declared Lithuania's annexation illegal. Such conduct was inconsistent with the provisions and spirit of the 24 December 1989 Resolution of the USSR Congress of People's Deputies. In this regard it is worth noting that Article 32 of the 2001 UN International Law Commission's Draft Articles on Responsibility of States for Internationally Wrongful Acts[49] clearly provides that the responsible State can not rely on internal law as justification for its failure to comply with, *inter alia*, the obligation to cease internationally wrongful acts. Furthermore, Article 3 reflects the well-known classical principle of international law that "the characterisation of an act of a State as internationally wrongful is governed by international law. *Such characterisation is not affected by the characterisation of the same act as lawful by internal law*" (emphasis added). Therefore, the corresponding conclusion is that in refusing to cease the illegal occupation and annexation of Lithuania as well as in trying to prevent the restoration of the

[49] *Supra* note 15.

independence of the Republic of Lithuania and in acting against the restored independence of Lithuania after 11 March 1990, under international law the Soviet Union could not justify its actions on the basis of its constitution or on any other laws, *inter alia*, the laws establishing the procedure of secession.

Thus, it can be concluded that, despite the non-compliance of the USSR with its international obligations towards the Republic of Lithuania, in accordance with the principle *ex injuria jus non oritur* the USSR had not obtained any sovereign rights to Lithuania from the 1940 aggression and under international law Lithuania was never a legitimate part of the USSR[50] (the Lithuanian SSR established in the territory of the Republic of Lithuania by the Soviet Union had been nothing more than a puppet Soviet creation).[51] A further conclusion following from the principle of *ex injuria jus non oritur*, and the most important one, is that the 1940 aggression and illegal annexation had not removed the State of Lithuania as a subject of international law, i.e. the Republic of Lithuania continued to exist as a State and an international legal person, despite the Soviet occupation of its territory and the destruction of State institutions.[52]

The legal continuity of the Republic of Lithuania, i.e. its continued existence *de jure* from 1940–1990, had been internationally recognised, which as a corollary also included the non-recognition of the illegal annexation of the Baltic States.[53] For instance, in the 29 September 1960

---

[50] *See* Žalimas, *supra* note 8, pp. 8–10 for more on the application of the principle *ex injuria jus non oritur* with regard to the illegal annexation of Lithuania.

[51] *See* K. Marek, *Identity and Continuity of States in Public International Law* (Librairie E. Droz, Geneve, 1954) p. 396.

[52] On the legal continuity of the Republic of Lithuania *see* Žalimas, *supra* note 8, pp. 10–19. For a general analysis on the continuity of the Baltic States and inapplicability of prescription with regard to the illegal annexation of the Baltic States *see* Malksoo, *supra* note 2, pp. 79–165.

[53] The principle of *ex injuria jus non oritur* also resulted in a general duty for the international community not to recognise the illegal situation, i.e. the duty of non-recognition of the Soviet annexation of the Baltic States. By the same token it also required the continued *de jure* recognition of the existence of the Baltic States. *See e.g.*, for a comprehensive review of State practice concerning non-recognition of the annexation of the Baltic States and the continued recognition of their legal existence: W. J. H. Hough III, 'The Annexation of the Baltic States and Its Effect on the Development of Law Prohibiting Forcible Seizure of Territory', 6:2 *New York Law School Journal of International and Comparative Law* (1985). Specifically on the US practice with regard to the Baltic States *see* T. D. Grant, 'United States Practice

Resolution No. 189(1960) on the Situation in the Baltic States on the Twentieth Anniversary of their Forcible Incorporation into the Soviet Union[54] the Parliamentary Assembly of the Council of Europe noted that "this *illegal annexation* (of the Baltic States) took place without any genuine reference to the wishes of the people" (emphasis added) and that "*the independent existence of the Baltic States is still recognised de jure by a great majority of the Governments of the nations of the free world*" (emphasis added). It is worth noticing that the 1975 Helsinki Final Act of the Conference for Security and Cooperation in Europe, which provided for the principle of the inviolability of borders, had not changed the policy of the non-recognition of the annexation of the Baltic States, as pursued by the majority of democratic States from 1940. The States adhering to the policy of non-recognition relied on the provision of the Helsinki Final Act which obliged States not to recognise any occupation or other territorial acquisition contrary to international law.[55] This is not surprising because, as it is enshrined in the Helsinki Final Act, all provisions of the Act should be interpreted as interrelated and in the context of each other, therefore, only legitimate borders can be recognised as inviolable. Such an interpretation can be also confirmed *inter alia* by the 13 January 1983 Resolution of the European Parliament,[56] adopted long after the Helsinki Final Act. In that Resolution the European Parliament expressly condemned the occupation of the Baltic States which had occurred pursuant to the Molotov-Ribbentrop Pact and was inconsistent with the 1920 peace treaties between the USSR and the Baltic States. It also noted that "the Soviet annexation of the three

---

Relating to the Baltic States, 1940–2000', 1 *Baltic Yearbook of International Law* (2001) pp. 23–110; R. A. Vitas, *The United States and Lithuania: the Stimson Doctrine of Non-recognition* (Praeger, New York, 1990). On the practice of France *see* R. Satkauskas, 'The Practice of France with Respect to the Baltic States', 1 *Baltic Yearbook of International Law* (2001) pp. 111–120.

[54] Council of Europe, Parliamentary Assembly, *On the Situation in the Baltic States on the Twentieth Anniversary of their Forcible Incorporation into the Soviet Union*, Resolution No. 189(1960), 29 September 1960, <assembly.coe.int/Main.asp?link=/ocuments/AdoptedText/ta60/ERES189.htm>, visited on 10 March 2006.

[55] That was the position expressly declared by the US President. *See* Malksoo, *supra* note 2, pp. 123–124. Similarly, "at the time of the signature of the Final Act at the Helsinki conference in 1975 the President of the Republic (of France), Valery Giscard d'Estaing, indicated that 'the text signed here does not imply the recognition of situations which it would not have recognised otherwise'". Cited in Satkauskas, *supra* note 53, pp. 112–113.

[56] *See* Hough, *supra* note 53, p. 439.

Baltic States has still not been formally recognised by most European States and the USA, Canada, the United Kingdom, Australia and the Vatican *still adhere to the concept of the Baltic States*" (emphasis added). More than 10 years after the Helsinki Final Act, the Parliamentary Assembly of the Council of Europe in the 28 January 1987 Resolution No. 872(1987) on the Situation of the Baltic Peoples[57] reiterated its previous position that "the incorporation of the three Baltic States into the Soviet Union was and still is a flagrant violation of the right to self-determination of peoples, and that *it remains unrecognised by the great majority of European States and many members of the international community*" (emphasis added).

For the purposes of the present article, it might be finally observed that from the standpoint of international law it is only logical that the 15 June 1940 Soviet aggression resulted in the illegal occupation of Lithuania. As a consequence of that illegal action, the subsequent annexation of Lithuania's territory, in accordance with the principle *ex injuria jus non oritur,* was null and void, therefore it had not changed the legal status of the Republic of Lithuania from 1940–1990 as an occupied State and territory. This conclusion is also supported by analogy with the 2004 Advisory Opinion of the International Court of Justice in *Legal Consequences of the Construction of a Wall in the Occupied Palestinian Territory* case.[58] In this case the Court noted that neither the annexation of a part of the occupied Palestinian territory, nor alleged partial autonomy of the occupied territory, nor any other legislative or administrative actions taken by the occupying State (Israel) could change the legal status of that occupied territory (paras. 75–78 of the Advisory Opinion). Thus, neither the creation of the Lithuanian SSR in the occupied territory of Lithuania, nor the alleged partial national autonomy of that puppet creation nor any other administrative measures of the USSR could ever change the legal status of the Republic of Lithuania. In line with that reasoning, the Parliamentary Assembly of the Council of Europe referred to the Baltic States as "the (formerly) occupied States".[59]

---

[57] Council of Europe, Parliamentary Assembly, *On the Situation of the Baltic Peoples*, Resolution No. 872(1987), 28 January 1987, <assembly.coe.int/ Main.asp?link=/Documents/AdoptedText/ta87/ERES872.htm>, visited on 10 March 2006.

[58] *Legal Consequences of the Construction of a Wall in the Occupied Palestinian Territory*, 9 July 2004, ICJ, Advisory Opinion, <www.icj-cij.org/icjwww/idocket/ imwp/imwpframe.htm>, visited on 1 March 2006.

[59] *See e.g.,* Council of Europe, Parliamentary Assembly, *On Russia's request for membership of the Council of Europe*, Opinion No. 193(1996), 25 January 1996, <assembly.coe.int/Main.asp?link=http://assembly.coe.int/Documents/AdoptedText/

This leads to the final conclusion concerning the position of Lithuania with regard to the Soviet Union from 1940–1990, that is during this period from the standpoint of international law the Republic of Lithuania and the USSR have always been different States and subjects of international law, although the former was illegally occupied by the latter. The period from 1940–1990 can also be described as a continuing breach by the USSR of its international obligation not to resort to force and refrain from any act of aggression.[60] That is, it can be concluded that the Soviet aggression against Lithuania from the 15 June 1940 armed invasion until 1990 continued in the form of an illegal occupation and annexation. It is not accidental that Article 3(a) of the Definition of Aggression approved by UN General Assembly Resolution No. 3314(XXIX) of 1974,[61] in comparison with the 1933 Convention on the Definition of Aggression (so called Litvinov Convention),[62] formally and logically expanded the previous exemplary list of the acts of aggression so as to include not only the invasion or attack by armed forces, but also possible consequences of such an invasion or attack – military occupation and annexation.

TA96/Eopi193.htm>, visited on 1 March 2006, para. 7.xii; Council of Europe, Parliamentary Assembly, *Honouring of obligations and commitments by the Russian Federation*, Resolution No. 1455(2005), 22 June 2005, <http://assembly.coe.int/Main.asp?link=/Documents/AdoptedText/ta05/ERES1455.htm>, visited on 1 March 2006, para. 14.iv.

[60] *E.g.*, relying on Article 14 of the 2001 UN International Law Commission's Draft Articles on Responsibility of States for Internationally Wrongful Acts Prof. I. Ziemele points out that the unlawful occupation of a State is a continuing breach of international law rather than only a consequence of a single unlawful act of armed intervention. *See* I. Ziemele, 'State Continuity, Succession and Responsibility: Reparations to the Baltic States and their Peoples?', 3 *Baltic Yearbook of International Law* (2003) p. 177.

[61] *See Resolutions Adopted by the General Assembly during its Twenty-ninth Session, 17 September – 18 December 1974*, Official Records of the UN General Assembly, Twenty-ninth Session, Supplement No. 31 (A/9619) (United Nations, New York, 1975) pp. 142–144.

[62] The 1974 Definition of Aggression had been prepared on the basis of the 1933 definition, however, it developed and supplemented the latter with new provisions reflecting the evolution of international law. *See* И. И. Лукашук and Д. Мэрфи, 'Преступления против мира', *Нюрнбергский процесс: право против войны и фашизма* (Институт государства и права РАН, Москва, 1996) p. 128.

3.1.2. The Situation after the Restoration of Lithuania's Independence

The 11 March 1990 restoration of the independence of the Republic of Lithuania changed the pre-existing situation between the USSR and the Republic of Lithuania in the sense that on that date the Soviet occupation of Lithuania ended. On the basis of *de jure* continuity, the State of Lithuania restored its independence (the execution of sovereign powers), regained control over its affairs and started to exercise State sovereignty as proclaimed by the 11 March 1990 Act on the Restoration of Independence. Thus, on 11 March 1990 the independent Lithuanian authorities (the first being the Supreme Council that was empowered by the people to implement the sovereign powers of the State) became the sole authorities on the territory of Lithuania exercising legislative, executive and judicial functions. At the same time the USSR lost the control necessary to continue its military occupation. The key role of that element of effective control and authority has been confirmed on several occasions by the International Court of Justice. For instance, in para. 172 of the 19 December 2005 Judgment in the *Case concerning Armed Activities on the Territory of the Congo*[63] the Court noted that "under customary international law, as reflected in Article 42 of the Hague Regulations of 1907, territory is considered to be occupied when it is actually placed under the authority of the hostile army, and the occupation extends only to the territory where such authority has been established and can be exercised" (here the Court also referred to its identical statement in para. 78 of the 2004 Advisory Opinion concerning *Legal Consequences of the Construction of a Wall in the Occupied Palestinian Territory*[64]). However, in para. 173 the Court stated that mere deployment and stationing of armed forces on a foreign territory without substitution of local authorities is not sufficient to consider the territory to be occupied. As evident from the factual circumstances,[65] as of 11 March 1990 the USSR neither had nor had been able to exercise any effective authority in Lithuania. Although the Soviet Armed Forces still remained in Lithuania illegally, they were unable to control the legislative, executive and judicial activities of the authorities of the Republic of Lithuania nor were they able to substitute the Lithuanian State institutions with their own. The Soviet Armed Forces had only been able to interfere with and impede the functioning of the

---

[63] *Case concerning Armed Activities on the Territory of the Congo*, 19 December 2005, ICJ, Judgment, Merits, <www.icj-cij.org/icjwww/idocket/ico/icoframe.htm>, visited on 1 March 2006.

[64] *Supra* note 58.

[65] *See* Section 2.1 of this article.

legitimate Lithuanian authorities, but those illegal attempts never suspended the activities of the Lithuanian State bodies.

However, the end of the occupation did not terminate the continuing breach of the USSR's international obligation not to resort to force and aggression. That continuing breach consisted, first and foremost, of the continuing illegal stationing of the Soviet Armed Forces in Lithuania which by the same token was also a consequence of the 15 June 1940 act of aggression. The International Law Commission in its commentary to Article 14 of the 2001 Draft Articles on Responsibility of States for Internationally Wrongful Acts provides the unlawful occupation of the territory of another State and "stationing armed forces in another State without its consent"[66] as examples of breaches of an international obligation of a continuing character.

Therefore, it can be concluded that, despite the end of the occupation on 11 March 1990, the continued illegal stationing of the Soviet Armed Forces in Lithuania must be regarded as a continuation of the 1940 aggression (the 15 June 1940 armed intervention). Indeed, in particular since from 1990 to 1991 those armed forces were involved in military operations against Lithuania, their presence on Lithuania's soil could be considered as an act of aggression *inter alia* in the sense of Article 3(e) of the 1974 Definition of Aggression by the UN General Assembly,[67] if interpreted and applied *mutatis mutandis* so as to comprise of the stationing of armed forces within the territory of another State without the consent of the latter, particularly when the stationed forces forcibly react against the legitimate measures of the territorial State.[68] This is exemplified in the *Case concerning Armed Activities on the Territory of the Congo*. In this case the International Court of Justice took into account the significant magnitude and long duration of

---

[66] Para. 3 of the UN International Law Commission's commentary to Article 14, *Responsibility of States for Internationally Wrongful Acts: commentaries*, Official Records of the UN General Assembly, Fifty-sixth session, Supplement No. 10 (A/56/10), chp. IV.E.2, <untreaty.un.org/ilc/texts/instruments/english/commentaries/_6_2001.pdf>, visited on 10 March 2006; J. Crawford, *The International Law Commission's Articles on State Responsibility: Introduction, Text and Commentaries* (University Press, Cambridge, 2002) p. 136.

[67] The 14 December 1974 UN General Assembly Resolution No. 3314(XXIX) on the Definition of Aggression, *supra* note 61.

[68] *E.g.*, restrictions on movement of the foreign armed forces or any other attempt to set the rules for those forces in order to ensure the sovereignty of the State within which they have been stationed. *See* C. Antonopoulos, *The Unilateral Use of Force by States in International Law* (Ant. T. Sakkoulas Publishers, Athens, 1997) p. 269.

the unlawful military intervention and the unilateral stationing of foreign armed forces and considered those acts to be not only a breach of the sovereignty and territorial integrity of the State on which soil those forces had been stationed, but also "*a grave violation* of the prohibition on the use of force expressed in Article 2, paragraph 4, of the (UN) Charter" (emphasis added).[69] It goes without saying that such a grave violation directed against the sovereignty and territorial integrity of a State amounts to aggression.[70]

3.2. The Soviet Actions of January 1991 – An Act of Aggression

Thus, taking into account the factual and legal background,[71] in particular the fact that the Republic of Lithuania has never ceased to be a State and an independent subject of international law, it is only logical to conclude that the January 1991 Soviet actions against Lithuania constitute an act of aggression. This is evident from the purposes, scale and nature of the actions of the Soviet military and other subversive activities.

Firstly, the purpose of the military attacks was clearly defined by the Soviet President M. Gorbachev in his address to the Supreme Council of Lithuania[72] made on 10 January 1990 (i.e. on the eve of the attacks). It was demanded that Lithuania "immediately and completely" renounce its sovereignty by revoking the 11 March 1990 Act on the Restoration of Independence and reinstate the constitutions of the USSR and the Lithuanian SSR. The statement also contained a threat to resort to "speedy measures" for "the re-establishment of (the Soviet) constitutional order", including "introduction of (the Soviet) presidential rule" to meet the alleged demands of people raised in "many appeals" to the Soviet Union[73] (actually those

---

[69] *Supra* note 63, para. 165.

[70] *See e.g.*, the definition of aggression under Article 1 of the Definition of Aggression, the 14 December 1974 UN General Assembly Resolution No. 3314(XXIX) on the Definition of Aggression, *supra* note 61.

[71] In particular, *see* Section 2.2 of this article.

[72] *Supra* note 28.

[73] The corresponding passage of the 'Telegram to the Supreme Soviet of the Lithuanian SSR' reads as follows:

"The situation has essentially reached an impasse. The necessity of finding a way out of the situation that has developed requires resorting to speedy measures. All-union bodies are receiving from the republic many appeals from public political organisations, industrial collectives, citizens of all nationalities. People are demanding the re-establishment of constitutional order, an assured guarantee of security and normal living conditions. Having lost faith in the policies of the current leadership, they are demanding introduction of presidential rule."

appeals had been a product of the activities of the CPL/CPSU and its 'Congress of Democratic Forces'). Those 'measures', indeed, were speedy as the military attacks were launched the morning of the next day (11 January 1990). On 12 January 1991 the so-called 'National Rescue Committee' declared that "all power" in Lithuania had been seized. Therefore, the declared purposes and the subsequent Soviet military activities in Lithuania clearly fall within the definition of aggression under Article 1 of the Definition of Aggression by the UN General Assembly,[74] that is the use of armed force by one State against the sovereignty, territorial integrity and political independence of another State.

Secondly, taking into account the material intensity and the geographical extension of the use of force as well as the numerical strength of the forces involved,[75] it can also be concluded that by their scale and nature, the January 1991 Soviet military activities fall within the meaning of acts of aggression under Article 3 (in particular, paras. a, b, e and g) of the Definition of Aggression approved by the UN General Assembly. Namely, it may be considered as an incursion by armed forces in an attempt to occupy the territory of another State, an attack on the territory of a State, illegal stationing of armed forces on the territory of another State without the latter's consent, and/or the sending by or on behalf of a State armed groups, bands and irregulars to carry out attacks against another State. This conclusion can be illustrated by the following aspects of the January 1991 Soviet military campaign against Lithuania:

- a large number of Soviet troops illegally stationed in Lithuania had been used which were supplemented by special forces units from the USSR,
- attacks occurred throughout Lithuania on people and property, in particular on strategic government buildings in the capital Vilnius,
- the armed groups, bands and irregulars (e.g., the so-called OMON and paramilitary groups operating under the framework of the so-called 'committees of citizens of the Lithuanian SSR') had been formed, supported and used,
- the alleged overthrow of the legitimate authorities had been announced,

[74] The 14 December 1974 UN General Assembly Resolution No. 3314(XXIX) on the Definition of Aggression, *supra* note 61.

[75] *See* on these criteria Antonopoulos, *supra* note 68, pp. 240–241.

- numerous other attempts to destabilise the situation in the Republic of Lithuania by military and forcible means had been made (e.g., the seizure of the Vilnius railway station and airport, the organisation of strikes in areas of economic importance, etc.).

The factual and legal circumstances arising out of particularities of the status of the Republic of Lithuania predetermine two *distinctive features* of the January 1991 Soviet act of aggression against Lithuania. The first one is related to the status of Lithuania from 1940–1990, while the second concerns the status of Lithuania from 11 March 1990.

The first distinctive feature is that the January 1991 Soviet act of aggression as well as the continued illegal stationing of the Soviet Armed Forces in Lithuania may be regarded as a continuation of the 1940 act of aggression. This may be concluded because the presence of the Soviet Armed Forces resulted from the 15 June 1940 act of aggression (armed invasion) against Lithuania, and Lithuania had never consented to the deployment of those forces and on the contrary, after the restoration of independence immediately demanded their withdrawal. Therefore, even though the restoration of Lithuania's independence had not taken place, that circumstance would not have changed the characterisation of the activities of the Soviet Union in Lithuania, i.e. from the standpoint of international law, all activities of the Soviet military in Lithuania after 15 June 1940 would be treated as a continuation of the aggression.

The second distinctive feature of the January 1991 Soviet act of aggression is the specific purpose of that act, namely, *to reoccupy Lithuania and regain control over its affairs*. For that purpose the Soviets attempted to restore the effective control and authority (i.e. the key element for the existence of military occupation) which was lost on 11 March 1990, when Lithuania restored independence. The purpose of the reoccupation is evidenced *inter alia* by the plan of the direct Soviet presidential ruling in accordance with which the Soviet military and the USSR Ministry of Defence were to take a decisive role in the administration of Lithuania after the overthrow of the Supreme Council and other legitimate authorities of the Republic of Lithuania. This proves intent to militarily occupy Lithuania that is even less masked than in June 1940.

Finally, from the above mentioned reasons it can be stated that the evaluation by the Lithuanian authorities of the January 1991 events as an act of "open military aggression"[76] rather than only an attempt to overthrow the constitutional order is correct from the standpoint of international law. Similarly, the European Parliament in its 22 January 1991 Resolution on the Situation in the Baltic States[77] declared that it was "profoundly shocked by the Soviet *military intervention* in the Baltic Republic of Lithuania . . . which *violates international law*" (emphasis added) and also strongly condemned "*the Soviet military aggression*" (emphasis added). In making that assessment the European Parliament was guided by the fact that "the Soviet Parliament declared that the Hitler-Stalin pacts concerning the annexation of the Baltic Republics were illegal" (i.e. the 24 December 1989 Resolution of the USSR Congress of People's Deputies).

Although not expressly referring to the act of aggression, in their reaction to the January 1991 events in Lithuania most third States had not used the political rhetoric typical when reacting to internal conflicts which generally includes expressions regretting violence and violations of human rights accompanied with assurances of respect for territorial integrity. Rather they condemned the Soviet activities of January 1991 as a violation of international law (the Helsinki Final Act in particular) and expressed their support for the legitimate aspirations of Lithuania and the other Baltic States.[78] The third States implied that they had treated the violence in Lithuania as an illegal use of force in international relations, i.e. as an armed attack by one State (the USSR) against another State (the Republic of Lithuania). This was evident in particular from the reaction of the Nordic States. For instance, on 10 January 1991 the Presidium of the Nordic Council demanded the Soviet Union cease military activities and start fair negotiations with Lithuania and the other Baltic States in implementing their aspirations for independence.[79] On 14 January 1991 the Althing (the

---

[76] *See e.g.*, the legal acts of the Supreme Council 11 January 1991 Statement, *supra* note 29; the 12 January 1991 Decision on Means to Defend the Republic of Lithuania, *supra* note 31; the 13 January 1991 Law on the Government of the Republic of Lithuania in Exile, *supra* note 32; the 14 January 1991 Decision on the Political and Legal Assessment of the so-called 'National Rescue Committee', *supra* note 36; *etc.*

[77] *The Road to Negotiations with the U.S.S.R.* (State Publishing Centre, Vilnius, 1991) pp. 232–233.

[78] *See e.g.*, *Lietuva, 1991.01.13* (Valstybinis leidybos centras, Vilnius, 1991) pp. 334–342.

[79] The 10 January 1991 Statement of the Presidium of the Nordic Council on the Situation in the Baltic States, *ibid.*, p. 338. On the same day a similar statement was

Parliament) of Iceland even requested recognition of the independence of Lithuania and other Baltic States, as, in its opinion, there were no other appropriate solutions to the problems facing the Baltic States.[80] The Althing also appealed to the Soviet Union to withdraw the Soviet Armed Forces from the Baltic States as well as to all nations and the Western countries in particular to promote the restoration of the independence of the Baltic States.

3.3. Attribution of the Soviet Communist Party's Actions in Lithuania to the USSR

As follows from the factual and legal circumstances,[81] under international law the activities of the CPL/CPSU as well as its puppet and subordinate organisations (including the 'Congress of Democratic Forces' and the 'National Rescue Committee') can not be separated and evaluated differently from the activities of the USSR because the 'Party' in fact had acted in the interests of the Soviet Union. First of all, it should be recalled[82] that the programme of the 'Party' clearly indicated that it was a part of the Communist Party of the Soviet Union (i.e. it was operating within 'the united Communist Party of the Soviet Union') and its task was to organise in Lithuania "the implementation of decisions adopted by the central structures of the CPSU", i.e. to actually perform Soviet government functions. In other words, the CPL/CPSU and in fact the whole CPSU attempted to retain by all means the leading role of the Communist Party within the organisation of the Soviet State.[83] As was rightly stated in the 28 December 2001 Judgment of

---

also made by the Prime Ministers of the Nordic countries gathered in the Nordic Council of Ministers.

[80] The 14 January 1991 Statement of the Parliament of Iceland, *ibid.*, p. 342.

[81] *See* Section 1 of this article.

[82] Established by the Lithuanian courts in the *January 13 Case*, *supra* note 4.

[83] That is why, the CPL/CPSU as the whole CPSU had belonged to the extreme reactionary political forces of the Soviet Union which, in line with the well known Bolshevik tradition, did not care about the real wishes of the people, were opposed to political pluralism and democratisation, sought to retain power and to preserve the communist system. Neither the popular voting in the 24 February 1990 elections nor massive support for independence in January 1991 and in the 9 February 1991 consultative plebiscite could persuade the CPSU, including its local branch in Lithuania (the CPL/CPSU), to change its objective of taking power and restoring the Lithuanian SSR by all possible means, first and foremost, by Soviet military force. Therefore, this 'Party' is considered to have been composed of neo-Bolsheviks who were willing to use any means to take and maintain power, including bloodshed.

the Supreme Court of Lithuania[84] in the *January 13 Case*, "the leading role of the Communist Party within the Soviet State followed Stalin's concept of government by merging the Communist Party and the State machinery into a single unit. Decisions of the highest Party authorities had been compulsory for all levels of the government institutions" (translation made by the author). While a certain degree of autonomy of the Soviet republics had formally existed under Soviet legislation, in fact the local sections within the united Communist Party ensured unconditional compliance by the local authorities with the decisions of the central structures of the Communist Party so no conflict would arise between the central and local Soviet authorities. However, the CPL/CPSU, being a part of the CPSU, also had a specific task: to serve as a tool of the Soviet Union (in which the Communist Party still controlled the State organs) to regain control over Lithuania where the Communist Party had already lost its power. This specific task was defined in the programme of the CPL/CPSU as the purpose "to reinstate in Lithuania the constitutions of the USSR and the Lithuanian SSR", i.e. to restore the puppet Lithuanian SSR as part of the USSR.

Secondly, it is also worth recalling that not only the programme slogans but also the actual activity of the CPL/CPSU demonstrated that it was exercising elements of the Soviet government authority.[85] All the time this 'Party', as a local branch of the CPSU, had been supported not only by the central party authorities, but also by the USSR government authorities, in particular the Soviet Armed Forces illegally stationed in Lithuania. For example, the sections and the central leadership of the CPL/CPSU included the military; the military also provided logistical and material support as well as a safe haven for the 'Party'. With support from the Soviet Union, the CPL/CPSU attempted to create the authorities of the Lithuanian SSR which had to operate under the control of the 'Party' and to substitute the legitimate authorities of the independent Republic of Lithuania in exercising

---

This is a point of view held by Lithuanian historians as reflected, *e.g.*, in *Lietuvos suvereniteto atkūrimas 1988-1991 metais* (Diemedis, Vilnius, 2000) pp. 220–226.

[84] *Supra* note 4.

[85] The principle that a party must be judged, above all, by the actions rather than only by its political programme was confirmed *inter alia* by the European Court of Human Rights in paras. 46 and 56 of the 3 February 2005 Judgment in *Partidul Comunistilor (Nepeceristi) and Ungureanu* v. *Romania*, 3 February 2005, ECHR, no. 46629/99, <cmiskp.echr.coe.int/tkp197/portal.asp?sessionId=6377704&skin=hudoc-en&action=request>, visited on 19 March 2006. *See also* para. 120 of the 16 March 2006 Judgment of the Grand Chamber in the *Ždanoka* v. *Latvia* case, *supra* note 1.

government functions. Soviet support of the CPL/CPSU was especially evident during the January 1991 aggression against Lithuania in both preparing and implementing the plan of the so-called direct Soviet presidential ruling. The 'Party' acted with approval and in close synchronisation and coordination with the President of the USSR M. Gorbachev, the USSR Government and other high-level leadership of the Soviet Union (in particular, in submitting identical ultimatums to the Supreme Council of the Republic of Lithuania and in resorting to force after the ultimatums were rejected). At the same time, with approval from the highest Soviet leadership the Soviet Armed Forces were placed at the disposal of the CPL/CPSU in carrying out the orders of its 'National Rescue Committee' (in particular, in capturing buildings, declaring the overthrow of the Republic of Lithuania and imposing a curfew). The actual activities of the CPL/CPSU ceased the moment the USSR was compelled to renounce its plans to re-establish the Lithuanian SSR and withdraw its armed forces from the illegally occupied buildings in Lithuania after the failure of the August 1991 military coup in Moscow.

Thus, it can be concluded that the CPL/CPSU can be regarded as a foreign organisation in Lithuania vested with elements of government authority of the USSR. In essence both the full control of the 'Party' by the Soviet authorities and its entitlement to exercise elements of Soviet government authority is also confirmed by the European Court of Human Rights in para. 120 of the 16 March 2006 Judgment in *Ždanoka* v. *Latvia*.[86] In this case, the Grand Chamber relied on the domestic courts' findings that "the unsuccessful attempted coups in the Baltic States in January 1991 and then in August 1991 *were organised and conducted* under the direction of the CPSU and its regional branches" (emphasis added). In addition, in para. 119 of the Judgment, the Court noted the same role of the CPSU and its regional branches in orchestrating and conducting the 1940 annexation of the Baltic States. These findings of the Court confirm the role of the CPSU and its local branches as entities exercising elements of Soviet government authority, otherwise they could not have been instrumental in the 1940 annexation and the 1991 act of aggression. Therefore, it is only logical to treat the CPL/CPSU as a kind of para-statal entity exercising elements of government authority[87] within the meaning of Article 5 of the 2001 UN

[86] *Supra* note 1.

[87] On para-statal organisations the conduct of which is attributable to the State *see* the UN International Law Commission's commentary to Article 5 of the 2001 Draft

International Law Commission's Draft Articles on Responsibility of States for Internationally Wrongful Acts.[88] In accordance with that Article, the conduct of this para-statal entity is attributable to the USSR without any need to demonstrate that the conduct was in fact carried out under the control of the Soviet State.[89]

In the alternative, even if it is presumed that the CPL/CPSU had not been empowered by Soviet internal law to exercise elements of government authority as required by Article 5 of the Draft Articles on Responsibility of States for Internationally Wrongful Acts, the conduct of that 'Party' would still be attributable to the Soviet Union under Article 8 of the Draft Articles. Article 8 attributes responsibility to a State for the conduct of a group of persons acting on the instructions of a State or under the direction and control of a State. It is clear that the factual circumstances demonstrate that the USSR had effective control over the activities of the CPL/CPSU which is required under international law to establish that a person or a group of persons can be regarded as an agent of the State. The degree of Soviet control clearly met the criterion of effective control as established in para. 115 of the 27 June 1986 Judgment of the International Court of Justice in the *Case concerning Military and Paramilitary Activities in and against Nicaragua*,[90] i.e. the Soviet Union through its governmental bodies, armed forces and the CPSU not only generally controlled (e.g., financing, organising, supplying) the activities of the CPL/CPSU, but also directed those activities and involved that 'Party' in concealing the January 1991 aggression. In other words, the USSR simply used the CPL/CPSU as a tool in the perpetration of the aggression, therefore the activities of the 'Party' must be seen as a part of the January 1991 Soviet act of aggression against Lithuania.

Articles on Responsibility of States for Internationally Wrongful Acts, *supra* note 66; Crawford, *supra* note 66, pp. 100–102.

[88] *Supra* note 15.

[89] This is the main difference from Article 8 of the Draft Articles which concerns the conduct of persons or groups of persons directed or controlled by a State, but not empowered by the internal law of that State to exercise elements of governmental authority. *See* paras. 3 and 7 the UN International Law Commission's commentary to Article 5, *supra* note 66; Crawford, *supra* note 66, pp. 100, 101–102.

[90] *Case concerning Military and Paramilitary Activities in and against Nicaragua*, 27 June 1986, ICJ, Judgment, Merits, <www.icj-cij.org/icjwww/icases/inus/inus_judgment/inus_ijudgment_19860627.pdf>, visited on 1 March 2006.

4. The Impact of the Failed Soviet Aggression on the Further Development of Events

Three main post-January 1991 developments can be observed as resulting from Lithuania's successful resistance to Soviet aggression: 1) the strengthening of Lithuania's position with regard to the Soviet Union; 2) the commencement and development of fruitful cooperation between Lithuania and Russia, then the largest part of the USSR; 3) international recognition of the restoration of Lithuania's independence.

4.1. Attempts to Resume Talks between Lithuania and the Soviet Union

The failure of the January 1991 Soviet act of aggression and the subsequent successful plebiscite on 9 February 1991 endorsing Lithuania's independence and democracy undoubtedly strengthened Lithuania's position in the preliminary talks with the Soviet Union which resumed in February 1991. The USSR was compelled to alter its position which regarded Lithuania as an ordinary Soviet republic. The Soviet Union had to accept Lithuania on an equal footing, which signified a shift back to the principles already declared in the 24 December 1989 Resolution of the USSR Congress of People's Deputies.

The most significant step towards this direction was the signing on 4 April 1991, by the authorised representatives of the Republic of Lithuania and the USSR, of the Protocol of the official meeting between delegations of the parties.[91] The Protocol provided for further discussions between the Parties aimed at increasing mutual confidence in the negotiation process. More importantly, the Protocol defined the underlying principles upon which eventual negotiations between the parties would be based: no preconditions, true equality between the parties, respect for human rights and the sovereignty of the parties, and impermissibility of illegal forms of pressure by both parties and respect for other universally recognised principles of law. Thus, it can be concluded that the USSR was obliged: 1) to withdraw all former preconditions for the start of negotiations with the Republic of Lithuania, including the demand to renounce or suspend the 11 March 1990 Act on the Restoration of Independence, 2) to respect the sovereignty of the Republic of Lithuania, including the 11 March 1990 Act on the Restoration of Independence, and 3) to refrain from any form of illegal pressure on

[91] *The Road to Negotiations with the U.S.S.R.* (State Publishing Centre, Vilnius, 1991) pp. 289–291.

Lithuania, including acts similar to the 1990 economic blockade and, in particular, the January 1991 act of aggression.

However, due to the domination of reactionary forces in the leadership of the USSR and the CPSU, the Soviet Union never had enough political will to move forward and start negotiations with Lithuania in accordance with the principles defined by the 4 April 1991 Protocol. It failed to comply with those principles by refusing to withdraw its armed forces from illegally occupied buildings and again resorted to force in July–August 1991. Only when weakened by the failed coup in Moscow did the Soviet Union actually start to comply with its obligations towards Lithuania (e.g., it withdrew the armed forces from the illegally seized buildings). However, it was too late to begin negotiations with Lithuania; on 6 September 1991 the USSR was compelled to recognise the restored independence of the Republic of Lithuania without any discussion on modalities as it could not prevent the growing international recognition of the restoration of independence of the Baltic States. In taking the Decision on the Recognition of the Independence of the Republic of Lithuania[92], the USSR Council of State referred "to the concrete historical and political situation that had existed before the entry of the Republic of Lithuania into the USSR", by this passage the Council was likely relying on the principles of the 24 December 1989 Resolution of the USSR Congress of People's Deputies.[93]

4.2. Mutual Recognition of Lithuania and Russia

The January 1991 Soviet aggression encouraged the Republic of Lithuania and other Baltic States to seek allies among the democratic forces within the Soviet Union. The counterbalance was found in the democratic leadership of Russia led by B. Yeltsin which competed with the central USSR Government and strongly opposed the leading role of the CPSU. The start of the political coalition between the Baltic States and democratic Russia began on 13 January 1991, when the heads of all four States issued a joint statement.[94] The statement condemned the USSR leadership for the use of

---

[92] A copy from the Archive of the Seimas of the Republic of Lithuania, reproduced in D. Žalimas, *Lietuvos Respublikos nepriklausomybės atkūrimas: pagrindiniai klausimai pagal tarptautinę teisę* (Rosma, Vilnius, 1997) pp. 202–203.

[93] Žalimas, *supra* note 8, p. 14.

[94] The 13 January 1991 Statement by the Chairmen of the Supreme Councils of the Republic of Estonia, the Republic of Latvia, the Republic of Lithuania and the Russian Soviet Federal Socialist Republic, *The Road to Negotiations with the U.S.S.R.* (State Publishing Centre, Vilnius, 1991) pp. 212–213.

force in Lithuania and other Baltic States and expressed their loyalty to the principles of democracy and the prohibition of the use of force as well as their readiness to assist each other in the event their sovereignty is threatened. However, most importantly Lithuania, Latvia, Estonia and Russia recognised the sovereignty of each other.

Guided by the principles proclaimed in the 13 January 1991 statement, Lithuania and Russia proceeded further towards full mutual recognition of each other and development of equal and mutually beneficial relations. On 29 July 1991 the Parties signed the Treaty on the Fundamentals of Interstate Relations,[95] whereby they recognised the sovereignty and independence of each other. In particular, by virtue of Article 1 Russia recognised the Republic of Lithuania as a fully-fledged subject of international law and a sovereign State under its State status defined in the fundamental acts of 11 March 1990. This means that Russia has recognised all the principles declared by those acts and the 11 March 1990 Act on the Restoration of Independence in particular, i.e. both the fact of the 1940 aggression against Lithuania and the illegality of the subsequent occupation and annexation as well as the legal continuity and identity of the Republic of Lithuania inherent in the acts of 11 March 1990. Thus, in general Russia accepted the concept of the State of Lithuania which was founded in 1918 and liberated on 11 March 1990 from Soviet occupation which began in 1940.

In the preamble of the Treaty Russia also expressed its conviction that the USSR had to remove the consequences of the 1940 annexation of Lithuania. This also implied that the USSR had to contribute to the restoration of the lawful situation by promoting the restoration of Lithuania's independence, recognising the restored independence, withdrawing the Soviet Armed Forces from Lithuania and making reparations for the damage sustained by Lithuania. Russia's stance, then the largest and the most influential part of the USSR, undoubtedly also contributed to the recognition by the USSR of Lithuania's restored independence after the failed August coup in Moscow. In that sense the recognition of Lithuania's independence by Russia, then a non-recognised entity and a part of the State that still refused to recognise the restored independence of Lithuania, "played a unique role in the history of recognition of states".[96] On the other hand, the

[95] The 29 July 1991 Treaty on the Fundamentals of Interstate Relations between the Republic of Lithuania and the Russian Soviet Federal Socialist Republic, *Lietuvos aidas*, 30 July 1991. *See* English text of the Treaty in 1 *Lithuanian Foreign Policy Review* (1998), <www.lfpr.lt/9801.phtml>, visited on 10 March 2006.

[96] R. Müllerson, *International Law, Rights and Politics: Developments in Eastern Europe and the CIS* (Routledge, London, 1994) p. 121.

recognition by Lithuania and the other Baltic States of the sovereignty of Russia also contributed to the growing role and future substitution by the latter of the Soviet Union. Thus, the mutual political support of the Baltic States and democratic Russia shook the very foundation of the Soviet empire.

4.3. Facilitation of International Recognition of the Government of Lithuania

The successful defence and massive popular support of the restored independence of Lithuania during the January 1991 Soviet aggression and the 9 February 1991 consultative plebiscite proved that the independence of the Republic of Lithuania had been irreversibly restored. This certainty encouraged other States to provide more political support to Lithuania and the other Baltic States rather than to only care about the fate of M. Gorbachev. This turning point announced the start of international recognition of Lithuania without worry as to Soviet reactions. No State had yet established diplomatic relations with the Government of Lithuania or recognised it *de jure* as appealed for by Lithuania on 8 and 11 January 1991.[97] However, this unfavourable attitude of the international community did not long remain the case after the 11–13 January attacks by the Soviet Union. In particular the Nordic States demanded the Soviet Union cease the violence and seek a fair solution of all issues arising in connection with the legitimate aspirations of the Baltic States. Not surprisingly, the first two countries to recognise Lithuania's restored independence were the Nordic States, Iceland and Denmark. On 11 February 1991 the Althing of Iceland (Icelandic Parliament) passed a special Resolution on this issue,[98] while on

---

[97] *See* the 8 January 1991 Letter to the Leaders of Governments of Democratic States from the Chairman of the Supreme Council of the Republic of Lithuania Vytautas Landsbergis and the 11 January 1991 Appeal of the Government of the Republic of Lithuania to the States of the World, *The Road to Negotiations with the U.S.S.R.* (State Publishing Centre, Vilnius, 1991) pp. 202–203, 209.

[98] *Ibid.*, p. 251. The full text of the Resolution reads as follows:

"The Althing resolves to confirm that *the recognition* by the Government of Iceland *in 1922* of the independence of the Republic of Lithuania *is fully valid.*

The Althing supports the Government's decision of 23 January 1991 to agree to the request of the *democratically elected authorities in Lithuania* to initiate talks concerning diplomatic relations.

The Althing calls upon the Government to bring this issue to a conclusion by *establishing diplomatic relations with Lithuania* as soon as possible." (Emphasis added).

28 February 1991 the Ministers of Foreign Affairs of Denmark and Lithuania signed the Joint Protocol on Cooperation between the Kingdom of Denmark and the Republic of Lithuania.[99] The joint protocol explicitly recognized the re-established bilateral cooperation and called for its promotion. It was the first treaty between the parties after World War II.[100]

A few important principles of the first two acts of recognition by Iceland and Denmark should be mentioned, in particular because they were followed by other democratic States in recognising the restored independence of the Baltic States after the failed August coup in Moscow. Namely, the legal continuity of the Republic of Lithuania inherent in the 11 March 1990 Act on the Restoration of Independence was recognised by the emphasis on the non-recognition of the 1940 illegal annexation and the full validity of the 1921–1922 pre-war recognition of the Republic of Lithuania. Consequently, it was recognition of the new legitimate Government (authorities of the State) of the Republic of Lithuania rather than recognition of the State.[101] There was no need to recognise the Republic of Lithuania as a State, since this State had been *de jure* recognised by the international community already in 1920–1922 and that recognition remained valid during the entire

---

[99] *Ibid.*, pp. 262–263.

[100] The most important passages of the Protocol read as follows:

"The Parties recalled that before the Second World War the Kingdom of Denmark and the Republic of Lithuania, which were both members of the League of Nations, had good and friendly relations, but that these were *interrupted for 50 years by the forcible incorporation of the Republic of Lithuania into the Soviet Union in 1940. Denmark, which recognised Lithuania in 1921, never recognised the legality of that incorporation.*

Denmark welcomed the fact that the people of Lithuania in the spring of 1990 had the opportunity to express themselves in free elections, which resulted in *a democratically elected Parliament and the subsequent formation of a legitimate Government*, which aims at creating a democratic society based on respect for human rights and fundamental freedoms. The Lithuanian Parliament decided on 11 March 1990 to re-establish the full national independence of the Republic of Lithuania and this decision was confirmed by the plebiscite of 9 February 1991 . . .

When the situation makes it possible, Denmark and Lithuania will seek *to re-establish diplomatic relations*." (Emphasis added).

[101] *E.g.*, on the day after the restoration of Lithuania's independence the spokesman of the White House confirmed that the United States of America had never recognised the forcible incorporation of the Baltic States into the USSR, therefore it was the new Lithuanian Government which had to be recognised rather than the State of Lithuania. *See* V. Lansbergis, *Laisvės byla* (Spindulys, Kaunas, 1992) pp. 40–41.

period of Soviet occupation from 1940–1990.[102] Due to the occupation the Lithuanian Government authority had been broken, therefore, it was the new Government of Lithuania, formed in the aftermath of the 1990 free elections and subsequent restoration of independence, which had to be recognised as the sole legitimate representative of the Republic of Lithuania in international relations with whom diplomatic relations had to be re-established.

5. International Legal Responsibility for the Soviet Aggression of January 1991

It is a paradox that Russia who initially supported Lithuania and the other Baltic States during the January 1991 Soviet aggression now bears the international legal responsibility for that act of aggression against Lithuania. Upon the dissolution of the USSR all of its international legal obligations, including those stemming from the responsibility for the January 1991 act of aggression against the Republic of Lithuania, automatically passed to Russia due to the fact that Russia continued the international legal personality of the USSR and therefore inherited the rights and obligations of the USSR. Furthermore, Russia took over responsibility for the Soviet Armed Forces illegally stationed in Lithuania and later withdrew those forces in accordance with international law.

The continuation by Russia of the USSR is clearly stated *inter alia* in the preamble of the 24 May 1999 Federal Law of the Russian Federation on the State Policy Regarding Compatriots Abroad[103] whereby it is proclaimed that the Russian Federation is both a successor and continuation ("*правопреемник и правопродолжатель*") of the Russian State, the Russian Republic, the Russian Soviet Federal Socialist Republic and the

[102] *E.g.*, on 12 March 1990 the Minister of Foreign Affairs of France Roland Dumas issued the press release, in which it was stated that "France *has never recognised the annexation of Lithuania* in 1940 and *the recognition granted* to Latvia and Estonia in 1921 and *to Lithuania in 1922 remains in force*; the legal personality of the Baltic States has survived the annexation, even though they were deprived of their sovereignty, and *consequently no additional act of recognition is required*." (Emphasis added). Cited in Satkauskas, *supra* note 53, p. 116.

[103] The text of the Law available on the Internet site of the State Duma (the lower chamber of the Parliament) of the Russian Federation: <www.duma.gov.ru>, visited on 8 May 2005.

USSR.[104] The legal continuity of Russia is a well-established fact that is evident from both objective and subjective facts,[105] moreover, Russia's continuity is not only claimed by Russia itself, but this claim has been generally accepted by the international community.[106] As the continuity of Russia is also undisputed in the legal doctrine, there is no need to explore this theme in this article.[107]

For the purposes of this article it is enough to recall that on 5 May 2005 Russia once more expressly acknowledged to be the State continuation of the USSR,[108] thereby also declaring to be bound by the 24 December 1989 Resolution of the USSR Congress of People's Deputies which implied that the 1940 occupation and annexation of Lithuania was illegal.[109] This is one more argument why Russia must acknowledge its responsibility for the failure of the USSR to comply with that Resolution by resorting to aggression in January 1991.

Thus, it is only logical that by the 13 June 2000 Law on Compensation of Damage Resulting from the Occupation by the USSR[110] the Republic of

---

[104] The Law actually reflects the point of view that the same international legal personality, the State of Russia, had been in existence under those different names. *See* Ziemele, *supra* note 2, p. 58.

[105] Müllerson, *supra* note 96, pp. 139–145.

[106] Ziemele, *supra* note 2, pp. 66–67, 69–70, 71–72, 75–76, 82–84, 87–88, 90–91, 92–93.

[107] For more generally about Russia's continuity and legal identity with the former USSR as a key subjective element of attribution for Russia's responsibility for the Soviet occupation of Lithuania and its consequences *see* Žalimas, *supra* note 42, pp. 126–133.

[108] On 5 May 2005 the Department of Information and Press of the Ministry of Foreign Affairs of the Russian Federation issued the Commentary on the statements by the national security advisor to the US President concerning a recommendation for Russia to denounce the Molotov-Ribbentrop Pact, whereby such a recommendation was rejected as illogical due to the fact that Russia considered all its obligations arising out of the 24 December 1989 Resolution of the USSR Congress of People's Deputies as valid because the State of Russia was a continuation of the USSR (*"Россия является <u>государством – продолжателем</u> Союза ССР*") (emphasis added). A copy of the Commentary is available from the internet site of the Ministry of Foreign Affairs of the Russian Federation <www.mid.ru>, visited on 8 May 2005.

[109] *See* more about the 24 December 1989 Resolution of the USSR Congress of People‘s Deputies in Section 3.1.1 of this article.

[110] *See* the English text of the Law in Žalimas, *supra* note 42, pp. 98–100; the Internet site of the Seimas of the Republic of Lithuania

Lithuania raised its claim for compensation of damage caused by the January 1991 Soviet act of aggression to Russia, as the State continuing the legal personality of the former USSR. In accordance with the principle of full reparation as reflected in Article 1 of the Law, this claim is a part of the whole claim for compensation of all damages resulting from the Soviet occupation of Lithuania and its consequences, including the continued illegal stationing of the Soviet Armed Forces in Lithuania and all attempts to reoccupy Lithuania after the restoration of its independence on 11 March 1990.[111]

6. Conclusion

To conclude, both the factual and legal circumstances demonstrate that under international law the January 1991 events in Lithuania (as well as in Latvia) were not an attempted internal *coup d'etat*. It was an act of aggression by the Soviet Union against the Republic of Lithuania because Lithuania had never been a legitimate part of the USSR. Rather from 1940–1990 the Republic of Lithuania had survived as a State and an independent subject of international law, notwithstanding the Soviet occupation of the entire territory and the destruction of its State structures in the aftermath of the 15 June 1940 act of aggression. Having in mind the 24 December 1989 Resolution of the USSR Congress of People's Deputies, whereby the seizure of the Baltic States was declared to be contrary to international law, even the Soviet Union must have realised that its armed forces were stationed in Lithuania illegally and therefore all their operations on Lithuania's soil had to be regarded as a continuation of the 1940 aggression.

Since the Soviet occupation of Lithuania ended on 11 March 1990 with the restoration of the independence of the Republic of Lithuania, the distinctive feature of the January 1991 Soviet act of aggression was its specific purpose to reoccupy Lithuania by overthrowing the legitimate authorities of the Republic of Lithuania and restoring the puppet entity of the Lithuanian SSR. For that purpose the local section of the CPSU (the CPL/CPSU) was used to conceal the involvement of the Soviet military. Therefore, once more the January 1991 events proved the criminal nature of the CPSU as the leading force of Soviet State machinery.

<www3.lrs.lt/pls/inter3/dokpaieska.showdoc_l?p_id=104885>, visited on 10 March 2006.

[111] *See* the commentary to Article 1 of the Law on Compensation for Damages Resulting from the Occupation by the USSR in Žalimas, *supra* note 42, pp. 149–151.

However, the January 1991 Soviet act of aggression brought about unexpected results for the USSR leadership. The failure of aggression demonstrated that the Soviet Union would not be able to escape its eventual collapse by military means. The Republic of Lithuania withstood the aggression and afterwards built a coalition with Russia, then a driving democratic force in the Soviet Union. The successful defence of the independence and democracy in Lithuania encouraged the first foreign States to break Lithuania's diplomatic isolation by recognising its legitimate authorities, thus shaking the foundations of the Soviet empire. The January 1991 success of the unprecedented civic resistance of the Baltic people against Soviet aggression could be reasonably placed alongside the success of the 'Solidarity' movement in Poland and the reunification of Germany.

Paradoxically, it is the Russian Federation who, being the State continuation of the USSR thereby assumes the USSR's rights and obligations, still bears the international legal responsibility for the January 1991 Soviet act of aggression against the Republic of Lithuania. It is part of the overall responsibility for the Soviet occupation of Lithuania. However, Russia not only denies its responsibility, but also refuses to cooperate with Lithuania in proceeding with further investigations of the *January 13 Case* as well as continuing to provide shelter for many persons wanted or even convicted by the Lithuanian judicial authorities for their active participation in the Soviet subversive activities from 1990–1991, which includes the January 1991 act of aggression, against the Republic of Lithuania. In line with the words of the current President of Russia V. Putin who has described the collapse of the Soviet Union as the greatest catastrophe in his life, Russia seems to ignore that it is supporting the people who then acted not only against Lithuania and the other Baltic States, but who also belonged to the Soviet reactionary forces fighting for the survival of the Soviet empire and against the sovereignty and democratic leadership of Russia. Thus, Russia's responsibility for the January 1991 Soviet aggression against Lithuania and the other Baltic States is not a purely legal or financial issue. First and foremost it is an issue of moral and political responsibility, an issue of sincere condemnation and renunciation of the imperialistic legacy. A fair settlement of this issue would significantly increase the level of confidence by the community of democratic States in Russia. Most likely the principled and uncompromising position of the international community on the assessment of the January 1991 events in the Baltic States, e.g. as laid down by the European Court of Human Rights in the *Ždanoka* v. *Latvia* case, will also contribute positively to that settlement.

Republic of Estonia Materials on International Law 2005

Edited by Leena-Maarja Kalda, Tanel Kerikmäe and Kari Käsper[*]

[Editorial Notes:

1. Republic of Estonia Materials on International Law 2005 (REMIL) have been classified according to the Recommendation (97) 11 of 12 June 1997 of the Committee of Ministers of the Council of Europe, as applied by the British Yearbook of International Law from the year 1997, which was also used in the Republic of Latvia Materials on International Law 2003.

2. The REMIL primarily concerns the opinions made by the institutions and officials of Estonia and provides the understanding of Estonian authorities of different aspects of international law. The editors do not necessarily share those opinions, understandings or interpretations. The editors do not claim that the content of the REMIL provides for universal or internationally common or even correct interpretations but only the understanding of the international law by Estonian institutions and officials.

3. Most of the materials provided in REMIL are taken from the speeches by relevant authorities either on certain occasions or in the parliament, *Riigikogu*, when presenting drafts of acts. In 2004 Estonia became a member of the European Union and the REMIL of 2004 thoroughly reflected the accession. In 2005 many of the changes in the Estonian legal system resulted from fulfilling the State's obligations under *aquis communautaire* and are not reflected in this issue.]

[*] All are legal experts at Supralaw, the Center for Supranational law. Jean Monnet professor Tanel Kerikmäe is the Dean of the Faculty of Law of International University Concordia Audentes and President of the Estonian European Community Studies Association.

Baltic Yearbook of International Law, Volume 6, 2006, pp. 347–381.

INDEX**

** The Baltic Yearbook provides the Index of State practice reports only in front of the first State report. – ed.

D. Procedure
E. Consequences of invalidity, termination or suspension of operation
V. State succession in respect of treaties
VI. Depositaries, notifications, corrections, and registration
VII. Consensual arrangements other than treaties

Part Four: Relationship between International Law and Internal Law

I. General
II. Application and implementation of international law in internal law
A. Treaties
B. Custom
C. Sources other than treaty and custom
III. Remedies under internal law for violations of international law
IV. Non-justiciability, including public interest immunity

Part Five: Subjects of International Law

I. States
A. Status and powers
1. Personality
2. Sovereignty and independence
3. Territorial integrity
4. Non-intervention in domestic jurisdiction
5. Equality of States
6. State immunity
7. Treaty-making power
8. Powers other than treaty making
B. Recognition
1. Acts of recognition
a) Recognition of States
b) Recognition of governments
2. Effects of recognition
3. Withdrawal of recognition
4. Non-recognition (including non-recognition of governments) and its effects
C. Types of States
1. Unitary States
2. Personal and real unions
3. Federal States and confederations
4. Protected States
5. The Holy See
D. Formation, identity, continuity, extinction and succession of States
1. Conditions for statehood

2. Formation
3. Identity and continuity
4. Extinction
5. Succession
   (a) Situations of State succession
      (i) Union with or without the demise of the predecessor State
      (ii) Dismemberment
      (iii) Separation
      (iv) Newly independent States
   (b) Effects of State succession
      (i) Territory and other areas under national jurisdiction
      (ii) Nationality
      (iii) Succession in respect of treaties
      (iv) Archives
      (v) Debts
      (vi) Property
      (vii) Responsibility
      (viii) Other rights and obligations

II. International organisations
A. General
1. Status and powers
   (a) Personality
   (b) Privileges and immunities of the organisation
   (c) Treaty-making power
   (d) Other powers
2. Participation of States and international organisations in international organisations and in their activities
   (a) Admission
   (b) Suspension, withdrawal, expulsion, and deportation
   (c) Obligations of membership
   (d) Representation of States and international organisations to international organisations, including privileges and immunities
3. Legal effect of the acts of international organisations
4. Personnel and experts of international organisations, including privileges and immunities
5. Responsibility of international organisations
6. Succession of international organisations

B. Particular types
1. Universal organisations
2. Regional organisations

3. Organisations constituting integrated (e.g. economic) communities
4. Other types

III. Entities or groups other than States and international organisations
A. Mandated and trust territories
B. Overseas territories and dependencies
C. Condominia
D. Special regimes
E. Self-determination units and the concept of self-determination
F. Insurgents
G. Belligerents
F. Others (e.g. indigenous people, minorities, national liberation movements)

Part Six: The Individual (including the Corporation) in International Law

I. Nationality
II. Diplomatic and consular protection
III. Aliens
IV. Members of minorities
V. Stateless persons
VI. Refugees
VII. Immigration and emigration, extradition, expulsion, asylum
A. Immigration and emigration
B. Extradition
C. Expulsion
D. Asylum
1. Territorial asylum
2. Diplomatic asylum

VIII. Human rights and fundamental freedoms
A. General concept
B. Under the United Nations treaty system
C. Under the Council of Europe treaty system
1. European Court of Human Rights
(a) Procedural issues
(b) Substantive issues
2. Other than the European Court of Human Rights
D. Other aspects of human rights and fundamental freedoms

IX. Responsibility of the individual

Part Seven: The State and its Organs

I. The composition of the State
A. Heads of State

B. Ministers
C. Governments
D. Departments of the State
E. Diplomatic missions and their members
F. Consulates and their members
G. Special missions
H. Trade and information offices, trade delegations, etc.
I. Armed forces, including visiting forces
J. Police and security services
II. Protecting powers
III. State property
IV. Privileges and immunities
A. State immunity (including Head of State immunity)
B. Diplomatic privileges and immunities
C. Consular privileges and immunities
D. Visiting forces
E. Other privileges and immunities

Part Eight: Jurisdiction of the State

I. Bases of jurisdiction
A. Territoriality
B. Personality (active and passive)
C. Protective principle
D. Universality
E. Other bases
II. Types of jurisdiction
A. Prescriptive
B. Adjudicative
C. Enforcement
III. Extra-territorial exercise of jurisdiction
A. General
B. Consular jurisdiction
C. Military and other personnel abroad
D. Other exercises (e.g. artificial islands, terrae nullius)
IV. Limitations upon jurisdiction (e.g. servitudes, leases)
V. Concurrent jurisdiction

Part Nine: State Territory

I. Territory
A. Elements of territory
1. Land, internal waters, lakes, rivers, and land-locked seas
2. Sub-soil

3. Territorial sea
4. Airspace

B. Good neighbourliness

II. Boundaries and frontiers

A. Delimitation
B. Demarcation
C. Stability

III. Territorial sovereignty

A. General
B. Acquisition and preservation
C. Transfer and loss

IV. Leased territory

Part Ten: International Watercourses

I. Rivers and lakes

A. Definition
B. Navigation
C. Uses other than navigation
D. Protection of the environment
E. Institutional aspects

II. Groundwaters

III. Canals

Part Eleven: Seas and Vessels

I. Internal waters, including ports and harbours

II. Territorial sea, including overflight

III. Straits, including overflight

IV. Archipelagic waters

V. Contiguous zone

VI. Exclusive economic zone

VII. Continental shelf

VIII. High seas

A. Freedoms of the high seas, including overflight
B. Visit and search
C. Hot pursuit
D. Piracy
E. Conservation of living resources

IX. Islands, rocks and low-tide elevations

X. Enclosed and semi-enclosed seas

XI. International Seabed Area

XII. Land-locked and geographically disadvantaged States

XIII. Protection of the marine environment

XIV. Marine scientific research
XV. Cables and pipelines
XVI. Artificial islands, installations, and structures
XVII. Tunnels
XVIII. Vessels
A. Legal regime
1. Warships
2. Public vessels other than warships
3. Merchant vessels
B. Nationality
C. Jurisdiction over vessels
1. Flag State
2. Coastal State
3. Port State
4. Exercises of jurisdiction other than by flag, coastal, and port State

Part Twelve: Air Space, Outer Space, and Antarctica

I. Air space
A. Status and limits
B. Uses
C. Legal regime of aircraft
II. Outer space and celestial bodies
A. Status and limits
B. Uses
C. Legal regime of spacecraft
III. Antarctica
A. Limits and status
B. Uses
C. Protection of the environment

Part Thirteen: International Responsibility

I. General concept (see part One: 2. 1/2 above)
II. Responsibility other than criminal
A. Responsible entities
1. States
(a) The elements of responsibility (e.g. wrongfulness of the act, imputability)
(b) Factors excluding responsibility (e.g. self-defence, necessity, counter-measures)
(c) Diplomatic and consular protection
(d) Nationality of claims
(e) Exhaustion of local remedies

2. States
(a) International organizations
(b) Entities other than international
III. Criminal responsibility
A. Definition and concept of an international crime
B. Responsible entities
1. States
2. Entities other States (e.g. individuals)
IV. Consequences of responsibility
A. Reparation
B. Consequences other than reparation

Part Fourteen: Peaceful Settlement of Disputes
I. The concept of an international dispute
II. Means of settlement
A. Negotiations
B. Good offices
C. Enquiry (fact-finding)
D. Mediation
E. Conciliation
F. Arbitration
1. Permanent Court of Arbitration
2. Arbitral tribunals and commissions other than the Permanent Court of Arbitration
G. Judicial settlement
1. International Court of Justice
2. Courts and tribunals other than the International Court of Justice
H. Settlement within international organisations
1. United Nations
2. Organisations other than the United Nations
I. Other means of settlement
III. Compensation arrangements

Part Fifteen: Coercive Measures short of the Use of Force
I. Unilateral measures
A. Retorsion
B. Counter-measures
C. Pacific blockade
D. Intervention
E. Other unilateral measures
II. Collective measures
A. United Nations

B. Outside the United Nations

Part Sixteen: Use of Force

I. Prohibition of the use of force

II. Self-defence

III. Use of force under the UN Charter

IV. Use of force other than self-defence and under the UN Charter

V. Disarmament and arms control

Part Seventeen: The Law of Armed Conflict and International Humanitarian Law

I. International armed conflict

A. Definition

B. Commencement

C. Distinction between combatants and non-combatants

D. Belligerent occupation

E. Termination, including armistices and treaties of peace

II. Non-international armed conflict

III. Aspects of the law of armed conflict

A. Sources

B. Rights and duties of participants

1. Land operations

2. Sea operations

3. Air operations

C. Mercenaries

D. Conventional weapons

E. Nuclear, bacteriological and chemical weapons

F. Protection of the individual (international humanitarian law)

G. Protection of property

H. Recognition of belligerency

I. War crimes

J. Belligerent occupation

K. Conventional, nuclear, bacteriological and chemical weapons

L. Treaty relations between combatants (cartels, armistices, etc.)

M. Termination of international armed conflict, treaties of peace

Part Eighteen: Neutrality and Non-belligerency

I. The laws of neutrality

A. Land operations

B. Sea operations

C. Air operations

II. Permanent neutrality

III. Neutrality in the light of the United Nations Charter

Part Two: III. Sources and Codification of International Law – Codification and progressive development of international law

2/1

> On 13 December 2005, Mr. Urmas Paet, Minister of Foreign Affairs of the Republic of Estonia explained to the *Riigikogu* on behalf of the Government of Estonia the country's role in international law making, "Estonia's interests are best served, in a quickly changing world, by a strong and dynamic European Union and NATO, based upon the principles of mutual solidarity. We support the further strengthening of the EU and NATO. NATO and the European Union are no longer 'they', but 'we'. When we criticize so-called 'Brussels bureaucracy' we should – especially in the case of a politician or government official – realize, that Estonia has also been able to influence the birth of those papers, that we also have a role to play in the creation of those regulations."

(Available at the internet site of the Foreign Ministry http://www.vm.ee/eng/kat_140/7168.html?arhiiv_kuup=arhiiv)

(See also under Part Five, II.B.3 Organizations constituting integrated communities)

Part Three: I. A. The Law of Treaties- Definition, conclusion and entry into force of treaties – Definition

3/1

It was decided that the *Constitutional Treaty of the EU* shall be treated as a treaty and therefore on 10 May 2005 the Government submitted it to the Parliament for ratification.

(The draft law 645 SE I together with the explanatory note are available at http://web.*Riigikogu*.ee/ems/sarosbin/mgetdoc?itemid=051320018&login =proov&password=&system=ems&server=ragne11)

(See also under Part Five, II.B.3 Organizations constituting integrated communities)

Part Three: I. B. The Law of Treaties – Definition, conclusion and entry into force of treaties – Conclusion, including signature, ratification, and accession

3/2

During the *Riigikogu* (Parliament) discussion of 20 April 2005, the Minister of Social Affairs Jaak Aab emphasized the importance of joining the World Health Organization (WHO) Convention on Reduction of Tobacco Consumption,

> "The Convention helps to protect the future generations from constant exposure to tobacco and tobacco products and therefore reduces the health risks derived from exposure. No country has managed to reduce the percentage of everyday smokers below 20. Due to its unique nature, tobacco harms health and creates addiction, thus it cannot be treated as any other product. The public has a right to be informed of the results of consumption. Estonia should ratify the said Convention in order to protect the health of the countries citizens."

(Available at the Internet site of the *Riigikogu* http://web.*Riigikogu*.ee/ems/plsql/stenograms.form, editors' translation)

3/3

(See *9/2*)

3/4

During the *Riigikogu* discussion of 14 December 2005, the Minister of Environment Villu Reilian argued for Estonia's accession to the Protocol on Heavy Metals accompanying the Convention on Long-range Transboundary Air Pollution on Persistent Organic Pollutants,

> "In order to reduce pollution and to establish appropriate measures to combat it, the Convention was signed in Geneva in 1979. Estonia ratified the said document in the year 2000. At the moment Estonia has ratified five out of the eight protocols accompanying the Convention. The Protocol on Heavy Metals was adopted in 1998 and it deals with the emissions of 3 mercury elements and other heavy metals. It is useful for Estonia to join the Protocol as we share the same goals as the other 35 States that have already done so. We wish for new technologies and innovation in order to reduce emissions.

> Here is an example – compared to 104.5 tonnes in 1990, Estonia has reduced its emissions to 39.3 tonnes in 2003. Lets be part of the international cooperation as our health is our common treasure."

(Available at the Internet site of the *Riigikogu* http://web.*Riigikogu*.ee/ems/plsql/stenograms.form, editors' translation)

Part Three: I. C. The Law of Treaties – Definition, conclusion and entry into force of treaties – Reservations, declarations and objections

3/5

During the *Riigikogu* discussion of 11 May 2005, the Minister of Communication and Economic Affairs, Edgar Savisaar explained the need for certain declarations in regard to joining the United Nations (UN) Convention on the Law of the Sea,

> "Estonia shall join the Convention, however we shall introduce two declarations in the process. Firstly, as an EU Member State, Estonia has delegated several of its powers in the area to the Community. The areas delegated include preservation of fish resources, international trade, scientific and technological cooperation and to a certain extent the safety at sea and sea pollution. The second declaration shall assign the International Court of Justice and the International Maritime Court as the institutions responsible for solving any disputes. These two declarations allow the country to join the Convention without breaching its obligations under EU legislation. Similar declarations have been made by all other EU Member States."

(Available at the Internet site of the *Riigikogu* http://web.*Riigikogu*.ee/ems/plsql/stenograms.form, editors' translation)

Part Three: II. A. The Law of Treaties – Observance, application and interpretation of treaties – Observance

3/6

During the *Riigikogu* discussion of 19 September 2005, Andres Lipstok as the president of the Bank of Estonia explained Estonia's duties under the Treaty establishing the European Community (ECT) with regard to joining the European Monetary Union (EMU),

> "I would like to start by providing you with some background information about some of the criteria Estonia is under an obligation to fulfill in order to

> be able to join the EMU. First are the Maastricht criteria. To become members of the EMU, all EU Member States must join the Exchange Rate Mechanism ERM2 and fulfill certain economic criteria: the government's budget deficit must remain below 3% of the GDP and the government's debt must remain smaller than 60% of the of the GDP. The country must be a member of the ERM 2 for at least two years during which it manages to keep its currency stable with regard to the Euro. As for price stability, the State's inflation rate cannot exceed by more than 1.5% the rates of the three best performers within the Community. In addition, all the States must bring their legislation into compliance with the ECT."

(Available at the Internet site of the *Riigikogu* http://web.*Riigikogu*.ee/ems/plsql/stenograms.form, editors' translation)

Part Three: II. B. The Law of Treaties – Observance, application and interpretation of treaties – Application

3/7

During the *Riigikogu* discussion of 21 February 2005, the Minister of Justice Ken-Marti Vaher responded to the inquiry by members of the *Riigikogu* in regard to the application of the UN Treaty to Outlaw Funding of Terrorism,

> "Funding of terrorism is considered a crime under Estonian legislation. The obligation to criminalize such funding derives from the 1999 UN Convention which was ratified in Estonia in 2002. It is important to remember that provisions on terrorism do not only cover such acts themselves but also the preparation of the crime. Funding terrorism is therefore covered by provisions on participating in the crime. No international agreement obliges the member of the Treaty to use the wording or the definitions of the document as long as the matters are clearly regulated. Minor differences in the application of the provisions do not hinder international cooperation as the main purpose of the agreement is to punish those responsible for the crime."

(Available at the Internet site of the *Riigikogu* http://web.*Riigikogu*.ee/ems/plsql/stenograms.form, editors' translation)

Part Three: II. C. The Law of Treaties – Observance, application and interpretation of treaties – Interpretation

3/8

During the *Riigikogu* discussion of 18 May 2005, the Minister of Social Affairs Jaak Aab emphasized the importance of joining the International Labour Organization (ILO) Convention concerning Discrimination in Respect of Employment and Occupation,

> "The Convention obliges its members to adopt policies that enhance equal treatment in respect of employment and occupation and that are oriented towards elimination of discrimination. According to the Convention any differentiation, exclusion or preference based on a persons race, skin color, sex, religion, political beliefs, nationality or social background is prohibited. Differentiation with regard to positions requiring special qualifications is not considered discrimination."

(Available at the Internet site of the *Riigikogu* http://web.*Riigikogu*.ee/ems/plsql/stenograms.form, editors' translation)

Part Three: II. D. The Law of Treaties – Observance, application and interpretation of treaties – Treaties and third States

3/9

On 7 September 2005, the Justice and Home Affairs Council discussed combating human trafficking with regards to the EU and third countries,

> "In connection with combating human trafficking, Estonia feels that cooperation with non-EU countries should definitely be enhanced. Only in cooperation with third countries can the fight against human trafficking be effective, because it is a crime that is very international by its nature", said Justice Minister Rein Lang. "We have to share our knowledge, experiences and skills with them to tackle the problems related to human trafficking. To that end we need to exchange experts and seize the possibilities of police cooperation. The third sector plays an important role in prevention of human trafficking and elimination of its consequences and the Member States of the European Union must support such efforts by non-profit associations. It is also important to increase people's awareness of the threats of human trafficking through the media and other channels."

(Available at the Internet site of the Ministry of Justice http://www.just.ee/19178)

Part Three: III. The Law of Treaties – Amendment and modification, derogation

3/10

During the *Riigikogu* discussion of 21 September 2005, the Minister of Finance Aivar Sõerd suggested amending and renewing the Treaty to avoid Double Taxation between Estonia and Lithuania,

> "The Double Taxation Treaty between Estonia and Lithuania has been in force since 1 January 1994. It is common practice for neighbouring countries with tight economic bonds to review and renew the existing treaties approximately every ten years. This is necessary to keep the agreements up to date in the fast developing economic world. Lithuania suggested certain changes already in 2002. Similarly to the previous agreement, the new agreement would be based on a OECD model contract, with the possibility to alter certain provisions upon agreement between the parties."

(Available at the Internet site of the *Riigikogu* http://web.*Riigikogu*.ee/ems/plsql/stenograms.form, editors' translation)

Part Four: II. A. Relationship between International Law and Internal Law – Application and implementation of international law in internal law – Treaties

4/1

The Constitutional Court, in case 3-4-1-1-05 of 19 April 2005 Petition of the Chancellor of Justice to declare § 70 of Local Government Council Election Act and § 1(1), the first sentence of § 5 (1) and § 6 (1) of Political Parties Act partly unconstitutional, expressed its views on the national level judicial review of acts allegedly in non-conformity with the European Union legislation,

> "Pursuant to Article 226 of the Treaty establishing the European Community, the Commission, if it considers that a Member State has failed to fulfill an obligation under this Treaty, including not bringing national law into conformity with the European Union law, may bring the matter before the Court of Justice. This does not mean that such abstract review procedure over national law should exist on the national level. Thus, the Supreme Court will not be able to examine the petition of the Chancellor of Justice to the extent that the Chancellor of Justice requests, on the basis of

> Article 19 of the Treaty establishing the European Community and directive 94/80/EC, that § 5(1) of PPA be declared invalid."

(Available at the Internet site of the Supreme Court of Estonia, http://www.nc.ee/english/).

Part Five II.A.2. Subjects of International Law – International organisations – General – Participation of States and international organisations in international organisations and in their activities

5/1

On 2 December 2005, the President of the Republic expressed the nation's views on participating in international organizations at the Forum of the Heads of State of the Baltic- Black Sea and Caspian Kiev Area,

> "Following the restoration of independence, Estonia set the accession to the European Union and NATO as its foreign policy priority. Today we can confirm that the membership in those organizations serves our national interests. It is a matter of common knowledge that one of the prerequisites for accession to the European Union and NATO is democratically arranged society.
>
> The force of gravity that the European Union and NATO have today has stabilizing and consolidating impact on the whole continent. At the same time, I would like to underscore that reforms should not be undertaken merely for the sake of the EU and NATO accession. The general rule is that whatever you do, do it for your own well-being. And therefore, while introducing reforms we should first of all have in mind our own national interests and goals."

(Available at the Internet site of the President of Estonia http://www.president.ee/ en/duties/speeches.php?gid=70706)

5/2

On 2 December 2005, the President of the Republic welcomed the Summit Declaration at the meeting of Heads of State and Government at the 60th Session of the UN General Assembly on 15 September 2005,

> "Five years ago, world leaders convened at the Millennium Summit to agree on the main goals for development in the 21st century. Today we are here to review the implementation of these goals, to set outlines for the

future and to take decisive steps for making the UN as an organization more efficient.

Estonia welcomes the Summit Declaration, which issues guidelines for the future. I believe that our discussion is a basis for the necessary reforms of the UN system, and for the accomplishment of the Millennium Development Goals.

Estonia, together with other European Union Member States, is consistently active in pursuing the increasing of resources devoted to development cooperation. Estonia is of the opinion that many development issues and humanitarian crises can be – also most efficiently – solved by means of multilateral organizations combining the resources and knowledge of individual nations. Therefore, we consider the supporting of the activities of the UN as well as other international development and humanitarian aid organizations to be extremely important, and we are also planning to increase our support in the future."

(Available at the Internet site of the President of Estonia http://www.president.ee/en/ duties/speeches.php?gid=67669)

Part Five: II. A. 3. Subjects of International Law – International organizations – General – Legal effect of the acts of international organizations

5/3

During the *Riigikogu* discussion of 8 November 2005, a member of the *Riigikogu*, Eiki Nestor, suggested that the legislator should rely on the ILO conventions when amending the Act on Collective Agreements,

> "Most collective agreements are traditionally bilateral, however no ILO convention forbids trilateral negotiations. It is true that agreements reached as mentioned through such negotiations are often not called collective agreements. However the name of the agreement is not important in itself. The ILO is perfectly aware of the trilateral negotiations regulated under the Estonian laws and would indeed notify the State about the mistake made. This has never been done.
>
> At the same time the trilateral negotiations have produced a number of excellent results in the Estonian labour market. The procedure has brought success in negotiations over the minimum salary, the pension schemes, the unemployment budget and there are many other examples."

(Available at the Internet site of the *Riigikogu* http://web.*Riigikogu*.ee/ems/plsql/stenograms.form, editors' translation)

Part Five: II. B. 1. Subjects of International Law – Particular types – Universal organizations

(also see *3/2*, *3/5*, *3/7*, *3/8*)

5/4

On 16 December 2005, H.E. Mr. Mart Laanemäe, Undersecretary of the Estonian Foreign Ministry elaborated on his views regarding Estonia's position in the World Trade Organization (WTO) at the WTO Ministerial Conference in Hong Kong,

> "Smaller countries can play a major role in strengthening the WTO, because all WTO members are equal. In turn, the WTO has much to offer smaller countries. For example, for a smaller country to have separate bilateral trade relations with many far-away states is difficult, simply because compared to larger countries, smaller countries lack the necessary resources. By making full use of the WTO, smaller countries can overcome this disadvantage of scale. This means there is a motivation for smaller countries to strive for WTO rules that are agreed, respected and followed by all, rules that will better enable the WTO to achieve its aims: to help producers of goods and services, exporters and importers conduct their business."

(Available at the Internet site of the Foreign Ministry http://www.vm.ee/eng/kat_140/7183.html?arhiiv_kuup=arhiiv)

Part Five: II. B. 2. Subjects of International Law – Particular types – Regional organizations

(also see *2/1*)

5/5

On 16 May 2005, the President of Estonia Arnold Rüütel discussed the success and role of the Council of Europe at the Third Council of Europe Summit Warsaw,

> "For more than half a century the Council of Europe has been defending European values and working in the name of a more unified, democratic and freer Europe. However, not all developments have been positive in

> Europe in recent years. The situation in Byelorussia is of concern, especially in the light of last year's elections. Moldova is still caught in the crisis in Transnistria. We have to consider that security risks have multiplied in the world over the recent years and Europe is not an exception. Terrorist attacks in Madrid last March and in Beslan in September bear tragic proof.
>
> Estonia welcomes the Council of Europe's leading role in the implementation of information technology in order to speed up democratic reforms. Estonia has rich experience to offer in this field and I am pleased to admit that Estonia's professionals are actively involved."

(Available at the Internet site of the President of Estonia http://www.president.ee/en/ duties/speeches.php?gid=62839)

Part Five: II. B. 3. Subjects of International Law – Particular types – Organizations constituting integrated (e.g. economic) communities

(see also *2/1*, *3/1*)

Part Six: III. The Individual (including the Corporation) in International Law – Aliens

(also see *6/5*)

6/1

During the *Riigikogu* discussion of 28 September 2005, the Social Minister Jaak Aab explained the need for a social insurance treaty between Estonia and Canada in relation to protecting aliens' social rights,

> "The purpose of the treaty is to establish a system that would accommodate the continuance of pension payments to people that have migrated to the other member State. The agreement would include those individuals who would lose their benefits in the event the insurance schemes are not modified and the dependants of such persons."

(Available at the Internet site of the *Riigikogu* http://web.*Riigikogu*.ee/ems/plsql/stenograms.form, editors' translation)

6/2

During the *Riigikogu* discussion of 9 February 2005, the Minister of Communication and Economic Affairs Andrus Ansip explained the legal implications related to adopting a Memorandum of Mutual Agreement between Estonia and Australia with regard to tourist visas enabling short term employment,

> "According to the Memorandum citizens aged 18–30 of either State can apply for tourist visas to the other country that also enable them to work there. The time span of the stay may last up to 12 months and the main aim of the trip has to be tourism while employment is secondary.
>
> In order to accommodate such an arrangement in the Estonian legal system, the Foreigners Act needs to changed, as there presently exists no possibility to work in the country while having just a tourist visa. It is possible to register the wish to work prior to applying for the visa, however that would not apply to situations covered by the Memorandum. The latter would cover situations where the person traveling does not even know where or if he will work.
>
> The agreement is beneficial for Estonia as it enables young people to travel and work more easily."

(Available at the Internet site of the *Riigikogu* http://web.*Riigikogu*.ee/ems/plsql/stenograms.form, editors' translation)

Part Six: VI. The Individual (including the Corporation) in International Law – Refugees

6/3

During the *Riigikogu* discussion of 26 October 2005, the Minister of Internal Affairs Kalle Laanet explained the need to adopt the Act on Providing International Protection for Foreigners and the protection measures introduced by the Act,

> "The need to adopt such an act derives from the EU Directives that regulate all forms of protection by the EU Member States with regard to citizens of third countries. The issues regulated are the refugee status, additional protection and temporary protection of individuals.
>
> A refugee is defined as a person who faces persecution due to his race, religion, nationality, political beliefs or social background. Additional protection is provided for people that do not qualify as refugees but who are nevertheless in real danger of torture, inhuman treatment and violence due to an armed conflict or if their lives are in danger.

> Temporary protection can be given to individuals who are also in real danger of systematic violations of their human rights or have fled their home countries due to armed conflicts. The latter however only applies in cases of mass evacuations under the guidance of international organisations.
>
> Inspired by the crisis in Kosovo, the EU has greatly increased the efficiency of such measures within the Community and has set minimum standards for providing temporary protection as well. The Community has also classified the categories of people entitled to protection. The duration of temporary protection is usually 1 year, however depending on the circumstances, that time limit may be extended to 3 years.
>
> In addition to the protection, the Act would also regulate the access of the individuals under protection to the local employment market."

(Available at the Internet site of the *Riigikogu* http://web.*Riigikogu*.ee/ems/plsql/stenograms.form, editors' translation)
(see also Part Five: II. B. 3.)

Part Six: VII. A. The Individual (including the Corporation) in International Law – Immigration and emigration, extradition, expulsion, asylum – Immigration and emigration

6/4

During the *Riigikogu* discussion of 6 April 2005, the Minister of Internal Affairs Margus Leivo introduced several changes to be implemented in the Estonian legislation with regard to refugees, border crossing and foreigners,

> "The Eurodac system specifies several categories of people whose fingerprints and other biological samples must be taken at the border upon entry into the Estonian territory. Such categories include asylum seekers and illegal immigrants. All such people must be at least 14 years old. The national laws also specify cases where such data must be collected from individuals under the age of 14. The latter is especially important in relation to the protection of children and combating human trafficking."

(Available at the Internet site of the *Riigikogu* http://web.*Riigikogu*.ee/ems/plsql/stenograms.form, editors' translation)

6/5

During the *Riigikogu* discussion of 28 September 2005, Jaan Õunapuu, a member of the *Riigikogu*, expressed his concerns related to the modification of the Estonian Foreigners Act, more specifically in relation to relaxed visa regulation,

> "I fear that the relaxing of requirements related to obtaining a visa increases the danger of unwanted illegal immigration. We should be aware firstly that people might not leave the country once their visa has expired and secondly people who might come to the country with the intention of working illegally. In addition we cannot forget about those who might enter Estonia in order to further move to a more developed EU Member State. These are the dangers that the Ministry of Internal Affairs should try to minimize."

(Available at the Internet site of the *Riigikogu* http://web.*Riigikogu*.ee/ems/plsql/stenograms.form, editors' translation)

Part Six: VIII. C. The Individual (including the Corporation) in International Law – Human rights and fundamental freedoms – Under Council of Europe treaty system

6/6

During the *Riigikogu* discussion of 19 October 2005, the Foreign Minister Urmas Paet discussed the nature of Protocol 14 of the European Convention for the Protection of Human Rights and Fundamental Freedoms (ECHR).

The Protocol changes the control system of the Convention with the aim to make the functioning of the European Court of Human Rights (ECtHR) more flexible and thus effective. The latter would enable the ECtHR to process the increasing number of applications within a reasonable time. At the moment 17 States have ratified the protocol,

> "The main changes introduced by the Protocol include extending the serving term of the judges to nine years without the possibility of re-election. The three member committee can from now on, in addition to deciding on the acceptance of the applications, give judgements on breaches of the convention in cases that follow similar firmly established precedents. The grounds of dismissing applications are also specified.
>
> The Protocol is in compliance with the Estonian Constitution and the EU legal acts, even though it lacks direct connection to the latter. All the EU Member States are members to the Convention. Ratifying the Protocol will provide the Estonian citizens with a faster and more efficient procedure at

> the ECtHR and hence will ensure more effective protection of the fundamental rights."

(Available at the Internet site of the *Riigikogu* http://web.*Riigikogu*.ee/ems/plsql/stenograms.form, editors' translation)

6/7

In the judgment of 15 February 2005, *Sulaoja* v. *Estonia* the ECtHR gave a decision with regards to the human right to a speedy and immediate trial under Article 5 § 3 of the European Convention on Human Rights:

> "Article 5 § 3 of the Convention reads, that everyone arrested or detained in accordance with the provisions of paragraph 1 (c) of this Article shall be brought promptly before a judge or other officer authorized by law to exercise judicial power and shall be entitled to trial within a reasonable time or to release pending trial. Release may be conditioned by guarantees to appear for trial.
>
> The Court reiterates that the question of whether or not a period of detention is reasonable cannot be assessed in the abstract. The reasonableness of the detention of an accused has to be assessed in each individual case according to its special features. Continued detention can be justified in a given case only if there are specific indications of a genuine requirement of public interest which, notwithstanding the presumption of innocence, outweighs the rule of respect for individual liberty laid down in Article 5 of the Convention.
>
> The Court finds that the mere absence of a fixed residence does not give rise to a danger of flight. Nor can it be concluded from the lack of a job or a family that a person is inclined to commit new offenses. The Court has doubts as to whether the grounds for the applicant's detention, as reflected in the perfunctorily reasoned court orders, retained their sufficiency for the whole period of the pre-trial detention.
>
> In that context, the Court would emphasize that under Article 5 § 3 the authorities, when deciding on the continuing detention of a person, are obliged to consider alternative measures of ensuring his appearance at trial. It should be recalled that this provision proclaims not only the right to 'trial within a reasonable time or to release pending trial' but also lays down that 'release may be conditioned by guarantees to appear for trial'."

(Available at the Internet site of the ECtHR http://cmiskp.echr.coe.int/tkp197/view.asp?item=1&portal=hbkm&action=html&highlight=estonia&sessionid=5582442&skin=hudoc-en)

6/8

In the judgment of 22 November 2005, *Taal* v. *Estonia* the ECtHR pronounced on the rights of the defence, the handling of the evidence and the questioning of witnesses under Article 6 §§ 1 and 3 (d) of the European Convention on Human Rights.

> "The Court reiterates that all the evidence must normally be produced in the presence of the accused at a public hearing with a view to adversarial argument. However, the use in evidence of statements obtained at the stage of the police inquiry and the judicial investigation is not in itself inconsistent with Article 6 §§ 1 and 3 (d) of the Convention, provided that the rights of the defence have been respected. As a rule these rights require that the defendant be given an adequate and proper opportunity to challenge and question a witness against him either when he was making his statements or at a later stage of the proceedings.
>
> Having regard to the fact that neither the applicant nor his representative were enabled to question any of the witnesses at any stage of the proceedings and that none of the witnesses were ever examined by the courts, the Court finds that the applicant's defence rights were restricted to an extent incompatible with the guarantees provided by Article 6 §§ 1 and 3 (d) of the Convention."

(Available at the Internet site of the ECtHR http://cmiskp.echr.coe.int/tkp197/view.asp?item=2&portal=hbkm&action=html&highlight=estonia&sessionid=5582442&skin=hudoc-en)

6/9

In the judgment of 21 June 2005, *Pihlak* v. *Estonia* the ECtHR gave a decision with regards to the pre- trial detention under Article 5 § 3 of the European Convention on Human Rights.

> "The applicant complained that the length of his pre-trial detention was in breach of Article 5 § 3 of the Convention, which provides:
>
> 'Everyone arrested or detained in accordance with the provisions of paragraph 1 (c) of this Article shall be brought promptly before a judge or other officer authorized by law to exercise judicial power and shall be entitled to trial within a reasonable time or to release pending trial. Release may be conditioned by guarantees to appear for trial.'
>
> The Court observes that the judicial orders authorizing the applicant's detention on remand were based on a brief standard formula that the

> detention was justified, namely that the applicant had committed new offenses while his earlier criminal case was pending in the City Court. In most of the court orders reference was also made to his previous convictions. In all instances it was concluded that he could commit further offenses while at liberty. No more elaborate reasons were put forward to justify the need for the protracted detention of the applicant.
>
> The Court agrees that the grounds for detention could initially be considered 'relevant' and 'sufficient' so as to justify the applicant's being again taken into custody under Article 5 § 3. However, the Court has doubts as to whether the grounds for the applicant's detention, as reflected in the perfunctorily reasoned court orders, retained their sufficiency for the whole period of the pre-trial detention."

(Available at the Internet site of the ECtHR http://cmiskp.echr.coe.int/tkp197/view.asp?item=3&portal=hbkm&action=html&highlight=estonia&sessionid=5582442&skin=hudoc-en)

6/10

In the judgment of 8 November 2005, *Alver* v. *Estonia* the ECtHR gave a decision with regards to the prohibition of torture and inhuman or degrading punishment under Article 3 of the European Convention on Human Rights.

> "Article 3 of the Convention enshrines one of the most fundamental values of democratic society. It prohibits in absolute terms torture and inhuman or degrading treatment or punishment, irrespective of the circumstances and the victim's behavior.
>
> The Court considers that the conditions of the applicant's detention as described above, in particular the overcrowding, inadequate lighting and ventilation, impoverished regime, poor hygiene conditions and state of repair of the cell facilities, combined with the applicant's state of health and the length of the period during which he was detained in such conditions, were sufficient to cause distress and hardship of an intensity exceeding the unavoidable level of suffering inherent in detention. Accordingly, there has been a violation of Article 3 of the Convention."

(Available at the Internet site of the ECtHR http://cmiskp.echr.coe.int/tkp197/view.asp?item=4&portal=hbkm&action=html&highlight=estonia&sessionid=5582442&skin=hudoc-en)

Part Seven: I. E. The State and its Organs – The composition of the State – Diplomatic missions and their members

7/1

During the *Riigikogu* discussion of 26 October 2005, the Foreign Minister Urmas Paet discussed the changes in the new Act of Foreign Service,

> "The first part of the Act deals with general definitions, the second regulates diplomatic posts, assignment of such posts, the status of the diplomats and the recalling of diplomats. The third part covers the administrative staff in foreign countries, the fourth regulates the rights of diplomats and their family members. The fifth part deals with different issues, the most important of which would be the assignment of a 'spouse salary'.
>
> The latter has been established in order to provide the non-working spouses of diplomats with the possibility to receive a decent pension once they have reached the appropriate age. In addition, changes to the previous act include the updating of the social insurance system and the specification of rules related to the foreign service."

(Available at the Internet site of the *Riigikogu* http://web.*Riigikogu*.ee/ems/plsql/stenograms.form, editors' translation)

Part Nine: I. A. 4. State Territory – Territory – Elements of territory – Airspace

9/1

During the *Riigikogu* discussion of 12 January 2005, the Defence Minister Jaak Jõerüüt explained the importance of the Treaty on Open Skies and expressed the government's position that Estonia should join the agreement,

> "The Treaty on Open Skies establishes an internal form of cooperation in the area of arms control known as the Confidence- and Security-Building Measures. Openness in such areas indicates and increases trust between States. The Treaty shall cover areas until now not covered by the European Armament Agreement as well as the Vienna documents.
>
> The main aim of the Treaty will be exchange of information and support between the Member States. Information shall be gathered by conducting surveillance flights with unarmed aircrafts whereby the State conducting the flights shall bear the related costs.

> Most of the OSCE Member States, including 24 NATO Member States have already joined the Treaty. All of the countries neighbouring Estonia have joined and by now 400 flights have been conducted. The Treaty was signed in 1992 and Estonia has participated in 8 trial flights, 6 of which were conducted in Estonian airspace. Joining the Treaty reflects Estonia's intent to participate in international cooperation in relation to arms control. The Treaty is extremely important at the international level, its provisions are in conformity with Estonia's interests and the Estonian Government considers it necessary for Estonia to join the agreement."

(Available at the Internet site of the *Riigikogu* http://web.*Riigikogu*.ee/ems/plsql/stenograms.form, editors' translation)

Part Nine: I. B. 2. State Territory – Good neighborliness – Boundaries and frontiers

9/2

On 18 May 2005 Estonia and Russia signed the Border Treaty, which the *Riigikogu* ratified on 20 June 2005 and which the President of the Republic proclaimed on 22 June 2005. On 27 June 2005 the Russian Federation withdrew its signature from the Treaty and called for new negotiations due to the preamble that the *Riigikogu* added to the ratification law:

> "Deriving from the legal succession of the Republic of Estonia, which was proclaimed on 24 February 1918 as it has been stated in the Constitution of the Republic of Estonia, the 20 August 1991 decision of the Supreme Council of the Republic of Estonia 'On Estonian national independence' and the declaration of the *Riigikogu* on 7 October 1992 'On restoration of constitutional State authority' and taking into account that the agreement named in § 1 of this Act [the ratification act] modifies partly in accordance with § 122 of the Estonian Constitution the Estonian border as it had been set in Article III (1) of the Tartu Peace Treaty from 2 February 1920 and does not modify the rest of the treaty not other bilateral issues that are not connected to the border treaties."

(Available at the Internet site of the Riigi Teataja https://www.riigiteataja.ee/rt/act.jsp?id=915915, editors' translation)

9/3

On 12 September 2005 at the opening of the 6th session of the *Riigikogu* Plenary Assembly, the President of the Republic expressed his regrets in regard to the unsuccessful negotiations over the Russian border treaty,

> "Estonia has worked towards cooperation based on mutual understanding with all its neighbours. Therefore it is rather regrettable that we have had a backlash on the accomplishment of signing the border treaty with Russia. I would like to emphasize that values and principles, which we acted upon in restoration of our independence and which were accepted by Russia through recognising of our independence form the foundation for cooperation with Russia. I believe that fair analysis of common history will help to eliminate shadows of the past, which cloud cooperation between our countries. "

(Available at the Internet site of the President of Estonia http://www.president.ee/en/duties/speeches.php?gid=67571)

Part Eleven: XVIII. A. 3. Seas and Vessels – Vessels – Legal regime-Merchant vessels

11/1

On 1 December 2005 Estonia signed the Merchant Shipping (Minimum Standards) Convention and the Protocol of 1996 to the Convention. The latter was adopted on 22 October 1996 at the 84th Maritime Convention of the International Labour Conference and it aims to promote the health and safety of workers, improve maritime safety and protect the marine environment. The 1996 Protocol to the Merchant Shipping Convention No. 147 includes in its additional annex Convention 180 concerning seafarers' hours of work and the manning of ships. The application of Convention 180 to ships flying the flag of third countries that call in at Community ports is possible only if the Member States ratify the Convention and the Protocol.

(Available on the Internet at http://europa.eu.int/scadplus/leg/en/cha/10821.htm)

Part Thirteen: IV. A. International Responsibility – Consequences of responsibility – Reparation

13/1

During the *Riigikogu* discussion of 12 October 2005, the Social Minister Jaak Aab explained the need to ratify the European Convention on Restitution to Victims of Violent Crimes and the consequences of such ratification for Estonia,

> "The European Convention on Restitution to Victims of Violent Crimes was adopted in Strasbourg on 24 November 1983 and came into force on 1 February 1988. So far 18 States have ratified the Convention and ten more, including Estonia have signed but have not yet ratified it. The main aim of the Convention is to establish minimum standards with regards to the compensation payable to the victims of violent crimes committed against them within the member States. The Convention shall ensure that foreigners from other member States will be compensated by the country in the territory in which the crime was committed.
>
> By ratifying the Convention, Estonia shall ensure equal treatment of its citizens with regard to the payment of compensation in other member States. At the same time the country will be obliged to compensate the citizens of other member States against whom violent crimes have been committed in Estonian territory. This means that the circle of possible recipients of compensation in Estonia grows considerably, as it includes all tourists who are citizens of other member States who fall victim to violent crimes in the territory of Estonia."

(Available at the Internet site of the *Riigikogu* http://web.*Riigikogu*.ee/ems/plsql/stenograms.form, editors' translation)

Part Fifteen: II. A. Coercive Measures short of the Use of Force – Collective Measures – United Nations

15/1

During the *Riigikogu* discussion of 23 November 2005, the Foreign Minister Jürgen Ligi suggested that Estonia should continue peacekeeping operations in Kosovo,

> "Estonian troops have taken part in peacekeeping missions in Kosovo since 1999. In 2003 BALTSQN started its operations under the direction of a Danish platoon. The *Riigikogu* should support the decision to continue the KFOR mission under NATO. Presently, the international community has decided to solve the problems existing in Kosovo with the support of the UN. KFOR is the most extensive NATO mission in the area with more than 17 000 peacekeepers from 35 countries. At the moment KFOR is being restructured whereby the static brigades are being replaced by the more mobile task forces. The restructuring of the mission should enable Estonia to reduce the number of peacekeepers in the area and set a limit of 150."

(Available at the Internet site of the *Riigikogu* http://web.*Riigikogu*.ee/ems/lsql/stenograms.form, editors' translation)

15/2

During the *Riigikogu* discussion of 23 November 2005, the Foreign Minister Jürgen Ligi suggested that Estonia should start peacekeeping operations in Kuwait, Qatar, Bahrain and Iraq,

> "I am suggesting to send up to 40 peacekeepers to a mission in Iraq for one year starting from 1 January 2006 with the aim of supporting the ongoing political processes and to improve the security situation in the country. Both Iraq and the UN Defence Committee have expressed their wish to extend the Estonian troops' presence in the region. Such pleads are not made without serious considerations, Iraq is in need and Estonia has the means to assist the country. The fight in Iraq is over ideals and values important to us. Most of the victims are civilians and it is morally right and humanly necessary to protect them."

(Available at the Internet site of the *Riigikogu* http://web.*Riigikogu*.ee/ems/plsql/ stenograms.form, editors' translation)

15/3

During the *Riigikogu* discussion of 19 October 2005, the Foreign Minister Urmas Paet elaborated on the importance of the Convention on the Safety of UN and Associated Personnel,

> "The Convention on the safety of UN and Associated Personnel is important for Estonia as it deals with issues important in the areas of foreign communication and international peacekeeping. Estonia as a UN member State is obliged to assist in achieving the above-mentioned aims of the organisation. Joining the Convention increases Estonia's international cooperation with the UN and the protection of associated personnel. It will create a situation where it is much simpler to prosecute individuals who have committed crimes against the personnel concerned. At the moment the Convention has been ratified by 78 States. Out of the 25 EU Member States only Estonia, Latvia and Malta have so far failed to do so."

(Available at the Internet site of the *Riigikogu* http://web.*Riigikogu*.ee/ems/plsql/stenograms.form, editors' translation)

15/4

On 23 September 2005, Mrs Tiina Intelmann, the Ambassador of the Estonian Permanent Representation to United Nations discussed Estonia's contribution to the UN peace keeping missions at the UN General Assembly,

> "Estonia also acknowledges the need to develop African peacekeeping and to provide better training for UN peace keepers. We hosted a UN peacekeeping 'train the trainers' course in Estonia a few months ago. This seminar was attended by peace keepers from roughly 30 countries.
>
> Over years, we have shown our continued commitment to UN activities, including peacekeeping, in a simple and unequivocal way – by regularly paying, on time, the full amount of assessed contributions."

(Available at the Internet site of the Foreign Ministry http://www.vm.ee/eng/kat_140/6998.html?arhiiv_kuup=arhiiv)

Part Seventeen: III. I. The Law of Armed Conflict and International Humanitarian Law – Aspects of the Law of Armed Conflict – War Crimes

17/1

On 24 July 2005 the President of the Republic expressed his views on the holocaust at the opening ceremony of a memorial to the victims of the Holocaust that had taken place on the territory of Estonia during World War II at the Klooga concentration camp,

> "The Holocaust was a horrific crime arising from misanthropic Nazi ideology. No other nation was subjected to such total and savage annihilation than the Jewish people were. Standing now at this place where so many innocent people had to meet humiliation, pain and death, it is difficult to find words. But it is our duty to talk about this.
>
> Estonia did not remain untouched by the Holocaust. The Nazis executed the Jews who had stayed in Estonia; those victims were people who had been residents and citizens of Estonian Republic where the rights of ethnic minorities were respected. Also thousands of Jewish people deported to Estonia from Czechoslovakia, Germany, France, Lithuania, and from elsewhere were murdered here. Today we do not know the exact numbers yet. It is a duty of Estonia to complete that research.
>
> To our nation caught up in the war, the occupation caused not only loss of freedom, but also the most barbarous massacre. Wars had ravaged Estonia also before, but during World War II we had to suffer from devastation caused by anti-human regimes. Those crimes do not expire with time nor have any justification."

(Available at the Internet site of the President of Estonia http://www.president.ee/ en/duties/speeches.php?gid=65655)

Appendix I A. Agreements signed by Estonia before 2005 which entered into force in 2005 – Bi-and multilateral agreements

Instrument and title	Date of Estonia's signature
Protocol Amending the Agreement on Baltic Parliamentary and Governmental Co-operation between the Republic of Estonia, the Republic of Latvia and the Republic of Lithuania	28.11.2003
Agreement between Denmark, Estonia, Finland, Iceland, Latvia, Lithuania, Norway and Sweden Concerning the Nordic Investment Bank	11.02.2004
Agreement between the Government of the Republic of Estonia and the Government of the Slovak Republic on mutual protection of classified information	09.09.2004
Agreement on the Taxation of Savings Income between the Republic of Estonia and the Isle of Man	19.11.2004
Agreement on the Taxation of Savings Income between the Republic of Estonia and Guernsey	19.11.2004
Agreement on the Taxation of Savings Income between the Republic of Estonia and Jersey	19.11.2004

Appendix I B. Agreements signed by Estonia before 2005 which entered into force in 2005 – Conventions

Instrument and title	Date of Estonia's signature
Protocol Amending the Agreement on Baltic Parliamentary and Governmental Co-operation between the Republic of Estonia, the Republic of Latvia and the Republic of Lithuania	26.11.2002

Appendix II A. Agreements signed by Estonia in 2005 – Bi-and multilateral agreements

Instrument and title	Date of Estonia's signature
Agreement between the Government of the Republic of Estonia and the Government of the Republic of Bulgaria on mutual	08.03.2005

protection and exchange of Classified Information	
Agreement between the Government of the Republic of Estonia and the Government of the Kingdom of Denmark on the Reciprocal Holding of Stocks of Crude Oil and Petroleum Products	07.04.2005
An Amendment to the Memorandum of Understanding between the Republic of Estonia and the Nordic Council of Ministers regarding the Status of the Tallinn Information Office for the Nordic Council of Ministers	26.04.2005
Agreement between the Government of the Republic of Estonia and the Government of Japan concerning the supply of Japanese language learning equipment to the Tallinn University	26.05.2005
Agreement between the Government of the Republic of Estonia and the Government of Ukraine concerning the temporary eradication of state fees charged for the processing of visa applications.	30.05.2005
Agreement between the Government of the Republic of Estonia and the Government of the Hashemite Kingdom of Jordan concerning the status of Estonian police officers deployed in the Kingdom of Jordan for the purpose of training Iraqi police forces	09.06.2005
Program on Cooperation in the Fields of Education and Culture between the Government of the Republic of Estonia and the Government of the Hellenic Republic for the Years 2005, 2006 and 2007	15.06.2005
Agreement between the Government of the Republic of Estonia and the Government of the Republic of Philippines on Cultural and Educational Co-operation	21.06.2005
Agreement between the Government of Republic of Estonia and Georgia on Visa Regime Liberalization	30.08.2005
Exchange Program between the Government of the Republic of Estonia and the Government of the Republic of Turkey in the fields of culture, education, science, youth and sports	06.09.2005
Project Agreement between the Government of the Republic of Estonia and the Government of the Republic of Finland concerning Kadrina Bark Boiler JI Project	20.10.2005
Agreement between the Government of the Republic of Estonia and the Government of Japan concerning the Improvement of Equipment for Exhibition and Preservation for the Art Museum of Estonia	18.11.2005

Appendix II B. Agreements signed by Estonia in 2005 – Conventions

Instrument and title	Date of Estonia's signature
Agreement between the Parties to the North Atlantic Treaty for the Security of Information	06.01.2005
Convention drawn up on the basis of Article K.3 (2) (c) of the Treaty on European Union on the fight against corruption involving officials of the European Communities or officials of Member States of the European Union	17.01.2005
NATO Agreement on the Communication of Technical Information for Defence Purposes	11.03.2005
Protocol for the Protection of Cultural Property in the Event of Armed Conflict	17.04.2005
Convention drawn up on the basis of Article K.3 of the Treaty on European Union, on the Protection of the European Communities' Financial Interests and the Protocols	04.05.2005
Treaty on Open Skies	23.05.2005
Agreement between the Republic of Estonia and the French Republic represented by the Delegation Interministerielle a la Ville, acting as Managing Authority and "la Caisse des Depots et Consignations", Paying Authority on the Implementation of the Community Initiative Programme "Urbact"	29.06.2005
Convention based on Article K.3 of the Treaty on European Union, on the Establishment of a European Police Office (Europol Convention)	01.07.2005
Protocol drawn up on the basis of Article K.3 of the Treaty on European Union, on the interpretation, by way of preliminary rulings, by the Court of Justice of the European Communities of the Convention on the establishment of a European Police Office	01.07.2005
Protocol drawn up, on the basis of Article K.3 of the Treaty on European Union and Article 41(3) of the Europol Convention, on the privileges and immunities of Europol, the members of its organs, the deputy directors and employees of Europol	01.07.2005
Protocol to the 1979 Convention on Long-range Transboundary Air Pollution on Persistent Organic Pollutants	09.08.2005
Convention established by the Council in accordance with Article 34 of the Treaty on European Union, on Mutual Assistance in	23.08.2005

Criminal Matters between the Member States of the European Union	
Convention defining the Statute of the European Schools	26.08.2005
United Nations Convention on the Law of the Sea	25.09.2005
Protocol of 1997 to amend the International Convention for the Prevention of Pollution from Ships, 1973, as modified by the Protocol of 1978 relating thereto	18.10.2005
Co-operation Agreement between the Republic of Estonia and the European Center for Medium-Range Weather Forecasts	07.11.2005
Merchant Shipping (Minimum Standards) Convention and the Protocol of 1996 to the Convention	01.12.2005
Agreement concerning specific stability requirements for ro-ro passenger ships undertaking regular scheduled international voyages between or to or from designated ports in North West Europe and the Baltic Sea	12.12.2005

Republic of Latvia Materials on International Law 2005

Edited by *Mārtiņš Paparinskis*[*]

[Editorial Note:

1. The Republic of Latvia Materials on International Law 2005 (RLMIL 2005) have been classified according to the Recommendation (97)11 of 12 June 1997 of the Committee of Ministers of the Council of Europe, as applied by the British Yearbook of International Law from the year 1997, with certain minor amendments.

2. Since the RLMIL mostly concern the opinions made by the institutions and officials of Latvia, if it has not been expressly provided for otherwise, the institutions and officials mentioned in the RLMIL are those of the Republic of Latvia.

3. The discussions surrounding the Treaty between the Republic of Latvia and the Russian Federation on the State Border of the Republic of Latvia and the Russian Federation involved very interesting issues of international law. The fundamental disagreement between Latvia and Russia was about a unilateral interpretative declaration that Latvia purported to attach to the Treaty upon its signature. Russia vehemently opposed the declaration on the grounds that it involved territorial claims by Latvia. Latvia explained that the declaration was necessary to make the proposed agreement compatible with the Satversme (Latvian Constitution). The narrower factual situation that Latvia and Russia had in mind evolved around the district of Abrene / Pitalova that had been taken away from Latvia after annexation by the Soviet Union. The broader legal implications involved the Latvian claim of State continuity and illegality of annexation as well as important questions of the

---

[*] LL.B. (University of Latvia), M.Jur. (Dist) (Oxon), M.Phil. (Oxon) student, Associate at Sorainen Law Offices. I am grateful for the provided materials and valuable suggestions about the relevant practice from Dainis Lasmanis, assistant to a Judge of the Administrative Matters Department of the Supreme Court Senate, and Gatis Melnudris, legal consultant at the Saeima Legal Bureau.

Baltic Yearbook of International Law, Volume 6, 2006, pp. 383–448.

law of treaties regarding distinctions between reservations and interpretative declarations. In the end Russia refused to sign and ratify the treaty in light of the interpretative declaration proposed by Latvia.[1]

4. The Constitutional Court has been judicially active this year in interpreting international law. In a landmark judgement, the Court reviewed the compliance of Latvia with obligations under Article 18 of the Vienna Convention on the Law of Treaties not to defeat the object and purpose of non-ratified treaties. In several cases the Court referred to the work of the International Law Commission on State responsibility and diplomatic protection. Addressing the sources of international law, the Court dealt with customary international law and twice considered *jus cogens* aspects of certain norms or situations. The Court also did not shy away from international case law and addressed the Permanent Court of International Justice case of *Albanian Minority Schools* and the International Court of Justice case of *Nottebohm.* It would seem that the year 2005 presented the opportunity for the Constitutional Court to make landmark pronouncements in many fields of international law.

5. The award in the case of *Nykomb* v. *Latvia* under the Energy Charter Treaty was rendered already at the end of 2003, but was released to the general public only in 2005. Substantial portions of the award have been reproduced in the relevant parts of the report. *Nykomb* is a landmark case as it is the first time Latvia fully argued the case (in the first investment case brought against Latvia, *SwemBalt* v. *Latvia,* Latvia did not participate in the proceedings).]

---

[1] Latvia acted on the basis of legal opinions of very eminent Latvian scholars of international and constitutional law. These opinions have not been made publicly available and as such will not be included in the RLMIL 2005. Consequently, only the bare practice will be shown, with the underlying legal reasoning and *opinio juris* largely remaining regrettably classified.

Part One: I. B. International law in general – Nature, basis, purpose – *Jus cogens*

1/1

The Constitutional Court in the judgment of 7 March 2005 in case No 2004-15-0106 considered whether constitutional norms guaranteed diplomatic protection:

> "Article 98 of the Satversme provides that **everyone having a Latvian passport shall be protected by the State when abroad**. It means that Latvia exercises diplomatic protection in respect of those persons having a Latvian passport. Diplomatic protection is not a fundamental right, but it is considered as a mechanism for enforcing human rights and can be carried out, for example, by providing access to consular institutions. The State has the discretion to carry out diplomatic protection in respect of the individual or not. However, the State may have an obligation to exercise diplomatic protection, if jus cogens norms have been breached in respect of the individual."[2]

(Available at the Internet site of the Constitutional Court, <www.satv.tiesa.gov.lv/ENG/spriedum.htm>, editor's translation)

1/2

The Constitutional Court in the judgment of 16 December 2005 in case No 2005-12-0103 considered a claim that the newly adopted rules on expropriation were in breach of constitutional rules on protection of property. In stressing the importance of the right to property, the Court remarked that:

---

[2] The Court further refers to the International Law Commission Draft Articles on Diplomatic Protection 2000. During that session, the Special Rapporteur had proposed, *de lege ferenda,* to include such a norm in the Articles on Diplomatic Protection. The proposal was rejected, *see* <http://www.un.org/law/ilc/reports/2000/english/chp5e.pdf>, paras. 447-456. It seems that the Court was more sympathetic towards Dugard's proposal than the International Law Commission had been. Although the judgment is not completely clear in this respect, an argument could be made that there could be an obligation enforceable in national law for Latvia to exercise diplomatic protection when the injury to the individual results from a breach of *jus cogens.*

"The special importance of the right to property has also been recognised by the Court of First Instance of the European Communities that has in its recent case law attributed a status of *jus cogens* to the arbitrary deprivation of the right to property, recognising that an arbitrary deprivation of property is contrary to a *jus cogens* norm (see*: T-306/01 Ahmed Ali Yusuf and Al Barakaat International Foundation v. Council of the European Union and Commission of the European Communities [2005]. http://europa.eu.int/eur-lex/lex/LexUriServ/LexUriServ.do?uri=CELEX:62001A0306:EN:HTML, para. 293).*"[3]

(Available at the Internet site of the Constitutional Court, <www.satv.tiesa.gov.lv/ENG/spriedum.htm>, editor's translation)

Part One: II. International law in general – History

1/3

On 12 January 2005, H. E. Dr. Vaira Vīķe-Freiberga, the President, made a declaration regarding 9 May 2005 and *inter alia* considered certain international law aspects of Latvian history in the second half of the 20th century:

"On May the 8th, Europe will also commemorate the 60th anniversary of the end of the Second World War . . .

. . . In my own country of Latvia, the Nazi Germans and their local accomplices carried out the most heinous and large-scale crimes against humanity to have ever been committed on Latvian soil. They annihilated over 90 % of Latvia's prewar Jewish community, as well as tens of thousands of other Jews whom they transported into Latvia from other parts of Europe. The Nazis also drafted tens of thousands of Latvian men into

[3] The Constitutional Court's reading of Case T-306/01 seems to be more expansive than that of the Court of First Instance itself. The CFI seems to address the *jus cogens* nature of arbitrary deprivation of right to property as a possibility ("it is only an arbitrary deprivation of that right that *might*, in any case, be regarded as contrary to jus cogens" (italics added), Case T-306/01 *Ahmed Ali Yusuf and Al Barakaat International Foundation* v. *Council of the European Union and Commission of the European Communities* [2005] ECR 00000). The language of the Constitutional Court is unconditional ("arbitrary deprivation *is* contrary to a *jus cogens* norm")(italics added). Of course, the remark was only *obiter dictum* and the Court did not expressly adopt it, but the expansive reading of the *Yusuf* case is certainly instructive.

their army ranks to serve as live cannon fodder, in a shameless violation of the Geneva Conventions regarding the rules of warfare.[4]

Latvia, together with the rest of Europe, rejoices at the defeat of Nazi Germany and its fascist regime in May of 1945. However, unlike the case in Western Europe, the fall of the hated Nazi German empire did not result in my country's liberation. Instead, the three Baltic countries of Latvia, Estonia and Lithuania were subject to another brutal occupation by another foreign, totalitarian empire, that of the Soviet Union.

. . . For Latvia, the beginning of the end of the Second World War arrived many decades later, on May the 4th, 1990. This was the date when my country's parliament passed a declaration of independence from the Soviet Union. This May, Latvians will be celebrating the 15th anniversary of that historic declaration.

. . . I will also be commemorating, with great sadness, the renewed Soviet occupation of my country, and the immense human loss and suffering that ensued as a result; not only in Latvia, but throughout the former captive nations of Central and Eastern Europe.

. . . Latvia invites Russia to display the same degree of conciliation to Latvia, Estonia, Lithuania, and to condemn the crimes of the Second World War, regardless of who committed them. All leaders of democratic nations should encourage Russia to express its regret over the post-war subjugation of Central and Eastern Europe, which ensued as a direct result of the Molotov-Ribbentrop pact.'

(Available at the Internet site of the Ministry of Foreign Affairs of Latvia, <www.am.gov.lv/en/news/speeches/> (01.01.2006))

1/4

On 14 January 2005, H. E. Dr. Vaira Vīķe-Freiberga, the President, addressed the foreign diplomatic corps in Riga and explained the aspects of the Second World War:

"For Latvia, the jubilation at the fall of Hitler will be tinged with sorrow at my country's further subjugation at the hands of the Soviet Union and the untold suffering that it imposed on our people as a result of inhuman persecution and mass deportations. But on May the 9th I will be expressing

[4] It would be more accurate to refer to the Hague Convention, since the relevant rule is found in Article 44 of the Annex to the Hague Convention 1899 (II) and 1907 (IV).

my sympathy to the Russian people as well for their losses and suffering. The Russian people played an important part in ridding Europe of one bloodthirsty tyrant – Hitler. But they, no more than people in Latvia and other countries, did not gain freedom from Stalinist tyranny and from the oppression of totalitarian Communism.

In attending the official events planned in Moscow on May the 9th, I will be extending a hand of friendship and reconciliation to the Russian people, while encouraging the present-day leadership of their country to denounce the crimes committed by the Stalinist regime in Latvia and elsewhere in Central and Eastern Europe. I believe it is the duty of all democratic countries to urge Russia to condemn the crimes that were committed during the Soviet era in the name of communism. Russia must face up and come to honest terms with its history, just as Germany did following the end of the Second World War, and just as my own country is doing today."

(Available at the Internet site of the Ministry of Foreign Affairs of Latvia, <www.am.gov.lv/en/news/speeches/> (01.01.2006))

1/5

On 18 January 2005, H. E. Dr. Vaira Vīķe-Freiberga, the President, made an address at Leiden University "A Larger Europe – A Stronger Europe?" where she considered *inter alia* similar issues as in her declaration of 9 January 2005.

(Available at the Internet site of the Ministry of Foreign Affairs of Latvia, <www.am.gov.lv/en/news/speeches/> (01.01.2006))

1/6

On 6 May 2005, H. E. Dr. Vaira Vīķe-Freiberga, the President, made a statement before the visit of the President of the United States of America where she considered *inter alia* similar issues as in her declaration of 9 January 2005.

(Available at the Internet site of the Ministry of Foreign Affairs of Latvia, <www.am.gov.lv/en/news/speeches/> (01.01.2006))

1/7

On 23 August 2005, Mr. Artis Pabriks, the Minister of Foreign Affairs, made an address to the Conference of the Konrad Adenauer Foundation on the "Hitler-Stalin Pact of 23 August 1939 and its Consequences" in Riga:

> "Unlike many other international agreements, this agreement [Hitler-Stalin Pact of 23 August 1939] was criminal both toward the people of the countries that signed it and to the people of the countries that it affected. That crime has still not been fully assessed, nor has it been unequivocally condemned so that it can serve as a lesson for future generations.
>
> This is a crime which has apparently been exposed, but the criminal has not been punished. Moreover, the criminal has not admitted any wrongdoing. How can we forgive when there has been no expression of regret or request for forgiveness? The essence of this heinous pact is evident not only in the context of the past and present, but also the future. Only when we consider the pact in the context of all these aspects together and at once are we able to arrive at the gist of things. Not all politicians from the countries which concluded the pact want to have a clear and comprehensive picture of the moral and historic significance of the pact; instead, they would rather look at it through a skewed prism.
>
> . . . Nonetheless, I express the hope that Russia will admit to the crimes of the Molotov-Ribbentrop Pact one day, be it in five, ten or fifty years.
>
> We are optimistic. We are a member of NATO and the European Union. In the context of the latest political developments with regard to the conclusion of agreements with our neighbouring state and concerning my actions as minister of foreign affairs and the actions of the ministry, I would like to emphasize that we are not hostages of our roots, of our past; the signing of one accord or another will not make a cardinal change in Russia's attitude. We must maintain a principled stance: we cannot make a short term concession for which we shall have to pay a severe price in the future."

(Available at the Internet site of the Ministry of Foreign Affairs of Latvia, <www.am.gov.lv/en/news/speeches/> (01.01.2006))

Part Two: I. A. Sources and codification of international law – Sources of international law – Treaties

2/1

The Constitutional Court in the judgment of 13 May 2005 in case No 2004-18-0106 considered the place of international law in the Latvian legal system:

> "It follows from Article 38 (1) of the UN International Court of Justice's Statute that primary sources of international law are international treaties, international customs and principles of law recognised by civilised nations. These sources of law are also applicable in the Latvian legal system. It is also confirmed by Article 1 (8) of the Administrative Procedure Law that provides that a norm of international law includes international treaties binding upon Latvia, customary international law and general principles of international law.
>
> However, each of these sources of international law becomes binding for Latvia in a different way. According to Article 68 (1) of the Satversme, all international treaties that deal with issues to be decided in a legislative manner require affirmation by the Saeima. To make such an international agreement binding upon Latvia, it must first be affirmed by Saeima."

(Available at the Internet site of the Constitutional Court, <www.satv.tiesa.gov.lv/ENG/spriedum.htm>, editor's translation)

Part Two: I. B. Sources and codification of international law – Sources of international law – Custom

2/2

The Constitutional Court in the judgment of 13 May 2005 in case No 2004-18-0106 considered different arguments why the minority educational programmes were unlawful. Among other things the court considered the possible customary nature of certain rules on minority protection:

> "During the judicial proceedings the counsel for the applicant admitted that Article 14 (2) of the Minority Convention [Framework Convention for the Protection of National Minorities] in reality does not impose obligations on the State to provide for the study of the educational content in the minority language. He also did not dispute that the Minority Convention has not become a norm of customary international law . . .

> . . . Moreover – it [Article 14 of the Minority Convention] cannot be binding as a norm of customary international law because the application of this Article in the Contracting Parties to the Minority Convention is too different. This article does not include unambiguous and precise obligations for the state that the state would have moreover considered as binding without the ratification of the Minority Convention."[5]

(Available at the Internet site of the Constitutional Court, <www.satv.tiesa.gov.lv/ENG/spriedum.htm>, editor's translation)

(See also *2/1*)

Part Two: I. D. Sources and codification of international law – Sources of international law – Unilateral acts (including acts and decisions of international organisations and conferences)

(See *2/2*)

Part Two: I. E. Sources and codification of international law – Sources of international law – Judicial decisions

2/3

The Constitutional Court in the judgment of 13 May 2005 in case No 2004-18-0106 considered different arguments why the minority educational programmes were unlawful. Among other things the applicants referred to the Advisory Opinion of the Permanent Court of International Justice in *Albanian Minority Schools*:

> "the case in question is not similar to the Advisory Opinion of the Permanent Court of International Justice of 6 April 1935 in the case about minority schools in Albania where the question was about Albania's obligations to allow the minorities to establish their own private schools. In 1993 Albania, relying on a respective constitutional amendment, decided to

[5] The last sentence seems to slightly confuse the issues of State practice and *opinio juris*. The content of the specific treaty provision would be relevant for the former, while the way a State could become bound by a custom for the latter. In considering the subjective criterion of custom, the Court seems to have adopted an extremely voluntaristic view, almost asking for an express statement of the State to be bound by the custom. An alternative reading of the judgment would be to read the first part of the sentence as rejecting the argument that Latvia is bound by a custom (because state practice is inadequate), while the second part as dealing with a possible argument that Latvia would have become bound by a unilateral statement.

close all – both Albanian and minority – private schools. The Court concluded that the closing of the private schools would not affect the ethnic and religious specifics of the majority, while the representatives of the minority would lose the institutions that are necessary for the maintenance of their specific requirements, rituals, etc. Albania consequently could not rely on the equal treatment of the representatives of the majority and minority, because the treatment of the minority needed to be different (see: *Minority schools in Albania. Advisory opinion of Permanent Court of Justice. http://www.icj-cij.org/cijwww/cdecisions/ccpij/serie_AB/AB_64/01_Ecoles_minoritaires_Avis_consultatif.pdf).*"

(Available at the Internet site of the Constitutional Court, <www.satv.tiesa.gov.lv/ENG/spriedum.htm>, editor's translation)

Part Three: I. C. The law of treaties – Definition, conclusion and entry into force of treaties - Reservations, declarations and objections

3/1

On 19 April 2005, the Government approved a declaration to be attached to the Treaty between the Republic of Latvia and the Russian Federation on the State Border of the Republic of Latvia and the Russian Federation ('Latvia-Russia Border Agreement'):

> "By signing the Border Agreement with the Russian Federation, Latvia, confirms its good will to promote good neighbourly relations with the Russian Federation and simultaneously expresses its satisfaction of the willingness of the Russian Federation to develop good neighbourly relations with Latvia.
>
> Latvia declares that by Article 1 of this Agreement it understands the *de facto* functioning line of demarcation dating from year 1990/1991, which is documented and technically described in the Annex of the Agreement. The only objective and subject of this Agreement is to document the abovementioned line of demarcation in order to ensure and to facilitate its practical functioning in the interests of both countries and their residents as well as in the mutual interests of the European Union and the Russian Federation.
>
> Latvia does not link this Agreement with the broader issue of the elimination of the consequences of the illegal occupation of Latvia. Latvia declares that this Agreement is not related and does not diminish, does not deprive the state of Latvia and its citizens of the rights and legal claims provided by the international law, including the Peace Treaty between

Latvia and Russia of August 11, 1920, and by state law of the Republic of Latvia pursuant to the international law.

Latvia stresses the fact that this Agreement is a result of the good will of both parties to the Agreement, provides reasons for optimism, and therefore it wishes to undertake efforts in order to solve the abovementioned issue in a way acceptable to both parties of the Agreement, and on the basis of these principles and in the interests of both countries to continue developing good neighbourly relations directed towards future and based on mutual respect and non-interference in the internal matters of the other state."

3/2

On 29 April 2005, Mr. Aigars Kalvitis, the Prime Minister, made a statement explaining the interpretative declaration by Latvia to the Latvia-Russia Border Agreement:

"Since regaining of independence governments of Latvia have consistently and clearly expressed readiness to sign the border treaty with Russia.

The declaration approved by the Government on last Tuesday does not present territorial claims against Russia. This issue is not on the agenda of Latvian – Russian relations. Latvia will respect the borders defined by the prepared and initialled treaty.

We are certain that Latvia's and Russia's differing opinions on the historic matters of the 20th century is the reason for the exasperated rhetoric between both countries. The true intention of Latvia is to do everything to find a common opinion on this issue in the future and thus create the basis for new relations with Russia that would be based on principles of democracy and international law.

Intended to serve this aim, the unilateral declaration of the Government of Latvia on the Latvian – Russian border treaty marks the historical keystones that Latvia sees as the fundamental basis for relations with Russia in the future.

Due to the complex questions concerning history and occupation in the 20th century, the Constitution of Latvia does not allow the Government of Latvia to sign the prepared border treaty in any other way than by adopting the mentioned unilateral declaration.

We are aware that at the moment, taking into account the processes in Russia, it is difficult to hope for a fast progress on the issue of occupation of the Baltic States; nevertheless, this does not allow us ignore our

> Constitution and history, which cannot be annulled or changed by decisions of the Government.
>
> The Government of Latvia once more reaffirms its willingness and readiness to sign the border treaty and at the same time invites the Russian side to an open and brave dialogue about history prior to or after the signing of the border treaty."

(Available at the Internet site of the Ministry of Foreign Affairs of Latvia, <www.am.gov.lv/en/news/policy/> (01.01.2006))

3/3

In an interview published on 9 June 2005, Mr. Artis Pabriks, the Minister of Foreign Affairs, explained how and why the declaration to the Latvia-Russia Border Treaty was formulated:

> "When I came to office last year, we made a decision to open [the treaty] to the public. The difference with Estonia is that we took the constitution. They had two different discussions on the border treaty in 1997 and 1999 in two different governments, and they had a legal analysis. This was not done by the previous governments in Latvia.
>
> So I did not inherit a legal analysis, and I asked for [one]. It came as a surprise. The legal analysis was not quickly made; we did not want to obstruct the negotiations, and we also knew that a unilateral declaration would not be binding to either side. We suggested to Russia that we make a unilateral declaration, and they could make their own. If our views do not correspond on what happened, then fine. So we could sign the border treaty with two unilateral declarations.
>
> At the very beginning we thought, after our consultations with lawyers, that we could attach the declaration later, but the problem was that sometime, two or three weeks before, Russia suggested opening the border treaty for technical checks. Which basically would be a challenge, and before we could do this we would have to go before the government. We were not sure we could keep this confidential anymore, so we also had to look at the border treaty.
>
> There have been some skeptics saying that we could have attached the declaration later. I would deny this. What has been our experience, looking at other similar situations – let's say Germany and the Soviet Union in 1965, the Helsinki Act of 1975 – we wanted to inform, and we have to inform the other sides of our unilateral views."

(Available at the Internet site of the Ministry of Foreign Affairs of Latvia, <www.am.gov.lv/en/news/speeches/> (01.01.2006))

Part Three: II. A. The law of treaties – Observance, application and interpretation of treaties – Observance

3/4

The Constitutional Court in the judgment of 13 May 2005 in case No 2004-18-0106 considered different arguments why the minority educational programmes were unlawful. Among other things the applicants argued that the minority legislation was in breach of Article 18 of the Vienna Convention on the Law of Treaties and the unratified Framework Convention for the Protection of National Minorities:

> "Article 18 of the Vienna Convention [on the Law of Treaties] among other things provides that a State is obliged to refrain from acts which would defeat the object and purpose of the treaty, if the State has signed a treaty subject to ratification.
>
> . . . The Satversme Court considers that the Vienna Convention is not an exception to the obligation of affirmation [by the Saeima] provided for in Article 68 of the Satversme. Obligations that are derived from both of these articles are different, and are not to be confused. First of all Article 18 of the Vienna Convention itself indicates that '[a] State . . . has signed a treaty . . . subject to ratification'.
>
> Upon ratification the international agreement with the legal norms included therein becomes binding and can be directly applied to the legal relations in the State, unless the State has simultaneously with the ratification made a reservation. On the contrary, the purpose of Article 18 of the Vienna Convention is to guarantee that the ratification of the treaty does not become futile, as for example in the case when the object of the treaty would not exist. This Article in no way imposes on the States an obligation to fulfil the obligations of a signed treaty that is not in force in respect of the State. Article 18 of the Vienna Convention imposes an obligation on the States not to defeat the object and purpose of the signed agreement before it comes into force. This obligation follows from the principle of good faith – not to make the fulfilment of treaty obligations impossible before the treaty norms become binding and consequently lead to a breach of the concluded agreement. Obligations imposed by Article 18 of the Vienna Convention are narrower than those that arise out of the ratification of the treaty."

(Available at the Internet site of the Constitutional Court,

<www.satv.tiesa.gov.lv/ENG/spriedum.htm>, editor's translation)

Part Three: II. D. The law of treaties – observance, application and interpretation of treaties – treaties and third States

(See *1/7*)

Part Four: II. A. Relationship between international law and internal law – Application and implementation of international law in internal law – Treaties

4/1

The Constitutional Court in the judgment of 7 March 2005 in case No 2004-15-0106 interpreted constitutional provisions by referring to international human rights law:

> "The right to leave the country provided for in Article 12(2) of the [International] Covenant [on Civil and Political Rights] applies to any person and not just to nationals of the respective State. Consequently, the content of the norm is applicable in determining the compatibility of the challenged norms with Article 98 of the Satversme.
>
> Article 12(4) provides for the right to return to one's own country. The Human Rights Committee has indicated that the rights provided for in this provision are to be interpreted considering the special link of a person with the State. The applicability of the rights provided for in this Article are not limited to the State of nationality in its formal meaning [see *Joseph S., Schultz J., Castan M. (ed.) The International Covenant in Civil and Political Rights. Cases, materials and commentary, 2nd ed., Oxford University Press, 2004, p. 366*]. Consequently, the content of the rights included in Article 12(4) of the Covenant is applicable in considering the compatibility of the challenged norms with Article 98 of the Satversme.
>
> Article 2(2) of Protocol 4 of the [European] Human Rights Convention provides for everybody's right to leave any country, including his own. The European Court of Human Rights has not as yet indicated that the rights provided for in this Article are applicable only to nationals of the relevant State. Consequently, this norm is applicable in interpreting everyone's rights to leave the country provided for in Article 98 of the Satversme.
>
> Article 3(2) of Protocol 5 of the Human Rights Convention provides that nobody shall be deprived of the right to enter the territory of the State of which he is a national. The European Court of Human Rights has recognised that 'the Convention does not guarantee person's rights to enter

> and reside in a country whose national the person is not, nor guarantees the right not to be expelled from this country. The Contracting Parties according to principle established in international law are entitled to control the entrance, residence and exit of such persons that are not its nationals (*non-nationaux*) (*Cour europeénne des Droits de l'Homme, Décision finale sur la recevabilité de la requête n° 50183/99 présentée par Aleksandr Kolosovskiy contre la Lettonie, le point B.c*).' Consequently this norm of the Convention guarantees rights only to the nationals of the relevant State and is not applicable to non-citizens, in interpreting the rights to return to Latvia provided for in Article 98 of the Satversme.
>
> From the abovementioned it follows that the scope of the rights provided for in the Pact and the Convention are different, but from the point of view of Latvian law the broader international human rights standard is binding upon Latvia."

(Available at the Internet site of the Constitutional Court, <www.satv.tiesa.gov.lv/ENG/spriedum.htm>, editor's translation)

4/2

The Administrative Matters Department of the Supreme Court in the judgment of 15 March 2005 in case no SKA-55 considering the degree of specificity that is necessary to make a provision sufficiently foreseeable. The lower court had found, relying on the case law of the European Court of Human Rights (ECtHR) and the German Constitutional Court, that the provision in question was not foreseeable enough. The Administrative Matters Department disagreed:

> "Legal norms cannot be recognised as such that raise doubts about possible arbitrary actions by the institution and possible non-predictability and unforseeability of such actions merely because they are general in nature.
>
> At the same time the reference to the judgments of the German Federal Constitutional Court and European Court of Human Rights is misguided. The Administrative Matters Department additionally draws attention to the fact that in the 'Goodwin v. United Kingdom' referred to by the Regional Court the journalist was obliged to reveal his source of information and since he did not reveal it, he was punished for contempt of court. In paragraph 33 of the judgment the European Court of Human Rights has stated that: '[t]he Court recognises that in the area under consideration it may be difficult to frame laws with absolute precision and that a certain degree of flexibility may even be desirable to enable the national courts to develop the law in the light of their assessment of what measures are

> necessary in the interests of justice'. In the specific case the formulation was not found to be too general in nature. Consequently, the European Court of Human Rights has accepted general formulations even in cases about the imposition of fines."

(Administrative Matters Department of the Supreme Court, Judgment SKA-55, para.14, editor's translation)

4/3

The Administrative Matters Department of the Supreme Court in the judgment of 19 April 2005 in case no SKA-94 considered the applicable onus probandi in VAT reclamation cases:

> "The Administrative Matters Department considers, similarly with the European Court of Justice that the cases when the tax rate is 0 per cent are to be interpreted narrowly, since they are exceptional from the general principle that all services that the taxpayer provides against remuneration are applied with VAT (cf. Judgment of the European Court of Justice of 18 November 2004 in the Case C-284/03 Belgium v. Temco Europe SA, para.17).
>
> In accordance with the generally accepted rules on principles of proof the burden of proof is on the person who alleges that he is covered by the exception (cf. Opinion of the Advocate General Poiare Maduro of 7 April 2005 in the Case C-446/03 Marks & Spencer plc v David Halsey, para.81). The obligation of the private person to provide the necessary evidence increases proportionally to the decision-making process being in the interest of the private person. In such cases it is natural and permissible to impose the burden of proof on the private person and not on the government as regards the facts that would facilitate the adoption of a beneficial decision (cf.: Nehl P.H. Principles of Administrative Procedure in EC Law. Oxford: Hart Publishing, 1999, pp.114–115)"

(Administrative Matters Department of the Supreme Court, Judgment SKA-94, para.10, editor's translation)

4/4

The Constitutional Court in the judgment of 13 May 2005 in case No 2004-18-0106 considered the argument that the change in the regulation of minority education was in breach of the obligation of Article 18 of the Vienna Convention on the Law of Treaties not to defeat the object and purpose of the signed treaty, i.e. the Framework Convention for the Protection of National Minorities:[6]

> "the counsel for the applicant insisted that the challenged norm is contrary to Article 18 of the Vienna Convention [on the Law of Treaties] because after signing the Minority Convention the minority rights to obtain education in native language have been diminished.
>
> The Constitutional Court agrees with the applicant's view that after signing the Minority Convention the minority rights to obtain education in native language have been diminished because at the moment of the signing the normative acts did not provide for mandatory use of State language in studying any courses. At the moment the challenged norm indeed provides a proportion of the study language.
>
> The signed Minority Convention is not binding upon Latvia because it is not ratified. The same applies to Article 14 of the Minority Convention . . . Even though the right to obtain education in native language as provided in the national rules has been diminished since the signing of the Minority Convention, the Constitutional Court agrees to the second argument of the applicant that this diminishing is not an obstacle for the ratification of the Minority Convention. The purpose of Article 18 of the Vienna Convention is exactly to address such obstacles that could endanger the ratification of an international treaty."

(Available at the Internet site of the Constitutional Court, <www.satv.tiesa.gov.lv/ENG/spriedum.htm>, editor's translation)

4/5

The Constitutional Court in the judgment of 13 May 2005 in case No 2004-18-0106 then considered the scope of the right to education provided in the European Convention for the Protection of Human Rights and Fundamental Freedoms (ECHR):

> "Article 2 of Protocol 1 of the ECHR provides that no person shall be denied the right to education. Although this article is formulated in a negative manner, that is 'no person shall be denied the right', there is no doubt that it still provides the 'right'. The negative formulation of the article is not accidental, and has certain legal consequences. This article does not impose any obligations on the State to provide from budgetary

[6] *See supra* at *3/4* the general analysis of Article 18 of the Vienna Convention on the Law of Treaties.

sources or to subsidize the education of any kind or level. Such a conclusion of the ECtHR is based on the fact that the Member States of the Council of Europe had already each established an education system. Consequently, Article 2 of Protocol 1 guarantees the right to a person to benefit from the already existing education system. To make the right to education effective, the beneficiary must be provided with the possibility to benefit from the obtained education, i.e., to obtain education one way or another in compliance with the regulations in force in the State, as well as to rely on official recognition of the finished education. (see: Grosz S., Beatson J., Duffy P. Human Rights. The *1998* Act and the European Convention. London*:* Sweet&Maxwell, 2000, p. 359–360*). The European Commission of Human Rights (hereinafter the Commission) has concluded that Article 2 of Protocol 1 is mostly addressed at primary education. The State can regulate the availability of other kinds of education without breaching Article 2 of Protocol 1. The Commission considers that the State is not obliged to provide the possibility to obtain a higher or specialized education* (*see, e.g., applications no. 5962/72 and no. 7671/76*).

At the same time it should be noted that Article 2 of Protocol 1 of the ECHR applies both to secondary education and higher education to the extent the relevant level of education is accessible in accordance with the relevant normative acts of the Contracting State. Although Article 2 of Protocol 1 is mainly addressed at primary education, this article also applies to other kinds and levels of education should they be created. For example, the Commission has concluded that it is permissible to limit the possibilities to obtain State sponsored higher education in such a way that the accessibility of the higher educational institutions would be barred for those students who have already achieved the academic level necessary for receiving maximum benefit from the education already obtained (see application no. 8844/80). The ECtHR and the Constitutional Court have similar case law in interpreting a person's rights to a fair trial. Namely, the ECHR does not impose an obligation to create a cassation instance court but, should such a court be established, its proceedings must comply with Article 6(1) of the ECHR and the first sentence of Article 92 of the Satversme . . .

The ECtHR has concluded that the content of the school programmes is, as a matter of principle, within the competence of the Contracting Parties (see the ECtHR judgment, 'Kjeldsen, Busk Madsen and Pedersen v. Denmark' 53. §). Although Article 2 of Protocol 1 neither directly nor indirectly refers to educational language, the right to education can become meaningless if it is not possible to exercise it due to a language barrier ('Case Relating to certain aspects of the laws on the use of languages in education in Belgium' v. Belgium (Merits) I. B. 3. §).

> The first sentence of Article 112 of the Satversme provides that everyone has a right to education is to be interpreted in the same way as Article 2 of Protocol 1 of the ECHR. The second and third sentences of Article 112 of Satversme, however, provide broader rights for individuals. Even though Article 2 of Protocol 1 of the ECHR does not impose on the State any obligation to create a specific system of education, the second sentence of Article 112 of Satversme demands provision of a right to obtain free primary and secondary education. The third sentence of this article even provides that primary education is mandatory.
>
> Since the system of secondary education has been established and exists in Latvia, the first and second sentence of Article 112 of Satversme without any doubt includes the accessibility of the secondary obligation. The challenged norm, considering the linguistic factors, could be a restriction of the rights provided for in this article."

(Available at the Internet site of the Constitutional Court, <www.satv.tiesa.gov.lv/ENG/spriedum.htm>, editor's translation)

4/6

The Administrative Matters Department of the Supreme Court in the judgment of 30 August 2005 in case no SKA-346 considered whether the State had to provide cost for counsel in the specific case:

> "In accordance with the first and fourth sentences of Article 92 of Satversme everybody is entitled to defend one's rights and legal interests in a fair court and everybody is entitled to be assisted by an attorney. From the right to fair trial follows the right of access to court. Effective access to court is connected to the person's possibility to receive legal services. Article 13 of the Recommendation of Committee of Ministers of the European Council of 14 May 1981 No R(81)7 'On measures facilitating access to justice' provides that cost for representation and experts should receive special attention so as not to become a bar to access to court. Consequently, the person's right to fair trial creates an obligation for the State to ensure the possibility for the person to receive legal services to the extent to ensure effective protection of the person's rights in the court. (see Judgment of the ECtHR of 9 September 1979 in Airey v. Ireland, para.26.)."

(Administrative Matters Department of the Supreme Court, Judgment SKA-346, para.8, editor's translation)

4/7

The Constitutional Court in the judgment of 17 October 2005 in case no 2005-01-01 considered the challenge of a norm prohibiting appeal about decisions of access to classified information. The applicant argued that this norm did not comply with the right to fair trial. The Court also relied on ECtHR judgments to confirm its interpretative conclusions:

> "The first sentence of Article 92 of the Satversme provides that 'anybody shall be entitled to defend their rights and legal interests in a fair court'. Analogous rights to fair trial have been provided in Article 10 of the UN Universal Declaration on Human Rights, Article 6 of the European Convention on the Protection of Human Rights and Fundamental Freedoms (hereinafter - Convention) and Article 14 of the International Covenant on Civil and Political Rights."

The Constitutional Court then reviewed its previous case law about the right to fair trial and stressed that this right has both a substantive and procedural aspect, including the right of access to the court. Then the Court referred to its case law to the effect that the right to fair trial might be limited even though Article 92 is not expressly included in the list of limitations in Article 116 of Satversme.

> "The ECtHR also has several times noted in its judgments that right to fair trial is not absolute and can be restricted and that such restrictions are permissible because the essence of the right asks for certain regulation from the state (see: Golder v. United Kingdom, no. 4451/70, para. 38, ECHR 1975, Ashingdane v. The United Kingdom, no. 8225/78, para. 57, ECHR 1985, Fogarty v. The United Kingdom, no. 37112/97, para. 33, ECHR 1999, Waite and Kennedy v. Germany, no. 26083/94, para. 59, ECHR 1999, Fayed v. The United Kingdom, no. 17101/90, para. 65, ECHR 1990).
>
> Consequently, the right of access to court is not absolute and can be restricted.
>
> For the restriction that the state has imposed on the person to be permissible, this restriction must be provided by law and it must pursue a legitimate aim that the state wants to achieve, and the restriction must be proportionate to the legitimate aim (see: Fayed v. The United Kingdom, no. 17101/90, para. 65, ECHR 1990)."

The Court concluded that the restriction was provided by law and moved on to consider the legitimate aim.

> "The purpose of the legislator in adopting the challenged norm was not only to protect the State interests and security of the society, but also other NATO Member Countries in this field.
>
> The ECtHR has recognised in several judgments that the protection of national security is a legitimate aim that can be a reason for restricting a person's right of access to court (see: *Devenny v. The United Kingdom, no. 24265/94, para. 26, ECHR 2002, Tinnelly & Sons Ltd and Other and McElduff and Others v. The United Kingdom, no. 62/1997/845/1052-1053, para. 76, ECHR 1998)*.
>
> . . . Consequently, the specific restriction has a legitimate aim."

The Court then applied the test of proportionality. It first considered the nature of the classified data and the high possibility of risk if the standard appeal proceedings were applied.

> "Certainly, if the person is barred from defending his rights in court, there is a necessity for such a decision-making process to be accessible to him to ensure effective protection of the person's rights. For this reason there is a necessity for alternative proceedings that would allow the person to exercise the protection of his rights at a maximally high level (see *Golder v. The United Kingdom, no. 4451/70, para. 57, ECHR 1975, Fogarty v. The United Kingdom, no. 37112/97, para. 33, ECHR 2001, Waite and Kennedy v. Germany, no. 26083/94, para. 59, ECHR 1999)*."

The Court concluded that it is possible in principle to devise alternative proceedings that would respect both the individual rights and protect the security interests. Applying the law to the facts of the case, the Court was satisfied that such a balanced system indeed existed and rejected the challenge.

(Available at the Internet site of the Constitutional Court, <www.satv.tiesa.gov.lv/ENG/spriedum.htm>, editor's translation)

Part Five: I. A. 2. Subjects of international law – States – Status and personality – Sovereignty and independence

5/1

On 23 January 2005, H. E. Dr. Vaira Vīķe-Freiberga, the President, made an address at the inauguration ceremony of President Viktor Yuschenko in Kiev, Ukraine, and stated that:

> "This Orange Revolution of Ukraine now takes its historic place alongside the Singing Revolution of Latvia, Lithuania and Estonia, it joins the Velvet Revolution of the former Czechoslovakia and other popular movements of Central and Eastern Europe.
>
> It joins the Rose Revolution of Georgia as a signal that sovereignty takes on its full meaning only when it rests on full democratic rights, the rule of law, responsibility and justice."

(Available at the Internet site of the Ministry of Foreign Affairs of Latvia, http://www.am.gov.lv/en/news/speeches/ (01.01.2006)

5/2

On 28 April 2005, Mr. Artis Pabriks, the Minister of Foreign Affairs, addressed the conference "Coming to terms with history: Building mutual cooperation and confidence in the Baltic Sea Region" and remarked that:

> "At the end of World War II, the Baltic States were in a peculiar situation: *de facto*, they simply did not exist."

(Available at the Internet site of the Ministry of Foreign Affairs of Latvia, <www.am.gov.lv/en/news/speeches/> (01.01.2006))

Part Five: I. D. 3. Subjects of international law - states – formation, identity, continuity, extinction, and succession of States – identity and continuity

(See *1/3–1/7*)

Part Five: II. B. 1. Subjects of international law – International organisations – Particular types – Universal organisations

5/3

On 14 January 2005, H. E. Dr. Vaira Vīķe-Freiberga, the President, addressed the foreign diplomatic corps in Riga and remarked that:

> "This year the United Nations will celebrate its 60th anniversary. Unfortunately, the challenge of establishing a collective security system for preventing the occurrence of widescale killings, systematic rapes and other crimes against humanity remains as acute as it was in 1945. Another pressing issue concerns the reform of the Security Council, which has been on the discussion table for the past 12 years. Although none of the proposed reform models is beyond reproach, Latvia believes that with sufficient

> political will, a workable agreement on a reformed Security Council could be attained during this anniversary year."

(Available at the Internet site of the Ministry of Foreign Affairs of Latvia, <www.am.gov.lv/en/news/speeches/> (01.01.2006))

5/4

On 15 March 2005, Mr. Artis Pabriks, the Minister of Foreign Affairs, addressed the 61st Session of the Commission on Human Rights in Geneva and elaborated on the work of the Commission, its reform proposals and more general improvements to be made to human rights mechanisms:

> "The Commission on Human Rights is the only Commission from all of ECOSOC, which is considered by the [High Level Panel] Report [on Threats, Challenges and Change], and that highlights its importance. Latvia shares the underlying concern expressed in the report regarding the composition of the CHR. At the same time, we are of the opinion, that before starting extensive discussion about the composition, the place of the CHR in current legal and institutional frameworks of the United Nations needs to be properly assessed. In our view, it would not make the work of the Commission more efficient, nor human rights more universal, if a body with universal membership would be subordinated to a body with limited membership, ECOSOC. At the same time, today we face the reality that a country's human rights record plays minor role in its election to the CHR. That, in our view, does not allow the Commission to address human rights issues adequately.
>
> Another area of Latvian interest is the work of the Sub-commission, which is an integral part of the UN Human Rights mechanisms. A CHR resolution on the Sub-commission, which will be introduced by Latvia this year, will contain some proposals which should improve its functioning.
>
> . . . Latvia, in particular, welcomes the activities of the Office towards the coordination of the work of treaty bodies, technical assistance programs and the efforts of the Commission's special procedures. Such coordination, in our view, will not only increase the effectiveness of the use of the Office's limited resources, but also will provide significant practical assistance to the countries themselves. In this manner, technical assistance programs would focus in those fields, which have been identified as most problematic by the Special Rapporteurs and Treaty bodies. At the same time, it would reduce the possibility that countries would receive different recommendations from the Treaty bodies and the Special Rapporteurs.

> We believe that one of the most valuable tools of the Commission, as well as the UN human rights system in general, is the periodic examination of State reports on the implementation of various human rights instruments. However, one has to acknowledge the difficulties faced by the treaty bodies now, particularly the failure of many States to honor their reporting obligations and the delays and backlogs in the work of various committees, which often consider reports long after they have been submitted.
>
> Latvia follows with interest the reform of treaty bodies and is delighted that tangible results have been achieved already at this stage, for example, the adoption of guidelines within the expanded core document.
>
> . . . The issue of anti-Semitism deserves our attention almost everywhere that human rights are not being adequately observed. Latvia will further support the initiatives of international organizations, whether universal or regional, to combat this form of intolerance. For example, Latvia considers the establishment of the post of Personal Representative of the Chairman in Office of the OSCE for anti-Semitism as an important initiative.
>
> . . . we welcome the activities and the report of the UN Special Rapporteur, Mr. Doudou Diene, on contemporary forms of racism, racial discrimination, xenophobia and related intolerance. The report gives a clear illustration that, more often than before, joint activities of the Special Rapporteur together with other rapporteurs, for instance, the Special Representative of the Secretary General on the situation of human rights defenders, are needed to address anti-Semitic activities carried out by neo-Nazi organizations."

(Available at the Internet site of the Ministry of Foreign Affairs of Latvia, <www.am.gov.lv/en/news/speeches/> (01.01.2006))

5/5

On 18 September 2005, Mr. Artis Pabriks, the Minister of Foreign Affairs, made an address to the 60th session of the UN General Assembly in New York:

> ". . . We need a United Nations that is more and more efficient in dealing with global challenges, and able to act effectively to prevent such horrors as the genocide in Rwanda, the ethnic cleansing in the Balkans, and the ongoing human tragedy in the Darfur region of Sudan. While such values and principles as national sovereignty, non-intervention and self-determination lie at the very core of the relations between the UN's member states, we also have to recognize our collective responsibility to protect innocent civilians from wide-scale abuse and suffering. It is our

duty to arrive at a common understanding of this responsibility to protect, so that the international community can act effectively to avert future mass killings and crimes against humanity. I encourage those UN member states that have not yet done so, to ratify the Rome Statute of the International Criminal Court and to support the court's endeavours to bring war criminals to justice.

. . . I am delighted that in some aspects we have succeeded in reaching a wide consensus, as for instance, on the necessity of creating a Peace-Building Commission . . .

. . . Latvia strongly supports the decision to establish a Human Rights Council, which recognizes human rights as a priority in the UN's agenda. I therefore encourage the delegations to work with vigour to ensure the smooth transformation of the Human Rights Commission into a Council, and to set the highest standards for its future members. A vital role in the realization of these standards will be played by the High Commissioner for Human Rights. I wish to confirm Latvia's support for the Commissioner and her Office, and welcome the decision to allocate a larger share of the regular UN budget to this important aspect of the UN's work.

My country fully supports the management reforms of the UN administration that have been put forth by the Secretary General . . .

Latvia has consistently endorsed the reform of the UN Security Council in order to render it more effective and representative. We believe that the Security Council should be enlarged to incorporate new permanent seats without veto rights. We also believe that permanent members of the Security Council should refrain from using the veto in cases of genocide, war crimes, ethnic cleansing and crimes against humanity. This promises to be one of the most difficult issues to resolve, but we should nevertheless not abandon our efforts to reach a feasible accord by the end of this year.

. . . A major step forward is our unequivocal condemnation of terrorism in all its forms and manifestations. My own country, Latvia, regained its freedom through peaceful and non-violent means. We triumphed due to our firm belief in historical justice, along with a great deal of persistence, patience, and hope.

Latvia welcomes the Secretary-General's counter-terrorism strategy. We need to arrive at a comprehensive convention on international terrorism, which would provide a legal framework for international cooperation in combating this modern-day scourge of humanity. The war against terrorism will only be won if it is fought while respecting basic human rights and remembering humanistic ethics.

> I express my profound disappointment that we could not achieve any consensus on disarmament and non-proliferation of weapons of mass destruction . . .
>
> Since the previous session of the General Assembly a year ago, the world has experienced natural disasters of an unprecedented scale of destruction . . . While there is nothing we can do to prevent earthquakes and tsunamis, scientists have warned us for years that our continued dependence and increasing consumption of fossil fuels is generating greenhouse gas emissions that are causing disruptive climate changes. Unless we diversify our sources of energy, we can expect to see more devastating hurricanes and floods in some parts of the world, along with drought and desertification in others."

(Available at the Internet site of the Ministry of Foreign Affairs of Latvia, <www.am.gov.lv/en/news/speeches/> (01.01.2006))

Part Five: II. B. 3. Subjects of international law – International organizations – Particular types of organizations – Organizations constituting integrated (e.g. economic) communities

5/6

On 9 June 2005, H. E. Dr. Vaira Vīķe-Freiberga, the President, made a keynote address at the Munich Economic Summit, explaining Latvia's position on freedom of movement and harmonisation of taxes:

> "We believe in the free movement of goods, people and services; and we believe in free and flexible labour markets. The removal of obstacles to the free movement of labour would assure that the principle of equality is truly observed within the Union. We believe in lightening the administrative burden on companies and in creating a business-friendly environment for all enterprises, and most particularly for small and medium enterprises, which account for 99% of all enterprises and two-thirds of all employment in Europe.
>
> What's more, services account for around 70% of added value in the European economy. Therefore it is in the EU's interest to conclude an agreement on a Service Directive that would facilitate the development of a dynamic service sector and promote an increase in European competitiveness.
>
> Regarding the harmonization of taxes, I have serious doubts about whether the imposition of a uniform company tax would add to the competitiveness of the Union. First of all, I don't believe that it would be fair to deprive the

> new member states of an important stimulus for promoting their economic growth. Secondly, if we raise the tax, then Latvia and the EU as a whole will lose investments which will flow elsewhere. Does the EU need that, and would this raise our overall competitiveness? Let us talk about tax harmonization once all the member states of the EU are equally strong and developed, and when the per capita income is no longer so different between the richer and the poorer EU nations."

(Available at the Internet site of the Ministry of Foreign Affairs of Latvia, <www.am.gov.lv/en/news/speeches/> (01.01.2006))

Part Six: I. The individual (including the corporation) in international law – Nationality and non-citizenship

6/1

On 10 March 2005, 5 MPs submitted a question to the Minister of Foreign affairs 'On Recommendations by UN Institutions'. The MPs referred to the Concluding Observations of the UN Committee on the Elimination of Rational Discrimination of 21 August 2003 and of the UN Human Rights Committee of 5 November 2003. In the Observation, the CERD and HRC had suggested limiting the list of positions not accessible for non-citizens and allowing non-citizens to participate in the municipal elections. The MPs asked:

> "In what way does the Ministry of Foreign Affairs plan to take into account the abovementioned recommendations by UN institutions?"

On 16 March 2005, the Minister of Foreign Affairs answered the question:

> ". . . Amendments have also been made to the Sea Code and the Aviation Law by removing nationality as a mandatory criterion for occupying certain positions.
>
> It should be noted that non-citizens in Latvia have been provided with many of the same rights as nationals. Several international organisations have recognised that Latvia fully complies with human rights as well as with minority rights.
>
> It should also be noted that international documents legally binding for Latvia do not impose an obligation to provide to non-citizens the right to vote in municipal elections."

(Question by the MPs of 10 March 2005 and answer by the Minister of Foreign Affairs of 16 March 2005, editor's translation)

6/2

The Constitutional Court in the judgment of 7 March 2005 in case No 2004-15-0106 elaborated on the concept of non-citizens (*nepilsoņi*):

> "To evaluate the conformity of the challenged norms with the Satversme and the norms of international law binding upon Latvia, one must analyse the historical and political aspects of the determination of the status of a non-citizen, as well as the legal consequences of the determination of the status of a non-citizen. To determine what are Latvia's international obligations towards Latvian non-nationals, one must consider the status of non-citizens and the extent to which the international community (foreign States and international organisations) have recognised them.
>
> The adoption of the Law on Non-Citizens was conditioned by the historical and political situation after the break-up of the USSR.
>
> The former republics of the USSR chose different ways of determining who qualified as a national. The nationals were determined by relying both on the territorial origin and the permanent residence in the relevant territory before the moment independence was regained. In some former republics of the USSR a note of residence was sufficient for automatic adoption of the nationality of the new state. In others, a certain number of years of permanent residence was considered as the main criterion. (see: Ziemele I. Pilsonība un cilvēktiesības valstu pēctecības kontekstā.// Likums un Tiesības, 2002, Nr. 8, 234. lpp.). If compared with other former Soviet republics, the Latvian and Estonian principles for the determination of nationality were different.
>
> The restoration of independence after the end of the Latvian occupation gave the legislature the opportunity to determine who were Latvian nationals. Continuity of Latvia as a subject of international law provided legal grounds for not granting automatic nationality to a certain group of persons.
>
> The legal grounds for Latvian continuity are established in the Declaration on the Restoration of Independence (hereinafter – the Declaration of Independence). It deals both with the status of Latvia in the meaning of international law as well as the basic question of State law.
>
> The preamble of the Declaration of Independence that includes the recital of historical facts and their legal evaluation among other things provides

that 'the incorporation of the Republic of Latvia in the Soviet Union is void from the point of view of international law, and the Republic of Latvia still exists as a subject of international law, recognised by more than 50 states of the world'.

The view expressed in the legal doctrine that the main function of the Declaration of Independence is the establishment of the Latvian State continuity doctrine in the Latvian legal system is well founded (see*: Levits E. 4. maija deklarācija Latvijas tiesību sistēmā.// 4. maijs. Rakstu, atmiņu un dokumentu krājums par Neatkarības deklarāciju, Rīga: Latvijas Universitātes žurnāla "Latvijas Vēsture" fonds, 2000, 57. lpp.*).

. . . Considering the continuity of Latvia as a subject of international law, there were reasons to restore the Latvian nationality as provided in the 1919 'Law On Nationality' (*'Likums par pavalstniecību'*). Consequently Latvia did not grant the right to nationality to persons who had it before the occupation of Latvia but only restored the rights of these persons *de facto.* (see*: Ziemele I. Starptautiskās tiesības un cilvēktiesības Latvijā: abstrakcija vai realitāte. Rīga: Tiesu namu aģentūra, 2005, 103. lpp.*).

Both the 1991 decision of the Supreme Council 'On the Restoration of the rights to nationality of the Republic of Latvia' and the Nationality Law of 1994 suggest that nationality is restored and not granted anew.

Consequently, the view is ill founded that Latvia had had the obligation to automatically grant nationality to those individuals and their successors who have never been Latvian nationals and have entered Latvia during the time of occupation. Additionally, these persons were given the right to obtain Latvian nationality by way of naturalisation.

. . . The grant of the status of non-citizen to a certain group of persons was a result of a complex political compromise. Additionally, when adopting the Law on Non-Nationals, Latvia had to comply with the international human rights standards that prohibit the increase of the number of stateless persons in the cases of State continuity.

Latvia has clearly indicated that non-citizens are not stateless persons, because the Law on Stateless Persons in Article 3(2) provides that persons who are subject to the law 'On the Status of Those Citizens of the Former USSR Who do not have the Citizenship of Latvia or Any Other Country' cannot be recognised as stateless persons. The representatives of Latvia in the international human rights institutions have also consistently defended the position that the status of a non-citizen can be equated to that of a stateless person.

> Non-citizens are not considered to be foreigners, because in accordance with Article 1 of the Immigration Law a foreigner is a person who is neither a citizen of Latvia nor a non-citizen of Latvia.
>
> The EU Network of Independent Experts on Fundamental Rights in the report on questions of fundamental rights in the European Union and its Member States also notes that the non-citizens provided for in the law 'On the Status of Those Citizens of the Former USSR Who do not have the Citizenship of Latvia or Any Other Country' are neither nationals nor foreigners nor stateless persons. The Network of Experts notes that Latvian non-citizens belong to a group of persons as yet unknown in international public law. (*Synthesis Report: Conclusions and Recommendations on the Situation of Fundamental Rights in the European Union and its Member States in 2003, 4 February 2004, p. 90*).

(Available at the Internet site of the Constitutional Court, <www.satv.tiesa.gov.lv/ENG/spriedum.htm>, editor's translation)

Part Six: II. The individual (including the corporation) in international law – Diplomatic protection

6/3

The Constitutional Court in the judgment of 7 March 2005 in case No 2004-15-0106 considered certain aspects of diplomatic protection:

> "Different views have been expressed as to whether diplomatic protection may be exercised only in respect of persons who are considered nationals of the respective state in the context of international law in the meaning of the Nottebohm case [*Nottebohm judgement* (*Liechtenstein* v. *Guatemala*), *Second Phase*, [1955] ICJ *Reports*] or if the permanent residence in the respective country is an equally important factor [see *Report of the International Law Commission on the work of its fifty-second session*, 1 *May* to 9 *June and* 10 *July* to 18 *August* 2000 (A/55/10), *Chapter* V; http://www.un.org/law/ilc/reports/2000/english/chp5e.pdf]."

(Available at the Internet site of the Constitutional Court, <www.satv.tiesa.gov.lv/ENG/spriedum.htm>, editor's translation)

Part Six: VIII. C. 1. (a) The Individual (including the Corporation) in International Law – Human rights and fundamental freedoms - – Under the Council of Europe treaty system –European Court of Human Rights – Procedural issues

6/4

On 16 May 2005, H. E. Dr. Vaira Vīķe-Freiberga, the President, made an address at the Third Summit of Heads of State and Government of the Council of Europe, Warsaw:

> "We still require measures to improve the effectiveness of the European Court of Human Rights.
>
> . . . one of the biggest challenges for the Council of Europe in the coming years will lie in optimizing the operations of the European Court of Human Rights and in reducing the tremendous backlog of cases that the Court is facing. If the Court is to operate effectively in the long term, then Protocol No 14 should be ratified without delay, and other measures agreed upon last year for improving human rights protection at the national level should be implemented. At the same time, we must not succumb to the temptation of releasing the Court from so-called 'less important' cases and leave it with only the challenging ones. While a repetitive or minor case may not be of great interest to international legal experts, it is of fundamental interest to the party concerned."

(Available at the Internet site of the Ministry of Foreign Affairs of Latvia, <www.am.gov.lv/en/news/speeches/> (01.01.2006))

6/5

The European Court of Human Rights (ECtHR) in *Sisojeva et al. contre la Lettonie* case considered an objection of the Government to the effect that the claimants had lost the status of 'victims' because the relevant authorities had altered their practices. The Court by a majority of five rejected the objection:

> *"Aux yeux de la Cour, la question qui se pose ici est celle de savoir si les requérants ont effectivement perdu leur statut de « victimes », au sens de l'article 34 de la Convention du fait des décisions prises par la Direction le 11 novembre 2003. Elle rappelle sa jurisprudence constante selon laquelle une décision ou une mesure favorable au requérant ne suffit en principe à lui retirer la qualité de « victime » que si les autorités nationales ont reconnu, explicitement ou en substance, puis réparé la violation alléguée*

de la Convention (voir, par exemple, Amuur c. France, arrêt du 25 juin 1996, Recueil 1996-III, p. 846, § 36, Dalban c. Roumanie [GC], n° 28114/95, § 44, CEDH 1999-VI, Labita c. Italie [GC], n° 26772/95, § 142, CEDH 2000-IV, et Ilaşcu et autres c. Moldova et Russie [GC] (déc.), n° 48787/99, 4 juillet 2001).

Dans la présente affaire, la Cour note que les autorités lettonnes n'ont ni reconnu, ni encore moins réparé les torts subis par les requérants. En effet, la décision de leur permettre de régulariser leur séjour ne constitue qu'une offre, soumises à des conditions strictes, qui ne correspond pas à leur demande initiale telle qu'elle avait été introduite dès 1993, à savoir de leur accorder le statut de résidents permanents et de les inclure dans le registre des résidents de la République de Lettonie, demande à laquelle le tribunal de première instance du district d'Alūksne avait, par ailleurs, fait droit à deux reprises. En outre, la décision de leur permettre de régulariser leur séjour n'a pas rendu inexistante la longue période d'incertitude et de précarité légale qu'ils ont vécue sur le territoire letton."

(*Sisojeva et al c. Lettonie,* n° 60654/00, Judgment of 16 June 2005, paras. 53–54)

Judge Vajič and judge *ad hoc* Briede disagreed with the majority and would have upheld the objection of the Government. In their joint dissenting opinion the judges explained why, in their view, the Court's decision was incompatible with established case law and with the admissibility decision in the case:

"a) En premier lieu, il y a remise en question de la jurisprudence établie par l'arrêt Vijayanathan et Pusparajah c. France (27 août 1992, série A, n° 241-B), dans lequel la Cour avait conclu qu'en l'absence d'ordre formel de reconduite à la frontière, donc en l'absence de risque imminent d'expulsion, les intéressés ne pouvaient se prétendre « victimes » de la violation alléguée. Dans la présente affaire, il n'y a jamais eu d'arrêté d'expulsion à l'encontre des requérants ; qui plus est, en 2003, la Direction les a officiellement informés qu'ils pouvaient régulariser leur séjour en Lettonie.

b) Il faut rappeler aussi que, dans la mesure où un étranger ou un apatride se plaint de son éloignement ou, d'une manière plus générale, de son statut irrégulier sur le territoire national, la délivrance d'un titre de séjour constitue en principe un redressement adéquat et suffisant (voir notamment Pančenko c. Lettonie (déc.), n° 40772/98, 28 octobre 1999 ; Bogdanovski c. Italie (déc.), n° 72177/01, 9 juillet 2002, ainsi que S.F. c. Suisse, n° 16360/90, décision de la Commission du 2 mars 1994, DR 76, p. 13, et

I.F. c. France, nº 22802/93, décision de la Commission du 11 décembre 1997, D.R. 91, p. 10). Cette règle vaut même si l'intéressé obtient satisfaction alors que la procédure est déjà engagée devant la Cour ; ainsi le veut le caractère subsidiaire du système des garanties de la Convention (voir, mutatis mutandis, Preikhzas c. Allemagne, nº 6504/74, rapport de la Commission du 13 décembre 1978, D.R. 16, p. 5, et Mikheyeva c. Lettonie (déc.), nº 50029/99, 12 septembre 2002).

Il est vrai que, même en l'absence de mesure formelle d'éloignement, les requérants se trouvent dans une situation d'incertitude plus ou moins précaire qui, en elle-même, peut poser problème sous l'angle de l'article 8 de la Convention. Cependant, dans les décisions Pančenko c. Lettonie (nº 40772/98, 28 octobre 1999) et Mikheyeva c. Lettonie (nº 50029/99, 12 septembre 2002), la Cour avait rappelé sa jurisprudence constante. Dans l'affaire Mikheyeva, elle avait ainsi déclaré :

> *« En particulier, dans la mesure où l'intéressé se plaint de son expulsion ou, d'une manière plus générale, de son statut irrégulier sur le territoire national, l'annulation de la mesure d'éloignement et la délivrance d'un titre de séjour sont en principe suffisants pour qu'il ne puisse plus se prétendre « victime » au sens de l'article 34 de la Convention. »*

Dans la même décision, la Cour avait précisé ce qui suit :

> *« Cette règle vaut même si l'intéressé obtient satisfaction alors que la procédure est déjà engagée devant la Cour ; ainsi le veut le caractère subsidiaire du système des garanties de la Convention. »*

c) Enfin, si l'on admet que les solutions proposées aux requérants par la Direction sont inadéquates pour remédier à leur grief, nous ne voyons pas comment concilier cette thèse avec la décision du 28 février 2002 sur la recevabilité de cette même affaire . . .

Certes, en l'occurrence, le deuxième requérant et la troisième requérante ne se sont pas vu offrir d'emblée un permis permanent. Toutefois, à notre avis, ce qui est décisif au regard des obligations découlant de la Convention, c'est le fait que les procédures de régularisation proposées par le Gouvernement permettraient aux requérants de vivre sans entraves sur le territoire letton, d'y mener une vie sociale normale et d'y jouir des droits garantis par l'article 8 de la Convention. Quant au choix des moyens concrets pour y parvenir, il incombe en premier lieu aux autorités de l'Etat défendeur, conformément au principe de subsidiarité qui sous-tend tout le système de la Convention. Il faut noter dans ce contexte que l'argument utilisé au paragraphe 54 de l'arrêt est contraire à la jurisprudence de la Cour, qui jusqu'ici n'a jamais affirmé que les requérants avaient le droit de

> *choisir le mode de régularisation de leur séjour sur le territoire d'un Etat partie à la Convention. Il en va de même pour l'argument de la majorité qui fait siennes (également au paragraphe 54) les décisions des tribunaux de première instance tout en sachant que les plus hautes juridictions du pays avaient par ailleurs décidé autrement.*
>
> *En l'espèce, malgré l'invitation à quitter le territoire national, exprimée dans les lettres de la Direction des 17 mai et du 26 juin 2000 et dépourvue en elle-même de caractère exécutoire, aucun arrêté d'expulsion n'a été pris à l'encontre des requérants (paragraphe 85 de l'arrêt ; pour une situation similaire, voir Vijayanathan et Pusparajah c. France, arrêt du 27 août 1992, série A, n° 241-B, p. 87, § 46). Au surplus, selon le Gouvernement les autorités lettonnes ont renoncé à l'idée d'expulser les requérants, et ce « pour des raisons de proportionnalité ». Compte tenu des circonstances de l'affaire, nous ne voyons aucune raison de mettre en doute cette déclaration."*

(*Sisojeva et al c. Lettonie,* n° 60654/00, Judgment of 16 June 2005, Joint dissenting opinion of judges Vajič and Briede, paras. 2–3)

The Government has requested that the case be referred to the Grand Chamber. The request has been granted with the hearing scheduled in 2006.

Part Six: VIII. C. 1. (a) The Individual (including the Corporation) in International Law - human rights and fundamental freedoms – under Council of Europe treaty system –European Court of Human Rights – Substantive issues

6/6

The ECtHR in the *Smolickis contre la Lettonie* case considered a claim that Article 4(1) of Protocol 7 had been breached. The Court considered that a dual conviction for a continuous crime did not violate the rule of *non bis in idem* and rejected the claim as manifestly unfounded:

> *"Le requérant estime avoir été condamné deux fois pour une seule et même infraction, au mépris du principe non bis in idem. Il se considère donc victime d'une violation de l'article 4 § 1 du Protocole n° 7 à la Convention, ainsi libellé :*
>
> > *« Nul ne peut être poursuivi ou puni pénalement par les juridictions du même Etat en raison d'une infraction pour laquelle il a déjà été acquitté ou condamné par un jugement définitif conformément à la loi et à la procédure pénale de cet Etat. »*

La Cour rappelle que l'article 4 du Protocole n° 7 a pour but de prohiber la répétition de poursuites pénales définitivement clôturées, en évitant qu'une personne soit poursuivie ou punie pénalement deux ou plusieurs fois pour la même infraction (voir Gradinger c. Autriche, arrêt du 23 octobre 1995, série A n° 328-C, p. 65, § 53). Cela étant, la protection du principe non bis in idem ne peut être invoquée que lorsqu'au moins deux procédures indépendantes et différentes, portant sur une seule et même accusation, aboutissent à plus d'une condamnation (voir, par exemple, Stanca c. Roumanie (déc.), n° 59028/00, 27 avril 2004).

Afin de conclure à l'applicabilité de l'article 4 du Protocole n° 7 dans chaque cas concret, la Cour doit s'assurer d'emblée que c'est effectivement une même infraction qui a été punie deux ou plusieurs fois (voir Ponsetti et Chesnel c. France (déc.), n°s 36855/97 et 41731/98, CEDH 1999-VI, et Garaudy c. France (déc.), n° 65831/01, CEDH 2003-IX). Dans l'arrêt Gradinger c. Autriche précité, la Cour a jugé que violait l'article 4 précité le fait de punir quelqu'un ayant commis un homicide par imprudence en état d'ébriété deux fois, par deux instances différentes ; en effet, la Cour a retenu qu'il y avait deux infractions, mais que les deux condamnations se sont fondées sur le même comportement. Dans l'affaire Franz Fischer c. Autriche (n° 37950/97, arrêt du 29 mai 2001), elle a conclu que la violation du principe non bis in idem ne pouvait pas être écartée sur le simple constat qu'une personne avait été poursuivie ou punie sur la base de deux infractions nominalement distinctes se fondant sur un seul et même comportement ; encore faut-il examiner si les deux infractions pour lesquelles elle a été poursuivie ne présentent pas en réalité les mêmes éléments essentiels (§ 25).

. . . A cet égard, la Cour considère que, si l'article 4 du Protocole n° 7 prohibe des condamnations répétées d'une seule et même personne pour un seul et même comportement, il ne saurait pour autant s'interpréter comme excluant des condamnations successives fondées sur des comportements manifestés à diverses reprises, même s'ils présentent en substance un caractère similaire ou identique (voir Raninen c. Finlande, n° 20972/92, décision de la Commission du 7 mars 1996, Décisions et rapports (DR) 84, p. 17). Aux yeux de la Cour, ceci est particulièrement vrai lorsqu'il s'agit d'infractions commises par voie d'inaction, c'est-à-dire du défaut de se conformer à une obligation prévue par la loi.

En résumé, les deux condamnations litigieuses ont trait à deux périodes bien distinctes entre lesquelles il n'y a aucun chevauchement, même si l'inertie de requérant au regard de la loi sur l'insolvabilité restait la même avant, pendant et entre ces deux périodes. Le requérant s'étant obstiné à ne pas déposer le bilan même après sa première condamnation, il y a lieu d'admettre que sa deuxième condamnation se fondait sur son refus répété, mais néanmoins distinct, de se conformer à la loi (voir, mutatis mutandis, la décision Raninen c. Finlande précitée). Par ailleurs, une approche contraire dans une pareille situation – c'est-à-dire en présence d'une obligation légale permanente pesant sur un individu – amènerait la Cour à conclure que la condamnation de l'intéressé au pénal pour ne pas avoir exécuté ladite obligation l'en libère définitivement et inconditionnellement, le soustrayant à tout risque de poursuites pénales dans l'avenir. Or, bien qu'une telle conclusion puisse être envisagée dans certains cas, elle ne saurait être étendue à l'ensemble des rapports juridiq0ues."

(*Smolickis c. Lettonie,* n° 73453/01, Decision of 27 January 2005)

6/7

The ECtHR in the *Sisojeva et al contre la Lettonie* case considered a possible breach of Article 8 in the context of immigration and expulsion proceedings. The Court by a majority of five to two (judge Vajič and judge *ad hoc* Briede having upheld the preliminary objection of the government) found that the private life aspect of Article 8 had been infringed:

"La Cour rappelle d'emblée que la Convention ne garantit pas, en tant que tel, le droit d'entrer ou de résider dans un Etat dont on n'est pas ressortissant et que les Etats contractants ont, en vertu d'un principe général de droit international et sans préjudice des engagements découlant pour eux de traités y compris la Convention, le droit de contrôler l'entrée, le séjour et l'éloignement des non-nationaux (voir, parmi beaucoup d'autres, Chahal c. Royaume-Uni, arrêt du 15 novembre 1996, Recueil des arrêts et décisions 1996-V, p. 1853, § 73, El Boujaïdi c. France, arrêt du 26 septembre 1997, Recueil 1997-VI, p. 1992, § 39, Baghli c. France, n° 34374/97, § 45, CEDH 1999-VIII, et Boultif c. Suisse, n° 54273/00, § 39, CEDH 2001-IX).

Les requérants soutiennent que, compte tenu de leur vécu personnel en Lettonie, le principe énoncé ci-dessus ne s'applique pas dans leur affaire. A cet égard, la Cour note que, dans le cadre matériel de la Convention, la seule disposition contenant une protection expresse contre un éloignement forcé du territoire national est l'article 3 du Protocole n° 4, dont le premier paragraphe prohibe l'expulsion, par un Etat, de ses propres ressortissants ; en revanche, ni la Convention, ni ses Protocoles ne prévoient aucune interdiction générale d'expulser des ressortissants étrangers ou des apatrides. Dans l'affaire Slivenko c. Lettonie précitée, la Cour a considéré que la question de savoir si l'intéressé est « ressortissant » (« national » dans la version anglaise) d'un Etat donné, devait en principe être déterminée d'après le droit interne de cet Etat. Elle a également estimé qu'au regard de la Lettonie, le statut de « ressortissant » au sens de l'article 3 du Protocole n° 4 était identique à la notion de « citoyenneté » ou de « nationalité », telle qu'elle est comprise par la loi lettonne respective (op. cit., §§ 77-78). Or, dans le cas d'espèce, il n'est pas contesté que les requérants n'ont à aucun moment été citoyens lettons après le 27 juin 1997, date d'entrée en vigueur de la Convention à l'égard de la Lettonie. Rien n'indique non plus qu'ils pouvaient légalement prétendre à la nationalité lettonne selon les lois de cet Etat ni que celle-ci leur ait été refusée arbitrairement.

Toutefois, la Cour rappelle que les décisions prises par les Etats en matière d'immigration peuvent, dans certains cas, constituer une ingérence dans l'exercice du droit au respect de la vie privée et familiale protégé par l'article 8 § 1 de la Convention, notamment lorsque les intéressés possèdent, dans l'Etat d'accueil, des liens personnels ou familiaux suffisamment forts qui risquent d'être gravement affectés en cas d'application d'une mesure d'éloignement. Pareille ingérence enfreint l'article 8, sauf si, « prévue par la loi », elle poursuit un ou plusieurs buts légitimes au regard du deuxième paragraphe dudit article et apparaît « nécessaire dans une société démocratique » pour les atteindre (voir, par exemple, Moustaquim c. Belgique, arrêt du 18 février 1991, série A n° 193, p. 18, § 36 ; Dalia c. France, arrêt du 19 février 1998, Recueil 1998-I, p. 91, § 52, et Amrollahi c. Danemark, n° 56811/00, § 33, 11 juillet 2002).

Dans le cas d'espèce, la Cour constate que les deux premiers requérants sont arrivés en Lettonie en 1969 et en 1968, c'est-à-dire, respectivement, à l'âge de vingt et de vingt-deux ans. Jusqu'à présent, ils ont toujours vécu en Lettonie. Quant à leur fille, la troisième requérante, elle est née en Lettonie en 1978 et y a toujours vécu. Cela étant, il ne prête pas à controverse qu'au cours de leur séjour sur le territoire letton, ils ont noué des relations personnelles, sociales et économiques qui sont constitutives de la vie privée de tout être humain. Force est à la Cour de conclure que la mesure imposée aux requérants a constitué une ingérence dans leur « vie privée », au sens de l'article 8 § 1 de la Convention (voir Slivenko c. Lettonie [GC], n° 48321/99, § 96, CEDH 2003-X).

En revanche, bien que les requérants eussent à l'évidence une « vie familiale » établie en Lettonie, la situation qu'ils dénoncent n'a pas pour effet de briser cette vie. En outre, les deux premiers requérants ne peuvent plus invoquer l'existence d'une « vie familiale » par rapport à la troisième requérante, qui est majeure ; il en est de même des liens unissant les trois requérants à la fille aînée de la famille, Mme Vizule (voir, mutatis mutandis, Kolosovskiy c. Lettonie (déc.), n° 50183/99, 29 janvier 2004). La Cour examinera donc le grief des requérants sous le volet de leur vie « privée » au sens de l'article 8 § 1 de la Convention.

Par ailleurs, la Cour note qu'aucun arrêté d'expulsion formel n'a été pris à l'encontre des requérants. Elle rappelle cependant qu'au même titre que toute autre disposition de la Convention ou de ses Protocoles, l'article 8 doit s'interpréter de façon à garantir des droits concrets et effectifs, et non théoriques et illusoires (voir, mutatis mutandis, Artico c. Italie, arrêt du 13 mai 1980, série A n° 37, p. 16, § 33, et Soering c. Royaume-Uni, arrêt du 7 juillet 1989, série A n° 161, p. 34, § 87). En outre, si l'article 8, relatif au droit au respect de la vie privée et familiale, tend pour l'essentiel à prémunir l'individu contre des ingérences arbitraires des pouvoirs publics, il ne se contente pas d'astreindre l'Etat à s'abstenir de pareilles ingérences : à cet engagement plutôt négatif peuvent s'ajouter des obligations positives inhérentes à un respect effectif de la vie privée et familiale (voir, par exemple, Gül c. Suisse, arrêt du 19 février 1996, Recueil 1996-I, pp. 174-175, § 38 ; Ignaccolo-Zenide c. Roumanie, n° 31679/96, § 94, CEDH 2000-I, et Mehemi c. France, n° 53470/99, § 45, CEDH 2003-X). En d'autres termes, il ne suffit pas que l'Etat d'accueil s'abstienne d'expulser l'intéressé ; encore faut-il qu'il lui assure, en prenant au besoin des mesures positives, la possibilité d'exercer sans entrave les droits en question.

Par conséquent, la Cour estime que le refus prolongé des autorités lettonnes de reconnaître aux requérants le droit de résider en Lettonie à titre permanent constitue une ingérence dans l'exercice de leur droit au respect de la vie privée. Reste à savoir si cette ingérence est conforme au deuxième paragraphe de l'article 8 de la Convention, c'est-à-dire si elle était « prévue par la loi », poursuivait un ou des buts légitimes qui sont énumérés dans cette disposition et était « nécessaire dans une société démocratique » pour atteindre le ou les buts en question."

The ECtHR agreed that the restriction was 'provided by law' in the meaning of Article 8 but was not persuaded that it was of the kind necessary in a democratic society, nor did it comply with the principle of proportionality:

"Quant à la question de savoir si la mesure litigieuse était « nécessaire dans une société démocratique », c'est-à-dire proportionnée au but légitime poursuivi, la Cour note que les requérants ont passé toute ou presque toute leur vie en Lettonie. Certes, ils ne sont pas d'origine lettone ; toutefois, il reste qu'ils ont noué en Lettonie des liens personnels, sociaux et économiques assez forts pour que l'on puisse dire qu'ils sont suffisamment intégrés à la société lettone, même si, comme le soutient le Gouvernement, leur niveau de connaissance du letton présente des lacunes (voir l'arrêt Slivenko c. Lettonie précité, § 124). De même, bien que les deuxième et troisième requérants aient la nationalité russe et qu'ils aient eu un domicile officiellement enregistré en Russie, il apparaît qu'aucun des

requérants n'y a noué des liens personnels similaires à ceux qu'ils ont établis en Lettonie (op.cit., § 125).

Dans ces circonstances, la Cour estime que seules les raisons particulièrement graves pourraient justifier le refus de régularisation, respectivement les conditions imposées aux requérants en vue d'obtenir leur régularisation; or, elle n'en a décelé aucune en l'espèce. Tout en reconnaissant le droit de chaque Etat de prendre des mesures effectives afin d'assurer le respect de la législation en matière d'immigration, elle considère qu'une mesure similaire à celle qu'ont subi les requérants ne pourrait être proportionnée qu'en présence d'agissements particulièrement dangereux de la part des intéressés. A cet égard, la Cour rappelle que la plupart des affaires similaires qu'elle a examinées sous l'angle de l'article 8 de la Convention portaient sur des situations où les requérants avaient été expulsés après avoir été condamnés pour des infractions pénales graves ; en revanche, dans la présente affaire, les requérants ne se sont vus infliger qu'une amende modérée, non qualifiée de pénale en droit letton (paragraphe 18 ci-dessus).

La Cour relève en outre que la régularisation des deuxième et troisième requérants dépend de celle de la première requérante (paragraphes 35 et 87-90 ci-dessus). En d'autres termes, si la première requérante ne profitait pas de l'opportunité offerte de légaliser son séjour, la situation de deux autres requérants resterait inchangée. La Cour estime qu'en subordonnant ainsi leur possibilité de mener une vie privée normale à des circonstances extérieures indépendantes de leur volonté, les autorités nationales, nonobstant leur marge d'appréciation, n'ont pas adopté les mesures que l'on pouvait raisonnablement exiger d'elles en l'occurrence.

Cela étant, eu égard à l'ensemble des circonstances, et en particulier compte tenu de la longue période d'incertitude et de précarité légale que les requérants ont vécue sur le territoire letton, la Cour estime que les autorités lettonnes ont outrepassé la marge d'appréciation dont jouissent les Etats contractants dans ce domaine, et qu'elles n'ont pas ménagé un juste équilibre entre le but légitime que constitue la défense de l'ordre et l'intérêt des requérants à voir protéger leurs droits au titre de l'article 8. Elle ne saurait donc conclure que l'ingérence litigieuse était « nécessaire dans une société démocratique »."

(*Sisojeva et al c. Lettonie,* n° 60654/00, Judgment of 16 June 2005, paras. 99–105, 107–110)

6/8

The ECtHR in the *Sisojeva et al contre la Lettonie* case also considered a possible breach of Article 34 by Latvia. After submitting the claim against Latvia, the applicant was approached by representatives of the Security Police who questioned her *inter alia* about the application. The Court firstly restated the general principles that:

> *"pour que le mécanisme de recours individuel instauré par l'article 34 de la Convention soit efficace, il est de la plus haute importance que les requérants, déclarés ou potentiels, soient libres de communiquer avec la Cour, sans que les autorités ne les pressent en aucune manière de retirer ou modifier leurs griefs (voir l'arrêt Akdivar et autres c. Turquie précité, p. 1219, § 105 ; Kurt c. Turquie, arrêt du 25 mai 1998, Recueil 1998-III, p. 1192, § 159 ; Ergi c. Turquie, arrêt du 28 juillet 1998, Recueil 1998-IV, p. 1784, § 105, et Salman c. Turquie [GC], n° 21986/93, § 130, CEDH 2000-VII).*
>
> *Par le mot « presse[r] », il faut entendre non seulement la coercition directe et les actes flagrants d'intimidation contre le requérant, sa famille ou ses représentants légaux, mais aussi les actes ou contacts indirects et de mauvais aloi tendant à dissuader ou à décourager l'intéressé de se prévaloir du recours qu'offre la Convention. Pour déterminer si des contacts entre les autorités et un requérant déclaré ou potentiel constituent des pratiques inacceptables du point de vue de l'article 34, il faut tenir compte des circonstances particulières de la cause. A ce propos, il faut envisager la vulnérabilité du plaignant et le risque que les autorités ne l'influencent (voir, par exemple, Petra c. Roumanie, arrêt du 23 septembre 1998, Recueil 1998-VII, pp. 2854-2855, § 43 ; Assenov et autres c. Bulgarie, arrêt du 28 octobre 1998, Recueil 1998-VIII, p. 3304, § 170, et Tanrıkulu c. Turquie [GC], n° 23763/94, § 130, CEDH 1999-IV)."*

(*Sisojeva et al c. Lettonie,* n° 60654/00, Judgment of 16 June 2005, paras. 120-121)

The Court found that the general nature of the questions posed and the previous interviews by the applicants alleging official corruption put the questioning in its proper context and that Article 34 had not been breached. Judge Kovler dissented from this finding and argued that the questioning by the police had reached the level necessary for finding a breach of Article 34.

Part Eleven: XV. Seas and vessels – Cables and pipelines

11/1

The Baltic Assembly during its 24th Session on 26 November 2005 in Tallin, Estonia, adopted a resolution "On the Dangers Connected with Construction of the Gas Pipeline in the Baltic Sea":

> The Baltic Assembly,
> **seeking** to achieve that
> - the Baltic Sea preserves its uniqueness;
> - the economic activity in the territorial waters and economic zone of coastal states of the Baltic Sea complies with the provisions of international law and laws and interests of the coastal states; and
> - environmental risk assessment of the Baltic Sea proceeds from the status of the Baltic Sea as a Particularly Sensitive Sea Area (PSSA);
> **being of the opinion** that
> - the realisation of large-scale energy infrastructure projects in the Baltic Sea region should proceed from the interest of guaranteeing energy supply security and safety of all states in the region, and that it is necessary to urgently make an integrated analysis of the energy situation of the EU member states in the Baltic Sea region which could serve as a basis for receiving the European Union's subsidies;
> - during the construction and in further exploitation of the gas pipeline along the Baltic Sea floor, any kind of dangers, especially those arising from the chemical weapons dumped in the Baltic Sea after World War II should be eliminated;
> - the construction of gas pipeline must not damage the ecosystems of the Baltic Sea or disturb the flora and fauna of the Baltic Sea as a Particularly Sensitive Sea Area;
> **draws** attention to the fact that simultaneously with solving the issues of seabed utilisation for economic or other activities, the reduction of harmful effects and risks caused by chemical weapons dumped into the Baltic Sea must be dealt with in international cooperation, and
> **calls** on the parliaments of the Baltic Sea states, the Baltic Council of Ministers and international organisations to focus their attention on the present situation and undertake measures to ensure that the assessment of all environmental impacts of the construction of the planned gas pipeline along the Baltic Sea floor is carried out in accordance with the Convention on Environmental Impact Assessment in a Transboundary Context (Espoo, 1991), the Convention on the Protection of the Marine Environment of the Baltic Sea Area (Helsinki, 1992), as well as the valid legal acts of the European Union.

(Available at the Internet site of the Baltic Assembly <http://www.baltasam.org/documents/index.htm> (01.01.2006))

Part Thirteen: II. A. 1. (a) International responsibility – responsibility other than criminal – Responsible entities – States – the elements of responsibility (e.g. wrongfulness of the act, imputability)

13/1

The *Nykomb Synergetics Technology Holding AB* v. *Republic of Latvia* award of 16 December 2003 rendered by an arbitration tribunal of the Arbitration Institute of the Stockholm Chamber of Commerce pursuant to the Energy Charter Treaty became publicly available in 2005. The dispute had arisen out of a contract between Nykomb and Latvenergo, a State owned company, about the purchase by the latter of energy produced in an environmentally friendly manner. Latvenergo had refused to pay according to the contract and Nykomb had instituted proceedings under the Energy Charter Treaty, alleging breaches of rules on expropriation, fair and equitable treatment, national treatment and an umbrella clause. The Tribunal initially addressed the question whether Latvenergo's actions where attributable to Latvia. Nykomb argued that Latvenergo's breach of contract was attributable to Latvia both according to customary international law rules of attribution and Article 22 of the Energy Charter Treaty. Latvia asked the Tribunal, as regards attributability, to adjuge and declare:

> "(ii) that Latvenergo's conducts are not attributable to Latvia".

It is not clear what Latvia argued as a matter of customary international law. Whatever the arguments, the tribunal was not persuaded and decided that Latvenergo's conduct was attributable to Latvia:

> "4.2. . . . the Arbitral Tribunal considers that Windau originally had both a statutory and a contractually established right to the double tariff for an eight year period.
>
> It is conceded by the Respondent that the Entrepreneurial Law in force at the time of Latvenergo and Windau entering into Contract No. 16/97 on 24 March 1997 gave Windau a *statutory right* to the double tariff during the first eight years of production. The Respondent has also conceded that Windau's acquired statutory right to the double tariff was taken away by successive legislative acts, first, possibly, with the amendment to the Entrepreneurial Law of 11 June 1997 (see section 3.5.4), then definitely by the repeal of the Entrepreneurial Law by the Energy Law with effect from 6 October 1998 and the Cabinet of Ministers' Regulation No. 425 of 31

October 1998 (see sections 3.5.5 and 3.5.6 above). These are acts for which the Republic is directly responsible.

With regard to a *contractually established* right to the double tariff the Arbitral Tribunal concludes that by entering into Contract No. 16/97 Latvenergo also gave Windau a contractual right to the double tariff for eight years, see section 3.8.d above. It is not contested that Latvenergo has never paid the double tariff for electricity delivered by Windau.

No explicit explanation or documentation has been given as to the reasons for Latvenergo's refusal to pay the double tariff, but apparently the immediate reason for Latvenergo's refusal to pay was the repeal of the statutory right to the double tariff. It is in evidence that Latvenergo had no authority of its own to decide or negotiate purchase prices for electric power produced in Latvia. The average price tariff at any time was determined by regulatory authorities, and the so called multipliers were determined by law, or according to law, with an obligation for Latvenergo to apply the relevant tariff and the multipliers determined by the public authorities. Failing any indication to the contrary, it may be assumed that Latvenergo felt it to be its duty to deny Windau the double tariff after the legislators' decision to repeal Windau's established statutory right to the double tariff.

However, Latvenergo must have been aware that Windau in all likelihood had a contractual right to the double tariff. As mentioned above, the Latvian Supreme Court in a judgement of 30 June 1999 decided, in the quite parallel case of Latelektro-Gulbene, that Latvenergo had a contractual obligation to pay according to the multiplier in force at the time of entering into the agreement, regardless of later changes in the legislation. Latvenergo also signed a new contract with Latelektro-Gulbene confirming payment of the double tariff during the eight year period.

The central government of Latvia was also fully aware of Latvenergo's refusal to pay the double tariff. After a meeting with the Prime Minister on 29 October 1999 the Cabinet of Ministers on 30 November 1999 issued a Resolution ordering the double tariff to be paid to Windau (see section 3.5.7 above). As explained, the Resolution was later invalidated by the Constitutional Court for constitutional reasons, but the incident is evidence of the central government's full knowledge of Latvenergo's failure to pay the double tariff. There is no evidence of the government taking any further steps to protect Windau's rights under the contract, or to reinstate Windau's statutory right to the double tariff, for instance in accordance with the Republic's obligations to protect foreign investments under the Energy Charter Treaty, see section 4.3.2 below.

It must therefore be concluded that the breach of Windau's contractual rights was allowed to continue, and in that sense was caused, by the government's failure to act in order to correct the situation.

The Arbitral Tribunal is also of the view that in the circumstances of this case, the Republic must be considered responsible for Latvenergo's actions under the rules of attribution in international law.

Latvenergo was established in 1991 as a state enterprise, and was in 1993 transformed into a joint stock company with the Republic as a 100 per cent owner. For a while the plans were to privatize the company, and the company was administered by the Latvian Agency for Privatization. But by a change in the Energy Law on 3 August 2000 it was decreed that:

'As a national economy object of the State importance, the Joint Stock Company "Latvenergo" shall not be privatized. All shares in the Joint Stock Company "Latvenergo" are owned by the State.'

By order of the Cabinet of Ministers of 9 August 2000 the supervision of the company was transferred to the Ministry of Economy.

Both before and after these organizational changes Latvenergo held a dominant position as a major domestic producer of electric power and as sole distributor of electricity over the national grid. It was clearly an instrument of the State in a highly regulated electricity market. In the market segment where Windau operated, Latvenergo had no commercial freedom. It had no freedom to negotiate electricity prices but was bound, and considered itself to be bound, by the legislation and the regulatory bodies' determination of the purchase prices to be paid for electric power produced by cogeneration plants. Latvenergo cannot be considered to be, or to have been, an independent commercial enterprise, but clearly a constituent part of the Republic's organization of the electricity market and a vehicle to implement the Republic's decisions concerning the price setting for electric power.

For this reason, whether Latvenergo's refusal to pay the double tariff was based on a misunderstanding of the legal situation, or whether it for other reasons ignored the legal framework under which it was operating, its actions concerning the purchase price are attributable to the Republic. Consequently, the Republic must be found responsible for Latvenergo's failure to pay the double tariff."[7]

---

[7] As was further explained by Nykomb's lawyers and legal experts, the Tribunal had "applied attribution principles under customary international law, influenced,

Having found that Latvenergo's actions were attributable according to customary law, the tribunal turned to the interpretation of Article 22 that provided in the relevant part that "Each Contracting Party shall ensure that any state enterprise which it maintains or establishes shall conduct its activities in relation to the sale or provision of goods and services in its Area in a manner consistent with the Contracting Party's obligations under Part III of this Treaty". Even though Latvia's arguments are not expressly elaborated in the award, from the legal commentaries of those involved in the arbitration it seems that Latvia argued for a narrow construction of the clause, seeing it as "a separate and independent obligation not subject to the investor-state arbitration resolution mechanism of the ECT, and thus outside the Tribunal's jurisdiction".[8] The Tribunal however did not find it necessary to address the issue.

> "The Tribunal will add that for this finding [of attributability] it is not necessary to rely on the supplemental rule in Article 22(1) of the Treaty contended by the Claimant".

(Available at <http://ita.law.uvic.ca/documents/Nykomb-Finalaward.doc> (01.01.2006))

---

perhaps, by Articles 5 and 8 of the Draft Articles. It found in the end, with no great difficulty, that the conduct at issue of the state-owned company was attributable to the state. The claimant had argued that any conduct that was not 'merely commercial', but had a significant element of governmental function, should result in attribution. The claimant relied expressly on the fact that the state-owned company did not negotiate commercially, but was under a legislative and government obligation to enter into the double tariff contracts, that it was a nationwide monopoly on which every supplier and purchaser of electricity depended and that it operated in a heavily regulated market. Other factors may have played a role as well, such as the fact that the state-owned company emerged out of a former Soviet government department, that there was a close political interconnection between the company and the political process, and the public service functions assigned to the electricity monopoly by the state", *see* T. Waelde and K. Hober, 'The First Energy Charter Treaty Arbitral Award' 22:2 *Journal of International Arbitration* (2005) pp. 90–91. K. Hober, 'State Responsibility and Investment Arbitration' 2:5 *Transnational Dispute Management* (2005) p. 21.

[8] J. Wetterfors, 'The First Investor-State Arbitration Award Under the 1994 Energy Charter Treaty', <http://www.iln.com/2004_newsletter/dec/Nykomb%20v%20 Latvia.pdf>, p. 5.

13/2

The Constitutional Court in the judgment of 14 January 2005 in case no 2004-10-01 considered several arguments why the rules prohibiting the appeal of arbitration awards are in breach of fundamental rights. While ultimately rejecting the challenge, the Court expressed its concern about certain aspects of the legal regulation of arbitration and indicated that the State may be internationally responsible for certain breaches:

> "by issuing a writ of execution of an arbitration award that has been made without complying with fundamental rights, both Article 92 of the Satversme and the State's international obligations to enforce human rights are breached. According to norms of customary international law on State responsibility, it arises in cases when a State adopts an action as its own, when the action would have been unlawful if committed by the State itself. This principle is codified in the Draft Articles on Responsibility of States for Internationally Wrongful Acts (see: Draft articles on Responsibility of States for Internationally Wrongful Acts 2001, UN Doc A/56/10 (2001) Ch IV.E.1, p. 43) that have been unanimously affirmed by the General Assembly of the United Nations. Not addressing the question of horizontal applicability of international human rights between subjects of private law, the Satversme Court agrees that State responsibility arises even in the case when the conduct adopted has been 'lawful so far as the original actor was concerned, or the actor may have been a private party whose conduct in the relevant respect was not regulated by international law' (see: Commentaries to the draft articles on Responsibility of States for Internationally Wrongful Acts 2001, UN Doc A/56/10 (2001) Ch IV.E.2, p. 122). Consequently, by issuing a writ of execution, the State becomes responsible for the breaches of human rights during the arbitration proceedings."

(Available at the Internet site of the Constitutional Court, <www.satv.tiesa.gov.lv/ENG/spriedum.htm>, editor's translation)

Part Thirteen: II. A. 1. (e) International responsibility – Responsibility other than criminal – Responsible entities – States – Exhaustion of local remedies

(See *6/4*)

Part Thirteen: III. A. International responsibility – Criminal responsibility– Definition and concept of international crime

(See *4/1/*)

Part Thirteen: III. B. 1. International responsibility – Criminal responsibility – Responsible entities – States

(See *1/3–1/7*)

Part Thirteen: IV. A. International responsibility – Consequences of responsibility – Reparation

13/3

The *Nykomb* v. *Latvia* Tribunal upheld the claim that Latvia had breached its obligation to act fairly and equitably by discriminating against the investor. The Tribunal then considered the consequences of the breach of the Energy Charter Treaty.

> "Article 13(1) of the Treaty spells out the principles of compensation in the special case of investments being nationalized, expropriated or subjected to measures having effect equivalent to nationalization or expropriation. As concluded in section 4.3.1 above, the Tribunal does not find that the refusal to pay the double tariff amounts to expropriation or the equivalent of an expropriation within the meaning of Article 13(1). The Tribunal considers that the principles of compensation provided for in Article 13(1) are not applicable to the assessment of damages or losses found to be caused by violations of Article 10, as in the present case.
>
> Another assessment rule is contained in Article 26(8), which provides that the awards of arbitration according to Article 26 may include an award of interest. The question of interest will be dealt with below.
>
> The Arbitral Tribunal holds, and it seems to be agreed between the parties, that the question of remedies to compensate for losses or damages caused by the Respondent's violation of its obligations under Article 10 of the Treaty must primarily find its solution in accordance with established principles of customary international law. Such principles have authoritatively been restated in The International Law Commission's Draft Articles on State Responsibility adopted in November 2001 (hereinafter referred to as the 'Articles ILC').
>
> According to Articles 34 and 35 ILC restitution is considered to be the primary remedy for reparation. Article 35 states:
>
> 'A State responsible for an internationally wrongful act is under an obligation to make restitution, that is, to re-establish the situation which existed before the wrongful act was committed, provided and to the extent that restitution:

(a) is not materially impossible;

(b) does not involve a burden out of all proportion to the benefit deriving from restitution instead of compensation.'

Restitution in the present case is conceivable, either through a juridical restitution of provisions of Latvian law ensuring Windau's right to the double tariff as it was ensured under the Entrepreneurial Law, or through a monetary restitution to Windau of the missing payments of the difference between the contractually established double tariff and 0.75 of the tariff actually paid. But even if damage or losses to an investment may be inflicted indirectly through loss-creating actions towards a subsidiary in the country of a Contracting State, restitution must primarily be seen as an appropriate remedy in a situation where the Contracting State has instituted actions directly against the investor. An award obliging the Republic to make payments to Windau in accordance with the Contract would also in effect be equivalent to ordering payment under Contract No. 16/07 in the present Treaty arbitration. The Arbitral Tribunal therefore finds the appropriate approach, for the time up to the time of this award, to be an assessment of compensation for the losses or damages inflicted on the Claimant's investments."

After setting the general principles, the Tribunal applied them to the case in question:

"The *Respondent* has argued, and the *Arbitral Tribunal* must agree, that the reduced flow of income into Windau obviously does not cause an identical loss for Nykomb as an investor. If one compares this with a situation where Latvenergo would have paid the double tariff to Windau, it is clear that the higher payments for electric power would not have flowed fully and directly through to Nykomb. The money would have been subject to Latvian taxes etc., would have been used to cover Windau's costs and down payments on Windau's loans etc., and disbursements to the shareholder would be subject to restrictions in Latvian company law on payment of dividends. An assessment of the Claimant's loss on or damage to its investment based directly on the reduced income flow into Windau is unfounded and must be rejected.

. . . Faced with the lack of further specifics, together with the undeniable finding that Nykomb as an investor has suffered economic loss or damage on its investment, the Arbitral Tribunal is compelled to make an assessment, taking into regard the requirements under applicable customary international law of causation, foreseeability and the reasonableness of the result.

The Tribunal finds that the best available basis for such an assessment is the calculated loss of electricity production in the 'dead-lock' period and the actual production of electric energy up to the time of this award. The Tribunal does not consider the asserted loss of heat production in the 'dead-lock' period to be helpful in connection with this, nor is it substantiated in any sufficient degree what net loss has been suffered on the non-production of heat. The only cost deducted in the Claimant's calculation of the net loss is the cost of natural gas required for the production.

The Tribunal considers that in the circumstances a discretionary award of one third of the estimated loss in purchase prices of electricity up to the time of this award may serve as a reasonable basis for quantification of the Claimant's assumed losses up to the time of this award, due to the Respondent's violations of its Treaty obligations."

(Available at <http://ita.law.uvic.ca/documents/Nykomb-Finalaward.doc> (01.01.2006))

Part Thirteen: IV. B. International responsibility – consequences of responsibility – consequences other than reparation

(See *1/3–1/7*)

Part Fourteen: II. F. 2. Peaceful settlement of disputes – Means of settlement – arbitration – arbitral tribunals and commissions other than the Permanent Court of Arbitration

14/1

The *Nykomb* v. *Latvia* Tribunal considered the jurisdictional objections of Latvia that the proper forum for the dispute should be the Latvian courts.[9] The Tribunal rejected the objection and affirmed its own jurisdiction:

"2.4. Lack of jurisdiction due to jurisdiction of local courts.

[9] It seems that Latvia's position was similar to that adopted by the majority in *SGS* v. *Phlippines*, suggesting that the amount under contract should be determined by local courts (ICSID Case No. ARB/02/6), <http://www.worldbank.org/icsid/cases/SGSvPhil-final.pdf>. Perhaps the *Nykomb* v. *Latvia* Tribunal was less impressed by such an argument because the amount under contract was not in dispute and the Supreme Court had already in a similar dispute affirmed the enforceability of the contract.

a) The *Respondent* requests, for several reasons all denied by the Claimant, that the Claimant's claims shall be dismissed in their entirety for lack of jurisdiction.

The Respondent notes that the Claimant's claims are based on the alleged breach of the agreements between Latvenergo and Windau, viz. Contract No. 16/97 and the agreement of 10 March 2000, and argues on that basis as follows:

- The Claimant is not party to these agreements, Windau's contract rights are not transferred to, nor can they be pursued by Nykomb even if it is a 100 per cent parent company. The claims are not owned by the Claimant;

- Both agreements contain a jurisdiction clause giving exclusive jurisdiction to Latvian courts;

- There is nothing to prevent Windau from suing for the same alleged breaches in a Latvian court, with a risk of double payment of the same claim; and

- When the Republic signed and ratified the Treaty, it did not contemplate that such claims as raised by the Claimant in this arbitration would be capable of being brought under Article 26 of the Treaty, and consequently has not agreed to this arbitration.

As for the first of these arguments, the Tribunal must agree that if the Claimant were to be understood as pursuing a contractual claim directly and exclusively based on the agreements between Latvenergo and Windau, such claims would not be admissible since Article 26 only allows arbitration of claims based on alleged breaches of the Treaty. However, as stated in section 1.2.3 above, the Claimant must be understood to claim for the losses or damages it has incurred *itself* as a result of the undelivered heat and electricity in the deadlock period and the refusal of Latvenergo to pay the double tariff during the eight year period, and such claims are alleged to constitute breaches of the Treaty.

As for the second argument, Nykomb is undeniably a legal entity separate from its subsidiary Windau. Nykomb is not a party to either of the two contracts in question and already therefore not bound by their jurisdiction clauses. Nor would Windau have any authority or power, by means of the contract clauses submitting its contract disputes to the jurisdiction of Latvian courts, to exclude Nykomb from pursuing its own claims in an arbitration under ECT Article 26, even in a situation where Nykomb's claims are based on alleged breaches of Windau's contracts.

The risk of double payment is admittedly an effect of the establishment of an arbitration facility also for alleged losses or damages suffered indirectly by an investor, for instance through violations against its subsidiary in a country that has adhered to the Treaty. No definite remedies have been developed at this stage, but clearly the Treaty based right to arbitration is not excluded or limited in cases where there is a possible risk of double payment. This risk of double payment is only likely to be resolved through the further development of the law in this area, such as by the means of new judgements, decisions, guidance or other relevant developments.

Finally, the Tribunal notes that the Republic did not file any reservations concerning the scope or interpretation of Article 26 when adhering to the Treaty. Clearly, the Republic must then be obliged to accept Treaty arbitration with such scope as follows from a proper interpretation of that Treaty provision.

b) The *Respondent* further argues that the dispute concerning the alleged breaches of the agreements between Latvenergo and Windau must first be settled by Latvian courts. In its brief of 4 September 2003 the Respondent states:

'Furthermore, Latvia's argument should not be understood (as do Nykomb and its expert) to advocate the principle of exhaustion of local remedies as a procedural requirement in the traditional sense of international law. Rather, Latvia's argument regarding Nykomb's claim for an alleged and contested breach of contract cannot be ascertained until the proper forum has first pronounced on the issue. There is no evidence to suggest that Windau has been prevented from pursuing such a course of action. It is in this sense that Latvia has presented its argument concerning the exhaustion of local remedies, which Nykomb and its legal expert persist in misunderstanding.

For the above reasons, Latvia is of the view that the Arbitral Tribunal lacks the jurisdiction to entertain Nykomb's claim for the double tariff. Whether such a tariff is due or not is a matter of dispute, and if contested (as seems to be the case here) can only be determined by the proper forum, and in accordance with the proper law of the contracts in question.'

The *Arbitral Tribunal* understands the quoted statement to the effect that the Respondent does not claim the existence of a general obligation under the Treaty or under international law that local remedies must be exhausted before arbitration can be requested under Article 26 of the Treaty. Nonetheless the Tribunal finds it appropriate to state that in the Tribunal's view, no such general obligation to exhaust local remedies can be derived from the Treaty or international law in general. On the contrary, according to ECT Article 26(4) the investor has the option of requesting Treaty arbitration even if it has agreed to the jurisdiction of a local forum – which, however, it has not done in the present case. As a preliminary issue, the Tribunal has come to the conclusion that it has jurisdiction to determine, as a preliminary matter, whether there has been a breach of the contract, insofar as it is necessary for its decision in relation to the claims raised on the basis of the Treaty."

14/2

Latvia also disputed the jurisdiction of the Tribunal on other grounds:

"2.5. Lack of jurisdiction due to limited scope of Treaty provisions

The *Respondent* has asserted several limitations to the scope of the Treaty provisions relied on by the Claimant, which under the circumstances of this case bring the Claimant's claims outside the jurisdiction of the Tribunal, primarily interpreted as follows:

a) Contract No. 16/97 was entered into on 24 March 1997, before the Treaty entered into force on 17 March 1998 and at a time when Windau had only Latvian shareholders. The Treaty does not apply retroactively to situations established prior to the entry into force of the Treaty;

b) The withdrawal of the right to the double tariff occurred before the Claimant's investments in Windau. The Treaty does not apply retroactively to situations established prior to the Claimant's investment;

c) Nykomb was aware of the price dispute, or ought to have been aware of it, before it bought the shares in Windau. Nykomb took a purely business or commercial risk when investing in Windau. The Treaty only protects against political risks and not against commercial or business risks;

d) Also, the Contract between Latvenergo and Windau for the purchase of electric power, upon which all the Claimant's claims are based, is a commercial contract and as such not protected by the Treaty. The Treaty protection only applies to investment contracts within the meaning of the Treaty."

The Tribunal rejected all of these objections:

"4.3.3. Limited scope of the Treaty provisions allegedly breached

. . . the Respondent has asserted several limitations to the scope of the Treaty provisions relied on by the Claimant:

a) The Treaty does not apply retroactively to contracts entered into before the Treaty entered into force:

It is undisputed that Contract No. 16/97 was entered into on 24 March 1997 and that the Energy Charter Treaty only came into force on 17 March 1998. However, none of the Claimant's claims are based on the date of the signing of the Contract. The claims are built on the repeal of Windau's statutory right to the double tariff, which took place in September/October 1998, and on the breach of the contractual obligation to pay the double tariff, which materialized in September 1999 when the Bauska plant was ready to go into operation, and which has been maintained since then, albeit in accordance with the interim agreement of 10 March 2000. Both the changes in the law and the breach of contract occurred after the entry into force of the Treaty. There is therefore no question of retroactive effects of the Treaty in this situation.

b) The Treaty does not apply retroactively to a withdrawal of the right to the double tariff which was effected before Nykomb's investment took place:

It is undisputed that the Claimant's first investment in Windau occurred by the contract of 11 March 1999, registered on 25 March 1999, for the purchase of 51 per cent of the shares in Windau. The withdrawal of Windau's statutory right to the double tariff took place in September/October 1998, which was before Nykomb's investment. But as pointed out in lit. a) above, the claims for losses or damages are also based on the breach of the Contract which occurred from September 1999, which is after Nykomb's first investment was made. At least in the latter situation there is no question of the retroactive effects of the Treaty.

c) Nykomb was aware of the price dispute, or ought to have been aware of it, and took a commercial risk not protected by the Treaty:

The Respondent also contends that Nykomb was aware of the price dispute, or ought to have been aware of it, before it bought the shares in Windau. Nykomb took a purely business or commercial risk when investing in Windau. The Treaty only protects against political risks and not against commercial or business risks.

This contention raises the question of what Nykomb knew, or ought to have known, about Latvenergo's refusal to pay the double tariff at the time of its investment. It also invites the question of whether a Contracting State to the Treaty can free itself from its Treaty obligations simply by informing a prospective foreign investor that it has established and intends to continue a discrimination of the foreign investment which would otherwise be a violation of the Treaty.

The Tribunal considered the facts of the case and concluded that:

"It must therefore be concluded that Nykomb was fully aware of the uncertainty and risk deriving from Latvenergo's position, but took its precautions in the share purchase agreement and took the risk that the Contract was valid and invested in the Windau shares.

Whether or not one would characterize the risk Nykomb was taking as a commercial risk, is in the Tribunal's view immaterial. It is the Tribunal's conclusion that Windau had entered into a purchase contract for the delivery of electric power that was, and is, legally valid and binding and gave Windau the right to the double tariff for eight years. Nykomb made its share investment relying on this contract. Latvenergo's contentions that Contract No. 16/97 was invalid and did not establish the right to the double tariff were legally unfounded. Nykomb's awareness of Latvenergo's contentions does not relieve the Republic of its obligations under the Treaty resulting from Latvenergo's refusal to pay the double tariff. Generally, a Contracting Party to the Treaty cannot be relieved of its obligations under the Treaty simply by letting it be announced that legally binding commitments, upon which the foreign investor is relying, will not be honored.

d) The Claimant's claims are based on a commercial contract not protected by the Treaty

Finally, the Respondent contends that the Contract between Latvenergo and Windau for the purchase of electric power, upon which all the Claimant's claims are based, is a commercial contract and as such not protected by the Treaty. The Treaty protection only applies to investment contracts within the meaning of the Treaty.

It follows from the remarks above that the Arbitral Tribunal cannot regard the purchase contract as purely commercial, nor can the action to refuse payment of the double tariff under the contract be considered as purely commercial.

As for the objection that the purchase contract is not an investment contract within the meaning of the Treaty, it suffices to note that such a contract clearly falls within the definition of investments in Article 1 of the Treaty."

(Available at <http://ita.law.uvic.ca/documents/Nykomb-Finalaward.doc> (01.01.2006))

14/3

The Tribunal considered the claim that the breach of contract by Latvenergo amounted to expropriation and rejected it:

> "*4.3.1. Expropriation*
>
> The Claimant does not contend that the non-payment of the double tariff amounts to a direct and formal expropriation meeting the requirements of Article 13 (1) (a)-(c), but rather that it constitutes an 'indirect' or 'creeping' expropriation. By taking away a substantial part of Windau's income from sales it makes the enterprise not economically viable and the Claimant's investment worthless.
>
> The Respondent denies that Latvenergo's non-payment amounts to the equivalent of an expropriation even in the wider sense developed under recent international treaty law and practice. First, no public authority is involved in Latvenergo's action under the contract, second, there is no taking of possession or control over the enterprise, and third, the payment of 0.75 rather than 2.00 of the tariff does not result in the investment becoming worthless. The Claimant itself admits that the pay-back time is only lengthened, but that does not amount to expropriation.
>
> The Arbitral Tribunal has considered the expert legal opinions and arbitral awards rendered under similar treaties presented in this case by the parties. The Tribunal finds that 'regulatory takings' may under the circumstances amount to expropriation or the equivalent of an expropriation. The decisive factor for drawing the border line towards expropriation must primarily be the degree of possession taking or control over the enterprise the disputed measures entail[10]. In the present case, there is no possession taking of Windau or its assets, no interference with the shareholder's rights or with

[10] In the light of the ongoing debate about the proper criteria for dealing with the cases of regulatory expropriation, it is interesting that the *Nykomb* v. *Latvia* Tribunal seems to consider the dividing line solely as a matter of effect of the measure. In general, two lines of case law have emerged, one of them focusing on the effect of the measure (the so-called 'sole effect' approach) while the other being more deferential to the regulator (the so-called 'purpose' approach), *see* R. Dolzer, 'Indirect Expropriations: New Developments', 11 *N.Y.U. Envtl L.J.* (2002-2003) p. 64, L. Yves Fortier and S. L. Drymer, 'Indirect Expropriation in the Law of International Investment: I Know It When I See It, or *Caveat Investor*', 19 *ICSID Review – Foreign Investment Law Journal* (2004) p. 293, Christoph H. Shreuer, 'The Concept of Expropriation under the ECT and other Investment Protection Treaties', 2 *Transnational Dispute Management* (2005). *Nykomb*, while rejecting the claim of expropriation, seemed to be clearly in favour of the effect oriented analysis.

the management's control over and running of the enterprise – apart from ordinary regulatory provisions laid down in the production licence, the off-take agreement, etc.

The Tribunal therefore concludes that the withholding of payment at the double tariff does not qualify as an expropriation or the equivalent of an expropriation under the Treaty."

The Tribunal then considered the claim of fair and equitable treatment including discrimination and upheld it:

"Article 10 (1) provides inter alia that

> '. . . no Contracting Party shall in any way impair by . . . unreasonable or discriminatory measures their [the Investor's Investments] . . . use, enjoyment or disposal'.

The Claimant contends that Windau has been subject to discriminatory measures by Latvenergo's refusal to pay the double tariff. Latvenergo has been, and still is, paying SIA 'Latelektro-Gulbene' and Joint Stock Company 'Liepãjas Siltums' the double tariff for its surplus electric power. There is no legitimate reason to treat Windau differently from the two aforementioned enterprises.

The Respondent does not deny the fact of the double tariff being paid to the two companies mentioned, but contends that the situations are not comparable. The Respondent has provided lists and some details concerning the 28 cogeneration power plants existing in Latvia, and asserted that they are in many respects different and therefore have been awarded different multipliers. An evaluation must take place in each case. No discrimination is demonstrated by the fact that the two above-mentioned plants have been granted the double tariff, whereas Bauska has not.

The Arbitral Tribunal accepts that in evaluating whether there is discrimination in the sense of the Treaty one should only 'compare like with like'. However, little if anything has been documented by the Respondent to show the criteria or methodology used in fixing the multiplier, or to what extent Latvenergo is authorized to apply multipliers other than those documented in this arbitration. On the other hand, all of the information available to the Tribunal suggests that the three companies are comparable, and subject to the same laws and regulations. In particular, this appears to be the situation with respect to Latelektro-Gulbene and Windau. In such a situation, and in accordance with established international law, the burden of proof lies with the Respondent to prove that no discrimination

> has taken or is taking place. The Arbitral Tribunal finds that such burden of proof has not been satisfied, and therefore concludes that Windau has been subject to a discriminatory measure in violation of Article 10(1)."

(Available at <http://ita.law.uvic.ca/documents/Nykomb-Finalaward.doc> (01.01.2006))

Part Sixteen: III. Use of force – Use of force under the UN Charter

16/1

On 22 June 2005, Mr. Artis Pabriks, the Minister of Foreign Affairs, made an address at an International Conference on Iraq in Brussels, remarking that:

> "Latvia will continue to contribute troops for the Multinational Force-Iraq until the Iraqi security forces will be able to assume full operational responsibilities.
>
> . . . Latvia itself has recently undergone the transition from being subjected to tyranny, to re-establishing freedom and democracy. We have experienced and appreciate the importance of international support. That is why we are participating in the EU and NATO training missions for Iraq, as well as continuing with bilateral assistance programmes.
>
> We have donated small arms and ammunition to the Iraqi security forces. We have offered training programme of Explosive Ordinance disposal personnel. We will continue to provide technical assistance in training for environmental and municipal management. We will continue to assist with the preservation of Iraq's rich cultural and historical heritage."

(Available at the Internet site of the Ministry of Foreign Affairs of Latvia, <www.am.gov.lv/en/news/speeches/> (01.01.2006))

16/2

On 10 November 2005, Ms. Udre, the Speaker of the Parliament, made a Statement that:

> "at the session of 10 November of this year the Saeima, in accordance with Article 1(2) and Article 5(1) of the Law on 'Participation of the National Armed Forces of Latvia in International Armed Operations', has extended until 31 December 2006 the term of participation of the Latvian National Armed Forces armed units in the peacekeeping operations in Iraq as part of

> the Polish Republic contingent of the Multinational Coalition's armed forces lead by the United States."[11]

(Published in Latvijas Vēstnesis (Latvian Herald), 17 November 2005, No 184, editor's translation)

Part Seventeen: III. B. 1. The law of armed conflict and international humanitarian law – Aspects of the law of armed conflict – Rights and duties of participants – Land operations

(See *1/3*)

Part Seventeen: III. J. The law of armed conflict and international humanitarian law – Aspects of the law of armed conflict – Belligerent occupation

(See *1/3*)

---

[11] "On 10 November 2005, the Saeima (the Parliament of Latvia) approved the extension of the Latvian soldiers' mission in Iraq to the end of next year, as agreed by the Latvian government on 1 November. On 8 November, the UN Security Council unanimously supported the Iraqi interim government's request to extend the mandate of the Multinational force in Iraq for the aforementioned time period", <http://www.am.gov.lv/en/news/press-releases/2005/november/11-5/>. It would seem that the decision was in effect formulated before the United Nations Security Council passed Resolution 1637 (2005). Even though complying with the deadline mentioned in the Resolution, the Statement does not refer to United Nations forces or any resolutions, unlike the previous statement of 19 May 2005. Consequently, Latvia's position in this context seems to suggest a shift of the legal emphasis from United Nations to less universal security measures.

Appedix I. Bilateral Agreements Signed By The Republic Of Latvia During The Period From 1 January 2005 To 31 December 2005

Instrument and Title	*Date of Latvia signature*
ANGUILLA (UNITED KINGDOM)	
Convention between the Government of the Republic of Latvia and the Government of Anguilla Concerning the Automatic Exchange of Information about Savings Income in the form of Interest Payments	03.02.2005
ARAB REPUBLIC OF EGYPT	
Agreement on Cultural Co-operation between the Government of the Republic of Latvia and the Arab Republic of Egypt	02.03.2005
AZERBAIJANI REPUBLIC	
Agreement between the Government of the Republic of Latvia and the Government of the Republic of Azerbaijan on Economic, Scientific, Technical and Cultural Cooperation	03.10.2005
Agreement between the Government of the Republic of Latvia and the Government of the Republic of Azerbaijan on Co-operation in Combating Terrorism, Illicit Trafficking In Narcotic Drugs, Psychotropic Substances and Precursors and Organised Crime	03.10.2005
Convention between the Government of the Republic of Latvia and the Government of the Republic of Azerbaijan for the Avoidance of Double Taxation and the Prevention of Fiscal Evasion with Respect to Taxes on Income and on Capital	03.10.2005
Agreement beween the Government of the Republic of Latvia and the Government of the	03.10.2005

Republic of Azerbaijan on the Promotion and Reciprocial Protection of Investments	
Agreement between the Government of the Republic of Latvia and the Government of the Republic of Azerbaijan Regarding Mutual Assistance in Customs Matters	03.10.2005
BALTIC STATES	
The Protocol to the Agreement between the Government of the Republic of Latvia, the Government of Estonia and the Government of Lithuania on Cooperation in Protection of Witnesses and Victims' Regarding the Procedure of Transfer	25.11.2005
BRITISH VIRGIN ISLANDS	
Agreement on the taxation of Savings Income between the Government of the British Virgin Islands and the Government of the Republic of Latvia	11.04.2005
CANADA	
Agreement on Social Security between the Republic of Latvia and Canada	29.06.2005
CAYMAN ISLANDS	
Agreement on the Taxation of Savings Income between the Cayman Islands and the Republic of Latvia	12.04.2005
GEORGIA	
Agreement between the Government of the Republic of Latvia and the Government of Georgia on Mutual Protection of Classified Information	06.07.2005
Agreement between the Government of the Republic of Latvia and the Government of Georgia for the Promotion and Reciprocal	05.10.2005

Protection of Investments

Agreement between the Government of the Republic of Latvia and the Government of Georgia on Economic, Industrial, Scientific and Technical Cooperation	05.10.2005
Air Services Agreement between the Government of the Republic of Latvia and the Government of Georgia	05.10.2005

KINGDOM OF SWEEDEN

Agreement between the Government of the Republic of Latvia and the Government of the Kingdom of Sweden on the Riga Graduate School of Law	07.11.2005

MONTSERRAT (UNITED KINGDOM)

Agreement on the Taxation of Savings Income between the United Kingdom Overseas Territory of Montserrat and the Republic of Latvia	07.04.2005

REPUBLIC OF ARMENIA

Agreement between the Government of the Republic of Latvia and the Government of the Republic of Armenia for the Promotion and Reciprocal Protection of Investments	07.10.2005
Agreement between the Government of the Republic of Latvia and the Government of the Republic of Armenia Regarding Mutual Assistance in Customs Matters	07.10.2005

REPUBLIC OF AUSTRIA

Convention between the Republic of Latvia and the Republic of Austria for the Avoidance of Double Taxation with Respect to Taxes on Income and on Capital	14.11.2005

REPUBLIC OF BULGARIA

Agreement on Cooperation in the Field of

Education, Science and Culture between the Government of the Republic of Latvia and Government of the Republic of Bulgaria	21.03.2005

REPUBLIC OF CROATIA

Agreement between the Government of the Republic of Latvia and the Government of the Republic of Croatia on Co-operation in the Field of Tourism	22.07.2005

REPUBLIC OF CYPRUS

Agreement between the Government of the Republic of Latvia and the Government of the Republic of Cyprus on Co-operation in Combating Terrorism, Illicit Trafficking in Narcotic Drugs, Psychotropic Substances and Precursors and Organized Crime	11.04.2005

REPUBLIC OF LITHUANIA

Agreement between the Government of the Republic of Latvia and the Government of the Republic of Lithuania on the Settlement of the Debt to the Republic of Latvia for the Maintenance of the Embassy of the Republic of Lithuania in Washington	15.02.2005

REPUBLIC OF SLOVENIA

Agreement between the Government of the Republic of Latvia and the Government of the Republic of Slovenia on Co-operation in Combating Terrorism, Organized Crime, Illicit Trafficking in Narcotic Drugs, Psychotropic Substances and Other Serious Crimes	13.10.2005

REPUBLIC OF TURKEY

Agreement between the Government of the Republic of Latvia and the Government of the Republic of Turkey on Co-operation in the Fields of Education, Science, Culture and Sports	19.04.2005

RUSSIAN FEDERATION

Protocol between the Government of the Republic of Latvia and the Government of the Russian Federation on Prolongation of the Agreement of 2 June 1993, on Regulation of Repatriation of Persons and Protection of the Rights of Repatriants	21.10.2005

SERBIA AND MONTENEGRO

Convention between the Government of the Republic of Latvia and the Council of Ministers of Serbia and Montenegro for the Avoidance of Double Taxation with Respect to Taxes on Income and on Capital	22.11.2005

SLOVAK REPUBLIC

Agreement between the Government of the Republic of Latvia and the Government of the Slovak Republic on Mutual Protection of Classified Information	02.02.2005

STATE OF ISRAEL

Memorandum of Understanding between the Government of the Republic of Latvia and the Government of the State of Israel Regarding Defence Industrial Cooperation	16.02.2005

SWISS CONFEDERATION

Agreement between the Republic of Latvia and Swiss Confederation on Police Cooperation in Combating Crime	23.05.2005

THE KINGDOM OF NORWAY

Bilateral Security Agreement between the Government of the Republic of Latvia and the Government of the Kingdom of Norway	26.09.2005

THE KINGDOM OF NETHERLANDS

Agreement between the Republic of Latvia and the Kingdom of the Netherlands Concerning the Privileges and Immunities of Liaison Officers	25.04.2005

TURKS AND CAICOS ISLANDS (UNITED KINGDOM)

Agreement on Taxation of Savings Income between the Turks and Caicos Islands and the Republic of Latvia	01.03.2005

UNITED MEXICAN STATES

Agreement between the Government of the Republic of Latvia and the Government of the United Mexican States on Co-operation in the Field of Education, Culture and Sport	15.04.2005

UNITED STATES OF AMERICA

Amendment to the Agreement between the Government of the Republic of Latvia and the Government of the United States of America Concerning Cooperation in the Area of Prevention of Proliferation of Weapons of Mass Destruction	14.02.2005
Agreement between the Government of the Republic of Latvia and the Government of the United States of America on Strengthening the State Defence Capabilities of Latvia	06.05.2005
Protocol to the Treaty between the Government of the Republic of Latvia and the Government of the United States of America on Mutual Assistance in Criminal Matters	07.12.2005
Extradition Treaty between the Government of the Republic of Latvia and the Government of the United States of America	07.12.2005

WORLD INTELECTUAL PROPERTY ORGANISATION	
Memorandum of Understanding between the Government of the Republic of Latvia and the World Intellectual Property Organization	07.04.2005

Appendix II. Multilateral Agreements signed by the Republic of Latvia during the period from 1 January 2005 to 31 December 2005

BALTIC STATES	
The Protocol to the Agreement between the Government of the Republic of Latvia, the Government of Estonia and the Government of Lithuania on Cooperation in Protection of Witnesses and Victims' Regarding the Procedure of Transfer	25.11.2005
HASHEMITE KINGDOM OF JORDAN	
Protocol to the Euro-Mediterranean Agreement establishing an Association between the European Communities and their Member States, and the Hashemite Kingdom of Jordan to take account of the accession of the new Member States to the EU	31.05.2005
KINGDOM OF MOROCCO	
Protocol to the Euro-Mediterranean Agreement establishing an Association between the European Communities and their Member States, and the Kingdom of Morocco to take account of the accession of the new Member States to the EU	31.05.2005
PEOPLE'S REPUBLIC OF CHINA	
Protocol amending the Agreement on maritime transport between the European Community and its Member States, and the Government of the People's Republic of China	05.10.2005

REPUBLIC OF CHILE

Additional Protocol to the Agreement establishing an association between the European Community and its Member States, and the Republic of Chile to take account of the accession of the new Member States to the EU	16.12.2005

REPUBLIC OF KOREA

Protocol to the Framework Agreement for Trade and Cooperation between the European Community and its Member States, and the Republic of Korea to take account of the accession of the new Member States to the EU	16.11.2005

REPUBLIC OF SAN MARINO

Protocol to the Agreement on Cooperation and Customs Union between the European Economic Community and the Republic of San Marino, regarding the participation, as contracting parties, of the new Member States to the EU	04.05.2005

REPUBLIC OF TUNISIA

Protocol to the Euro-Mediterranean Agreement establishing an association between the European Communities and their Member States, and the Republic of Tunisia, to take account of the accession of the new Member States to the EU	31.05.2005

Republic of Lithuania Materials on International Law 2005

Edited by prof. Saulius Katuoka[*]
in cooperation with Loreta Šaltinytė LL.M.[**]

[Editorial Notes:

1. The Republic of Lithuania Materials on International Law 2005 (RLMIL 2005) have been classified according to Recommendation (97)11 of 12 June 1997 of the Committee of Ministers of the Council of Europe, as applied by the British Yearbook of International Law from the year 1997.

2. Since the RLMIL mostly concern the opinions made by the institutions and officials of Lithuania, in case it has not been expressly provided for otherwise, the institutions and officials mentioned in the RLMIL are those of the Republic of Lithuania.

[*] Chair of the Department of International law at Mykolas Romeris University. Teaches international law and the law of the sea at Mykolas Romeris University. Appointed member of the Permanent Court of Arbitration since 2005.

[**] Doctoral candidate at Mykolas Romeris University, Lithuania; LL.M. (Riga Graduate School of Law (2003), Master of Law (Vilnius University Faculty of law, 2003). Currently a lecturer on international and EU law at Mykolas Romeris University.

Baltic Yearbook of International Law, Volume 6, 2006, pp. 449–478.

Part One: I. A. International Law in general – Nature, basis, purpose – In general

1/1

On 23 February 2005 the Minister of Foreign Affairs issued a public statement commenting on an evaluation of the Molotov-Ribbentrop Pact made by the Russian President Vladimir Putin in an interview to Slovak Radio 'Radio slovensko' and the TV station STV on 22 February 2005. The statement reads, in part, as follows:

> "In the interview the Russian President claimed that the Soviet Union signed the so-called Molotov-Ribbentrop Pact in order to 'safeguard its interests and security of its western borders'. However, the protection of one's interests may not serve as an excuse for annexation of another sovereign country.
>
> The Ministry of Foreign Affairs of the Republic of Lithuania reminds that the Congress of the People's Deputies of the USSR gave its political and legal evaluation of this notorious pact on 24 December 1989, whereby the Congress condemned the secret protocols and declared them void. Therefore an attempt to 'explain' the legitimacy of the Molotov-Ribbentrop Pact may be regarded as an attempt to once again turn over the already closed page of history and thus to review the decision of the Congress of the People's Deputies of the USSR.
>
> The Ministry of Foreign Affairs of the Republic of Lithuania is surprised with the comparison drawn by the Russian President that the 1938 Munich agreements with Great Britain and France were signed by Adolf Hitler personally while the 1939 agreement with the Soviet Union was signed 'only' by the Foreign Minister of Hitler's Germany.
>
> The Ministry of Foreign Affairs of the Republic of Lithuania draws attention to the fact that the 1938 Munich conspiracy is by no means an excuse to justify the secret agreement between the USSR and the Government of Hitler's Germany, which infringed on Lithuania's sovereign rights.
>
> Present intergovernmental relations between the Republic of Lithuania and the Russian Federation are based on the treaty of 1991, whereby both parties acknowledged the fact of the annexation of the Republic of Lithuania by the USSR and the Russian Federation committed to eliminate the consequences of annexation.

The Ministry of Foreign Affairs would like to emphasize that this agreement has paved the way for the development of friendly Lithuanian-Russian relationship based on the interests of both states and their citizens and corresponding to the universally accepted international norms.

The citizens of Lithuania would greatly appreciate the reassurance by the Russian President that political will of the present Russian authorities will be based on the provisions of that agreement. Speculations about 'those willing to rewrite the history' hardly contribute to good neighbourly relations and mutual understanding. History is such as it is and it may not be changed overnight.

The Ministry of Foreign Affairs of the Republic of Lithuania will make every effort to ensure that interpretations of the history will not cast a shadow over aspirations of both States to cherish good relationships and mutual commitments to do so. The Ministry will further seek to jointly solve the most urgent European and global issues of security, economic and social development."[1]

1/2

President Adamkus turned down President Vladimir Putin's invitation to attend the commemoration of the 60th anniversary of the victory over Nazi Germany in Moscow on 9 May, as the victory was followed by the nearly half century long Soviet occupation of the Baltic States.

1/3

On 26 April 2005 *Seimas* (the Parliament) adopted a statement on the Evaluation of the Consequences of the End of World War II in Europe, urging Russia to recognize the Soviet occupation of the Baltic States. The declaration reads, in part:

"World War II was the result of the concerted aggression of Nazi Germany and Bolshevik Soviet Union. In 1939 Germany and the Soviet Union occupied Poland. This prompted the formation of the Western Antihitlerite Coalition which was later joined by the Soviet Union.

World War II claimed millions of lives primarily of the Soviet Union people. Millions of residents of other countries perished too. During the War, the Jewish people were subjected to the most brutal genocide and

---

[1] Statement available at <www.urm.lt>.

> suffered an extremely great loss. The tragic consequences of the War befell on Lithuania: many people were deported for forced labour in the Third Reich, others perished while actively fighting in the anti-Nazi underground. Therefore, the historical significance of the victory over Nazism is unquestionable and there is no doubt that victory over Nazism means halting aggression. However, something that prolonged occupation of other states, caused countless losses and trampled on expectations of democracy may not be regarded as victory.
>
> [...]
>
> Having evaluated the actual consequences of World War II, the Seimas of the Republic of Lithuania states that:
>
> 1) the end of World War II in Europe meant the annihilation of Nazism - one of the greatest evils of civilisation, which also brought about a decades-long occupation of Lithuania and other Baltic States and its painful consequences;
>
> 2) it is high time that all good-will states together with Russia, which is seeking to get closer to the united and democratic Europe, should see and recognise the aspects of both the annihilation of Nazism and occupation of the Baltic States, and pay their respects both to the victims of Nazism and Bolshevism;
>
> 3) not forgetting all victims of World War II, the Holocaust, post-war resistance and repressions, we should hope that forbearance and tolerance will become the universal principle of communication between the states and their residents."[2]

1/4

On 5 May 2005 regarding the occupation of the Baltic States by the Soviet Union in 1940 President Putin's Spokesman on European Affairs Sergei Yastrzhembsky stated that:

> "There was no occupation. There were agreements at the time with the legitimately elected authorities in the Baltic countries."[3]

---

[2] Full text available in English, Russian and Lithuanian at <www.lrs.lt>.

[3] BBC News, available at <http://news.bbc.co.uk/go/pr/fr/-/2/hi/europe/4517683.stm>.

1/5

On 12 May 2005 the European Parliament adopted a resolution recognizing the fact of Soviet occupation. The document reads that the end of the war did not mean the end of tyranny in all European countries. President V. Adamkus made the following comments on the resolution:

> "It is very important for us that the European Community recognizes the fact that not all of the liberated countries regained their freedom after Hitler's Germany had been defeated. The commemoration of the end of the Second World War has given us the possibility to remind the world of the fact that the Soviet Union kept the Baltic countries under occupation for many decades."[4]

1/6

On 22 July 2005 the House of Representatives of the USA passed a concurrent resolution with respect to the Soviet occupation of the Baltic States. The resolution reads, in full:

> "Expressing the sense of Congress that the Government of the Russian Federation should issue a clear and unambiguous statement of admission and condemnation of the illegal occupation and annexation by the Soviet Union from 1940 to 1991 of the Baltic countries of Estonia, Latvia, and Lithuania.
>
> Whereas the incorporation in 1940 of the Baltic countries of Estonia, Latvia, and Lithuania into the Soviet Union was an act of aggression carried out against the will of sovereign people;
>
> Whereas the United States was steadfast in its policy of not recognizing the illegal Soviet annexation of Estonia, Latvia, and Lithuania;
>
> Whereas the Russian Federation is the successor state to the Soviet Union;
>
> Whereas the Molotov-Ribbentrop Pact of 1939, including its secret protocols, between Nazi Germany and the Soviet Union provided the Soviet Union with the opportunity to occupy and annex Estonia, Latvia, and Lithuania;

---

[4] Report of the Ministry of Foreign Affairs. Available at <www1.urm.lt/data/15/EF52171152_nf860.htm>.

Whereas the occupation brought countless suffering to the Baltic peoples through terror, killings, and deportations to Siberian concentration camps;

Whereas the peoples of Estonia, Latvia, and Lithuania bravely resisted Soviet aggression and occupation;

Whereas the Government of Germany renounced its participation in the Molotov-Ribbentrop Pact of 1939 and publicly apologized for the destruction and terror that Nazi Germany unleashed on the world;

Whereas in 1989, the Congress of Peoples' Deputies of the Soviet Union denounced the Molotov-Ribbentrop Pact of 1939 and its secret protocols;

Whereas President Putin recently confirmed that the statement of the Congress of Peoples' Deputies remains the view of the Russian Federation;

Whereas the illegal occupation and annexation of the Baltic countries by the Soviet Union remains unacknowledged by the Russian Federation;

Whereas a declaration of acknowledgment of the illegal occupation and annexation by the Russian Federation would lead to improved relations between the people of Estonia, Latvia, and Lithuania and the people of Russia, would form the basis for improved relations between the governments of the countries, and strengthen stability in the region;

Whereas the Russian Federation is to be commended for acknowledging grievous and regrettable incidents in the Soviet era, such as the massacre by the Soviet regime of Polish soldiers in the Katyn Forest in 1939;

Whereas the truth is a powerful weapon for healing, forgiving, and reconciliation, but its absence breeds distrust, fear, and hostility; and

Whereas countries that cannot clearly admit their historical mistakes and make peace with their pasts cannot successfully build their futures: Now, therefore, be it

Resolved by the House of Representatives (the Senate concurring), That it is the sense of Congress that the Government of the Russian Federation should issue a clear and unambiguous statement of admission and condemnation of the illegal occupation and annexation by the Soviet Union from 1940 to 1991 of the Baltic countries of Estonia, Latvia, and Lithuania, the consequence of which will be a significant increase in good will among the affected peoples and enhanced regional stability."[5]

---

[5] H. CON. RES. 128, 1st session in the Senate of the United States.

Part Three: I. B. The Law of Treaties – Conclusion, including signature, ratification, and accession

3/1

On 7 July 2005 the Law on Treaties was amended so that the procedure of granting powers to conclude international agreements was clarified. By the same act, the Seimas agreed to amend the law on treaties specifying that the agreements not requiring ratification shall be approved by the Government. The new edition of the relevant Articles reads:

> "Article 6. Procedure for Granting Powers to Conclude Treaties of the Republic of Lithuania
>
> 1. The powers to perform the acts relating to the conclusion of treaties of the Republic of Lithuania referred to in Article 7 of this Law, with the exception of international mixed agreements, shall be granted by the President of the Republic of Lithuania on the recommendation of the Government.
>
> 2. The powers to perform the acts relating to the conclusion of international mixed agreements shall be granted by the Prime Minister of the Republic of Lithuania with the consent of the President of the Republic of Lithuania, on the recommendation of the ministry or Government agency within whose competence falls the drawing-up of the treaty, and with the consent of the Ministry of Foreign Affairs.
>
> 3. The powers to perform the acts relating to the treaties of the Republic of Lithuania which are not subject to the ratification procedure under the Constitution of the Republic of Lithuania, this Law or the treaty itself, however, the conclusion of which, according to the procedure laid down in Article 9 of this Law, is approved by the Government of the Republic of Lithuania, shall be granted by the Prime Minister of the Republic of Lithuania on the recommendation of the ministry or Government agency within whose competence falls the drawing-up of the treaty, provided the Ministry of Foreign Affairs has given its consent thereto.
>
> 4. The powers for concluding treaties of the Republic of Lithuania which enter into force on the date of the signing thereof shall be granted by the Government of the Republic of Lithuania on the recommendation of the ministry or Government agency within whose competence falls the drawing up of the treaty, provided the Ministry of Foreign Affairs has given its consent thereto.

5. By the resolution of the Government of the Republic of Lithuania, the Ministry of Foreign Affairs shall be instructed to conclude treaties which enter into force from the date of exchange of diplomatic notes.

6. Upon the granting of the powers referred to in paragraphs 1–4 of this Article, full powers shall be issued by the Ministry of Foreign Affairs.

7. Information about full powers shall be stored and administered at the Ministry of Foreign Affairs.

[…]

Article 9. Approval of Treaties of the Republic of Lithuania

1. The treaties of the Republic of Lithuania for which ratification procedure is not provided for in the Constitution of the Republic of Lithuania, this Law or the treaty itself shall be approved by the Government of the Republic of Lithuania. This requirement shall not apply to the treaties of the Republic of Lithuania referred to in paragraphs 4 and 5 of Article 6 of this Law."[6]

Part Three: II. B. The Law of Treaties – Observance, application and interpretation of treaties – Application

(see also *1/1* above, *3/4*, *6/1* below)

3/2

The Supreme Court has continued to develop its theory on direct application of the CMR convention. In *UAB Senukų prekybos centras* v. *UAB 'EM Trans'*, Case No. 3K-3-3/2005 (decision of 5 January 2005) the Court stated as follows:

"Article 41(1) of the Convention on the Contract for the International Carriage of Goods by Road (hereinafter CMR) establishes that the provisions of the Convention are imperative. This principle has been consistently followed in the practice of the foreign courts. Pursuant to Article 41(1) and subject to the provisions of Article 40, any stipulation which would directly or indirectly derogate from the provisions of this Convention shall be null and void. Article 41(1) does not permit derogation or elimination on the basis of national law or the agreement of the parties. Therefore any agreement on higher liability of a carrier than that provided under the Convention should be considered null and void. Also, due to the

[6] Official translation. Available at <www.lrs.lt>.

imperative nature governing the rights and duties of the parties to the carriage contract of the CMR convention, different agreements, pursuant to which a carrier undertakes additional duties, *inter alia*, a duty of a carrier to accept the documents received from the sender, and to check their credibility should be considered invalid *ab initio*, therefore the courts should find them void and determine their legal consequences *ex officio* (Article 1.78(5) of the Civil Code). Since nullity of these contractual provisions does not involve the nullity of the other provisions of the contract, the court hearing the case must apply the provisions of the CMR instead of the contractual provisions, contradicting the Convention."[7]

3/3

On 16 September 2005 the Supreme Administrative Court of Lithuania issued a judgment in the *Tomkus* case (Supreme Administrative Court judgment No. N^3-1603-05). The facts of the case raised issues that Tomkus, an editor of a Lithuanian daily, "Respublika", beginning in 20 February 2004 to 12 March 2004 wrote and published in Respublika a series of articles titled "Who rules the world?", which spurred protests in Lithuania and throughout Europe for alleged incitement of racial hatred against Jews and discrimination against homosexuals. The prosecution reacted by initiating a criminal case against Tomkus for encouraging racial hatred. The case was subsequently terminated for lack of evidence of Tomkus' intent to incite hatred. The prosecution viewed the articles as "humour" and "irony". Afterwards, the administrative procedure for the same acts was initiated. The district court found Tomkus guilty and ordered him to pay a fine of 3000 Lt. The Supreme Administrative Court heard the case on appeal and overruled it because of its incompatibility with the principle *non bis in idem*, as enshrined in the European Convention on Fundamental Rights and Freedoms. The relevant excerpts from the judgment read (in part):

"*Non bis in idem* is a general principle of law which finds expression in *inter alia* Article 31(5) of the Constitution and Article 4(1) of Protocol No.7 to the European Convention on Human Rights and Fundamental Freedoms.

The concept of 'crime' which is used in the Lithuanian text of the Convention is not an accurate reflection of the authentic version which uses the concept of 'offence' (Fr. – *infraction*). Under the Convention, the concept of 'criminal' (offence or procedure) has an autonomous meaning and has a wider scope than is common to Lithuanian law. Article 4 of

---

[7] Editor's translation. Full judgment is available at <www.lat.lt> in Lithuanian.

> Protocol No.7 should be understood and applied in light of the case law of the European Court of Human Rights on criminal charges (Article 6(1)) and the concepts of criminal offence and punishment (Article 7). For the purposes of the Convention, in order to decide whether a certain offence is a crime, it needs to be established whether it is defined as such under the legal system of the respondent State. If it is not, the rule needs to be analyzed on the basis of additional criteria, i.e. 1) the nature of the offence 2) the nature of the punishment and its severity. Thus, if it is established that the nature of the offence is criminal and the punishment would be similar to criminal punishments in light of its nature or degree of severity it will be deemed criminal.
>
> Offences that are punished with criminal sentences seeking inter alia to deter and which generally are in the form of fines or imprisonment, are generally considered criminal within the meaning of the Convention. When a penalty is a fine, it should be considered whether it seeks to compensate for damages suffered or to punish the wrongdoer. Only in the latter case is the violation likely to fall under the criminal sphere. The amount of the fine should also be taken into consideration, however the size of the fine does not of itself deprive the offence from the penal area. If the questionable offence is criminal under these criteria, cases for these violations should equally be considered as penal. ('Teismų praktika' Nr. 21, l. 300-301 [Lithuanian Supreme Court bulletin], Decision of the Supreme Court in Penal case No. 2K-322/2003 of 29 April 2003).

The Supreme Administrative court has consistently noted that the rules of the Convention are of an abstract nature and in order to understand their meaning the courts need to take into consideration the case law of the European Court of Human Rights. (decision in case No. A3 -750-04 of 9 November 2004).

Having discussed the practice of ECtHR on the principle of *non bis in idem*, the Court considered whether the scope and nature of the two rules invoked against the appellant were similar within the meaning of the European Convention on Human Rights. It concluded that they were and further found that the appellant was charged for violating each of those provisions on the basis of the same facts. The Court further noted that the criminal investigation in Tomkus' case was halted due to lack of evidence that by publishing the series of articles Tomkus intended and wanted to defile Jews and gays, and to incite hatred and discrimination against these groups. The formal basis to cease criminal investigation was lack of evidence supporting Tomkus' guilt. The Court then proceeded:

> "In the administrative case at hand V. Tomkus is criminally prosecuted (within the meaning of the Convention) for the same acts, on the basis of identical charges, and legal qualification of his acts is essentially identical. A number of circumstances subject to establishing in the case at hand have already been established in the criminal investigation which has been ceased. In light of these circumstances the Court concludes that the decision of the prosecutor to cease criminal investigation against V. Tomkus also precludes administrative proceedings against him in this case. The decision of the public prosecutor to cease criminal investigation against V. Tomkus has not been declared invalid, therefore by punishing the applicant [District Administrative] the Court violated Article 4 of Protocol No.7 of the European Convention on Human Rights and Fundamental Freedoms which enshrines a right not be tried or punished twice for an offence for which he has already been convicted or acquitted in accordance with the law and penal procedure of a relevant State.
>
> Therefore the decision of the [District Administrative] Court is held invalid and the administrative prosecution is terminated as it violates Article 4 of the Protocol No. 7 of the European Convention on Human Rights and Fundamental Freedoms."[8]

Part Four: II. A. Relationship between International Law and Internal Law – Application and implementation of international law in internal law – Treaties

(see also *6/1*)

3/4

With its decision of 25 May 2005 in *Svenska Petroleum* v. *Geonafta and the Government of the Republic of Lithuania* (Case No. 3K-7-268/2005) the expanded chamber of the Supreme Court continued a contradictory trend which was started in *Parekss banka* case of 16 December 2004 (see *Parekss banka* v. *Parex Lizingas*, Case no. 3K-7-552/2004). Pursuant to it, a case on the enforcement of the arbitral award may be suspended until a separate case concerning the validity of an arbitration clause is pending. The reasoning behind the decision is related to interpretation of the 1958 New York Convention on Recognition and Enforcement of Foreign Arbitral Awards, however, it is open to argument whether this interpretation is in line with the object and purpose of the Convention. The relevant paragraphs of the decision read:

---

[8] Editor's translation. The full judgment is available at <www.lvat.lt> in Lithuanian.

"The expanded chamber of the Supreme Court Division of civil cases on 16 December 2004 in a civil case AS "Parekss banka" . . . formulated a rule of interpretation and application of procedural law, pursuant to which the general grounds and rules for suspension of cases governed by Articles 163 and 164 of the Code of Civil Procedure [hereinafter: CCP] must be applied also when the requests for recognition and enforcement of the arbitral award in Lithuania is considered, because the procedure of enforcement is governed by the rules of the CCP, as far as it is not governed by the rules of the 1958 New York Convention (Article 163 1(3) CCP). Therefore the proceedings may be suspended on the basis of Article 163 1(3) CCP if it is not possible to determine the relevant circumstances that might decide prejudicial issues in a case under consideration. Consequently, before a case on validity of a contract, which contains an arbitration clause is decided, it is not possible to conclude whether a request on recognition and enforcement of an arbitral award would be contrary to public policy and it is not possible to consider whether an arbitration clause was validly concluded.

[...]

The expanded chamber of justices considers that the circumstances determined in the civil case on validity of the Articles of Association and on the validity of an arbitration clause contained therein will have prejudicial force for the question on whether the arbitration award is enforceable. Furthermore, the Court may pronounce on whether an arbitration clause which includes contradictory provisions corresponds to the Lithuanian law and whether it is compatible with public policy. The Court does not agree that the latter issue may be decided only by the Court of Appeals when it considers a question of recognition and enforcement of an arbitral award. This argument raised by Svenska Petroleum Exploration AB narrows down the possibilities of judicial protection when an agreement contains an arbitration clause. Following the logic of this statement, even if the Articles of Association or its part containing an arbitration clause were found to be invalid, the Court of Appeals would need to decide the question on public policy de novo. This would deny the prejudicial force of a court's judgment, and this would contradict the principles of Civil Procedure."[9]

[9] Editor's translation. Full judgment is available at <www.lat.lt> in Lithuanian.

Part Five: II. B. 1. Subjects of International Law – International organisations – Particular types – Universal organisations

5/1

On 16 September 2005 the President Valdas Adamkus addressed the United Nations High Level Meeting on Implementation of the Millennium Goals. The excerpts of the address are reproduced here.

> "The world has changed significantly since the foundation of the United Nations. Our organization must change accordingly, in order to be able to fully and effectively respond to the expectations of our nations. I therefore believe that the implementation of the Millennium Declaration and a comprehensive reform of the organisation must go hand in hand.
>
> Courage to change must be an essential attribute of this summit. Courage to embrace a UN reform that reaffirms and locks in the intrinsic link between development, security, and human rights. Courage to implement to the fullest the purpose of the United Nations 'to be a centre for harmonizing the actions of nations in the attainment of common ends'.
>
> [...]
>
> The United Nations, created to deal with the legacy of World War Two, must now stand up to these new threats and challenges. To be able do so, a comprehensive reform of the United Nations is necessary, including a major management overhaul ensuring greater accountability, transparency, efficiency, and professionalism.
>
> Also, we can no longer delay the reform of the Security Council, an essential body which should be fully equipped and enjoy requisite legitimacy to operate in a world of increasingly challenging tasks. Lithuania has consistently maintained that the Security Council should be expanded in both categories of membership, with the inclusion of new major international actors as permanent members.
>
> [...]
>
> It is essential that we reaffirm our previous commitments. But we must go much further. We must build a United Nations for the twenty-first century. Insisting on status quo of this most inclusive multilateral organization will not protect us from the horrors of poverty, extremism, weapons of mass

destruction getting into the hands of terrorists, or the ever more threatening effects of environmental degradation."[10]

Part Six: VIII. B. The Individual (including the Corporation) in International Law – Human rights and fundamental freedoms – Under United Nations treaty system

6/1

On 22 February 2005 the Supreme Court of Lithuania delivered a judgment in a criminal case against two persons indicted with genocide of Lithuanian guerrilla fighters committed in the aftermath of World War II. The legal basis for conviction was Article 99 of Lithuanian Penal Code which includes a wider definition of genocide than that provided by the 1948 Genocide Convention.

As concerns the argument that it is erroneous to apply a broader definition of genocide under Lithuanian Penal Code because it contradicts international law, the Supreme Court replied:

> "It is correct that Article 99 of the Penal Code includes a wider definition of genocide than Article 2 of the [Genocide] Convention. Article 99 defines as genocide any act which is performed with a purpose to physically destroy a group or members of a group of a social or political character. Pursuant to Article 2 of the Convention these groups are not covered by the definition of genocide.
>
> By becoming a party to the Convention, Lithuania undertook to ensure its application in its jurisdiction. Therefore by acceding to the Convention, Lithuania undertook to punish any act by which it is intended to kill, destroy or exterminate groups or members of a group on a national, ethnic, racial or religious basis or a failure to take measures to prevent such acts. Accession to a convention does not preclude a State from defining the crimes itself and to prohibit them. Furthermore, Article 5 of the Convention establishes that the Contracting Parties, each acting on the basis of their constitutions, undertakes to adopt the legislation necessary for the entry into force of the Convention and to provide for effective penalties for the acts of genocide and other acts defined by Article 3. This provision was enforced in Lithuania on 9 April 1992, by adoption of law no. I-2477 on responsibility for genocide of Lithuanian residents. This act

[10] Full text available at <www.president.lt/en/news.full/5944> ; site last accessed on 27 July 2006.

served as a basis of accession of Lithuania to the Convention. Article 1 of this law defines genocide, and this definition is in line with Article 2 of the Convention. Under Article 2 of the same act the Supreme Council of Lithuania established that the acts of killing or torturing of Lithuanian people, deportation of its residents during the period of German or USSR occupation and annexation corresponds to the definition of Genocide under international law. On 21 April 1998 the Criminal Code of Lithuania was supplemented with Articles 62^1, 71 and 8^1, 24, 25, 26, 35, 49, 54^1, 89, and the definition of genocide encompassed activities which were intended to physically destroy a group or members of a group on social or political grounds. This definition of genocide was maintained in Article 99 of the Penal Code [of 2003]. It is apparent that by supplementing the definition of genocide with acts which are intended to physically destroy or exterminate a group or members of a group on social or political grounds the legislator sought to enforce Article 2 of the law of 9 April 1992 on responsibility for genocide of Lithuanian residents. Therefore there is no basis to dispute the correctness of interpretation of the definition of genocide as applied by the courts." (Editor's translation)

6/2

On 28 February 2005 the Supreme Court considered a question on the criteria for the determination of the amount of money to be paid by a parent for child caree. Regarding this, the Court stated:

"The duty of parents to take care of a child, to bring him up and to support him is derived from their natural duty to be responsible for the well-being of a child until he attains majority. Lithuania has ratified the UN Convention on the Rights of the Child which enshrines a universally recognized principle that every child has a right to the standard of living adequate for his physical, mental, spiritual, moral and social development and that the parents' primary responsibility is to secure, within their abilities and financial capacity, the conditions of living necessary for the child's development (Article 27(1) and 27(2)). Similarly under Article 3.192(2) of the Civil Code the amount of money for child care must be proportional to the needs of the child and the financial capacity of his parents. It needs to ensure the standard of living adequate for the child's development. This principle of proportionality between the needs of the child and the financial capacity of his parents means that the amount required for the care of the child is directly dependent on his parents' financial capacity. Also, for the purposes of determining the amount of money required for care of the child the principle of the primary interest to protect and ensure the rights of the child needs to be taken into consideration (Article 23.3(1) of the Civil Code). Essentially this means that the court needs to primarily take into consideration the interests of the child when determining the amount due for child care. The principle serves as an underlying reason for the developing approach of the courts that in order to ensure the development of the child the form and amount of maintenance cannot be limited to satisfaction of the minimal (physiological) needs. [...] consequently, if the financial capacity of the parents objectively permits granting an adequate amount of money for maintenance necessary for the development of the child, this amount must be granted. It is a consistent practice of the courts that any doubts on the size of the amount for maintenance must be decided in the interests of the child." (Supreme Court Case No. 3K-3-286/2004 of 19 April 2004).[11]

Part Six: VIII. C. The Individual (including the Corporation) in International Law – Human rights and fundamental freedoms – Under Council of Europe treaty system

6/3

On 7 July 2005 the European Court of Human Rights delivered its judgment in the *Karalevičius* v. *Lithuania* case (Appl. No. *53254/99*, 7.4.2005) finding a violation of Articles 3, 5 and 8. The factual circumstances of the case are similar to the earlier *Valašinas* (with respect to Articles 3 and 8, Appl. no. 44558/98, 24.7.2001), *Jėčius* (Article 5) and *Puzinas* (Article 8, *Appl. no.* 44800/98, 14.03.2002) cases.

The applicant complained that the living space in the Šiauliai Remand prison were unsatisfactory due to their small size (1.5 square metres per prisoner); they also lacked adequate ventilation and had a strong smell due to the inmates' smoking and toilet use. Furthermore, the cells were humid and cold, and the inmates were permitted to stroll outside only for one hour per day. The applicant had shower access only once in 15 days. He was kept in these conditions for more than three years (from 2 January 1997 until 22 September 1999 and from 28 September 1999 until 6 March 2000).

The Court found that this treatment of the prisoner amounted to a violation of an obligation to ensure freedom from inhuman or degrading treatment. The living conditions in question were similar to those complained of by Valašinas, where the Court on the contrary held that they did not amount to inhuman or degrading treatment. The Court distinguished the case at hand

---

[11] Editor's translation. Full text is available in Lithuanian <at www.lat.lt>.

from the *Valašinas* case because in the latter case freedom of movement of prisoners was not restricted during the daytime.

The Court also found a violation of Article 8. The applicant complained of his treatment on the basis of the applicable Detention on Remand Act 1996 and the Remand Prisons Internal Rules 1996, pursuant to which his letters were subject to censorship.

According to Rule 75 of the Remand Prisons Internal Rules, the remand centre administration could not open letters of detainees addressed to the European Court of Human Rights if those letters were given to the administration to be sent in a closed envelope.

Pursuant to Rule 83 the remand prison administration was under an obligation to familiarise the detainee with a reply to his correspondence within three days following receipt of the letter addressed to the detainee. As a consequence, all letters received by the detainees would not be given to them and would be kept in their files by the remand centre administration. The Court found that this constituted violation of Article 8 of the Convention.

Finally, the Court found a violation of Article 5, since the national courts sanctioned the applicant's detention without specifying the period of his detention.

The relevant paragraphs of the judgment read:

> "36. The Court observes that the applicant spent more than three years and one month in the Šiauliai Remand Prison, which according to the Government was overcrowded by more than 100 percent from the point of view of the relevant domestic requirements (see §§ 23 and 30 above). For most of that time the applicant was afforded less than 2 square metres of space, of which more than one year and a half was spent by the applicant being restricted to 1.51 m^2 of space, in a cell of 16.65 m^2 together with 10 other inmates (see § 23 above). The Government have not contested the applicant's statement that the possibility to have a stroll or outside exercise was limited to one hour per day. The Court considers it established that the applicant was thus confined to his cell for 23 hours daily. In these circumstances, the extreme lack of space weighs heavily as an aspect to be taken into account for the purpose of establishing whether the impugned detention conditions were 'degrading' from the point of view of Article 3. By contrast, in the *Valašinas* case cited above, no violation of Article 3

was found in view *inter alia* of the fact that the somewhat restricted space in the sleeping facilities was counterbalanced in the Court's assessment by the unlimited freedom of movement enjoyed by the detainees during the day (*loc. cit.*, §§ 103 and 107).

[...]

39. Hence, as in those cases, the Court considers the extreme lack of space as a central factor in its analysis of compliance of the applicant's detention conditions with Article 3. The fact of the applicant being obliged to live, sleep and use the toilet in the same cell with so many other inmates was itself sufficient to cause distress or hardship of an intensity exceeding the unavoidable level of suffering inherent in detention, and arouse in the applicant the feelings of fear, anguish and inferiority capable of humiliating and debasing him (see above; also see, *mutatis mutandis*, the aforementioned *Peers* and *Kalashnikov* cases (*ibid.*); *Kudla v. Poland* [GC], no. 30210/96, § 92, ECHR 2000-XI).

40. Finally, while in the present case it cannot be established in principle that the ventilation, heating, lighting or sanitary facilities in the Šiauliai Remand Prison were unacceptable from the point of view of Article 3, the Court none the less notes the Government's admission that no toilet paper was given to the inmates during the whole of the applicant's stay there, that until the renovation of 1999–2000 the possibility to use the bath had been restricted to less than one time a week, and that until 2000 no adequate facilities had existed for laundry of the inmates' belongings and bedding (see §§ 23 and 31 above). These factors, while not as such capable of justifying the notion of 'degrading' treatment, are none the less relevant in addition to the focal factor of the severe overcrowding, to show that the impugned detention conditions of the applicant went beyond the threshold permitted by Article 3 of the Convention.

Regarding the violation of Article 8 of ECHR:

59. The Court notes that the Government did not deny that all of the applicant's correspondence with the Convention organs had been opened up and read in his absence by the prison administration. They only submitted that the applicant could have been himself responsible for the censorship of part of that correspondence, namely his letters to Strasbourg which he had not given to the prison administration in a sealed envelope.

60. The Court further notes the parties' argument as to whether the censorship had been permitted by the domestic law applicable at the material time. However, the Court does not consider it necessary to answer this question because, even assuming that the censorship had a basis in

domestic law and that it pursued the legitimate aim of prevention of crime, the measures of control of the applicant's correspondence with the Convention organs were not 'necessary in a democratic society', the Government having presented no valid reason to justify the interference (see, *mutatis mutandis*, *Valašinas* cited above, §§ 128–130). The Court only emphasises in this respect that the fact of the applicant not having given some of his letters in a sealed envelope is not as such sufficient to justify the censorship of the letters by the prison administration. Nor has there been any justification for the control of the letters addressed to the applicant by the Court."

6/4

The issue of censorship of correspondence of prisoners was also addressed in *Jankauskas v. Lithuania* (Appl. No. *59304/00*, 24 February 2005). The applicant was convicted for abuse of office and bribery and sentenced for eight years of imprisonment. He complained that throughout the period of two years (beginning with March 1999 through July 2001) of his detention at Šiauliai detention centre his letters to NGOs, European Court of Human Rights, his family, friends and legal counsel (in total – 362 letters) were opened up and read in his absence and that this constituted a violation of his right to privacy. The relevant excerpt from the judgment is (footnotes omitted):

"20. The Court notes that the Government do not contest the substance of the applicant's allegation that all his letters had been subject to censorship by the remand prison administration. Indeed, and in view of the domestic statutes as well as the factual evidence submitted by the applicant . . . the Court considers it established that a substantial number of the letters written by the applicant as well as an equally important number of the letters received by the applicant were opened up and read in his absence, to be later put and classified in his prison file. There was, therefore, an interference with the applicant's right to respect for his correspondence under Article 8 of the Convention, which can only be justified if the conditions of the second paragraph of the provision are met. In particular, such interference must be 'in accordance with the law', pursue a legitimate aim and be necessary in a democratic society in order to achieve that aim . . .

21. The interference in the present case had a legal basis, namely the provisions of Article 15 of the Detention on Remand Act and Rule 72 of the Remand Prisons Internal Rules, and the Court is satisfied that it pursued the legitimate aim of 'the prevention of disorder or crime'. However, as regards the necessity of the interference, the Government have

> not explained why the control of all the applicant's letters addressed to and coming from the outside world was indispensable. The reason put forward in this respect by the Government – namely the fear of the applicant's absconding or influencing trial . . . – may have been relevant for the purpose of justifying his remand in custody or even giving basis for a certain form of interference with part of his correspondence, such as, for example, checking of some correspondence of non-legal nature or his correspondence with certain persons of dangerous character . . .
>
> 22. However, this fear alone could not be sufficient to grant the remand prison administration an open licence for indiscriminate, routine checking of all of the applicant's correspondence. This is particularly so in connection with the censorship of the applicant's letters addressed to and coming from his legal counsel, the confidentiality of which must be respected – save for reasonable cause (see, the *Campbell v. the United Kingdom* judgment of 25 March 1992, Series A no. 233, pp. 16-21, §§ 32–54). The Court also does not find any reason to justify the censorship by the prison administration of the applicant's letters to the State authorities whereby he may have complained about his detention conditions, or may have made other submissions unrelated to the criminal case against him. All in all, the Government have not presented sufficient reasons to show that such a total control of the applicant's correspondence with the outside world was 'necessary in a democratic society'."

6/5

On 7 April 2005 the European Court of Human Rights adopted a judgment in the *Rainys and Gasparavičius* v. *Lithuania* case (*Appl. Nos. 70665/01 and 74345/01*). The case concerned a law on the Evaluation of the USSR State Security Committee (NKVD, NKGB, MGB, KGB) and the Present Activities of Former Permanent Employees of the Organisation. The facts of the case are very similar to those of *Sidabras and Džiautas* (appl. nos. 55480/00 and 59330/00), decided in 2004, where the Court found a violation of Article 14 of the Convention, in conjunction with Article 8, to the extent that the Act precluded those applicants from employment in the private sector on the basis of their former 'KGB officers' status under the Act. The Rainys and Gasparavičius complaints were wider, because the applicants were actually dismissed from existing employment in the private sector, as opposed to an earlier case, which concerned the hypothetical inability to apply for certain private sector jobs until 2009. The Court adopted a similar reasoning and found a violation of Article 14, taken in conjunction with Article 8 of the Convention.

6/6

On 7 April 2005 the Court found in *Užkurėlienė and others* v. *Lithuania* (appl. *no. 62988/00*) that Lithuania was not in breach of Article 6 or the right to property protection. The facts of the case raised an issue of delay in establishing restitution of rights to property nationalized by the Soviet authorities in the 1940s, and was similar to the earlier decided *Jasiūnienė* v. *Lithuania* case (Appl. No. 41510/98, 6.3.2003). The applicants in essence complained of a failure to execute a judgment of the Supreme Court of Lithuania adopted in their case which demanded that a decision be made "to restore the [applicants'] property rights to the land which belonged to [their father] prior to the nationalisation" (para 18) and in which the Court found that although the applicants could not have a certain part of land returned to them, the applicants were entitled to compensation for the impugned portion of land in accordance with the provisions of the Property Restitution Act. Since it took the authorities more than two years to adopt the necessary decisions executing this judgment, the applicants asked the Court to find that Lithuanian executive authorities had failed to return the whole of the original land in kind or offer adequate compensation in due time. The Court agreed that the execution of a judgment must be regarded as an integral part of the "trial" for the purposes of Article 6 of the Convention and noted that delay may be justified in particular circumstances, but that delay may not be such as to impair the essence of the right protected under Article 6 (para. 31). Nevertheless, the applicant lost on the facts, since in the view of the Court the period of two years after the court's judgment until the final offer of compensation "was regrettable" (para. 36), but was not comparable with the facts in the *Jasiūnienė* case where the period approximated 8 years. In light of this, the Court found:

> "In view of the above considerations, and in particular on account of the lack of activity established on the part of the applicants themselves, the Court considers that the delays in the execution of the judgment of 22 May 2000 were not such as to infringe upon the essence of the applicants' right to a court guaranteed by Article 6 of the Convention." (para. 36)

The Court accordingly also dismissed a claim concerning a violation of Article 1 of the Protocol 1 of the Convention.

Part Six: VIII. D. The Individual (including the Corporation) in International Law – Human rights and fundamental freedoms – Other aspects of human rights and fundamental freedoms

6/7

On 24 November 2005 the *Seimas* adopted a statement commemorating the victims of political repression and starvation in Ukraine from 1932 to 1933, which reads in part as follows:

> "The Seimas of the Republic of Lithuania,
>
> [...]
>
> **condemning** war crimes, genocide and crimes against humanity,
>
> **notes** that the Ukrainian famine/genocide, which had been planned and executed by the totalitarian communist regime under Stalin to crush the resistance of the Ukrainian people to the Soviet collectivisation of agriculture and to destroy the cultural and ethnic singularity of the Ukrainian people, caused the deaths of over seven million Ukrainians in 1932–1933. One fifth of the Ukrainian population perished as a result of this deliberate atrocity. During the famine/genocide organised and executed by the Communists in 1932–1933, approximately 25 thousand people died daily in Ukraine, while the Soviet authorities exported approximately 1.7 million tons of grain from the country to the West. It must be noted that the Soviet Union had for decades covered up and denied the atrocities planned and executed in Ukraine in 1932–1933 by the totalitarian communist regime under Stalin;
>
> [...]
>
> **recognises** that in 1932–1933, the totalitarian communist regime under Stalin carried out a deliberate and carefully planned genocide of the Ukrainian people [...]."

The full text of the resolution is available in Lithuanian, English and Russian at www.lrs.lt.

6/8

On 15 December 2005 the *Seimas* of the Republic of Lithuania issued a resolution recognizing the genocide of the Armenian people. The resolution reads as follows:

> "The Seimas of the Republic of Lithuania,
>
> Commemorating the 90th anniversary of the genocide of the Armenian people,
>
> Denouncing genocide committed in 1915 by the Turkish Ottoman empire,
>
> Encourages the Republic of Turkey to recognize this historical fact."[12]

Part Nine: I. B. State Territory – Territory – Good neighbourliness

9/1

On 31 August Lithuanian Ambassador to Belarus Mr. Petras Vaitiekūnas met Leonyi Horuzhek, a Minister of Natural Resources and Environment, and informed him of Lithuania's plans to construct a storage site for radioactive waste. Belarus was informed that a study was undertaken to list alternatives concerning the storage site and that the public would be informed of the results of the study.

The project of radioactive waste storage was discussed by the Minister of Foreign Affairs Mr. Antanas Valionis with his Latvian counterpart Mr. Artis Pabriks. Valionis ascertained that the project will be open for public discussion, furthermore, constant scientific research on environmental impact will be undertaken and the public will be informed of the results.

9/2

On 29 September 2005 the Seimas adopted a resolution on the Continuity of Nuclear Energy and Updating of the National Energy Strategy. The resolution reads, in part, as follows:

> "The Seimas of the Republic of Lithuania, States:
>
> […]

---

[12] Editor's translation. Full text is available at <www.lrs.lt> in Lithuanian.

2) although certain EU Member States have announced a nuclear energy moratorium, the requirements of the Kyoto Protocol and the prices of oil and gas, as well as the problems of reliability of supply call for a revision of the earlier adopted decisions;

3) the necessity to address the problems of environmental protection and reliability of energy supply creates favourable preconditions for the development of nuclear energy. Therefore, the European Union is expected to make a positive revision of the nuclear energy prospects;

declares:

1) recognising the necessity of primary energy resources, including nuclear energy, the Seimas of the Republic of Lithuania will seek that Lithuania remain a nuclear power state and continue generating electricity in a nuclear power plant which meets all modern requirements;

2) the Seimas of the Republic of Lithuania will support, legally and politically, investment into construction of a new reactor;"[13]

Part Eleven: XIII. Seas and Vessels – Protection of the marine environment

11/1

The Standing Committee of the Council of Europe Parliamentary Assembly meeting on 1 September in Monaco unanimously and without amendments adopted a resolution No. 1461 on the Curonian Spit, oil and environment. The oil rig D-6 is located in the Baltic sea near the UNESCO protected Curonian Spit. The oil rig is utilized by the Russian oil company "Lukoil". The resolution reads, in part, as follows:

"5. The Assembly has noted the good operating conditions of the oil rig off the Curonian Spit, its modern technology, its skilled staff and its environment protection and accident prevention measures. It has, however, also noted the increased risk represented by its proximity to the highly vulnerable coasts of the Curonian Spit, the need to reinforce the material and human resources to respond to any accident affecting the coast and the lack of co-ordination of both countries' accident response services, as well as the unresolved issue of compensation in the event of an accident.

6. Should an accident occur, it recommends application of the "polluter pays" principle on the basis of a bilateral agreement on the payment and

---

[13] The resolution is available at <www.lrs.lt> in Lithuanian and English.

reimbursement of the clean-up costs incurred and of lost earnings, if applicable within the framework of a general agreement on protection of the Baltic Sea environment and on liability in the event of an accident. It also notes the importance of the transparency of information, the role of the media, the provision of information to the public and the training of the staff concerned.

7. The Assembly welcomes the progress noted in co-operation between Russia and Lithuania on the protection of the Curonian Spit natural site and particularly the agreement concluded on the conduct of an environmental impact assessment of oil exploitation and exploration in the Baltic Sea which has enabled UNESCO to refrain from including the Curonian Spit on its List of World Heritage in Danger.

8. Consequently, the Assembly recommends that Baltic member states develop their co-operation on environmental matters with a view to protecting the Baltic Sea and its coasts both through transfrontier initiatives and through regional co-operation, inter alia in the framework of the Helsinki Convention and the Council of the Baltic Sea States.

9. In this respect, the Assembly wishes particularly to emphasise the importance that must be attached to the prevention of accidents and ecological disasters, particularly those involving hydrocarbon pollution through:

9.1. the exercise of particular vigilance by the supervisory authorities and local authorities as to the proper operation of oil installations, their regular inspection, the strict application of the regulations and the provision of information to the public about any failure with the potential to jeopardise health or the environment;

9.2. the provision, by the responsible authorities and also by the media, of full and transparent information to the public about the dangers of oil exploitation, the risks of pollution and the way to behave in the event of an accident, especially in the most exposed areas;

9.3. ongoing training for the staff involved both in the extraction, transport and refining of oil and in the emergency accident response services;

9.4. the adoption of response protocols appropriate to emergency situations resulting from oil pollution, giving the responsible local authorities broad scope for action;

9.5. the permanent availability of adequate human and material resources for immediate and co-ordinated action in the event of an emergency;

9.6. transfrontier co-operation agreements on emergency action, providing for the necessary resources and specifying the procedures for intervention and the authorities responsible in the event of an accident.

10. With more particular reference to the Curonian Spit, the Assembly calls on Lithuania and Russia to continue their co-operation so as to reach an intergovernmental agreement on the fight against pollution of the Baltic Sea by hydrocarbons or other dangerous substances and, in particular, on the question of the evaluation of any environmental damage and the compensation for any oil spill affecting the coast, also taking account, if applicable, of the liability of the oil company exploiting oil field D-6, in accordance with the international regulations in force.

11. To this end, the Assembly invites member states, particularly Lithuania and Russia, to sign and/or ratify:

11.1. the International Convention on Liability and Compensation for Damage in Connection with the Carriage of Hazardous and Noxious Substances by Sea (HNS);

11.2. the Council of Europe Convention on Civil Liability for Damage resulting from Activities Dangerous to the Environment (CETS No. 150);

11.3. the Council of Europe Convention on the Protection of Environment through Criminal Law (CETS No. 172).

12. The Assembly particularly invites the Council of the Baltic Sea States and the riparian member states to:

12.1. consider a moratorium on the exploitation of new oil fields or new oil drilling rigs in the Baltic Sea;

12.2. develop a system of oil pipelines enabling movements of hydrocarbons across the Baltic Sea by ship to be restricted;

12.3. consider setting up a guarantee fund for the Baltic Sea to cover the expenses connected with accidental hydrocarbon pollution, into which payments could be made by the riparian states, the oil companies concerned and companies shipping hydrocarbons."

Part Twelve: I. B. Air Space, Outer Space, and Antarctica – Air space – Uses

12/1

On 15 September 2005 a Russian warplane breached Lithuanian airspace and crashed on the territory of Lithuania. On 13 October 2005 reacting to the incident the *Seimas* adopted a resolution, which reads, in part:

> "Noting that Russian Federation does not ensure safe navigation of its armed warplanes and that the closeness of these flights to the airspace of Lithuania and other EU and NATO allies poses a threat,
>
> Expressing its support for demilitarization of the Kaliningrad region,
>
> Emphasising the exceptional importance of the NATO air police mission,
>
> Seeking to avoid similar incidents in the future,
>
> Suggests that the Government of the Republic of Lithuania:
>
> Seeks to strengthen the NATO air police mission over the Baltic states and that it become permanent;
>
> [...]
>
> To improve and strengthen the national and regional airspace system of monitoring, control and management and to provide the necessary funds."[14]

Part Thirteen: IV. A. International Responsibility – Consequences of responsibility – Reparation

(see also *6/7* above)

13/1

On 14 April 2005 the *Seimas* of the Republic of Lithuania issued a resolution commemorating the Katyn massacre. The relevant parts of the resolution read as follows:

> "The Seimas of the Republic of Lithuania,

[14] Editor's translation. Available in Lithuanian and Russian at <www.lrs.lt>.

Expressing condolence and solidarity with the Polish people, commemorating the 65th anniversary of the Katyn massacre,

Expressing support for the decision of Seimas of the Polish Republic of 22 March 2005 and its demand that the surnames of all persons who massacred more than 20 000 Polish prisoners of war in Katyn and other places are made public, and that Polish law enforcement authorities be granted access to the material of the case collected in Russia,

Protesting the decision of Russian Federation General Prosecutor's Office to discharge the investigation of this crime and its qualification as a civil crime subject to a statute of limitations and failure to disclose the burial location of a significant number of those massacred,

Emphasising that the Katyn massacre was a continuation of the Molotov-Ribbentrop pact,

Encourages the Government of the Republic of Lithuania,

Requests disclosure of the list of polish officers who were massacred in Katyn and other USSR locations in April and May 1940 in order to ascertain whether there were Lithuanian nationals among them or relatives of current Lithuanian nationals,

Invites Lithuanian nationals, who could provide evidence of this massacre, to assist Lithuanian law enforcement authorities or the Institute of Commemoration of the Polish People, which decided to initiate an independent investigation of the case."[15]

13/2

On 30 June 2005 the *Seimas* adopted a resolution "On the Commemoration of the 65th Anniversary of the Soviet Occupation of Lithuania and the First Mass Deportation of the Residents of Lithuania". The resolution reads, in part, as follows:

> "*[E]xpressing* great concern over and disapproval of the attempts made by the officials of the Russian Federation to justify or even deny the fact of Soviet occupation acknowledged in the Treaty on the Foundations of Inter-State Relations between the Republic of Lithuania and the Russian Soviet Federal Socialist Republic, which was signed on 29 July 1991 and came into effect on 4 May 1992;

[15] Official translation. Full text available in Lithuanian and English at <www.lrs.lt>.

welcoming the resolutions of the European Parliament, the Congress of the United States of America and the Parliamentary Assembly of the Council of Europe, which condemn fascism and communism as well as the occupation of the Baltic States;

[...]

acknowledging that even today, after fifteen years of the functioning of the Independent State of Lithuania, a part of former deportees and political prisoners feel themselves socially insecure and there are those to whom the immovable property seized by the occupation government has not been returned yet;

[...]

underlining the importance of preserving and honouring the horrifying historical experience because reconciliation is impossible if historical truth and the memory of innocent victims are denied,

invites the Russian Federation to declassify, at least now, 65 years after the occupation, the burial places of the leader of Lithuanian partisans Jonas Žemaitis-Vytautas and other resistance fighters as well as those of public figures of Independent Lithuania and to transfer their remains to Lithuania;

expects that the Russian Federation will return the KGB and other archives as well as cultural property removed from Lithuania and will co-operate in providing legal information in the criminal cases of the occupation period;

proposes that, by 2009, i.e. the celebration of the millennium of the mention of the name of Lithuania, the Government of the Republic of Lithuania and the Vilnius City Council erect in Vilnius, Lukiškių Square, a monument to Lithuanian fighters for the freedom and independence of Lithuania and build a Memorial to the Nation's Struggle for Freedom and Suffered Losses in the complex of the former KGB buildings."[16]

---

[16] Official translation. Available in Lithuanian, Russian and English at <www.lrs.lt>.

Part Fourteen: II. H. 2. Peaceful Settlement of Disputes – Means of settlement – Settlement within international organisations – Organisations other than the United Nations

14/1

On 25 May 2005 the Minister of Foreign Affairs Mr. A.Valionis addressed the Euro Atlantic Partnership Council.

> "Good neighbourly relations, political dialogue, and, most important, an ability to seek compromise – those are a few of the most important criteria for success, which helped us to integrate with NATO. I strongly believe that the measures like enforcement of the Membership action plan and the development of the process of Vilnius 10 were the most efficient means to ensure peace and stability on our continent. A recent GUAM summit meeting is a similar example of exemplary regional cooperation. I am certain that the cooperation will not cease and that NATO and the EU will continue to encourage it. Closer cooperation provides better opportunities to solve regional conflicts which at first glance seem to be insolvable."[17]

[17] Editor's translation. Full text in Lithuanian is available at <www.urm.lt/index.php?-519572490>.

Book Reviews

S. Chesterman, *Just War or Just Peace? Humanitarian Intervention and International Law*, Oxford University Press, Oxford, 2001. ISBN13: 978-0-19-925799-7, ISBN10: 0-19-925799-X, 295 pages, price: USD 35.

The topic of the legality of humanitarian intervention is perhaps as old as the issue of the prohibition of the use of force in international relations itself. Thus it is not to be described as novel or lacking the attention of scholars. Despite the amount of ink spilled on this area it will remain true for decades if not centuries to come that consensus of States on it is highly unlikely. And still, in light of the changing State practice the controversies concerning the obligation to protect human rights on the one hand and the prohibition of the use of force on the other are looming.

In "Just War or Just Peace?" Dr. Chesterman analyses whether a so-called right of humanitarian intervention is a part of customary international law. Having described it as a question which "at first blush is a simple one" (in light of the presence of Article 2(4) in the UN Charter), the purpose of the book is later identified as "to use humanitarian intervention to reflect on the manner in which international law deals with a 'hard case'" (p. 6). Indeed, the author is not particularly interested in the question of whether there is or is not a right of humanitarian intervention in customary international law as in the implications of its presence on the world order and international morality (p. 6). His main concern, as he has put it, is to deliver a message that "incorporating a 'right' of intervention would lead to more such interventions being undertaken in bad faith, it would be incoherent as a principle, and it would be inimical to the emergence of an international rule of law" (p. 6).

The book is divided into six chapters, the final one also serving as a conclusion. In the first chapter, the author discusses the origins of humanitarian intervention. Despite the interest that this issue provokes of its own, the reason behind introduction of this chapter is a need to address the arguments that the right of humanitarian intervention pre-existed the Charter. In this chapter scholarly writings are discussed, including the writings of Hugo Grotius, Gentili, Christian Wolff and Hegel, followed by coverage of instances of State practice relating to humanitarian intervention until the adoption of the UN Charter.

The second chapter discusses the relationship between arguments for a right to humanitarian intervention and the law of the Charter. This chapter raises particular interest by its very scope since Article 2(4) of the Charter continues to be the central category of disagreement concerning the legality of humanitarian intervention between the pluralists, realists and solidarists.

The analysis then continues with the issue of the customary status of humanitarian intervention. A part of this chapter is dedicated to an analysis of legal arguments supporting the right of humanitarian intervention introduced by Richard

Baltic Yearbook of International Law, Volume 6, 2006, pp. 479–481.

Lillich, Fernando Teson and Michael Reisman. As might be expected, the author dismisses them all as lacking credibility and it takes him only some five pages. He then proceeds to the issue whether a right of humanitarian intervention might be considered to be as a newly developed norm. This part is then followed by a factual description and evaluation of selective State practice where humanitarian motives seem to be relevant, and, finally, a less than one page conclusion: support of States to a right of humanitarian intervention is not likely, thus "it will remain at most in a legal penumbra – sometimes given legitimacy by the Security Council, sometimes merely tolerated by states" (p. 87).

The book includes a whole separate third chapter on the question of intervention to promote democracy where US interventions in Panama and Grenada are discussed.

Chapters four and five cover the topic of the role of Security Council in sanctioning the use of force. Chapter four covers the changing meaning of the concept of 'threat to international peace and security' in the practice of Security Council. Here two trends are identified– the first being 'arbitrariness' in the use of force, the second – lack of coherence in the Security Council mandate (pp. 161–162). The main idea of this chapter is reflected by the statement "by blurring the boundaries of the exception to the prohibition of the use of force established by Chapter VII [the trends of State practice in the period 1990–9] threaten to undermine this cardinal legal principle of the international legal order" (p. 112). A similar idea in the context of enforcement actions is delivered in Chapter five. Perhaps the climax of chapter five is a discussion of the circumstances of the imposition of the no-fly zones in Northern and Southern Iraq as well as the NATO operation in Kosovo.

The book ends with a general conclusion that unilateral decisions to use force in the name of morality is a recipe for bad policy, bad law and a bad international order.

The book should be an interesting read to anybody who wants to learn about current scholarly approaches to humanitarian intervention. The fact that this book has won a certificate of merit from the American Society of International Law speaks for itself. It may be described as defending the views of realist and pluralist schools of international relations, and represents a perfect accumulation of arguments against humanitarian intervention. It may also serve as a reference for students seeking to learn the main factual details of the most important instances of State practice on humanitarian intervention.

However, those expecting a more profound and thought-provoking analysis of humanitarian intervention or one which would encompass arguments for and against it are likely to be disappointed – the author is apparently a realist and his analysis is clearly, though not entirely persuasively oriented towards dismissing any opposite point of view. Although very pedantically outlined, the arguments nonetheless at times appear circular and are not always coherent enough to lead to what is identified as a general conclusion.

Having read the book one still will not get an answer to a number of questions directly related with the topic considered. The impact on law of changes in international relations in the 1990s is barely considered. It seems to be an important omission, since it has been argued this period may have given rise to a new permissive rule of customary international law concerning humanitarian intervention. Thus it also remains dubious whether the scope of Article 2(4) remains the same as it was in 1945.

Another issue not considered is the content of the rule of international law governing humanitarian intervention. For example, it is not to be disputed that the means of intervention in Kosovo in 1999 were not the most effective in ensuring that ethnic cleansing did not occur in Kosovo. However, what if the NATO countries decided to risk the lives of their soldiers and use ground forces for the purpose of protecting Kosovo civilians from the attacks by Serbian forces, and the much criticised consequences were avoided, would it still be argued that legally speaking this was a violation of Article 2(4)? The author would most likely dismiss such an action as an exception from the rule, never to be repeated again and his final answer would remain that the introduction of the right of humanitarian intervention would be "a recipe for bad policy, bad law and a bad international order". It is not entirely clear why, because the author does not waste his energy on hypotheticals, he only lists the suggested criteria for humanitarian intervention and then again simply dismisses all of them for the reason that no incidents considered in his book would satisfy all listed requirements (pp. 228–229).

Nonetheless, it is beyond doubt that this book is an important contribution to the criticism directed against the sole remaining superpower and the way the Security Council has been used after the Cold War.

Loreta Šaltinytė[*]

[*] Lecturer of international and EU law at Mykolas Romeris University, Vilnius.

N. J. Wheeler, *Saving Strangers. Humanitarian Intervention in International Society*, Oxford University Press, Oxford, 2000. ISBN-10: 0-19-829621-5, ISBN-13: 978-0-19-829621-8, 336 pages, price: GBP 47.50.

The discussion of humanitarian interventions in East Pakistan, Cambodia, Uganda, Iraq, Somalia, Rwanda and Kosovo are found in a variety of works. However, there are a number of issues that distinguish Wheeler's contribution on humanitarian intervention from others. Wheeler argues in favour of recognition of a right to humanitarian intervention and in doing so he builds on R. Vincent's contributions on humanitarian intervention written in the 1980s, and further develops the case for the legitimacy of humanitarian intervention discussed in the writings of Fernando Teson. "Saving Strangers" discusses incidents of humanitarian interventions from a comparative and theoretical perspective. The author provides a detailed and coherent discussion of the factual circumstances leading to interventions, legitimating reasons for the action as invoked by the interveners, reactions of the other States and the possible motives behind them, and, finally, an evaluation of whether a specific incident of intervention could be treated as a case of genuine humanitarian intervention.

Arguing that humanitarian intervention should be permitted in the face of sovereignty, non-intervention and the prohibition of the use of force, the author focuses on two areas – State practice (i.e. discussion of seven selected incidents) and the normative dimension of the issue.

In the first chapter the normative dimension of humanitarian intervention is set out. The author initially discusses the arguments of realist and pluralist schools of international relations, and then sets out a solidarist case for humanitarian intervention. The starting point for this is that States need to legitimize their actions, and that legitimization is indispensable to States because it grants them security (p. 4). Thus State actions will be constrained if they cannot be justified in terms of a plausible legitimating reason (p. 4). The correlative assumption is also that States, and this applies even to the most powerful ones, are not free to create legitimacy for their actions. To illustrate this point, a resort is made to the theory of Charles Manning, who was the first to liken international relations to a game with self-contained rules. States are players in this game, and, quoting Pierre Bourdeu, "nothing is simultaneously freer and more constrained than the action of the good player". From this statement, several implications follow which serve as the basis of the book reviewed: firstly, successful players recognize the constraints that membership of international society imposes, and, secondly, when the rules become disputed among the players, the referee will have the task of not only finding a rule, but also of determining its substantive content, and this, according to Rosalyn Higgins, requires making choices between alternative legal claims which cannot be divorced from wider political and social considerations (p. 25). The author intimates that recent State practice on humanitarian intervention may suggest that

Baltic Yearbook of International Law, Volume 6, 2006, pp. 483–486.

humanitarian intervention is gaining legitimacy and, perhaps, even legality. Briefly outlined, this represents the underlying rationale on which the theme of the book – legitimacy of humanitarian intervention in international society – is developed.

The chapter is particularly interesting to read since the discussion of legitimacy of humanitarian intervention is not limited to policy arguments for and against it: any humanitarian intervention needs to satisfy as a minimum four criteria in order to be legitimate: firstly, it has to be initiated for a just cause, secondly, the decision to use force must be a last resort, thirdly, the action should be proportionate, and, lastly, there must be a high probability that the intervention will achieve a positive humanitarian outcome (p. 33). Several criteria that have been suggested earlier by other writers are not included in this list, of which the most well known is the requirement of a Security Council resolution as well as a requirement that the primary motives of the intervening State should be humanitarian. The position of Wheeler is that the key question for legitimacy of the humanitarian intervention is not the purity of motives, but the relationship between motives and humanitarian outcomes (pp. 37–39, 47). As to the sanction of the Security Council, Wheeler considers that States should seek to obtain the sanction of the Security Council as much as possible, and if the sanction is obtained, this would further increase the standard of legitimacy of the action. The author explicitly admits that in certain instances failure to obtain the mandate from the Security Council would not be a de-legitimating factor if the minimum four discussed criteria were satisfied (p. 309).

This normative framework is perfectly applied to seven selected instances of State practice. It is argued that the interventions in North Pakistan, Cambodia and Uganda qualify as humanitarian interventions, though at that time the international community was not prepared to accept them as legitimate exceptions from the rule prohibiting the use of force. Although the Tanzanian intervention in Uganda, in author's opinion, qualifies as the most legitimate action among the three examples, (i.e. humanitarian motives were explicitly invoked in this action), nonetheless it is argued that both Vietnam's intervention in Cambodia and India's intervention in Pakistan also fulfil the minimum threshold criteria in order to qualify as humanitarian interventions and should have been accepted as such by other States. Especially in the case of Cambodia, "failure to do so discloses the moral bankruptcy of pluralist international society" (p. 110). Although the author is critical of this reaction by States, nonetheless he agrees that in the 1970s the States did not consider that humanitarian intervention was a legitimate practice.

For the first time the 'voice of solidarism' became heard in 1991, when no-fly zones over northern Iraq were established for the protection of the Kurds. Though the means chosen by the actors were not effective enough to protect the civilians from attacks by the Iraqi government forces, Wheeler describes this incident as a legitimate humanitarian intervention. He claims though that in this case, the right of humanitarian intervention was a limited one, in that it required a supporting Security Council resolution which was restricted to bringing "relief and redress in human rights emergencies". However, in the words of Wheeler, it cannot be argued that this action supports the existence of a customary norm of humanitarian intervention (p. 169), since the *opinio iuris* of States was lacking.

Neither could the uniform Security Council action in the case of Somalia provide support for the existence of a custom, since arguably the total collapse of government in Somalia did not involve the issue of sovereignty at all. Discussion of the failure to act in Rwanda serves as natural supporting evidence that international society should permit humanitarian interventions. Disregarding the general indecisiveness to intervene, no Security Council member invoked the sovereignty of the Rwandan government as the reason why intervention was not feasible.

Finally, the chapter on the case of Kosovo is of immense significance for Wheeler's thesis. The decision of the NATO countries to begin the air strikes even without Security Council authorization was the first case since the founding of the UN that a group of States explicitly justified their use of force against another State on humanitarian grounds. Apart from that, an attempt to condemn the action as a violation of Articles 2(4), 24 and 53 of the UN Charter by a Security Council resolution failed when six members of the Council joined NATO countries and Slovenia in voting against it. In evaluating the legitimacy of this instance of intervention, Wheeler disagrees with Ken Boothe who qualifies it as a failure because it did not save lives and was counterproductive. Instead, he considers that the contradiction between the means employed and the positive humanitarian outcome can hardly serve as a clear de-legitimating factor: "the moral judgment here is a complex one and it can in the nature of things be only an interim assessment" (p. 284). Nonetheless, he finally concludes that the NATO decision to act preventatively was the right thing to do, although the means invoked were wrong (*id.*).

This stimulating discussion finally leads to the conclusion that the problem with the legitimacy of humanitarian intervention is not so much sovereignty and non-intervention into internal affairs but the fact that State leaders are too reluctant to take human and other risks that humanitarian intervention might require. This practice might be accepted as legitimate (and perhaps also legal) as soon as there is a change in the moral consciousness of public opinion (pp. 309–310).

The book will be equally interesting to experts and beginners in international relations and international law interested in humanitarian intervention. Though strictly speaking it is not a legal treatise where numerous materials of international law are covered, it is a compelling study of State practice presented in a concise though accurate normative framework. However, it seems that the in-depth analysis of the normative framework for humanitarian intervention could have been enriched with a brief discussion of the concepts of 'legitimate' and 'legal'. This might have provided a link between the approach of analysis by an international political theorist and an international lawyer.

The study is persuasive enough to return hope to those who consider that international law fails to meet its purpose of constraining the actions of States, especially the United States, as well as those who have lost hope in expecting that States will act whenever moral considerations dictate action. This well-written book is a strong and compelling work on humanitarian intervention, a must-read to anyone as a source of intellectual inspiration and challenge.

Loreta Šaltinytė[*]

[*] Lecturer of international and EU law at Mykolas Romeris University, Vilnius.

Information: Legal Journals in the Baltic States

Legal Scientific Journal TEISĖ (LAW)

Jevgenij Machovenko[*]

Short History

The journal *Teisė* (*Law*) ISSN 1392-1274 is the first scientific legal journal in Lithuania. It was established by the Faculty of Law at Vilnius University in 1957. The first volume came out with the title *Teisės mokslų klausimai* (*Questions of the legal sciences*) as a result of scientific cooperation with the Faculty of Economy. The second volume was prepared by the Faculty of Law independently and came out in 1961 with the title *Teisė* (*Law*).

Until 1990 Lithuanian legal science and its journal *Teisė* were developed according to Soviet standards. For the most part Lithuanian legal science was structured and run in accordance with the needs of the Soviet Union, it had a strictly centralized governance structure which gave no priority to the needs of Lithuania. Vilnius University, its Faculty of Law and the Journal were controlled by different governing bodies, such as the Ministry of Higher Education, the Lithuanian Academy of Sciences, and various ministries of either Lithuania or the former Soviet Union. The main research areas were Soviet criminal law, criminology and criminal procedure, constitutional law and administrative law. From 1957 to 1990 the Journal has published about 230 articles (60 per cent) in Russian and only 150 articles (40 per cent) in Lithuanian. Scientists at the Faculty aspired to investigate national Lithuanian laws adopted until 1940. As a result, 81 articles (21 per cent) focusing on the history of Lithuanian law have been published in the Journal from 1957 to 1990.

In 1990, after regaining independence, it was clear that a new Lithuanian legal system would be created and many teachers and researchers would be involved in public work and activities of various governmental bodies and private institutions in the coming years. Therefore, it was necessary to safeguard the research potential of the faculty, as well as to direct the research to fulfill the needs of Lithuanian society and to integrate the Lithuanian legal system and legal science into the legal system and legal science of the European Union. The *Law on Research and Higher Education* adopted in 1991 was very important for legal research at Vilnius University. The Law enforced the principles of autonomy, academic freedom,

[*] Executive Secretary of the Journal, Dr., Assoc. Professor of the Faculty of Law, Vilnius University

Baltic Yearbook of International Law, Volume 6, 2006, pp. 487–490.

integration of research and higher education; it described the then structure of the country's scientific system and also protected research activities of higher education institutions. The contents of the Journal reflect the development of Lithuanian legal science. After 1990 many vital questions have been discussed in the journal such as: the problems of codification of the Lithuanian labor law; problems of developing a new Lithuanian code of civil procedure; dismissal from employment due to the dissolution and reorganization of enterprises; prospects of criminological research in Lithuania; the regime of the protected territories in Lithuania in the context of legal reform; the legal status of foreigners in Lithuania. The Journal provided Lithuanian students with the opportunity to explore these legal issues at a time when there did not exist textbooks or other scientific literature on contemporary national law issues. Later, the Editorial Board was reorganized – some teaches and researchers from foreign and national higher education schools and scientific institutions were co-opted. Scientific co-operation in the field of legal research between Lithuanian and foreign higher education schools and scientific institutions has become one of the priorities of the Journal.

The Content

Since 1999 the Journal has been published quarterly. Each volume of the journal consists of 140 to 180 pages. Structurally it is divided into two parts. The main part (without title) consists of research papers (scientific articles) prepared in accordance with the requirements of the Science Council of Lithuania. Articles are reviewed by recognized professors and scientists in the relevant field. All articles included in the main part have comprehensive summaries (up to one page) in English, German, French or Russian. This part of the Journal is recognized by the Science Council of Lithuania as a generally recognized and reviewed scientific publication. The second part of the Journal with the title *Teisės aktualijos* (*Problems of Law*) is devoted to such issues as book reviews, current issues, discussion, events, and legal education, etc.

Fifty-seven volumes of the Journal have been published from 1957 to 2005. They consist of 882 articles by 325 authors. Five hundred and forty five articles have been published in Lithuanian and 337 in English, German, French, Polish or Russian. The Journal covers all branches of law in Lithuania: 153 articles concern civil law and procedure; 89 labor law and social security; 134 history of law; 44 theory of law, legal sociology and legal philosophy; 44 international and European Union law; 98 constitutional and administrative law; 175 criminal law; 88 criminology and criminal procedure; 57 in other fields of legal science. Among them are 99 articles by 88 foreign scientists from Germany, Poland, Ukraine, Russia, Latvia, Estonia, Hungary, Italy, Canada, Finland, Switzerland, Great Britain, Czech Republic, the United States of America, France, Sweden and Belarus. Each volume includes articles by highly esteemed researchers in private and public law. The Journal is also open to young authors in order to promote their ideas and provide a forum for their often progressive views on legal issues – 183 articles by postgraduate students have been published since 1990.

Now in accordance with the research program *Integration of the Lithuanian legal system into the legal system of the European Union* the Editorial Board is primarily interested in articles concerning the development of the Lithuanian legal system and legal doctrine in the processes of integration to the European Union, as well as the legal problems of membership of Lithuania in the European Union and NATO. The Journal also discusses theoretical and practical problems of interpreting, applying and creating civil law and civil procedure law, problems implementing a new criminal code and criminal procedure code, the impact of the constitutional principles on the development of subsystems of public law, and problems of legal regulation of collective and individual labour relations.

The Editorial Board

The contents of the Journal are determined by the Editorial Board which consists of three teachers from foreign universities -- Professor Habil. Dr. Peter Gilles (Johann Wolfgang Goethe University, Frankfurt on the Main, Germany), Professor Habil. Dr. Uldis Krastinš (University of Latvia) and Professor Habil. Dr. Valerian Sanetra (Bialostok University, Poland); 11 teachers from Vilnius University (Editor-in-Chief Professor Dr. Ipolitas Nekrošius, Executive Secretary Assoc. Professor Dr. Jevgenij Machovenko, Assoc. Professor Dr. Armanas Abramavičius, Assoc. Professor Dr. Juozas Galginaitis, Assoc. Professor Dr. Gintaras Goda, Assoc. Professor Dr. Danutė Jočienė, Professor Dr. Antanas Marcijonas, Assoc. Professor Dr. Ilona Michailovič, Professor Habil. Dr. Valentinas Mikelėnas, Professor Habil. Dr. Vytautas Nekrošius and Professor Dr. Egidijus Šileikis) and three teachers and researchers from other national universities and research institutions – Dr. Algimantas Čepas (Law Institute, Lithuania), Professor Habil. Dr. Mindaugas Maksimaitis (Mykolas Romeris University, Lithuania) and Professor Dr. Alvydas Pumputis (Mykolas Romeris University, Lithuania). Vice-dean of the Faculty of Law Assoc. Professor Dr. Tomas Davulis, Head of the Department of International and European Union Law Assoc. Professor Dr. Dainius Žalimas, Head of the Department of Civil Law and Procedure Assoc. Professor Dr. Vytautas Mizaras and Head of the Department of Criminal Law Assoc. Professor Dr. Gintaras Švedas are also involved in structuring the content of the Journal.

To Authors and Readers

The Editorial Board is open to co-operation and welcomes articles in English, German, French, Lithuanian or Russian. They can be sent to the Editorial Office at Saulėtekio al. 9, I rūmai, LT-10222 Vilnius, Lithuania or submitted by e-mail to teises_fakultetas@tf.vu.lt. Articles should be nine to fifteen pages in length. Longer articles are accepted at the discretion of the Editorial Board. A list of sources and bibliography must be appended to the manuscript. The article shall be structured in a style typical of scientific works which includes the object of investigation, purpose and methods, results of the investigation and conclusions. Other information to be provided includes the date on which the article was sent to the Editorial Office, the authors' place of occupation, duties, degrees, title, postal and e-mail addresses. The article shall include an abstract, which will be translated into Lithuanian and posted on the Internet.

The Journal is now published by the non-governmental organization Vilnius University Publishing House in co-operation with Vilnius University. All articles published by the Journal since 2003 can be found on the Vilnius University Publishing House's site at www.leidykla.vu.lt. Additionally, English translations of titles, contents and summaries of articles since 1998 are posted on this website. In Lithuania subscriptions to the Journal are administered by *AB Lietuvos Paštas* (www.post.lt).

The readership of the Journal is varied. The Journal is an important source of legal analyses and comments for civil servants, attorneys-at-law, notaries and other practicing lawyers. Most readers are associated with foreign and national higher education schools, research institutions, courts, administrative institutions and local governments. Among them are law students and teachers at the Johann Wolfgang Goethe University (Frankfurt on the Main, Germany), Max Plank Institute (Germany), Cologne University (Germany), Kiel University (Germany), Bialostok University (Poland), Warsaw University (Poland), Krakow University (Poland), Vytautas Magnus University (Lithuania), Mykolas Romeris University (Lithuania), the Law Institute (Lithuania), as well as judges of the Supreme Court of Lithuania, the Constitutional Court of Lithuania, etc. The *Teisė* plays a significant role in the development of Lithuanian legal science and education and offers lawyers a forum for discussion. It aspires to promote democracy, the rule of law and innovative legal thinking in accordance with European legal standards and principles which are of great importance in Lithuania.

List of Contributors

Antony Anghie	The Samuel D. Thurman Professor of International Law at the S.J.Quinney School of Law at the University of Utah, USA
Oriol Casanovas	Professeur à l'Université Pompeu Fabra, Barcelone, Espagne
Monique Chemillier-Gendreau	Professeur émérite à l'Université Paris VII-Denis Diderot, France
Barbara Delcourt	Professor at the Faculty of Social, Political and Economic Sciences and at the Institute of European Studies and Associate Member of the Centre of International Law (Free University of Brussels), Belgium
Olivier De Schutter	Professeur à la Faculté de Droit de l'UCL, Belgique
Lauri Hannikainen	Professor of International Law, University of Turku (Åbo), Finland
Emmanuelle Jouannet	Professeur à l'Université Paris I (*Panthéon-Sorbonne*), France
Leena-Maarja Kalda	Legal expert at Supralaw, the Center for Supranational law, Estonia
Saulius Katuoka	Chair at the Department of International law at Mykolas Romeris University, Lithuania; Member of the Permanent Court of Arbitration since 2005
Tanel Kerikmäe	LL.Lic,; LL.M.; Dean of the Faculty of Law of International University Concordia Audentes; President of the Estonian European Community Studies Association; Senior expert at SupraLaw, the Centre for Supranational Law
Jevgenij Machovenko	Executive Secretary of the Journal, Dr., Assoc. Professor of the Faculty of Law, Vilnius University

Iulia Voina-Motoc	Professor of Public International Law, University of Bucharest
Lauri Mälksoo	Dr.iur., Associate Professor of International Law, Faculty of Law, University of Tartu, Lithuania
Mārtiņš Paparinskis	LL.B. (University of Latvia), M.Jur. (Dist) (Oxon), M.Phil. (Oxon) student, Associate at Sorainen Law Offices, Romania
Alain Pellet	Professeur à l'Université de Paris X-Nanterre, France; Membre et ancien Président de la Commission du droit international (C.D.I.)
Gaetano Pentassuglia	Dott.re in Giurisprudenza, PhD, Senior Lecturer in Law, Liverpool Law School, University of Liverpool, the United Kingdom
W. Michael Reisman	Myres S. McDougal Professor of International Law, Yale Law School, USA
August Reinisch	Prof. Dr.; Department of European, International and Comparative Law, University of Vienna, Austria; Professorial Lecturer at the Bologna Center of SAIS/Johns Hopkins University in Bologna, Italy
Loreta Šaltinytė	Doctoral candidate at Mykolas Romeris University, Lithuania; LL.M. (Riga Graduate School of Law (2003), Master of Law (Vilnius University Faculty of law, 2003). Currently a lecturer on international and EU law at Mykolas Romeris University
Bruno Simma	Judge at the International Court of Justice; First President of the European Society of International Law
Dainius Žalimas	Associate Professor, the Head of the Department of International Law and the European Union Law, Faculty of Law, Vilnius University, Lithuania

Information for Authors

1. All contributions are refereed. The editors reserve the right to suggest modifications and/or additions to submitted contributions, and further reserve the right to reject or to revoke acceptance.

2. Languages: Contributions must be submitted in English. Authors should ensure that their contribution is reviewed by a person who is competent in English, and edited as necessary. Contributions accepted for publication may, at the discretion of the editors, be linguistically revised. Contributions in German and French may be considered for publication.

3. Proofs: The authors may receive proofs for correction. Authors are requested to keep corrections to a minimum, with the exception of taking into account important material or references not previously available, or development of notes. Substantial modifications other than those described are permitted at the discretion of the editors.

4. Manuscripts should not exceed 25 pages. They should be typed, double-spaced with wide margins, and presented in Microsoft Word format. The editors are unable to accept non-IBM or MS DOS manuscripts.

5. Manuscripts should be submitted via e-mail attachment (virus scanned) or floppy disc. If the article is submitted on diskette, the latter shall be properly labelled with the title, author, operating system and software used. Always keep a copy of the submission.

6. Authors should check for errors before submitting their work. They are responsible for providing complete and correct references, for accuracy of quotations, and for obtaining any permission necessary for quoting another author's material.

7. Manuscripts must adhere to guidelines on format, spelling and style available from the editors, *especially*; U.K. English must be the language selection tool for Microsoft Word.

8. Book reviews: The editor will accept reviews of books published internationally and locally and in another languages than English. Book reviews shall not exceed 5 pages. They should be submitted to Dainius Žalimas, Book Review Editor, at DainiusZ@pastas.kam.lt.

9. Copyright and Permissions: Copyright is established in the name of Kluwer Law International. Submission of a paper for publication implies that copyright reverts to the publisher from the author and that the article has not been published elsewhere, and is not being considered for publication elsewhere. Consent to Publish and Transfer of Copyright forms will be sent to authors whose work has been accepted for publication.

10. Fees: Authors will not receive a fee, but will be presented with a copy of the Yearbook and twenty-five offprints of each article free of charge. Ordering information for additional offprints will be sent to each author as publication nears.

Submissions should be addressed to Carin Laurin, Publications Officer, at Carin.Laurin@rwi.lu.se or on diskette via post to Raoul Wallenberg Institute, P.O. Box 1155, 221 05 Lund, Sweden, by January 15th of each year for publication the same year. Further information and enquiries should be directed to the same also via phone at +46 (0)46 222 12 47 or fax at +46 (0)46 222 12 22.

Authors are requested to follow the guidelines below in the preparation of their manuscripts:

1. British English spelling should be used.
2. The preferred reference source is the Oxford English Dictionary.
3. The preferred font and size for text and footnotes are Times New Roman 12 pt and Times New Roman 10 pt, respectively.
4. Do not use bold or underline formats to emphasise a word or sentence. Words should only be emphasised using italics, sparingly.
5. When beginning a new section the first paragraph should not be indented, however, subsequent paragraphs should be indented.

Punctuation

1. One space after each punctuation mark is sufficient. That is, after a full stop (.) there should only be one space.

Figures and Numerals

1. Spell out the numbers from one to ten (except in pages, legislation, dates and other similar references); use numerals for numbers 11 and higher. Also use numerals throughout for dates and times.

2. For percentages spell out the word per cent. For example, eight per cent, not 8%.
3. Spell out fractions. For example, two-thirds or three-quarters.
4. Page ranges should be separated by an en dash. For example, pp. 26–46.

Foreign and Latin Words
1. Foreign and Latin words should be italicised.

Italicising
1. Italics are used for emphasis. Do not use bold or underline formatting for emphasis.
2. Italics should be used sparingly. If they are used too often the emphasis will be weakened.
3. Foreign and Latin words should be italicised.
4. All case names should be italicised, however, the word case and the v. should not be italicised. For example, *Hermes* v. *FHT Marketing* case.
5. All signals should be italicised in footnotes. Such signals include *see*, *see also*, *cf.*, *contra*, *but see*, *but cf.*, *see generally*, *et seq.*, and *e.g.*

Monetary Amounts
1. Do not use dollar signs, use USD (US dollars), SEK (Swedish Kronor), EUR (Euro), etc. This abbreviation should be placed directly before the amount it refers to. For example, EUR 100.

Dates and Time
1. For dates including day, month and year use the following format, 1 January 2003.
2. If only month and year is included use the following format, January 2003.
3. If only month and day is used use the following format, 1 January.
4. Years should be separated by an en dash. For example, 1980–1986.

Headings
1. Authors are asked to use only three levels of headings, although four can be accommodated. They should be numbered consecutively and formatted as in the example. The first letter of all words should be *capitalised*, except prepositions and articles.

Example: 1. **Democracy within States**
1.1. *Key Principles and Institutions*
1.1.1. Civil and Political Rights

Quotations

1. *Direct* quotations should be enclosed in double quotation marks (“ ”) and run on in the text.
2. Single quotation marks (‘ ’) are used to distinguish words, concepts or short phrases under discussion.
3. For larger sections of quoted text (*i.e.*, anything over five lines) use block quotes: set these off from other text by adding a blank line above and below the section, and indent the block of text on the left and right by five points. Reduce type size to 10 pt. These larger sections, or ‘block quotes’, should be enclosed in quotation marks.
4. Quotation marks should come before all punctuation, except where the whole sentence is a quotation.

Example: He said “I agree with you”. “Don’t do it.”

5. Where the quoted material begins with a capital but is being placed in the middle of a sentence and the letter should grammatically be lower case, place the letter in square brackets and change to lower case.

Example: As explicitly stated in Article 20 “[a]ny propaganda for war shall be prohibited by law”.

6. Omission points
    a. Use to designate that the quoted material has omitted information (usually only in a sentence).
    b. Should be styled as three spaced points (full stops), with a space before the first point and a space after the last point.
    c. When used within quotations, omit all punctuation (including full stops) immediately prior to the omission points.
    d. It is *unnecessary* to include omission points at the beginning of a quote if the first letter of the quoted material is in lower case. The lower case letter denotes that the quote comes from the middle of a sentence.

       Example: Article 6 also states that the right to life “shall be protected by law”.

       Article 50 states that the “. . . Covenant shall extend to all parts of federal States without any limitations or exceptions”.

Citations

- When citing the following general guidelines should be observed:
- When in doubt, provide all information – it is easier and faster to cut than to hunt down minutiae.
- If there is one footnote in a sentence the footnote should follow all punctuation. However, when there is more than one footnote the

footnotes should be placed after the idea, quote, article, etc, *except* for the last footnote, which should follow all punctuation.
Examples: Article 6 can be said to predate the Covenant by many years.[12]

Both case law[13] and customary practice illustrate this point[14]

- Do not use endnotes; use footnotes (bottom of page).
- All footnotes should end with a full stop.
- Footnotes should be in Times New Roman 10 pt.
- Do not make reference within the text to other parts of the text using page numbers. Use section headings, numbers/letters, or a prose description of the part of the text you wish to refer to.
- The following abbreviations should be used:
  - pp. = pages
  - p. = page
  - para. = paragraph
  - paras. = paragraphs

  Example: pp. 25–27.
- *et seq*. is preferred to ff.
- All signals should be italicised in footnotes. Signals (for example: *see, see also, cf.*, *but see*, etc.) should not be separated from the rest of the citation by a comma, except for *e.g.*

  Examples: *See Rispoli* v. *Italy,* 30 October 2003 . . .

  E.g., J. Klabbers, '*The Concept of Treaty* . . .

References and Cross References

1. When referring to a previously cited work use the following format: author's surname, *supra* note . . . and give the number of the footnote in which the work was first cited.

Example: Bogdan, *supra* note 8.

2. When referring to a previously cited case use the following format: case name, *supra* note . . . and give the number of the footnote in which the case was first cited. Note: long case names should be shortened appropriately.

Example: *Lockerbie* case, *supra* note 2.

3. When referring to a previously cited work or case but referring to a different page or paragraph than what was originally cited indicate the page or paragraph referred to.

Examples: Crawford, s*upra* note 10, p. 25.

Rispoli v. *Italy*, *supra* note 6, para. 18.

4. When referring to a work cited *immediately above* the citation in question, and with the same page number, use the following: *Ibid.* Remember: use *ibid.* only for immediately preceding references, otherwise, use *supra* note.
5. In cases such as no. 4 above, but with a different page number indicate the page referred to.

Example: *Ibid.*, p. 4.

References – Examples
References should adhere to the specifications below, in accordance with the publisher's requirements. Most importantly, our ability to furnish missing bibliographic information on sources is limited by time constraints. The guidelines below have been simplified greatly with respect to the publisher's guidebook in order to facilitate adherence.
1. ***Website/Internet references***
For journal articles, books, case law, newspaper articles, and other documents accessed via the Internet simply cite as normal adding the URL (website address) in angle brackets (omitting http://) and the date the material was accessed *to the end of the citation*. For example:

Legality of the Threat or Use of Nuclear Weapons, 8 July 1996, ICJ, Advisory Opinion, paras. 61–63, <www.icj-cij.org/icjwww/icases/iunan/iunanframe.htm>, visited on 29 October 2003.

If the material does not lend itself to the above mentioned citation format provide the following information in this order:
The capitalised initial of the author's first name and middle name (if applicable), followed by the author's surname (If relevant) *and/or* issuing institution, group, etc. (if relevant)
Title of document in italics.
URL (website address) in angle brackets omitting http://.
Date that the material was accessed.

2. ***Articles in journals***
The following information should be contained in this order:
The capitalised initial of the author's first name and middle name (if applicable), followed by the author's surname.
The name of the article enclosed in single quotation marks.
The volume number.
The name of the journal in italics.
The year in parentheses.

Page(s)/paragraph(s) directly referred to or the page range of the article.

Examples:
R. O'Keefe, 'The Admission to the United Nations of the Ex-Soviet and Ex-Yugoslav States', 1 *Baltic Yearbook of International Law* (2001) p. 170.

O. Spiermann, 'Humanitarian Intervention as a Necessity and the Threat or Use of *Jus Cogens*', 71:4 *Nordic Journal of International Law* (2002) pp. 530–534.

3. ***Books***
The following information should be contained in this order:

a. The capitalised initial of the author's first name and middle name (if applicable), followed by the author's surname. If an article has two authors their names should be separated by the word and. If an article has more than two authors, list only the first author, followed by *et al.*
b. The title of the book in italics.
c. The publisher, the place of publication and the year of publication in parentheses.
d. Editor and editors should be specified as: (ed.) and (eds.) respectively.
e. Page(s) or paragraph(s) referred to (if applicable).

Example:
L. Holmström (ed.), Concluding Observations of the UN Committee on the Elimination of Racial Discrimination (Kluwer Law International, The Hague, 2002) pp. 77–79.

4. ***Chapters in books***
The page reference at which the cited chapter begins should always be specified *or* specify the specific page(s) referred to.

Example:
A. Eide, 'Cultural Rights and Minorities: Essay in Honour of Erica-Irene Daes', in G. Alfredsson and M. Stavropoulou (eds.), *Justice Pending: Indigenous Peoples and Other Good Causes* (Kluwer Law International, The Hague, 2002) p. 83.

5. ***Case law***:

The following information should be contained in this order:

a. Case name in italics, excluding ‘v.’ which should be in roman.
b. Parties to the case if *not* included in case name, in parentheses.
c. Date of judgement.
d. Issuing court, this can be abbreviated if the court is well known internationally. For example, ECHR, ICJ, etc.
e. In the absence of any indication to the contrary the cited case is a judgement on the merits. Any variation from that should be stated. For example, advisory opinion, a dissenting opinion, provisional measures or if it has some other unique characteristic.
f. Reference or application number (if applicable).
g. Source, however, if accessed by Internet cite appropriately, see above.
h. Page(s) or paragraph(s) referred to (if applicable).

Examples:
International Court of Justice:
Arrest Warrant of 11 April 2000 (Democratic Republic of the Congo v. *Belgium),* 8 December 2000, ICJ, Provisional Measures, *I.C.J. Reports 2000*, p. 182.

Legality of the Threat or Use of Nuclear Weapons, 8 July 1996, ICJ, Advisory Opinion, paras. 61–63, <www.icj-cij.org/icjwww/icases/iunan/iunanframe.htm>, visited on 29 October 2003.

European Court of Human Rights:
Rispoli v. *Italy,* 30 October 2003, ECHR, no. 00055388/00, para. 26, <hudoc.echr.coe.int/hudoc/ViewRoot.asp?Item=1&Action=Html&X=1030183728&Notice=0&Noticemode=&RelatedMode=1>, visited on 29 October 2003.

Velikova v. *Bulgaria*, 18 May 2000, ECHR, no. 41488/98, *Reports of Judgments and Decisions 2000-VI*, para. 92.

Inter-American Court of Human Rights:
The Case of the Mayagna (Sumo) Awas Tingni Community v. *Nicaragua*, 31 August 2001, Inter-American Court of Human Rights, Series C No. 79, para. 164, <www.corteidh.or.cr/seriecing/serie_c_79_ing.doc>, visited on 29 October 2003.

6. ***UN documents, publications, and resolutions***
The following information should be contained in this order:

a. Author/agency/body (if necessary).
b. Title in italics (if necessary).
c. Document symbol or publication sales number in parentheses.
d. Specific page(s) or paragraph(s) referred to (if applicable).

7. ***Newspaper articles***
The following information should be contained in this order:

a. The capitalised initial of the author's first name and middle name (if applicable), followed by the author's surname.
b. Title of article.
c. Newspaper.
d. Date.
e. Page or section.

Example:
S. Kishkovsky, 'The Most Dangerous Place in Europe for Journalists', *The International Herald Tribune*, 24 October 2003, p. 2.